DeathQuest

An Introduction to the Theory and Practice of Capital Punishment in the United States

4th Edition

DeathQuest

An Introduction to the Theory and Practice of Capital Punishment in the United States

4th Edition

Robert M. Bohm

AMSTERDAM • BOSTON • HEIDELBERG • LONDON • NEW YORK • OXFORD
PARIS • SAN DIEGO • SAN FRANCISCO • SINGAPORE • SYDNEY • TOKYO

Anderson Publishing is an imprint of Elsevier

Acquiring Editor: Pamela Chester
Development Editor: Ellen S. Boyne
Project Manager: Danielle S. Miller
Designer: Joanne Blank

Anderson Publishing is an imprint of Elsevier
225 Wyman Street, Waltham, MA 02451, USA

Notices

Knowledge and best practice in this field are constantly changing. As new research and experience broaden our
understanding, changes in research methods or professional practices may become necessary. Practitioners
and researchers must always rely on their own experience and knowledge in evaluating and using any information
or methods described herein. In using such information or methods they should be mindful of their own safety
and the safety of others, including parties for whom they have a professional responsibility.

To the fullest extent of the law, neither the Publisher nor the authors, contributors, or editors, assume any liability
for any injury and/or damage to persons or property as a matter of product liability, negligence or otherwise,
or from any use or operation of any methods, products, instructions, or ideas contained in the material herein.

Library of Congress Cataloging-in-Publication Data
Application submitted

British Library Cataloguing-in-Publication Data
A catalogue record for this book is available from the British Library.

ISBN: 978-1-4377-3493-5

For information on all Anderson publications
visit our website at www.elsevierdirect.com

Printed in the United States of America

11 12 13 14 15   10 9 8 7 6 5 4 3 2 1

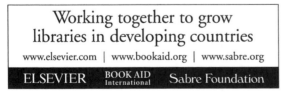

Working together to grow
libraries in developing countries

www.elsevier.com | www.bookaid.org | www.sabre.org

ELSEVIER   BOOK AID International   Sabre Foundation

To my nieces and nephews: Lisa, Traci, Allie, Daniel, Kami, Blythe, Weston, Kyler, Kallie, Jackson, Bella, and Layla

Contents

Foreword

Vengeance is mine, saith the Lord; and that means that it is not the Lord Chief Justice's.

—George Bernard Shaw, 1922

On an oppressively humid July night in 1987, I stood at the window of the gas chamber at the Mississippi State Penitentiary, staring at Connie Ray Evans. Strapped into a cold, steel chair nicknamed the "Black Death" by some forlorn, condemned prisoner many years before I became warden, I was preparing to give the order that would end Connie Evans's life. This was my second execution in just 5 weeks. Still numb from the first one, I realized as I gazed into the eyes of this next victim that my senses were all but dulled. This one, I knew, would be even more difficult than the first. I had permitted myself to become close to Connie Ray Evans. I came to recognize him as more than just a prison number waiting his turn on death row. In the end, standing there that hot summer night, I realized I was about to execute a friend. My mind was haunted by questions: How had Connie Ray Evans and I gotten there? What goes so wrong that a normal 18-year-old kid spends the last 7 years of his life awaiting a date with the executioner?

At a 1790s meeting of the American Philosophical Society held at the home of longtime friend Benjamin Franklin, Dr Benjamin Rush delivered a paper condemning the young nation's embrace of capital punishment. Rush, signer of the Declaration of Independence, father of American psychiatry, and social reformer, asked the same question: How had America arrived at the use of such a barbaric sanction? He dared to believe that we could be better than that.

Two centuries later, on a sweltering August day in Boston, champion libertarian and death penalty opponent Henry Schwarzschild delivered a message eerily similar to Rush's earlier admonition. Insisting that it is useless to discuss a hypothetical society that applies capital punishment in a fair, rational, consistent manner, Schwarzschild asserted that such an idyllic society is nonexistent. It is necessary, then, to remember that people are not infallible, therefore rendering the legal system imperfect. For this reason alone, he concluded that the use of capital punishment should be relegated to the writings of historical scholars.

DeathQuest would win the wholehearted approval of both Rush and Schwarzschild, indeed no small achievement. Professor Bohm has crafted an exhaustive introductory work that should be required reading, not just for students of criminal justice but for any thoughtful, enlightened citizenry as well. Absent the emotional histrionics that characterize so much capital punishment literature, this work forges a detailed, fact-based discussion of what many believe to be the most contentious social issue in America today. While the quality of Professor Bohm's book is unassailable, of even greater importance to the reader is the manner in which he "tells the story." This is not a textbook filled with charts, graphs, and data, however impressive and necessary we perceive such material to be. It is, in the final analysis, a book about people—people not so very different from the rest of us. America's death rows are filled with hope and despair, dreams and nightmares, optimism and resignation. While the purpose of this work is not to beatify death row prisoners, it does force the reader to come to grips with the stereotypical images that we so often assign to them.

As any thoughtful reader will quickly conclude, Professor Bohm has skillfully succeeded in painting the death penalty issue in realistic hues and shades of gray. Very rarely can we attribute consummate good or evil to any particular individual or community, and so it is with those on death row.

The death penalty has been a force in every major civilization since the dawn of history. So have the debate and controversy that surround it. For our part, executions are not new to the American scene. They have been part of our machinery of justice since the precolonial era, brought to Jamestown, Plymouth, and Boston by the earliest European settlers. Capital punishment is not a topic of discussion that falls within the purview of researchers or policy makers alone. The major religious denominations, civil rights organizations, and other social- and reform-minded groups have all focused attention on the troublesome issues that arise from the capital punishment debate.

This book will foster renewed, vigorous examination of the multiple realities that are capital punishment, and the impact the execution process has each time America leads one of its citizens to the execution chamber. Whether discussing the early history of executions in this country, retributive arguments, or our present enthrallment with sanitized lethal injection, Professor Bohm writes with acuity and a forcefulness that compels the reader to revisit long-held beliefs. This is not, after all, a book of abstract ideas or fictitious characters. Rather, when Professor Bohm forces us to confront the stark reality of the gallows, the grisly nature of the electric chair, or the sterility of the lethal injection table, he engages us in a self-examination of who we are as a society. The calculated, methodical, politically convenient approach to justice that has long been part of the execution protocol is laid bare in this book, in all of its disturbing reality.

This work will ensure that we never view state-ordered killing in quite the same way again.

Donald A. Cabana
Professor, University of Southern Mississippi
Author of *Death at Midnight: The Confession of an Executioner*
Former warden at various correctional facilities throughout the South

Acknowledgments

I would like to thank all of my friends and colleagues for their support, help, understanding, and inspiration. Although there are too many people to list here by name, many of them are cited in the pages of this book. The others know who they are.

About the Author

Robert M. Bohm is a Professor of Criminal Justice at the University of Central Florida in Orlando. He has also been a faculty member in the Departments of Criminal Justice at the University of North Carolina at Charlotte (1989–1995) and at Jacksonville State University in Alabama (1979–1989). In 1973–1974, he worked for the Jackson County Department of Corrections in Kansas City, Missouri, first as a corrections officer and later as an instructor/counselor in the Model Inmate Employment Program, a Law Enforcement Assistance Administration sponsored work-release project. He received his PhD in Criminology from Florida State University in 1980.

Professor Bohm has published numerous journal articles and book chapters in the areas of criminal justice and criminology. In addition to being the author of *DeathQuest: An Introduction to the Theory and Practice of Capital Punishment in the United States*, 4th ed. (2012), he is the author of *Ultimate Sanction: Understanding the Death Penalty Through Its Many Voices and Many Sides* (2010) and *A Concise Introduction to Criminal Justice* (2008). He is coauthor (with Keith N. Haley) of *Introduction to Criminal Justice*, 7th ed. (2012), and (with Brenda L. Vogel) *A Primer on Crime and Delinquency Theory*, 3rd ed. (2011). He is also the editor of *The Death Penalty Today* (2008) and *The Death Penalty in America: Current Research* (1991), and coeditor (with James R. Acker and Charles S. Lanier) of *America's Experiment with Capital Punishment: Reflections on the Past, Present, and Future of the Ultimate Sanction*, 2nd ed. (2003), and (with Jeffery T. Walker) *Demystifying Crime and Criminal Justice* (2006).

Professor Bohm has been active in the American Society of Criminology, the Southern Criminal Justice Association, and especially the Academy of Criminal Justice Sciences, having served in the latter organization as President (1992–1993). In 1989, the Southern Criminal Justice Association selected him as the Outstanding Educator of the Year. In 1999, he became a Fellow of the Academy of Criminal Justice Sciences; in 2001, he was presented with the Founder's Award of the Academy of Criminal Justice Sciences; and, in 2008, he was presented with the Bruce Smith Sr. Award by the Academy of Criminal Justice Sciences.

Introduction

At one level, the death penalty is a minor issue. The media keep the public aware of all sorts of horrible crimes, but relatively few people are directly affected by these crimes, either as perpetrators or victims or as family and friends of the perpetrators and victims. Very few people are sentenced to die for their crimes, and fewer people, still, are ever executed. The approximately 3,300 inmates currently on death rows throughout the United States represent less than two-tenths of 1 percent of the approximately 2.4 million inmates in all prisons and jails. Moreover, the only reason there are as many as 3,300 death row inmates is that some of them have been awaiting execution for more than 30 years.

Certainly, for me, the death penalty was a minor issue prior to the mid-1980s, and I am a criminal justice professor! I had not given much thought to the issue because other subjects, such as the causes and prevention of crime, were more important to me. (I suppose that even then I did not believe that the death penalty was an important tool in preventing crime.) Then, one day, an article in the local newspaper caught my eye. It mentioned a Gallup poll that showed that 75 percent of the American public supported the death penalty. What struck me as interesting was that such a large percentage of the public agreed about anything. Soon thereafter, I began my effort to understand why the death penalty in the United States was so strongly supported. I wanted to know what was motivating the "deathquest" of the American people.

Not long into my investigation, I became aware that, at another level, the death penalty represents two profound concerns of nearly everyone: the value of human life and how best to protect it. I also discovered that people differ greatly in the ways they believe these concerns should be addressed. For most people who support the death penalty, the execution of killers (and people who commit other horrible acts) makes sense. Death penalty supporters frequently state that executions do prevent those executed from committing heinous crimes again and that the example of executions probably prevents most people who might contemplate committing appalling crimes from doing so. In addition, many death penalty supporters simply believe that people who commit such crimes deserve to die, that they have earned their ignominious fate.

For opponents, the death penalty issue is about something else entirely. It is a benchmark of the "developing moral standards" of American civilization.[1] As Winston Churchill once said, "The mood and temper of the public with regard to the treatment of crime and criminals is one of the most unfailing tests of the civilization of any country." Put somewhat differently, for many opponents, the level of death penalty support in the United States is a rough estimate of the level of maturity of the American people. The not-so-subtle implication is that a mature, civilized society would not employ the death penalty. Opponents maintain that perpetrators of horrible crimes can be dealt with effectively by other means and that it makes little sense to kill some people, however blameworthy they are, to teach other people not to kill. These opponents argue that although the perpetrators of terrible crimes may deserve severe punishment, the punishment need not be execution.

The death penalty issue can be and has been addressed on many different levels. Only superficially is it a minor issue. Rather, it is a complex concern that encompasses fundamental questions of who we are as a people and how we deal with some of our most vexing social problems.

One of the more unexpected findings of my research is that most people have a relatively strong opinion about the death penalty, even though they know little about it. What they think they know, moreover, is often wrong. For these reasons, I decided to prepare and teach a college class on the death penalty. Not only did I believe that such a class would be a good vehicle for teaching critical-thinking skills in general, but also I was curious to know whether information about the death penalty (an entire semester's worth) would have any effect on people's opinions about it.

This book is a product of more than two decades of preparing and teaching my class. My principal goal, both in teaching and in writing this book, is to educate students so that whatever their death penalty opinions are, they are informed ones.

I believe it only fair to admit that I am an opponent of the death penalty. Years of study have convinced me that it is a penal practice we can do without. However, as I do in my classes, I will present in this book, as best I can, both sides of all issues. I will let the reader decide whether I have succeeded in the effort and interpret what I write in light of my biases. The reader should be forewarned that most of the literature and research on the death penalty has been produced by its opponents. For the most part, supporters have not felt the need to justify their position. As noted previously, for most of them, supporting the death penalty is just common sense.

The book is divided into 12 chapters. The first six are the least controversial, as they present mostly facts about the death penalty in the United States. The first chapter traces the history of the death penalty in the United States from 1608 until the mid-1960s—which may be called the premodern death penalty period. The second chapter focuses on the role of the US Supreme Court in the premodern practice of capital punishment. Although some of the premodern death penalty cases set precedent for modern capital jurisprudence, other cases, perhaps most of them, are mostly of historical interest. All of them, however, reveal troubling flaws in the premodern death penalty systems of many jurisdictions. Chapter 3 describes the constitutional attack on capital punishment's legality that culminated with the Supreme Court's 1972 landmark decision in *Furman v. Georgia*. It also examines the tremendous public backlash to *Furman* and the Court's reinstatement of the death penalty 4 short years later in *Gregg v. Georgia*. Chapter 4 presents many of the Court's decisions that have shaped death penalty jurisprudence during the modern period. The chapter reveals the Court's ongoing effort to regulate the penalty of death. The fifth chapter addresses the death penalty systems of the federal government and the military. Similarities and differences between these two systems and the systems of the 34 death penalty states are highlighted. The fifth chapter also examines the death penalty from a global perspective. The sixth chapter provides a detailed analysis of execution methods employed in the United States, outlines the legal history of the concept of "cruel and unusual punishment," and briefly describes the execution process and what it is like to witness an execution.

Chapters 7 through 11 examine the arguments and counterarguments employed by proponents and opponents of the death penalty. The seventh chapter addresses the issue of general deterrence. People who believe in the general deterrent effect assume that either the threat of executions or executions themselves prevent other people from committing capital crimes. Incapacitation and the economic costs of capital punishment are the subjects of the eighth chapter. Incapacitation refers to the goal of execution preventing convicted murderers or other capital offenders from committing other crimes. In the second section of this chapter, the economic costs of capital punishment are compared to the economic costs of alternative punishments, especially life imprisonment without opportunity of parole, or LWOP. The ninth chapter explores the subject of miscarriages of justice in capital cases. Incidents of wrongful arrests, wrongful charges or indictments, wrongful convictions, wrongful sentences, and wrongful executions are discussed, as are the reasons for miscarriages of justice. The chapter ends with suggestions about what can be done about them. Chapter 10 addresses two major problems the Supreme Court found with premodern death penalty statutes: that they did not prevent the death penalty from being imposed arbitrarily and in a discriminatory fashion. The major focus of the chapter is the modern record and whether the procedural reforms that have been implemented since *Furman v. Georgia* was decided in 1972 have, indeed, eliminated arbitrary and discriminatory application of the death penalty. Chapter 11 examines the subjects of retribution and religion in relation to the death penalty. Emphasized in the section on retribution are the effects of capital punishment on the families of murder victims and death row and executed inmates.

The twelfth and final chapter of the book, focuses on American death penalty opinion. This chapter is divided into three major sections. The first section provides the history of death penalty opinion, describing what is called here "the too simple and, therefore, misleading death penalty opinion question period." The second section surveys the present period and chronicles "the more complex and revealing death penalty opinion question period." This section begins with a description of research that tested the hypothesis that death penalty support is largely a product of ignorance about the way capital punishment is actually administered. The final section, and the conclusion to the book, addresses the future of American death penalty opinion and the effect it may have on the practice of capital punishment in the United States.

Three remarks about terminology should prove helpful. First, the terms "death penalty" and "capital punishment" are used interchangeably. They refer to the same thing. Second, frequent use is made of the terms "pre-*Furman*" (premodern) and "post-*Furman*" (modern) to denote different historical periods. *Furman* refers to the 1972 landmark Supreme Court decision, *Furman v. Georgia*—the first time that capital punishment was held to be unconstitutional. The pre-*Furman* era, for purposes of this book, spans the period from 1608, the year the first person in America was executed by legal authority, to the mid-1960s, when the legal assault on capital punishment began. The "modern" era of capital punishment, the post-*Furman* period, covers everything about the death penalty in the United States that has occurred since June 29, 1972. Third, the term "death eligible" is used frequently. The definition provided by law professors Baldus and Woodworth is employed: "A death-eligible case refers to one in which the facts are sufficient under state law to sustain a capital murder conviction and death sentence, whether or not the state actually seeks a death sentence or the jury actually imposes a death sentence in the case."[2]

Notes

1. See, for example, Kohlberg and Elfenbein (1975).
2. Baldus and Woodworth (1998, p. 386).

History of the death penalty in the United States: The premodern period

THE DEATH PENALTY IN COLONIAL TIMES

Captain George Kendall, a councilor for the Virginia colony, was executed in 1608 for being a spy for Spain – and so began America's experience with capital punishment.[1] The death penalty was just another one of the punishments brought to the New World by the early European settlers.

DEATH PENALTY LAWS

The crimes for which the death penalty was legally imposed varied from colony to colony. At one extreme was the law of the Puritans of the Massachusetts Bay Colony, which listed 12 death-eligible crimes: (1) idolatry, (2) witchcraft, (3) blasphemy, (4) murder, (5) manslaughter, (6) poisoning, (7) bestiality, (8) sodomy, (9) adultery, (10) man stealing, (11) false witness in capital cases, and (12) conspiracy and rebellion.[2] Each of these capital crimes, except conspiracy and rebellion, was accompanied by a Biblical quotation as justification. For example, following murder was this Biblical passage, in the language of the statute: "If any person committ any wilfull murther, which is manslaughter, committed upon premeditated mallice, hatred, or Crueltie, not in a mans necessarie and just defence, nor by meere casualtie against his will, he shall be put to death."[3]

At the other extreme was the law of the Quakers who were far less punitive than their neighbors to the north. In the Royal Charter of South Jersey (1646), capital punishment was originally forbidden altogether, but the prohibition ended in 1691.[4] William Penn's Great Act of 1682 (Pennsylvania) allowed capital punishment only for treason and murder.[5] The Quakers, however, were the exception. Most of the British colonies had statutes similar to those of the Massachusetts Bay Colony.

Today it may seem as if the statutes of the colonies listed too many capital crimes (crimes for which death could be imposed), but for colonial times, the number was relatively modest. In Great Britain, death could be imposed for more than 50 crimes, including burglary, robbery, and larceny. Later, during the reign of George II (1727–1760), the number of capital crimes was increased to nearly 100, and under George III (1760–1820), the death penalty could be imposed for almost 150 capital crimes (some authorities maintain it was closer to 200 capital crimes).[6] Moreover, for some of the moral or religious offenses, such as blasphemy, idolatry, adultery, sodomy, and bestiality, few offenders were ever executed in the colonies.[7] The main reason for the relatively small number of capital crimes in colonial America was the great need for able-bodied workers. It made little sense to execute people at a time when workers were so scarce, and people could be made to work. The British colonies might have had even fewer capital crimes if long-term confinement facilities had been available.[8] (The first prison was not established until 1790.)

EXECUTIONS AND SAVING SOULS

Executions in colonial America, though rare events, had a significant religious component that they lack today. They provided an especially dramatic occasion for saving souls. To be sure, executions served other purposes as well. They were considered just retribution – "an eye for an eye" – and a general deterrent to crime. They were also a stark reminder of what the state had the power to do to people who violated its laws. However, their role in saving souls was part of a morality lesson central to the clergy's social control of the colonists.[9]

The twin beliefs that human beings were inherently depraved, victims of original sin or the fall from grace, and that they could be influenced by the devil or demons anchored the religious view of the world that dominated colonial America. Believers were taught that, to avoid eternal damnation, they must spend their lives fending off devilish enticements, controlling their evil natural urges, and seeking salvation. Fortunately, for sinners, religious doctrine guaranteed that repentance was possible for anyone, anytime prior to death, no matter how despicable their behavior. In this view, capital punishment both hastened a criminal's effort to repent and expiated the community's collective guilt for past crimes.[10]

It was primarily for these religious reasons that condemned offenders typically were not executed for a week or two or, in some cases, several weeks, after conviction.[11] So important was repentance and assuaging the community's collective guilt that the government was willing to forfeit some of the retributive and deterrent effect of the punishment by temporally separating the connection between the crime and the punishment. The delay was also costly to the government because it had to house and feed the condemned person during the interim and it increased the possibility that the condemned person would escape. Another reason for delaying the execution was to provide authorities a chance to publicize the impending execution, allowing spectators to make plans to attend.[12]

A minister would regularly visit the condemned prisoner while the prisoner awaited execution (as could anybody else who wanted to do so). The minister's purpose was to prepare the condemned prisoner for death and the afterlife. If the minister were successful, as he apparently frequently was, the condemned prisoner would repent and accept Christ as his or her savior.[13] Condemned prisoners were usually allowed to attend church on the day of worship just prior to their execution, where they were often the subjects of the sermon.[14] As part of the ritual, condemned prisoners would often rise during the service and confess their guilt and proclaim their newfound faith to the congregation and especially its most influential members. Not only did such proclamations please the ministers who convinced condemned offenders to make them, but they also gave condemned prisoners their best opportunity of receiving executive clemency. (Influential congregants might petition the executive on behalf of the condemned person.) However, having nothing to lose by making the declarations, there was always some question about the condemned person's sincerity.[15] Some pardoned convicted murderers were still branded on the thumb.[16]

The ritual continued on hanging day beginning with the procession to the gallows, followed by a sermon (or sermons), sometimes the singing of hymns, and the condemned prisoner's last words.[17]

The entire ceremony was public and outdoors, and could take several hours to complete.[18] No other public event in colonial America drew larger crowds than executions, and unlike public executions in the nineteenth century that were criticized for being drunken, irreverent, and rowdy events, public executions in colonial America were generally solemn occasions.[19] They were considered a particularly wholesome experience for children.[20] Having an audience many times larger than they normally had, ministers took advantage of public hangings to preach about the consequences of sin and the power of salvation.[21] They also used the occasion to instruct spectators (and others who might later read about it) about the perils of resisting religious and secular authority.[22] The same messages were also frequently conveyed by the condemned prisoner's last words. Ministers often took great pride in their execution day activities. For example, Cotton Mather, the famed Puritan minister, remarked in his diary following his sermon at the simultaneous execution of two condemned women that "'one of the greatest Assemblies, ever known in these parts of the World, was come together' to hear him preach."[23] He also noted his "later satisfaction of seeing his sermon 'immediately printed, greedily bought up, and afterwards reprinted in London.'"[24] The sermon remained a part of the execution ritual until public executions were finally abandoned in the twentieth century, although by 1820, accounts of many executions indicate that the minister's participation was limited to a brief prayer.[25] Allowing the condemned prisoner to make a final statement is a ritual that is still practiced today.

Penitence is no longer an ostensible goal of capital punishment. The reason is that during the colonial period criminals were not viewed as fundamentally different from the rest of the population, as they are more likely to be today. The belief prevalent during the colonial period was that everyone was inherently evil, plagued by the curse of original sin, and that criminals were simply less able to control their primal urges or fend off the devil. Crime was considered a failure of will. Because crime triggered collective guilt, criminal repentance was a common goal. Today, criminals are routinely viewed as lacking the virtue of law-abiding citizens, fundamentally different, and alien to the rest of society. No longer is there a sense of collective guilt when a crime is committed; therefore, penitence is no longer such a major concern. In addition, with the current separation of church and state, religion no longer has the influence in secular affairs as it did during colonial times.[26]

THE DEATH PENALTY IMPOSED

Although Captain Kendall's was the earliest recorded lawful execution in America, his punishment and the circumstances surrounding it differed from most of those that followed. First, his was an execution for a relatively unusual offense (spying/espionage), and second, he was shot instead of hanged.[27] More than 20 years passed before the first murderer, John Billington, was executed in 1630. He was executed in the Massachusetts colony. In between Kendall and Billington, Frank Daniell (1622), Cornish Richard (1624), and Hayle Thomas (1626) were executed for theft, sodomy (buggery/bestiality), and rape, respectively. All four men were hanged in the Virginia colony.[28] Of the 162 colonists executed in the seventeenth century (for which the offense is known – 85 percent of the total), nearly 40 percent were executed for murder, about 25 percent for witchcraft, and nearly 15 percent for piracy. No other crimes accounted for more than 8 percent of all executions. Most of the executed were hanged (88%), 10 percent were shot, an alleged witch was pressed to death, and a convicted arsonist was burned.[29]

Since Kendall's execution in 1608, more than 19,000 executions, performed in the United States under civil (as opposed to military) authority, have been confirmed by M. Watt Espy, the leading historian of capital punishment in the United States. Espy estimated that between 20,000 and 22,500 people have been executed by legal authority since 1608.[30] This estimate does not include the approximately 10,000 people lynched in the nineteenth century.[31] Only 1,553 of the 19,000 executions – less than 10 percent of the total – occurred during this country's first two centuries. Compared to more recent times and using only total executions, colonial Americans appear to have used the death penalty sparingly. More executions were conducted in the 1930s (1,676) than in the entire 1600s (162) and 1700s (1,391).[32] However, if rates of execution are compared, colonial Americans executed many more people per capita than Americans at any other time in their history; in fact, in relation to population, the colonists' use of the death penalty was comparable to Britain's use of the death penalty during the same period.[33] Viewed historically, from 1608 to the present, there has been a long-term decline in the rate of executions.

Nearly all the people executed from the seventeenth century to the present in America have been adult men; only about 3 percent (approximately 569) have been women.[34] Ninety percent of the women were executed under local, as opposed to state, authority, and the majority (87%) was executed prior to 1866.[35] A quarter of all women executed met their fates during the 1600s (42) and 1700s (100).[36] The first woman executed in America was Jane Champion in the Virginia colony in 1632.[37] She was hanged for murdering and concealing the death of her child, who allegedly was fathered by William Gallopin and not her husband.[38] The most women executed in any single year in America were the 14 women hanged for witchcraft in Massachusetts in 1692.[39] The number of women executed declined dramatically with the decline in the prosecution of moral offenses. Adultery was last punished with legal execution in the 1640s, and executions for witchcraft ended in 1692.[40]

About 2 percent (approximately 366) of the people executed have been juveniles, that is, individuals who committed their capital crimes prior to their 18th birthdays.[41] Most of them (69%) were black, and nearly 90 percent of their victims were white.[42] The first juvenile executed in America was 16-year-old servant boy Thomas Graunger. He was executed in 1642 for the crime of bestiality – genital copulation with a mare and a cow.[43] The citizens of the Plymouth Colony first condemned to death and then executed the mare, the cow, the cow's calves, and the young Mr. Graunger, in that order. His prosecution was based on the scriptures, Leviticus 20:15: "And if a man shall lie with a beast, he shall surely be put to death: and ye shall slay the beast."[44] The youngest nonslave executed in the United States was Hannah Ocuish, who was hanged for a murder she committed when she was 12 years old. Ocuish was executed in New London County, Connecticut, on December 20, 1786.[45] The apparently retarded girl was the daughter of an alcoholic Pequot Indian mother and an unknown white father and was notorious "for robbing and harassing local citizens." Ocuish was convicted and sentenced to death for killing the 6-year-old daughter of a prominent white family following a quarrel over strawberries. Reports of her execution indicate that she displayed great fear but remained polite, "thanking the sheriff for his kindnesses to her as she stepped forward to be hanged."[46] The execution of a child as young as 12 was rare, although at the time the Bill of Rights was ratified in 1791, American law only prohibited the execution of children under the age of seven. Besides murder, juveniles in America have been executed for sodomy with animals, arson, robbery, assault, and rape. The U.S. Supreme Court ended the practice of executing juvenile capital offenders on March 1, 2005, when, in the case of *Roper v. Simmons* (543 U.S. 551), it ruled that executing capital offenders under the age of 18 violated the U.S. Constitution's Eighth and Fourteenth Amendments (more about this later).

DEATH PENALTY ABOLITIONISTS

There have probably always been people opposed to capital punishment, but even though their numbers have often been small, they have not been without influence. Quakers, for example, have always opposed capital punishment, and because of their early presence and influence in Pennsylvania, that state, and especially the city of Philadelphia, may be considered the birthplace of the American death penalty abolitionist effort.

Among the first people in the United States to organize others against the death penalty was Dr Benjamin Rush (1747–1813), a Philadelphia physician and signer of the Declaration of Independence.[47] Rush was among the founders (in 1787) of the Philadelphia Society for Alleviating the Miseries of Public Prisons.[48] (In 1833, the Philadelphia society changed its name to the Pennsylvania Prison Society. The same organization exists under the changed name today.) Rush questioned the Biblical support for capital punishment and the belief that it was a general deterrent to crime. He did not believe that the example of executions dissuades people from carrying out crimes they have contemplated committing. To the contrary, he thought that capital punishment might increase crime.[49] This made Rush one of the first Americans to suggest that the death penalty might have a counter-deterrent or "brutalizing effect" (more about this in Chapter 7). Reflecting Enlightenment philosophy, Rush maintained that the social contract was violated whenever the state executed one of its citizens. He was greatly influenced by Cesare Beccaria's argument against the death penalty in *On Crimes and Punishments*, first published in Italy in 1764 and translated and published in New York in 1773.[50] People had opposed the death penalty for centuries, but Beccaria gave abolitionist sentiment an authoritative voice and renewed energy.[51]

In the late eighteenth century, Rush attracted the support of such prominent Americans as Benjamin Franklin and William Bradford, who was Pennsylvania and later U.S. attorney general. Other prominent Americans who opposed the death penalty early on were James Madison; DeWitt Clinton, future governor of New York; and Thomas Jefferson, who opposed the death penalty for all crimes except murder.[52] It was at Franklin's home in Philadelphia that Rush became one of the first Americans to propose confinement in a "House of Reform" as an alternative to capital punishment.[53] According to one commentator, the paper delivered by Rush at Franklin's home was "the first reasoned argument in America favoring the abolition of capital punishment."[54] The Houses of Reform envisioned by Rush would be places where criminals could learn to be law-abiding citizens through moral education. At least in part because of the efforts of Rush and his colleagues, in 1790, the Walnut Street Jail in Philadelphia was converted into the world's first penitentiary – an institution devoted primarily to reform.[55]

Pennsylvania became the first state in legal proceedings to consider degrees of murder based on culpability, largely as a result of Bradford's efforts.[56] Before this change, the death penalty was mandated for anyone convicted of murder (and many other crimes), regardless of circumstance. Like Rush, Bradford did not believe that capital punishment deterred crime, citing the example of horse stealing, which at the time was a capital offense in Virginia and the most frequently committed crime in the state. Because of the penalty's severity, convictions for the crime were hard to obtain.[57] Pressure from abolitionists also caused Pennsylvania in 1794 to repeal the death penalty for all crimes except first-degree murder.[58]

Many people were drawn to Rush's ideas, and petitions to abolish the death penalty were introduced in several state legislatures. Between 1794 and 1798, Virginia and Kentucky joined

Pennsylvania in abolishing the death penalty for all crimes except first-degree murder; New York and New Jersey abolished the penalty for all crimes except murder and treason.[59] At the time, New York and New Jersey had not yet divided murder into degrees, as had the other three states.[60] Because treason against a state rarely occurred and has never been prosecuted at the state level, in practice, murder was the only capital crime in those two states.[61] Virginia and Kentucky, both slave states, confined the reforms to free people; slaves in those states were still subject to a long list of capital crimes.[62] When New Jersey, Virginia, and Kentucky severely restricted the scope of capital punishment, they also appropriated funds for the construction of their first prisons; Pennsylvania and New York had established prisons earlier.[63] Still, half a century would pass before the first state abandoned capital punishment entirely.

A driving force of the abolitionists' efforts was the belief that the death penalty was no longer needed. Although conceding that the death penalty may have been necessary in the more barbaric past, abolitionists argued that society had progressed to a higher stage of civilization rendering the death penalty obsolete. This idea was not peculiar to the United States. It was a sensibility held by death penalty abolitionists throughout Europe and Russia as well.[64] The American abolitionists bolstered their position by pointing out that the newly created prisons could accomplish whatever purposes capital punishment had previously served.[65] Indeed, the prison was crucial to the abolitionist argument because it provided a legitimate alternative to capital punishment.[66] If prisons had not been available, the abolitionist position would have been much weaker. Death penalty proponents, on the other hand, were less sanguine about humanity and the possibility of progress. They were pessimistic about human nature and generally assumed that neither the individual nor society could improve enough to safely eliminate the death penalty from society's arsenal of punishments.[67] They were distrustful of the prison's ability to protect them and did not believe that long-term imprisonment was punishment enough for the most heinous crimes.

It is important to keep in mind that the histories of the death penalty and the death penalty abolitionist movement in the United States are the same in many places because all the significant changes in the practice of capital punishment – culminating in its complete abolition in some jurisdictions – are the result of abolitionist efforts. The efforts created: (1) degrees of murder, which distinguish between murders heinous enough to warrant death and those murders that do not; (2) a reduction in the number of offenses warranting the death penalty (except for the federal government, as described in Chapter 5); (3) the hiding of executions from public view; and (4) a decreased annual number of executions. Although abolition of the death penalty has been their unremitting goal, abolitionists have been far more successful reforming its practice.

THE DEATH PENALTY IN THE NINETEENTH CENTURY

Between 1800 and 1865, use of the death penalty increased significantly. The number of executions rose almost 60 percent over the number from the entire seventeenth and eighteenth centuries (from 1,553 to 2,443). Although after the Civil War, and until 1880, the number of executions dropped by two-thirds (to 825), from 1880 until the turn of the century, the number of executions increased to about a thousand each decade.[68]

In 1812, New Hampshire joined the five states that had limited the death penalty to murder and treason between 1794 and 1798. Ohio followed suit in 1814.[69] However, most of the death penalty legislation during the first quarter of the nineteenth century was in the opposite direction. For example, in 1807, rape, arson, and horse stealing were made capital crimes in Indiana. It added receiving a stolen horse to the list in 1808.[70] New York, which had limited the death penalty to murder and treason in 1796, added residential arson to its list of capital crimes in 1808 and, following a prison riot, arson in a prison in 1817.[71] Pennsylvania legislators refused to abolish the death penalty for all crimes when the governor proposed it in both 1809 and 1811.[72]

The period between 1825 and 1850 was a time of reform in America. The increase in the number of executions, plus general abolitionist sentiment, spurred anti–death penalty activity, resulting in the organization of several abolitionist societies (especially along the eastern seaboard) and the founding of the American Society for the Abolition of Capital Punishment in 1845.[73] Two of America's greatest poets wrote anti–death penalty poems during the 1840s. John Greenleaf Whittier penned, "The Human Sacrifice," in 1843, and Walt Whitman's "The Dialogue: A Brief Statement of the Argument for the Abolition of the Death Penalty" was published in a popular magazine in 1845.[74] By the late 1840s, death penalty opposition became so prevalent in some northern states that it had become difficult to empanel juries in capital cases. Horace Greeley, the influential founder and editor of *The New York Tribune* and ardent death penalty and slavery opponent, delighted in reporting that 80 percent of the people in a capital case jury pool were dismissed because of their opposition to the death penalty.[75] By 1850, death penalty abolitionist societies were working in Tennessee, Ohio, Alabama, Louisiana, Indiana, and Iowa.[76] Two other reform movements – antisaloon and antislavery – also gave a boost to the death penalty abolitionists.

HIDING EXECUTIONS FROM THE PUBLIC

Between 1800 and 1850, American death penalty abolitionists helped change public sentiment about public executions, especially among many northern-state social elites. Whereas in 1800, public hangings were mostly solemn events regularly attended by members of all social classes and touted as having important educational value, by mid-century, members of the upper classes were staying away from them because in their minds they had become tasteless, shocking, rowdy, sometimes dangerous, carnival-like spectacles.[77] This view, however, may have been more a matter of perception than reality, as eyewitness accounts suggested that decorum at public executions had not changed that much.[78] In any event, the elite began to view those who attended executions as contemptible "rabble out for a good time" and concluded that any educational value public hangings once had was being lost on the less respectable crowd.[79] Another problem with public hangings during this period was that attendees were increasingly sympathizing with the condemned prisoners, weakening the position of the state. Indeed, some of those who met their fate on the gallows became folk heroes.[80] Still, another change was increasing acceptance of the belief that public executions were counterproductive because of the violence they caused. Stories were circulated about the violent crimes being committed just before or just after a pubic hanging by attendees of the event.[81]

For these reasons, Connecticut, in 1830, became the first state to ban public executions. Pennsylvania became the second state to do so in 1834.[82] In both states, only a few authorized officials and the relatives of the condemned were allowed to attend. By 1836, New York, New Jersey, Massachusetts, Rhode Island, and New Hampshire had enacted similar policies.[83] By 1860, all northern states and Delaware and Georgia in the South had shifted the site of executions from the public square to an enclosed jail yard controlled by the sheriff and deputies.[84] By 1890, some states had moved executions to inside the jail or a prison building.[85] Some states were so intent on hiding executions from the public that they banned members of the media from attending them, and those people who were allowed to witness executions were expressly forbidden to divulge to anyone what they had seen. State statutes stipulated that anyone who disclosed or published anything about the execution, "beyond the statement of the fact that such convict was on the day in question duly executed according to law," committed a misdemeanor subject to fine or incarceration.[86] These were not trivial changes because executions were among the best-attended public events and continued to be well into the nineteenth century in states that had not banned public executions.[87] The last public execution was held in Galena, Missouri, in 1937.[88]

In states that hid executions from the public, apparently, legislators were willing to sacrifice any general deterrent effect of witnessing executions to escape the "public disorder, rioting, and even murder" that sometimes accompanied the public spectacles, especially the botched executions and last-minute reprieves.[89] This accusation may be a bit overblown, however, because the movement to ban public executions coincided with other developments that were substitutes, albeit less dramatic substitutes, for personally witnessing an execution. The most important arguably was the proliferation of newspapers – the so-called "penny press."[90] In those states that allowed journalists to attend, the newspapers carried vivid descriptions of jail-yard hangings, allowing the public to at least experience the executions vicariously.[91] A second development was a dramatic increase in the number of people who attended capital trials. Observing a capital trial in a way replaced witnessing a public hanging. For people unable to attend the trials, the newspapers carried daily accounts that helped to satisfy their curiosity.[92] The third development was increased public participation in the clemency process. In the eighteenth century, only a few prominent citizens typically signed clemency petitions, but by the middle of the nineteenth century, the process had become more democratic. It was not unusual for governors to receive clemency petitions, both for and against, signed by hundreds or even thousands of people.[93] In sum, although most people were banned from personally witnessing public hangings, early nineteenth century Americans still could participate indirectly in the execution process by reading about it in newspapers, attending or reading about capital trials, and signing petitions for clemency.[94]

FROM MANDATORY TO DISCRETIONARY CAPITAL PUNISHMENT STATUTES

In 1837, Tennessee became the first state to enact a discretionary death penalty statute for murder; Alabama did the same 4 years later, followed by Louisiana 5 years after that.[95] All states before then employed mandatory death penalty statutes that required anyone convicted of a designated capital crime to be sentenced to death. The reason for the change, at least at first and in the South, undoubtedly was to allow all-white juries to take race into account when deciding whether death was the appropriate penalty in a particular case.[96] Between the Civil War and the end of the nineteenth century, at least 20 additional jurisdictions changed their death penalty laws from mandatory to discretionary ones. Illinois was the first northern state to do so in 1867; New York was the last state to make the change in 1963.[97] The reason most northern states switched from mandatory to discretionary death penalty statutes, and another reason for southern states to do so, was to prevent jury nullification, which was becoming an increasing problem.[98] Jury nullification refers to a jury's knowing and deliberate refusal to apply the law because, in this case, a mandatory death sentence was considered contrary to the jury's sense of justice, morality, or fairness.[99] Many jurors during this period were being influenced by new scientific claims that criminality was not freely chosen but rather a product of biological and environmental factors beyond the criminal's control.[100] If this were true, it seemed unfair to hold offenders completely responsible for criminal behavior they could not fully control. Discretionary death penalty statutes allowed juries the option of imposing a sentence of life in prison instead of death.[101] For the same reason, the insanity defense was being increasingly used (some critics contended overused) in capital cases to allow defendants to escape the death penalty without being acquitted outright.[102] This new deterministic view of criminal behavior that was coming from university-based social scientists in the late nineteenth century not only undermined the retributive and deterrent bases for capital punishment but also challenged the legitimacy of the death penalty itself.[103] In the case of retribution, how could it be just to execute a person for a crime he or she did not freely choose to commit? In the case of deterrence, how could people be prevented from committing crime if crime were caused by uncontrollable biological, especially genetic, factors?[104] By 1963, as noted, mandatory capital punishment laws were removed from all penal codes, except for a few rarely committed crimes in a handful of jurisdictions.[105]

This change from mandatory to discretionary death penalty statutes, which introduced unfettered sentencing discretion into the capital-sentencing process, was considered, at the time, a great reform in the administration of capital punishment. Ironically, it was unfettered sentencing discretion that the Supreme Court declared unconstitutional in its *Furman* decision in 1972.[106] (The *Furman* decision is discussed in detail in Chapter 3.)

STATES ABOLISH THE DEATH PENALTY

In 1846, the state of Michigan abolished the death penalty for all crimes, except treason, and replaced the penalty with life imprisonment. The law took effect the next year, making Michigan, for all intents and purposes, the first English-speaking jurisdiction in the world to abolish capital punishment.[107] Sociology professor John Galliher and his colleagues relate that the mostly puritan–Yankee colonists and later citizens of Michigan have always had an aversion to capital punishment and that aversion contributed to the state's eventual abolition of the death penalty.[108] Prior to abolition, what became the state of Michigan only conducted 11 executions. Eight of the 11 executions occurred in the 1770s under colonial rule, the other three while Michigan was a U.S. territory. Two of the latter three executed were Native Americans, and both were executed in 1821. The other, Stephen Simmons, was executed in 1830, 7 years before Michigan gained statehood. Simmons in a drunken rage killed his wife in Detroit. A public outcry against the death penalty followed Simmons's execution, while the execution of the Native Americans drew little interest. Simmons, incidentally, is the only non–Native American ever executed in Michigan under state or territorial authority.[109] Michigan has resisted the death penalty despite high murder rates and large minority and immigrant populations.[110]

The first state to outlaw the death penalty for all crimes, including treason, was Rhode Island, in 1852; Wisconsin was the second state to do so a year later.[111] Although no other states abolished the death penalty during this period, by 1860, no northern state punished by death any crime except for murder and treason. Furthermore, those states that had divided the crime of murder into degrees limited the death penalty to first-degree murders.[112] The last person executed for the crime of rape in the northern states was probably Horace Carter, a white man hanged in Massachusetts in 1825.[113]

Opponents of the death penalty, who initially benefited from general abolitionist sentiment, saw concern with capital punishment wane as the Civil War approached, and attention shifted to the growing antislavery movement.[114]

Not until well after the Civil War did Iowa, in 1872, and Maine, in 1876, become the next states to abolish the death penalty. Legislatures in both states reversed themselves, however, and reinstated the death penalty in 1878, in Iowa, and in 1883, in Maine. Maine reversed itself again in 1887 and abolished capital punishment and, to date, has not reinstated it.[115] Colorado abandoned capital punishment in 1897, but the move apparently was unpopular with many of its citizens. At least partially in response to three lynchings of blacks by whites within 2 years of abolition, the death penalty was restored in 1901.[116]

FROM LOCALLY AUTHORIZED TO STATE-AUTHORIZED EXECUTIONS

A major change took place in the legal jurisdiction of executions during the time of the Civil War. Before the war, all executions were conducted locally – generally in the jurisdiction in which the crime was committed – but on January 20, 1864, Sandy Kavanagh was executed at the Vermont State Prison. He was the first person executed under state, as opposed to local, authority.

This shift in jurisdiction was not immediately adopted by other states. After Kavanagh, there were only about two state-authorized or federally authorized executions per year well into the 1890s; the rest were locally authorized.[117] This pattern shifted dramatically during the next 30 years. In the 1890s, about 90 percent of executions were imposed under local authority, but by the 1920s, about 90 percent were imposed under state authority.[118] By 1905, 23 states, none of them in the South, imposed executions under state authority; eight southern states did so between 1906 and 1925.[119] However, Louisiana and Mississippi continued to carry out executions at the local level into the 1950s.[120] Today, all executions are imposed under state authority, except those conducted in Delaware and Montana and by the federal government and the military.

THE DEATH PENALTY IN THE FIRST HALF OF THE TWENTIETH CENTURY

As the United States entered the twentieth century, a new age of reform began. It was called the "Progressive Period."[121] Death penalty abolitionists benefited from the critical examination of American society that characterized the era and achieved a series of successes, albeit in most cases, temporary ones.[122]

STATES ABOLISH AND REINSTATE THE DEATH PENALTY

During the first two decades of the twentieth century, six states outlawed capital punishment entirely (Kansas, 1907; Minnesota, 1911; Washington, 1913; Oregon, 1914; South Dakota, 1915; Missouri, 1917), and three states (Tennessee, 1915; North Dakota, 1915; Arizona, 1916) limited the death penalty to only a few rarely committed crimes, such as treason or the first-degree murder of a law enforcement official or prison employee. Tennessee also retained capital punishment for rape.[123] In addition, 17 other states nearly abolished the death penalty or at least seriously considered abolition, some of them several times. They included California, Connecticut, Colorado, Illinois, Indiana, Massachusetts, Nebraska, New Hampshire, New Jersey, New York, North Carolina, Ohio, Pennsylvania, Utah, Vermont, Virginia, and West Virginia.[124] The momentum, however, failed to last. By 1920, five of the states that had abolished the death penalty earlier had reinstated it (Arizona, 1918; Missouri, 1919; Tennessee, 1919; Washington, 1919; Oregon, 1920).[125]

The Progressive era death penalty abolition movement in eight of the abolition states has been attributed to the support of the state's governor, the state's press, or both during a time of economic prosperity.[126] Some of the abolition-state governors were affiliated with the Anti-Capital Punishment Society of America.[127] On the other hand, the press apparently played little role in the states that restored the death penalty other than by publicizing taunts made by nonrepentant convicted murderers. In each of the states that reinstated the death penalty, a convicted murderer acknowledged that he might not have killed had there been a death penalty. After being sentenced to life imprisonment, others bragged that the state would have to feed and care for them the rest of their lives.[128] These types of remarks angered many citizens who began pushing for the death penalty's reinstatement. The movement to reestablish the death penalty was also a function of the reluctance of some states to abolish the death penalty in the first place. In Oregon and Arizona, for example, legislatures passed death penalty abolition bills by very small margins.[129] Some states considered abolition an experiment, which many people thought was failing.[130] Lynching played a major role in at least four states. State officials began to believe that vigilante violence was a reaction to the death penalty's abolition and that without capital punishment lynchings were bound to occur. In those states, many state officials considered the death penalty the lesser of two evils.[131] Another factor that has been used to explain the death penalty's reinstatement during this period is the post–World War I economic depression. During this time there were frequent complaints about job shortages and the threat of unemployed workers.[132] Punitive attitudes toward criminals tend to increase during periods of economic hardship.[133] The economic recession also exacerbated the fear of minorities. Three of the states that restored the death penalty (Tennessee, Arizona, and Missouri) had the largest minority populations, while two of the states that did not reinstate the death penalty (South Dakota and Minnesota) had the smallest nonwhite populations.[134]

In the South, the white establishment undoubtedly used the death penalty to terrify and subdue the black population. As the seventeenth century English philosopher John Locke noted early on, political power is "a right of making laws with penalties of death."[135] Most of the capital crimes in the southern states at the beginning of the Civil War remained capital crimes for nearly a century, long after they had been removed from the penal codes of the northern states.[136] For example, as of 1954, rape was a capital crime in 18 states, 16 of them in the South; robbery was a capital crime in nine states, eight of them in the South; arson was a capital crime in five states, all of them in the South; and burglary was a capital crime in four states, again all of them in the South.[137] Persons executed for those crimes were overwhelmingly black. For example, between 1870 and 1950, 701 of the 771 people (whose race was known) executed for rape were black, 31 of the 35 executed for robbery were black, and 18 of the 21 executed for burglary were black.[138] Although the racial disparity was smaller for those executed for murder, blacks still outnumbered whites.[139] Also, augmenting capital punishment in the South was lynching, which reached its peak in the late nineteenth and early twentieth centuries.[140] Lynch mobs killed at least 4,743 people, more than 90 percent of the lynchings occurred in the South, and African Americans comprised three-quarters of the people lynched.[141] At its zenith, lynchings outnumbered executions: 82 to 6 during the 1870s and 92 to 40 during the 1890s.[142] Since the Civil War, the nationwide legal execution rate did not rise higher than the lynching rate until the first decade of the twentieth century.[143] The last public mass lynching in the United States occurred in northeast Georgia in 1946.[144] The U.S. Congress never passed a law against lynching.[145] A recent study suggests that "states with the largest black populations and the most substantial inclinations to use vigilante violence [lynching] in the past now are more likely to impose the death penalty."[146]

Finally, it has been argued that the reinstatement of capital punishment during this period was at least partly the result of a media-inspired panic about the threat of revolution.[147] The Russian Revolution occurred in 1917, the same year the United States entered World War I. Just before the war, the United States had experienced intense class conflict as socialists, and especially the IWW or Industrial Workers of the World ("Wobblies") increased in number and mounted the first serious challenge to capitalist dominance.[148] Within this frenzied atmosphere, a crime in 1920 involving two foreign anarchists received unprecedented worldwide media coverage. Nicola Sacco and Bartolomeo Vanzetti maintained their innocence but nevertheless were convicted of a robbery and murder. They were electrocuted in 1927. Surrounding circumstances and the trial record suggest that Sacco and Vanzetti were indeed innocent and that they were sentenced to death because they were anarchists and foreigners.[149] According to at least one observer, the threat of the death penalty has been used to terrify and subdue dissidents,[150] and this may have been a motivating factor in the case against Sacco and Vanzetti.

The death penalty abolitionist movement fell on hard times during Prohibition and the Great Depression (roughly 1920–1940). Only the determined efforts of members of the American League to Abolish Capital Punishment, founded in 1925, and a few high-profile abolitionists, such as Attorney Clarence Darrow, newspaper publisher William Randolph Hearst, industrialist Henry Ford, and Lewis E. Lawes, the abolitionist warden of New York's Sing Sing State Prison, kept the movement alive.[151] Death penalty abolitionists also received unexpected support from Franklin D. Roosevelt, who, during his first term as president, publicly expressed his opposition to capital punishment.[152] Despite the efforts of determined abolitionists, more capital offenders were executed during the 1930s than in any other decade in American history; the average was 167 executions per year.[153] The most executions in any single year occurred in 1935, when 199 offenders were put to death.[154] This was a dramatic reversal from earlier in the century when the number of executions fell from 161 in 1912 to 65 in 1919. The 65 executions in 1919 were the fewest in 50 years.[155] Furthermore, of the 10 states that abolished capital punishment for all crimes after 1850, only three – Minnesota, Maine, and Wisconsin – had not restored the death penalty entering the 1950s.[156] No state abolished the death penalty between 1918 and 1957. In contrast, after World War II, most of the advanced western European countries abolished the death penalty or severely restricted its use. Great Britain did not join them until 1969.[157]

THE DEATH PENALTY FROM 1950 TO THE MID-1960s

Beginning in the 1950s, partly as a result of the lingering horrors of World War II and the movement by many allied nations either to abolish the death penalty or to restrict its use, the number of executions in the United States began to drop precipitously – from 1,289 in the 1940s to 715 during the 1950s[158] – and there were only 191 executions from 1960 through 1976.[159] In its 1967 report, the

National Crime Commission observed that the decline in executions was due to the loss of will on the part of those charged with administering the death penalty.[160] The American abolitionist movement was able to claim some modest achievements in the late 1950s. Besides resurrecting debate in some state legislatures, the (then) territories of Alaska and Hawaii abolished the death penalty in 1957.[161] Delaware did the same in 1958, only to reinstate it 3 years later in 1961.[162] However, the degree to which these victories can be attributed directly to the efforts of death penalty abolitionist organizations themselves is questionable.[163] To be sure, abolitionists such as Sara Ehrmann, Donal MacNamara, Hugo Bedau, and Doug Lyons worked tirelessly for the cause during this period, but they did so more as individuals than members of strong and effective death penalty organizations.[164] The fact is that death penalty abolitionist organizations during this period and, for that matter, throughout history have been largely impotent primarily because of a lack of funding. It is hard to raise money for a cause that benefits one of the most despised groups in society whose media images are overwhelmingly negative.[165] The drive to abolish the death penalty in the 1960s was spearheaded by the American Civil Liberties Union and, especially, the NAACP Legal Defense and Educational Fund (LDF), neither of which was a death penalty abolitionist organization. Thus, Haines attributes death penalty abolitionism during this period more to the civil rights movement (because of the lead of LDF attorneys) than to prior death penalty abolitionist efforts.[166] (More about the role of the LDF will be discussed later.) Also during the 1950s, because of the extraordinary media attention devoted to them, two cases in particular influenced the ways in which many Americans viewed capital punishment. What is interesting is that the two cases had very different effects. The *Rosenberg* case, involving alleged treason, seemed to influence the public toward favoring capital punishment. The *Chessman* case, on the other hand, had the opposite and, for the time, the more sustained effect.

THE CASE OF ETHEL AND JULIUS ROSENBERG

Ethel and Julius Rosenberg were prosecuted for espionage during the summer of 1950 in an atmosphere of anti-Communist hysteria,[167] allegedly having given atomic bomb secrets to Soviet agents. Their guilt, and especially the evidence against them, continues to be the subject of much debate. There was a worldwide campaign of protest following their convictions. Among the notables who championed their cause were Albert Einstein, Jean-Paul Sartre, Pablo Picasso, and the sister of Bartolomeo Vanzetti. Appeals to both President Truman, just before he left office in 1953, and President Eisenhower were turned down. At the last moment, Supreme Court Justice Douglas granted a stay of execution, and Chief Justice Vinson sent out special jets to return the vacationing justices to Washington. The full court canceled Douglas's stay, and the Rosenbergs were executed on June 19, 1953.

The paradox of the Rosenberg executions is reflected in American death penalty opinion of 1953. Between the first and fifth of November 1953, Gallup queried the public about the death penalty for the first time in 16 years.[168] Results of the poll indicated that 70 percent of Americans favored the death penalty, 29 percent opposed it, and 1 percent had no opinion. The 70 percent figure was the highest level of support for the death penalty in the United States to that date, and it remained the highest level until the 1980s. To what extent the Rosenberg executions influenced that opinion can only be speculated. What seems clear is that the executions did not generate immediate and overwhelming sympathy for the Rosenbergs or have a dampening effect on American death penalty opinion.

THE CASE OF CARYL CHESSMAN

The decade-long case of Caryl Chessman began in 1948 when, at age 26, he was convicted on 17 counts, including robbery, kidnapping, sexual abuses, and attempted rape. Under California's "Little Lindbergh" law, capital punishment was mandatory for kidnapping "with bodily harm."[169] Chessman was "self-taught in law" and defended himself. He admitted committing many crimes, but he denied guilt in the kidnappings for which he was sentenced to death.[170]

Chessman had an unusually long stay on death row due to the death penalty postconviction process. A relatively large segment of the public found this well-publicized experience with capital punishment objectionable and turned against the death penalty.

For purposes of this account, Chessman's story begins on May 3, 1954, a day that held both good and bad news for him. The good news was that his book, *Cell 2544, Death Row*, was published. The book was the first of four and would receive critical acclaim, become a best seller (more than 500,000 copies sold), be translated into many languages, and bring to Chessman's situation unprecedented worldwide attention. The bad news was that California Governor Goodwin J. Knight denied Chessman a reprieve from his execution, scheduled for May 14.[171] The day before he was scheduled to die in San Quentin's gas chamber, however, Chessman won a writ of habeas corpus "on grounds that a false transcript of his first trial had been presented to an appeals court."[172] A writ of habeas corpus claims that a federal constitutional right has been violated and, thus, the claimant is being held illegally.[173] The writ was subsequently denied, and Chessman was rescheduled to die on July 30. The day before this execution, to allow the U.S. Supreme Court the opportunity to act on Chessman's petition for a writ of review, California Supreme Court Justice Jesse W. Carter granted him a stay.

On March 3, 1955, San Quentin Warden Harley O. Teets impounded the manuscript of Chessman's second prison-written book, *Trial by Ordeal*. Teets charged that Chessman violated regulations when he attempted to send the book out of the prison without official clearance.[174] The book nevertheless was published by Prentice-Hall on July 11.[175] Criminologist Robert Johnson relates that the book was a study of "the media distortion of capital offenders, particularly of the type likely to enrage decent citizens."[176] In the book, Chessman "summarized the public image of the condemned fostered by sensationalist journalism."[177] Chessman had been given the moniker the "Red Light Bandit" because he allegedly "posed as a police officer while robbing men and raping women in lovers' lanes in Los Angeles."[178] Chessman denied he was the "Red Light Bandit."[179]

The Supreme Court granted Chessman a new hearing in San Francisco's U.S. District Court on October 17, 1955. The court ruled five to three that "Chessman's plea that his 1948 trial records had been 'fraudulently prepared' should not have been summarily dismissed."[180] Nearly a year later, on November 22, 1956, to prevent the setting of an execution date and to allow Chessman to make another appeal to the U.S. Supreme Court, the U.S. Circuit Court of Appeals in San Francisco granted Chessman a stay of mandate.[181]

State authorities had banned Chessman's writing for publication.[182] When a manuscript of his third book, *The Face of Justice*, was found in his cell on February 14, 1957, Chessman, then 35, was placed in solitary confinement. Another copy of the manuscript, however, was smuggled out of prison to his literary agent.

On April 8, 1957, the Supreme Court granted Chessman another hearing, to be held on May 13. This hearing would decide whether Chessman had been denied due process of law, as guaranteed by the Fourteenth Amendment, on the issue of his alleged fraudulent trial transcript. Then, on June 10, the U.S. Supreme Court granted him another stay of execution so that a lower court could review Chessman's lack of representation by an attorney at a federal district court hearing the previous year.[183] (That was the hearing to determine whether the state court records of his first trial were fraudulent.) Superior Judge Walter R. Evans ruled in Los Angeles on February 28, 1958, that the record of Chessman's original trial was "adequate for purposes of appeal," and Chessman lost his chance for a new trial on this issue.[184]

By the time Chessman lost another appeal to the U.S. Supreme Court for release on a writ of habeas corpus on April 6, 1959, his execution had been stayed six times, and he was running out of legal maneuvers.[185] On July 7, the California Supreme Court upheld the 11-year-old death verdict by denying his latest appeal for a rehearing, and on August 10, Chessman was ordered to die on October 23.[186] California Governor Edmund G. Brown rejected Chessman's plea for clemency 4 days before the scheduled execution.

It looked like the end of the line for Chessman, but he had not yet run out of luck. Two days before his execution, the U.S. Supreme Court granted his seventh stay to allow him to file a petition challenging the California Supreme Court's decision on July 7 to affirm his conviction.[187] On December 14, though, the Supreme Court, by an eight to zero vote, rejected that petition. The Court also dismissed a November 30 appeal for a new trial filed by psychiatrist Karl Menninger, writer Aldous Huxley, and 21 others. In Los Angeles, on December 21, Judge Herbert V. Walker ordered Chessman to be executed on February 19, 1960. It was Chessman's eighth execution order.[188]

On February 19, just 10 hours before Chessman was to die, Governor Brown gave Chessman, then 38, a 60-day reprieve. Brown's reasons for granting an eighth stay in 12 years were twofold. First, Brown had received a telegram from Assistant Secretary of State Roy R. Rubottom Jr. relaying a Uruguayan government warning that, if Chessman were executed, President Eisenhower might encounter hostile demonstrations there during his upcoming visit. Second, as a death penalty opponent, Brown wanted the state legislature to consider abolishing capital punishment in California.[189]

Brown's action was decried. Senator Clair Engle and others protested that "justice to an individual should be based on the facts of the case and 'not rest on international reaction.'" But throughout the United States, Latin America, and western Europe, opponents of the death penalty continued to protest on Chessman's behalf, and the Vatican newspaper, *L'Osservatore Romano*, pleaded for Chessman's life – but to no avail. Appeals for a stay of execution were rejected by U.S. Supreme Court Justice Hugo L. Black on February 13, the U.S. Circuit Court of Appeals in San Francisco on February 15, and the California Supreme Court on February 17 and 18.[190] Chessman was finally executed in the gas chamber at San Quentin on May 2, 1960.[191] The same year, Chessman's fourth book was published. *The Kid Was a Killer* was Chessman's only work of fiction.

Denying his guilt to the end, Chessman won the support of death penalty opponents universally. Pleas to save his life were made not only by Menninger and Huxley, but also by Albert Schweitzer, Pablo Casals, Brigitte Bardot, and thousands of others.[192] The execution cost California around half a million dollars, and it prompted anti–United States demonstrations throughout the world.[193] Additionally, in each of Gallup's death penalty polls following Chessman's execution, the percentage of

Americans in favor of the penalty declined (and the percentage opposed increased) until, in 1966, public support for capital punishment reached an all-time low of 42 percent.[194] In addition to the case of Caryl Chessman, the civil rights movements of the 1960s also helped galvanize abolitionist sentiment as protests against the misuse of government authority continued to grow. Four states abolished the death penalty (Michigan, in 1963, for treason; Oregon, 1964; Iowa, 1965; and West Virginia, 1965), and two states (New York, 1965, and Vermont, 1965) sharply reduced the number of death-eligible crimes.[195] In 1965 alone, legislatures in 20 states debated bills to abolish the death penalty.[196]

CONCLUSION

Despite the long history of the American death penalty abolitionist movement, a serious challenge to the death penalty's constitutionality did not materialize until the late 1960s. Until then, the death penalty, for most Americans, was an abstract concept made real only by the occasional well-publicized execution of a particularly heinous offender. Rarely did the penalty or the process touch the lives of ordinary Americans. Still, the efforts of death penalty abolitionists did result in many reforms of the death penalty's administration.

Prior to the late 1960s, the U.S. Supreme Court was unwilling to meddle in a state's use of the sanction. Even when a state abrogated fundamental constitutional principles in its administration of the death penalty, the Court was reluctant to interfere. As a result, states were able to employ the death penalty with virtually no outside regulation. Chapter 2 examines the Supreme Court's role in the death penalty during the premodern period, Chapter 3 describes the legal challenge to the death penalty beginning in the 1960s, and Chapter 4 addresses the Supreme Court's willingness to assume the role of ultimate regulator in the death penalty's administration.

DISCUSSION QUESTIONS

1. What general lessons can be learned from the history of the death penalty in the United States?
2. Should religion play as large a role in capital punishment as it did in colonial America? Why or why not?
3. Should the death penalty be reserved primarily for adult men? Why or why not?
4. Why do people oppose capital punishment? How could they be so wrong?
5. Why do people support capital punishment? How could they be so wrong?
6. Should the public be allowed to view executions? Should executions be televised? Why or why not?
7. Which are fairer: mandatory or discretionary death penalty laws? Why?
8. Should executions be carried out in the local jurisdictions where capital defendants are convicted and sentenced or at some other location in the state? Defend your answer.
9. Is the threat of the death penalty in the United States used to terrify and subdue political dissidents? Explain.
10. Why is the United States the only western industrialized nation to routinely employ capital punishment?
11. What can be learned from the cases of Ethel and Julius Rosenberg and Caryl Chessman?

Notes

1. Espy and Smykla (1987). Another source claims that Kendall was shot for mutiny, see Allen and Clubb (2008, p. 9, fn. 1).
2. Bedau (1982, p. 7) and Vila and Morris (1997, pp. 8–9).
3. Exodus 21.12; Numbers 35.13, 14, 30, 31 (cited in Vila and Morris, 1997, p. 8).
4. Bedau (1982, p. 7).
5. Ibid.
6. Bedau (1982, p. 6), Thompson (1975, pp. 22–23), and Vila and Morris (1997, p. 8); for the 200 number, see Banner (2002, p. 7).
7. Banner (2002, pp. 6–7).
8. Filler (1967, p. 105).
9. See, for example, Banner (2002).
10. Ibid., pp. 14–15.
11. Ibid., p. 17.
12. Ibid.
13. Ibid., pp. 18–19.
14. Ibid., p. 19.
15. Ibid., pp. 19–20.
16. Steelwater (2003, p. 53).
17. Ibid., p. 24.
18. Ibid.
19. Ibid., pp. 25 and 27.
20. Ibid., p. 28.
21. Ibid., pp. 33–34.
22. Ibid., pp. 34–35.
23. Ibid., p. 40.
24. Ibid.
25. Banner (2002, p. 35) and Steelwater (2003, p. 47).
26. Banner (2002, pp. 22–23).
27. Espy and Smykla (1987).
28. Ibid.
29. Ibid. Allen and Clubb (2008, p. 40) claimed that only a little more than 1% of the executions in colonial America were for witchcraft, and most of them occurred in Salem.
30. Updated from personal correspondence.
31. Bedau (1982, p. 3).
32. Schneider and Smykla (1991, p. 6, Table 1.1).
33. See Allen and Clubb (2008, pp. 16–19 and 28).
34. Streib (2006).
35. Schneider and Smykla (1991, p. 14).
36. Ibid., Table 1.7.
37. Ibid., p. 14.
38. Schwarz (1999).
39. Streib (2002).
40. Steelwater (2003, p. 41).
41. Streib (2005).
42. Streib (1989, p. 39).

43. Streib (1987, p. 73).
44. Ibid.
45. Ibid.
46. Streib (1987, pp. 74–75).
47. Bedau (1982, p. 13).
48. Filler (1967).
49. Gorecki (1983, p. 85); also see Filler (1967, p. 106).
50. Filler (1967, p. 105); but see Kania (1999) for a different view of the social contract.
51. Ancel (1967, pp. 5–6).
52. Banner (2002, p. 88).
53. Bedau (1982, p. 13) and Ralph (1996, p. 413).
54. Filler (1967, p. 106).
55. See Bedau (1982) and Grimes (1996, p. 494).
56. Filler (1967, p. 107) and Paternoster (1991, p. 6).
57. Filler (1967, pp. 106–107).
58. Banner (2002, p. 98), Bedau (1982, p. 4), Bowers (1984, p. 7), and Hood (2002, p. 9).
59. Banner (2002, p. 98).
60. Ibid., pp. 98–99.
61. Ibid., p. 99; Steelwater (2003, p. 65).
62. Banner (2002, p. 99).
63. Ibid.
64. Ibid., pp. 107–108.
65. Ibid., pp. 100–101.
66. Ibid., p. 110.
67. Ibid., pp. 106–107.
68. Schneider and Smykla (1991, p. 6, Table 1.1).
69. Banner (2002, p. 131).
70. Ibid.
71. Ibid.
72. Ibid.
73. Bedau (1982, p. 21).
74. Atwell (2004, p. 3).
75. Haney (2005, pp. 101–102) and Vila and Morris (1997, pp. 62–65). Apparently, Greeley and other abolitionists did not consider what effect these dismissals would have on the verdicts of the jurors who remained.
76. Filler (1967, p. 112).
77. Banner (2002, p. 146).
78. Ibid., pp. 152–153.
79. Ibid.
80. Ibid., p. 148.
81. Ibid., p. 149.
82. Banner (2002, p. 154). There is some discrepancy about the first state to ban public executions; Banner cites Connecticut in 1830, while Bowers (1984, p. 8) and Filler (1967, p. 109) cite Pennsylvania in 1834.
83. Banner (2002, p. 154).
84. Ibid., pp. 146 and 154.
85. See, for example, *Holden v. Minnesota*, 137 U.S. 483 (1890).

86. See, for example, *In re Medley* [Colorado], 134 U.S. 160 (1890); *Holden v. Minnesota*, 137 U.S. 483 (1890).
87. Banner (2002, p. 25).
88. Bedau (1982, p. 13). Some controversy surrounds this issue. Author Perry Ryan contends that the last public execution took place not in Galena, Missouri, in 1937 but in Owensboro, Kentucky, in 1936. Perry reasons that because a stockade was built around the scaffold in Galena, Missouri, to keep children out and adults had to get tickets from the sheriff (they were free to any adult who wanted one), the execution in Galena, Missouri, was not truly a public one. Banner (2002, p. 156) cites Perry and writes that the last person publicly executed in the United States was Rainey Bethea in Owensboro, Kentucky, in 1936. Criminologist Robert Johnson (1990, p. 19) claims that there were public executions in Mississippi in the 1940s. Former Mississippi Prison Warden Don Cabana corroborates Johnson's claim that the last public execution in Mississippi was held in the late 1940s. Cabana adds that the condemned was strapped into the portable electric chair set up in the Jackson County courthouse. Anyone who could get into the courtroom could view the execution (personal communication, September 29, 2005).
89. Bowers (1984) and Denno (1994, p. 564).
90. Banner (2002, p. 162).
91. Ibid.
92. Ibid., pp. 163–164.
93. Ibid., pp. 164–165.
94. Ibid., p. 166.
95. Ibid., pp. 214–215, see note 14.
96. Ibid, p. 215.
97. Ibid.
98. Ibid.
99. Garner (2000, p. 694).
100. Banner (2002, p. 208).
101. Ibid., p. 214.
102. Ibid.
103. Ibid., pp. 208–211.
104. Ibid., p. 217.
105. Ibid. and Acker and Lanier (1998).
106. Acker and Lanier (1998, p. 85).
107. Bedau (1982, p. 21), Bowers (1984, p. 9), and Filler (1967, p. 113).
108. Galliher, Koch, Keys, and Guess (2002, p. 11).
109. Ibid., pp. 11–12.
110. Ibid., pp. 12–14.
111. Bedau (1982), Bowers (1984), and Galliher et al. (2002); Hood (2002, p. 9) writes that Rhode Island retained the death penalty for murder of a prison guard by a convict serving a life sentence.
112. Banner (2002, p. 131).
113. Ibid., p. 132, and Gorecki (1983, p. 86).
114. Bowers (1984, p. 10).
115. Ibid.
116. Bedau (1982, p. 24).
117. Bowers (1984, pp. 43 and 50).
118. Ibid., pp. 54–55.
119. Allen and Clubb (2008, p. 75).
120. Ibid.

121. Zinn (1990, p. 341).
122. For one of the most comprehensive examinations of the history of capital punishment in a single state (Texas, 1923–1990), see Marquart, Ekland-Olson, and Sorensen (1994).
123. Bedau (1982, p. 23, Table 1–2) and Bowers (1984, p. 10).
124. Banner (2002, pp. 222–223).
125. Bedau (1982, p. 23, Table 1–2) and Bowers (1984, p. 10).
126. Galliher, Ray, and Cook (1992, p. 559).
127. Ibid.
128. Ibid., p. 574.
129. Ibid.
130. Ibid.
131. Ibid.
132. Ibid., p. 575.
133. See Rothman (1980) and Rusche and Kirchheimer (1968).
134. Galliher et al. (1992).
135. Locke (1988, p. 268).
136. Banner (2002, p. 228).
137. Ibid., pp. 228–229.
138. Ibid., p. 230.
139. Ibid.
140. Ibid.
141. Bright (2006, p. 215); also see Allen and Clubb (2008, p. 81).
142. Banner (2002, p. 230).
143. Steelwater (2003, p. 196).
144. Haines (2006).
145. Steelwater (2003, p. 185).
146. Jacobs, Carmichael, and Kent (2005, p. 671).
147. See, for example, Filler (1967, p. 119) and Galliher et al. (1992).
148. Zinn (1990, p. 350).
149. Ibid., p. 367.
150. Ancel (1967, pp. 13–14).
151. See Banner (2002, p. 224), Filler (1967, pp. 119–120), and Haines (1996, pp. 10–11).
152. Banner (2002, p. 224).
153. Gorecki (1983, p. 92) and Schneider and Smykla (1991, p. 7).
154. Paternoster (1991, p. 10, Table 1–2).
155. Banner (2002, p. 223).
156. See Bedau (1982).
157. Zimring and Hawkins (1986, p. 12).
158. Schneider and Smykla (1991, p. 6, Table 1–1).
159. Bedau (1982, p. 25, Table 1–3); Banner (2002, p. 208) notes that the rate of executions had been declining since the 1880s.
160. Cited in Lain (2007a, p. 13, n. 42).
161. Bedau (1982, p. 23, Table 1–2) and Bowers (1984, p. 10).
162. Ibid.
163. Haines (1996, p. 42).
164. Ibid.
165. Ibid., p. 43.

166. Ibid.
167. See Zinn (1990, pp. 424–426).
168. See Bohm (1991, p. 116, Table 8.1).
169. Facts on File, hereafter abbreviated FOF (1961, p. 156).
170. FOF (ibid.; 1955, p. 152).
171. Ibid.
172. FOF (1955, p. 168).
173. Bohm and Haley (1997, p. 234).
174. FOF (1956, p. 80).
175. FOF (1955, p. 243).
176. Johnson (1989, p. 23).
177. Ibid.
178. Duffy (1962, p. 145).
179. Ibid., p. 146.
180. FOF (1956, p. 345).
181. FOF (1957, p. 400).
182. FOF (1958, p. 60).
183. Ibid., p. 192.
184. FOF (1959, p. 76).
185. FOF (1960, p. 123).
186. Ibid., p. 308.
187. Ibid., p. 348.
188. Ibid., p. 439.
189. Ibid., p. 68.
190. Ibid.
191. FOF (1961, p. 156).
192. Ibid.
193. On the cost of the execution, see Bedau (1982, p. 193, fn. 21); on the demonstrations, see FOF, ibid.
194. See Bohm (1991).
195. Bedau (1982, p. 23, Table 1–2).
196. Banner (2002, p. 244).

Capital punishment and the Supreme Court: The premodern period

JUDICIAL REVIEW AND THE REGULATION OF CAPITAL PUNISHMENT

For more than 150 years, the U.S. Supreme Court ("the Court") has exercised its responsibility to regulate capital punishment in the United States and its territories. The Court's authority is given in the U.S. Constitution, Article III, Section 1, and the Judiciary Act of September 24, 1789. Article III, Section 1, of the Constitution states, "The judicial Power of the United States, shall be vested in one supreme court, and in such inferior Courts as the Congress may from time to time ordain and establish." The Court was officially organized on February 2, 1790, and handed down its first opinion in 1792.[1]

The Court's appellate jurisdiction in death penalty cases originally derived from its power of judicial review. Judicial review refers to "a court's power to review the actions of other branches or levels of government; esp., the courts' power to invalidate legislative and executive actions as being unconstitutional."[2] Although the U.S. Constitution does not provide for it, there was precedent for judicial review before the Constitution was adopted. For example, prior to 1789, state courts had ruled against legislation that conflicted with state constitutions.[3] Moreover, many of the founding fathers expected the Court to engage in judicial review. For instance, in the "Federalist Papers," both Alexander Hamilton and James Madison emphasized its importance. Hamilton wrote, "Through the practice of judicial review the Court ensured that the will of the whole people, as expressed in their Constitution, would be supreme over the will of a legislature, whose statutes might express only the temporary will of part of the people."[4] Madison averred, "Constitutional interpretation must be left to the reasoned judgment of independent judges rather than to the tumult and conflict of the political process."[5] He added, "If every constitutional question were to be decided by public political bargaining, the Constitution would be reduced to a battleground of competing factions, political passion and partisan spirit."[6] The Court's power of judicial review was formally confirmed in 1803, when Chief Justice John Marshall invoked it in *Marbury v. Madison* (5 U.S. 137). Marshall argued, "The Supreme Court's responsibility to overturn unconstitutional legislation was a necessary consequence of its sworn duty to uphold the Constitution. That oath could not be fulfilled any other way."[7] He famously asserted, "It is emphatically the province of the judicial department to say what the law is."[8]

The Court received additional review authority with the ratification of the Fourteenth Amendment in 1868. In part, the amendment reads as follows: "No State shall make or enforce any law which shall abridge the privileges or immunities of citizens of the United States, nor shall any State deprive any person of life, liberty, or property, without due process of law; nor deny to any person within its jurisdiction the equal protection of the laws." The main purpose of this "Civil War Amendment" was to extend all the rights of citizenship to African Americans. Whether the Fourteenth Amendment extended the procedural safeguards described in the Bill of Rights to people charged with crimes at the state level was debatable. Before the passage of the amendment, the Bill of Rights applied only to people charged with federal crimes; individual states were not bound by its requirements. It was not until the 1960s that the Court began to selectively incorporate most of the procedural safeguards contained in the Bill of Rights and apply them to the states. Before then, many Supreme Court justices, perhaps a majority of them, did not believe that the Fourteenth Amendment applied the Bill of Rights to the states. There are at least three explanations for this state of affairs.[9] First, there is little evidence that supporters of the Fourteenth Amendment intended it to incorporate the Bill of Rights. Second, by 1937, a series of court decisions had established the precedent that the due process clause of the Fourteenth Amendment did not require states to follow trial procedures mandated at the federal level by provisions in the Bill of Rights. The Court had held that due process was not violated if procedures followed in state courts were otherwise fair. Third, there was the states' rights issue. Because the administration of justice is primarily a state and local responsibility, many people resented what appeared to be unwarranted interference by the federal government in state and local matters. Indeed, the Constitution, for the most part, leaves questions about administering justice to the states, unless a state's procedure violates a fundamental principle of justice. This last qualification explains why some of the early appeals in state death penalty cases cited Fourteenth Amendment violations.

Finally, appellate jurisdiction has been conferred on the Court by various statutes under authority given Congress by the Constitution.[10] These statutes give appellate jurisdiction to the Court in cases appealed from federal courts of appeals, federal district courts in certain circumstances, and the high court of a state, providing the claim involves a federal law or the Constitution.

PREMODERN DEATH PENALTY CASES

Prior to 1968, only two capital cases reviewed by the Court challenged the constitutionality of capital punishment itself: *Louisiana ex rel. Francis v. Resweber* (329 U.S. 459, 1947), which permitted a state to attempt a second execution by electrocution after the first attempt failed, and *Solesbee v. Balkcom* (339 U.S. 9, 1950), which allowed a governor to determine an inmate's sanity where finding an inmate insane would prevent his or her execution.[11] A more concerted challenge would come later.

Compared to the number of postmodern cases, the Court was relatively reticent when it came to interfering in the practice of capital punishment during the earlier period. Two additional points are worth noting. First, throughout its history, the Court has rejected as unworthy of review the vast majority of cases appealed to it. Appeals to the Court are heard at the discretion of the Court, in contrast to appeals to the U.S. circuit courts, which review cases as a matter of right. Second, there are many noncapital cases (i.e., cases that did not involve either a capital charge or a death sentence) that have influenced death penalty jurisprudence. None of the premodern cases reviewed here are noncapital cases.

The premodern death penalty cases are grouped into categories and presented in chronological order within the categories. They provide a good summary of the types of death penalty issues that the Court was willing to address during the premodern period. The categories are (1) clemency, (2) jurisdiction, (3) methods of execution, (4) ex post facto, (5) sentencing, (6) the Fifth Amendment (double jeopardy), (7) juries, and (8) the Fourteenth Amendment (equal protection and due process). Unless indicated otherwise, the case descriptions come from the court decisions.

CLEMENCY

What were probably the first two death penalty cases reviewed by the Court involved clemency. In the case of *United States v. Wilson* (32 U.S. 150), decided by the Court in 1833, the issue was whether a capital defendant could refuse to accept a pardon. George Wilson and an accomplice had been indicted on six counts of robbing the U.S. mail and, in some of these counts, putting the life of the mail carrier in jeopardy. The U.S. attorney refused to prosecute three of the counts but proceeded on one of them. At the arraignment, both Wilson and his accomplice pleaded not guilty to the charges. They were subsequently tried, found guilty, and sentenced to death. Wilson's accomplice was executed about a month later. Following Wilson's sentencing, he withdrew his not-guilty plea and pleaded guilty to all counts except those the U.S. attorney elected not to prosecute. Before Wilson's date with the executioner, President Andrew Jackson had received numerous petitions from respected citizens to grant Wilson executive clemency. Jackson pardoned Wilson, stipulating that the pardon was only for the crime for which Wilson was sentenced to death. Jackson attached the condition knowing that Wilson could still be sentenced to 20 years' imprisonment for the crimes for which he pleaded guilty and an even more severe punishment in the criminal courts of Pennsylvania.

At Wilson's subsequent sentencing hearing for a crime for which he changed his plea to guilty (that crime was on the same day, at the same place, and on the same carrier as the crime for which he was previously sentenced to death, except in the latter case the carrier's life was not put in jeopardy), the court asked Wilson whether he wanted to avail himself of his presidential pardon. The court was confused as to whether the crime before it was the same crime for which Wilson had received a pardon or a different crime. Wilson answered that he was not interested in using his pardon to avoid sentence in this particular case, presumably because it only could be punished by imprisonment and a fine. Wilson's response befuddled and divided the court, so it sought clarification from the Court. The Court ruled that if a defendant does not bring the fact of his or her pardon to the attention of the Court by way of plea, motion, or otherwise, the Court cannot recognize the pardon nor can it affect the judgment of law.

In *Ex parte Wells* (59 U.S. 307), decided in 1855, the issue was whether the president of the United States had the authority to grant conditional pardons or commutations as opposed to absolute pardons. The Court held that he did. The president's power of pardon is given in Article II, Section 2, of the U.S. Constitution, the relevant portion of which is: "The President … shall have the Power to grant Reprieves and Pardons for Offences against the United States, except in Cases of Impeachment." William Wells was convicted of murder in the District of Columbia in December 1851 and was sentenced to be hanged on April 23, 1852. On the day of his scheduled execution, President Fillmore granted Wells a conditional pardon, commuting his death sentence to life imprisonment in the penitentiary in Washington. On the same day, Wells signed a document, witnessed by the jailer and warden, accepting the pardon with its condition. While in prison, Wells petitioned the District of Columbia circuit court for a writ of habeas corpus, which was granted. After hearing the arguments of counsel, the circuit court upheld the president's power to commute Wells's death sentence to life imprisonment and ordered that Wells be remanded to the penitentiary. Wells then sought a writ of habeas corpus from the Court, which the Court granted, deciding to hear his claim as an appeal from the circuit court. Wells's attorney claimed that his client's pardon was absolute, the pardon's condition was null and void, and Wells was entitled to be discharged from prison. Wells's attorney reasoned

> … that a President granting such a [conditional] pardon assumes a power not conferred by the constitution – that he legislates a new punishment into existence, and sentences the convict to suffer it; in this way violating the legislative and judicial powers of the government, it being the province of the first, to enact laws for the punishment of offences against the United States, and that of the judiciary, to sentence convicts for violations of those laws, according to them.

The Court responded,

> We think this [interpretation] is a mistake arising from the want of due consideration of the legal meaning of the word pardon. It is supposed that it was meant to be used exclusively with reference to an absolute pardon, exempting a criminal from the punishment which the law inflicts for a crime he has committed. But such is not the sense or meaning of the word, either in common parlance or in law.

The Court affirmed the circuit court's refusal of Wells's application for the writ of habeas corpus and, in doing so, affirmed the president's right to grant conditional pardons or commutations to people convicted of federal offenses.

In *Biddle v. Perovich* (274 U.S. 480, 1927), the Court ruled that President Taft had the authority to commute Perovich's sentence from death to life imprisonment, without the defendant's consent.

JURISDICTION

The Court appears to have reviewed its third death penalty case, *Ex parte Milligan* (71 U.S. 2), in 1866. The issue before the Court in this case was the problem of military power over civilians. Lambdin P. Milligan was a southern sympathizer living in Indiana as a civilian during the Civil War.[12] Milligan was a member of the "Copperheads," a northern political group that sought peace at any price, and was believed to be a member of a secret society known as the Order of American Knights or Sons of Liberty, whose purpose was "overthrowing the Government and duly constituted authorities of the United States." He was arrested by the military in 1864, and later that month a military commission tried him on five charges: (1) "Conspiracy against the Government of the United States"; (2) "Affording aid and comfort to rebels against the authority of the United States"; (3) "Inciting insurrection"; (4) "Disloyal practices"; and (5) "Violation of the laws of war." At trial, Milligan objected to the authority of the military commission to try him. The objection was overruled, the military commission found him guilty of all five charges, and sentenced him to death by hanging.

Milligan sought release from military custody through habeas corpus. Although President Lincoln had authorized such military tribunals during the Civil War, the Court held that trials of civilians by military commissions unauthorized by congressional authority are unconstitutional in jurisdictions where the civil courts are operating constitutionally. Milligan could have been tried in a federal court in Indiana. The Court ordered that "Milligan was to be delivered from military custody and imprisonment, and if found probably guilty of any offence, to be turned over to the proper tribunal for inquiry and punishment; or, if not found thus probably guilty, to be discharged altogether." Milligan was released, whereupon he sued the military for false imprisonment. He won the suit and was awarded five dollars in damages.[13]

METHODS OF EXECUTION

The Eighth Amendment, which prohibits "cruel and unusual punishment," was not incorporated and made applicable to the states until 1962 (*Robinson v. California*, 370 U.S. 660). For this reason, in none of the premodern cases (nor in any case since) was a particular execution method declared cruel and unusual by the Court.[14] Neither, as law professor Deborah Denno observes, did the Court review any evidence regarding whether a particular punishment was cruel and unusual.[15] That is, until 2008, when in the case of *Baze et al. v. Rees* (553 U.S. 35), the Court ruled that lethal injection was not cruel and unusual punishment.

The first case involving the constitutionality of execution methods was *Wilkerson v. Utah* (99 U.S. 130, 1878), wherein the Court declared that shooting is not a cruel and unusual punishment. However, as Denno points out, the Court did not examine any evidence as to whether the shooting was cruel because the plaintiff did not raise the issue. Wilkerson instead challenged the application of Utah's death penalty statute on the grounds that the statute did not specify the method of execution. The Court emphasized that for a punishment to be considered cruel and unusual in violation of the Eighth Amendment it had to involve torture or unnecessary cruelty, something that the Court apparently opined shooting did not.

Electrocution as a permissible form of execution was the subject of *In re Kemmler* (136 U.S. 436, 1890). Although admitting that electrocution was unusual, since it had never been used before, a unanimous Court decided that: "The punishment of death is not cruel, within the meaning of that word as used in the Constitution." The Court's decision specified what constitutes "cruelty" in connection with legal punishments. According to the Court, "punishments are cruel when they involve torture or lingering death.... [i]t implies there [is] something inhuman and barbarous, something more than the mere extinguishment of life." The Court also provided examples of punishments it would consider as manifestly cruel and unusual: "burning at the stake, crucifixion, breaking on the wheel, or the like."

In a related case, *Louisiana ex rel. Francis v. Resweber* (329 U.S. 459, 1947), the Court held that a second electrocution, conducted after the first one had failed to kill the defendant, is not in violation of the Eighth Amendment's prohibition. The case involved the botched execution of Willie Francis, a 16-year-old black youth sentenced to die in Louisiana's electric chair for the murder of a popular white druggist.[16] Francis was strapped into the state's portable electric chair, but when the switch was thrown, the device malfunctioned (it did not produce enough current) and death did not result. Francis was removed from the chair and returned to his prison cell. The chair was fixed and his execution rescheduled. Francis stated:

> [T]he experience was in all "plumb miserable." His mouth tasted "like cold peanut butter," and he saw "little blue and pink and green speckles." Added Francis: "I felt a burning in my head and my left leg, and I jumped against the straps."[17]

Francis challenged Louisiana's plan for a second attempt, arguing that it would constitute both torture and the degradation of a human being. The Court denied Francis's claim and maintained that the botched execution was "an unforeseeable accident," "an innocent misadventure," and unintentional on the part of the state – and therefore not a form of torture prohibited by the Eighth Amendment. Justice Burton dissented, seeming to agree with Francis that executing a person after a first attempt had failed was nothing less than imposing "death by installments."

EX POST FACTO

Ex post facto refers to having a retroactive effect. In a legal context, it (1) declares criminal an act that was not illegal when it was committed, (2) increases the punishment for a crime after it is committed, or (3) alters the rules of evidence in a particular case after the crime is committed. Although the first meaning of the term is the most common, the cases in this section involve the second meaning. Article I, Sections 9 and 10, of the U.S. Constitution forbid ex post facto laws.

In the case of *In re Medley* (134 U.S. 160, 1890), James J. Medley had been sentenced to death in Colorado for murdering his wife. He applied to the Court for a writ of habeas corpus, claiming that the state's new death penalty law, enacted in 1889, varied substantially from the death penalty law in force at the time the crime was committed. He complained that the changes in the new law under which he was sentenced were prejudicial and injurious to him and, therefore, ex post facto in violation of Article I, Section 10, of the U.S. Constitution.

The Court addressed two of his complaints. The first dealt with the provision in the new statute that allowed the state of Colorado to hold Medley in solitary confinement pending his execution. On this issue, the Court held that holding Medley in solitary confinement "was an additional punishment of the most important and painful character" and is forbidden by the ex post facto provision of the U.S. Constitution. The second complaint addressed that part of the new statute that required

> the particular day and hour of the execution of the sentence within the week specified by the warrant shall be fixed by the warden, and he shall invite to be present certain persons named, to-wit, a chaplain, a physician, a surgeon, the spiritual adviser of the convict, and six reputable citizens of the state of full age, and that the time fixed by said warden for such execution shall be by him kept secret, and in no manner divulged except privately to said persons invited by him to be present as aforesaid, and such persons shall not divulge such invitation to any person or persons whomsoever, nor in any manner disclose the time of such execution; and … that any person who shall violate or omit to comply with the requirements of … the act shall be punished by fine or imprisonment.

The Court objected that under the new law the prisoner was "to be kept in utter ignorance of the day and hour when his mortal life [was to] be terminated by hanging, until the moment arrive[d] when this act [was] to be done." The Court ruled that this provision was "a departure from the law as it stood before," and was "an additional punishment to the prisoner [causing an immense mental anxiety], and therefore ex post facto." It added, "it confers upon the warden of the penitentiary a power which had heretofore been solely confided to the court and is therefore a departure from the law as it stood when the crime was committed." The Court concluded that Colorado's new death penalty statute, as applied to crimes committed before it came into force, violated the U.S. Constitution. It, therefore, ordered the release of Medley from his current sentence, warrant, and the custody of the warden of the Colorado penitentiary.

In *Rooney v. North Dakota* (196 U.S. 319, 1905), John Rooney, who had been convicted of murder during a robbery, complained of changes in North Dakota's new death penalty statute of 1903, which was enacted between the time he committed his crime, the verdict was rendered, and the time he was sentenced to death. Specifically, in the new law, "close confinement in the penitentiary for not less than six months and not more than nine months, after judgment and before execution, was substituted for confinement in the county jail for not less than three months nor more than six months after judgment and before execution." In addition, the new law substituted "hanging within an inclosure [sic] at the penitentiary, by the warden or his deputy … for hanging by the sheriff within the yard of the jail of the county in which the conviction occurred."

The Court ruled that the two changes in the new statute of which Rooney complained were "not repugnant to the constitutional provision declaring that no state shall pass an ex post facto law." The Court surmised that the provisions at issue "did not create a new offense, nor aggravate or increase the enormity of the crime for the commission of which the accused was convicted, nor require the infliction upon the accused of any greater or more severe punishment than was prescribed by law at the time of the commission of the offense." The substitution of close confinement in the penitentiary prior to execution for confinement in the county jail, the Court maintained, was immaterial. They both amounted to the same thing: "such custody, and only such custody, as [would] safely secure the production of the body of the prisoner on the day appointed for his execution." "Close confinement" was not "solitary confinement." The Court also believed that at least one of the changes in the law actually was favorable to Rooney. He was to receive three more months of life. Not only was that a benefit in its own right, the extra time gave Rooney additional opportunity to obtain a pardon or commutation from the governor.

In 1912, Joe Malloy was found guilty without a recommendation for mercy of a murder he committed in 1910. He was sentenced to die by electrocution under South Carolina's new death penalty statute of 1912. The state supreme court affirmed the judgment. In *Malloy v. South Carolina* (237 U.S. 180, 1915), Malloy sought a reversal on the ground that the new death penalty statute had materially changed the punishment for death, making his punishment ex post facto in violation of Article I, Section 10, of the U.S. Constitution.

At the time Malloy committed his crime, the punishment for murder without a recommendation of mercy in South Carolina was "death by hanging within the county jail, or its inclosure [sic], in the presence of specified witnesses." The new law, as noted, prescribed electrocution instead of hanging and also fixed the place of execution inside the penitentiary and allowed more invited witnesses than had the previous statute. The Court ruled that the new statute did not increase the punishment for murder without a recommendation of mercy; it only changed the method of producing death, which abated "some of the odious features incident to the old method." Other changes in the statute, the Court opined, were "nonessential details in respect of surroundings." Consequently, the Court affirmed the judgment of the state supreme court.

SENTENCING

In *Calton v. Utah* (130 U.S. 83, 1889), the jury was instructed as to what constituted murder in the first and second degrees. It was not informed, however, of its right, under the penal code of Utah, to recommend life imprisonment at hard labor in the penitentiary in place of the punishment of death. The

Court opined that if the jury's attention had been called to the statute, it may have made such a recommendation, and thereby enabled the court to reduce the punishment to life imprisonment. The Court ruled that the trial court erred in not directing the attention of the jury to the alternative sentence and reversed the judgment, with directions for a new trial, and for such further proceedings as may not be inconsistent with its opinion.

In *Craemer v. Washington* (168 U.S. 124, 1897), Henry Craemer had been charged by information with murder in the first degree, murder in the second degree, and manslaughter. Only the first charge carried the death penalty. In convicting Craemer of murder in the second degree and manslaughter, the jury returned a verdict of simply "guilty as charged." Before he was sentenced, Craemer, alleging that he could not be tried upon an information for his life, appealed his conviction to the Washington Supreme Court and, when unsuccessful there, to the U.S. Supreme Court, which denied his appeal. In the meantime, the original judge in the case had been replaced. The new judge sentenced Craemer to death. Craemer was unable to appeal the sentence to the Washington Supreme Court because the next term of the court did not start until after the date Craemer was to be executed. The only course of action open to Craemer was to appeal his sentence to the federal circuit court, which refused his writ of habeas corpus. The Court affirmed the decision of the federal circuit court, but Craemer apparently escaped execution, anyway.[18]

The petitioner in *Robinson v. United States* (324 U.S. 282, 1945) was indicted and convicted in a federal district court for violating the Federal Kidnapping Act by transporting in interstate commerce a person whom he had kidnapped and held for a reward. The jury recommended and the court imposed the death penalty. The circuit court of appeals affirmed, and the Court granted certiorari on the sole question of the court's statutory authority to impose the death sentence. The act authorizes the death sentence when recommended by a jury "provided that the sentence of death shall not be imposed by the court if, prior to its imposition, the kidnapped person has been liberated unharmed." The indictment charged, and there was evidence before the jury, to the effect that the kidnapping victim yielded to capture only after the petitioner had twice violently struck her on the head with an iron bar; that while held in custody her lips were abrased and made swollen by repeated applications of tape on her mouth; and that wounds resulting from these assaults were not healed when she was liberated after 6 days' captivity. No evidence was introduced, nor did the indictment charge, that the injuries inflicted were permanent or that the victim still suffered from them when Robinson was sentenced 9 years after commission of the offense. The trial court charged the jury that, in determining whether the victim had been "liberated unharmed," they were limited to a consideration of her condition at the time she was liberated and they were not authorized to recommend the death penalty if at the time of her liberation she had recovered from her injuries. The Court had to determine only whether the injuries inflicted had to be permanent or in existence at the time of sentence to authorize the infliction of the death sentence. While the Court admitted that Congress did not make clear what it meant by harm, that is, it did not unmistakably mark some boundary between a pinprick and a permanently mutilated body, it did not doubt that a kidnapper who violently struck the head of his victim with an iron bar came within the group Congress had in mind. The Court therefore ruled that the trial court committed no error of which the petitioner could complain.

In *Williams v. New York* (337 U.S. 241, 1949), a jury in a New York state court found Williams guilty of murder in the first degree. The jury recommended life imprisonment, but the trial judge imposed a sentence of death. In giving his reasons for imposing the death sentence, the judge discussed in open court the evidence upon which the jury had convicted, stating that he had considered this evidence in the light of additional information made available to him through the court's "Probation Department, and through other sources." Consideration of this additional information was pursuant to the New York Criminal Code, which provides: "Before rendering judgment or pronouncing sentence the court shall cause the defendant's previous criminal record to be submitted to it, including any reports that may have been made as a result of a mental, phychiatric [sic] or physical examination of such person, and may seek any information that will aid the court in determining the proper treatment of such defendant." The New York Court of Appeals affirmed the conviction and sentence over the contention that as construed and applied the controlling penal statutes are in violation of the due process clause of the Fourteenth Amendment in that the sentence of death was based upon information supplied by witnesses with whom the accused had not been confronted and as to whom he had no opportunity for cross-examination or rebuttal. The Court held that the due process clause does not render a sentence void merely because a judge gets additional out-of-court information to assist him in the exercise of his awesome power of imposing the death sentence. Note that in this case a Fourteenth Amendment violation was claimed; therefore, the case could have been included in the section of Fourteenth Amendment cases. It was included here because it dealt with a sentencing issue.

THE FIFTH AMENDMENT (DOUBLE JEOPARDY)

In 1916, Robert Stroud (the "Bird Man of Alcatraz") was convicted of first-degree murder and sentenced to hang for the killing of a prison guard at the Leavenworth Federal Penitentiary in Kansas. Stroud was serving the remainder of a 12-year sentence he received for his 1908 conviction in Alaska for killing the man who had beaten his female companion. Stroud originally had been serving his sentence at McNeil Penitentiary in Seattle but was transferred to Leavenworth in 1912 for stabbing another inmate who had allegedly stolen food from him and for generally being disobedient.[19] Stroud appealed the judgment of the federal district court in his 1916 trial to the circuit court of appeals, which reversed judgment and granted Stroud a new trial after the U.S. district attorney confessed error. Stroud's new trial was held in 1917. The new trial jury found him "guilty as charged in the indictment without capital punishment." Stroud then appealed this judgment to the Court and, after the U.S. solicitor general confessed to error, the judgment of the district court was reversed and the case was remanded for further proceedings. The district court vacated the former sentence and ordered a new trial. Stroud's third trial ended with the jury finding Stroud guilty of first-degree murder but made no recommendation about dispensing with capital punishment. The judge sentenced Stroud to death.

Stroud appealed to the Court, alleging that the results of the last trial placed him in double jeopardy in violation of the Fifth Amendment. In *Stroud v. United States* (251 U.S. 15, 1919), the Court observed that the convictions and sentences in the former trials were reversed only after Stroud had appealed those judgments. Once error was found in those proceedings, the Court continued, the only recourse for the appellate courts was to award new trials. The Court concluded that because Stroud himself initiated the actions that resulted in new trials, he was not placed in second jeopardy within the meaning of the Constitution.

As a postscript, Stroud was never executed. Through the tireless work of his mother, who had gained the support of several women's organizations, President Woodrow Wilson commuted Stroud's death sentence to life in prison in solitary confinement. He was transferred to Alcatraz in his 26th year of confinement, in 1942, and died at the age of 73 after serving 54 years in prison, the last 42 in solitary confinement.[20]

JURIES

Winston v. United States, Strather v. United States, and *Smith v. United States* (172 U.S. 303, 1899) were three cases of indictments returned and tried in the District of Columbia Supreme Court for murders committed after the passage of the act of Congress of January 15, 1897. The act stipulated, in part, that "in all cases where the accused is found guilty of the crime of murder or of rape … the jury may qualify their verdict by adding thereto 'without capital punishment'; and whenever the jury shall return a verdict qualified as aforesaid the person convicted shall be sentenced to imprisonment at hard labor for life." Upon review, the Court maintained that the instructions of the judge to the jury in each of the three cases led the jury to understand that the act of Congress did not intend or authorize the jury to qualify their verdict by the addition of the words "without capital punishment," unless mitigating or palliating circumstances were proved. The Court held that the instructions were erroneous in matter of law, as undertaking to control the discretionary power vested by Congress in the jury, and as attributing to Congress an intention unwarranted either by the express words or by the apparent purpose of the statute. The Court reversed the judgment in each of the three cases and remanded them to the court of appeals, with directions to reverse the judgment of the District of Columbia Supreme Court and to order a new trial.

Alfred Aldridge, a black man, was convicted by an all-white jury and sentenced to death in the District of Columbia Supreme Court for the first-degree murder of one of the District's white police officers. The conviction was affirmed by the court of appeals, and the Court granted certiorari on the question about the trial court's voir dire of prospective jurors. In this interracial case, the trial court refused to ask prospective jurors whether they had racial prejudices. In *Aldridge v. United States* (283 U.S. 308, 1931), the government argued "that it would be detrimental to the administration of the law in the courts of the United States to allow questions to jurors as to racial or religious prejudices." To which the Court replied,

> We think that it would be far more injurious to permit it to be thought that persons entertaining a disqualifying prejudice were allowed to serve as jurors and that inquiries designed to elicit the fact of disqualification were barred. No surer way could be devised to bring the processes of justice into disrepute. We are of the opinion that the ruling of the trial court on the voir dire was erroneous.

The Court reversed the judgment.

In the case of *Norris v. Alabama* (294 U.S. 587, 1935), Clarence Norris, a black man and one of the "Scottsboro Boys" (discussed later in *Powell v. Alabama*), moved at the onset of his trial to quash his indictment for rape and his trial venire because qualified "Negroes" were systematically excluded from both his grand and petit juries, "solely because of their race and color" – a long-standing, though unconstitutional practice in the counties in which he was indicted and tried. Norris was indicted in Jackson County and, because of a change of venue, was tried in Morgan County. The trial judge denied both motions, and Norris was convicted and sentenced to death. On appeal, the Alabama Supreme Court affirmed the judgment of the trial court. The U.S. Supreme Court granted certiorari and, after reviewing the evidence and arguments, reversed the judgment of the Alabama Supreme Court, asserting that the practice violated the equal protection clause of the U.S. Constitution's Fourteenth Amendment and remanded the cause for further proceedings not inconsistent with its opinion.

The same issue was raised again in *Patton v. Mississippi* (332 U.S. 463, 1948). Patton, a black man, was indicted for the murder of a white man in the Lauderdale County, Mississippi, circuit court, by an all-white grand jury. He was convicted by an all-white petit jury and sentenced to death by electrocution. He filed a timely motion to quash the indictment alleging that, although there were blacks in the county qualified for jury service, the venires for the term from which the grand and petit juries were selected did not contain the name of a single black person. He claimed that the absence of any blacks on the venires was due to the "systematic, intentional, deliberate and invariable practice on the part of administrative officers [of the county] to exclude Negroes from the jury lists, jury boxes and jury service, and that such practice has resulted and does now result in the denial of the equal protection of the laws to this defendant as guaranteed by the 14th amendment to the U.S. Constitution." The petitioner introduced evidence showing "without contradiction that no Negro had served on the grand or petit criminal court juries for thirty years or more." According to the U.S. Census, the 1940 adult black population of Lauderdale County was 12,511 (36%) out of a total adult population of 34,821. The trial court overruled the motion to quash, and the Mississippi Supreme Court affirmed the trial court's decision.

Upon review, the Court held:

> ... the State wholly failed to meet the very strong evidence of purposeful racial discrimination made out by the petitioner upon the uncontradicted showing that for thirty years or more no Negro had served as a juror in the criminal courts of Lauderdale County. When a jury selection plan, whatever it is, operates in such way as always to result in the complete and long-continued exclusion of any representative at all from a large group of negroes, or any other racial group, indictments and verdicts returned against them by juries thus selected cannot stand ... our holding does not mean that a guilty defendant must go free. For indictments can be returned and convictions can be obtained by juries selected as the Constitution commands.

The Court reversed the judgment of the Mississippi Supreme Court and remanded the case for proceedings that were not inconsistent with its opinion. This case also could have been reviewed in the Fourteenth Amendment category.

THE FOURTEENTH AMENDMENT (EQUAL PROTECTION AND DUE PROCESS)

The Court reviewed many Fourteenth Amendment challenges charging violations of due process of law. In many cases, appeals on Fourteenth Amendment grounds served as unofficial proxies for alleged violations of provisions of the Fourth, Fifth, Sixth, and Eighth Amendments. The reason is conveyed by the Court, which frequently wrote: "It has been well settled for years that the first ten amendments apply only to the procedure and trial of causes in the federal courts, and are not limitations upon those in state courts."[21]

In *McElvaine v. Brush* (142 U.S. 155, 1891), Charles McElvaine, who was sentenced to death for murder in New York, contended that being held in solitary confinement pending his execution, as provided by the New York death penalty statute, constituted cruel and unusual punishment in violation of the federal Constitution's Eighth Amendment. In his petition, McElvaine acknowledged that the first ten amendments to the U.S. Constitution "were not intended to limit the powers of the states in respect of their own people, but to operate on the federal government only." Nevertheless, he argued that,

> so far as those amendments secure the fundamental rights of the individual, they make them his privileges and immunities as a citizen of the United States, which cannot now, under the fourteenth amendment, be abridged by a state; that the prohibition of cruel and unusual punishments is one of these; and that that prohibition is also included in that "due process of law" without which no state can deprive any person of life, liberty, or property.

The Court responded that the "general rule of decision is that this court will follow the adjudication of the highest court of a state in the construction of its own statutes, and there is nothing in this case to take it out of that rule." It added that "the record does not disclose that the petitioner is restrained of his liberty in violation of the constitution and laws of the United States."

James W. Finley was tried, convicted, and sentenced to death for violating Section 246 of the California state penal code: "Every person undergoing a life sentence in a state prison of this state, who, with malice aforethought, commits an assault upon the person of another with a deadly weapon or instrument, or by any means or force likely to produce great bodily injury, is punishable with death." The California Supreme Court affirmed the sentence. In *Finley v. California* (222 U.S. 28, 1911), Finley argued that "246 is repugnant to the 14th Amendment of the U.S. Constitution in that it denies to him the equal protection of the laws, because it provides an exceptional punishment for life prisoners." The California Supreme Court "sustained the law on the ground that there was a proper basis for classification between convicts serving life sentences in the state prison, as defendant was when he committed the crime … and convicts serving lesser terms." In affirming the judgment of the state supreme court, the Court reasoned that for convicts serving life sentences, there "manifestly" "could be no extension of the term of imprisonment as a punishment for crimes they might commit, and whatever other punishment should be imposed was for the legislature to determine."

In 1913, 29-year-old pencil factory manager Leo Frank was tried, convicted, and sentenced to death in Atlanta, Georgia, for the murder of his 13-year-old employee Mary Phagan. The day after he was sentenced, his counsel filed a written motion for a new trial, which was amended about 2 months later to include 103 different grounds. Among them were several contending that Frank did not have a fair and impartial trial because it was conducted in a charged atmosphere of virulent anti-Semitism. The motion argued that the disorder both inside and outside the courtroom "amounted to mob domination" that intimidated the presiding judge and the jury. The trial court denied the motion, whereupon the cause was appealed to the state supreme court, which affirmed the conviction. After the decision by the Georgia Supreme Court, an "extraordinary motion" was made on Frank's behalf on the basis of newly discovered evidence. This motion was refused, and again the case was brought before the state supreme court, which again affirmed the action of the trial court. Other motions were then brought before various state courts and a petition was made to the Court, all without success. Persevering, a petition for a writ of habeas corpus was presented to the U.S. District Court for the northern district of Georgia on the ground that Frank was being confined in violation of the U.S. Constitution, "especially that clause of the 14th Amendment which declares that no state shall deprive any person of life, liberty, or property without due process of law." The district court refused to award the writ. This decision was appealed to the Court and, in *Frank v. Mangum* (237 U.S. 309, 1915), the Court affirmed the decision of the district court. But the legal maneuverings did not end there.

Facing execution, Frank sought clemency from Georgia Governor John Slaton, who, after reviewing the trial transcripts and knowing he was committing political and perhaps actual suicide, commuted Frank's death sentence to life imprisonment.[22] Following his decision, Governor Slaton, who had found numerous discrepancies in the trial transcript, stated "he would rather live in fear of his life than have a guilty conscience." Community members burned the governor in effigy, threatened his life, and eventually forced him to leave Georgia. As for Frank, on the night of August 16, 1915, a group of armed men forcibly took Frank from the prison where he was being held and lynched him. Later, it was discovered that another man's lawyer told the judge in Frank's original trial that his client, Jim Conley, also an employee of the pencil factory, had confessed to him several times that he, and not Leo Frank, had killed Mary Phagan. The judge kept this information to himself during Frank's trial and sentenced Frank to death anyway. In 1982, Alonzo Mann, who was a 14-year-old pencil factory employee at the time of Phagan's murder, told investigators that he had witnessed Conley commit the murder but kept silent because Conley threatened to kill him if he revealed what he saw. In 1986, Frank was issued a posthumous pardon by the state of Georgia because of "blatant due-process violations."[23] No one was ever charged with a crime for Frank's lynching.[24]

In *Moore v. Dempsey* (261 U.S. 86, 1923) the Court responded to an appeal from an order of the District Court for the Eastern District of Arkansas dismissing a writ of habeas corpus. The appellants were five black men who were convicted of first-degree murder and sentenced to death by an Arkansas court. The ground of the petition for the writ was that the defendants did not receive a fair trial, that they "were hurried to conviction under the pressure of a mob without any regard for their rights and without according to them due process of law."

The circumstances of the original case were as follows: On the night of September 30, 1919, a number of black people were meeting in a church to discuss hiring an attorney to protect them from being extorted by white landowners. During the meeting, a group of white men, presumably representing the white landowners, attacked and shot at the blacks. In the disturbance that followed, a white man was killed. The news of the killing incited white community members, who went on a rampage killing many black people. During the rampage, a white man, Clinton Lee, was killed. The five black defendants were indicted for Lee's murder. The black defendants claimed that other whites killed Lee.

The governor, in the meantime, appointed a "Committee of Seven" to investigate what the committee called the "insurrection" in the county. All the while, the newspapers were daily publishing inflammatory articles. In one of the articles, it was made public that at least one member of the committee believed that what had occurred was "a deliberately planned insurrection of the negroes against the whites, directed by an organization known as the 'Progressive Farmers' and 'Household Union of America' established for the purpose of banding negroes together for the killing of white people."

Shortly after the five black men were arrested, a lynch mob marched to the jail but was prevented from lynching the black men by the presence of U.S. troops and "the promise of some of the Committee of Seven and other leading officials that if the mob would refrain ... they would execute those found guilty in the form of law." The Committee's own statement indicated that mob violence was prevented because the "Committee gave our citizens their solemn promise that the law would be carried out."

The Court reversed the district court's dismissal of the writ of habeas corpus and ordered the district court to conduct a hearing. In doing so, the Court wrote: "… it does not seem to us sufficient to allow a Judge of the United States to escape the duty of examining the facts for himself when if true as alleged they make the trial absolutely void."

Powell v. Alabama (287 U.S. 45, 1932) involved the so-called Scottsboro Boys – nine young black men, ranging in age from 13 to 21, arrested for the alleged rapes of two white women.[25] One remarkable aspect of the case was that it took only one week to arrest, indict, arraign, try, convict, and sentence the defendants to death.[26] Another conspicuous aspect was that none of the defendants was represented by counsel until the day of the trial. Even then, it was not until the morning of the trial that a reluctant Scottsboro attorney offered to represent the young men.

On appeal, the Alabama Supreme Court reversed the conviction of one of the defendants but affirmed the convictions of the other seven (see note 26). Those defendants appealed their convictions to the Court, which reversed all seven convictions, holding that because of the special circumstances involved ("the ignorance and illiteracy of the defendants, their youth, the circumstances of public hostility, the imprisonment and the close surveillance of the defendants by the military forces, the fact that their friends and families were all in other states and communication with them necessarily difficult, and above all they stood in deadly peril of their lives"), the defendants were denied their right to the effective assistance of counsel required by the due process clause of the Fourteenth Amendment. Upon retrial, however, the eight Scottsboro Boys were reconvicted and, although they escaped execution, five of the eight served between 10 and 20 years in prison.[27] The *Powell* decision was narrowly drawn – it applied only to cases in which defendants were indigent, incapable of defending themselves because of their ignorance, illiteracy, or other similar handicap, and the death penalty was a possible sentence – but it was still important because it was the first in a series of cases that would extend the Sixth Amendment right to the effective assistance of counsel.

The question in *Brown v. Mississippi* (297 U.S. 278, 1936) was whether convictions based solely on coerced confessions violated due process of law as required by the Fourteenth Amendment. Three black men were indicted on March 30, 1934, for a murder committed 5 days earlier. They were arraigned the next day, and all three pleaded not guilty. Their trial commenced the following day and ended one day later. All three defendants were convicted and sentenced to death. Their convictions were based solely on their confessions, which, according to their testimony during the trial, were false and obtained through physical torture.

One of the suspects was taken from his home by a deputy sheriff accompanied by several white men to the house of the murdered man. There they accused him of the crime, which he vehemently denied committing, whereupon they hung him by the neck to a tree. After letting him dangle for a few moments, they cut him down and again asked him if he had committed the crime, which again he denied. They then hung him again, cut him down after a few moments, and posed the question to him anew. Again, he protested his innocence. After that, they tied him to a tree and whipped him, but he still refused to confess. They finally released him and with some difficulty he returned home. A day or two later, the aforementioned deputy sheriff together with another officer went to the suspect's home again, this time to arrest him. Following the arrest, the two deputies transported the suspect to a jail in an adjoining county. Along the way, the deputies stopped the car, removed the suspect, and severely whipped him again, declaring that they would continue to whip him until he agreed to confess to the murder, which he did. The suspect was then transported to the jail. The other two suspects were arrested and taken to the same jail. There the same deputy sheriff, along with the jailer and other white men, made the suspects strip and lean over chairs, whereupon their backs were cut by leather straps with buckles on them. The deputy sheriff advised the suspects that the beatings would continue until they agreed to confess to the murder, which they did. The next day the sheriff, some deputies, and other men came to the jail to hear the "free and voluntary confessions" of the three suspects.

In court, the sheriff testified that he had heard about the beatings but stated that he had no personal knowledge of them. He also admitted that one of the defendants was limping badly and did not sit down when making his confession because, as the defendant told it, he was strapped so badly he could not sit down. Finally, the sheriff noted that the rope burns around one of the defendant's neck were visible for anyone to see. During the trial the defendants were called to testify as to how the confessions were obtained, which they did truthfully. Interestingly, the deputy sheriff and two others who had administered the beatings were put on the stand and admitted to their roles in the torture. Not a single witness who was introduced denied that the beatings took place. Nevertheless, the so-called "free and voluntary confessions" were admitted in evidence over the objections of the defendants' counsel, who, incidentally, was only appointed the previous day. As noted, all three defendants were convicted and sentenced to death based solely on their confessions. The trial court's decision was challenged in the state supreme court as a violation of the Fourteenth Amendment's due process clause. The state supreme court upheld the lower court's judgment and chose not to enforce the defendants' constitutional rights. However, the Court reversed the state supreme court's judgment citing a violation of a fully established federal right.

Frank Palko was indicted in Connecticut for first-degree murder. The jury in his case found him guilty of second-degree murder, and he was sentenced to life imprisonment. The state of Connecticut appealed and won a new trial. At the new trial, Palko was convicted of first-degree murder and sentenced to death. Before the jury was impaneled for the new trial, as well as during later stages of the case, Palko objected that the second trial effectively put him twice in jeopardy for the same offense and, thus, violated the Fourteenth Amendment. The trial judge overruled his objections. The Connecticut Supreme Court affirmed the judgment, which Palko then appealed to the Court. In *Palko v. Conneticut* (302 U.S. 319, 1937), the Court held that the Fourteenth Amendment's due process clause absorbed fundamental rights and applied them to the states. The Court concluded, however, that the protection from double jeopardy was not a fundamental right, as the freedoms of speech, press, religion, and peaceable assembly were, and affirmed the judgment.

In *Watts v. Indiana* (338 U.S. 49, 1949), the Court elected to review a case after the Indiana Supreme Court rejected the petitioner's claim that "confessions elicited from him were procured under circumstances rendering their admission as evidence against him a denial of due process of law." Robert Watts was arrested on November 12, 1947, on suspicion that he had committed a criminal assault earlier that day. Later the same day, a dead woman was found near where Watts allegedly committed the assault. The police immediately suspected that Watts had committed the murder and began questioning him about it. They took him from the county jail to state police headquarters, where six to eight officers questioned him in relays off and on for 6 days, with only a break on Sunday. During the lengthy interrogation, he did not receive much food, and he was deprived of sleep. On the sixth day, Watts finally made an incriminating statement. However, the statement did not satisfy the prosecutor who had been called in, so the prosecutor turned Watts over to another interrogator for additional questioning, which produced a more incriminating statement from Watts.

Although Indiana law required that Watts be given a prompt preliminary hearing before a magistrate, "with all the protection a hearing was intended to give him," Watts was denied the preliminary hearing during the entire time he was being interrogated. He also "was without friendly or professional aid and without advice as to his constitutional rights."

In reversing the decision of the Indiana Supreme Court, the Court held that the due process clause of the Fourteenth Amendment bars "police procedure which violates the basic notions of our accusatorial mode of prosecuting crime and vitiates a conviction based on the fruits of such procedure." It opined:

> A confession by which life becomes forfeit must be the expression of free choice. A statement to be voluntary of course need not be volunteered. But if it is the product of sustained pressure by the police it does not issue from a free choice. When a suspect speaks because he is overborne, it is immaterial whether he has been subjected to a physical or a mental ordeal. Eventual yielding to questioning under such circumstances is plainly the product of the suction process of interrogation and therefore the reverse of voluntary.

It added that, while "mindful of the anguishing problems which the incidence of crime presents to the States … the history of the criminal law proves overwhelmingly that brutal methods of law enforcement are essentially self-defeating, whatever may be their effect in a particular case."[28]

In *Alcorta v. Texas* (355 U.S. 28, 1957), a Texas state court had convicted Alvaro Alcorta of murdering his wife and sentenced him to death. At his trial, Alcorta admitted he had killed his wife but claimed it occurred in a fit of passion when he saw his wife, whom he had already suspected of marital infidelity, kissing another man in a parked car late at night. Had the jury believed him, it could have returned a verdict of guilty of "murder without malice," which, under Texas law, carried a maximum sentence of 5 years' imprisonment. The jury did not believe him and sentenced him to death. At the trial, the other man testified that he and Alcorta's wife were simply friends and that their "relationship" amounted to nothing more than his driving her home from work a few times. The Texas Court of Criminal Appeals affirmed the judgment and sentence. However, in a subsequent habeas corpus proceeding, the other man confessed to having had sexual intercourse with Alcorta's wife several times. He also testified that he had told the prosecutor about it before the trial and that the prosecutor advised him not to volunteer the information unless he was asked and then he should tell the truth. The prosecutor admitted that these statements were true. Nevertheless, both the trial court and the Texas Court of Criminal Appeals denied Alcorta's petitions for writs of habeas corpus. Having exhausted state remedies, Alcorta appealed to the Court, which held that he had been denied due process of law. It reversed the judgment denying the writ of habeas corpus and remanded the cause to the Texas Court of Criminal Appeals.

In *Ciucci v. Illinois* (356 U.S. 571, 1958), Vincent Ciucci, a Chicago grocery store owner, was charged in four separate indictments with murdering his wife and three children, all of whom were found dead in a burning building with bullet wounds in their heads. In three successive trials, Ciucci was convicted of the first-degree murder of his wife and two of his children. At each of the trials the prosecution introduced into evidence the details of all four deaths. At the first two trials, involving the death of the wife and one of the children, the jury fixed the penalty at 20 and 45 years' imprisonment, respectively. At the third trial, which involved the death of the second child, the penalty was fixed at death. Before the third trial, Ciucci objected that he was being subjected to double jeopardy and moved to exclude testimony about the other deaths. The trial court overruled both objections. On appeal, the state supreme court affirmed the conviction. Ciucci then appealed to the Court, claiming that his third trial violated the due process clause of the Fourteenth Amendment. In his brief, Ciucci appended several articles from Chicago newspapers describing how the prosecutor was dissatisfied with the prison sentences in the first two trials, and his intention to prosecute Ciucci until he obtained a death sentence. However, none of that material was part of the record certified to the Court from the state supreme court, so the Court could not consider it in the appeal. In affirming the judgment of the state supreme court, the Court ruled "the State was constitutionally entitled to prosecute these individual offenses singly at separate trials, and to utilize therein all relevant evidence, in the absence of proof establishing that such a course of action entailed fundamental unfairness." It added, "Prosecution is allowed to try the accused with repeated trials (three) and convictions on the same evidence, until it achieves its desired result of a capital verdict." The Court did leave open the opportunity for Ciucci to institute "such further proceedings as may be available to him for the purpose of substantiating the claim that he was deprived of due process."

Leslie Irvin, an Evansville, Indiana, pipe fitter, was tried, convicted, and sentenced to death for the murder, in 1954, of gas station attendant Whitney Wesley Kerr. Shortly after Irvin's arrest, the prosecutor of Vanderburgh County and Evansville police officials issued widely publicized press releases stating that Irvin had confessed to six murders that had recently been committed in the Evansville area. The local news media had extensively covered the six murders, which had created quite a stir throughout Vanderburgh County, where Evansville is located, and in adjoining Gibson County. When Irvin was indicted in Vanderburgh County, his appointed attorney sought a change of venue, which was granted, but to adjoining Gibson County. Irvin's attorney then moved for a change of venue from Gibson County, claiming that the widespread and inflammatory publicity had also highly prejudiced the residents of that county against Irvin, but that motion was denied. The jury pool for Irvin's trial consisted of 430 persons, 268 of whom were excused for cause because they had already decided that Irvin was guilty. Of the 12 who were finally selected to serve on the jury, eight had admitted that they thought Irvin was guilty, but each indicated that he or she could still render an impartial verdict. After the state supreme court sustained Irvin's conviction, he applied to a federal district court for a writ of habeas corpus, claiming that he had not received a fair trial in violation of the Fourteenth Amendment. The district court denied his application for the writ on the ground that he had not exhausted his state remedies. The Seventh Circuit Court of Appeals affirmed the dismissal. After another round in the federal courts, the Court granted certiorari. In *Irvin v. Dowd* (366 U.S. 717, 1961), the Court held that Irvin was "not accorded a fair and impartial trial, to which he was entitled under the due process clause of the 14th Amendment." The Court voided his conviction and vacated the judgment denying him the writ of habeas corpus. It remanded the case to the district court for further proceedings affording the state a reasonable time to retry Irvin. The case is important because it was the first time the Court overturned a murder conviction because of pretrial publicity.[29]

Edward Griffin was convicted and sentenced to death in California for the first-degree murder of Essie Mae Hodson, the female companion of one of his drinking buddies, after he sexually assaulted her.[30] On automatic appeal, the California Supreme Court affirmed the judgment. The judgment was appealed to the Court on the ground that the prosecutor's comments and the trial judge's instructions to the jury about Griffin's failure to take the stand and testify during the guilt stage of his trial violated the self-incrimination clause of the Fifth Amendment, made applicable to the states by the Fourteenth Amendment in *Malloy v. Hogan* (378 U.S. 1, 1964). In *Griffin v. California* (380 U.S. 609, 1965), the Court reversed the California Supreme Court's affirmation of Griffin's conviction and death sentence.

"Skinny" Gilbert was tried, convicted, and sentenced to death for a 1964 armed robbery of a California bank and the murder of a police officer who entered the bank during the robbery. The California Supreme Court affirmed the judgment. The Court granted certiorari to hear Gilbert's allegations about four constitutional errors made in his case. Specifically, Gilbert claimed that (1) the admission of handwriting exemplars taken from him after arrest violated his Fifth and Sixth Amendment rights; (2) the admission during the guilt stage of his trial of his codefendant's pretrial statements to the police detailing his (Gilbert's) role in the crimes – statements that in his codefendant's appeal were held to have been improperly admitted – violated his right to due process of law; (3) the admission of testimony identifying him from photographs seized by police from his locked apartment pursuant to a warrantless search was a violation of his Fourth Amendment rights; and (4) the admission of witness testimony that identified him at a lineup, which occurred 16 days after his indictment and after appointment of counsel, who was not notified, violated his Sixth Amendment right to have counsel present during a pretrial lineup.

In *Gilbert v. California* (388 U.S. 263, 1967), the Court ruled on the four claims. First, it held that the taking of handwriting exemplars did not violate Gilbert's constitutional rights. The Court reasoned that a handwriting exemplar, as opposed to the content of what is actually written, is not protected by the Fifth Amendment's privilege against compelled self-incrimination. It also maintained that Gilbert's Sixth Amendment right to counsel was not violated because the taking of handwriting exemplars is not a "critical" stage of criminal proceedings entitling him to the assistance of counsel. Second, regarding the admission of his codefendant's statements, the Court found no problem with the California Supreme Court's judgment that any error involving the statements was harmless. Third, as for the claim of a Fourth Amendment violation in the search and seizure of the photographs from his apartment, the Court observed that the facts submitted were not clear enough to permit resolution of that question. Therefore, it vacated certiorari on that issue as improvidently granted. Fourth, the Court determined that the admission of the in-court identifications of Gilbert without first ascertaining whether they were tainted by the illegal lineup procedure was constitutional error. The Court opined that a postindictment pretrial lineup is a "critical" stage in criminal proceeding and the denial of counsel at that stage violates the Sixth Amendment's right to counsel. However, the Court added that because the record did not allow an informed judgment about whether the in-court identifications at the two stages of the trial (the guilt stage and the penalty stage) had an independent source, Gilbert was entitled only to a vacation of his conviction, "pending proceedings in California courts allowing the State to establish that the in-court identifications had an independent source or that their introduction in evidence was harmless error." As for the witnesses' testimony that they identified Gilbert at the lineup, which was a direct result of an illegal procedure, the Court ruled that "the State [was] not entitled to show that such testimony had an independent source but the California courts must, unless 'able to declare a belief that it was harmless beyond a reasonable doubt.' grant [Gilbert] a new trial if such testimony was at the guilt stage, or grant appropriate relief if it was at the penalty stage." (See Chapter 9 for a discussion of harmless and serious or prejudicial errors in capital cases.)

CONCLUSION

Some of the premodern death penalty cases set precedent for post-*Furman* capital jurisprudence, but other cases, perhaps most of them, are mostly of historical interest. All of them, however, revealed troubling flaws in the death penalty systems of many jurisdictions. After *Furman v. Georgia* (1972) and *Gregg v. Georgia* (1976), the issues addressed by the Court were very different from most of those reviewed during the premodern period. [*Furman* and *Gregg*, which are discussed at greater length in the next chapter, are the cases in which the Court held that existing death penalty statutes were unconstitutional (in *Furman*) and approved new death penalty statutes (in *Gregg*).] In the premodern period, the issues involved (1) clemency, (2) jurisdiction, (3) methods of execution, (4) ex post facto, (5) sentencing, (6) the Fifth Amendment (double jeopardy), (7) juries, and (8) the Fourteenth Amendment (equal protection and due process). After the *Furman* and *Gregg* decisions, the Court has dealt primarily with issues pertaining to the new death penalty statutes, such as (1) the constitutionality of the new death penalty statutes, (2) what crimes are capital, (3) mitigating circumstances, (4) aggravating circumstances, (5) the appellate process, (6) capital juries, (7) who may or may not be executed, and (8) assistance of counsel. These issues and the cases in which they are raised are examined in Chapter 4.

DISCUSSION QUESTIONS

1. At the time of the Supreme Court's *Marbury v. Madison* decision (1803), many Americans opposed judicial review. Why?

2. Why do you suppose the Warren Court broke with long-established precedent and incorporated most of the Bill of Rights and made them applicable to the states in the 1960s?

3. Do you agree with the Court's decision in *Louisiana ex rel. Francis v. Resweber*? Why or why not?

4. What can be learned about the criminal justice process in the United States prior to the 1960s from a review of the cases in this chapter?

Notes

1. Supreme Court of the United States, "About the Supreme Court," "A Brief Overview of the Supreme Court" at http://www.supremecourt.gov/about/briefoverview.aspx
2. Garner (2000).
3. Supreme Court of the United States, "About the Supreme Court," "The Court and Constitutional Interpretation," http://www.supremecourt.gov/about/constitutional.aspx
4. Ibid.
5. Ibid.
6. Ibid.
7. Ibid.
8. Ibid.
9. Cox (1987, pp. 239–249).
10. Supreme Court of the United States, "About the Supreme Court," "A Brief Overview of the Supreme Court," at http://www.supremecourt.gov/about/briefoverview.aspx

11. See Liebman (2007, p. 14, n. 42).
12. See the Supreme Court Historical Society, "History of the Court," "The Chase Court, 1864–1873" at http://www.supremecourthistory.org/02_history/subs_history/02_c06.html
13. Ibid.
14. Denno (1997) notes that courts have relied on *In re Kemmler* to dismiss challenges not only to electrocution but to the other four methods of execution as well. See the discussion of *In re Kemmler* below and in Chapter 6. In October 2001, the Georgia Supreme Court by a vote of 4–3 became the first appellate court in the United States to rule that electrocution violated the Eighth Amendment's prohibition against cruel and unusual punishment. The Court held that electrocution "inflicts purposeless physical violence and needless mutilation that makes no measurable contribution to accepted goals of punishment," http://www.clarkprosecutor.org/html/death/updates.htm; Georgia bans the electric chair. (2001, October 6). *The Orlando Sentinel*, p. A19.
15. Denno (1997, 1998).
16. See Denno (1994, pp. 607–612) and Paternoster (1991, p. 39).
17. Andersen (1983, p. 32).
18. Craemer's name was not listed in the Espy File; see Espy and Smykla (1987).
19. Gaddis (1979).
20. Ibid.
21. See, for example, *Gaines v. Washington*, 277 U.S. 81 (1928), and *Spies v. Illinois*, 123 U.S. 131 (1887) and cases cited.
22. See Radelet, Bedau, and Putnam (1992, p. 304) and Dinnerstein (1968).
23. Radelet et al. (1992, p. 304).
24. Bedau (1987, p. 218, fn. 6).
25. See Carter (1969) and Paternoster (1991, p. 68, fn. 3). It is generally believed that the charges against the Scottsboro Boys were fabricated. See Haines (1996, p. 210, n. 1).
26. Only eight of the suspects were indicted; the 13-year-old was not.
27. Haines (1996).
28. Also see *Turner v. Pennsylvania* (388 U.S. 62, 1949) for a similar decision under similar circumstances.
29. The Indiana Law Blog (2005).
30. *People v. Griffin*, 60 Cal. 2d 182.

The challenge to capital punishment's legality

3

THE CHALLENGE BEGINS

Although specific methods of execution had been legally challenged as early as 1890, and procedural issues before that, the fundamental legality of capital punishment itself was not subject to challenge until the 1960s.[1] It had long been argued that the Constitution or, more specifically, the Fifth Amendment authorized capital punishment and that a majority of the framers of the Constitution did not object to it. The Fifth Amendment reads as follows:

> No person shall be held to answer for a *capital*, or otherwise infamous *crime*, unless on a presentment or indictment of a grand jury, except in cases arising in the land or naval forces, or in the militia, when in actual service in time of war or public danger; nor shall any person be subject for the same offense to be twice put in *jeopardy of life* or limb; nor shall be compelled in any criminal case to be a witness against himself, nor be *deprived of life*, liberty, or property, without due process of law, nor shall private property be taken for public use without just compensation (emphasis added).

The three explicit references to capital punishment in the amendment have not only been taken as prima facie evidence that the framers of the Constitution did not object to its use, but they also show that the framers expected it to be used because of the guidelines they provided (i.e., "with due process of law").

Referral to capital punishment and the aforementioned guidelines is repeated in the Fourteenth Amendment, which was ratified shortly after the Civil War. The Fourteenth Amendment states in part:

> No State shall make or enforce any law which shall abridge the privileges or immunities of citizens of the United States; nor shall any State *deprive any person of life*, liberty, or property, without due process of law; nor deny to any person within its jurisdiction the equal protection of the laws (emphasis added).

Given such evidence, it made little sense to argue that capital punishment violated the Constitution. This conventional wisdom was challenged in 1961.

In an article published in the *University of Southern California Law Review*, Los Angeles antitrust lawyer Gerald Gottlieb, an affiliate with his local American Civil Liberties Union branch, suggested that "the death penalty was unconstitutional under the Eighth Amendment because it violated contemporary moral standards, what the U.S. Supreme Court in *Trop v. Dulles* (356 U.S. 86, 1958) referred to as 'the evolving standards of decency that mark the progress of a maturing society.'"[2] In *Trop* and in *Weems v. United States* (217 U.S. 349), the latter decided in 1910, the Court departed from the fixed or historical meaning it had always used in deciding whether a particular punishment was cruel and unusual in violation of the Eighth Amendment. The court opined in *Weems* that the cruel and unusual punishment provision "would only offer paper, illusory protection if it was restricted solely to the intent of the Framers."[3] The Court consequently declared that the meaning of the Eighth Amendment is not limited by the Framers' intent but that it changes with evolving social conditions—specifically, "the evolving standards of decency that mark the progress of a maturing society."[4] Neither *Trop* nor *Weems* was a death penalty case. Gottlieb applied to the practice of capital punishment the Court's logic from two cases not concerned with the death penalty. The key question raised by Gottlieb's interpretation, of course, was whether the United States, in fact, had evolved or progressed to the point where standards of decency no longer permitted capital punishment. A problem with the "evolving standards" doctrine, recognized by both the plurality and the dissent in *Stanford v. Kentucky* (1989), was the tendency of evolving standards "to evolve toward a Justice's personal views."[5]

Gottlieb took an extreme position toward the death penalty, calling for its complete abolition. Most of the other attacks on the penalty during this period were more moderate, seeking only its reform. A 1961 *University of Texas Law Review* article by Walter Oberer criticized the common practice of "death qualifying," a process that eliminates death penalty opponents from capital juries.[6] Oberer argued that death qualification "purged the jury of its more compassionate members and produced a homogenous jury more likely to convict."[7]

In addition, in 1961, in a speech delivered at Villanova Law School, Supreme Court Justice Tom Clark voiced his opposition to capital punishment. Such a public declaration by a sitting justice was not unprecedented. Robert Jackson had done it in 1946, and Felix Frankfurter did it in 1948 and again in 1950.[8] Politicians were also expressing their opposition to the death penalty. In the 1960s, there was not much political liability to taking a principled public stand against capital punishment.[9]

Two years before the Gottlieb and Oberer articles were published, in 1959, drafters of the American Law Institute's Model Penal Code suggested two legal reforms in the way capital punishment was administered.[10] The first was a bifurcated (two-part) trial consisting of a guilt phase, where guilt or innocence was the principal issue to be determined, and a penalty phase, where the imposition of either a life or death sentence was the sole issue. California had implemented such a trial process in 1957; the only other states to have split trials by the early 1960s were Connecticut, New York, Pennsylvania, and Texas.[11] The second reform was the use of enumerated aggravating and mitigating circumstances to guide and restrict the sentencing authority's (judge or jury) discretion during the penalty phase of the bifurcated trial. Both these procedural reforms would later be incorporated into the new, that is, post-*Furman*, death penalty statutes (examined in detail later).

THE *RUDOLPH* CASE

Problems with the administration of capital punishment had long been a focus of attack by death penalty opponents, but they were also a source of consternation to proponents of the penalty who wanted it "done right." By the 1960s, some reform in the process of putting capital offenders to death seemed necessary, as at least three members of the Supreme Court agreed. In a rare published dissent from a denial of certiorari in Alabama and Virginia rape cases, *Rudolph v. Alabama* and *Snider v. Cunningham*, 375 U.S. 889 (1963) (hereafter referred to as the *Rudolph* case), Justice Arthur Goldberg, joined by Justices Brennan and Douglas, suggested that the entire Court ought to determine whether the death penalty for a rapist who has not taken a life was unconstitutional under the Eighth

Amendment.[12] (A writ of certiorari is an order from a higher court to a lower court whose decision is being appealed to send the records of the case forward for review. It is a dominant avenue to the U.S. Supreme Court.)

Rudolph's attorneys chose not to challenge the constitutionality of capital punishment for rape, but Justice Goldberg felt compelled to comment anyway. In his written dissent from the certiorari denial, he posed three questions he thought the Court should address:

1. "In light of the trend both in this country and throughout the world against punishing rape by death, does the imposition of the death penalty by those States which retain it for rape violate 'evolving standards of decency that mark the progress of [our] maturing society,' or 'standards of decency more or less universally accepted'?"

2. "Is the taking of human life to protect a value other than human life consistent with the constitutional proscription against 'punishments which by their excessive ... severity are greatly disproportioned to the offenses charged'?"

3. "Can the permissible aims of punishment (e.g., deterrence, isolation, rehabilitation) be achieved as effectively by punishing rape less severely than by death (e.g., by life imprisonment); if so, does the imposition of the death penalty for rape constitute 'unnecessary cruelty'?"[13]

Goldberg's position in *Rudolph* was part of a broader strategy to get his colleagues on the Court to either restrict the death penalty or abolish it.[14] He personally considered the death penalty an abomination, maintaining that it was applied arbitrarily, haphazardly, capriciously, and in a discriminatory way against disadvantaged minorities.[15] In the summer of 1963, less than a year after he joined the Court, he asked his new law clerk, Alan Dershowitz, who later would become a Harvard law professor, to research precedent to support an argument that the death penalty constituted cruel and unusual punishment in violation of the Eighth Amendment. With Dershowitz's help, Goldberg prepared and circulated a memorandum imploring his fellow justices to grant a review of six pending death penalty appeals (four murders and two rapes) so that they could rule on the death penalty's constitutionality. Unfortunately for Goldberg, a majority of the Court was not prepared for such a drastic move.[16] Chief Justice Earl Warren was particularly irate because he believed the memorandum, if published, would turn the public against the Court and jeopardize its desegregation decisions.[17] If not for that, Warren probably would have been sympathetic to a review of the death penalty. He revealed after his retirement in 1968 that he had been repulsed by the death penalty all his life.[18] Even justices Brennan and Douglas, who joined Goldberg in the *Rudolph* dissent, did not vote to review the cases.[19] Thus, Goldberg's ruminations in *Rudolph* had little immediate effect, but they did hearten a small group of abolitionist lawyers with the NAACP Legal Defense and Educational Fund (LDF) by suggesting that the Supreme Court might be ready at a later date to consider the constitutionality of the death penalty for rape where the victim does not die. For the LDF lawyers it seemed the appropriate time to begin preparing for a test case on the matter.[20]

THE NAACP LEGAL DEFENSE AND EDUCATIONAL FUND LAWYERS

The NAACP Legal Defense and Educational Fund, founded in 1939 by the National Association for the Advancement of Colored People (NAACP), is a coalition of lawyers, clients, staff, consultants, and expert advisors that had as its original goals to dismantle racial segregation and attack racial discrimination in the United States through the courts.[21] It played a major role in the black civil rights movement of the 1950s and 1960s by winning challenges to protective covenants that segregated neighborhoods by race and the segregation of public schools from elementary schools to universities.[22] From 1940 until 1961, future U.S. Supreme Court Justice Thurgood Marshall headed the Fund. When John F. Kennedy appointed him to the U.S. Court of Appeals for the Second Circuit in 1961, Marshall handed off the reins of the fund to Jack Greenberg, a white man who received his law degree from Columbia Law School.[23]

Fund lawyers turned their attention to the death penalty in the 1960s primarily because of the racially discriminatory way it was being administered. Hugo Adam Bedau has called their efforts "the final act of the Civil Rights movement."[24] Later, however, when they began accepting clients actually facing execution, they realized that they needed to raise issues having nothing to do with race. With this change in focus, there was no longer any reason not to take on the cases of white death row inmates too, so they did.[25] In attempting to achieve judicial abolition of the penalty, Fund lawyers Michael Meltsner, Frank Heffner, and LeRoy Clark plotted a general strategy to convince the Court that the death penalty was employed in a discriminatory way against minorities and to otherwise block all executions by challenging the legal procedures employed in capital cases (the "moratorium strategy").[26] If successful, their plan would accomplish three goals. First, it would make those who were still executed appear to be unlucky losers in a death penalty lottery. Second, if the death penalty were used only rarely, it would show that the penalty was not really needed for society's protection. Third, if all executions were blocked, the resulting logjam of death row inmates would lead to an inevitable bloodbath if states ever began emptying their death rows by executing en masse. The LDF lawyers did not believe the country could stomach the gore and would demand abolition of the penalty.[27] The Fund's ambitious plan would be very expensive but, fortunately for the Fund attorneys and other cooperating lawyers, Greenberg was able to use a million-dollar grant from the Ford Foundation to help finance the project.[28] In 1967, Greenberg appointed Jack Himmelstein, a 26-year-old Harvard Law School graduate, to manage the capital project.[29]

The intellectual leader and "front man" of the capital project was Anthony G. Amsterdam. Amsterdam had become acquainted with the LDF lawyers at a 1963 conference at which he lectured about the legal defense of civil rights demonstrators. Amsterdam had graduated from the University of Pennsylvania Law School in 1960 and was the first non-Harvard Law School graduate to clerk for U.S. Supreme Court Justice Felix Frankfurter.[30] In 1961, he served as an assistant U.S. attorney in the District of Columbia and, in 1962, he joined the faculty of the University of Pennsylvania Law School.[31] Amsterdam has been described as "a man of rare intelligence and force" and as "a well-programmed legal computer"—a "lawyer's lawyer."[32] He served as an "advisor-at-large" to hundreds of civil rights and civil liberties lawyers; was involved in lawsuits and projects supported by the American Civil Liberties Union, the Lawyer's Committee for Civil Rights Under Law, and the Lawyer's Constitutional Defense Fund; and served as a consultant to the American Law Institute, the President's Commission on Law Enforcement and Administration of Justice (the National Crime Commission), the National Advisory Commission on Civil Disorders (the Kerner Commission), and the American Bar Association—to name a few.[33] He became an LDF consultant after 1963 and between 1965 and 1972 managed the LDF's growing docket of capital cases.[34] From 1963 until 1972, Amsterdam and/or LDF attorneys represented more than 300 death row inmates.[35] Amsterdam and Himmelstein's first joint project for the LDF was the creation of a "how-to" manual dubbed the "Last Aid Kit." The "Kit" included petitions for habeas corpus, applications for stays of execution, and legal briefs that contained every significant constitutional argument against the death penalty—everything a lawyer would need to present to a court to postpone an execution. The "Kit" was distributed to hundreds of lawyers.[36]

THE *MAXWELL* CASE

The defendant selected for the LDF's first test case was William L. Maxwell, a 22-year-old black man who in 1961 was charged in Arkansas with the rape of a white woman.[37] Maxwell was convicted of the crime and sentenced to die the following year. His initial appeal to the Arkansas Supreme Court claimed that there was a pattern of racial discrimination in the way Arkansas juries handled rape cases. The appeal was denied. Maxwell's attorney, with the help of LDF lawyers, then drafted a writ of habeas corpus for review by the federal courts. In each of the courts—first the U.S. District Court, then the Court of Appeals for the Eighth Circuit, and, finally, the U.S. Supreme Court—the writ was rejected. All this occurred during 1964 and 1965.

In 1966, a second writ of habeas corpus was presented to the U.S. District Court on Maxwell's behalf and, this time, the court agreed to a hearing. Although his lawyers were able to show, using social scientific evidence, that there was a pattern of racial discrimination in death cases for rape in some Arkansas counties, the result was the same. The court rejected all of Maxwell's claims and refused his request for a stay of execution. The court's ruling was affirmed by the Court of Appeals for the Eighth Circuit. Maxwell, however, was not finished. In 1967, he won a stay of execution from the U.S. Supreme Court, and the Court sent the case back to the Eighth Circuit Appellate Court for further review. In 1968, the appellate court again denied Maxwell's claim and upheld his death sentence.[38]

Still, Maxwell persevered. In 1968, Maxwell petitioned the U.S. Supreme Court a third time, and the Court agreed to hear arguments about Arkansas's lack of guidelines in jury sentencing and its single-verdict procedure. Amsterdam and his LDF team of Jack Greenberg, James M. Nabrit III, Michael Meltsner, and Elizabeth DuBois wrote the brief, and Amsterdam argued the cause on March 4, 1969. Following oral arguments, the Court voted 8-1 to declare Arkansas's death penalty unconstitutional, but the decision was never announced, and no one outside the court knew of it.[39] Because of unusual circumstances (the unexpected resignation of Justice Abe Fortas on May 14, 1969, and the retirement of Chief Justice Earl Warren that June), the court ordered *Maxwell v. Bishop* to be reargued at the beginning of the next term on October 13, 1969.[40] The reargument, however, was postponed until May 4, 1970, when President Richard Nixon had trouble getting his first two nominees to replace Fortas confirmed. The Senate rejected both Clement Haynsworth, chief judge of the Fourth U.S. Circuit Court of Appeals, and G. Harrold Carswell, a U.S. District Court judge from Tallahassee, Florida. The Senate finally confirmed Nixon's third nominee for the post, Judge Harry A. Blackmun of the Eighth U.S. Circuit Court of Appeals. However, Blackmun had written the Eighth Circuit's opinion in *Maxwell v. Bishop*, so he could not sit on the case as a Supreme Court justice. Thus, the court was left with only eight justices to decide *Maxwell*.[41]

One of the consequences of the *Maxwell* case, as well as two other death penalty cases decided by the Supreme Court in 1968 (*Witherspoon v. Illinois* and *United States v. Jackson* – both discussed below), was the unofficial suspension of all executions until some of the more problematic issues with the death penalty could be resolved. The last execution in the United States was held in June of 1967, when Luis Jose Monge was executed in Colorado's gas chamber.[42] The moratorium on executions would last 10 years, until 1977, when Gary Gilmore requested to be executed by the state of Utah (more about this in Chapter 5).

The U.S. Supreme Court finally determined William Maxwell's fate on June 1, 1970 (*Maxwell v. Bishop*, 398 U.S. 262). The Court, however, did not directly address Maxwell's principal claim that racial discrimination on the part of jurors, who had total discretion in the sentencing decision, infected death cases for rape in at least some Arkansas counties. Instead, the Court vacated Maxwell's death sentence on the more narrow grounds that several prospective jurors in Maxwell's case were improperly removed during voir dire because of their general opposition to the death penalty. As for the problem of juror discretion and, presumably, the racial discrimination that it sometimes allowed, the Court, in footnote 4 of the *Maxwell* decision, announced that it would address the issue early in the 1970 term. The Court had already granted certiorari in the two test cases: *Crampton v. Ohio* and *McGautha v. California*. What the Court could not know at this time was that it was embarking on a road that would eventually lead to the complete abolition of capital punishment in the United States. Before turning to *Crampton* and *McGautha*, however, three cases—two decided in 1968 and one decided in 1969—that would help set the stage for the abolition to come are considered.

UNITED STATES V. JACKSON AND WITHERSPOON V. ILLINOIS

The Supreme Court decided two cases in 1968 that dealt with the discretionary roles of the prosecutor and the jury in the processing of a capital case. The problem addressed in the first case, *United States v. Jackson* (390 U.S. 570, 1968), was the provision in the federal kidnapping statute that required a jury recommendation to impose the death penalty.[43] Congress made kidnapping punishable by death in 1934, following a rash of professional kidnappings, the most notorious of which was the 1932 kidnapping of the Lindbergh child (the kidnapping statute was known as the "Lindbergh law").[44] Under the statute, a defendant could escape a death sentence by waiving the right to a jury trial or by entering a guilty plea. By being able to dangle the prospect of a death sentence before a defendant, prosecutors gained considerable leverage in the plea bargaining process and, apparently, still do.[45] The court opined that the provision impermissibly encouraged defendants, particularly innocent defendants, to waive their right to a jury trial to escape the chance of a death sentence. The court ruled the provision unconstitutional.

In *Witherspoon v. Illinois* (391 U.S. 510, 1968), the Court rejected the common practice of excusing prospective jurors simply because they were opposed to capital punishment.[46] In Witherspoon's case, 47 jurors, nearly half the jurors called for the trial, were successfully challenged for this reason.[47] Witherspoon, who was convicted in 1960 of killing a Chicago police officer,[48] argued that such a practice—referred to as "death qualification"—deprived him of his right to a jury that was representative of the community.[49] Research shows that death-qualified jurors are less concerned with due process and more inclined to believe the prosecution than are excludable jurors. Death-qualified jurors are also significantly less knowledgeable and have more misconceptions about the death penalty and the death-sentencing process than do excludable jurors. Death-qualified jurors are more likely to believe that the focus of the penalty phase of a bifurcated trial should be only on the nature of the crime rather than mitigation and that the death penalty deters murder. They are less likely to believe that innocent people are convicted of capital crimes, that the death penalty is unfair to minorities, and that life without parole really means that a prisoner will not be released from prison. Most troublesome, death-qualified jurors have been found to be more conviction prone.[50]

Little of this evidence was available when the Court decided *Witherspoon*, but the Court, nonetheless, agreed with Witherspoon's argument and held that prospective jurors could be excused only for cause. That is, jurors could be excused only if they would automatically vote against imposition of the death penalty, regardless of the evidence presented at trial, or if their attitudes toward capital punishment prevented them from making an impartial decision on the defendant's guilt. The *Witherspoon* decision was especially important because it drew attention to the composition of capital juries. The discretion exercised by such juries was frequently identified as a principal source of the arbitrariness and discrimination that occurred in the imposition of the death penalty.[51] During the 1980s, the Supreme Court would reconsider its *Witherspoon* decision three different times.

BOYKIN V. ALABAMA

The same day that Amsterdam argued the appeal in *Maxwell v. Bishop* (March 4, 1969), the U.S. Supreme Court heard the appeal of Edward Boykin Jr.[52] Boykin, a 27-year-old black man, had been sentenced to death after pleading guilty to five counts of robbery committed during the spring of 1966. At the time, Alabama was one of the few states that still provided the death penalty as the maximum punishment for robbery. On appeal, Boykin's new attorney (his original court-appointed attorney dropped out of the case after sentencing) maintained that to execute a person for robbery constituted cruel and unusual punishment in violation of the Eighth Amendment. Another argument made on Boykin's behalf was that the trial judge failed to make sure that Boykin understood the possible consequences of his guilty plea. On February 8, 1968, the Alabama Supreme Court rejected both arguments, and 6 months later the U.S. Supreme Court agreed to review the Alabama court's decision.[53] Amsterdam and his legal team (Jack Greenberg, James A. Nabrit III, Michael Meltsner, and Melvyn Zarr) wrote an amicus curiae brief urging reversal.[54] In June of 1969, the Supreme Court granted Boykin a new trial. In doing so, however, the Court bypassed the Eighth Amendment claim and ruled more narrowly that the trial judge had erred in not inquiring about Boykin's understanding of the nature and consequences of his guilty plea.[55]

The *Boykin* appeal is important for two reasons. First, it was the first time the U.S. Supreme Court agreed to consider the constitutionality of the death penalty itself and not simply the procedures used to impose it.[56] Second, the LDF attorneys hoped that the arguments set forth in the *Boykin* brief would eventually become the basis for the death penalty's complete abolition on Eighth Amendment grounds.[57] In the brief, Amsterdam argued:

> The American people ... accept the death penalty only on the statute books—in theory, that is, but not in practice. The evidence demonstrates that Americans will not in fact tolerate its general, even-handed application. Our society accepts the death penalty ... solely because it is applied "sparsely, and spottily to unhappy minorities." The numbers selected are so few, their plight so invisible, and their background so unappealing, that "society can readily bear to see them

suffer torments which would not for a moment be accepted as penalties of general application to the populace."[58]

MCGAUTHA V. CALIFORNIA AND CRAMPTON V. OHIO

Dennis McGautha was sentenced to death for killing a store owner's husband during an armed robbery; James Crampton, for the first-degree murder of his wife.[59] Oral arguments in the cases were heard before the full Supreme Court in November of 1970. A final decision was rendered on May 3, 1971.

The defendants' lawyers argued that unfettered jury discretion in imposing death for murder resulted in arbitrary or capricious sentencing (i.e., sentences not governed by principle; fickle or fanciful sentencing) and, hence, violated the Fourteenth Amendment right to due process of law. McGautha's trial-court judge, following the procedure used in California at the time, instructed the jury as follows: "Now, beyond prescribing the two alternative penalties [death or life imprisonment], the law itself provides no standard for the guidance of the jury in the selection of the penalty, but, rather, commits the whole matter of determining which of the two penalties shall be fixed to the judgment, conscience, and absolute discretion of the jury."[60]

Jurors in Crampton's case were instructed to "consider all the evidence and make your finding with intelligence and impartiality, and without bias, sympathy, or prejudice, so that the State of Ohio and the defendant will feel that their case was fairly and impartially tried."[61] They were also instructed that, unless they recommended mercy, a conviction for first-degree murder would result in a death sentence. The importance of Crampton's case to the issue at hand was not so much the jury instructions, though they provided little guidance on how to arrive at a decision, but, rather, whether bifurcated trials were required in capital cases. McGautha's trial was bifurcated; Crampton's was not.[62]

McGautha's claim, which was joined for decision with Crampton, was rejected by a vote of 6-3. In rejecting the claim, the Court tacitly approved (1) unfettered jury discretion in death sentencing and (2) capital trials in which guilt and sentence were determined in one set of deliberations. Regarding unfettered jury discretion, Justice Harlan, for himself, Chief Justice Burger, and Justices Stewart, White, Black, and Blackmun, reasoned that: "In light of history, experience, and the present limitations of human knowledge, we find it quite impossible to say that committing to the untrammeled discretion of the jury the power to pronounce life or death in capital cases is offensive to anything in the Constitution."[63] This conclusion was based on the underlying belief that it was impossible to adequately guide capital sentencing discretion:

> Those who have come to grips with the hard task of actually attempting to draft means of channeling capital sentencing discretion have confirmed the lesson taught by … history…. To identify before the fact those characteristics of criminal homicides and their perpetrators which call for the death penalty, and to express these characteristics in language which can be fairly understood and applied by the sentencing authority, appear to be tasks which are beyond present human ability.[64]

Abolitionists were disappointed but not surprised by the decision. Some abolitionists remained hopeful because in the majority opinion there was a suggestion that the Court had not foreclosed entirely the possibility of a successful Eighth Amendment challenge.[65] Indeed, on June 28, 1971, less than 60 days after its *McGautha* decision, the Supreme Court agreed to review four cases that challenged the death penalty's constitutionality. In its review orders, the Court stipulated that it would entertain only one question: "Does the imposition and carrying out of the death penalty in this case constitute cruel and unusual punishment in violation of the Eighth and Fourteenth Amendments?"[66] The four test cases were *Aikens v. California, Branch v. Texas, Furman v. Georgia,* and *Jackson v. Georgia.*

AIKENS, BRANCH, FURMAN, AND JACKSON

The four test cases were not selected at random. The Court had chosen them from the nearly 200 pending death penalty appeals.[67] *Aikens* and *Furman* were murder cases; *Jackson* and *Branch* were rape cases.[68] All four of the defendants were black, while all their victims were white.[69] *Aikens, Furman,* and *Jackson* were chosen because LDF attorneys represented them; thus, the Court knew their Eighth Amendment challenges would be well presented.[70] Jackson was also picked because the victim had suffered no special injury, thus making his death sentence appear disproportionately severe for rape.[71] By choosing both murder and rape cases, the Court left itself the option of declaring the death penalty unconstitutional for rape but not for murder.[72]

Earnest James Aikens, Jr. was indicted in California on first-degree murder charges for the stabbing deaths of Kathleen Nell Dodd and Mary Winifred Eaton. Dodd, a 25-year-old pregnant housewife with two small children, was raped and murdered in 1962. Eaton, in her sixties, was raped and murdered in 1965. Aikens pleaded not guilty to both charges. He, his court-appointed counsel, and the district attorney agreed to consolidate the two cases and try them before a judge. At his trial in 1969, he was found guilty on both charges and sentenced to death for the Eaton murder, but , under California law, could only be sentenced to life in prison for the Dodd murder because he was only 17 years old at the time of the murder. In addition, during the sentencing phase of the trial, the state introduced evidence of a third rape and murder he allegedly had committed in 1962 for which he was neither charged nor convicted.[73]

Elmer Branch was sentenced to die in Texas for raping a 65-year-old woman. He did not have a weapon when he raped her and did not make any threats, but he did press his arm against her throat when she tried to scream. Following the rape, he asked her for money, and she gave him the contents of her purse. Before he left, they had a brief conversation about her feelings toward black people, and he told her that if she told anyone, he would come back and kill her. Branch had an IQ of 67 and the equivalent of 5½ years of grade school education.[74]

William Henry Furman was sentenced to die on September 20, 1968, in Savannah, Georgia, for the August 1967 murder of William J. Micke, Jr., a 30-year-old Coast Guard petty officer and the father of four children and the stepfather of six others. Furman, 25 years old at the time of the murder and with an IQ of 65, shot Micke during a burglary attempt at Micke's home.[75] It is instructive to note that Furman's court-appointed trial attorney was paid a total of $150 to defend him. The trial judge denied his attorney's request for additional funds to hire an investigator and to pay for the additional time and expenses needed to prepare Furman's defense. The entire trial—from jury selection to the jury's rendering a death sentence—was completed in one day, between 10:00 a.m. and about 5:00 p.m. Furman's trial attorney made no mention of his client's mental impairments. (Furman was diagnosed as "mentally deficient" with convulsive disorder and psychotic episodes.) According to Justice Brennan, "the jury knew only that he [Furman] was black and that, according to his statement at trial, he was 26 years old and worked at 'Superior Upholstery.'"[76]

Lucious Jackson Jr was sentenced to die in Georgia for the rape of a 20-year-old woman in 1968. At the time of the crime, he was an escaped convict from a prison work gang. He was serving a 3-year sentence for auto theft. He entered the victim's home after her husband had left for work, held scissors against her neck, and demanded money. When she could find none, they battled over the scissors. She lost the battle, and he raped her, holding the scissors against her throat. During the 3 days Jackson was at large, he had committed other crimes—burglary, auto theft, and assault and battery.[77]

FURMAN V. GEORGIA

On January 17, 1972, less than 9 months after the *McGautha* decision, Furman's lawyers argued to the Supreme Court that unfettered jury discretion in imposing death for murder resulted in arbitrary or capricious sentencing. However, Furman's lawyers, per the Court's stipulation and unlike McGautha's, claimed that unbridled jury discretion violated both their client's Fourteenth Amendment right to due process and his Eighth Amendment right not to be subjected to cruel and unusual punishment. Furman's challenge proved successful and, on June 29, 1972—the last day of the term—the U.S. Supreme Court set aside death sentences for the first time in its history. Furman's sentence was commuted to life imprisonment. He was paroled in 1984.

In September 2006, Furman, age 64, was indicted on a 2004 burglary charge. He had broken into a house in Macon, Georgia, that was occupied by a mother and her 10-year-old daughter. The mother, unbeknown to Furman, called 911. When the police arrived, they arrested him. Furman had a pair of the girl's panties in his pocket. He was denied bond because of a bail-jumping charge related to a 2005 possession of burglary tools arrest. Since his 1984 release from prison, Furman has worked in construction in Macon, Georgia, and has had a few arrests for alcohol and weapons violations.[78]

In its decision in *Furman v. Georgia*, *Jackson v. Georgia*, and *Branch v. Texas* (all three cases were consolidated under 408 U.S. 238, 1972, and are referred to here as the *Furman* decision; the *Aikens* case had been dropped on June 7 and will be discussed later), the Court held that the capital punishment statutes in the three cases were unconstitutional because they gave the jury complete discretion to decide whether to impose the death penalty or a lesser punishment in capital cases. Although nine separate opinions were written (a very rare occurrence), the majority of five justices (Douglas, Brennan, Stewart, White, and Marshall) pointed out that the death penalty had been imposed arbitrarily, infrequently, and often selectively against minorities. (Actually, only a few pages of the massive decision addressed racial discrimination.[79]) The majority agreed that the statutes provided for a cruel and unusual punishment in violation of the Eighth and Fourteenth Amendments. (The four dissenters—all Nixon appointees—were Chief Justice Burger and Justices Blackmun, Powell, and Rehnquist. Justices Burger and Blackmun noted, however, that had they been legislators they would have voted to abolish or severely restrict the death penalty.[80]) The *Furman* decision totaled 50,000 words and 243 pages and at the time was one of the longest decisions in Supreme Court history.[81] A practical effect of *Furman* was the Supreme Court's voiding of 40 death penalty statutes and the sentences of more than 600 death row inmates in 32 states.[82] Depending on the state, the death row inmates received new sentences of life imprisonment, a term of years, or, in a few cases, new trials.[83]

An interesting question is why the Supreme Court entertained the *Furman* challenge to unbridled jury discretion in capital cases in the first place, having just the year before rejected the same claim made in *McGautha*. The answer lies in the constitutional right that was challenged. As Raymond Paternoster relates:

> The position that the plurality in *Furman* appeared to be taking … was that while the process of having defendants sentenced to death by juries lacking formal guidance is consistent with the Fourteenth Amendment's requirement of due process, the product, an arbitrary and freakish pattern of death sentencing, is condemned by the Eighth Amendment.[84]

The argument was persuasive enough to change the positions of Justices White and Stewart, who voted against *McGautha* (who lost by a 6-3 margin) but in favor of *Furman* (who won on a 5-4 vote). Making no difference was the change in the composition of the Court between the two cases. Although Lewis Powell replaced Hugo Black and William Rehnquist replaced John Harlan, Powell and Rehnquist voted against *Furman* just as Black and Harlan voted against *McGautha*.

Another factor that may have influenced the Court's *Furman* decision was the Fourth U.S. Circuit Court of Appeals' decision in *Ralph v. Warden* (438 F.2d 786, 4th Cir. 1970). On December 11, 1970, the court became the first federal court to declare the death penalty unconstitutional in violation of the Eighth Amendment's prohibition of cruel and unusual punishment.[85] William Ralph had been convicted of rape in Maryland in 1961 and sentenced to die. Although he did not employ violence, and the victim showed no visible signs of trauma, Ralph did threaten to kill her and her young son, who was asleep in another room, if she resisted.[86] Following years of litigation, Ralph's court-appointed attorney, supported by Amsterdam and an LDF amicus brief, presented the Eighth Amendment claim to the appeals court.[87] In deciding the case, the Court relied on Amsterdam's *Boykin* theory of the Eighth Amendment (that the public would be appalled by the less arbitrary application of the death penalty).[88] The Court concluded that the death penalty was not necessarily unconstitutional for all rapes, but it was for rapes where the victim's life was neither taken nor endangered.[89] It also pointed out that death was an excessive penalty for rape because only a few jurisdictions authorized it, and even in those it was seldom imposed.[90] The Court's *Ralph* opinion only applied to death row inmates convicted of certain forms of rape. Some critics questioned whether the victim, in fact, was not endangered. What if the victim had not submitted voluntarily, and what about pregnancy and disease? Despite the criticism, the *Ralph* case did demonstrate that the Eighth Amendment's cruel and unusual punishment prohibition could be applied successfully in capital cases.[91]

Also consequential to the *Furman* decision may have been California's preemptive action. Between *McGautha* and *Furman*, the California Supreme Court decided *People v. Anderson* (6 Cal.3d 628, 493 P.2d 880, 1972), in which by a vote of 6-1 it ruled the state's death penalty cruel and unusual, in violation of the state constitution. The decision not only invalidated the state's death penalty, but it rendered moot the *Aikens v. California* appeal to the U.S. Supreme Court.[92] Because he no longer faced execution, the Court granted an LDF motion to dismiss Aikens's appeal.[93] Nevertheless, *Aikens* probably influenced *Furman* by allowing Aikens's legal team to continue to hone its arguments in preparation for *Furman*. Amsterdam argued the cause for both petitioners, and five of the eight members of his legal team who helped with the *Aikens* brief also assisted on the six-member team that wrote the *Furman* brief. The five members of both teams were LDF lawyers Michael Meltsner, Jack Greenberg, James M. Nabrit III, Jack Himmelstein, and Elizabeth B. DuBois.[94] Thus, another factor that may have influenced the *Furman* decision was Amsterdam and his team's skilled advocacy. As one commentator put it, they simply convinced the justices to change their minds.[95]

Finally, law professor Corinna Lain argues that *"Furman* was a decision the Justices wanted to make, not one they had to make (or even had substantial support for making). The Court invalidated the death penalty because five Justices were convinced it was the right thing to do."[96]

It is important to note that the Court did not declare the death penalty itself unconstitutional. It held as unconstitutional only the statutes under which the death penalty was then being administered. Actually, the five justices in the majority split on this issue. Justices Brennan and Marshall maintained that capital punishment itself violated the Eighth and Fourteenth Amendments. Justices Douglas, Stewart, and White, on the other hand, rejected the position that capital punishment was inherently unconstitutional and argued that only the way it was being applied under current statutes made it unconstitutional. The Court seemed to be implying that if the process of applying the death penalty could be changed to eliminate the problems cited in *Furman*, then it would pass constitutional muster. Both Justices White and Burger believed that mandatory or automatic death sentences were still probably constitutional.[97] Justice Stewart, on the other hand, was fairly certain that the states would not reenact the old, "barbaric" mandatory death penalty statutes[98]—the last of which (except for a few rarely committed crimes in a few jurisdictions) was abolished in 1963.

Ignoring for the moment the Court's suggestion that the death penalty could be salvaged, death penalty opponents were jubilant on that June day in 1972. LDF lawyers knew their work did not end with *Furman*. There was still much to do to ensure that states followed the Court's directive. They understood that capitulation to the Court's decree would not come automatically, and that it would have to be fought for in most of the states that had their capital punishment statutes invalidated. To implement *Furman* and to make sure the death sentences of all death row inmates were vacated, each state's highest court had to take action, which in many states required the prodding of the LDF lawyers and those that assisted them throughout the country.[99] Nevertheless, LDF attorneys could take pride in what they had accomplished. In 7 years of hard work, they had achieved what had eluded American abolitionists for two centuries.[100] Many people believed, as Justices Stewart and Burger predicted privately, that there would never be another execution in the United States.[101]

Justices Stewart and Burger and all those who shared their belief, of course, were wrong! The backlash against *Furman* was immediate and widespread. Many people, including those who had never given the death penalty issue much thought, were incensed at what they perceived as the Supreme Court's arrogance in ignoring the will of the majority and its elected representatives. They clamored to have the penalty restored. Obliging their constituents, the elected representatives of 35 states proceeded to adopt new death penalty statutes designed to meet the Court's objections. Florida was the first jurisdiction to reinstate the death penalty after *Furman*. The Florida legislature met in special session to approve the new law in December of 1972, only 5 months after the *Furman* decision.[102] By May 1973, 13 states had enacted new death penalty statutes, including New Mexico, which had abolished the death penalty in 1969 prior to *Furman* (New Mexico abolished the death penalty again in 2009). By *Furman*'s 1-year anniversary, 20 states had reinstated the death penalty, and by 1976, 35 states had done so.[103] (Currently, 36 jurisdictions, which includes 34 states, the federal government, and the military, have death penalty statutes; 17 jurisdictions, including 16 states and the District of Columbia, do not.) The new death penalty laws took two forms. Twenty-two states removed all discretion from the process by mandating capital punishment upon conviction for certain crimes ("mandatory" death penalty statutes).[104] Other states provided specific guidelines that judges and juries were to use in deciding if death was the appropriate sentence in a particular case ("guided discretion" death penalty statutes).[105] Georgia was the first jurisdiction to impose a post-*Furman* death sentence. Chester Thomas Atkins was sentenced to death in early May 1973, about 6 weeks after Governor Jimmy Carter signed the state's post-*Furman* "guided discretion" death penalty statute into law. Atkins's death sentence was overturned 6 months later by the state supreme court.[106] Although the sentence was one of only a few imposed in 1973, the floodgates began to open in 1974, when a three-decade high of 149 death sentences were imposed. In 1975, the number of death sentences increased to 298—at the time, the highest year-end number ever recorded.[107]

The legislative response to *Furman* caused the LDF lawyers to begin preparing to take on the new death penalty statutes. In doing so, their immediate mission was to extend the then 5-year-old moratorium, but their ultimate goal was to abolish the death penalty once and for all.[108] There was reason to be optimistic about both goals. In the first place, it was unlikely the Court would approve the new "guided discretion" statutes when, just a few years earlier, Justice Harlan maintained in *McGautha* that it was humanly impossible to create adequate guidelines to channel juror discretion. Second, because of the moratorium and the subsequent growth of the death row population, a resumption of executions could cause a bloodbath—something few people wanted. Third, the Court was getting weary of deciding death penalty cases every year. Fourth, as noted previously, Justices Stewart and Burger did not think there would be any more executions in the United States. Fifth, Justice Powell, who voted with the *Furman* minority, believed that either Justice Stevens, who was new to the Court since *Furman*, or Justice Blackmun would join the four justices left from the *Furman* majority and vote to bring closure to the issue. Sixth, Justice Powell also assumed that Justices Stewart and White, who, in their *Furman* decisions, voted to strike down the death penalty, as then applied, but expressed their belief that it could be fixed, would vote to totally abolish the death penalty if given another chance.[109] How could the death penalty be reinstated under these circumstances? The answer is that it could and it was. As it turned out, each of the reasons was wrong. In retrospect, the legal strategy backfired. It produced only a fleeting victory. Given the scope of the public reaction to *Furman*, the Court was put in a difficult position when the new death penalty laws were challenged 4 years later. The LDF lawyers' strategy of invoking an "evolving standards" argument was hard to defend in light of the backlash.[110] The Court's institutional authority was also challenged by the public backlash to *Furman*. Following *Furman*, 17 members of Congress began promoting a constitutional amendment to restore the death penalty. By 1976, it appeared that they had the votes to succeed. However, even if the constitutional amendment effort had failed, the attempt to override the Court would have undermined the Court's power and legitimacy.[111] With the public in favor of the death penalty by a 2-1 margin, both political parties aligned on the issue, and Solicitor General Robert Bork's request that the Court overrule its *Furman* decision, the Court's decision to follow the solicitor general's recommendation is not difficult to understand.[112] Had the public response to *Furman* been milder, perhaps the outcome in the subsequent cases might have been different.[113] Justices Stewart and White suggested as much in later decisions.[114] The lesson of *Furman* was that death penalty abolition had to be won in the legislatures and not in the courts.

Another response to the *Furman* decision, though its importance probably was not fully appreciated at the time, was the enactment of the first true life without opportunity of parole (LWOP) statutes. Afraid of the prospects of a punishment scheme without a capital option and responding to public dissatisfaction with murderers sentenced to "life" being paroled early, law-and-order legislators, with the support of prosecutors, pushed through the first LWOP statutes in Alabama, Illinois, and Louisiana.[115] Other states followed. At this writing, all states but Alaska have LWOP statutes, and Alaska does not have a death penalty.[116] Passage of the LWOP statutes following *Furman* soon became a classic case of "be careful of what you wish for." When the death penalty was reinstated in 1976, prosecutors no longer wanted the LWOP statutes because they wanted to use the possibility of parole to convince jurors to sentence defendants to death. Prosecutors frequently used the possibility of parole as a scare tactic by warning jurors that if a capital defendant was not executed, he or she would pose a future danger to society. At the same time, death penalty abolitionists began to realize that LWOP could be promoted as a viable option to death sentences.[117]

WOODSON V. NORTH CAROLINA AND *GREGG V. GEORGIA*

The constitutionality of the new death penalty statutes was quickly challenged, and on July 2, 1976, the Supreme Court announced its rulings in five test cases. The five cases were chosen because they were "relatively straightforward," the facts were clear, and there were no side issues, such as racial prejudice.[118] All five cases involved felony murders, none of which was especially brutal and, perhaps most important, each case was selected from a state that had one of the five different types of new death penalty laws.[119] In *Woodson v. North Carolina* (428 U.S. 280) and *Roberts v. Louisiana* (428 U.S. 325), the Court rejected, by a vote of 5-4, mandatory statutes that automatically imposed death sentences for defined capital crimes. In the North Carolina case, the state's brief defending the law pointed out that the state enacted the law to eliminate "all sentencing discretion" so that "there would be no successful *Furman*-based attack" on it.[120] Justice Stewart explained why the Court rejected the mandatory statutes. First, Stewart admitted that "it is capricious to treat similar things differently," and that mandatory death penalty statutes eliminated that problem.[121] He added, however, that it also "is capricious to treat two different things the same way."[122] Therefore, to impose the same penalty on all convicted murderers, even though all defendants are different, is just as capricious as imposing a penalty randomly.[123] To alleviate the problem, then, some sentencing guidelines were necessary.[124] Thus, in *Gregg v. Georgia* (428 U.S. 153), *Jurek v. Texas* (428 U.S. 262), and *Proffitt v. Florida* (428 U.S. 242) (hereafter referred to as the *Gregg* decision), the Court, by a vote of 7-2 (Justices Marshall and Brennan dissented), approved guided discretion statutes that set standards for juries and judges to use when deciding whether to impose the death penalty. Justice Harlan's *McGautha* opinion notwithstanding, the Court's majority concluded that the guided discretion statutes struck a reasonable balance between giving the jury some direction and allowing it to consider the defendant's background and character and the circumstances of the crime. In doing so, they would respect the defendant's basic human dignity, as required by the Eighth Amendment, and prevent jury nullification—the practice of a jury's refusal to convict guilty defendants to avoid imposing unjust death sentences.[125]

Not all the justices were happy with their decisions in *Gregg*. For example, Justice White, who cast his lot with the majority, complained, "Mistakes will be made and discriminations will occur which will be difficult to explain."[126] Lain maintains that one of the great ironies of both *Furman* and *Gregg* (and several other subsequent death penalty cases) is that "the litigant with the law on its side lost. In *Furman*, conventional sources of constitutional law supported the death penalty, but the Court still invalidated it. In *Gregg*, precedent finally cut against the death penalty, but the Court reinstated it anyway."[127] She concludes, "Both cases make sense only when viewed in light of the larger historical context in which they were decided."[128] Lain's point—a point she shares with many Court observers—is that extralegal factors (e.g., "broader social and political forces"), rather than the law, frequently guide the justices' decisions.

The Court also approved three other major procedural reforms in *Gregg*: bifurcated trials, automatic appellate review of convictions and sentences, and proportionality review. Proportionality review is a process whereby state appellate courts compare the sentence in the case before it with sentences imposed in similar cases in the state. Its purpose is to identify sentencing disparities and aid in their elimination.[129] Ironically, in the case that would set the standards for the modern death penalty, no mitigating evidence was presented during the new, special sentencing hearing. Mitigating evidence, along with aggravating evidence (to be discussed later), is the hallmark of guided discretion statutes. The jury heard absolutely nothing about Gregg's background and character. In fact, in a trial that lasted only 4 days, Gregg's court-appointed attorney presented no evidence at all (except to put Gregg on the witness stand to testify that he did not commit the murders with which he was charged).[130]

In any event, the primary justification for the unique procedural safeguards approved in *Gregg* was the "death-is-different" principle created by Supreme Court Justice William Brennan and first articulated in *Furman v. Georgia*.[131] In *Furman*, the Court observed that death is "an unusually severe punishment, unusual in its pain, in its finality, and in its enormity."[132] Later, in *Gardner v. Florida* (420 U.S. 349, 1977), the Court elaborated:

> [F]ive Members of the Court have now expressly recognized that death is a different kind of punishment from any other which may be imposed in this country. From the point of view of the defendant, it is different both in its severity and its finality. From the point of view of society, the action of the sovereign in taking the life of one of its citizens also differs dramatically from any other legitimate state action. It is of vital importance to the defendant and to the community that any decision to impose the death sentence be, and appear to be, based on reason rather than caprice or emotion.[133]

As a result of these decisions, the death penalty, unlike any other punishment prescribed by law, requires special procedures that ensure its lawful application. Law professor Margaret Jane Radin refers to these special procedures as "super due process."[134]

Paternoster has noted that the Court in *Gregg* and *Woodson* attempted to cleverly reconcile two seemingly irreconcilable goals: consistency in application and consideration of individual circumstances.[135] Whereas in *Woodson*, mandatory statutes would guarantee consistency in application; they would preclude "individualized" sentencing decisions. In *Gregg*, guided discretion statutes would allow for the consideration of factors peculiar to the case but would necessarily produce disparities in sentencing. If one of the two goals had to be sacrificed for the other, the Court apparently opted (if it ever considered the dilemma) for the consideration of individual circumstances over consistency in application.[136] Inconsistency in application, however, was one of the problems cited by the Court in *Furman*.

It is also noteworthy that the Court approved the guided discretion statutes on faith, assuming that the new statutes and their procedural reforms would rid the administration of the death penalty of the problems cited in *Furman*. Because guided discretion statutes, automatic appellate review, and proportionality review had never been required or employed before in death penalty cases, the Court could not have known whether they would make a difference. Now, more than 30 years later, it is possible to evaluate the results. Steiker and Steiker claim that the statutes have not made much (positive) difference:[137]

> The Supreme Court's death penalty law, by creating an impression of enormous regulatory effort, while achieving negligible effects, effectively obscures the true nature of our capital sentencing

system. The pre-Furman world of unreviewable sentencer discretion lives on, with much the same consequences in terms of arbitrary and discriminatory sentencing patterns.[138]

Newly retired Supreme Court Justice John Paul Stevens would agree. In a 2010 interview, Justice Stevens confessed that he particularly regretted one vote during his 35 years on the Court—his 1976 vote to uphold the death penalty in *Gregg v. Georgia*.[139] He stated, "I thought at the time … that if the universe of defendants eligible for the death penalty is sufficiently narrow so that you can be confident that the defendant really merits that severe punishment, that the death penalty was appropriate." "But, over the years," he continued, "the Court constantly expanded the cases eligible for the death penalty, so that the underlying premise for my vote has disappeared, in a sense." He lamented, "I really think that the death penalty today is vastly different from the death penalty that we thought we were authorizing." Indeed, Justices Stevens, Blackmun, and Powell—all of whom voted with the majority in *Gregg*—have changed their minds about the death penalty and no longer believe it is constitutional. Had those justices voted differently in *Gregg*, the Court would have abolished the death penalty in 1976 by a vote of 5-4.

One of the problems was that the Court, which endorsed the aforementioned reforms, did virtually nothing to guarantee that defendants benefited from them. For example, despite the emphasis placed on the presentation of mitigation evidence during the penalty phase of the bifurcated trial, the Court ignored the fact that many attorneys in capital cases lacked the training, experience, and resources to do so effectively.[140]

The Court actually accepted several different types of guided discretion statutes that varied in the restrictions placed on judges and juries. Some of those statutes were modeled after ones proposed in the American Law Institute's Model Penal Code of 1959.[141] Two of the most common types of guided discretion statutes are "aggravating versus mitigating" and "aggravating only"; a third type, "structured discretion," is one of the most frequently used types of guided discretion statutes.[142] Aggravating circumstances (or factors) or "special circumstances," as they are called in some jurisdictions, refer "to the particularly serious features of a case, for example, evidence of extensive premeditation and planning by the defendant, or torture of the victim by the defendant."[143] Mitigating circumstances (or factors), or "extenuating circumstances," refer "to features of a case that explain or particularly justify the defendant's behavior, even though they do not provide a defense to the crime of murder" (e.g., youth, immaturity, or being under the influence of another person).[144] An example of each type of statute is presented next.

AGGRAVATING VERSUS MITIGATING DEATH PENALTY STATUTES

Florida's current death penalty statute is an example of the "aggravating versus mitigating" type. It is the most widely used type of death penalty statute.[145] Under it, at least one aggravating factor must be found before death may be considered as a penalty. If one or more aggravating factors are found, they are weighed against any mitigating factors. If the aggravating factors outweigh the mitigating factors, then the sentence is death. If the mitigating factors outweigh the aggravating factors, the sentence is life imprisonment without possibility of parole. If the aggravating and mitigating factors are of equal weight, a death sentence may be imposed.[146]

Following are the aggravating and mitigating circumstances listed in Florida's death penalty statute.

Aggravating circumstances

1. The capital felony was committed by a person previously convicted of a felony and under sentence of imprisonment or placed on community control or on felony probation.
2. The defendant was previously convicted of another capital felony or of a felony involving the use or threat of violence to the person.
3. The defendant knowingly created a great risk of death to many persons.
4. The capital felony was committed while the defendant was engaged, or was an accomplice, in the commission of, or an attempt to commit, or flight after committing or attempting to commit, any: robbery; sexual battery; aggravated child abuse; abuse of an elderly person or disabled adult resulting in great bodily harm, permanent disability, or permanent disfigurement; arson; burglary; kidnapping; aircraft piracy; or unlawful throwing, placing, or discharging of a destructive device or bomb.
5. The capital felony was committed for the purpose of avoiding or preventing a lawful arrest or effecting an escape from custody.
6. The capital felony was committed for pecuniary gain.
7. The capital felony was committed to disrupt or hinder the lawful exercise of any governmental function or the enforcement of laws.
8. The capital felony was especially heinous, atrocious, or cruel.
9. The capital felony was a homicide and was committed in a cold, calculated, and premeditated manner without any pretense of moral or legal justification.
10. The victim of the capital felony was a law enforcement officer engaged in the performance of his official duties.
11. The victim of the capital felony was an elected or appointed public official engaged in the performance of his official duties if the motive for the capital felony was related, in whole or in part, to the victim's official capacity.
12. The victim of the capital felony was a person less than 12 years of age.
13. The victim of the capital felony was particularly vulnerable due to advanced age or disability, or because the defendant stood in a position of familial or custodial authority over the victim.
14. The capital felony was committed by a criminal street gang member, as defined in s. 874.03.
15. The capital felony was committed by a person designated as a sexual predator pursuant to s. 775.21 or a person previously designated as a sexual predator who had the sexual predator designation removed.
16. The capital felony was committed by a person subject to an injunction issued pursuant to s. 741.30 [domestic violence] or s. 784.046 [repeat violence, sexual violence, or dating violence], or a foreign protection order accorded full faith and credit pursuant to s. 741.315 [domestic violence], and was committed against the petitioner who obtained the injunction or protection order or any spouse, child, sibling, or parent of the petitioner.

Mitigating circumstances

1. The defendant has no significant history of prior criminal activity.
2. The capital felony was committed while the defendant was under the influence of extreme mental or emotional disturbance.

3. The victim was a participant in the defendant's conduct or consented to the act.
4. The defendant was an accomplice in the capital felony committed by another person and his or her participation was relatively minor.
5. The defendant acted under extreme duress or under the substantial domination of another person.
6. The capacity of the defendant to appreciate the criminality of his or her conduct or to conform his or her conduct to the requirements of law was substantially impaired.
7. The age of the defendant at the time of the crime.
8. The existence of any other factors in the defendant's background that would mitigate against imposition of the death penalty.[147]

Two issues about Florida's death penalty statute in particular, and aggravating versus mitigating death penalty statutes in general, are worthy of note. First, Florida is one of only three death penalty states (the others are Alabama and Delaware) where a jury's sentencing recommendation is only advisory.[148] In other words, a judge is legally entitled to ignore the jury's recommendation and impose the sentence (either life or death) that he or she believes is most appropriate; the only stipulation is that a judge must give the jury verdict "great weight."[149] Thus, between 1972 and 2002, for example, Florida judges overruled 167 jury decisions to sentence defendants to life in prison and instead sentenced the defendants to death. However, most Florida judges stopped overruling juries, even though the law allowed it, because so many of those death sentences had been overturned on appeal by the Florida Supreme Court.[150] In Alabama, more than 20 percent of recent death row inmates were sentenced to death by trial judges who overrode jury sentences of life without parole.[151] None of this may matter anymore, because in June 2002, the U.S. Supreme Court ruled in *Ring v. Arizona* (536 U.S. 584) that the Sixth Amendment right to a jury trial requires that juries and not judges determine whether death is the appropriate penalty in a capital case. This decision may end the practice in Florida, Alabama, and Delaware of making the jury's decision in capital cases only advisory. As of this writing, however, all three states have withstood several *Ring* challenges to their override provisions.

The second issue is that the weighing of aggravating versus mitigating factors was not intended as a simple exercise in adding and subtracting. Jurors are not supposed to count the number of aggravating factors and then subtract them from the number of mitigating factors, or vice versa. Not all factors necessarily count equally. It is conceivable that a single aggravating factor could outweigh several mitigating factors, or, again, vice versa. A problem with this weighing process is that it gives the sentencing authority tremendous discretion—something the guided discretion statutes were meant to control. Without any rules guiding how much weight should be given to specific aggravating and mitigating factors, judges and jurors are forced to use their "common sense" in making their sentencing decisions.[152]

AGGRAVATING-ONLY DEATH PENALTY STATUTES

Georgia's post-*Furman* capital statute is an example of the "aggravating-only" type. In Georgia, if a jury finds at least one statutory aggravating factor, then it may, but need not, recommend death. Two exceptions are the offenses of aircraft hijacking or treason, for which the death penalty may be imposed without finding at least one of the statutory aggravating factors. In all capital cases, the jury may also consider any mitigating factor, although mitigating factors are not listed in the statute as they are in some states. The judge must follow the jury's recommendation.[153] The aggravating factors listed in Georgia's death penalty statute are similar to those in Florida's death penalty statute.

STRUCTURED DISCRETION STATUTES

Texas's current death penalty statute is an example of the "structured discretion" type. It is the most unusual type of guided discretion statute, employed only in Texas, Oregon, and Virginia.[154] In Texas, for a defendant to be convicted of capital murder, the state must prove beyond a reasonable doubt that the defendant committed murder with at least one of nine statutorily enumerated aggravating circumstances. If the state fails in the effort, then the sentencing authority may still convict the defendant of murder or any other lesser-included offense. If the defendant is convicted of capital murder, then during the sentencing phase of the trial, the state and the defendant or the defendant's counsel may present evidence as to any matter that the court deems relevant to sentence, that is, any aggravating or mitigating factors, as long as they have not been secured in violation of the U.S. or Texas constitutions. The court then submits the following issues to the jury:

1. whether there is a probability that the defendant would commit criminal acts of violence that would constitute a continuing threat to society; and
2. (if raised by the evidence) whether the defendant actually caused the death of the deceased or did not actually cause the death of the deceased but intended to kill the deceased or another or anticipated that a human life would be taken.

During penalty deliberations, juries in Texas must consider all evidence admitted at the guilt and penalty phases. Then, they must consider the two aforementioned issues. To answer "yes" to the issues, all jurors must answer "yes"; to answer "no" to the issues, 10 or more jurors must answer "no." If the two issues are answered in the affirmative, jurors are then asked if there is a sufficient mitigating factor (or factors) to warrant that a sentence of life imprisonment without parole rather than a death sentence be imposed. To answer "no" to this issue, all jurors must answer "no"; to answer "yes," 10 or more jurors must agree. If the jury returns an affirmative finding on the first two issues and a negative finding on the third issue, then the court must sentence the defendant to death. If the jury returns a negative finding on either of the first two issues or an affirmative finding on the third issue, then the court must sentence the defendant to life imprisonment without parole.[155]

Answering the first issue in the affirmative might prove difficult for many people. Despite decades of trying, social scientists remain incapable of predicting, with a reasonable degree of accuracy (a debatable standard), future human behavior, criminal or otherwise. Given what might seem the difficulty in getting all 12 jurors to answer "yes" to the two issues of aggravation and "no" to the issue of mitigation, one might surmise that states with structured discretion statutes would have a hard time sentencing offenders to death. This conclusion, however, would be wrong: Texas has executed more people than any other state under its structured discretion statute, executing more than four times as many people as any other state.[156] Apparently, getting all members of a jury to answer in the ways necessary to return a death sentence can be relatively easy.

AUTOMATIC APPELLATE REVIEW

Each of the guided discretion statutes approved in *Gregg* also provided for automatic appellate review of all convictions and death sentences. This reform was added to ensure that death sentences were applied in a constitutionally acceptable manner. Prior to *Furman*, many death row inmates did not take advantage of the appellate process. During the 1960s, for example, one-quarter of the prisoners executed had no appeals at all, and two-thirds of their cases were never reviewed by a federal court.[157]

The review is typically conducted by the state's highest appellate court. In an effort to reduce delays in capital cases, the Florida legislature has written into its capital punishment statute instructions that every effort is to be made to ensure "that all appeals and postconviction actions in capital cases are resolved within 5 years after the date a sentence of death is imposed in the circuit court."[158]

At the end of 2009, 33 of the now 34 states with capital punishment statutes provided for an automatic review or direct appeal of all death sentences, regardless of the defendant's wishes.[159] South Carolina allows the defendant to waive sentence review if the court deems the defendant competent; also, the federal jurisdiction does not provide for automatic appellate review. Most of the 33 states automatically review both the conviction and the sentence. Idaho, Montana, Oklahoma, South Dakota, and Tennessee require review of the death sentence only. In Idaho, review of conviction has to be filed through appeal or forfeited. In Indiana and Kentucky, a defendant can waive review of the conviction. In Virginia, a defendant can waive an appeal of trial court error but cannot waive a review of the death sentence for arbitrariness and proportionality. Mississippi has not addressed whether a defendant can waive the right to automatic appellate review. In Wyoming, neither case law nor statute precludes waiver of appeal. Arkansas requires review of specific issues relating to both capital convictions and sentences.[160] The rationale for not allowing defendants to waive the automatic review is that the state has an independent interest in making sure that the death penalty is administered lawfully. On the other hand, the rationale for waivers is that the defendant's autonomy and freedom of choice ought to prevail. If either the conviction or the sentence is overturned, then the case is usually sent back to the trial court for additional proceedings or for retrial. It is possible that the death sentence may be reimposed as a result of this process. Although the Supreme Court does not require it (*Pulley v. Harris*, 465 U.S. 37, 1984), some states, as noted previously, provide for proportionality review during the review process.

A NOTE ON THE APPELLATE PROCESS UNDER POST-*FURMAN* STATUTES

In addition to automatic appellate review, direct appeal, or direct review, defendants sentenced to death also have a dual system of collateral review; that is, they may challenge their convictions and/or sentences through both state postconviction proceedings and federal habeas corpus petitions.[161] Steps in the dual system of collateral review in death penalty cases are:[162]

Stage 1: Direct appeal
    Step 1: Trial and sentence in state court

Step 2: Direct appeal to state appeals court (state supreme court)
Step 3: U.S. Supreme Court for writ of certiorari (discretionary)

Stage 2: State postconviction review
Step 1: Trial court
Step 2: State court of appeals (state supreme court)
Step 3: U.S. Supreme Court for writ of certiorari (discretionary)

Stage 3: Federal postconviction review
Step 1: Petition for writ of habeas corpus in U.S. District Court
Step 2: U.S. Circuit Court of Appeals
Step 3: U.S. Supreme Court for writ of certiorari (discretionary)

A state appellate court has at least five options when a conviction and/or death sentence has been appealed to it: (1) it can vacate the conviction (and therefore the sentence) and remand the case to the trial court for additional proceedings or for retrial, (2) it can affirm the conviction and remand the case to the trial court for resentencing, (3) it can reduce the sentence to life imprisonment or life imprisonment without opportunity of parole, (4) it can affirm both the conviction and the sentence,[163] or (5) it can reverse both the sentence and conviction and order the defendant to be freed, although this option occurs rarely. If the state appellate court affirms both the conviction and the sentence, an appeal may be made to the U.S. Supreme Court through a writ of certiorari. If the appeal to the Supreme Court is unsuccessful, the capital defendant may then return to state postconviction proceedings and begin the appeals process anew. Even if the defendant's appeal is denied in the state appellate courts, because of the dual system of collateral review, the defendant may appeal to the appropriate U.S. District Court through a writ of habeas corpus. If the appeal is denied in the U.S. District Court, that decision may be appealed to the appropriate U.S. Circuit Court of Appeals. However, in order to appeal a district court's decision to a federal court of appeals, either the district court or the court of appeals must grant the inmate permission in the form of a certificate of appealability, or COA.[164] If the COA is granted but relief in the court of appeals is denied, a third appeal may be made to the U.S. Supreme Court.

Until recently, it was possible for people sentenced to death to employ this dual system of collateral review numerous times (see, e.g., the case of Caryl Chessman in Chapter 1). Now, however, because of Supreme Court decisions, the passage of the Antiterrorism and Effective Death Penalty Act of 1996, and similar measures by state legislatures, access to both the federal and state appellate courts has been made more difficult. Proponents of these types of decisions and legislation believe that most appeals are frivolous and are simply delaying tactics, and they hope that the new rules will greatly reduce the long delays in executions and the high costs associated with the entire capital punishment process.[165] They point to death row inmates such as James Hitchcock, who was sentenced to death in 1977 for the rape and murder of his stepniece. Hitchcock still sits on Florida's death row even though he has had three resentencings, four death sentences upheld, and 19 appeals.[166] But what if many of the appeals are not frivolous and delaying tactics? What if the delays in executions are greatly reduced because death row inmates are unable to have their claims heard in the federal courts?

At least 30 percent and as many as 68 percent of all convictions or sentences in death penalty cases from 1973 through 2009 have been overturned on appeal.[167] Many appeals may, indeed, be frivolous and delaying tactics, but the evidence shows that many of them are not. The reversals, as described in more detail in Chapter 9, have resulted from fundamental constitutional errors such as coerced confessions; ineffective assistance of counsel; denial of the right of an impartial jury; prosecutors withholding exculpatory evidence, suborning perjury, and using tainted evidence; and unconstitutional jury instructions.[168] The percentage of death penalty cases overturned by the appellate courts since the reestablishment of capital punishment has far exceeded the percentage of appellate reversals of all other noncapital felony cases—in most states, this probably does not exceed 1 percent.[169] However, the number of death penalty appeal reversals has been decreasing dramatically in recent years, not because of greater fairness in the system or fewer constitutional errors, but rather because death row inmates are simply less likely to prevail. Nearly all constitutional errors today are subject to harm analysis and "proving that an error was harmful is difficult or impossible."[170]

In sum, despite a very elaborate process that includes guided discretion statutes and bifurcated trials, a large number of convictions and/or sentences in death penalty cases are reversed on appeal or during postconviction review—a reversal rate many times higher than that in noncapital cases. The errors that are discovered, moreover, are not insignificant legal technicalities but are the result of violations of fundamental constitutional protections. Under such circumstances, a likely result of restricting the access of death row inmates to the appellate process is miscarriages of justice. In other words, without the ability to challenge arrests, charges, indictments, convictions, sentences, and pending executions in the appellate courts, there likely will be an increase in the number of innocent people or people not legally eligible for execution involved in the capital punishment process. The subject of miscarriages of justice in capital cases is examined in detail in Chapter 9.

CONCLUSION

On June 29, 1972, the U.S. Supreme Court, for the first and only time in American history, declared the death penalty unconstitutional. In 7 short years, LDF attorneys, led by attorney extraordinaire Anthony Amsterdam, had accomplished the goal that had eluded American abolitionists for two centuries. Unfortunately for the abolitionists, their accomplishment was short-lived and, in retrospect, turned out to be a pyrrhic victory. The public backlash to the *Furman* decision was overwhelming and swift. Only 4 years after *Furman*, the Court reversed itself and reinstated capital punishment. The Court approved capital punishment statutes that the majority believed would rid the death penalty of the problems cited in its *Furman* decision. Based on the death-is-different principle, the Court approved what would be called "super due process." Super due process consisted of a guided discretion process that requires juries to consider aggravating and mitigating evidence presented during the sentencing phase of a bifurcated trial. (The first phase in the bifurcated trial is the guilt phase.) In addition, super due process included automatic appeal usually of both the conviction and the sentence and proportionality review, though neither process is constitutionally required.

As noted, the Court's majority believed that super due process would rid the death penalty of the problems cited in *Furman*. This leap of faith on the Court's part was not based on any evidence because there was none. However, now, it is possible to determine whether the Court's faith in super due process was justified. Several of the subsequent chapters of this book review the evidence that has been amassed in the more than three decades since the death penalty was reinstated. Before turning to that evidence, however, the next chapter examines the Court's massive effort to regulate capital punishment's administration under super due process.

DISCUSSION QUESTIONS

1. Do you agree with the Court's *Witherspoon* decision?
2. Do you agree with Justice Harlan in *McGautha* that it is impossible to adequately guide capital sentencing discretion?
3. Do you agree with the Court's *Furman* decision?
4. Which are fairer: mandatory or discretionary death penalty laws?
5. Do you agree with Justice Brennan that "death is different"?
6. Does the death penalty require "super due process"?
7. Do the guided discretion death penalty statutes adequately reconcile the goals of consistency in application and consideration of individual circumstances?
8. Which type of guided discretion death penalty statute is fairest?
9. Is automatic appellate review necessary?
10. What are the steps in the dual system of collateral review?
11. Should we be concerned about the reversal rate of convictions and death sentences in capital cases?

Notes

1. The challenges to specific methods of execution addressed whether such methods as electrocution violated the "cruel and unusual punishment" standard of the Eighth Amendment. See Chapter 2. For early procedural challenges, also see Chapter 2.
2. Banner (2002, p. 248), Gottlieb (1961), Meltsner (1973, p. 23), and Paternoster (1991, p. 41).
3. Paternoster (1991, p. 51).
4. Ibid., p. 52.
5. Lain (2007a, p. 28).
6. Meltsner (1973, p. 24) and Paternoster (1991, p. 41).
7. Paternoster (1991, p. 41).
8. Banner (2002, pp. 238–239).
9. Ibid., p. 241.
10. Meltsner (1973, p. 21) and Paternoster (1991). The American Law Institute (ALI) is an organization comprising about 4000 judges, lawyers, and law professors, who synthesize and shape the law in statements and model codes that provide structure and coherence in a federal legal system that might otherwise consist of 50 different approaches to everything. The ALI in its Model Penal Code created the framework for the modern death penalty—a framework the Supreme Court largely adopted in *Gregg v. Georgia*. In October 2009, the ALI pronounced its death penalty structure a failure and abandoned efforts to reform it. Its decision was a compromise. Some members wanted the ALI to take a stand against the death penalty but the effort failed. Liptak (2010).
11. Meltsner (1973, p. 109).
12. Meltsner (1973, p. 28) and Paternoster (1991, p. 42).
13. *Rudolph v. Alabama*, 375 U.S. 889 (1963).
14. Meltsner (1973, pp. 31–32).
15. Ibid., p. 32; Banner (2002, p. 248).
16. Meltsner (1973, pp. 32–33).

17. Banner (2002, p. 250).

18. Ibid., p. 239.

19. Banner (2002, p. 250) and Meltsner (1973, p. 33).

20. Meltsner (1973, pp. 30 and 60). For a fascinating description of the "road to *Furman*" by one of the LDF lawyers who was there from the beginning, see Meltsner (1973).

21. Ibid.

22. See Banner (2002, p. 247).

23. Meltsner (1973).

24. Bedau (2009, p. 617).

25. Banner (2002, pp. 251–252).

26. Meltsner (1973, pp. 60 and 65–66).

27. Ibid.

28. Ibid., p. 109.

29. Ibid., pp. 110–111.

30. Ibid., pp. 78–79.

31. Ibid., pp. 79–80.

32. Ibid., p. 80.

33. Ibid., pp. 83–84.

34. Ibid., pp. 84–86.

35. Ibid., pp. 85–86.

36. Ibid., "About the Author."

37. Ibid., p. 112.

38. See Paternoster (1991, pp. 42–45).

39. Banner (2002, p. 255). In *The Brethren* (Woodward & Armstrong, 1979, pp. 205–206), the authors wrote that the vote was 6-3, not 8-1.

40. Meltsner (1973, pp. 186–187).

41. Ibid., pp. 186–197.

42. Coyne and Entzeroth (1994, p. 95).

43. See Nakell and Hardy (1987, p. 20).

44. Meltsner (1973, p. 115).

45. See Leyte-Vidal and Silverman (2006, p. 271).

46. Nakell and Hardy (1987).

47. Meltsner (1973, p. 119).

48. Ibid., p. 118.

49. Death qualification received judicial approval as early as 1820. In *United States v. Cornell* (25 F. Cas. 650, 1820), Circuit Justice Joseph Story reluctantly denied a motion for a new trial in this murder case. One of the exceptions raised by counsel was that two potential jurors disqualified themselves because they were Quakers and had conscientious scruples about "taking away life." The two Quakers stated that they could not be impartial in a capital case. In response to the counsel's exception and endorsing death qualification, Justice Story wrote: "To insist on a juror's sitting in a case when he acknowledges himself to be under influences, no matter whether they arise from interest, from prejudices, or from religious opinions, which will prevent him from giving a true verdict according to law and evidence, would be to subvert the objects of a trial by jury, and to bring into disgrace and contempt, the proceedings of courts of justice."

50. See Haney (2005, p. 109); also see Bronson (1970), Cowan, Thompson, and Ellsworth (1984), Dillehay and Sandys (1996), Fitzgerald and Ellsworth (1984), Goldberg (1970), Gross (1984), Haney (1984), Horowitz and Seguin (1986), Jurow (1971), Luginbuhl and Middendorf (1988), Moran and Comfort (1986), Sandys (1998), and Thompson (1989).

51. See Nakell and Hardy (1987, p. 20).
52. Meltsner (1973, p. 168).
53. Ibid., pp. 169–170.
54. *Boykin v. Alabama*, 395 U.S. 238 (1969).
55. Meltsner (1973, p. 184).
56. Ibid., p. 170.
57. Ibid., p. 185.
58. Ibid., p. 182.
59. Paternoster (1991, pp. 45–46).
60. *McGautha v. California*, 602 U.S. 183 at 190 (1971).
61. Ibid., p. 195.
62. Acker (1996, pp. 143–144). In 1971, only six states used bifurcated trials in capital cases: California, Connecticut, Georgia, New York, Pennsylvania, and Texas; see *McGautha v. California*, 602 U.S. 183 at 208, n. 19.
63. *McGautha v. California*, 602 U.S. 183 at 207.
64. Ibid., p. 204.
65. Meltsner (1973, p. 242).
66. Ibid., p. 246.
67. Banner (2002, p. 258).
68. Meltsner (1973, p. 246).
69. Ibid.
70. Banner (2002) and Meltsner (1973, p. 246).
71. Banner (2002).
72. Ibid.
73. See *People v. Aikens*, 70 C.2d 369 (1969).
74. *Furman v. Georgia*, 408 U.S. 238 (1972); Meltsner (1973, p. 248).
75. *Savannah Morning News* (1967, August 12), p. 8B; (1968, September 21), p. 1A.
76. Haney (2005, p. 21).
77. *Furman v. Georgia*, 408 U.S. 238 (1972); Meltsner (1973).
78. Sturrock (2006).
79. Steiker and Steiker (2009, p. 108).
80. Meltsner (1973, p. 305).
81. Woodward and Armstrong (1979, p. 220) reported that at the time it was the longest decision in Supreme Court history. However, Cheever (2006, p. 276, n. 24) noted that *Dred Scott v. Sandford* (60 U.S. 393, 1857), the case that upheld slavery in the United States, was 109,163 words—more than twice as long as *Furman*. More recently, *McConnell v. Federal Election Commission* (540 U.S. 93, 2003), a federal campaign finance reform case, was 89,694 words.
82. Andersen (1983, p. 38) and Meltsner (1973, pp. 292–293). Cheever (2006, p. 589) claimed that the death sentences of 589 death row inmates were voided by the *Furman* decision. Woodward and Armstrong (1979, p. 430) wrote that the *Furman* decision "struck the laws in 35 states."
83. Meltsner (1973, p. 293).
84. Paternoster (1991, p. 54).
85. Meltsner (1973, p. 231).
86. Ibid., p. 232.
87. Ibid.
88. Ibid., p. 231.
89. Ibid., p. 232.

90. Ibid.
91. Ibid., pp. 232–233.
92. *Aikens v. California*, 406 U.S. 813 (1972).
93. Meltsner (1973, p. 287).
94. See *Aikens v. California* (1972) and *Furman v. Georgia* (1972).
95. See Banner (2002, p. 266).
96. Lain (2007a, p. 12).
97. Woodward and Armstrong (1979, pp. 217 and 220).
98. Ibid., p. 218.
99. Haines (1996, p. 50).
100. Ibid., p. 44.
101. Woodward and Armstrong (1979, pp. 218–219).
102. Cole (1984).
103. Lain (2007b, p. 48).
104. See Bowers and Steiner (1999, p. 612, n. 25); Haines (1996, p. 46) reported that 16 states enacted "mandatory" death penalty statutes following *Furman*.
105. Haines (1996) indicated that 13 states enacted "guided discretion" death penalty statutes following *Furman*.
106. Liebman, Fagan, and West (2000, n. 136).
107. Lain (2007b, p. 48).
108. Haines (1996, p. 50). On extending the moratorium, Amsterdam and the LDF attorneys fought each individual death sentence and were successful in blocking all executions until January 1977, when Gary Gilmore, at his own request, was executed by the state of Utah. The first "non-volunteer" executed was John Spinkelink, who was executed by Florida in May 1979. Woodward and Armstrong (1979, p. 442).
109. Woodward and Armstrong (1979, p. 432).
110. Haines (1996, p. 54).
111. Lain (2007a, p. 23; 2007b, p. 63).
112. Lain (2007a, p. 23; 2007b, p. 62–63).
113. Haines (1996, p. 44).
114. Ibid., p. 54.
115. "A Matter of Life and Death" (2006).
116. Death Penalty Information Center, "Life Without Parole."
117. "A Matter of Life and Death" (2006).
118. Woodward and Armstrong (1979, p. 431).
119. Ibid.
120. Ibid., p. 439.
121. Ibid.
122. Ibid.
123. Ibid.
124. Ibid.
125. Acker (1996, p. 145).
126. *Gregg v. Georgia*, 428 U.S. 153 at 226 (1976).
127. Lain (2007a, p. 24).
128. Ibid.; Lain (2007b, pp. 7 and 30).
129. For a detailed examination of proportionality review, see Bienen (1996).
130. Haney (2005, p. 22).

131. Also see Bedau (1987) and Steiker and Steiker (1998, p. 55).
132. *Furman v. Georgia*, 408 U.S. 238 at 287–289 (1972).
133. *Gardner v. Florida*, 420 U.S. 349 at 357 (1977). Also see *Woodson v. North Carolina*, 428 U.S. 280 (1976), and *Gregg v. Georgia*, 428 U.S. 153 (1976).
134. Radin (1980).
135. Paternoster (1991, pp. 75–76); also see Steiker and Steiker (1998). Culbert (2008, p. 30) observed that "since Aristotle, the two principles of equality and difference have defined the poles between which the practice of judgment has been stretched to achieve justice."
136. For a more nuanced view, see Culbert (2008, pp. 41–47).
137. Steiker and Steiker (1998); also see Acker (1996) and Mello (1989).
138. Steiker and Steiker (1998, p. 70). Much of the death penalty research that has been conducted over the past 30-plus years on this matter is presented in subsequent chapters of this book.
139. Totenberg (2010).
140. Haney (2005, pp. 21 and 24).
141. Acker and Lanier (1998) and Nakell and Hardy (1987).
142. Acker and Lanier (1998, p. 89) remark, "It is futile in the post-*Furman* era to embark on a discussion of 'the death penalty' from a procedural standpoint, for there are almost as many variations on capital sentencing laws as there are capital-punishment jurisdictions."
143. Baldus and Woodworth (1998, p. 394).
144. Ibid.
145. Acker and Lanier (1998, p. 101). Twenty-one of the 38 death penalty states have some type of balancing statute, see Bowers and Steiner (1999, p. 618, n. 49).
146. See *Kansas v. Marsh* (2006).
147. Online Sunshine View Statutes (2010a).
148. See Acker and Lanier (1998, p. 98) and Bowers and Steiner (1998, p. 309).
149. Until June 2002, juries were excluded entirely from the capital sentencing process in five states—Arizona, Colorado, Idaho, Montana, and Nebraska. This practice was held to be unconstitutional by the Supreme Court in *Ring v. Arizona*. Only a few states (e.g., Kentucky and Texas) give juries sentencing responsibility in noncapital cases, see Acker and Lanier (1998) and Bowers and Steiner (1998).
150. Gibson (2002) and Stevenson (2004, p. 110, n. 65).
151. Stevenson (2004, p. 89).
152. See Culbert (2008, pp. 58–59); also see Lain (2007b, pp. 58–59).
153. Coyne and Entzeroth (1994, pp. 264–265).
154. Acker and Lanier (1998, p. 103).
155. Texas Code of Criminal Procedure. Article 37.071. Procedure in Capital Case (last amended September 1, 2009). Retrieved December 15, 2010, from http://www.statutes.legis.state.tx.us/Docs/CR/htm/CR.37.htm#37.071.
156. See Death Penalty Information Center, "Executions." Retrieved December 14, 2010.
157. Andersen (1983).
158. Online Sunshine View Statutes (2010b).
159. Snell (2010b).
160. Ibid.
161. Paternoster (1991, p. 202).
162. Adapted from Paternoster (1991, p. 202); also see Cook and Slawson (1993, p. 19) and Freedman (1998, p. 418).
163. See Liebman et al. (2000, n. 44) and Paternoster (1991, pp. 202–204).
164. Dow (2002b, p. 18).

165. It has been claimed that "in a capital case, the lawyer for the accused has a professional obligation to assert at every level of the proceedings what otherwise might be deemed a frivolous claim" if that claim "might conceivably persuade even one judge in an appeals court or in the Supreme Court" or "might increase the chances of a desirable plea agreement or might favorably influence a governor or other official in making a decision regarding clemency," see Freedman (2003).

166. Lundy and McClure (2009).

167. Approximately 8100 death sentences were imposed in the United States from 1973 through 2009. See Snell (2006, 2007, 2008, 2009, 2010a) for the lower figure and Liebman et al. (2000) for the higher figure. State reversal rates vary widely, from highs of 54 percent in Mississippi and 53 percent in North Carolina to lows of 13 percent in Texas and 5 percent in Virginia, see Lofquist (2002, pp. 1513–1514). Dow (2002b, pp. 14 and 27) claims that since the late 1980s more than 90 percent of the death penalty cases have been affirmed by state courts of appeals (i.e., fewer than 10% have been reversed), and in Texas and Virginia, the number exceeds 98 percent (i.e., fewer than 2% have been reversed). Hammel (2002, pp. 116–117) also notes the dramatic decrease in appellate reversals in Texas. From 1974 to 1995, according to Hammel, the reversal rate in Texas death penalty appeals was about 30 percent compared to the low single digits in more recent years.

168. Liebman et al. (2000), Paternoster (1991, pp. 208–209), and Scheck Neufeld, and Dwyer (2001).

169. White (1987, p. 10).

170. Dow (2005, pp. xxii–xxiii and 44).

Capital punishment and the Supreme Court: The modern period

4

This chapter is devoted to many (but not all) of the Supreme Court cases decided after capital punishment was reinstated in 1976. Since then, the Court has been engaging in a time-consuming effort to fine tune the way capital punishment is applied. According to Franklin Zimring, in the century before *Furman*, the Supreme Court "only rarely reviewed state death sentences," but in the two decades after 1976, "the substantive law and procedure in state death penalty cases became the most frequent business of that court."[1] Some of the issues have been so controversial that the Court has changed positions on them several times. The cases address nine basic and, frequently, interrelated issues: (1) the constitutionality of death penalty statutes, (2) what crimes are capital, (3) mitigating circumstances, (4) aggravating circumstances, (5) the appellate process, (6) capital juries, (7) who may or may not be executed, (8) assistance of counsel, and (9) other procedural issues. Many of the cases addressed multiple issues, but generally only the most important issue is examined. For the most part, cases in each subsection are presented in chronological order and only brief descriptions of the Court's holdings are provided.

THE CONSTITUTIONALITY OF DEATH PENALTY STATUTES

Not long after the Supreme Court rendered its decisions in *Woodson* and *Gregg*, the constitutionality of the new death penalty statutes was challenged in *Harry Roberts v. Louisiana* (431 U.S. 633, 1977). The Supreme Court had rejected mandatory death penalty statutes as unconstitutional in *Woodson v. North Carolina* (1976) and *Roberts v. Louisiana* (1976), but the new rewritten Louisiana statute still mandated the death penalty for the killing of a special category of victim: a police officer. Consistent with its earlier ruling, the Court held that even mandatory death penalty statutes that are confined to a special category of victim are unconstitutional.

Ten years later, in *Sumner v. Shuman* (483 U.S. 66, 1987), the Court considered the death penalty mandated for a special category of offender. The Nevada legislature had (1) established the punishment of LWOP, and (2) amended its death penalty statute to require the penalty for a murder committed by an inmate serving LWOP. In *Sumner v. Shuman*, the Court declared the provision unconstitutional. The Court's decisions in *Harry Roberts v. Louisiana* and *Sumner v. Shuman* seem to confirm the Court's opposition to mandatory death penalty statutes, even if they are confined to a special category of victim or offender.

Still, the Court is not necessarily opposed to mandatory provisions in otherwise nonmandatory statutes. In *Blystone v. Pennsylvania* (494 U.S. 299, 1990), for example, the Court upheld Pennsylvania's statute that mandates a death sentence if the jury finds at least one aggravating circumstance and no mitigating circumstance.

71

The most sweeping challenge to the constitutionality of the new death penalty statutes was *McCleskey v. Kemp* (481 U.S. 279, 1987) wherein the Court considered evidence of racial discrimination in the application of Georgia's death penalty statute. Recall that in the *Furman* decision, racial discrimination was cited as one of the problems with the pre-*Furman* statutes. The most compelling evidence were the results of an elaborate statistical analysis of post-*Furman* death penalty cases in Georgia. This analysis showed that Georgia's new statute produced a pattern of racial discrimination based on both the race of the offender and the race of the victim. In *McCleskey*, the Court opined that evidence such as the statistical analysis – which showed a pattern of racial discrimination – is not enough to render the death penalty unconstitutional. By a vote of 5–4, it held that state death penalty statutes are constitutional even when statistics indicate that they have been applied in racially biased ways.[2] The Court ruled that racial discrimination must be shown in individual cases – something McCleskey did not show in his case. For death penalty opponents, the *McCleskey* case represented the best, and perhaps last, chance of having the Supreme Court again declare the death penalty unconstitutional.

In 2008, the Court tackled the constitutionality of lethal injection. In *Baze et al. v. Rees* (553 U.S. 35), the Court held that Kentucky's three-drug lethal injection protocol, which is similar to the execution protocol of most other death penalty states, does not violate the Eighth Amendment as "cruel and unusual" because it does not pose a "substantial" or "objectively intolerable" risk of severe harm, and that Kentucky employs sufficient safeguards to ensure that the protocol is followed properly. Additionally, Kentucky's failure to adopt proposed alternatives to its lethal injection protocol does not violate the Eighth Amendment because other states have not adopted such protocols and the comparative efficacy of those alternative methods has not been established.

WHAT CRIMES ARE CAPITAL

The Supreme Court has repeatedly emphasized that the death penalty should be reserved for the most heinous crimes. In 1977, in *Coker v. Georgia* (433 U.S. 584), the Court ruled that the death penalty is not warranted for the crime of rape of an adult woman in cases in which the victim is not killed. The Court held that the death penalty for such a rape was "grossly disproportionate and excessive punishment." At the time of the decision, Georgia was the only state that authorized the death penalty for the rape of an adult woman and, in nine out of 10 rape convictions in Georgia since 1973, juries had not imposed the death penalty. Then in 2008, in *Kennedy v. Louisiana* (554 U.S. 407), the Court extended its *Coker* decision to the rape of a child, ruling that the rape of a child is unconstitutional under the Eighth and Fourteenth Amendments because it is disproportionate to the crime where the crime did not result, and was not intended to result, in the death of the child. Also, in 1977, in *Eberheart v. Georgia* (433 U.S. 917), the Court, for the same reasons, held that the death penalty is not warranted for the crime of kidnapping in cases in which the victim is not killed. Traditionally, both rape and kidnapping have been capital crimes, regardless of whether the victim died. Thus, for all intents and purposes, the three cases have limited the death penalty to only "aggravated" or capital murders. (To date, all post-*Furman* executions have been for that type of murder.)

The federal 1994 Violent Crime Control and Law Enforcement Act expanded the federal death penalty to about 50 crimes – 46 of which involved murder. The four exceptions were treason; espionage; drug trafficking in very large amounts; and attempting, authorizing, or advising the killing of any public officer, juror, or witness in a case involving a continuing criminal enterprise – regardless of whether such a killing actually occurs. As of 2011, Congress reduced the number of capital crimes to 41, with only 3 offenses not necessarily involving murder: espionage, treason, and mailing of injurious articles with intent to kill (or resulting in death).[3] (The 41 federal capital crimes are listed in Chapter 5.)

As of 2009, eight states had death penalty statutes that listed capital crimes that do not necessarily involve murder. They were:

- Arkansas: treason
- California: sabotage and treason
- Colorado: treason
- Florida: capital drug trafficking
- Georgia: aircraft hijacking and treason
- Idaho: first-degree kidnapping
- Kentucky: kidnapping with aggravating factors
- Louisiana: treason[4]

If and when the statutory provisions are challenged, it seems unlikely that the Supreme Court would allow the execution of offenders convicted of any of the crimes.

MITIGATING CIRCUMSTANCES

One of the changes to death penalty statutes approved by the Court in *Gregg* was the requirement that sentencing authorities (either juries or judges) consider mitigating circumstances before determining the sentence. The main purpose of considering mitigating factors is to temper the desires for retribution and punishment with mercy, to realize that all people who kill do not deserve the death penalty.[5] Some states list mitigating circumstances in their death penalty statutes, and some states do not. Among those states that list mitigating factors, Colorado lists the most with 12; Arizona lists the fewest with five.[6] The average number of mitigating circumstances among states that list them is eight. Seven states – Connecticut, Delaware, Georgia, Idaho, Oklahoma, Oregon, and Texas – do not list mitigating factors in their death penalty statutes but, instead, provide a broad statement that sentencing authorities must consider any mitigating circumstances proffered by the defense, as long as the mitigating factors are supported by evidence.

The requirement to consider mitigating factors has been the subject of several challenges. The first test was in 1978 in the cases of *Lockett v. Ohio* (438 U.S. 586) and *Bell v. Ohio* (438 U.S. 637). In these cases, one of the issues was whether defense attorneys could present only mitigating circumstances that were listed in the death penalty statute. The Court held that trial courts must consider any mitigating circumstances that a defense attorney presents, and not just those listed in the statute.

In *Eddings v. Oklahoma* (455 U.S. 104, 1982), the trial judge refused to consider three mitigating circumstances: a turbulent family history, beatings by a harsh father, and serious emotional disturbance. The only mitigating circumstance the judge found was Eddings's youth; he was 16 at the time of the crime. The judge held that the single mitigating circumstance did not outweigh the aggravating circumstances, and sentenced Eddings to death. The Court reversed and remanded, maintaining that although the sentencer and reviewing court could determine the weight given to any mitigating circumstance, they could "not give it no weight by excluding it from their consideration."

The issue before the Court in *Skipper v. South Carolina* (476 U.S. 1, 1986) was the admissibility of a specific mitigating circumstance: the defendant's good behavior in jail while awaiting trial. Such testimony by correctional officers is very persuasive with jurors because it shows that if they choose LWOP rather than death, the defendant is not likely to pose a future danger and may even contribute positively to the prison environment.[7] Consistent with its earlier rulings in *Lockett*, *Bell*, and *Eddings*, the Court held that convicted murderers trying to escape a death sentence in favor of life in prison may present such evidence and it must be considered a legitimate mitigating circumstance in sentencing deliberations.

A year later, in *Hitchcock v. Dugger* (481 U.S. 393, 1987), the Court revisited *Lockett*, *Bell*, and *Eddings* when a Florida court refused to consider evidence of nonstatutory mitigating circumstances. The Court reemphasized that the sentencing authority may not refuse to consider any relevant mitigating evidence. Also, in 1987, the Court heard *California v. Brown* (479 U.S. 538), in which the petitioner challenged the trial judge's instruction that the jury not be swayed by "mere sympathy, passion, prejudice or public opinion." The petitioner argued that such an instruction undermined his ability to present mitigating evidence and, hence, violated both his Eighth and Fourteenth Amendment rights. The Court rejected the argument.

In 1988, in *Mills v. Maryland* (486 U.S. 367), the Court considered jury instructions that required the jury to be unanimous in its finding of a mitigating circumstance. In other words, before a Maryland juror (and jurors in other "weighing" states as well) could weigh a mitigating circumstance against aggravating circumstances, all 12 members of the jury had to agree that the mitigating circumstance did exist. If they did not, the mitigating circumstance could not be used in sentencing deliberations. The Court ruled that jury unanimity on the presence of a mitigating circumstance is not required before an individual juror may weigh it against aggravating factors. The issue arose again in 1990 in the case of *McKoy v. North Carolina* (494 U.S. 433), and the Court held that sentencing instructions that prevent the sentencing jury from considering any mitigating factor that the jury does not unanimously find do violate the Eighth Amendment.

In *Walton v. Arizona* (497 U.S. 639, 1990), the Court ruled that states may adopt a preponderance-of-the-evidence standard for proving mitigating factors (as Arizona did), though such a standard is not required. Preponderance of the evidence is evidence that outweighs the opposing evidence, or sufficient evidence to overcome doubt or speculation. It is a less stringent standard of proof than beyond a reasonable doubt (which is required for proving aggravating circumstances). In *Walton*, the Court determined that a state may adopt any standard for proving mitigating factors so long as the adopted standard does not lessen the prosecution's burden of proving all the elements of its case beyond a reasonable doubt. Most death penalty states have adopted the preponderance-of-the-evidence standard.

In *Parker v. Dugger* (498 U.S. 308, 1991), the issue, in part, was whether appellate courts must independently (of trial courts) consider mitigating circumstances. The Florida Supreme Court reviewed Parker's death sentence and disallowed two of the aggravating circumstances on which the trial judge based his sentencing decision. However, relying on the trial court's finding of no mitigating circumstances and the existence of other aggravating circumstances, the Florida court upheld Parker's death sentence. The Florida court would have found that the trial record supported a showing of nonstatutory mitigating circumstances had it independently reviewed the evidence. The U.S. Supreme Court held that the Florida Supreme Court and, by implication, other reviewing courts, must conduct an independent reweighing of mitigating (and aggravating) evidence before rendering a decision.

In *Delo v. Lashley* (507 U.S. 272, 1993), the Court considered a Missouri case in which no evidence was presented to support the existence of a mitigating circumstance – the defendant's lack of prior criminal activity. The trial court judge refused to instruct the jury about the mitigating circumstance following the penalty phase of the trial because defense counsel provided no supporting evidence. The Supreme Court denied relief, holding that without supporting evidence, the Missouri trial court is not required to instruct the jury of the mitigating circumstance.

In *Deck v. Missouri* (544 U.S. 622, 2005), the Court ruled that the Fifth and Fourteenth Amendments are violated when a capital defendant is made to wear visible shackles during a capital trial's penalty phase, as Deck was made to do, unless that use is "justified by an essential state interest" such as courtroom security, which it was not. The problem, according to the Court, is that "the offender's appearance in shackles almost inevitably implies to a jury that court authorities consider him a danger to the community (which is often a statutory aggravator and always a relevant factor); almost inevitably affects adversely the jury's perception of the defendant's character; and thereby inevitably undermines the jury's ability to weigh accurately all relevant considerations when determining whether the defendant deserves death." The same rule also applies to the use of visible shackles during a capital trial's guilt phase for similar reasons.

In *Oregon v. Guzek* (546 U.S. 517, 2006), the Court held that nothing in the Eighth and Fourteenth Amendments granted the petitioner the right to present alibi evidence at the sentencing stage of his trial. He had presented the evidence at the guilt phase, so the evidence had already been litigated and, thus, the matter was no longer an issue. The Court emphasized that evidence contradicting guilt does not have to be considered at the sentencing phase of a capital trial.

In sum, this line of cases clearly shows that the U.S. Supreme Court requires trial courts to consider any mitigating circumstances that a defense attorney presents, whether or not a mitigating circumstance is listed in a state's death penalty statute. The only qualification to this requirement is that the mitigating circumstance must be supported by evidence. Although the requirement serves the desired purpose of narrowing death eligibility, it also "invites arbitrary and even invidious decisionmaking."[8] The problem, according to Steiker and Steiker, is that the "unconstrained consideration of any kind of mitigating evidence ... gives those with a mind to discriminate the opportunity to discriminate."[9] They further claim that, "although such discretion cannot be used to render a defendant death-eligible contrary to community standards, it can be used to exempt favored defendants from the death penalty or to withhold severe punishment for crimes against despised victims."[10]

AGGRAVATING CIRCUMSTANCES

The "trigger" for any death sentence is the finding of at least one aggravating circumstance, generally "beyond a reasonable doubt."[11] Without such a finding, death may not be imposed. Death penalty states vary in the number of aggravating circumstances listed in their statutes. Connecticut, Kansas, Kentucky, Mississippi, and Oklahoma have the fewest with eight; California and Delaware have the most with 22.[12] The average number of aggravating circumstances is 13, but the trend is toward an increase in the number of statutory aggravating circumstances.[13] It is important to note that aggravating circumstances differ widely in their significance; therefore, their content is more important than how many there are in determining the number of death-eligible offenses.[14] There are three broad types of aggravating circumstances: (1) those that focus on offender characteristics, (2) those that focus on the manner in which the murder was committed, and (3) those that focus on victim characteristics.[15]

As was the case with mitigating circumstances, the aggravating circumstance requirement has generated a series of constitutional challenges. Ironically, although the aggravating circumstance requirement, like the mitigating circumstance requirement, was intended to narrow death eligibility, it has not done so very well. Steiker and Steiker observe, "States have adopted, and the Court has sustained, aggravating circumstances that arguably encompass every murder."[16] Research shows that "virtually all persons sentenced to death in Georgia before *Furman* would have been deemed death eligible under Georgia's post-*Furman* statute."[17]

Law professor Jonathan Simon and public defender Christina Spaulding suggest that aggravating circumstances also have a largely unrecognized but important symbolic role.[18] Simon and Spaulding contend that the aggravating factors in all current death penalty statutes serve not only their ostensible legal purpose of narrowing the range of offenders eligible for the death penalty but also the legislative purpose of recognizing and valorizing certain kinds of subjects and situations. In the latter context, aggravators have symbolic capital as "tokens of our esteem" as they validate the worth of potential victims. Types of potential victims "honored" in this way include public employees (such as peace officers, parole agents, and government investigators), private employees (such as newspaper reporters in the state of Washington),[19] and victims of crimes that have caused particular angst for some groups, such as drive-by shootings, carjackings, or gang activity. This is what had occurred with the aggravating factors in Illinois's death penalty statute, for example, which had ballooned from seven in the 1977 statute to 21 before it abolished its death penalty in 2011.[20] Simon and Spaulding argue that public employees and other people not specifically covered by the aggravators are being dishonored by exclusion. This "popular punitiveness" or "punitive kitsch," as Simon and Spaulding call it, is being promoted for a popular audience to evoke empathy for people "just like me" and vengeance against those who threaten "us." A practical effect of these new aggravators is the forcing of prosecutors to seek the death penalty in cases where it ordinarily might not be pursued.[21]

One of the first tests involving aggravating circumstances was *Godfrey v. Georgia* (446 U.S. 420, 1980). The Court held that the aggravating factor under which Godfrey had been sentenced to death (his offense, in the language of the statute, was "outrageously or wantonly vile, horrible or inhuman in that it involved torture, depravity of the mind, or an aggravated battery to the person") was too broad and vague, and as a result, it reversed Godfrey's death sentence. It is worth noting that the Court did not rule that the statutory aggravating factor was unconstitutional on its face (many other states have similar aggravating circumstances in their statutes), only in the way it was applied in Godfrey's case. The problem was twofold. First, the trial judge did not explain the meaning of the aggravating circumstance to the jury, and second, the Georgia Supreme Court did not apply a clarifying interpretation of the meaning it had developed in earlier cases. Thus, in the words of the Court, "There is no principled way to distinguish this case, in which the death penalty was imposed, from the many cases in which it was not." For such a statutory aggravating circumstance to withstand constitutional challenge, a state high court must adequately clarify its meaning and that meaning must be applied independently to the facts of the case, as the Tennessee Supreme Court has done with the "especially heinous, atrocious, or cruel" aggravating circumstance in its statute (see *Bell v. Cone*, 543 U.S. 447, 2005).

In *Shell v. Mississippi* (498 U.S. 1, 1990), the Court held that the limiting instruction defining the "especially heinous, atrocious, or cruel" aggravating circumstance as "extremely wicked," "outrageously wicked and vile," and "designed to inflict a high degree of pain" was not constitutionally deficient.

In *Barefoot v. Estelle* (463 U.S. 880, 1983), the Court addressed the issue of using psychiatric evidence to predict future dangerousness. Such a prediction is a component (and aggravating circumstance) in Texas's post-*Furman* death penalty statute. Barefoot claimed that (1) "psychiatrists, individually and as a group, are incompetent to predict with an acceptable degree of reliability that a particular criminal will commit other crimes in the future and so represent a danger to the community"; (2) "psychiatrists should not be permitted to testify about future dangerousness in response to hypothetical questions and without having examined the defendant personally" (as they did in Barefoot's case); and (3) "in the particular circumstances of this case, the testimony of the psychiatrists was so unreliable that the sentence should be set aside." The Supreme Court rejected all three claims and held that such psychiatric evidence predicting future dangerousness is admissible. Subsequent examination of 155 Texas death penalty cases in which prosecutors used experts to predict defendants' future dangerousness showed that the experts were wrong 95 percent of the time.[22] Another more recent study of 145 LWOP-sentenced capital offenders who entered the Federal Bureau of Prisons from August 1991 through November 2005 found that among those inmates for whom the government argued that the inmate would pose a future danger if not executed, only 10 percent had been cited for a serious assault during an average of 6 years (the range was 6 months to 15 years).[23] None of the assaults was life-threatening, and none of them was committed against a member of the correctional staff. Additionally, 28 percent of the inmates whom the government argued would pose a future danger if not executed had no disciplinary infractions. Currently, Texas is one of only three death penalty states in which the prediction of future dangerousness plays a significant role in juries' life and death decisions. In five other death penalty states, the prediction of future dangerousness has a limited role, and in the other 26 death penalty states, the prediction of future dangerousness has no role in capital sentencing procedures.[24]

The Court considered two other cases in 1983 involving aggravating circumstances. In *Zant v. Stephens* (462 U.S. 862), the issue was whether a death sentence must be vacated if one of the three statutory aggravating circumstances found by the jury was subsequently held to be unconstitutional, even though the two other aggravating circumstances were valid. The Court noted that the answer depended on the function of aggravating circumstances in a particular state's death penalty statute. In Georgia, for example, where the case originated, the jury is instructed not "to give any special weight to any aggravating circumstance, to consider any multiple aggravating circumstances any more significant than a single such circumstance, or to balance aggravating against mitigating circumstances pursuant to any special standard." Consequently, "in Georgia, the finding of an aggravating circumstance does not play any role in guiding the sentencing body in the exercise of its discretion, apart from its function of narrowing the class of persons convicted of murder who are eligible for the death penalty." For those and other reasons, the Supreme Court did not vacate the death sentence in the Georgia case. The outcome likely would have been different had the case occurred in a state in which aggravating circumstances played a more important role.

In *Barclay v. Florida* (463 U.S. 939, 1983), the principal issue was whether a nonstatutory aggravating circumstance was admissible. The nonstatutory aggravating factor in this case was racial hatred. Barclay was a member of the Black Liberation Army, whose avowed purpose was "to kill white persons and to start a revolution and a racial war." The Court upheld Barclay's death sentence, implying that the sentencing authority may consider virtually any factor in aggravation (that would be properly before it) once it has found at least one statutory aggravating circumstance.

In 1987, the Court addressed for the first time the use of victim-impact statements in death penalty cases. The case was *Booth v. Maryland* (482 U.S. 496). Victim-impact statements typically describe the harm done to and the suffering of victims and their family members. In accordance with Maryland law, victim-impact information was contained in the presentence investigation report. Booth's defense attorney moved to suppress the victim-impact statement, claiming it was both irrelevant and unduly inflammatory and, thus, its use violated the Eighth Amendment. The trial court judge denied the motion. The Supreme Court ruled 5–4 to vacate Booth's death sentence, holding that the introduction of victim-impact statements at the sentencing phase of a capital trial risked arbitrary and capricious imposition of the death penalty and, thus, violated the Eighth Amendment. The Court opined that victim-impact statements improperly refocused the death decision from the defendant and his or her crime to the "character and reputation of the victim and the effect on his family." Two years later, in *South Carolina v. Gathers* (490 U.S. 805, 1989), the Court, again by a 5–4 decision, reversed Gathers's death sentence. It reasoned that the prosecutor's argument that the death penalty should be imposed because of the personal characteristics of the victim – that he was a religious person and a registered voter – violated *Booth v. Maryland*. By 1991, however, the composition of the Court had changed. Justices Souter and Kennedy had replaced Justices Brennan and Powell. Consequently, in *Payne v. Tennessee* (501 U.S. 808, 1991), this time by a 6–3 decision, the Court reversed itself in both *Booth v. Maryland* and *South Carolina v. Gathers*. Justices Souter and Kennedy joined the *Booth* and *Gathers* minority, while the *Booth* and *Gathers* majority had lost Justices Brennan and Powell. The Court ruled that the introduction of victim-impact evidence and prosecutorial argument on that subject at the sentencing phase of a capital trial does not violate the Eighth Amendment. The Court decided that "evidence about the victim and about the impact of the murder on the victim's family is relevant to the jury's decision as to whether or not the death penalty should be imposed." The Court reasoned that it was only fair that the defendant's mitigating evidence be counterbalanced by evidence about the loss of the victim to his or her family and to society as a whole. What the Court failed to appreciate in *Payne* are additional problems with victim-impact evidence. Because victims testify about states of consciousness, that is, their pain and suffering, in their victim-impact statements, their statements cannot be refuted. It is conceivable that victims may pretend to suffer more than they actually do, hoping that their testimony will convince the sentencing authority that the defendant should be punished as severely as possible.[25] Alternatively, some victims may not be able to express their pain and suffering as well as other victims, making their testimony less effective than the testimony of more eloquent victims.[26] Both problems could lead to unfair results.

It is important to note that *Payne* allows victim-impact statements but does not require them. At this writing, 30 of the 34 death penalty states, the U.S. government, and the military authorize the use of victim-impact statements, although Indiana and Mississippi have limited admissibility.[27] Most of these jurisdictions have no limitations on their use other than the Court's admonition in *Payne* that a statement not be so "unduly prejudicial that it renders the trial fundamentally unfair."[28] Based on data from the Capital Jury Project, victim-impact evidence has been used in about half of all capital trials since the *Payne* decision in 1991. Research findings are mixed on the influence of victim-impact evidence on sentencing outcomes.[29]

In *Brown v. Sanders* (546 U.S. 212, 2006), the Court created a new rule for the handling of a subsequently invalidated aggravating circumstance in a jury's weighing process. In this case, the jury found four aggravating circumstances and sentenced Sanders to death. The California Supreme Court invalidated two of the aggravating circumstances on direct appeal but still affirmed the conviction and sentence. The federal district court rejected Sanders's claim that the jury's consideration of an invalid aggravating circumstance rendered his death sentence unconstitutional, but the Ninth Circuit reversed the district court's decision and held that Sanders had been deprived of an individualized death sentence. Upon review, the U.S. Supreme Court concluded that the consideration of the two invalidated aggravating circumstances in Sanders's case did not give rise to a constitutional violation, reversed the court of appeals, and remanded the case for further proceedings consistent with its opinion. The Court held, "An invalidated sentencing factor … will render the sentence unconstitutional by reason of its adding an improper element to the aggravation scale in the weighing process unless one of the other sentencing factors enables the sentencer to give aggravating weight to the same facts and circumstances," which the two valid aggravating circumstances did.

THE APPELLATE PROCESS

Many of the capital cases that address the appellate process involve the Court's effort to reduce the amount of time between imposition of sentence and execution. This time interval in 2009 averaged more than 14 years.[30] The Court first signaled its intention in *Barefoot v. Estelle* (463 U.S. 880, 1983). Not only did *Barefoot* allow psychiatric evidence predicting future dangerousness, it also approved acceleration of the appeals process in capital cases. Specifically, it allowed courts of appeal to deny an application for a stay of execution on habeas appeal – something they rarely did before *Barefoot*. The Court also provided detailed procedural guidelines for handling such appeals.

Haines is among those who consider 1983 a pivotal year in the struggle against the death penalty. In the 7 years between *Gregg* and *Barefoot*, the Supreme Court decided in favor of 14 of the 15 death-sentenced inmates whose appeals were fully argued before it.[31] Haines argues that by 1983 a majority of the Supreme Court justices had become frustrated trying to regulate death-sentencing procedures.[32] Those justices were no longer interested in telling states how to administer the penalty phase of capital trials.[33] The Court's *Barefoot* decision was only one among a number of cases that signaled the Court's new attitude. For at least a decade after 1983, most of the cases decided by the Supreme Court went against death row inmates.[34] However, during the first few years of the twenty-first century, the Court's attitude appears to have changed, and it seems willing again to police the capital process.[35]

In *Pulley v. Harris* (465 U.S. 37, 1984), as mentioned previously, the Court decided that there was no constitutional obligation for state appellate courts to provide, upon request, proportionality review of death sentences. Recall that proportionality review, as required in Georgia's post-*Furman* death penalty statute, and as recommended in *Gregg* as a desirable reform, is a means by which the appellate court can compare the sentence in the case before it with penalties imposed in similar cases in the state. Its purpose is to reduce arbitrariness and discrimination in death sentencing. Since *Pulley*, many states have eliminated the proportionality review requirement from their statutes, while some states simply no longer conduct the reviews. Other states continue to conduct proportionality reviews but never find a death sentence to be disproportionate.[36] For example, as of the mid-1990s the Georgia Supreme Court had found only one death sentence to be disproportionate in the more than 300 it had reviewed, and it had not found any death sentences to be disproportionate since *Pulley*.[37] A recent examination of Georgia's death penalty system found its proportionality review process deficient because the Georgia Supreme Court "only reviews cases in which a death sentence has been imposed [a valid proportionality review also requires comparing sentences in which the death penalty was sought but not imposed and cases in which the death penalty could have been sought but was not], only expands that review to cases where the death penalty was not imposed upon a claim by the defendant that his/her sentence is disproportionate to that of his/her co-conspirator, and explains its proportionality review in a cursory manner."[38]

Further streamlining was accomplished in *Antone v. Dugger* (465 U.S. 200, 1984). In this case, the Court announced that it would no longer consider issues raised for the first time pursuant to last-minute pleas for stays of execution when the issues could have been raised on previous petitions for habeas relief. The Court's ruling was aimed at the popular practice employed by some appellate attorneys of stalling executions by raising constitutional issues one at a time.

In 1989, in *Murray v. Giarratano* (492 U.S. 1), the Court hastened the process by ruling that neither the Eighth nor the Fourteenth Amendment requires the appointment of counsel to indigent death row inmates seeking state postconviction relief. Chief Justice Rehnquist, writing for the majority, explained that the right to counsel at the trial stage and for an initial appeal of the judgment and sentence of the trial court does not carry over to discretionary appeals. He reasoned that "the additional safeguards imposed by the Eighth Amendment at the trial stage of a capital case are … sufficient to assure the reliability of the process by which the death penalty is imposed." Nevertheless, by 1995, all states with death row inmates had passed legislation providing appointed counsel for indigent death row inmates in state habeas corpus postconviction proceedings.[39] In state habeas corpus postconviction proceedings, unlike in direct-appeal proceedings, a new lawyer, who is not associated with the previous proceedings, is allowed to thoroughly examine the trial's fairness by looking outside the formal record of the case.[40]

In the 1990s, the Supreme Court made it more difficult for innocent defendants to obtain relief. For example, in 1992, in *Sawyer v. Whitley* (505 U.S. 333), the Court ruled that to show "actual innocence" on a successive petition for a writ of habeas corpus, a defendant must show, by clear and convincing evidence, that "but for a constitutional error, no reasonable juror would have found the [defendant] eligible for the death penalty." In 1993, in *Herrera v. Collins* (506 U.S. 390), the Court decided that a claim of actual innocence based on newly discovered evidence is not grounds for granting a further hearing in federal court. Chief Justice Rehnquist maintained that judges are not empowered "to correct errors of fact," even if a mistake could lead to the execution of an innocent person, and that the federal courts should intervene only when state courts violate constitutional procedures. The proper procedure for making claims of actual innocence after the "judicial process has been exhausted" is by filing a request for executive clemency. Clemency, wrote Rehnquist, "is the historic remedy for preventing miscarriages of justice"; it has "provided the 'fail safe' in our criminal justice system."

In dissent, Justice Blackmun, who was joined, in part, by Justices Stevens and Souter, responded that "nothing could be more contrary to contemporary standards of decency, or more shocking to the conscience, than to execute a person who is actually innocent." Justice Blackmun argued that to rely on executive clemency to correct miscarriages of justice is to "make judicial review under the Eighth Amendment meaningless." He further suggested that "to obtain relief on a claim of actual innocence, the petitioner must show that he probably is innocent." Justice Blackmun ended his dissent with a warning to those who would reduce procedural safeguards to speed up the process:

> Of one thing, however, I am certain. Just as an execution without adequate safeguards is unacceptable, so too is an execution when the condemned prisoner can prove that he is innocent. The execution of a person who can show that he is innocent comes perilously close to simple murder.

In 1995, in *Schlup v. Delo* (513 U.S. 298), the Court abandoned the "clear and convincing" standard for demonstrating actual innocence and replaced it with the new standard of "probable innocence." "Probable innocence" means that it is "more likely than not" that the inmate is innocent.

The Court made it harder for federal judges to overturn tainted convictions and sentences in state courts again in 2000, in *Williams (Terry) v. Taylor* (529 U.S. 362). A 5–4 majority held that it is not enough that a state court acted incorrectly. The law requires a hands-off approach by federal judges unless a state court clearly is wrong about some Supreme Court precedent or "unreasonably applies that principal to the facts of the prisoner's case." In other words, a federal court can save a prisoner from execution only if the state court decision against the prisoner was not only wrong but unreasonably wrong.

CAPITAL JURIES

Challenges involving capital juries have occupied a considerable amount of the Court's time. Among the first was *Beck v. Alabama* (447 U.S. 625, 1980), in which the issue was whether a conviction-minded jury must be allowed to consider a verdict of guilt of a lesser-included noncapital offense. Under Alabama's death penalty statute, the trial judge was prohibited from giving the jury this option. Instead, the jury was given the choice of either convicting the defendant of the capital crime, in which case it was required to impose the death penalty, or acquitting the defendant. [In Alabama, if the defendant is convicted and the death penalty is imposed, the trial judge must hold a hearing to consider aggravating and mitigating circumstances. After hearing the evidence, the judge may refuse to impose the death penalty and, instead, may sentence the defendant to LWOP. As noted previously, this jury-override provision may change as a result of *Ring v. Arizona* (2002) but, so far, it has withstood constitutional challenge.] The Court held in *Beck* that the death penalty may not be constitutionally imposed after a jury verdict of guilt of a capital offense when the jury was not permitted to consider a verdict of guilt of a lesser-included noncapital offense when the evidence would have supported such a verdict. In *Hopper v. Evans* (456 U.S. 605, 1982), the Court qualified its ruling in *Beck*, holding that *Beck v. Alabama* applies only when the evidence supports a verdict of a lesser sentence and not in the case where the defendant makes it crystal clear that he or she killed the victim, intended to kill the victim, and would do the same thing again in similar circumstances.

The Court further qualified its *Beck* decision in *Hopkins v. Reeves* (524 U.S. 88, 1998). In this case, the Court held, "*Beck* does not require state trial courts to instruct juries on offenses that are not lesser-included offenses of the charged crime under state law." Prior to jury deliberations in his felony-murder case, Reeves, who was attempting to escape a death sentence, asked the trial court to instruct the jury to consider convicting him of second-degree murder or manslaughter instead of felony murder. The trial court refused on the ground that the Nebraska Supreme Court had consistently ruled that the two crimes are not lesser-included offenses of felony murder. Reeves was convicted and sentenced to death. After exhausting state remedies, Reeves filed a federal habeas corpus petition claiming that the trial court's failure to give the requested instructions violated *Beck*. As noted, the Court ruled that it did not. The Court explained that this case differed from *Beck* in two important respects. In *Beck*, Alabama law prohibited instructions on offenses that state law clearly recognized as lesser-included offenses of the charged crime. Nebraska law, on the other hand, did not provide for second-degree murder or manslaughter as lesser-included offenses for felony murder. Second, in Alabama, juries were restricted to a choice between conviction of a capital offense and death or acquittal. In Nebraska, on the other hand, the jury did not impose sentence (which will change as a result of *Ring v. Arizona*, 2002), and the three-judge sentencing panel had a choice between death or life imprisonment.

The Court revisited its *Witherspoon* decision in a series of cases. Recall that in *Witherspoon v. Illinois* (1968) the Court held that during the voir dire, prospective jurors may not be removed from the jury for cause simply because they voiced general objections to the death penalty or expressed conscientious or religious scruples against its imposition. In the first case, *Adams v. Texas* (448 U.S. 38, 1980), the Court decided that prospective jurors can be excluded from capital juries if their views on capital punishment would not allow them to obey their oath and follow the law of Texas without conscious distortion or bias. Texas law at that time required prospective jurors to state under oath that the mandatory penalty of death or life imprisonment would not affect their deliberations on any issue of fact. The law mandated a sentence of life imprisonment or death on conviction of a capital felony.

In *Wainwright v. Witt* (469 U.S. 412, 1985), the Court reconsidered its decisions in *Witherspoon* and *Adams* and held that potential jurors in capital cases should be excluded from jury duty in a manner no different from how they are excluded in noncapital cases. The Court opined that no longer does a juror's automatic bias against imposing the death penalty have to be proved with unmistakable clarity. Instead, the question of exclusion from a jury should be determined by the interplay of the prosecutor and the defense attorney and the decision of the judge based on his or her first-hand observations of the prospective juror. If the judge determines that a prospective juror's beliefs would bias the juror's ability to impose the death penalty, then the juror should be excluded.

Further clarification was offered in *Lockhart v. McCree* (476 U.S. 162, 1986). In this case, the Court ruled that prospective jurors whose opposition to the death penalty is so strong that it would prevent or substantially impair the performance of their duties as jurors at the sentencing phase of the trial may be removed for cause. Stated differently, as long as jurors can perform their duties as required by law, they may not be removed for cause because they are generally opposed to the death penalty.

Finally, in *Uttecht v. Brown* (551 U.S. 1, 2007), the Court held that even where a potential juror offers no objection to the death penalty and states clearly that he or she will follow the applicable law, it is not contrary to clearly established federal law to exclude the juror for cause under the *Witherspoon–Witt* "substantially impaired" standard. In this case potential jurors were instructed that Brown was eligible only for death or LWOP. The transcript showed that the juror in question (Juror Z) seriously misunderstood his juror responsibilities and had an attitude about capital punishment that could have prevented him from voting for death based on the facts of the case. He was instructed four times that Brown could not be released from prison and responded six times that he could obey the law. He also gave contradictory statements such as he would consider a death sentence only if there were no possibility that Brown would be released to offend again. The state challenged Juror Z, arguing that he was confused about the conditions under which the death penalty could be imposed and apparently believed it was only appropriate when there was a risk of release and recidivism. The defense did not object to Juror Z's removal. Thus, Juror Z was dismissed because he was "substantially impaired" based on his demeanor, which is a legitimate basis for evaluating a juror. The Court noted that the law requires reviewing courts to give deference to a trial court's assessment of a potential juror's demeanor.

This series of cases modifying the Court's *Witherspoon* decision addressed the issue of what to do with prospective jurors who are opposed to capital punishment. Another interesting issue is what to do with prospective jurors who would automatically impose the death penalty following a defendant's conviction in a capital case. This issue was considered in *Morgan v. Illinois* (504 U.S. 719, 1992).

During jury selection, Morgan's attorney requested the judge to ask all prospective jurors the following question: "If you found Derrick Morgan guilty, would you automatically vote to impose the death penalty no matter what the facts are?" The judge refused to ask the jurors this "life-qualifying" or "reverse-*Witherspoon*" question. The jury found Morgan guilty and sentenced him to death. Morgan appealed the court's refusal to ask the reverse-*Witherspoon* question, and the Supreme Court reasoned that "a juror who will automatically vote for the death penalty in every case will fail in good faith to consider the evidence of aggravating and mitigating circumstances as the instructions require him to do." Thus, ruled the Court, a prospective juror who would automatically vote for the death penalty may be challenged for cause.

In *Bullington v. Missouri* (451 U.S. 430, 1981), the Court considered the issue of whether a death sentence could be imposed following a retrial when a jury had imposed life imprisonment at the first trial. The Court held that it could not because to do so would violate the Fifth Amendment's prohibition of double jeopardy. In *Sattazahn v. Pennsylvania* (537 U.S. 101, 2003), the Court considered a similar issue. During the penalty phase of Sattazahn's capital trial, the jury reported to the trial judge that it was hopelessly deadlocked 9–3 for life imprisonment. The court discharged the jury and entered a life sentence as Pennsylvania law required. Sattazahn then appealed his first-degree murder conviction to the Pennsylvania Superior Court, which reversed the conviction and remanded for a new trial. At his second trial, Sattazahn was convicted and sentenced to death. The Pennsylvania Supreme Court affirmed the death sentence, noting that the death sentence in the second trial, after he was sentenced to life imprisonment in the first trial, neither violated the Fifth Amendment's double-jeopardy clause nor the Fourteenth Amendment's due process clause. In a 5–4 ruling, the Supreme Court agreed, opining that "the life sentence at issue did not amount to an acquittal based on findings sufficient to establish legal entitlement to the life sentence or that the government failed to prove one or more aggravating circumstances beyond a reasonable doubt." The Court also maintained that the Fourteenth Amendment's due process clause does not provide greater double-jeopardy protection than does the double-jeopardy clause of the Fifth Amendment.

In *Spaziano v. Florida* (468 U.S. 447, 1984), the jury-override provision of Florida's death penalty statute was challenged. Recall that in Florida (as well as in Alabama, Delaware, and Indiana at the time), a trial judge was allowed to overrule the jury and impose a death sentence, even if all jurors voted for a life sentence, or impose a life sentence, even if all jurors voted for a death sentence. A majority of jurors in Spaziano's case recommended life imprisonment after he was found guilty of first-degree murder. The trial judge, however, who conducted his own independent weighing of the aggravating and mitigating circumstances in the case, overrode the jurors' recommendation and sentenced Spaziano to death. On appeal, the Supreme Court upheld Florida's override provision, maintaining that a sentencing judge may disregard the jury's recommendation of life imprisonment and impose the death penalty. In *Harris v. Alabama* (513 U.S. 504, 1995), the Court upheld Alabama's override provision.

However, in *Ring v. Arizona* (536 U.S. 584, 2002), the constitutionality of the jury-override provisions in the capital punishment statutes of Florida, Alabama, and Delaware (Indiana had since eliminated jury override from its death penalty statute) were thrown into doubt. In a 7–2 decision, the Court ruled that the Sixth Amendment right to a jury trial requires that juries and not judges determine whether death is the appropriate penalty in a capital case. This means that a jury and not a judge (in a jury trial) must find capital aggravating factors beyond a reasonable doubt. The decision invalidated the death-sentencing statutes in Arizona, Idaho, Montana, Colorado, and Nebraska, which gave the trial judge or sentencing judges (in Colorado and Nebraska a three-judge panel decided the sentence) sole responsibility for determining the appropriate sentence. The fate of the 168 death row inmates in those five states at the time of the decision was uncertain. Some were likely either to have their sentences commuted to life imprisonment or to be resentenced. Others, however, would get no relief. In *Schriro v. Summerlin* (542 U.S. 348, 2004), the Court ruled that *Ring* did not apply retroactively to cases already final on direct review. The Court maintained that a new rule, as created in *Ring*, applies to convictions that are final only in limited circumstances. According to the Court, "New substantive rules generally apply retroactively, but new procedural rules generally do not," and *Ring* created a procedural rule. *Ring* altered neither the range of conduct nor the class of persons subject to the death penalty in Arizona. It only changed the method of determining whether the defendant engaged in that conduct. The only procedural rules that can be applied retroactively are "watershed rules" that address "the fundamental fairness and accuracy of the criminal proceeding," and *Ring* did not announce a watershed rule of criminal procedure. At this writing, it is not entirely clear what the effect of the *Ring* decision will be on the death-sentencing practices of Florida, Delaware, and Alabama, but, as mentioned previously, all three states have withstood several *Ring* challenges to their override provisions.

The issue in *Caldwell v. Mississippi* (472 U.S. 320, 1985) was whether a death sentence is valid when the sentencing jury is led to believe that responsibility for determining the appropriateness of a death sentence rests not with the jury but with the appellate court which later reviews the case. The prosecutor at Caldwell's trial urged the jury not to view itself as determining whether the defendant would die because a death sentence would be reviewed for correctness by the state supreme court. The Court vacated the petitioner's sentence, arguing that the prosecutor's suggestion to the sentencing jury that the appellate court would correct an inappropriate death sentence created an intolerable risk of unreliable sentencing.

Another series of cases in this area deals with procedures that may contribute to unacceptable forms of juror discrimination in the imposition of the death penalty. In *Batson v. Kentucky* (476 U.S. 79, 1986), a non-death penalty case, the Court considered the relatively common prosecutorial practice of using peremptory challenges to eliminate black people from trial juries in capital cases involving black defendants. This practice resulted in black defendants frequently being tried by all-white juries. In *Batson*, the Court held that "the Equal Protection Clause forbids the prosecutor to challenge potential jurors solely on account of their race or on the assumption that black jurors as a group will be unable impartially to consider the State's case against a black defendant." Thus, under *Batson*, once the defendant establishes a prima facie case showing race was a factor in a prosecutor's decision to exercise a peremptory challenge, the burden shifts to the prosecutor to provide a neutral, legitimate explanation to justify his or her striking of the juror. However, in *Purkett v. Elem* (514 U.S. 765, 1995), another non-death penalty case, the Court held that once the prosecutor provided a race-neutral explanation, the trial court must decide whether the opponent of the strike has proved purposeful racial discrimination. According to the Court, this does not demand an explanation by the prosecutor that is persuasive or even plausible, only one that is facially valid. If discriminatory intent is not inherent in the prosecutor's explanation, then the explanation offered is considered race-neutral.

Batson and *Elem* were put to the test in the case of *Miller-El v. Dretke* (545 U.S. 231, 2007, 2005). In this case, the Court ruled that Thomas Miller-El, a black defendant, was entitled to a new trial because of strong evidence of racial bias during jury selection at his original trial. Prosecutors peremptorily struck 10 of 11 qualified black venire members. The Court found the prosecutors' race-neutral explanations for striking the black venire members improbable and a pretext designed to conceal racial bias. Also indicative of decisions based on race were the prosecution's shuffling of the venire panel (rearranging the order in which venire panel members were seated and questioned), its asking different questions to black and nonblack panel members about their views on the death penalty and minimum acceptable sentences, and, perhaps most telling, the widely known practice of the Dallas County District Attorney's Office to exclude black venire members from juries – a practice that had been going on for decades. The Court surmised that some of the evidence is open to judgment calls, but when viewed cumulatively "its direction is too powerful to conclude anything but discrimination."

In *Thaler v. Haynes* (130 S. Ct. 1171, 2010), the Court, in rejecting a demeanor-based explanation for a peremptory challenge under *Batson*, held that a judge did not have to personally observe the aspect of the juror's demeanor on which the explanation is based. In this Texas death penalty case, two judges presided at different stages. Judge Harper presided during voir dire, when prospective jurors were questioned individually, and Judge Wallace took over when peremptory challenges were exercised. Haynes's attorney raised a *Batson* objection when the prosecutor struck an African American juror named Owens. Judge Wallace determined that Haynes's attorney had made a prima facie case under *Batson*, but the prosecutor offered a race-neutral explanation based on Owens's demeanor during individual questioning. The prosecutor argued that Owens had been "somewhat humorous" and not "serious" and that her "body language" had belied her "true feeling." He concluded that she "had a predisposition" and would not consider the possibility of imposing a death sentence "in a neutral fashion." Haynes's attorney did not object to the prosecutor's characterization of Owens's demeanor but noted that her answers on the jury questionnaire "show[ed] that she was a juror who [was] leaning toward the State's case." Thus, without observing Owens himself during voir dire, Judge Wallace denied the *Batson* objection, ruling that the prosecutor's reason for striking Owens was "race-neutral."

The Court applied its *Batson* logic to the selection of grand juries in *Vasquez v. Hillery* (474 U.S. 254, 1986). In this case, the Court ruled that indictment by an all-white grand jury from which black individuals were systematically excluded created an intolerable risk that a defendant's indictment was a result of discrimination, thereby violating the Equal Protection Clause. The Court added that even though a defendant is subsequently lawfully convicted, that fact does not cure the taint attributed to a grand jury selected on the basis of race.

At issue in the case of *Turner v. Murray* (476 U.S. 28, 1986) was whether a defendant in an interracial murder case has a right to question prospective jurors about racial prejudice. In this case, the defendant was denied that opportunity. The Court ruled on appeal that failure to voir dire a jury about racial bias in an interracial murder case created an intolerable risk of discrimination.

In *J.E.B. v. Alabama* (511 U.S. 127, 1994), a noncapital case, the Equal Protection Clause was held to prohibit discrimination in jury selection on the basis of gender, or an assumption that an individual will be biased in a particular case solely because that person happens to be a woman or a man. The Court's decision suggests that the Court will not tolerate gender discrimination in capital jury selection for the same reason it will not tolerate racial discrimination.

At issue in *Simmons v. South Carolina* (512 U.S. 154, 1994) was South Carolina's new sentencing option in capital cases: life imprisonment without possibility of parole. Research shows that citizens are confused and skeptical about this sentencing option. Many citizens believe that even when offenders are sentenced to LWOP, they may still be paroled. Concerned that the jury might not understand that "life imprisonment" did not carry with it the possibility of parole in Simmons's case, his defense attorney asked the trial judge to clarify the issue by defining the term "life imprisonment" in accordance with the South Carolina statute. The judge refused. On appeal, the Court ruled that a defendant has a right to inform the jury of the real consequences of a "life" sentence when the state argues that the defendant would be dangerous in the future (as the state did in Simmons's case), and "life" means LWOP, as a matter of state law. However, in *Ramdass v. Angelone* (530 U.S. 156, 2000), the Court made clear that where an offender may some day be paroled, the state is under no obligation to explain to the jury what a life sentence means. In addition, in *California v. Ramos* (463 U.S. 992, 1983), the Court held that a capital sentencing instruction about the governor's power to commute an LWOP sentence (a "Briggs Instruction") did not violate the Constitution. The Court suggested that focusing the jury's attention on a defendant's probable future dangerousness if ever released was a desirable goal.

The Court reiterated its decision in *Simmons v. South Carolina* in 2001 in *Shafer v. South Carolina* (532 U.S. 36). In *Shafer*, the Court maintained that whenever a defendant's future dangerousness is raised by the prosecution, the defendant has the right to an accurate jury instruction that a life sentence means no possibility of parole. The jury in *Shafer* was given the ambiguous instruction that "life imprisonment means until death of the offender," and that "[p]arole eligibility or ineligibility is not for your consideration." The Court returned Shafer's case to South Carolina because the instructions misled the jury.

In yet a third South Carolina case, *Kelly v. South Carolina* (534 U.S. 246, 2002), the Court in a 5−4 decision held that a South Carolina trial court again had violated *Simmons v. South Carolina* by refusing to inform Kelly's sentencing jury that he would never be eligible for parole if the jury sentenced him to life imprisonment instead of death. During the sentencing phase of Kelly's trial, the prosecution did not state outright that Kelly posed a future danger but rather told the jury that "murderers will be murderers" and that Kelly had planned jail escapes when previously incarcerated. On appeal, Kelly contended that the issue of future dangerousness had been raised by the state. The South Carolina Supreme Court believed otherwise and maintained that escape attempts were not the type of evidence of future dangerousness intended by *Simmons*. The Supreme Court reversed that decision and ordered a new sentencing trial for Kelly.

Note that when a state does not argue that a defendant would be dangerous in the future, there is no obligation to explain to sentencing juries parole eligibility and minimum sentence requirements associated with life imprisonment sentences. Only a few death penalty statutes have such a requirement.[41]

In another case dealing with sentencing instructions the issue was how far a judge must go to clarify jury questions. After 4 hours of deliberation, a confused jury asked the judge, "If we believe that Lonnie Weeks, Jr. is guilty of at least 1 of the [aggravating factors], then is it our duty as a jury to issue the death penalty? Or must we decide … whether or not to issue the death penalty, or one of the life sentences? What is the rule? Please clarify?" The defense asked the judge to instruct the jury that it could impose a life sentence even if it found an aggravating factor beyond a reasonable doubt. The judge refused, stating that he did not think he could answer the question any clearer than the instruction. The jury deliberated for another 2 hours and returned a death sentence. In *Weeks v. Angelone* (528 U.S. 225, 2000) the Court decided that a trial judge's refusal to do more than to refer the jury to pattern instructions he had given before deliberations was permissible and constitutionally sound. Pattern instructions are a uniform set of scripted instructions. Justice Rehnquist, writing for the five-member majority, conceded that "there exists a slight possibility that the jury considered itself precluded from considering mitigating evidence … [but] a jury is presumed to follow its instructions [and] to understand a judge's answer to its question." As proof of that understanding, Justice Rehnquist cited the 2 hours of jury deliberation following the judge's [lack of] response to the jury's question. One can only wonder how the 2 hours of deliberation can be taken as proof of understanding, or how Justice Rehnquist and the Court's majority could presume the jury's understanding despite the jury's seeking clarification and not getting it.

In a related case, the Court held in *Buchanan v. Angelone* (552 U.S. 269, 1998) that the Eighth Amendment does not require that a capital jury be instructed on the concept of mitigating evidence generally, nor that any definitional instruction be given on any particular mitigating circumstances. In this Virginia death penalty case, Buchanan was convicted of killing his father, stepmother, and two brothers. The aggravating factor in the case was that the crime was vile. The sentencing phase of the trial took 2 days, during which there was testimony about Buchanan's troubled family background and mental and emotional problems. Both the prosecutor and defense counsel made lengthy arguments about the mitigating evidence and what role it should play in sentencing. The jury was instructed that if it found beyond a reasonable doubt that Buchanan's crime was vile "then you may fix the punishment ... at death," but "if you believe from all the evidence that ... death ... is not justified, then you shall fix the punishment ... at life imprisonment." Buchanan's attorney requested the judge to give four additional instructions on specific statutory mitigating factors and a general instruction on the concept of mitigating evidence. The judge refused. The Court affirmed the judge's decision based on the context in which the instructions were given. Given the extensive consideration of mitigating evidence and the instruction to base their decision on "all the evidence," opined the Court, it was unlikely the jurors understood the instructions to preclude consideration of relevant mitigating evidence.

WHO MAY OR MAY NOT BE EXECUTED

The Supreme Court has established limits on who may or may not be executed and has adopted the principle that the Eighth Amendment requires at least a rough correspondence between the punishment imposed, the harm done, and the blameworthiness of the defendant.[42] In the extreme, this means that the Court would not allow an execution for jaywalking, however intentional. The cases that the Court has decided were not as easy. The first of the cases addressed the issue of whether a participant in a felony murder who did not kill, attempt to kill, or intend to kill may be executed. Many states include the crime of felony murder in their homicide statutes. In a felony murder, it is possible to find a defendant guilty of murder even though he or she did not intend to kill and may or may not have caused a death. Many states hold such a defendant guilty of first-degree murder because he or she committed a specified felony that caused a death. For example, prior to Governor Ryan's mass commutation in 2003, 60 percent of Illinois's death row inmates had been convicted of a felony murder.[43] Illinois's felony-murder statute lists 16 felony-murder offenses punishable by death.[44] It has been estimated that, nationwide, about 40 percent of all capital indictments are for felony murder.[45]

The Supreme Court first addressed the issue in *Enmund v. Florida* (458 U.S. 782, 1982). Enmund was the driver of the getaway car in a robbery in which the victims were murdered. Enmund did not himself kill and was not present at the killings, but the fact that he helped the killers escape was enough under Florida law to make him "a constructive aider and abettor and hence a principal in first-degree murder upon whom the death penalty could be imposed." Enmund was sentenced to death for his role in the crime. In addressing Enmund's blameworthiness, the Court ruled that to impose the death penalty on someone who did not kill or intend to kill violated the Eighth Amendment. The Court reversed the judgment upholding Enmund's death penalty and remanded the case for further proceedings in light of its ruling.

The Court revisited its *Enmund* decision in 1987 in the case of *Tison v. Arizona* (481 U.S. 137). As in *Enmund*, Raymond Tison and Ricky Tison were participants in felony murders – in this case, involving robbery and kidnapping. Also like Enmund, the Tison brothers did not do the killing or intend to kill. Unlike Enmund, however, the Tisons were major participants in the crimes and showed a "reckless indifference to human life." The Court held that even though the killing and intent to kill were absent, the other circumstances were sufficient to support a judgment of death.

In 1986, in *Ford v. Wainwright* (477 U.S. 399), the Court considered the issue of whether states may execute people who have literally gone crazy on death row. Writing for the majority, Justice Marshall noted that the Court had never decided whether the Constitution forbids the execution of the insane, even though for centuries no jurisdiction has approved the practice. This does not mean that insane persons have never been executed. To the contrary, as attorney Stephen Bright observes, "'insane' has been so narrowly defined as to allow people with severe mental illness to be put to death."[46] Justice Powell defined insanity for Eighth Amendment purposes as the condition under which people "are unaware of the punishment they are about to suffer and why they are to suffer it." In a Florida case, a circuit judge acknowledged the mental health problems of the death row inmate in the case before him, but concluded that they were not severe enough to prevent his impending execution. The judge opined that to meet the threshold of incompetency to be executed the inmate "would have to virtually be unable to clean himself, feed himself, or otherwise function."[47] Nevertheless, consistent with common-law heritage, the Court in *Ford* held that states are barred from executing people who have become insane while on death row. The implication is that death row inmates must first be cured of their insanity before they are executed.[48]

An important question raised by the *Ford* decision is whether a state can forcibly medicate death row inmates who have become insane while on death row for the sole purpose of rendering them competent for execution. However, when a case (*Singleton v. Norris*, 540 U.S. 832, 2003) addressing this question was appealed to the U.S. Supreme Court, the Court refused to grant certiorari. As a result, Charles Singleton was executed in Arkansas on January 6, 2004, and the Eighth U.S. Circuit Court of Appeals' decision in the case (*Singleton v. Norris*, 319 F.3d 1018, 8th Cir. 2003) remains precedential.[49] The Eighth Circuit ruled:

> In order to justify the forcible medication of an inmate when that medication would render the prisoner competent for execution, the state must (1) present an essential state interest that outweighs the individual's interest in remaining free from medication, (2) prove that there is no less intrusive way to fulfill the essential interest, and (3) prove by clear and convincing evidence that the medication is medically appropriate. Medication is medically appropriate where it is in the best medical interest of the inmate, where the medication is likely to render the inmate competent, and where the severity of the side effects of the medication does not overwhelm its benefits.

The Court held that "the interest in carrying out Singleton's capital punishment sentence outweighed Singleton's substantial liberty interest in remaining free of unwanted medication," despite Singleton's argument "that medication could not be in his best interest when it would ultimately render him eligible for execution." Although the state has an essential interest in exacting punishment, the decision has been criticized because the state's interest may be achieved by another punishment besides the death penalty, such as LWOP.[50] In dissent, one of the Eighth Circuit judges observed:

> At the end of the day, the state executed a person who was mentally ill. Artificial sanity is not the same as true sanity. Treatment is not synonymous with being cured; antipsychotic drugs merely mask mental illness. Competency in Singleton's case was a fiction maintained only by powerful antipsychotic medications.[51]

In *Panetti v. Quarterman* (551 U.S. 930, 2007), the Court expanded its definition of insanity for Eighth Amendment purposes. The Court held that it is not enough to consider only whether the death row inmate is aware that he is going to be executed and why, without considering delusions that may prevent him from comprehending the meaning of the punishment. In 1992, Scott Panetti was convicted of the capital murders of his parents-in-law and sentenced to death despite his well-documented history of mental illness. Nevertheless, during his initial state and federal proceedings, Panetti did not argue that mental illness rendered him incompetent to be executed. However, when his execution date was set, Panetti for the first time filed a motion claiming that he was incompetent to be executed because of mental illness. The trial court judge dismissed the motion, and the Texas Court of Criminal Appeals dismissed Panetti's appeal for lack of jurisdiction. Panetti then filed a habeas appeal, but the federal district court did not grant relief, arguing that Panetti was competent to be executed because he knew he was going to be executed and why. The Fifth Circuit affirmed. For technical reasons dealing with the Antiterrorism and Effective Death Penalty Act of 1996's restriction on successive habeas petitions, the Court reviewed the lower courts' decisions and concluded that although Panetti knew he was going to be executed, he believed the reason for his execution was a sham. Panetti thought that the state of Texas was working in legion with the devil and sought his execution to stop him from preaching the gospel. The Fifth Circuit had decided that the delusion was irrelevant. The Court disagreed, maintaining that the Fifth Circuit's decision was inconsistent with *Ford v. Wainwright* and that Panetti's delusion caused by severe mental illness was so far removed from reality that the punishment could serve no proper purpose. The Court reversed and remanded.

The issue in *Penry v. Lynaugh* (492 U.S. 302, 1989) was whether the Eighth Amendment categorically prohibits the execution of a capital offender who is mentally retarded. Court testimony indicated that Penry, who was 22 years old when he allegedly committed the brutal rape and murder for which he was convicted and sentenced to death, had the reasoning capacity of a 7-year-old. The Court provided the following rationale in upholding Penry's death sentence:

> In sum, mental retardation is a factor that may well lessen a defendant's culpability for a capital offense. But we cannot conclude today that the Eighth Amendment precludes the execution of any mentally retarded person of Penry's ability convicted of a capital offense simply by virtue of his or her mental retardation alone. So long as sentencers can consider and give effect to mitigating evidence of mental retardation in imposing sentence, an individualized determination whether "death is the appropriate punishment" can be made in each particular case. While a national consensus against execution of the mentally retarded may someday emerge reflecting the "evolving standards of decency that mark the progress of a maturing society," there is insufficient evidence of such a consensus today.

By 2002, a national consensus against the execution of the mentally retarded had emerged. Results of a 2002 Gallup poll showed that only 13 percent of respondents favored the death penalty for the mentally retarded who are convicted of capital crimes, 82 percent opposed it, and 5 percent did not know or refused to answer. Among subgroups, only 18 percent of males, 9 percent of females, 13 percent of whites, and 14 percent of nonwhites favored the death penalty for mentally retarded capital offenders.[52] Furthermore, by 2002, 18 death penalty states had prohibited the execution of the mentally retarded. In 1989, when *Penry* was decided, only Maryland and Georgia prohibited their execution. The Court was swayed by these developments and in June 2002, in the case of *Atkins v. Virginia* (536 U.S. 304), ruled 6–3 that it is cruel and unusual punishment to execute the mentally retarded. The Court reasoned that the death penalty's two social purposes – retribution, that is, "just deserts," and deterrence of capital crimes by prospective offenders – are not served by the execution of mentally retarded capital offenders. Regarding retribution, the Court believed the lesser culpability of mentally retarded offenders by virtue of their cognitive and behavioral impairments did not merit that form of retribution; regarding deterrence, the Court averred that these impairments make it less likely they can process the information of execution as a possible penalty and, therefore, control their behavior based on the information. The Court also surmised that exempting the mentally retarded from execution would not lessen the death penalty's deterrent effect for offenders who are not mentally retarded. The Court was especially concerned that mentally retarded offenders faced a special risk of wrongful execution because they might unwittingly confess to crimes they did not commit, be less able to meaningfully assist their attorneys, and be poor witnesses, and their demeanor may create an unwarranted impression that they lacked remorse for their crimes.

A problem with the *Atkins* decision is that the Court did not set a standard for what constitutes mental retardation. That issue was left to the states to decide. In *Schiro v. Smith* (546 U.S. 6, 2006), the Court held that states can develop their own methods of determining an inmate's mental competency and cannot be compelled to conduct a jury trial with regard to the issue of mental retardation. It is presumed that the standard definition of mental retardation, which is an IQ of 70 or below and significant limitations in adaptive skills, will be used. The decision is likely to spare the lives of dozens, if not hundreds, of convicted killers. It is estimated that 12–20 percent of the death row population is mentally retarded, and that at least 27 mentally retarded defendants have been executed under post-*Furman* statutes.[53] Ironically, on August 5, 2005, a Virginia jury found Daryl Atkins (the petitioner in *Atkins v. Virginia*) mentally competent, despite his IQ of 59, and he was rescheduled for execution.[54] In January 2008, a state court judge, citing prosecutorial misconduct, commuted Atkins's death sentence to life in prison.[55]

In 1988 and 1989, the Court decided three cases that dealt with the age of the offender at the time the crime was committed. At issue was the question of whether the Constitution permitted the execution of juveniles, that is, individuals who committed their capital crimes prior to their eighteenth birthday. The Court held in *Thompson v. Oklahoma* (487 U.S. 815, 1988) that the Constitution prohibited the execution of a person who was under 16 years of age at the time of his or her offense. In this particular case, the Court stipulated that the decision applied only when a state had not specifically legislated the death penalty for such minors. The next year, in the cases of *Stanford v. Kentucky* and *Wilkins v. Missouri* (collectively as 492 U.S. 361), the Court determined that the Eighth Amendment did not prohibit the execution of persons who were 17 (in *Stanford*) or 16 (in *Wilkins*) years of age at the time of their offenses. The three decisions together meant that the Supreme Court would allow the executions of 16- and 17-year-olds but would not allow the execution of persons who were under 16 years of age at the time of their offenses.

By 2002, however, it was clear that a national consensus had developed about the desirability of executing juveniles. In a 2002 Gallup poll, for example, only 26 percent of respondents favored the death penalty for juveniles, 69 percent opposed it, and 5 percent did not know or refused to answer. Among subgroups, only 31 percent of males, 21 percent of females, 25 percent of whites, and 29 percent of nonwhites favored the death penalty for juveniles.[56] However, the Supreme Court was slow to move. Toward the end of 2002, the Court by a 5–4 vote declined to hear another appeal by Kevin Stanford (the appellate in *Stanford v. Kentucky*) who had been sentenced to die for abducting, sodomizing, and killing a gas-station attendant when he was 17.[57] Nevertheless, by 2005, 18 death penalty states prohibited the death penalty for juveniles, and the 20 death penalty states that had not prohibited it infrequently imposed it. In addition, by 2005, the death penalty in general, and the juvenile death penalty in particular, had become politically embarrassing to the United States and a major impediment in its international relations.[58] Perhaps most importantly, by 2005, Justice Anthony Kennedy had changed his mind on the issue. Based on these developments, the Court, in *Roper v. Simmons* (543 U.S. 551, 2005), affirmed by a 5–4 vote the decision of the Missouri Supreme Court and ruled that the Eighth and Fourteenth Amendments forbid the imposition of the death penalty on offenders who were under the age of 18 at the time their crimes were committed. The Missouri Supreme Court had accepted Simmons's claim that the Court's reasoning in *Atkins v. Virginia* applied to the execution of juveniles. The Court identified three differences between juvenile offenders and adult offenders that diminished the former's culpability: (1) "Juveniles' susceptibility to immature and irresponsible behavior means 'their irresponsible conduct is not as morally reprehensible as that of an adult'"; (2) "Their own vulnerability and comparative lack of control over their immediate surroundings mean juveniles have a greater claim than adults to be forgiven for failing to escape negative influences in their whole environment"; and (3) "The reality that juveniles still struggle to define their identity means it is less supportable to conclude that even a heinous crime committed by a juvenile is evidence of irretrievably depraved character." The Court concluded:

> When a juvenile commits a heinous crime, the State can exact forfeiture of some of the most basic liberties, but the State cannot extinguish his life and his potential to attain a mature understanding of his own humanity. While drawing the line at 18 is subject to the objections always raised against categorical rules, that is the point where society draws the line for many purposes between childhood and adulthood and the age at which the line for death eligibility ought to rest.

Until recently, the Court allowed states to sentence juveniles as young as 13-years-old to life imprisonment without opportunity of parole (JLWOP), even for nonhomicide offenses. Indeed, until recently, 37 states, the District of Columbia, and the federal government allowed such sentences in some circumstances. Research by the Court found that, nationwide, 129 juvenile offenders were serving JLWOP sentences for nonhomicide crimes. However, on May 17, 2010, in a 5–4 decision, the Court, in *Graham v. Florida* (No. 08-7412), ruled that a juvenile offender may not be sentenced to JLWOP for a nonhomicide crime, thus restricting JLWOP to juvenile homicide offenders.

ASSISTANCE OF COUNSEL

Not only do capital defendants have a Sixth Amendment right to counsel, they also have the right to the "effective assistance of counsel."[59] It was not until 1984, however, that the Court provided any guidelines for determining when counsel is ineffective. The case was *Strickland v. Washington* (466 U.S. 668).

Strickland's claim of ineffective assistance of counsel was denied, but the Court did create a two-pronged test for determining when counsel is ineffective at either the guilt or penalty phase of a bifurcated capital trial. First, the defendant must show (and the burden of proof is on the defendant) that his or her attorney's performance was deficient based on "prevailing professional norms." The Court emphasized, however, that:

> Judicial scrutiny of counsel's performance must be highly deferential, and a fair assessment of attorney performance requires that every effort be made to eliminate the distorting effects of hindsight, to reconstruct the circumstances of counsel's challenged conduct, and to evaluate the conduct from counsel's perspective at the time. A court must indulge a strong presumption that counsel's conduct falls within the wide range of reasonable professional assistance.

If the Court agrees with the defendant on this first claim, then the defendant must also show that his or her attorney's deficient performance contributed to the adverse outcome of the case. The Court stressed that "the ultimate focus of inquiry must be on the fundamental fairness of the proceeding whose result is being challenged." Thus, "a court need not first determine whether counsel's performance was deficient before examining the prejudice suffered by the defendant as a result of the alleged deficiencies. If it is easier to dispose of an ineffectiveness claim on the ground of lack of sufficient prejudice [i.e., adverse outcome], that course should be followed." Paternoster observes that the second prong of the test "requires that a court reviewing an attorney's performance for effectiveness must, with hindsight, determine if the outcome of the trial would have been different had counsel not been incompetent."[60] In Strickland's case, this was easy. Strickland had pleaded guilty to three capital murder charges. In cases in which the defendant does not plead guilty, however, it may be more difficult to show. In sum, the Court's holding in *Strickland* seems to suggest that it is unnecessary for defense lawyers in capital cases to be effective; it is only necessary for them not to be ineffective.[61]

In *Burger v. Kemp* (483 U.S. 776, 1987), the petitioner claimed that his well-respected and experienced court-appointed trial lawyer was constitutionally inadequate because, in part, he failed to develop and present any mitigating evidence at either of the two state court sentencing hearings. The evidence that might have been disclosed would have shown that Christopher Burger had "an exceptionally unhappy and unstable childhood." After talking with a psychologist retained by the trial lawyer, as well as Burger's mother and other people who knew his client, Burger's trial lawyer decided his client's interests would not be served by presenting what mitigating evidence was available. He also decided that it would not be wise to put his client, his client's mother, or the psychologist on the witness stand and expose them to cross-examination. Burger had never expressed remorse for his crime, and the psychologist believed that Burger might have bragged about it on the witness stand. The trial lawyer did not think his client's mother's testimony would be helpful and might even be counterproductive. As it was, no evidence had been produced at trial establishing that Burger had any prior criminal record. His mother, however, knew her son had committed at least one prior petty offense, had been involved with drugs, had a violent temper, and had other problems with law enforcement officers. All this could have come out during cross-examination. Citing *Strickland v. Washington*, the Court concluded that petitioner had not established "in light of all the circumstances, the identified acts or omissions [of counsel] were outside the wide range of professionally competent assistance." It further noted that petitioner did not show that "the justice of his sentence was rendered unreliable by a breakdown in the adversary process caused by deficiencies in counsel's assistance."

In *In re Berger* (498 U.S. 233, 1991), the Court determined that appointed counsel representing a capital defendant before the U.S. Supreme Court is limited to $5000 in fees, even though 21 U.S.C. § 848 (q) (10) prescribes no such limitation.

In *Wiggins v. Smith* (539 U.S. 510, 2003), the Court held, "The performance of Wiggins' attorneys at sentencing violated his Sixth Amendment right to effective assistance of counsel." The principal concern of the Court was not whether trial counsel should have presented a mitigation case (according to the Court, they presented a "halfhearted mitigation case") but whether trial counsel's investigation supporting their decision not to introduce mitigating evidence about the severe physical and sexual abuse Wiggins suffered at the hands of his alcoholic, absentee mother and a series of foster parents; his time spent homeless; and his diminished mental capacities was reasonable under prevailing professional norms. The Court concluded that counsel did not conduct a reasonable investigation and that their failure to investigate thoroughly "stemmed from inattention, not strategic judgment." Wiggins's trial attorneys chose not to hire a forensic social worker at the state's expense to investigate his background. The only significant mitigating factor the jury heard was that Wiggins had no prior convictions. The Court reasoned that had the jury heard about the other mitigating factors, it may have returned with a sentence other than death.

In the case of *Florida v. Nixon* (543 U.S. 175, 2004), Nixon's public defender was faced with overwhelming evidence of his client's guilt. Therefore, he adopted the strategy of conceding his client's guilt at the guilt phase of the capital trial to preserve credibility for penalty-phase evidence of his client's mental instability and defense pleas to save his client's life. When he attempted to explain his strategy to his client, Nixon was unresponsive, neither approving nor protesting the proposed strategy. Nixon gave little, if any, assistance or direction to his attorney in the preparation of his case. Nixon was convicted and sentenced to death. The Florida Supreme Court reversed holding that conceding that a defendant is guilty without the defendant's express consent automatically constitutes ineffective assistance of counsel requiring a new trial. The Court ruled that the Florida Supreme Court erred and reversed its decision, noting, "Counsel's failure to obtain the defendant's express consent to a strategy of conceding guilt in a capital trial does not automatically render counsel's performance deficient." In explaining its ruling and, at the same time, acknowledging the special problems faced by defense attorneys in capital trials, the Court wrote:

Attorneys representing capital defendants face daunting challenges in developing trial strategies: Prosecutors are more likely to seek the death penalty, and to refuse to accept a plea to a life sentence, when the evidence is overwhelming and the crime heinous. Counsel therefore may reasonably decide to focus on the trial's penalty phase, at which time counsel's mission is to persuade the trier that his client's life should be spared. Defense counsel must strive at the guilt phase to avoid a counterproductive course. Mounting a "defendant did not commit the crime" defense risks destroying counsel's penalty phase credibility and may incline the jury against leniency for the defendant. In a capital case, counsel must consider in conjunction both the guilt and penalty phases in determining how best to proceed. When counsel informs the defendant of the strategy counsel believes to be in the defendant's best interest and the defendant is unresponsive, counsel's strategic choice is not impeded by any blanket rule demanding the defendant's explicit consent.

In *Rompilla v. Beard* (543 U.S. 1086, 2005), the Court held: "Even when a capital defendant and his family members have suggested that no mitigating evidence is available, his lawyer is bound to make reasonable efforts to obtain and review material that counsel knows the prosecution will probably rely on as evidence of aggravation at the trial's sentencing phase." In this case, the Court found defense attorneys deficient because they failed to carefully examine the court file of Rompilla's prior rape and assault conviction even though they knew the prosecution intended to seek the death penalty by proving that Rompilla had a prior history of violent felony convictions. Had they carefully examined the file, which was a public record readily available at the courthouse, they would have discovered, just like Rompilla's postconviction attorney did, a number of mitigation leads that were not identified by the defendant or his family members. The mitigation evidence, then, taken as a whole, might have convinced the jury to return a verdict other than death.

In its 2009 and 2010 terms, the Court decided a series of cases dealing with the issue of ineffectiveness of counsel. In *Porter v. McCollum* (130 S. Ct. 447, 2009), the Court ruled that penalty-phase counsel provided ineffective assistance by failing to investigate any mitigating evidence about the defendant's mental capacity, family background, or military service.

In *Wong v. Belmontes* (130 S. Ct. 383, 2009), the Court held that penalty-phase counsel, who presented substantial mitigating evidence, including testimony from nine witnesses regarding the defendant's terrible childhood, the abuse he suffered, and the defendant's religious conversion, was not ineffective under *Strickland*.

In *Bobby v. Van Hook* (130 S. Ct. 13, 2009), the Court ruled that counsel's penalty-phase investigation was not ineffective at the time of his client's trial and that it was inappropriate for the court of appeals to rely on American Bar Association guidelines that were announced 18 years after the defendant's trial.

In *Sears v. Upton* (130 S. Ct. 3259, 2010), the Court held that the proper prejudice standard for evaluating ineffective assistance in the context of a penalty-phase mitigation investigation requires a "probing and fact-specific analysis" of the totality of the available mitigation evidence, including reliable hearsay evidence and speculation as to the effect of new mitigation evidence.

In *Wood v. Allen* (130 S. Ct. 841, 2010), the Court held that the state court's factual determination that defense counsel made a strategic decision not to pursue or present evidence of defendant's mental deficiencies was not unreasonable.

In *Smith v. Spisak* (130 S. Ct. 676, 2010), the Court reversed the Sixth U.S. Circuit Court of Appeals, holding that, contrary to the Sixth Circuit's judgment, Spisak's trial attorney's closing argument did not prejudice Spisak for purposes of ineffective assistance of counsel. In other words, a better closing argument by his defense attorney would not have made a difference in the outcome of the case. At the guilt phase of his trial, Spisak's attorney put his client on the stand to demonstrate Spisak's mentally defective condition. In front of the jury, Spisak confessed that he indeed committed three murders and two attempted murders at Cleveland State University in 1982. He said he committed the crimes because he was a follower of Adolph Hitler, his "spiritual leader," in a "war" for "survival" of "the Aryan people." He added that "he had hoped to 'create terror' at Cleveland State University, because it was 'one of the prime targets' where the 'Jews and the system … are brainwashing the youth.'" The Court also rejected Spisak's claim that instructions and jury forms at the penalty phase unconstitutionally required the jury to consider in mitigation only those factors that the jury unanimously found to be mitigating in violation of *Mills v. Maryland*. The Court explained that the Ohio courts considered the claim and rejected it on its merits. The Court noted that federal law allows a federal court to reach a contrary decision only if the state court decision "was contrary to, or involved an unreasonable application of, clearly established Federal law, as determined by the Supreme Court of the United States." Contrary to the Sixth Circuit, the Court concluded that Spisak's claim did not meet this standard.

OTHER PROCEDURAL ISSUES

Other procedural issues that do not fit well into any of the other categories are briefly described in this last section. The first three cases involve the role of psychiatrists in capital cases. In *Estelle v. Smith* (451 U.S. 454, 1981), the Court held that a defendant's statements to a psychiatrist during a competency evaluation may not be used against the defendant in a capital sentencing proceeding unless, prior to the evaluation, the defendant was "informed of his right to remain silent and the possible use of his statements." In *Ake v. Oklahoma* (470 U.S. 68, 1985), the issue was whether the Constitution requires an indigent defendant to have access to psychiatric examination and assistance necessary to prepare an effective defense based on his or her mental condition, when sanity at the time of the offense is seriously in question. In *Ake*, the Court held that "when a defendant has made a preliminary showing that his insanity at the time of the offense is likely to be a significant factor at trial, the Constitution requires that a State provide access to a psychiatrist's assistance on this issue if the defendant cannot otherwise afford one." In *Powell v. Texas* (492 U.S. 680, 1989), the Court ruled that the Sixth Amendment is violated if a state psychiatrist conducts a pretrial evaluation without notice to defense counsel.

In *Darden v. Wainwright* (477 U.S. 168, 1986), the Court decided that a Florida prosecutor's reference to a capital murder defendant as "an animal" at a sentencing trial did not violate the defendant's right to a fair trial.

In *Minnick v. Mississippi* (498 U.S. 146, 1990), the Court held that once counsel is requested, police interrogation must cease, and any reinitiation of interrogation without presence of counsel, irrespective of whether the accused has consulted with counsel, is prohibited.

The facts in *Arizona v. Fulminante* (499 U.S. 279, 1991) were as follows. After Fulminante's 11-year-old stepdaughter was murdered in Arizona, Fulminante left the state. He was subsequently convicted of an unrelated federal crime and imprisoned in New York. A fellow inmate, who was really a government agent posing as an organized crime figure, told Fulminante that Fulminante was getting rough treatment from other inmates because of rumors that he was a child murderer and promised to protect him in exchange for the truth. Fulminante confessed to the government agent that he had killed his stepdaughter and provided details of the crime. Subsequently, Fulminante was indicted in Arizona for first-degree murder. The trial court denied his motion to suppress his confession, and he was convicted and sentenced to death. On appeal, the Arizona Supreme Court held that the confession was coerced in violation of the Fifth and Fourteenth Amendments and remanded the case for a new trial without the confession. The Court affirmed the decision but also noted that the erroneous admission of a coerced confession may, in some cases, be a harmless error, but that under the circumstances of this case, it was not. (For a discussion of errors in capital cases, see Chapter 9.)

CONCLUSION

As the list of cases indicate, over the past three-plus decades the Supreme Court has been actively refining the procedures approved in *Gregg*. Its faith in its ability to make the system of capital punishment a just and constitutionally acceptable one remains strong. With Justices Marshall and Brennan no longer members of the Court, it is only on rarest of occasions that any doubts are expressed – but they are expressed. On February 22, 1994, for example, in a rare written dissent from the Court's refusal to hear the appeal of a Texas inmate scheduled to be executed the next day, Justice Harry A. Blackmun asserted that he had come to the conclusion that "the death penalty experiment has failed" and that it was time for the Court to abandon the "delusion" that capital punishment could be administered in a way that was consistent with the Constitution. Blackmun proclaimed, "From this day forward, I no longer shall tinker with the machinery of death." What is interesting is that, unlike Justices Marshall and Brennan, who always opposed capital punishment, Justice Blackmun, despite personally opposing the penalty, had supported the administration of capital punishment for more than 20 years.[62] He believed the death penalty was "basically a legislative discretionary matter."[63] Similarly, on May 9, 2008, in comments made to about 50 judges and 800 attorneys at a conference of the Sixth U.S. Circuit Court of Appeals in Chattanooga, Tennessee, Justice John Paul Stevens stated for the first time that he now thinks the death penalty is unconstitutional.[64]

Justices Blackmun and Stevens are the exceptions. The majority of the current Court continues to make adjustments to the process. To summarize the general elements of the process: Bifurcated trials are required in capital cases. Guided discretion statutes are constitutional; mandatory statutes of any kind are not. For practical purposes, capital punishment is permissible only in cases of aggravated murder. (At the state level it is also permissible for a few other rarely committed crimes, such as treason. At the federal level, it is authorized for 41 crimes.) It is not a permissible penalty unless there is at least one aggravating circumstance, generally proved "beyond a reasonable doubt." A person who participated in a crime that resulted in death but who did not actually kill or plan to kill anyone may be found guilty of aggravated murder if he or she was a major participant and showed a reckless disregard for the value of human life. Juries must be allowed to convict a capital defendant of an included noncapital offense instead of the capital one. During the penalty phase of bifurcated trials, courts must allow the presentation of any mitigating evidence that is supported by evidence and victim-impact statements. The presentation of aggravating evidence is initially limited only to factors listed in the statutes. However, after one statutory aggravating factor has been found, any factor in aggravation can be considered. Automatic appellate and proportionality reviews, though desirable, are not required. Death penalty opponents may be excluded from juries in capital cases if they are opposed to the death penalty, no matter what the circumstances. Prospective jurors who would automatically vote for the death penalty may be challenged for cause. Executing people who have gone crazy on death row or who are mentally retarded is not permitted. Execution of persons who were under 18 years of age at the time of their offense is prohibited. Execution by lethal injection, firing squad, hanging, electrocution, or lethal gas is not cruel and unusual punishment and, thus, is allowable for capital crimes.

DISCUSSION QUESTIONS

1. Do you agree with the Court's decision in *McCleskey v. Kemp*?
2. Should any crimes besides aggravated murder be death eligible?
3. Do you agree with Steiker and Steiker that the "unconstrained consideration of any kind of mitigating evidence … gives those with a mind to discriminate the opportunity to discriminate

... [by exempting] favored defendants from the death penalty or [by withholding] severe punishment for crimes against despised victims"?

4. Has the requirement of finding at least one statutorily enumerated aggravating circumstance adequately narrowed death eligibility?
5. Can future dangerousness be accurately and adequately predicted?
6. Should a prediction of future dangerousness be a basis for sentencing someone to death?
7. Should victim-impact statements be admissible at the penalty phase of a capital trial?
8. Should proportionality review be required of all death penalty jurisdictions?
9. Should appointment of counsel be required for appeals beyond the automatic appeal?
10. Should a person's opinion about the death penalty (either in favor or opposed) affect whether he or she serves as a juror in a capital case?
11. Should a judge be allowed to overrule a jury sentence in a capital case (as is allowed in Alabama, Delaware, and Florida)?
12. Should a participant in a crime in which a capital murder is committed be death eligible, even though the participant did not kill or intend to kill?
13. Should inmates who have become insane while on death row be executed anyway?
14. Should a state be able to forcibly medicate death row inmates who have become insane while on death row for the sole purpose of rendering them competent for execution?
15. At what age should a person be death eligible? Should there be an age limit for death eligibility?
16. Should mentally retarded offenders be death eligible? At what IQ level, if any, should a capital offender be death eligible?
17. What, if anything, should be learned from Justice Blackmun's recent mea culpa?
18. What are the general elements of the capital punishment process in the United States?

Notes

1. Zimring (2003, p. 9). Law professor James Liebman (2007, p. 14, n. 42) writes that "between 1972 and 2006, the Court issued at least 209 opinions in capital cases in which capital-specific issues were raised."
2. Justice Powell, who wrote the opinion in *McCleskey*, has since stated that his vote in *McCleskey* was his biggest and most regrettable mistake as a Supreme Court justice. See Cavender (1995, p. 128).
3. ProCon.org at http://deathpenalty.procon.org/view.resource.php?resourceID=001172 (accessed April 29, 2011).
4. Snell (2010a).
5. Sundby (2005, p. 14).
6. Derived from an analysis of the 2009 or 2010 statutes of all death penalty jurisdictions, except the U.S. military. Thanks to Tim Colyer for conducting the analysis.
7. Sundby (2005, p. 19).
8. Steiker and Steiker (1998, p. 63).
9. Ibid.
10. Ibid.
11. Acker and Lanier (1998, p. 102); *Tuilaepa v. California* (512 U.S. 967, 1994).
12. Derived from an analysis of the 2009 or 2010 statutes of all death penalty jurisdictions, except the U.S. military. Thanks to Tim Colyer for conducting the analysis.
13. Ibid.
14. Acker and Lanier (1998, p. 92).

15. Ibid., pp. 92–93.
16. Steiker and Steiker (1998, p. 57).
17. Ibid., p. 58.
18. Simon and Spaulding (1999).
19. Sundby (2005, p. 11).
20. Turow (2003, pp. 67–68).
21. Simon and Spaulding (1999).
22. Texas Defender Service (2004, p. xiii).
23. Cunningham, Reidy, and Sorensen (2008).
24. Texas Defender Service (2004, p. xii). Updated November 16, 2010.
25. Culbert (2008, p. 106–107).
26. Ibid., p. 108.
27. The Death Penalty Information Center. Retrieved November 21, 2010, from http://www.deathpenaltyinfo .org/legal-issues-states-allow-victim-impact-statements.
28. Logan (2006, p. 163); also see Lanier and Breslin (2006) and Karp and Warshaw (2006). In some jurisdictions, prosecutors have not allowed co-victims to make victim-impact statements because the co-victims are opposed to the death penalty (Reed and Blackwell, 2006, pp. 261–262). Some states, such as Delaware, Georgia, Idaho, and Indiana, allow members of the victim's family to sit with the prosecution at the counsel table during a capital trial (Stevenson, 2004, p. 101, n. 4).
29. For findings that show that victim-impact statements do influence sentencing decisions, see Paternoster and Deise (2011). For findings that show that victim-impact evidence is less or not influential on sentencing decisions, see Eisenberg, Garvey, and Wells (2006, pp. 298 and 304) and Karp and Warshaw (2006, pp. 283 and 290).
30. Snell (2010a, Table 12).
31. Haines (1996, p. 74).
32. Ibid., p. 73.
33. Ibid., p. 74; also see Weisberg (1983).
34. Haines (1996, p. 75).
35. Steiker and Steiker, 2006.
36. Bright (1997, p. 14).
37. Ibid.
38. American Bar Association (2006).
39. Dow (2005, p. 22).
40. Ibid., p. 61.
41. Acker and Lanier (1998, pp. 99–100).
42. See McCord (2000) about the Court's attempt to minimize "overinclusion," and Hoffmann (1993, p. 124) for the correspondence between the punishment and the blameworthiness.
43. Turow (2003, p. 68).
44. Ibid., p. 69.
45. Walker (2006, p. 267). The Constitution Project (2005, pp. xvii and xxv) recommends that felony murder should not be death eligible or an aggravating circumstance.
46. Bright (1997, p. 19).
47. Cox (1999).
48. For a detailed description of the *Ford* case, see Miller and Radelet (1993).
49. Brunsvold (2004).
50. Ibid., p. 1306.
51. Ibid., pp. 1309–1310.

52. Jones (2002).
53. Bright (1997, p. 17) and Owens (2002).
54. Lindsey (2005).
55. Liptak (2008).
56. Jones (2002); also see Vogel and Vogel (2003).
57. McCaffrey (2002).
58. Lain (2007a, p. 33).
59. See *McMann v. Richardson*, 397 U.S. 759 at 771, n. 14 (1970).
60. Paternoster (1991, p. 88).
61. Ibid., p. 89; also see Mello and Perkins (1998).
62. *Callins v. Collins*, 510 U.S. 1141 (1994); Meltsner (1973, p. 198).
63. Ibid.
64. "Stevens alters stance on lethal-injection methods" (2008).

The death penalty at the federal level, in the military, and globally

5

It is important to understand that there are 36 separate death penalty systems in the United States. Thirty-four states have a death penalty system, as do the federal government and the military. No two systems are exactly alike. In this chapter, the death penalty systems of the federal government and the military are examined. Also briefly explored is the international context in which the death penalty in the United States exists.

THE DEATH PENALTY AT THE FEDERAL LEVEL

Except for the judicial branch, the federal government (i.e., the executive and legislative branches) historically has played a limited role in the administration of capital punishment in the United States. Its principal responsibility has been the execution of offenders found guilty of committing federal capital crimes. In addition, the president has granted an occasional pardon or commutation, and Congress has tinkered with federal death penalty legislation. Beginning in the 1990s, however, Congress has become much more active in death penalty matters. Two major initiatives have been the expansion of the number of federal crimes punishable by death and the changing of the ways capital crimes are handled. The congressional initiatives will be examined following a brief description of the role of the federal courts in capital punishment.

CAPITAL PUNISHMENT AND THE FEDERAL COURTS

The federal courts represent one half of the dual court system in the United States.[1] The other half is the state court system. The federal court system consists of three levels of courts. At the bottom are 94 district courts. The U.S. district courts are further divided into 13 circuits, with at least one federal district court in each state, one each in the District of Columbia and the Commonwealths of Puerto Rico and the Northern Mariana Islands, and one each in the U.S. territories of the Virgin Islands and Guam. Violations of federal capital punishment statutes are first adjudicated in federal district courts, as are claims first made in federal postconviction proceedings.

The middle level of the federal court system comprises 13 U.S. circuit courts of appeals. Twelve of them have jurisdiction over death penalty appeals from U.S. district courts in the particular geographic areas assigned to them. The Court of Appeals for the Federal Circuit is the only court of appeals that does not hear appeals in death penalty cases.

At the top of the federal court system is the U.S. Supreme Court—the "court of last resort." Under its appellate jurisdiction, the Court hears death penalty cases appealed from U.S. circuit courts of appeals or from the high court of a state. It hears appeals from the high court of a state only when claims under federal law or the Constitution are involved. This means that the Supreme Court rules only on death penalty cases in which (1) the constitutionality of a state or federal death penalty statute is challenged, or (2) a capital defendant claims that his or her constitutional rights were violated. Such violation might be improper guilt phase or penalty phase court procedures or improper procedures of the appellate court.

For a case to be heard by the Supreme Court, at least four of the nine justices must vote to hear the case (the "rule of four"). (It takes five justices to stay, or stop, an execution.) The Court next issues a writ of certiorari to the lower court whose decision is being appealed, ordering it to send the records of the case forward for review. The Court will issue a writ of certiorari only if the defendant in the case has exhausted all other avenues of appeal and the case involves a substantial federal question as defined by the appellate court.

When the Supreme Court decides a case it has accepted on appeal, it can take one of four actions:

1. Affirm the verdict or decision of the lower court and "let it stand";
2. Modify the verdict or decision of the lower court, without totally reversing it;
3. Reverse the verdict or decision of the lower court, requiring no further court action; or
4. Reverse the verdict or decision of the lower court and remand the case to the court of original jurisdiction, for either retrial or resentencing.

Appeals to the Supreme Court are heard at the discretion of the Court, in contrast to appeals to the U.S. circuit courts, which review cases as a matter of right. The high court's refusal to hear a case generally ends the process of direct appeal.

In some cases, a death row inmate whose appeal has been denied may still try to have the Supreme Court review his or her case on constitutional grounds by filing a writ of habeas corpus. A writ of habeas corpus is a court order directing a law officer to produce a prisoner in court to determine if the prisoner is being legally detained or imprisoned. The habeas corpus proceeding does not test whether the prisoner is guilty or innocent. Recent changes making it more difficult to get habeas petitions heard by the Court are discussed in a later section of this chapter.

FEDERAL CAPITAL CRIMES

Prior to the 1990s, the most significant act of Congress regarding the death penalty may have been its effort to reduce the number of federal capital crimes. In the latter part of the nineteenth century, Congress reduced the number of federal crimes punishable by death from 60 to only three nonmilitary offenses: murder, rape, and treason.[2] A hundred years later, it has reversed course and added numerous new crimes. The 1994 federal crime bill (the Violent Crime Control and Law Enforcement Act), for example, expanded the number of federal crimes punishable by death to about 50. (Estimates vary depending on whether statutes or offenses are counted, and how offenses are counted.) The bill also reinstated the death penalty for federal crimes already on the books that likely would have been held unconstitutional had they been tested. The new law brings the earlier statutes into compliance with guidelines established by the Supreme Court (see the discussion in Chapter 2). The 41 federal crimes for which the death penalty is available as a sentencing alternative are (as of year-end 2009):[3]

- Murder related to the smuggling of aliens.
- Destruction of aircraft, motor vehicles, or related facilities resulting in death.
- Murder committed during a drug-related drive-by shooting.
- Murder committed at an airport serving international civil aviation.
- Retaliatory murder of a member of the immediate family of law enforcement officials.
- Civil rights offenses resulting in death.
- Murder of a member of Congress, an important executive official, or a Supreme Court justice.
- Espionage.
- Death resulting from offenses involving transportation of explosives, destruction of government property, or destruction of property related to foreign or interstate commerce.
- Murder committed by the use of a firearm during a crime of violence or a drug-trafficking crime.
- Murder committed in a federal government facility.
- Genocide.
- First-degree murder.
- Murder of a federal judge or law enforcement official.
- Murder of a foreign official.
- Murder by a federal prisoner.
- Murder of a U.S. national in a foreign country.
- Murder by an escaped federal prisoner already sentenced to life imprisonment.
- Murder of a state or local law enforcement official or other person aiding in a federal investigation; murder of a state correctional officer.
- Murder during a kidnapping.
- Murder during a hostage taking.
- Murder of a court officer or juror.
- Murder with the intent of preventing testimony by a witness, victim, or informant.
- Retaliatory murder of a witness, victim, or informant.
- Mailing of injurious articles with intent to kill or resulting in death.
- Assassination or kidnapping resulting in the death of the president or vice president.
- Murder for hire.
- Murder involved in a racketeering offense.
- Willful wrecking of a train resulting in death.
- Bank robbery–related murder or kidnapping.
- Murder related to a carjacking.
- Murder related to rape or child molestation.
- Murder related to sexual exploitation of children.
- Murder committed during an offense against maritime navigation.
- Murder committed during an offense against a maritime fixed platform.
- Terrorist murder of a U.S. national in another country.
- Murder by the use of a weapon of mass destruction.
- Murder involving torture.
- Treason.
- Murder related to a continuing criminal enterprise or related murder of a federal, state, or local law enforcement officer.
- Death resulting from aircraft hijacking.

FEDERAL CAPITAL PUNISHMENT PROCEDURES

When the Supreme Court in *Furman* (1972) invalidated existing death penalty statutes, it also invalidated the federal death penalty law. Congress did not create procedures that would meet the requirements of *Furman* until 1988 in a new statute that allowed the death penalty for murder in the course of a drug kingpin conspiracy. Six people have subsequently been sentenced to death under this conspiracy law; only one of them, Juan Raul Garza (discussed later), as of April 30, 2011, has been executed.[4] Using the long record of reforms summarized in Chapter 4, Congress incorporated into its new law many of the desirable features of state death penalty statutes already approved by the Supreme Court. Congress further refined federal death penalty procedures in the Federal Death Penalty Act of 1994. Among the features the current federal death penalty law shares with some states are:

- Requiring a minimum of two attorneys be appointed to represent federal capital defendants (at least one of the attorneys must have experience in capital defense work)
- Requiring the government to inform the defendant of its intention to seek death within a reasonable time before trial or before the court accepts a defendant's guilty plea
- Requiring the government, before trial or plea, to list the aggravating circumstances that it proposes to prove to justify a death sentence
- The weighing of statutorily enumerated aggravating and mitigating circumstances (no method or standard for weighing is prescribed)
- Giving the government the burden of establishing aggravating circumstances beyond a reasonable doubt
- Requiring unanimity on the part of jurors in the finding of an aggravating circumstance
- Requiring that a sentence other than death be imposed if no aggravating circumstance is found to exist
- Requiring only a single juror to find a mitigating circumstance before it can be weighed
- Allowing victim-impact evidence
- The right to appeal both the conviction and the death sentence*
- Exempting from the federal death penalty persons less than 18 years of age at the time of the offense, mentally retarded and insane persons, and pregnant women (but only while they are pregnant)

A few features unique to the federal death penalty statute are:

- Requiring authorization from the U.S. attorney general before federal prosecutors can file capital charges
- Requiring the court to consider the federal public defender's recommendation about which attorneys are qualified for appointment in capital cases
- Three different sets of aggravating circumstances: those for espionage and treason; those for homicide; and those for nonhomicide drug offenses

---

*There are three grounds for appeal: (1) the death sentence was imposed under the influence of passion, prejudice, or any other arbitrary factor, (2) the admissible evidence and information adduced does not support the special finding of the existence of the required aggravating factor, or (3) the proceedings involved any other legal error requiring reversal which was properly preserved for appeal under the rules of criminal procedure. No relief may be provided for any error that the government proves to be harmless beyond a reasonable doubt.

- Requiring federal judges in capital sentencing proceedings to instruct the jury that "in considering whether a sentence of death is justified, it shall not consider the race, color, religious beliefs, national origin, or sex of the defendant or of any victim"
- Requiring a jury that recommends death to furnish the court with a certificate signed by each juror swearing that discrimination played no part in the decision and that the same sentencing recommendation would have been made regardless of the race, color, religious beliefs, national origin, or sex of the defendant or any victim
- Restricting the federal government's ability to impose the death penalty on Native Americans (capital prosecution of persons subject to the criminal jurisdiction of an Indian tribal government where federal jurisdiction is based solely on Indian country and where the offense occurred within the boundaries of Indian country is prevented, unless the governing body of the Indian tribe waives its sovereign immunity)

FEDERAL EXECUTIONS

After the U.S. government was founded, more than a decade would pass before it conducted the first federal execution. On June 25, 1790, Thomas Bird was hanged for murder in Maine.[5] Until recently, federal prisoners were usually executed in the state where the crime occurred because the federal government did not have its own site for executions. Prior to 1937, all federal prisoners were hanged but, after that date, they were executed using the method of the state in which the crime was committed.[6] In states without a death penalty, a federal judge could choose another state to conduct the execution. All this changed in 1995, when the Federal Bureau of Prisons converted an old cellblock at the U.S. Penitentiary in Terre Haute, Indiana, into the first national death row facility in American history.

Renovations of the two-story housing unit of the redbrick federal prison built in the 1940s were made at a cost of $475,000.[7] The special unit was designed to confine male offenders sentenced to death by the federal courts. It includes 50 single cells, upper-tier and lower-tier corridors, an industrial workshop, indoor and outdoor recreation areas, a property room, a food preparation area, attorney and family visiting rooms, and a video-teleconferencing area that is used to facilitate inmate access to the courts and their attorneys. The small brick death house, where executions are conducted, is located near the housing unit and is surrounded by chain-link fencing and razor wire. The death row facility did not become operational until July 13, 1999, the date it received the first group of death row inmates. The government delayed opening the facility until then because it decided that it took at least 20 inmates to be cost-effective. Henceforth, most federal executions will take place in Terre Haute. However, in some cases, federal executions will still be conducted near the jurisdiction in which the crime was conducted.[8] As of April 30, 2011, only three people have been executed at the Terre Haute facility: Timothy McVeigh on June 11, 2001; Juan Raul Garza on June 19, 2001; and Louis Jones, Jr. on March 18, 2003.

Since Bird's execution in 1790, and including McVeigh, Garza, and Jones, the U.S. government has executed 339 men and four women. Although most of those executed were convicted of murder or crimes involving murder, some were convicted of rape, kidnapping, rioting, piracy, spying, and espionage. McVeigh, Garza, and Jones were executed by lethal injection, the only method now used by the U.S. government. The 340 other federal executions were by hanging (81%), electrocution (17%), and lethal gas (2%).

The execution of McVeigh was the first federal execution in nearly 40 years. The last federal execution before him occurred on March 15, 1963, when Victor H. Feguer was hanged at Iowa State Penitentiary for kidnapping and murdering an Iowa physician. The prison billed the U.S. government $28.75 for the rope. Between 1931 and 1963, the U.S. government executed 68 people (about 20% of the total), two of whom were women. (This includes more than 30 people executed under federal jurisdiction because their crimes occurred in the District of Columbia.) Between 1871 and 1910, by contrast, the U.S. government executed 175 people (more than 50% of the total). Between 1790 and 1870, there were 71 federal executions (about 20% of the total), and between 1911 and 1931, there were 26 executions (8%). Under its modern death penalty statute, the federal government has executed relatively few capital or potentially capital offenders. For example, from 1995 through 2000, 682 cases eligible for the federal death penalty were submitted to the U.S. attorney general, who authorized prosecutors to seek the death penalty in 159, or 23 percent, of the cases. Of the 159 cases, 51, or 32 percent, were resolved through a plea bargain. The remaining cases were tried, but most defendants avoided the death penalty.[9]

Of the three most recent people executed by the federal government, Timothy McVeigh is by far the more infamous.[10] In interviews for the book *American Terrorist: Timothy McVeigh & the Oklahoma City Bombing*, by Lou Michel and Dan Herbeck, McVeigh confessed to the April 19, 1995, bombing of the Alfred P. Murrah Federal Building in Oklahoma City, Oklahoma. The death toll from the 9:02 a.m. explosion was 168, including 19 children. More than 500 other people were wounded. Until the horrific tragedy of September 11, 2001, the disaster at Oklahoma City was considered the worst act of domestic terrorism in American history and McVeigh the worst mass murderer in American history.

McVeigh's trial began on April 24, 1997, in a federal courthouse in Denver, Colorado. (The trial was moved from Oklahoma because of a concern that McVeigh could not get a fair trial there.) He was convicted on June 2, 1997, of all 11 counts for which he was indicted: conspiracy to use a weapon of mass destruction, use of such a weapon, destruction of government property with explosives, and eight counts of first-degree murder—one for each of the eight federal law enforcement officers killed in the blast. The jury sentenced McVeigh to death on June 13, 1997, and the trial judge did so 2 months later on August 15.

Not coincidentally, the explosion in Oklahoma City occurred on the 2-year anniversary of the government debacle at Waco, Texas, which left some 80 people dead. Revenge for Waco and the tragedy at Ruby Ridge, Idaho, in 1992 was the principal motivating factor in the bombing. However, McVeigh had been compiling a list of grievances against the U.S. government for years. Among them were U.S. military actions against smaller nations, no-knock search warrants, crooked politicians, overzealous government agents, high taxes, political correctness, and gun laws. McVeigh believed that the bombing was necessary to send a message to an out-of-control U.S. government that he claimed was using military tactics to turn the United States into a police state. He was concerned about a new American tyranny and wanted to teach the U.S. government a lesson. It has been estimated that the McVeigh case cost taxpayers more than $100 million (the defense spent nearly $20 million, and the government spent more than $80 million).

Juan Raul Garza, the second person executed by the federal government in nearly 40 years, was the first person executed under the 1988 federal "drug kingpin" statute, which allows the death penalty to be imposed on murders resulting from large-scale illegal drug operations.[11] Garza was sentenced to death in Texas in August 1993 for murdering a man by shooting him five times in the head and neck and ordering the murders of two other men. The victims, like Garza, were drug traffickers; the murders were motivated by Garza's desire to gain control of marijuana distribution networks.

President Clinton twice delayed Garza's execution within a week of his scheduled execution date (the second time just 3 days before he left office) because of concern about the results of a Justice Department study that showed large racial and geographical disparities in the application of the federal death penalty. The study revealed that 80 percent of federal defendants charged with capital offenses between 1995 and 2000 were minorities; half of them were African American. The study also found that just five of the 94 U.S. attorney districts accounted for about 42 percent of all cases in which prosecutors sought the death penalty. Deputy Attorney General Eric Holder remarked that he could not "help but be both personally and professionally disturbed by the numbers ... [and] that no one reading [the] report [could] help but be disturbed, troubled, by [the] disparity."[12] Though not part of the study, Garza's attorney in court filings cited 26 cases involving similar crimes to Garza's where prosecutors did not seek the federal death penalty.

Garza's petition for clemency was considered and denied by newly elected President George W. Bush. Following the clemency denial, newly appointed Attorney General John Ashcroft told the press that besides the three murders for which he was convicted, Garza was responsible for at least five more deaths, including four in Mexico for which he was not prosecuted. Ashcroft also stated that there was no racial bias in Garza's case, pointing out that the prosecutor was Hispanic as were seven of the eight victims. As for the racial disparities found in the aforementioned Justice Department study, Ashcroft explained that they were not the result of racial bias but were rather a product of legitimate law enforcement strategies and differing policies in the nation's 94 federal districts. According to Ashcroft, "In areas where large-scale, organized drug trafficking is largely carried out by gangs whose membership is drawn from minority groups, the active federal role in investigating and prosecuting these crimes results in a high proportion of minority defendants in potentially capital cases...."[13] What Ashcroft failed to note was that black and Hispanic gang members frequently face death sentences, while white mobsters almost never do. According to a Federal Death Penalty Resource Counsel study, since 1988, when the federal death penalty was restored (and until 2000), 700 defendants had been charged with potentially death-eligible federal crimes; the attorney general authorized 211 (30%) of them to be prosecuted as death penalty cases. At least 40 of the death penalty cases (nearly 20%) involved black or Hispanic gang members, but only one of the cases involved a white mobster. Because of the high priority given to organized crime by the FBI in recent years, 1500 organized crime figures have been convicted since 1996. Not one of them faced a death sentence, even when multiple murders were committed.[14] (Chapter 10 provides an extended discussion of arbitrary and discriminatory application of the death penalty at the state level.)

As of March 31, 2011, 58 people were under a federal death sentence. All but two of them were male, 45 percent were black, 40 percent were white, 14 percent were Latino, and 2 percent were Native American.[15]

THE RACIAL JUSTICE ACT AND THE FAIRNESS IN DEATH SENTENCING ACT

Justice Powell suggested in the *McCleskey* decision (described in Chapter 4) that claims of racial discrimination would be best presented to legislative bodies for corrective action. Congress thereupon commissioned a review of research on racial discrimination in capital charging and sentencing. The resulting General Accounting Office (GAO) report confirmed that such discrimination was a problem—especially when it was based on the race of the victim.[16] (Findings of the GAO report are described in more detail in Chapter 10.) In an effort to rectify the situation, two pieces of legislation were proposed: the Racial Justice Act and the Fairness in Death Sentencing Act.

The legislation was intended to give offenders sentenced to death the right to challenge as racially discriminatory their individual death sentences, much in the same way that individuals may challenge racially discriminatory outcomes under federal employment or housing laws.[17] The two pieces of legislation would allow a black defendant or a defendant whose victim was white the opportunity to present evidence showing a pattern of racially discriminatory charging or sentencing. The state could rebut the evidence by showing, by a preponderance of the evidence, that the pattern of racially discriminatory charging or sentencing could be explained by identifiable and pertinent nonracial factors. If the state failed in its rebuttal, the defendant would be entitled to have his or her death sentence set aside.[18]

Both proposals were vigorously opposed by state attorneys general and by prosecutors who claimed that (1) racial discrimination did not exist, making legislation unnecessary, and (2) passage of the legislation would result either in the use of quotas or in the de facto abolition of the death penalty.[19]

The Racial Justice Act stalled and was set aside. The House of Representatives passed the Fairness in Death Sentencing Act in 1990 and again in 1994, but the Senate in a House–Senate Conference Committee rejected the act both times.[20] When Congress enacted death penalty measures as part of the Violent Crime Control and Law Enforcement Act later in 1994, it included no provisions regarding racial discrimination in charging or sentencing.[21]

THE ANTITERRORISM AND EFFECTIVE DEATH PENALTY ACT OF 1996

In the mid-1990s, Congress turned its attention to what some of its members believed was the abuse of the writ of habeas corpus in death penalty cases. Recall that a writ of habeas corpus claims that a federal constitutional right has been violated and, thus, the claimant is being held illegally. It is a primary avenue to the U.S. Supreme Court. Critics maintain that abuse of the writ has contributed to the long delays in executions (currently averaging more than 14 years after conviction) and to the high costs associated with capital punishment.

In part to speed up the process and reduce costs, Congress passed the Antiterrorism and Effective Death Penalty Act of 1996, and President Clinton signed it into law on April 24. The law requires that second or subsequent habeas petitions be dismissed when the claim has already been made in a previous petition. It also requires that new claims be dismissed unless the Supreme Court hands down a new rule of constitutional law and makes it retroactive to cases on collateral review. Under the act, the only other way the Supreme Court will hear a claim made for the first time is when the claim is based on new evidence not previously available. Even then, the new evidence must be of sufficient weight, by a clear and convincing standard of proof, to convince a judge or jury that the capital defendant was not guilty of the crime or crimes for which he or she was convicted.

The act made the federal appellate courts "gatekeepers" for second or subsequent habeas corpus petitions. Now, to file a second or subsequent claim, a capital defendant must first file a motion in the appropriate appellate court, announcing his or her intention. A panel of three judges must hear the motion within 30 days and decide whether the petitioner has a legitimate claim under the act. If the claim is denied, the new law prohibits any review of the panel's decision, either by a rehearing or by a writ of certiorari to the Supreme Court. So far, the U.S. Supreme Court has upheld the constitutionality of the new law.[22]

THE INNOCENCE PROTECTION ACT OF 2004

The issues of innocent people being wrongly convicted of capital crimes and inadequate legal representation of capital defendants fared better in Congress than did the issue of racial discrimination in the administration of the death penalty. On October 30, 2004, President Bush signed into law a crime bill dubbed the "Justice For All Act of 2004." The Innocence Protection Act of 2004 is a part of the crime bill. The Innocence Protection Act was not an easy sell. Senator Patrick Leahy of Vermont first introduced it in the Senate, albeit in a much tougher form, in early 2000. Leahy's motivation for introducing the legislation was what he called "the growing national crisis in the administration of capital punishment."[23] He noted that, since the reinstatement of capital punishment in the 1970s, 85 people [at the time] had been released from death rows after being found innocent. He implored his colleagues to join him in finding ways to minimize the risk of executing innocent people. It took 4 years for what critics contend is a watered-down version of Leahy's original bill to become law.

The Innocence Protection Act has three major sections. The first is entitled "Exonerating the Innocent Through DNA Testing." This section "establishes rules and procedures governing applications for DNA testing by inmates in the Federal system."[24] According to these rules and procedures:

> A court shall order DNA testing if the applicant asserts under penalty of perjury that he or she is actually innocent, and the proposed DNA testing may produce new material evidence that supports such assertion and raises a reasonable probability that the applicant did not commit the offense. Motions filed more than 5 years after enactment and 3 years after conviction are presumed untimely, but such presumption may be rebutted upon good cause shown. Penalties are established in the event that testing inculpates the applicant. Where test results are exculpatory, the court shall grant the applicant's motion for a new trial or resentencing if the test results and other evidence establish by compelling evidence that a new trial would result in an acquittal.[25]

In addition, this section "prohibits the destruction of DNA evidence in a Federal criminal case while a defendant remains incarcerated, with certain exceptions."[26] Specifically:

> The government may destroy DNA evidence if the defendant waived the right to DNA testing; if the defendant was notified after his conviction became final that the evidence may be destroyed and did not file a motion for testing; if a court has denied a motion for testing; or if the evidence has already been tested and the results included the defendant as the source. If the evidence is large or bulky, the government may remove and preserve a representative sample. Intentional violations of these evidence-retention provisions to prevent evidence from being tested or used in court are punishable by a term of imprisonment. Nothing in this section supersedes any law requiring that evidence be preserved.[27]

This section also includes "The Kirk Bloodsworth Post-Conviction DNA Testing Grant Program" and "Incentive Grants to States to Ensure Consideration of Claims of Actual Innocence." The former, named after the first death row inmate to be exonerated by DNA evidence, authorized $5 million in grants through 2009 to help states pay for the costs of postconviction DNA testing. The latter provides states with funding to establish procedures for providing postconviction DNA testing and preserving DNA evidence.[28]

The second major section of the Innocence Act is entitled "Improving the Quality of Representation in State Capital Cases." Its purpose is to increase the reliability of capital trial verdicts. The first part of this section "authorizes a grant program, to be administered by the Attorney General, to improve the quality of legal representation provided to indigent defendants in State capital cases."[29] The second part "authorizes grants to improve the representation of the public in State capital cases," that is, to improve the work of prosecutors in capital cases. Congress authorized $75 million a year for 5 years to implement these programs. Each one has an evaluation component.[30]

The Innocent Act's third major section is entitled "Compensation of the Wrongfully Convicted." This section "increases the maximum amount of damages that the U.S. Court of Federal Claims may award against the United States in cases of unjust imprisonment from a flat $5,000 to $50,000 per year in non-capital cases, and $100,000 per year in capital cases."[31] The section also "expresses the sense of Congress that States should provide reasonable compensation to any person found to have been unjustly convicted of an offense against the State and sentenced to death."[32]

THE DEATH PENALTY IN THE MILITARY

Information on the military's use of the death penalty is scarce. What little is available suggests that, historically, the military has used the death penalty mostly for crimes committed during wartime.[33] In this section of the chapter, three topics are addressed: (1) the history of military executions, (2) military capital offenses, and (3) military capital punishment procedures.

MILITARY EXECUTIONS

Although there are no official records on the subject, it is believed that executions by the military were relatively common during both the American Revolution and in the early years of the nation. It is also believed that many death sentences were never carried out because of subsequent pardons. It is presumed that the crime for which most soldiers were sentenced to death during this period was desertion.

Official War Department records of military executions were first kept during the Civil War by the Union Army. The records show 267 executions for the following offenses: desertion (141), murder (72), rape (23), mutiny (20), theft (4), multiple offenses (4), and spying (3). The list shows that more than half of the executions were for desertion. More Union soldiers would have been executed for desertion had President Lincoln not pardoned many of them, deciding "to take the risk on the side of mercy." There is no record of executions by the Confederate Army. Either no such record was kept or they were destroyed before the war's end.

During World War I, the U.S. military executed 35 of the 145 soldiers sentenced to death. All of the soldiers executed were black. They were executed for murder and mutiny (19), rape (11), murder and rape (3), and murder (2). Ten of the executions were conducted in France and the remaining 25 in the United States. All executions took place at dawn following the day the trial ended. Because executions were carried out so quickly, there was no time to review the records of a case, as required by law, or there was not enough time for condemned soldiers to petition the president for clemency or a pardon.

During World War II, the Army executed 147 soldiers. The Navy, the Air Force, and the Marine Corps executed none. The crimes for which soldiers were executed were murder (76), rape (52), murder and rape (18), and desertion (1). Although only one soldier was executed for desertion, 2,864 soldiers were tried for the offense and 49 of them were sentenced to death. All those death sentences, except the one, were later commuted to life imprisonment. The one execution involved what has been called "the most widely publicized [case] of cowardice and desertion in modern times." The soldier violated Articles of War #52—desertion to avoid hazardous duty—and was executed by firing squad in France on January 31, 1945. In addition to American soldiers, 14 German prisoners of war were hanged at the U.S. Disciplinary Barracks, Fort Leavenworth, Kansas, in July and August 1945, for murdering other prisoners of war.

Criminologist J. Robert Lilly has researched the records of 18 American soldiers executed by the U.S. Army in England from 1943 to 1945.[34] Eight of the executions were for murder, six were for rape, and four were for murder and rape.[35] Fifty-six percent (10) of the 18 soldiers executed, and 80 percent of all U.S. soldiers executed in the European Theater, were African American even though African Americans comprised no more than 10 percent of the soldiers in the European Theater and in the Army, generally.[36] Combined with the three Latinos executed, minorities accounted for 72 percent (13) of the 18 executions studied by Lilly. He found that only nonwhite soldiers were executed for rape. He also discovered evidence of racial discrimination at nearly every stage of the process.[37]

After World War II and until 1961, the military executed only 12 soldiers, although many more had been sentenced to death. All but the 12 had their sentences commuted. Eleven of the 12 executed were African American.[38] The U.S. military's last execution was on April 13, 1961. Private John Bennett was hanged at the U.S. Disciplinary Barracks, Fort Leavenworth, Kansas, for the rape and attempted murder of an 11-year-old Austrian girl. Bennett was the 464th Army soldier executed since 1861. By contrast, the Navy has executed no more than 26 sailors during its history (not counting deaths from flogging which was outlawed in 1850). The last executions by the Navy were in 1849, when two sailors were hanged for mutiny. Similarly, the Air Force has executed only three airmen in its history: one in 1948 and two in 1954. The Coast Guard has carried out no executions, and no information is available on the Marines.

The military's death row is currently a pod in the U.S. Disciplinary Barracks' "Special Housing Unit" at Fort Leavenworth, Kansas. The U.S. Disciplinary Barracks at Fort Leavenworth, Kansas, is the only maximum-security correctional facility in the Department of Defense. As of July 1, 2009, eight soldiers occupied the military's death row: all were male, six were African American, one was white, and one was Asian.[39] So far, the military has not executed anyone since 1961.

MILITARY CAPITAL OFFENSES

Offenses for which death is a potential punishment in the military can be divided into three general categories: (1) offenses that could be committed at any time, (2) offenses committed during the time of war, and (3) offenses that are "grave breaches" of the law of war. There are 10 potentially capital offenses that could be committed at any time:

1. Mutiny or sedition
2. Misbehavior before the enemy
3. Subordinate compelling surrender
4. Forcing a safeguard
5. Aiding the enemy
6. Espionage
7. Improperly hazarding a vessel
8. Premeditated murder
9. Felony-murder
10. Rape

The five potentially capital offenses committed during time of war are:

1. Desertion
2. Assaulting or willfully disobeying a superior commissioned officer
3. Improper use of countersign
4. Spying
5. Misbehavior of sentinel

For purposes of the military's death penalty, "time of war" refers to a period of war declared by Congress or the factual determination by the president that the existence of hostilities warrants a finding that a "time of war" exists (examples of the latter are the Korean and Vietnam wars). The death penalty is mandatory for soldiers convicted of spying in time of war; however, given the Supreme Court's consistent post-*Furman* record of rejecting mandatory death penalty statutes, it is doubtful that the military's mandatory provision could withstand constitutional scrutiny if ever challenged.

The third category of offenses for which the death penalty is a possible sanction is "grave breaches" of the law of war. The law of war to which this provision refers is the Geneva Convention Relative to the Treatment of Prisoners of War. Potentially capital crimes under the law of war are:

1. Willful killing, torture, or inhuman treatment, including biological experiments
2. Willfully causing great suffering or serious injury to body or health
3. Unlawful deportation or transfer or unlawful confinement of a protected person
4. Compelling a protected person to serve in the forces of a hostile power
5. Willfully depriving a protected person of the rights of fair and regular trial prescribed in the present Convention
6. Taking of hostages and extensive destruction and appropriation of property, not justified by military necessity and carried out unlawfully and wantonly

MILITARY CAPITAL PUNISHMENT PROCEDURES

The Supreme Court has upheld the military death penalty process in *Loving v. United States* (1996).[40] Private Loving had been sentenced to death in 1988 for the murder of two taxi drivers. He appealed, arguing that his death sentence violated the Eighth Amendment's prohibition against cruel and unusual punishment and the separation-of-powers doctrine. The latter requires that Congress, and not the president, set military death penalty policy. The statute under which Loving was convicted and sentenced contained a list of aggravating factors—at least one of which had to be found before a death sentence could be imposed—issued by President Reagan in 1984 by executive order. President Reagan was responding to the ruling of the Court of Military Appeals in *U.S. v. Matthews* (1983), wherein the Court held the military's death penalty unconstitutional because it was imposed in an arbitrary manner. Specifically, the statute "failed to narrow effectively the class of defendants eligible for capital punishment." Recall that the Supreme Court reached the same conclusion about the civilian death penalty in *Furman v. Georgia* in 1972. President Reagan issued the aggravating factors to satisfy the Court on this issue. In *Loving*, the Court ruled 9–0 that Congress had granted the president that power in 1951 under the Uniform Code of Military Justice, and it denied Private Loving's claim.

The military's death penalty process has much in common with some of the schemes approved by the Supreme Court in *Gregg*. Chief among them is that the members of the military court (the military's counterpart to the civilian jury) must unanimously find, beyond a reasonable doubt, at least one statutorily enumerated aggravating factor before it may consider a death sentence. Any aggravating factor that is found must be weighed against any mitigating circumstances that are presented at trial. Like its civilian counterpart, the military court must allow the presentation of any mitigating circumstance that is supported by evidence. If the members of the military court unanimously find that the aggravating factor or factors substantially outweigh any mitigating circumstances, then a death sentence may be imposed; if the mitigating circumstances are found to outweigh the aggravating factor or factors, then a death sentence may not be imposed.

The military's aggravating factors, many of which are unique to the military, are:

1. That the offense was committed before or in the presence of the enemy, except that this factor shall not apply in the case of a violation of Article 118 [premeditated murder and felony-murder] or 120 [rape];
2. That in committing the offense the accused—
   (A) Knowingly created a grave risk of substantial damage to the national security of the United States; or
   (B) Knowingly created a grave risk of substantial damage to a mission, system, or function of the United States, provided that this subparagraph shall apply only if substantial damage to the national security of the United States would have resulted had the intended damage been effected;
3. That the offense caused substantial damage to the national security of the United States, whether or not the accused intended such damage, except that this factor shall not apply in case of a violation of Article 118 [premeditated murder and felony-murder] or 120 [rape];
4. That the offense was committed in such a way or under circumstances that the life of one or more persons other than the victim was unlawfully and substantially endangered, except that this factor shall not apply to a violation of Articles 104 [aiding the enemy], 106a [espionage], or 120 [rape];
5. That the accused committed the offense with the intent to avoid hazardous duty;
6. That, only in the case of a violation of Article 118 [premeditated murder and felony-murder] or 120 [rape], the offense was committed in time of war and in territory in which the United

States or an ally of the United States was then an occupying power or in which the armed forces of the United States were then engaged in active hostilities;

7. That, only in the case of a violation of Article 118(1) [premeditated murder]:
   (A) The accused was serving a sentence of confinement for 30 years or more or for life at the time of the murder;
   (B) The murder was committed: while the accused was engaged in the commission or attempted commission of any robbery, rape, aggravated arson, sodomy, burglary, kidnapping, mutiny, sedition, or piracy of an aircraft or vessel; or while the accused was engaged in the commission or attempted commission of any offense involving the wrongful distribution, manufacture, or introduction or possession, with intent to distribute, of a controlled substance; or, while the accused was engaged in flight or attempted flight after the commission or attempted commission of any such offense;
   (C) The murder was committed for the purpose of receiving money or a thing of value;
   (D) The accused procured another by means of compulsion, coercion, or a promise of an advantage, a service, or a thing of value to commit the murder;
   (E) The murder was committed with the intent to avoid or to prevent lawful apprehension or effect an escape from custody or confinement;
   (F) The victim was the president of the United States, the president-elect, the vice president, or, if there was no vice president, the officer in the order of succession to the office of president of the United States, the vice-president-elect, or any individual who is acting as president under the Constitution and laws of the United States, any member of Congress (including a delegate to, or resident commissioner in, the Congress) or member-of-Congress elect, justice or judge of the United States, a chief of state or head of government (or the political equivalent) of a foreign nation, or a foreign official … if the official was on official business at the time of the offense and was in the United States or in a place described in Mil. R. Evid….;
   (G) The accused then knew that the victim was any of the following persons in the execution of office: a commissioned, warrant, noncommissioned, or petty officer of the armed services of the United States; a member of any law enforcement or security activity or agency, military or civilian, including correctional custody personnel; or any firefighter;
   (H) The murder was committed with intent to obstruct justice;
   (I) The murder was preceded by the intentional infliction of substantial physical harm or prolonged, substantial mental or physical pain and suffering to the victim. For purposes of this section, "substantial physical harm" means fractures or dislocated bones, deep cuts, torn members of the body, serious damage to internal organs, or other serious bodily injuries. The term "substantial physical harm" does not mean minor injuries, such as a black eye or bloody nose. The term "substantial mental or physical pain or suffering" is accorded its common meaning and includes torture;
   (J) The accused has been found guilty in the same case of another violation of Article 118 [premeditated murder and felony-murder];
   (K) The victim of the murder was less than fifteen years of age;
8. That only in the case of a violation of Article 118(4) [felony-murder], the accused was the actual perpetrator of the killing or was a principal whose participation in the burglary, sodomy, rape, robbery, or aggravated arson was major and who manifested a reckless indifference for human life;

9. That, only in the case of a violation of Article 120 [rape]:
    (A) The victim was under the age of 12; or
    (B) The accused maimed or attempted to kill the victim;
10. That, only in the case of a violation of the law of war, death is authorized under the law of war for the offense;
11. That, only in the case of a violation of Article 104 [aiding the enemy] or 106a [espionage]:
    (A) The accused has been convicted of another offense involving espionage or treason for which either a sentence of death or imprisonment for life was authorized by statute; or
    (B) That in committing the offense, the accused knowingly created a grave risk of death to a person other than the individual who was the victim.

Other key features of the military's capital punishment procedure are listed next. Some of the procedures are the same as those in other death penalty jurisdictions, and some of them are unique to the military.

- Before arraignment, the prosecution must provide written notice to the defense of aggravating factors that the prosecution intends to prove.
- Court members (the military's equivalent to civilian jurors) do not need to possess any specific requirements other than being the best qualified by reason of age, education, training, experience, length of service, and judicial temperament. They do not have to hold any particular rank.
- Although the UCMJ requires only five court members, including a military judge, a 12-person panel is required in a capital case.
- Capital defendants are entitled to individual military counsel, preferably one with experience defending capital cases. They may also retain civilian counsel. The military is not required to appoint "ABA qualified" civilian defense counsel at government expense.[41]
- A guilty plea may not be accepted for an offense for which the death penalty may be adjudged.
- The panel members must find unanimously that the accused is guilty of a death-eligible offense.
- The panel members must find unanimously beyond a reasonable doubt that at least one qualifying aggravating factor exists.
- The panel members must unanimously concur that any aggravating factors substantially outweigh any mitigating factors.
- The panel members must unanimously vote for the death penalty as the sentence for the accused. (It is the duty of the military judge in a capital case to ensure that the members are informed and understand that they may propose lesser sentences and, if so propose, must vote on such sentences before reaching a vote for death.)
- If death is adjudged, the president (military judge and one of the court members) shall announce which aggravating factors were found by the members.
- A death sentence includes a dishonorable discharge or dismissal, as appropriate. Confinement is a necessary incident of a death sentence but not part of it.
- Convictions and death sentences may be appealed first to the particular branches' court of criminal appeals (e.g., the Army Court of Criminal Appeals); next, to the U.S. Court of Appeals for the Armed Forces; and finally, to the U.S. Supreme Court.
- The president of the United States must approve all military executions. The president may also grant a commutation or pardon.
- Execution is by lethal injection.

The Uniform Code of Military Justice was recently amended to provide LWOP as an alternative to the death penalty for any soldier whose capital crime occurred on or after November 17, 1997. Prior to the LWOP alternative, a soldier sentenced to life imprisonment was eligible for parole in 10 years.[42]

A STUDY OF THE MILITARY'S MODERN DEATH PENALTY

The time frame of this study is from January 24, 1984, the year the military's modern death penalty system took effect, until December 31, 2006.[43] During the study period, 47 court-martial cases were tried capitally. A "capital court-martial" was defined "as a case that remained death-eligible at the conclusion of the presentation of evidence on the merits."[44] Not included are "cases that were initially referred capitally but, for various reasons including pretrial agreements, did not result in a death-eligible trial" or "known cases of inadvertent capital referrals."[45] Of the 47 capital cases, the Army tried 18, the Marine Corps 13, the Air Force 10, the Navy six, and the Coast Guard none.

Forty-five of the 47 capital cases were tried between 1984 and 1998, no capital cases were tried between 1998 and 2005, two capital cases were tried in 2005, and no capital cases were tried in 2006. Among the factors that may account for the gap in capital trials between 1998 and 2005 were our allies' objections to the military's holding capital courts-martial in their countries. At least nine capital courts-martial were conducted in European countries between 1984 and 1990. Another factor may have been increasing litigation costs, caused, for example, by the use of civilian mitigation specialists. A third factor may have been increased preparation time for capital trials. In one case, *United States v. Akbar*, the time between apprehension and trial was 2 years. One last factor may have been the availability of LWOP sentences for offenses committed after November 18, 1997.

Fifteen death sentences were imposed in the 47 capital prosecutions (32%). However, in two of the 15 cases, the convening authority commuted the death sentence: in one case to life imprisonment plus a dishonorable discharge, and in the other case to confinement for natural life. Both soldiers were Marines. Not including the two commutations, only about 28 percent of the 47 capital prosecutions resulted in an approved death sentence. Of the remaining 13 death sentences, the Army imposed six, the Marine Corps five, the Air Force two, and the Navy zero.

The 13 cases in which a death sentence was imposed and not commuted entered the military appellate system. As previously noted, for capital cases, two levels of mandatory appeals are provided by the military appellate system: the particular branch's court of criminal appeals (e.g., the Army Court of Criminal Appeals), which is equivalent to a civilian intermediate court of appeals, and the U.S. Court of Appeals for the Armed Forces (CAAF), the military's highest court. The particular branch's court of criminal appeals, like the civilian appellate courts, conducts a sentence appropriateness review but, unlike the civilian appellate courts, also conducts a factual sufficiency review. Another significant difference between the military appellate system and the civilian appellate system is, in the civilian appellate system, facts outside the trial record that can be used to attack a conviction or sentence, such as ineffective assistance of counsel or discovery violations by the prosecutor, are not generally raised on direct appeal but rather are raised during postconviction review. In the military appellate system, by contrast, there is no postconviction review. Facts outside the trial record are routinely raised on direct appeal, usually through a motion to attach an affidavit.

During the study period, nine of the 13 appealed cases completed direct appellate review. In six of the cases reviewed by a particular branch's court of criminal appeals, a death sentence was affirmed. In four of the cases, the CAAF reversed the lower appellate court and set aside the death sentence, and in the other two cases, CAAF affirmed the death sentences. In one case, the CAAF reversed a part of the lower appellate court's ruling but still affirmed the lower court's decision to set aside the death sentence. In the two remaining cases, the CAAF affirmed the relief granted by the lower appellate court. The reasons for reversing a death sentence at one of the two appellate stages were: (1) acceptance of what amounted to a prohibited guilty plea to the capital offense of felony-murder, (2) a military judge's faulty instructions about the procedures for voting on a death sentence, (3) ineffective assistance of counsel, and (4) a military judge's erroneous application of case law limiting the removal of members (the equivalent of jurors) based on moral or religious concerns about the death penalty. The reversals in military death penalty cases are probably due primarily to the unfamiliarity of trial-level litigators and military judges with death penalty practice.

When the military's mandatory appellate process has been concluded, the president of the United States must decide whether to approve the death sentence. Without the president's explicit approval, the death sentence may not be carried out. No president has acted on a military death sentence since 1962, when President John F. Kennedy commuted a sailor's death sentence. Since then, only two death sentences have been affirmed on appeal. The U.S. Supreme Court affirmed the death sentence of Army Private First Class Dwight Loving in 1996, and denied certiorari in the case of Army Specialist Ronald Gray, whose death sentence was affirmed by the CAAF. As of this writing, both cases await presidential action.

Were the president to approve a military death sentence, the condemned would be eligible for habeas corpus review by an Article III court, which is a federal court. (Article III refers to Article III of the U.S. Constitution, which reads: "The judicial Power of the United States, shall be vested in one supreme Court, and in such inferior Courts as the Congress may from time to time ordain and establish.") No military death row inmate has filed a habeas corpus petition with an Article III court since 1961.

THE DEATH PENALTY IN A GLOBAL CONTEXT[46]

Globally, the death penalty is trending toward abolition. At the beginning of the twentieth century, only three countries—Costa Rica, San Marino, and Venezuela—had abolished the death penalty for all crimes. By 1977, only 14 countries had abolished the death penalty for all crimes. Another two countries had abolished it for all but exceptional capital crimes, such as those committed during wartime. As of December, 2010, 96 countries had abolished the death penalty for all crimes; another nine countries had abolished it for all but exceptional crimes; and 34 countries had abolished it in practice (i.e., they retain the death penalty but have not carried out an execution for at least 10 years and are believed to have a policy or established practice of not using the death penalty). More than 50 countries have abolished the death penalty since 1990. The most recent is Gabon, which abolished the death penalty for all crimes in 2010. Since 1985, only four abolitionist countries have reintroduced the death penalty. Two of those countries, Nepal and the Philippines, have since abolished it again; and the other two, Gambia and Papua New Guinea, have not executed anyone since reintroducing the penalty. So, as of this writing, more than 70 percent of the countries in the world—139 of them—have abolished the death penalty in law or practice.

On the other hand, only 58 countries have retained the death penalty. However, the number of countries that actually execute anyone in a given year is much smaller. Law professor Carol Steiker offers 10, in many cases interrelated, theories that may account for American exceptionalism regarding capital punishment.[46] She also provides critiques of most of them.

1. The United States has a much higher homicide rate than any of its western European or other peer counterparts (the most common theory).
2. Strong public support for capital punishment in the United States.
3. Crime and punishment ("law and order") are top issues in political agendas at all levels of government in the United States (the most persuasive reason).
4. Populism in American politics compared to the elitism in European politics.
5. Populist influence and control in American criminal justice.
6. Criminal law-making and law enforcement in the United States are primarily a state and local concern.
7. The exceptionalism of the American South based on racial inequality and prejudice, Protestant fundamentalism, a subculture of violence, and the strength and resistance to the civil rights movement of the 1950s and 1960s.
8. European exceptionalism against capital punishment due to the World Wars, ethnic conflicts, and state abuses of power.
9. The United States' (and not just the American South's) subculture of violence, as portrayed in the media and the ownership of guns.
10. Historical contingency, that is, the United States' failure to abolish capital punishment was a historical accident (the "failure" of *Furman v. Georgia*).

EXECUTIONS WORLDWIDE

In 2010, at least 527 prisoners were executed in 23 countries, and in 67 countries, at least 2,024 people were sentenced to death. This does not count China, which does not report death sentences or executions but is believed to have sentenced and executed thousands. Of the 527 known executions that took place in 2010, at least 83 percent were carried out in five countries: 48 percent in Iran, 11 percent in North Korea, 10 percent in Yemen, 9 percent in the United States, and 5 percent in Saudi Arabia. Besides China, Iran, North Korea, Yemen, the United States, and Saudi Arabia, other countries to execute at least one person in 2010 were Bahrain, Bangladesh, Belarus, Botswana, Egypt, Equatorial Guinea, Iraq, Japan, Libya, Malaysia, the Palestinian Authority, Singapore, Somalia, Sudan, Syria, Taiwan, and Vietnam. The methods of execution used in 2010 were hanging, shooting, beheading, electrocution, and lethal injection. Iran used stoning as a method of execution in 2009.

INTERNATIONAL TREATIES PROHIBITING THE DEATH PENALTY

In recent years, many countries have committed to abolishing the death penalty by ratifying international treaties prohibiting the practice. Currently, there are four such treaties:

- The Second Optional Protocol to the International Covenant on Civil and Political Rights, which was adopted by the UN General Assembly (UNGA) in 1989. Seventy-two countries have ratified this treaty. An additional three countries have signed the protocol, indicating their intention to become parties to it at a later date.

- The Protocol to the American Convention on Human Rights to Abolish the Death Penalty, which was adopted by the General Assembly of the Organization of American States in 1990. This treaty has been ratified by 11 countries.
- Protocol No. 6 to the European Convention for the Protection of Human Rights and Fundamental Freedoms (known as the European Convention on Human Rights), which was adopted by the Council of Europe in 1982. It has been ratified by 46 European countries and signed by one other.
- Protocol No. 13 to the European Convention for the Protection of Human Rights and Fundamental Freedoms (the European Convention on Human Rights), which was adopted by the Council of Europe in 2002. It has been ratified by 42 European countries and signed by three others.

Protocol No. 6 to the European Convention on Human Rights is an agreement to abolish the death penalty in peacetime. Its influence on the international debate about the death penalty is considered enormous because it has provided "the foundation for external judgments about the penal policies of other nations."[48] The Second Optional Protocol to the International Covenant on Civil and Political Rights and the Protocol to the American Convention on Human Rights provide for the total abolition of the death penalty but allow states wishing to do so to retain the death penalty in wartime as an exception. Protocol No. 13 to the European Convention on Human Rights provides for the total abolition of the death penalty in all circumstances with no exceptions permitted. The United States has taken reservations to the death penalty abolition provisions of treaties that it has ratified or signed. Reservations are statements that modify or exclude the applications or certain provisions for that country.

In addition, three human rights treaties that have been ratified by the United States ban arbitrary and discriminatory punishments. The International Covenant on Civil and Political Rights, mentioned above, prohibits any arbitrary use of the death penalty. The UN Convention Against Torture and Other Cruel, Inhuman or Degrading Treatment or Punishment bans torture and the infliction of severe pain or suffering based on any kind of discrimination. The International Convention on the Elimination of All Forms of Racial Discrimination (the Race Convention), as the name implies, forbids racial discrimination in the law's administration. International agencies and courts have found the United States in violation of each of these treaties. The United States, in turn, has adamantly denied the accusations.

THE DEATH PENALTY VIEWED GLOBALLY

The UN Commission on Human Rights has repeatedly condemned the death penalty in the United States. It has implored the U.S. government to halt all executions until states are brought into compliance with international standards and laws. In December 2007, the UN General Assembly (UNGA) called for a worldwide death penalty moratorium with the goal of abolishing executions. One hundred four member countries voted in favor of the resolution, 54 nations opposed it, and 29 nations abstained.[49] In December 2008, the UNGA adopted a second resolution calling for a worldwide death penalty moratorium. This time 106 countries voted in favor of the resolution, 46 countries voted against it, and 34 countries abstained.[50] In November 2010, the UNGA adopted a third resolution calling for a worldwide moratorium with 107 countries in favor, 38 countries opposed, and 36 abstentions.[51] The UNGA resolutions are not legally binding, but they do carry considerable moral and political weight. They are also indicative of the international trend to abolish the death penalty.

In Europe, the death penalty is viewed as a human rights violation. Admittance into the European Union requires abolition of the death penalty, and membership in the Council of Europe necessitates renouncing it. In 2001, the Council of Europe's 602-member parliamentary assembly passed a resolution to remove the United States and Japan as observers at the organization unless significant progress toward abolishing executions and repealing the death penalty was made by January 1, 2003. When both countries failed to comply by that date, the Assembly passed another resolution requiring the United States and Japan "to make more of an effort" to place a moratorium on executions "with a view to abolishing the death penalty," or risk losing their observer status. By 2008, neither the United States nor Japan had complied, so the parliamentary assembly passed yet another resolution to "intensify its political dialog with Japan and the United States, to urge both countries to finally place an immediate moratorium on executions, [and] to abolish the death penalty as soon as possible."[52] As of this writing, neither country has complied.

The European Union also considers a universal moratorium on executions and the death penalty's abolition as key factors in relations between the European Union and third countries. Member countries are to take this into account when finalizing agreements with third countries. Consequently, some foreign businesses, particularly those operated by governments, may make economic decisions based on a state's use of the death penalty. In a 1998 letter to then–Texas Governor George Bush, a European Union official wrote, "Many companies, under pressure from shareholders and public opinion to apply ethical business practices, are beginning to consider the possibility of restricting the investment in the U.S. to states that do not apply the death penalty."

The most direct way in which the United States has been alienating its allies is the execution of foreign nationals, especially when they have not been accorded their rights under the Vienna Convention on Consular Relations. The United States, along with almost all of the other countries of the world, has long been a party to the Vienna Convention. Article 36 of this convention requires officials in the United States and other countries that have ratified the convention to inform foreign nationals placed under arrest of their rights to confer with their home country's consular officials. This provision is binding on all states under the U.S. Constitution but has been systematically ignored, partly because the police generally are unaware of the law. Cases in which countries fail to comply with Article 36 can be referred to the International Court of Justice (ICJ, also known as the world court), which can forward the cases to the UN Security Council for "appropriate action"—whatever that means. In February 2005, President Bush signed a memorandum affirming that the United States would comply with the 2004 decision of the ICJ to have state courts review and reconsider the effect of Vienna Convention violations in the cases of 51 Mexican nationals on U.S. death rows. Mexico had sued the United States on behalf of its 51 citizens. According to Bush's memo, compliance was required despite state laws governing challenges to criminal convictions. However, in *Sanchez-Llamas v. Oregon* (548 U.S. 331, 2006), the U.S. Supreme Court ruled that "the Vienna Convention did not preclude the application of state default rules." One of the 51 Mexican nationals was Jose Ernesto Medellin, who had been convicted of raping and killing two teenage girls. He was sentenced to death in a Texas state court. Based on the ICJ's decision and President Bush's memo, Medellin filed an application for a writ of habeas corpus in state court. The Texas Court of Criminal Appeals dismissed Medellin's application as an abuse of the writ because under state law Medellin had failed to raise his Vienna Convention claim in a timely manner. The Court granted certiorari and, in *Medellin v. Texas* (552 U.S. 491, 2008), ruled 6–3 that neither the ICJ's decision nor President Bush's memorandum preempted state limitations on the filing of successive habeas petitions. Thus, ignoring the ICJ's decision and President Bush's memo, the state of Texas executed Medellin on August 5, 2008. A spokesperson for Texas Governor Rick Perry remarked, "The world court has no standing in Texas and Texas is not bound by a ruling or edict from a foreign court. It is easy to get caught up in discussions of international law and justice and treaties. It's very important to remember that these individuals are on death row for killing our citizens."[53] As of July 28, 2010, 131 foreign citizens representing 34 nationalities were imprisoned on U.S. death rows.

Until March 2005, when the Supreme Court decided *Roper v. Simmons* (543 U.S. 551), the most flagrant U.S. deviation from the consensus of international law was its execution of juvenile offenders. The execution of offenders who were under 18 years of age at the time of their crime is directly prohibited by the International Covenant on Civil and Political Rights, the UN Convention on the Rights of the Child, and the American Convention on Human Rights. So broad is the acceptance of this prohibition that it is widely considered a norm of customary international law.

Ironically, former Supreme Court Justice Sandra Day O'Connor, during a speech in 2003, argued that international law was important in American jurisprudence and that the United States needed to improve its image abroad. She noted how the Supreme Court cited international law in its recent decision banning the execution of the mentally retarded, as it had done in many cases over its history.[54] Justice O'Connor stated, "I suspect that over time we will rely increasingly, or take notice at least increasingly, on international and foreign courts in examining domestic issues." She added that doing so "may not only enrich our own country's decisions, I think it may create that all important good impression."

The U.S. position on the death penalty is also affecting the war on terrorism. In 2000, the European Union adopted the Charter of Fundamental Rights, which, among other things, prohibits the extradition of offenders to any country where the death penalty might be imposed unless a firm guarantee is given that the death penalty will not be imposed. This includes those suspected of carrying out terrorist acts against the United States after September 11. This impediment to extradition may cause the United States to expand the practice of forcibly taking suspects from other countries without resort to the courts, a practice referred to as "rendition."

Countries that have retained the death penalty, such as the United States and Japan, continue to oppose death penalty abolitionist efforts. They resent attempts to make the issue one of international morality. They consider such attempts as insulting and culturally imperialistic. In the United States, Supreme Court Justice Antonin Scalia, in his dissent in *Atkins v. Virginia* (536 U.S. 304, 2002), called the practices of the "so-called 'world community'" irrelevant, maintaining that its "notions of justice are (thankfully) not always those of our people." Death penalty proponents in the United States argue that European and other countries have a convoluted interpretation of human rights. As one death penalty advocate has put it:

> What the DP is, is a punishment for a human rights violation, not a human rights violation itself. Anyone with any amount of moral judgment and coherence would recognize and respect that difference. All abolitionists are trying to do is protect human rights violators at the expense of

their victims by trying to pass off the just punishment of human rights violations as a human rights violation itself, an analysis that one would have to be totally lacking in sound moral judgement [*sic*] to accept since it is so obviously contradictory as well as morally and logically skewed.[55]

Death penalty opponents, on the other hand, counter that the views expressed above are arrogant and dismissive of the position of most countries of the world, including most of our allies. They observe that the U.S. position on the death penalty is especially important because other retentionist countries can point to the United States as a champion of human rights that continues to impose the death penalty.

The international movement away from the death penalty raises serious questions for the United States:

- How likely is it that sanctions will be invoked against the United States if it continues to ignore the growing international consensus?
- What damage is being done to the United States' leadership and credibility in the field of human rights?
- Are the rights of U.S. citizens abroad being endangered because the United States has failed to follow international treaties and the decisions of international courts?

The answers to these questions may profoundly affect the United States' place in the world community and the course of human rights for years to come.

CONCLUSION

With the exception of the federal courts, neither the federal government nor the military plays a significant role in the practice of capital punishment. At this writing, the federal government, which has executed three people under post-*Furman* statutes, and the military, which has executed none, account for less than 0.3 percent of all post-*Furman* executions. Yet, together, they have made many more crimes death eligible than has any of the states.

The position of the United States on the death penalty is contrary to the position of all other western industrialized nations and most U.S. allies. Retaining the death penalty may have significant political and economic repercussions. As law professor Richard Wilson observes, "[T]he United States risks bitter resentment and legitimate claims of hypocrisy by the community of nations if it continues to aggressively apply the death penalty while asserting a commitment to human rights at home and abroad."[56]

DISCUSSION QUESTIONS

1. What are four actions the Supreme Court can take when it decides a case it has accepted on appeal?
2. Do you agree with the list of federal capital crimes? Should any of the crimes be removed from the list? Should any crimes be added to the list?
3. Should the federal government have executed Timothy McVeigh and Juan Raul Garza? Why or why not?

4. Do you agree with the changes in federal habeas corpus made in the Antiterrorism and Effective Death Penalty Act of 1996?
5. What are the major procedural differences among the death penalty statutes of the death penalty states, the federal government, and the military?
6. What accounts for the differences identified in question five?
7. Should the United States be concerned about world opinion about its use of the death penalty? Why or why not?
8. Why does the United States remain the only western industrialized nation in the world to employ the death penalty?

Notes

1. Material in this section is from Bohm and Haley (2007, Chap. 8).
2. Filler (1967, p. 117) and Gorecki (1983, p. 86).
3. Snell (2010a, Table 3).
4. Death Penalty Information Center. Retrieved April 10, 2006, and December 16, 2010.
5. Material about *Bird* and pre-*Furman* federal executions is from Death Penalty Information Center (2010). Retrieved from http://www.deathpenaltyinfo.org/federal-death-penalty?scid=29&did=147; Gillespie (2003, pp. 91–102) and Santich (2001).
6. Banner (2002, p. 189).
7. Material about the national death row facility is from Michel and Herbeck (2001, pp. 371–373).
8. In the case of *United States v. Sampson*, 300 F. Supp. 2d 278 (D. Mass. 2004), for example, the court selected New Hampshire as the place of execution because Massachusetts, where the trial took place, does not have a death penalty or execution facility. Also see 18 U.S.C. § 3596 (a).
9. Word (2002).
10. More than 1,000 reporters registered for credentials to cover McVeigh's execution; only 75 reporters registered for credentials for Garza's execution. Most of the material about McVeigh is from Michel and Herbeck (2001); also see Gillespie (2003, pp. 91–97).
11. Material about Garza is from http://www.aclu.org/death-penalty/garza_factsheet.html; http://ccadp.org/juanraulgarza.htm.
12. For a copy of the federal study, see http://www.usdoj.gov/dag/pubdoc/dpsurvey.html.
13. Study: No racial bias in executions. (2001, June 7). *The Orlando Sentinel*, p. A3.
14. Death penalty often a subjective pursuit. (2001, June 14). *The Orlando Sentinel*, p. A16; for information about the Federal Death Penalty Resource Counsel, see http://www.capdefnet.org.
15. Death Penalty Information Center. Retrieved April 30, 2011.
16. U.S. General Accounting Office (1990).
17. Acker (1996, pp. 150–151) and Baldus and Woodworth (1998, p. 410).
18. Ibid.
19. Baldus and Woodworth (1998, pp. 410–411).
20. Acker (1996, pp. 150–151) and Baldus and Woodworth (1998, p. 410).
21. Acker (1996, p. 151).
22. See *Felker v. Turpin*, 518 U.S. 1051 (1996).
23. Leahy (2004a).
24. "Justice For All Act of 2004: Section-By-Section Analysis" at (Leahy, 2004b).
25. Ibid.
26. Ibid.

27. Ibid.
28. Ibid.
29. Ibid.
30. Ibid.
31. Ibid.
32. Ibid.
33. Unless indicated otherwise, information in this section is from Einwechter (1998), Montgomery (1994), Sullivan (2006), Turney (2000), and Wyble (1985).
34. Lilly (1996).
35. Ibid., p. 497, Table 1.
36. Ibid., p. 497; Lilly, Davies, and Ball (1995, p. 2).
37. Lilly (1993, p. 13).
38. Lilly (1997, p. 11).
39. Death Row USA (Summer 2009).
40. The following account of the *Loving* case is from Lilly (1996, pp. 511–512); also see Visger (2005), for a discussion of the military capital process.
41. ABA (American Bar Association) guidelines require lead trial defense counsel in capital cases to have at least 5 years' criminal defense experience, to have tried no fewer than nine jury trials of serious and complex cases (one of which was a capital case), or to have completed in the last year a CLE (Continuing Legal Education) course in defending capital cases.
42. Death Penalty Information Center. (2010). The U.S. military death penalty. Retrieved December 16, 2010, from http://www.deathpenaltyinfo.org/us-military-death-penalty.
43. All information about this study is from Sullivan (2006).
44. Ibid., p. 11.
45. Ibid.
46. Unless indicated otherwise, material in this section is from Amnesty International. Retrieved May 2, 2011, from http://www.amnesty.org/en/death-penalty.
47. Steiker (2002).
48. Zimring (2003, p. 29).
49. Radelet (2009, p. 19).
50. Amnesty International (2010).
51. Ibid.
52. Council of Europe (2010).
53. Turner and Ruiz (2008).
54. Wilson (2003).
55. Pro Death Penalty Web page from http://www.wesleylowe.com/cp.html.
56. Wilson (2003, p. 150).

Methods of execution

6

INTRODUCTION: CRUEL AND UNUSUAL PUNISHMENT

Human beings historically have been quite creative in the methods they have legally employed to put people to death. At one time or another, execution methods have included "flaying and impaling, boiling in oil, crucifixion, pulling asunder, ... burying alive, and sawing in half."[1] None of these methods has ever been used legally in the United States, but beheading, pressing to death, drawing and quartering, breaking on the wheel, drowning, and burning at the stake were used as late as the eighteenth century.[2] The last execution method—burning at the stake—was reserved for two classes of crimes, both referred to legally as "petit treason." The first class included the murdering of an owner by a slave or a slave plotting a revolt; the second was the murder of a husband by a wife. Both classes of crimes had in common a challenge to traditional hierarchical authority and were considered especially disruptive of the social order. Burning was employed infrequently.[3]

As noted in Chapter 1, deterrence was a primary goal of the death penalty during the colonial period. To increase deterrence, colonial Americans sometimes employed "enhancements" to an execution. The "gibbet" was one of these enhancements. If a crime were particularly heinous and authorities wanted to magnify and extend the deterrent message beyond the actual execution, they might take the corpse from the gallows and cover it in tallow or pitch to slow down the body's decomposition.[4] Then they would enclose the corpse in a "gibbet"—an iron cage with bars that permitted easy viewing—and hang it in a public place, subjecting it to the weather, insects, and birds of prey.[5] People, as they engaged in their daily routines, would pass the hanging corpse and literally watch it decompose. Sometimes, executions would be followed by dismemberment of the body— another "enhancement." A head might be severed from a corpse and placed on the end of a pole for public viewing, or, in some cases, not only would the head be severed from the body but also the remaining body would be cut into quarters. The body parts would be displayed in different parts of the county, allowing more people to be exposed to the message being conveyed.[6] These death penalty "enhancements," along with burning the body, were especially terrifying to most colonial Americans and, thus, presumably effective deterrents to crime because, according to Christian theology, if the integrity of a person's corpse had been violated and the corpse had not been properly buried, that person would be denied resurrection at the final judgment.[7]

Commenting on these early methods of execution, Hugo Adam Bedau observed, "It is curious that any of these barbarous and inhumane methods of execution survived so long, for the English Bill of Rights (1689) proscribed "cruel and unusual punishments."[8] Several American state constitutions and the Eighth Amendment of the U.S. Constitution also prohibited such punishments.

A FIXED OR HISTORICAL MEANING

For approximately 120 years after the adoption of the Bill of Rights, the Supreme Court employed a fixed or historical meaning for the concept of cruel and unusual punishment. The Court interpreted the concept's meaning in light of the practices authorized and used at the time that the Eighth Amendment was adopted in 1791. Thus, only the most barbarous punishments and tortures were prohibited. Capital punishment itself was not prohibited because there was explicit reference to it in the Fifth Amendment, and it was in use when the Eighth Amendment was adopted.

The Court, in *Wilkerson v. Utah* (1878), provided examples of punishments that were prohibited by the Eighth Amendment because they involved "torture" or "unnecessary cruelty." They included punishments in which the criminal "was emboweled alive, beheaded, and quartered." The Court expanded the meaning of cruel and unusual punishment in *In re Kemmler* (1890) to include punishments that "involve torture or lingering death ... something more than the mere extinguishment of life," such as "burning at the stake, crucifixion, breaking on the wheel, or the like."

A NEW MEANING

In 1910, in the noncapital case of *Weems v. United States*, the Court abandoned its fixed or historical interpretation of cruel and unusual punishment and created a new one. Weems was a U.S. Coast Guard disbursing officer in the Philippines convicted of making two false accounting entries amounting to 612 pesos (equivalent to about U.S.$14 in 2010).[9] He was fined and sentenced to 15 years of hard labor and forced to wear chains on his ankles and wrists. After completing his sentence, he was to be under surveillance for the rest of his life, he was to lose his rights to parental authority and guardianship of persons and property, he was to notify public authorities whenever he changed his place of residence, and he was to lose his voting rights and the right to hold office as well. Weems argued that his punishment was disproportionate to his crime and, therefore, cruel and unusual.[10]

The Court agreed with Weems and broke with tradition, holding "that (1) the meaning of the Eighth Amendment is not restricted to the intent of the Framers, (2) that the Eighth Amendment bars punishments that are excessive, and (3) that what is excessive is not fixed in time but changes with evolving social conditions."[11] Thenceforward, the Court no longer used the fixed or historical interpretation; it chose instead to interpret the concept in the context of "evolving social conditions."

The Court further clarified its position nearly 50 years later in another noncapital case, *Trop v. Dulles* (1958). As punishment for desertion during World War II, Trop was stripped of his U.S. citizenship.[12] The Court reviewed the case on appeal and ruled that the punishment was cruel and unusual because it was an affront to basic human dignity. It noted that the "dignity of man" was "the basic concept underlying the Eighth Amendment," and it held that Trop's punishment exceeded "the limits of civilized standards." Referring to the earlier *Weems* case, the Court emphasized that "the limits of civilized standards ... draws its meaning from the evolving standards of decency that mark the progress of a maturing society." The evolving standards are, in turn, determined by "objective indicators, such as the enactments of legislatures as expressions of 'the will of the people,' the decisions of juries, and the subjective moral judgments of members of the Supreme Court itself."[13] In short, it appears that as long as a punishment has been enacted by a legislature, imposed by a jury, and approved of by the Supreme Court, it will not be considered cruel and unusual. The Supreme Court has never declared an execution method cruel and unusual punishment.[14]

WHAT ABOUT LONG STAYS ON DEATH ROW?

Do long stays on death row constitute cruel and unusual punishment? According to the U.S. Supreme Court, apparently not. In November 1999, the Court refused to hear appeals from two convicted killers who claimed that their long stays on death row subjected them to cruel and unusual punishment. Carey Dean Moore had been on Nebraska's death row for 19 years, while Askari Abdullah Muhammad had been a resident of Florida's death row for 24 years. Justice Stephen Breyer, who voted to hear the appeals, wrote: "Where a delay, measured in decades, reflects the state's own failure to comply with the Constitution's demands, the claim that time has rendered the execution inhuman is a particularly strong one." On the other hand, Justice Clarence Thomas, who voted not to hear the appeals, blamed his colleagues for making the review of capital punishment cases so time-consuming. Thomas argued that "[c]onsistency would seem to demand that those who accept our death penalty jurisprudence as a given also accept the lengthy delay between sentencing and execution as a necessary consequence."[15] Similar unsuccessful claims had been made earlier by Clarence Lackey (in 1995), who had served 17 years on Texas's death row, and William Elledge (in 1998), who had been confined on Florida's death row for 23 years.[16] A provocative argument has been made that the lengthy delays on death row serve the prison bureaucracy's interests of achieving a smooth execution process by rendering condemned inmates completely docile, unwilling to resist being executed.[17]

WHAT ABOUT THE EXECUTION OF ELDERLY AND INFIRM DEATH ROW INMATES?

The Supreme Court also has ruled that it is not cruel and unusual punishment to execute elderly and infirm death row inmates. In 2004, 74-year-old James Hubbard was executed in Alabama for a murder he had committed in 1977, shortly following his release from prison after serving 19 years for a 1957 killing. Hubbard's lawyer argued to the Supreme Court that to execute someone so old and mentally incompetent was cruel and unusual.[18] After serving 20 years on Mississippi's death row, 77-year-old John Nixon, Sr. was executed in 2005, for a murder he was convicted of committing in 1985. He did not pursue an appeal based on his age.[19] Finally, in 2006, 76-year-old Clarence Ray Allen was executed in California after being sentenced to death in 1982 for hiring a hit man who killed a witness and two bystanders. Allen was blind and mostly deaf, had diabetes, and almost died of a heart attack a few months prior to his execution. Four large correctional officers had to assist him into the death chamber, where they lifted him out of his wheelchair and placed him on the gurney. The Supreme Court had rejected Allen's requests for a stay of execution, and Governor Schwarzenegger had rejected his clemency appeal. Allen's lawyer had argued unsuccessfully to the Supreme Court that his client's execution would constitute cruel and unusual punishment because Allen was a frail old man, who had spent 23 years on death row.[20]

WHAT ABOUT CONDITIONS ON DEATH ROW?

Conditions of death row confinement are another area that has been subjected to Eighth Amendment claims. In *Rhodes v. Chapman* (1981), the Supreme Court held that "the Constitution does not mandate comfortable prisons." Conditions may be "restrictive and even harsh." To rise to the level of an Eighth Amendment violation, prison conditions must "involve the wanton and unnecessary infliction of pain." The Court established a two-part analysis to govern Eighth Amendment challenges to conditions of confinement. First, under the objective component, an inmate must show that the condition of which he complains is sufficiently serious to violate the Eighth Amendment, that it is "extreme," and that it "poses an unreasonable risk of serious damage to his future health."[21] It also must be so grave that it violates contemporary standards of decency.[22] Second, under the subjective component, an inmate must show that prison officials "acted with a sufficiently culpable state of mind," that they acted with "deliberate indifference."[23] In other words, a prison official can be held liable under this standard if he or she "knows of and disregards an excessive risk to inmate health or safety; the official must both be aware of facts from which the inference could be drawn that a substantial risk of serious harm exists, and he must draw the inference."[24]

In two cases decided by federal appellate courts in 2004, death row conditions were challenged on Eighth Amendment grounds. The first case, *Gates v. Cook*, addressed death row conditions at the Mississippi State Penitentiary in Parchman. In the class-action suit, it was claimed that "prisoners housed on Death Row are knowingly and deliberately subjected to profound isolation, lack of exercise, stench and filth, malfunctioning plumbing, high temperatures, uncontrolled mosquito and insect infestations, a lack of sufficient mental health care, and exposure to psychotic inmates in adjoining cells." Reiterating the trial court's findings of fact, the Fifth U.S. Circuit Court of Appeals described in detail the conditions in which Mississippi death row inmates had to live:

1. Sanitation – Inmates have been subjected to cells that were extremely filthy with chipped, peeling paint, dried fecal matter and food encrusted on the walls, ceilings, and bars, as well as water from flooded toilets and rain leaks. Inmates are routinely moved from cell to cell and are forced to clean their new cells that may have been left in horrendous sanitation by the prior occupants, especially if the occupant were mentally ill. Adequate cleaning supplies and equipment are not routinely made available for inmates to clean their cells. These filthy conditions contribute to the infestation of pests and play a role in the mental well-being of inmates.

2. Heating and Cooling – The summer temperatures in the Mississippi Delta average in the nineties with high humidity, and Death Row is primarily not an air-conditioned facility. There are industrial-type fans in the hallways to help with air circulation, and most inmates have smaller fans. Relief from the heat can be obtained by keeping the windows open in the cell using fans. But keeping the windows open increases the mosquito population in the cells since there are holes in the cell window screens and the screen gauge is not sufficient to keep mosquitoes out. The ambient temperature in the cells is within reasonable limits except during the summer months. The ventilation is inadequate to afford prisoners a minimal level of comfort during the summer months. The probability of heat-related illness is extreme on Death Row and is dramatically more so for mentally ill inmates who often do not take appropriate behavioral steps to deal with the heat. Also, the medications often given to deal with various medical problems interfere with the body's ability to maintain a normal temperature. The inmates are not afforded extra showers, ice water, or fans if they do not have fans when the heat index is 90 or above. The heat problem extends to all of Death Row and possibly throughout Parchman.

3. Pest Control – The heat problem also exacerbates the problem of pest control. Mosquitoes in Mississippi, and the Delta in particular, are a problem that cannot be eliminated. But the

problem must be addressed and the impact lessened, especially with the incidence of West Nile virus, a mosquito-borne disease increasing in Mississippi. Inadequate screening on the cell windows causes the inmates to choose between suffering from the heat or increasing the mosquitoes in their cells. The problems of heat and mosquitoes must be addressed to provide the inmates with conditions that would meet minimal constitutional standards. The problem of roaches and other vermin will be met by adhering to the ACA [American Correctional Association] standards and by meeting the sanitation goals the court will set.

4. "Ping-Pong" Toilets and Plumbing – Fecal and other matter flushed by a toilet in one cell will bubble up in the adjoining cell unless the toilets are flushed simultaneously. This has been a problem since the unit opened. Parchman officials have identified the problem as one of calibration, especially if the water is shut off. The toilets must be recalibrated to work properly. Recalibration has helped, but not eliminated, the problem of ping-pong toilets. No one in civilized society should be forced to live under conditions that force exposure to another person's bodily wastes.

5. Lighting – The lighting in the cells is grossly inadequate. While 20 foot-candles [a foot-candle is a unit of measure of the intensity of light falling on a surface] is the appropriate level of lighting for the cells, the maximum foot-candles was 7 or 8, with the typical cell being in the 2-4 foot-candle range.

6. Laundry – The inmates' laundry is returned foul smelling, necessitating the inmates to wash their clothes in their cells.

7. Mental Health Issues – The extremely psychotic prisoners [on Death Row] scream at night, throw feces, and generally make life miserable for the other inmates and guards… The mental health care afforded to the inmates on Death Row is grossly inadequate… What mental health services are provided generally take place at the inmate's cell within hearing of other inmates and guards. This results in the failure of inmates to tell the mental health specialists anything of substance. Moreover, comprehensive mental health evaluations are consistently inadequate. Inmates are also prescribed psychotropic drugs with only sporadic monitoring. This can result in life-threatening situations due to the toxicity of these drugs.

8. Exercise – The exercise facilities provided are adequate. While, in general, the use of "flip-flops" is understandable as a security measure, such shoes do not allow effective exercise. The inmates should be given access to sneakers prior to entering the exercise pen and should be given access to water and shade while exercising.

The trial court concluded that the aforementioned conditions constituted Eighth Amendment violations and ordered injunctive relief. The appeals court vacated in their entirety three of the injunctions, vacated four of the injunctions to the extent they did not apply exclusively to conditions on death row, and affirmed three of the injunctions. Following are the injunctions affirmed by the court:

1. If defendants wish to continue the practice of moving inmates from cell to cell [on Death Row], they will insure that the cell to which an inmate is moved is clean prior to the move. While an inmate should be required to keep his own cell clean, he should not be required to clean the cell of another inmate in order to inhabit it.

2. Adequate cleaning supplies and equipment shall be provided to inmates in order that they may clean their cells at least weekly.

3. The defendants shall insure that the new vendor for medical services complies with the ACA and the National Commission on Correctional Health Care medical and mental health standards. Each inmate on Death Row shall be given a comprehensive mental health examination in private. These

comprehensive examinations shall be conducted on a yearly basis. Those inmates diagnosed with psychosis and severe mental health illnesses shall be housed separately and apart from all other inmates. The medication levels of all inmates receiving psychotropic medications shall be monitored and assessed in accordance with appropriate medical standards. All inmates receiving mental health counseling or evaluation shall meet with the mental health professionals in a private setting.

In the other case, the class-action suit, *Chandler v. Crosby*, the Eleventh U.S. Circuit Court of Appeals ruled against 365 Florida death row inmates at Union Correctional Institution in Raiford. The inmates claimed that the high temperatures in their cells during the summer months combined with high humidity and inadequate ventilation amounted to cruel and unusual punishment in violation of the Eighth Amendment. To deal with the heat, inmates would stand in toilets, drape themselves in wet towels, and sleep naked on the concrete floors.[25] In the ruling the court observed "while no one would call the summertime temperatures at the Unit pleasant, the heat is not unconstitutionally excessive." It cited the district court's finding that "the building mass remains at a relatively constant temperature" during July and August, "between approximately eighty degrees at night to approximately eighty-five or eighty-six degrees during the day." Furthermore, temperatures during the 2 months climbed past 90° only 9 percent of the time in 1998 and 1999. During the same time period, the temperature reached 95° or higher only seven times, and there were no recorded temperatures that exceeded 100°. The court noted, "at the hottest times of the day, it is cooler in the cells than it is outdoors." It concluded that "the temperatures and ventilation on the … Unit during the summer months are almost always consistent with reasonable levels of comfort and slight discomfort which are to be expected in a residential setting in Florida in a building that is not air-conditioned."

Death row in Oklahoma also has no air conditioning, despite very hot summer temperatures. However, in Oklahoma, the entire death row facility is underground, which undoubtedly gives relief from the summer heat but allows for no natural light. Thus, a death sentence in Oklahoma means never seeing sunshine again. This may help explain why about one-third of all Oklahoma death row inmates do not pursue any appeals.[26]

Turning to methods of execution, for a century after the ratification of the Eighth Amendment, hanging was the only legally authorized method of execution in the United States. The one exception was that spies, traitors, and deserters convicted under federal statutes could be shot.[27] Five methods of execution are currently authorized in various jurisdictions in the United States: (1) hanging, (2) firing squad, (3) electrocution, (4) lethal gas, and (5) lethal injection.

HANGING

Hanging was one of the first lawful execution methods used in the United States. Although its use declined dramatically after the introduction of the electric chair in 1890, more people—at least 70 percent of the total—have been executed by hanging than by any other method.[28]

In colonial America, hanging had a dual role. Its primary role, of course, was as an execution method. However, it also was employed as a means of mitigating a death sentence, which, at the time, was the sentence for most serious crimes.[29] The second use for hanging—"simulated hanging"—was first employed in the Massachusetts colony in 1693 for offenders convicted of a second burglary or robbery.[30] Such offenders were required to sit upon the gallows for an hour with a noose around their necks, after which they were taken down and whipped.[31] If they were convicted of either offense a third time, they were executed.[32]

The slow and agonizing deaths caused by hangings prior to the nineteenth century were meant to be instructive for the public and degrading to the person executed. Quicker and more dignified methods of execution were firing squad and beheading.[33] In the nineteenth century, British master hangmen discovered the "long drop"—a fall sufficiently long to break the neck and cause relatively quick and painless death.[34] The long drop proved a more humane technique than the previous strangulation method, but in some cases it still took up to 20 minutes to cause death.[35]

Until they eventually abolished capital punishment, England and other European countries employed professional hangmen who were often pariahs in their own communities.[36] The American colonies tried several different arrangements. For example, in the seventeenth century, the Massachusetts colony excused Thomas Bell from taking his turn on the night watch in exchange for his serving as the colony's hangman.[37] Maryland had such a hard time appointing a hangman that it finally employed convicted criminals to serve in the position for a number of years or for life in exchange for death sentence reprieves.[38] However, by the end of the seventeenth century, all of the colonies had made executions the responsibility of the county sheriff, the arrangement that most colonies had adopted in the first place.[39] The sheriff was responsible for the entire execution, from building the gallows to disposal of the corpse.[40] When the sheriff could not induce someone with money or liquor to serve as hangman, he did the job himself.[41]

There were numerous botched hangings. At least 170 legal hangings performed in the United States between 1622 and 2002 were botched.[42] Before routine use of the long drop, most of the flawed hangings resulted in slow and painful strangulation. An improperly administered long drop (that is, if the drop were too long) could cause decapitation. As late as the 1960s, for example, at the state prison in Walla Walla, Washington, a hanging resulted in the inmate's head nearly being torn off and witnesses to the execution being spattered with blood.[43]

Two states (New Hampshire and Washington) still allow hanging;[44] however, both states also authorize lethal injection. New Hampshire authorizes hanging only if lethal injection cannot be given (see note 93). In Washington, the choice is the condemned prisoner's to make. If the prisoner fails to choose, the method is hanging. In March 2010, the state announced an option for inmates to choose a one-drug protocol. The first person executed by hanging in the United States since 1965 was child-killer Westley Allan Dodd, on January 5, 1993, in the state of Washington.[45]

FIRING SQUAD

Execution by firing squad currently remains an option in two states: Oklahoma and Utah.[46] In Oklahoma, firing squad is authorized only if both lethal injection and electrocution are held to be unconstitutional. In Utah, execution by firing squad is available for those inmates who chose that option before legislation passed in March 2004 banned it.

Firing squads in Utah consisted of five volunteer marksmen. Four of them were given rifles with live rounds, and one of them was given a rifle with blanks.[47] The rifle with blanks maintained the fiction that none of the shooters would know who fired the fatal shot. In reality, the kick produced by live rounds is easily distinguishable from the kick produced by blanks, and any firearms expert would have no trouble telling the difference. The inmate was seated and strapped to a chair with a hood over his head and a bull's-eye over his heart. Following a signal from the warden, the shooters fired at the bull's-eye. There is no solid evidence, but it is presumed that a competently performed execution by firing squad caused a quick death with little or no pain. When given a choice between death by firing squad and death by hanging, most inmates chose the former. Botched executions by firing squad were rare.

The most celebrated recent execution by firing squad was the January 17, 1977, execution of Gary Gilmore in Utah.[48] Gilmore was the first person executed in the United States in a decade and the first person executed under post-*Furman* statutes. Unlike most death row inmates, Gilmore had voluntarily waived his right to appeal and demanded that the state of Utah carry out his sentence. His case was appealed anyway without his consent, and he received three stays of execution. While in prison, he twice tried to commit suicide. His last words were "Let's do it."

The last person executed by firing squad in the United States was Ronnie Lee Gardner, in June 2010. He was also executed in Utah. Gardner was convicted in 1985 of the courthouse killing of Attorney Michael Burdell during an escape attempt. He chose the firing squad over lethal injection for the notoriety. He was the first person to be executed by firing squad since Utah executed John Albert Taylor in 1996.[49] Fewer than 150 people have been executed legally by firing squad in the United States since 1608.[50]

ELECTROCUTION

In October 2001, the Georgia Supreme Court by a vote of 4–3 became the first appellate court in the United States to rule that electrocution violated the Eighth Amendment's prohibition against cruel and unusual punishment. The court held that electrocution "inflicts purposeless physical violence and needless mutilation that makes no measurable contribution to accepted goals of punishment."[51] A year earlier the U.S. Supreme Court refused to review a challenge to Alabama's use of the electric chair, and canceled its review of Florida's practice after the state legislature passed new legislation providing for lethal injection as the primary means of execution. Alabama then followed Florida's lead and gave condemned inmates the option of lethal injection or electrocution.[52] The last state to abandon electrocution as a primary means of execution was Nebraska when, on February 8, 2008, the Nebraska Supreme Court by a vote of 6–1 declared electrocution unconstitutional under the Nebraska Constitution.[53] The decision did not invalidate Nebraska's death penalty statute, although it left the state with no means to implement the penalty.[54] That problem was resolved in May 2009, when the Nebraska legislature adopted lethal injection as its method of execution.[55] Electrocution remains an option in nine other states.[56] Alabama, Florida, South Carolina, and Virginia authorize a choice of electrocution or lethal injection.[57] On July 20, 2006, murderer and rapist Brandon Hedrick was executed by electrocution in Virginia. Hedrick, who chose electrocution because he was afraid of lethal injection, was the first person in the United States to die in the electric chair in 2 years.[58] Arkansas, Kentucky, and Tennessee offer the same choice to death row inmates whose offenses occurred before July 4, 1983; March 31, 1998; and January 1, 1999, respectively. For those whose capital offenses occur after those dates, there is no choice—execution is by lethal injection. Finally, Illinois and Oklahoma authorize electrocution if lethal injection is ever held to be unconstitutional. (If both electrocution and lethal injection are ever held to be unconstitutional, Oklahoma authorizes firing squad, as previously noted.[59]) Although many states have recently abandoned electrocution, between 1930 and 1972 it was the method employed by 25 states; hanging was employed in 13 states and lethal gas in 11.[60] During the twentieth century, more people were executed by electrocution than by any other method.[61]

The history of electrocution as a method of capital punishment is both fascinating and instructive.[62] The electric chair is an American invention and an unintended product of a corporate battle between the Westinghouse and Edison companies. In the late 1880s, competition was fierce over which of the two companies would provide electricity to American cities. Westinghouse was successfully touting its alternating current (AC), while Edison was promoting, somewhat less successfully than Westinghouse, its direct current (DC). A problem with Edison's DC was that low transmission voltages reduced its range to just a mile beyond the generator that produced it. There was no such problem with AC. In addition, AC proved cheaper than DC to transmit. Trying to beat its competition, Edison staged public demonstrations during which animals were electrocuted with Westinghouse's AC to show how dangerous their competitor's product was.

The governor of New York, meanwhile, dissatisfied with hanging as the state's method of execution, appointed a three-member commission to determine and recommend to the legislature "the most humane and practical method [of execution] known to modern science." One of the commission members was Alfred P. Southwick, a dentist from Buffalo, who believed that electrocution would be preferable to hanging. Before his appointment to the commission, Southwick (later known as the "father of electrocution") had witnessed a man touch an electric generator and die what appeared to be a fast and painless death. Southwick also witnessed and conducted the electrocution of animals in demonstrations like those performed by the Edison company. Southwick enlisted the help of Edison, who already was an American hero, to persuade the other commission members to endorse electrocution as the new method of execution. Edison personally opposed capital punishment, but he agreed to help Southwick, who had convinced him that the issue was not whether capital punishment should be employed but rather what form it should take.

The commission did recommend that hanging be replaced with electrocution. Interestingly, the commission also considered lethal injection (as well as the guillotine and the garrote) as an alternative to hanging but rejected injection because of protests from the medical profession. Doctors feared that people would associate death with the hypodermic needle and the practice of medicine. On June 4, 1888, the legislature, with little opposition, enacted New York's Electrical Execution Act. The act provided that anyone sentenced to die after January 1, 1889, would be electrocuted instead of hanged. The act did not, however, stipulate what type of current would be employed. That matter was left to the Medico-Legal Society of New York to decide. Following a number of experiments on animals, it was decided that Westinghouse's AC would be used.

William Kemmler became the first person to die by legally authorized electrocution on August 6, 1890. Kemmler had been convicted of the brutal first-degree murder of his girlfriend, who he believed was involved with another man. Although there was little doubt about his guilt, his appeals drew much public interest. In an effort to block the ultimate test of AC's lethality, Westinghouse retained for Kemmler one of the nation's leading lawyers, W. Bourke Cockran, and reportedly spent more than $100,000 on the appeals.

The case ultimately reached the Supreme Court. Kemmler's lawyer, however, failed to convince the Court that death by electrocution was cruel and unusual. The Court refused to decide Kemmler's claim, arguing that the Eighth Amendment did not apply to the states [*In re Kemmler* (1890)].[63] By taking this position, the Court did not have to scrutinize the New York state legislature's conclusion that electrocution produced "instantaneous, and, therefore, painless death."

Eyewitness reports of Kemmler's execution belie the legislature's conclusion. Kemmler did not die "instantaneously"[64]—a second jolt of electricity had to be administered 4.5 minutes after the first one. During the second jolt, witnesses observed Kemmler's hair and flesh burning and blood on his face. His body emitted a horrible stench. Whether his death was a "painless" one is uncertain. Electricians blamed faulty equipment for the botched execution. Among the problems were the failure to provide enough power, an uninterrupted current, and adequate contact between the electrodes and Kemmler's body. Reaction to the bungled execution was mixed. Some commentators argued that death by electrocution was worse than hanging; others believed it was not. It was even suggested that the execution was intentionally sabotaged to deter further use of AC. Not surprisingly, Westinghouse stated that "[t]hey could have done better with an axe." Experts on electricity, such as Thomas Edison and Nikola Tesla, publicly debated whether electrocution was so horrible that it should never have been invented. Both proponents and opponents of capital punishment called for repeal of New York's Electrical Execution Act, but to no avail.

Nearly a year after Kemmler's execution, New York electrocuted four men in one day and a fifth man later that year. Despite continued reports of flawed electrocutions, numerous other states were quick to adopt the new method, and as noted at the beginning of this section, electrocution became the method used by a majority of executing states between 1930 and 1972.[65]

Botched electrocutions are not a thing of the past. Following are three more recent newspaper accounts:[66]

- The state's [Georgia's] first try at executing Alpha Otis Stephens in the electric chair failed today, and he struggled to breathe for eight minutes before a second jolt carried out his death sentence.[67]
- [In Michigan City, Indiana] five jolts of electricity instead of the prescribed two were needed today to execute William E. Vandiver…. A prison doctor said Vandiver, 37, was still breathing after the first round of 2,300 volts and second of 500 volts were applied at 12:03 a.m. Three more blasts of current were applied before he was pronounced dead 17 minutes later.[68]
- The replacement of a worn sponge in the headpiece of the electric chair by two maintenance workers at Florida State Prison led to the botched execution of Jesse Tafero. Their action triggered an eruption of smoke and flames from Tafero's head…. When the first jolt of 2,000-volt electricity hit Tafero, the sponge in the headpiece gave off a combustible gas, which shot smoke and flames from the top of the leather hood hiding Tafero's face. The flames—described as 3 inches to a foot long—horrified witnesses. Tafero's attorney described the flawed execution as torture…. Between the jolts, witnesses observed Tafero seemingly gasping for air.[69]

LETHAL GAS

Seeking a more humane method of execution, in 1921 the Nevada legislature passed a "Humane Death Bill."[70] The legislation replaced hanging with death by lethal gas, which had gained attention because of its use in World War I. The condemned inmate was to be executed in his or her cell, while asleep and without any warning. Governor Emmet Boyle, who personally opposed the death penalty, nevertheless signed the legislation, believing that, upon challenge, it would be ruled unconstitutional as a cruel and unusual punishment.

The first person sentenced to die under the new legislation was Gee Jon, who was convicted of a gangland murder. Jon was a member of a "tong," in this case an organized Chinese crime association. Jon appealed his death sentence to the Nevada Supreme Court, which, to the surprise of Governor Boyle, upheld the constitutionality of lethal gas. When prison officials realized the impracticality of executing Jon in his cell while he slept, they quickly built a chamber for the purpose, and on February 8, 1924, Jon became the first person to be lawfully executed with a lethal dose of cyanide gas.

By 1937, Arizona, California, Colorado, North Carolina, and Wyoming had passed legislation requiring executions to be carried out using lethal gas. By 1970, 10 states (which, in addition to the aforementioned, included Maryland, Mississippi, Missouri, and New Mexico) used lethal gas as their sole method of execution, but by 1992, Maryland was the only state to do so.[71] Maryland abandoned lethal gas for lethal injection in 1994, except for inmates whose sentence was imposed before the change in statute. They have a choice between lethal gas and lethal injection.

Clinton Duffy, longtime warden of California's San Quentin prison, provided the following description of a lethal gas execution:

The gas chamber was an octagonal enclosure containing two chairs and considerable mechanical equipment. It had windows on all sides, through which the witnesses viewed the execution. A long, narrow door, similar to that on a bank vault, led into it. This faced a small corridor off which were two holding cells.

Death in the gas chamber was caused by dropping cyanide from a container into a mixture of sulphuric acid and distilled water in a well under each chair. The poisonous fumes that resulted caused almost instant loss of consciousness, although it took anywhere from thirteen to fifteen minutes for death actually to occur. Watch officers who had worked both at hangings and gas executions told me the latter was far preferable. The executioner liked it better, too, mostly, I think, because he didn't feel so directly responsible for the death of the condemned. Death by lethal gas was more mechanical, which made it less personal.

On the morning of an execution the executioner got two pounds of cyanide from the prison armory and took it to a mix room off the gas chamber. Regardless of whether there was to be one execution or two, he carefully measured out into little gauze bags one pound of cyanide for each chair. These bags were placed on hooks directly under the chairs, hanging down toward the wells a few inches below.

About ten minutes before the prisoner was to be brought in, the executioner put a gallon of distilled water into each of two jars, then added sulphuric acid, letting it stand in the mix room until it was time for the actual execution. Tubes ran from these jars into the wells beneath the chairs. After the chamber was tested for leaks, the prisoner, with a stethoscope strapped to his chest, was taken from the holding cell. When he was seated in one of the chairs, his hands and feet were strapped and the stethoscope was hitched to a tube connected with a valve outside the chamber, where the attending physician could listen to the man's heart beats and report the time of death.

When the door was sealed with the prisoner inside, the executioner pulled a lever controlling a suction fan that drew some of the air out of the chamber. He then signaled an assistant in the mix room, who opened the valves releasing the sulphuric acid from the jars into the wells beneath the chairs. After the valves were closed, the executioner informed the warden, standing beside him outside a window to the left of the condemned man, that everything was in readiness. At the warden's nod, the executioner pulled another lever which lowered the cyanide into the sulphuric acid, causing gas fumes to rise. The whole operation took less than two minutes.

In order to make death as quick and painless as possible, the condemned man was instructed to take deep breaths at the warden's signal. This would be a few seconds after the cyanide and sulphuric acid came together. Without the inhalations, loss of consciousness would take longer and choking might result.

… To make sure that death had actually occurred, the body was left in the sealed chamber at least half an hour after the heart stopped beating. Then the poison gas was pumped out through a smoke stack on top of the north cell block. At the same time, fresh water flushed the sulphuric-acid residue out of the wells beneath the two chairs into pipes leading to the bay.

It took another half hour before it was safe for attendants to open the big iron door, but even then they had to be careful. Before touching the body, they sprayed it thoroughly with liquid ammonia to neutralize any gas that might have been caught in the folds of the dead man's clothing or in any parts of his body. Once that had been done, the body was placed in a wooden casket and taken to the prison morgue for later burial.[72]

Lethal gas is currently an option in only four states.[73] California and Missouri authorize both lethal gas and lethal injection.[74] If the condemned inmate refuses to choose, the method is lethal gas. Arizona authorizes lethal injection for persons whose capital sentence was imposed after November 15, 1992; for those who were sentenced before that date, the condemned prisoner may select lethal injection or lethal gas. If the condemned prisoner refuses to choose, the method is lethal injection. Wyoming authorizes lethal gas if lethal injection is ever held to be unconstitutional.

A newspaper account of the 1979 execution of Jesse Bishop in Nevada describes death by lethal gas:

After a metal door to the 10-by-10 death chamber clanged shut, three volunteer guards flipped switches to activate the device that lowered cyanide pellets into acid beneath the death seat. Only one of the switches was live, so none of the guards knew which one would kill Bishop…. [Then the] cyanide pellets fell into the acid bath, unleashing deadly gas, Bishop wrinkled his nose, seemed to search the room and breathed deeply several times. His eyes rolled upward, his head fell on his chest and then snapped back. He took another deep breath and closed his eyes—for the last time. Bishop's face reddened, saliva ran from his mouth and his body shuddered. After a series of convulsive jerks, it was over.[75]

LETHAL INJECTION

In the continuing quest to find more humane and publicly acceptable methods of execution, Oklahoma became the first jurisdiction in the United States to authorize lethal injection as an execution method.[76] The legislation, passed on May 11, 1977, replaced electrocution with the "continuous, intravenous administration of a lethal quantity of an ultrashort-acting barbiturate in combination with a chemical paralytic agent."[77] The three chemicals most commonly used in lethal injections are (1) sodium thiopental or sodium pentothal, a common anesthetic used in surgery, which is the ultrashort-acting barbiturate that is supposed to induce a deep sleep and loss of consciousness in about 20 seconds, (2) pancuronium bromide, also known as Pavulon, a total muscle relaxant, which in sufficient dosages stops breathing by paralyzing the diaphragm and lungs, and (3) potassium chloride, which induces cardiac arrest and stops the inmate's heartbeat permanently.[78] Economic matters played a major role in Oklahoma's change to lethal injection. Legislators were concerned that the electric chair, which had not been used since 1966, would be too expensive to return to good working order. The cost of fixing the chair was estimated to be $62,000.[79] Execution by lethal gas was rejected because of the estimated $300,000 cost of a gas chamber.[80] Lethal injection was estimated to cost less than $15 per execution.[81] Also favoring the use of lethal injection was the argument that persons executed by this method could donate all of their bodily organs for medical transplants. Other execution methods limited this possibility.

Oklahoma's adoption of lethal injection was also motivated by the realization on the part of state representative Bill Wiseman that the state's use of the electric chair was losing public support because of some high-profile botched executions where flesh had been burned off the bodies of condemned inmates or the inmates had caught on fire.[82] Representative Wiseman and state senator Bill Dawson sought the help of the Oklahoma Medical Association to devise a drug protocol for lethal injection, but the association was not interested mainly because it did not want to be a part of a procedure designed to end human life. However, two doctors agreed to participate: Jay Chapman, Oklahoma's chief medical examiner, and Stanley Deutsch, a faculty member in Oklahoma Medical School's anesthesiology department. Wiseman and Dawson first contacted Chapman, who informed the legislators that he was willing to help, but that he had no expertise in the fields of anesthesia or toxicology. Chapman explained to Wiseman and Dawson that he "was an expert in dead bodies but not an expert in getting them that way." As for the position of the Oklahoma Medical Association, Chapman told the legislators: "To hell with them: let's do this."

Together, Chapman and Wiseman proceeded to create a lethal injection protocol. In a later interview, Chapman related that they settled on "a lethal quantity of an ultra-short acting barbiturate or other similar drug in combination with a chemical paralytic to cause death." He added that he "didn't care which drug killed the prisoner, as long as one of them did." Chapman and Wiseman chose not to be specific about the drugs to be used because they were concerned about unforeseen consequences and the availability of any suggested drug. When asked how he arrived at the two-drug strategy, Chapman replied, "I didn't do any research. I just knew from having been placed under anesthesia myself, what was needed. I wanted to have at least two drugs … that would kill the prisoner, to make sure that if one didn't kill him, the other would." At about the same time that Chapman and Wiseman were working on their drug protocol, Senator Dawson telephoned Deutsch and asked him to devise a drug protocol. Deutsch, like Chapman, proposed "an ultra-short acting barbiturate (for example, sodium thiopental) in combination with a neuromuscular blocking drug (for example, pancuronium bromide) to create a long duration of paralysis." Deutsch believed that his drug combination would be a "rapidly pleasant way of producing unconsciousness leading to death."

How the third drug—potassium chloride—became a part of the mixture is not entirely clear. One commentator suggests that the reason Chapman added the second and third drugs to his protocol was "to accelerate the execution process by stopping the heartbeat within minutes; a large overdose of a single drug would take up to 45 minutes or even longer to cause death."[83] Perhaps the best explanation is that Chapman simply decided to add it. When asked about it, Chapman responded, "Why not.... You wanted to make sure the prisoner was dead at the end, so why not just add a third drug. I didn't do any research ... it's just common knowledge. Doctors know potassium chloride is lethal. Why does it matter why I chose it?" This, then, is how the three-drug protocol for lethal injections used in nearly all death penalty jurisdictions in the United States was created—not as the result of a deliberate process by a panel of medical and scientific experts, but rather as the consequence of an informal and ad hoc process involving two physicians with no special expertise in the relevant subject matters and two politicians bent on saving Oklahoma's death penalty.

Despite its questionable origins, Texas, Idaho, and New Mexico were quick to follow Oklahoma in adopting lethal injection as their method of execution. In Florida, however, a 1979 bill calling for the replacement of electrocution with lethal injection was defeated in the state legislature. Opposed to the legislation were medical doctors, and especially anesthesiologists, who argued that, among other things, no assurances could be given that the barbiturates would not wear off before death occurred, causing the condemned inmate to wake up and slowly suffocate to death. (The Florida legislature grudgingly approved lethal injection as an option to electrocution in January 2000. The legislature wanted to avoid legal challenges to the use of the electric chair.[84]) The 1980 annual meeting of the American Medical Association (AMA) saw a resolution passed urging doctors not to be participants in executions by lethal injection beyond pronouncing an inmate dead. Later, the AMA prohibition was expanded to include declaring death; as well as selecting injection sites; starting intravenous lines; prescribing, administering, or supervising the use of lethal drugs; and monitoring vital signs, on site or remotely. To participate in a lethal injection execution, according to the AMA, constitutes a violation of the Hippocratic Oath and international medical principles, and would represent "a corruption and exploitation of the healing profession's role in society." The AMA's resolution is mostly symbolic, however, because no state's death penalty statute requires that a licensed doctor perform the lethal injection, and most doctors are not members of the AMA. Nevertheless, a 1994 study by the American College of Physicians, Human Rights Watch, the National Coalition to Abolish the Death Penalty, and Physicians for Human Rights found that 29 of the then 37 capital punishment states required the presence or participation of a physician at all executions, and that no licensing boards in any of the states were enforcing the prohibition.[85] In a survey published in the *Annals of Internal Medicine* in 2001, 41 percent of the 413 doctors who responded to the survey indicated that they would perform at least one of 10 functions of administering a lethal injection and 25 percent would perform five or more.[86] Thus, it appears that many doctors would be willing to participate in an execution despite the fact that it violates the Hippocratic Oath to do no harm and is prohibited by medical societies. For doctors willing to participate in executions, several death penalty states provide them with a handy rationalization. The laws in at least eight death penalty states stipulate that the medical techniques used in lethal injection executions are not medical techniques, and the medical personnel who participate in them are not medical personnel for the purpose of executing prison inmates.[87] In 2006, the state of Georgia enacted a statute that reads: "Participation in any execution of any convicted person carried out under this article shall not be the subject of any licensure challenge, suspension, or revocation for any physician or medical professional licensed in the State of Georgia."[88] Arizona and Oregon have similar statutes.[89]

The first person executed by lethal injection was Charles Brooks, Jr., in Texas, on December 7, 1982. He was sentenced to die on December 14, 1976, for the murder of David Gregory in Forth Worth. Brooks was also the first black man to be executed in the United States since 1967 and the first person executed in Texas since 1964.[90]

Until recently, the only challenge to lethal injection as an execution method that the Supreme Court has been willing to hear was *Heckler v. Chaney* (470 U.S. 821, 1985). In this case, inmates in Oklahoma and Texas claimed that the Food and Drug Administration (FDA), as required by law, had not approved the drugs used in lethal injections for this purpose. The plaintiffs claimed that to use approved drugs for unapproved purposes violates the misbranding prohibition of the Federal Food, Drug, and Cosmetic Act. The plaintiffs wanted the FDA to approve the drugs for the purpose of human execution; the FDA refused to do so. The Court dodged the issue, maintaining that the FDA's discretionary authority in refusing the plaintiffs' demands was not subject to judicial review.

Lethal injection has now become the sole or principal method of execution in all executing jurisdictions in the United States. However, there is no uniform policy for conducting lethal injections among executing jurisdictions. There are differences in procedure, in the number of drugs used, in the amount of drug used, who performs the injections, how well the executioners are trained, and how much the executioners are paid—to name just a few differences.[91] In some jurisdictions, lethal injections are performed on a table attached to the floor with wings on the sides of the table for the inmate's arms. South Carolina uses a gurney with wings that is wheeled into the same execution chamber that contains the state's electric chair. A curtain is used to separate the two. North Carolina requires that the inmate's arms be flat against his or her body while lying on a hospital-like gurney. Some jurisdictions begin the procedure only after all appeals and requests for a stay of execution have been exhausted. Other jurisdictions insert the tubes while the inmate is awaiting final word from the governor and the U.S. Supreme Court. In some jurisdictions prisoners make their final statements in their cells before they are taken to the execution chamber; in other jurisdictions final statements are made on the table in the execution chamber minutes before execution.

Most jurisdictions employ prison employees with some emergency medical training to insert the needles. A common problem with inmates who have been intravenous drug users is finding suitable veins. Frequent drug injections can leave scarring on the blood vessels. Minor surgery is sometimes needed to expose a viable vein. However, generally, the execution team just keeps searching the inmate's body until a viable vein is found. In Texas, condemned inmates have had to help the execution team find a viable vein, and in Louisiana the execution team had to insert the needle into an inmate's neck after failing to find a viable vein in the inmate's arm. On September 15, 2009, Ohio prison officials tried unsuccessfully for nearly 2 hours to find a usable vein in 53-year-old Romell Broom, who had been convicted of the 1984 rape and murder of a 14-year-old girl.[92] Witnesses reported that Broom sobbed with pain while prison officials repeatedly stuck him with a needle and inserted a shunt in his leg. Ohio Governor Ted Strickland finally halted Broom's execution and granted him a 1-week reprieve. Broom's lawyers filed an appeal arguing that Ohio's attempt to execute Broom a second time was cruel and unusual punishment. As of February 2011, Broom remained alive on Ohio's death row.

Some jurisdictions employ lethal injection machines; in other jurisdictions the warden or governor selects the executioners who inject the drugs. When executioners are used to inject the drugs, their identities are kept confidential. They generally perform their duties from behind a curtain or a one-way glass mirror, or inside a separate room. In North Carolina, each of three executioners has a syringe. Each of the executioners injects each of the three drugs (as discussed earlier), but with each drug one of the injections is detoured into a "dummy bag" instead of the inmate's body. This practice conceals who is actually administering the lethal drugs to the inmate. Oklahoma pays three executioners $300 each per execution, while Florida pays its lone executioner $150 per execution.

Most jurisdictions use the three aforementioned lethal drugs. North Carolina also uses the three drugs, but its death penalty statute only requires the use of two drugs: sodium thiopental and pancuronium bromide. Ohio and Washington use only one drug—traditionally sodium thiopental, although Ohio has also used pentobarbital. Louisiana injects all three drugs into one IV inserted into the left arm, which is closest to the heart. If a problem arises, a second IV is inserted into the right arm. Texas and Florida insert IVs into both arms, but inject the drugs only into the left arm unless there is a problem, in which case they are injected into the right arm. Oklahoma inserts IVs into both arms and alternates the injection of the three drugs from arm to arm—left, right, left. Arizona injects all three drugs into both arms. It is standard procedure to flush the IV lines with a saline solution between injections to prevent the chemicals from crystallizing before they reach the inmate's bloodstream. In some jurisdictions the entire procedure takes only a few minutes, while in other jurisdictions the procedure can take 30 minutes or longer. An inmate is usually pronounced dead within 5–10 minutes following the injection. Because medical ethics, as noted previously, prohibit doctors from participating in executions, most jurisdictions use doctors only to verify the inmate's death. In Texas, this practice allows the prison system to avoid an autopsy that is otherwise required by state law.

Theoretically, death by lethal injection should be a more humane method of execution than any of the other methods that have been used. The popular image is one in which the condemned inmate painlessly falls asleep (forever) on a hospital gurney. Perhaps the New York legislature of 100 years ago, in its rejection of lethal injection as a less humane method of execution than electrocution,[93] showed an insight still valid today. Despite the creation of elaborate machines to administer the lethal drugs, problems still arise.[94] Consider, for example, the following newspaper account of the 1988 execution of Raymond Landry in Texas:

> Prison officials began administering the lethal dosage [to Landry] at 12:21 a.m. Landry was not pronounced dead until 24 minutes later. In between, a tube attached to a needle inside his right arm began leaking, sending the lethal mixture shooting across the death chamber toward witnesses. "There was something of a delay in the execution because of what officials called a 'blowout'.... The syringe came out of the vein and the warden ordered the (execution) team to reinsert the catheter into the vein." The leak occurred two minutes after the injections began.[95]

Another problem that could occur in lethal injections, although it would be nearly impossible to detect, is that an inadequate dose of sodium pentothal (the anesthetic used in lethal injections) would cause the inmate to retain consciousness and suffer great pain during the injections of the second and third chemicals.[96] A similar problem would occur if the three chemicals were administered out of sequence. These problems are not hypothetical. Consider, for example, Florida's lethal injection execution of Angel Nieves Diaz on December 13, 2006:

> Mr. Diaz took 34 minutes to die and was seen to be struggling for breath, moving, attempting to speak, and grimacing in pain for the first 24 minutes of the procedure. At his autopsy the medical examiner discovered 11- and 12-inch blisters on his right and left arms, respectively. The problem was that when the execution technician inserted the IV, he pushed the needle through the vein into the surrounding soft tissue. Because the mistake delayed the absorption of the lethal chemicals, Mr. Diaz was administered a second dose.... According to several other ...

medical doctors, the blisters on the arms of Mr. Diaz were classic signs of sodium thiopental entering muscle/flesh, as opposed to the bloodstream, meaning that little or no anesthetic was delivered to his central nervous system before the suffocating drug and the caustic potassium chloride were introduced into his bloodstream.... These same doctors came to a general consensus that the inmate probably died in agony.[97]

The problem of an inadequate dose of sodium pentothal and its interaction with pancuronium bromide was the subject of recent challenges to lethal injection in Florida and California. Both challenges followed the April 2005 publication of an article in *The Lancet*, a prominent British medical journal, that claimed "methods of lethal injection are flawed and some inmates might experience awareness and suffering during execution."[98] The article's authors reported that toxicology reports from Arizona, Georgia, North Carolina, and South Carolina "showed that post-mortem concentrations of [sodium] thiopental in the blood were lower than that required for surgery in 43 of 49 executed inmates (88%); 21 (43%) inmates had concentrations consistent with awareness."[99] A problem is that most death penalty states specify the same dosage of thiopental for every condemned inmate rather than calculating the proper dosage based on the inmate's weight. Virginia, for example, injects 2 grams of thiopental regardless of the inmate's weight, while Florida and California use 5 grams.[100] The researchers noted "without [the proper amount of] anesthesia, the condemned person would experience asphyxiation, a severe burning sensation, massive muscle cramping, and finally cardiac arrest" because of the other drugs commonly used in executions.[101] Following their examination of protocol information from Texas and Virginia, whose officials refused to provide toxicology reports, the authors also found that "executioners had no anesthesia training, drugs were administered remotely with no monitoring for anesthesia, data were not recorded and no peer-review was done."[102] The authors added, in contrast to medical applications, "anaesthesia in execution has not been subjected to clinical trials, governmental regulation, extensive training of practitioners, standardization, or the supervision of peer-review and medico-legal liability."[103] Critics have questioned the study's methodology and the conclusion that some inmates might have experienced awareness and suffering during the execution.[104] The major criticism is that concentrations of sodium pentothal in the blood as long as 12 hours after an execution (at the time autopsies were performed) do not accurately reflect the concentrations of the drug at the time of death, that concentrations decrease over time. In a reply to their critics, the authors of the original study countered that research shows that after death, concentrations of sodium pentothal in the blood actually increase, not decrease. They surmised, "post-mortem concentrations of [sodium] pentothal in blood, including those taken after execution, might actually overestimate concentrations in life."[105]

In Florida, Clarence Hill's January 24, 2006, execution was halted just moments before the deadly chemicals were to be injected into his body, when U.S. Supreme Court Justice Anthony Kennedy issued a temporary stay. The next day the full Court confirmed the stay and agreed to hear Hill's civil rights claim (in *Hill v. McDonough*) that Florida's lethal injection method caused inmates to suffer excessive pain during the procedure and, thus, violated the U.S. Constitution's Eighth Amendment. Recall that the Court had previously ruled that any execution method that involved "something more than the mere extinguishment of life" constituted cruel and unusual punishment. Hill's attorneys argued that if a condemned inmate were not unconscious because of an inadequate dose of sodium pentothal, then the pancuronium bromide, which paralyzes muscles, would render the inmate helpless to respond to his or her suffocating and the excruciating pain caused by the potassium chloride. It would also make it impossible for those witnessing the execution to recognize and prevent the gratuitous pain and suffering.[106] In other words, the pancuronium bromide's role is primarily cosmetic, creating the serene appearance of dying associated with lethal injection executions. It is instructive to note that the American Veterinary Medical Association has banned pancuronium bromide for animal euthanasia because it can conceal any signs of whether the anesthetic has failed to work.[107]

In California, Michael Morales's lawyers made a similar claim in the U.S. District Court (*Morales v. Hickman*) and, as a result, on February 21, 2006, his execution was postponed indefinitely. Federal Judge Jeremy Fogel, who heard the case, rather than wait until the Supreme Court decided the Florida case, ruled that the state could execute Morales either with an overdose of barbiturates alone (something no other state did) administered by someone medically qualified to give intravenous drugs or, if the state wanted to use the standard three-drug combination, a qualified anesthetist had to be present at the execution. To comply with the judge's order, prison officials hired two anesthetists (one for backup), but, just hours before the execution, they both refused to participate when they learned that they would have to intervene if Morales regained consciousness. They had believed their role was only to verify that the execution protocol was humane. After the anesthetists' refusal to participate, prison officials tried to find a medical professional willing to administer the barbiturate overdose before Morales's death warrant expired. They were unable to do so. Consequently, the federal judge declared he would hold a hearing on California's lethal injection protocol at a later date.[108] The hearing was held on December 15, 2006, after which Judge Fogel issued a memorandum order stating "unless California made substantial revisions to its protocol, [Fogel] would declare it unconstitutional."[109] The state of California filed a detailed response on May 15, 2007. However, Judge Fogel did not lift the injunction halting the execution of death row inmates until September 2010, which allowed the scheduled execution of Albert Greenwood Brown on September 29. But before Brown's execution, Governor Schwarzenegger issued a temporary reprieve to permit the courts to review California's new execution protocol fully. The U.S. Court of Appeals for the Ninth Circuit ordered Fogel to reconsider his decision to lift the injunction using different legal standards. Judge Fogel then gave the California attorney general 6 hours to provide a detailed description of the similarities and differences between the old and the new execution protocols and a recommendation of whether the state should execute Brown as scheduled. On September 28, Judge Fogel canceled Brown's execution because he did not have enough time to decide the constitutional issues Brown raised before his execution. Even if Judge Fogel decides against Brown, it appears that California will not be able to execute any death row inmates for several months because of a shortage of sodium thiopental—the first and arguably the most crucial of the three drugs used in an execution.[110] As of this writing, the more than 700 inmates on California's death row—by far the most inmates on any death row in the United States—await Judge Fogel's decision.

The judicial decisions in Florida and California have influenced impending executions in other jurisdictions. For example, on March 7, 2006, a U.S. District Court judge for the District of Columbia issued a stay of execution, pending the outcome of the Florida case, for three codefendants on federal death row, who were scheduled to die in May.[111] Also, on April 10, 2006, a U.S. District Court judge ordered North Carolina prison officials to provide medically trained personnel to supervise the execution of Willie Brown, Jr., who was scheduled to die on April 21.[112] Stays of executions have also been granted to inmates in Maryland and Missouri, and another inmate in Florida for similar reasons. Among the problems revealed in the Missouri case (*Taylor v. Crawford*) was that the doctor who had supervised 54 post-*Furman* executions was dyslexic, and his dyslexia impaired his ability to properly mix the drugs, which he did without supervision.[113] A *Saint Louis Post-Dispatch* investigation also found that the doctor had 20 malpractice suits filed against him, had his privileges revoked at two hospitals, and was publicly reprimanded by the Board of Healing Arts.[114] Other inmates who have raised lethal injection challenges have been denied and executed.[115] Even Clarence Hill, who made the initial challenge, was executed by lethal injection (using the controversial three-chemical cocktail) in Florida on September 20, 2006, after the Supreme Court, by a 5−4 vote, refused to grant him another stay. His latest challenges had been rejected as "stalling tactics," with the clear message that complicated issues should not be raised at the last minute.[116] Also, in 2007, a Tennessee federal district court, following the precedent set in California, declared Tennessee's revised death penalty protocol unconstitutional because "the new protocol presents a substantial risk of unnecessary pain" (*Harbison v. Little*).[117]

By September 25, 2007, the status of lethal injection had become so controversial that the U.S. Supreme Court decided to grant certiorari in a Kentucky case—*Baze et al. v. Rees*—to review the issue. The selection of the Kentucky case was an odd one for several reasons, not the least of which was that Kentucky had conducted only one post-*Furman* execution and had scant evidentiary and execution data. Cynics argued that the Court deliberately chose the case because the challenge was weak, and it wanted to dispose of the issue before more state and federal courts were saddled with lethal injection challenges.[118] What Kentucky did have was the same three-drug cocktail used by most other lethal injection jurisdictions and a relatively standard execution protocol. The Court's decision to hear *Baze* initiated what turned out to be a 7-month de facto moratorium on executions.

The petitioners in the case, Kentucky death row inmates Ralph Baze and Thomas C. Bowling, had both been sentenced to death for double homicides. They conceded that if Kentucky's lethal injection procedure were implemented as intended, the result would be a humane death. They claimed, however, that there was a substantial risk that the execution protocol might not be properly followed and the result would be significant pain in violation of the Eighth Amendment's prohibition of cruel and unusual punishment. They also proposed another protocol—a one-drug protocol using only sodium thiopental or another barbiturate with trained personnel to monitor the drug's effectiveness—that they acknowledged had not been adopted by any other state and had never been tried. On April 16, 2008, the Court announced its 7−2 decision and held that the petitioners had "not carried their burden of showing that the risk of pain from maladministration of a concededly humane execution protocol, and the failure to adopt untried and untested alternatives, constitute cruel and unusual punishment." The Court's decision ended the de facto moratorium.

Legal commentators, including U.S. Supreme Court justices John Paul Stevens and Clarence Thomas, predict that the Court's decision in *Baze* will not end legal challenges to lethal injection for two reasons. First, the decision was splintered. Seven separate opinions were written (including six by the majority), and none of them garnered more than three votes. The justices provided a number of explanations, concerns, and qualifications.[119] Second, the decision applied only to Kentucky and its particular protocol. Although the Court maintained that its decision applies to all lethal injection jurisdictions that have protocols substantially similar to Kentucky's, it provided no guidelines as to what constitutes "substantially similar."[120]

Justices Stevens, Thomas, and the other legal commentators were prescient. Less than 2 months after the Court's *Baze* decision, an Ohio state court judge ruled in *State v. Rivera* that Ohio's use of the standard three-drug combination for lethal injection executions violated Ohio's lethal injection statute and due process.[121] The Ohio court, contradicting *Baze*, ruled that the two drugs—pancuronium bromide and potassium chloride—created "an unnecessary and arbitrary risk that the condemned [would] experience an agonizing and painful death."[122] The court concluded that "a sufficient dosage of sodium thiopental [would] cause death rapidly and without the possibility [of] causing pain to the condemned."[123] Law professor Deborah Denno explains that Ohio's death penalty statute requires "a lethal injection of a drug or combination of drugs of sufficient dosage to quickly and painlessly cause death [and] because the duty of the state to the individual is mandatory, a property interest is created in the benefit; [that is] the statute confers on the condemned person a property interest in a painless death."[124] Because the court found that the three-drug cocktail carried an unnecessary risk of causing an agonizing or excruciatingly painful execution, the court held that Ohio's use of the three-drug cocktail violated the due process clause of the Fifth and Fourteenth Amendments.[125] As a result, the Ohio court ordered that the words "or combination of drugs" be removed from the Ohio statute and that only one anesthetic drug be used.[126] The major difference between the Ohio statute and the Kentucky statute (and *Baze*) was that Kentucky did not mandate that the execution be painless.[127] Thus, *Rivera* is the first case in which a court has ordered a state to utilize a single anesthetic drug. On December 8, 2009, Ohio became the first death penalty jurisdiction in the United States to use a single drug in an execution, when it executed with one dose of sodium thiopental Kenneth Biros, 51, at Southern Ohio Correctional Facility. Biros died in 10 minutes.[128] On March 10, 2011, Ohio executed Johnnie Baston with a single dose of pentobarbital, an animal tranquilizer that is normally used in conjunction with other drugs.[129] Ironically, the one-dose, barbiturate-only procedure was rejected in 1977 by Jay Chapman, the creator of Oklahoma's three-drug cocktail, because he did not believe that the public would accept an execution method for humans modeled after the method used by veterinarians for euthanizing animals.[130]

The latest controversy with lethal injection involves the first drug in the lethal cocktail—the barbiturate sodium thiopental or Pentothal.[131] Death penalty states were obtaining sodium thiopental from its sole U.S. manufacturer, an Illinois-based company called Hospira, Inc., which was making the drug at its plant in Italy. However, the Italian Parliament objected to Hospira's manufacturing an execution drug in Italy, so Hospira stopped making it in 2009, and announced in 2011 that it would stop selling the drug altogether. Most other suppliers of the drug have also buckled under international pressure. Ironically, Hospira (allegedly) had sent letters annually for at least the past decade to all death penalty states with this disclaimer: "Hospira provides these products because they improve or save lives and markets them solely for use as indicated on the product labeling. As such, we do not support the use of any of our products in capital punishment procedures."

Death penalty states have had to scramble to find a new source for the drug, and federal law severely restricts its importation. As a result, death penalty states began swapping the drug with each other. For example, Arkansas corrections officials obtained the drug from a company in England after learning about it from Georgia corrections officials. They have since given the drug to corrections officials in Mississippi, Oklahoma, and Tennessee free of charge. Arkansas corrections officials have also obtained the drug from their counterparts in Texas. The sodium thiopental received by Georgia and later Arkansas came directly from British supplier Dream Pharma, a wholesaler that operated out of the back room of a London driving academy offices. Obtaining drugs from the wholesaler rather than ordering them through a state health care company and receiving them from a local pharmacy may violate federal law. The Drug Enforcement Agency (DEA) seized Georgia's supply of sodium thiopental in March 2011, and in April 2011, Kentucky and Tennessee voluntarily turned over their supplies to the DEA. Another problem is that sodium thiopental has a shelf life of about two years, so the last batch made in 2009 is set to expire in 2011. The sodium thiopental crisis is likely to be short lived despite some inevitable legal challenges, as Oklahoma, Texas, and Ohio have already substituted the barbiturate pentobarbital for sodium thiopental in their execution processes. Pentobarbital is widely available and manufactured in the United States. Recall that pentobarbital is most commonly used in euthanizing animals.

As noted, lethal injection is the method of execution provided by the most states (34), at least as an option, as well as by the U.S. military and the U.S. government.[132] For the military, the government, and in the following 20 states, it is the sole method of execution: Colorado, Connecticut, Delaware, Georgia, Idaho, Indiana, Kansas, Louisiana, Mississippi, Montana, Nebraska, Nevada, North Carolina, Ohio, Oklahoma, Oregon, Pennsylvania, South Dakota, Texas, and Wyoming. In Arkansas, lethal injection is the authorized mode of execution for those convicted after July 4, 1983; for Arizona, after November 15, 1992; for Kentucky, after March 31, 1998; for Maryland, after March 25, 1994; for New Hampshire, if it can be given; for Tennessee, after December 31, 1998; and for Utah, after May 3, 2004. Lethal injection is one of two options in the following seven states: Alabama, California, Florida, Missouri, South Carolina, Virginia, and Washington.

Lethal injection is also the method by which most people have been executed under post-*Furman* statutes (since 1976). As of April 12, 2011, 1,246 people had been executed in the United States under post-*Furman* statutes. The number of executions by method employed was as follows: lethal injection, 1,072; electrocution, 157; lethal gas, 11; hanging, 3; and firing squad, 3.[133]

THE EXECUTION PROCESS

The execution process varies somewhat among states, the federal government, and the U.S. military. Below is a generic description of most executions' basic elements. The procedures of specific states are used to illustrate some of the elements.

THE DEATH WARRANT

In all death penalty jurisdictions, a death or execution warrant instigates the execution process. A death warrant, which typically sets the date and place for a prisoner's execution, usually is issued by a state's governor, or the president of the United States in federal death penalty cases, and authorizes a warden or other prison officials to carry out a death sentence. In Texas, a district court judge sets the execution date. A death warrant commonly lists the execution as a homicide and absolves the executioner of criminal responsibility. The length of time before a death warrant expires and has to be reissued varies from a few days to several months. Florida no longer issues multiple death warrants (after previous warrants expire) as other states do, but instead issues one death warrant and multiple execution dates as needed.

DEATHWATCH

A condemned inmate and all of his belongings generally are moved from his death row cell to the deathwatch or holding cell after prison officials receive the death warrant. Depending on the state and the execution date, the move may be made as early as immediately after the death warrant is received and read to the inmate or as late as 24 hours before the execution, or anytime in between. In some states, inmates are given the choice of immediately moving to the holding cell or delaying the move until prison officials say it is time to move. Inmates will be moved immediately when their security is in jeopardy, for example, if they appear suicidal or if it is believed that another inmate aims to preempt the execution by killing the condemned inmate.

During the deathwatch, there is a corrections officer either in the holding cell with the inmate or right outside the holding cell 24 hours a day (some states assign two or three officers to the holding cell). The primary goal of the deathwatch officers is to keep the inmate calm and under control. The officer keeps a detailed log of all the inmate's actions. The inmate is allowed to make collect phone calls if prison officials approve them. A log is kept of all outgoing and incoming calls. The holding cell usually is equipped with a television and a VCR, and most inmates pass the time watching movies on video. In some states, an inmate on deathwatch (at least those who are there for relatively short periods of time) also can get free items from the commissary. Popular items are soft drinks, snacks, and cigarettes.

Many states maintain a liberal visitation policy during the deathwatch. For security purposes, the inmate generally is allowed only two visitors at a time. Besides his attorneys, family, and friends, ministers or religious advisors may also visit the inmate. As for the length of visits, many prison officials try to be flexible. This is especially true for the day of the execution.

EXECUTIONS

The death warrant does not specify the actual time of execution, which is left to the warden's discretion. However, executions normally have been conducted at 12:01 a.m. The reason is fivefold. First, it has become the traditional time for executions. Second, it provides extra security. At that time of night, all inmates are locked down. Third, the early hour deters some demonstrators. Fourth, adverse publicity is reduced because the execution takes place after the 11 o'clock TV news and past the deadline for the morning newspapers. Fifth, it allows the state a full 24 hours to carry out the death sentence. Between 1977 and 1995, in excess of 80 percent of all executions took place between 11:00 p.m. and 7:00 a.m., and half of them were scheduled for between midnight and 1:00 a.m.[134] Sometimes, events, such as a stay of execution, require the execution to be conducted at a later time.

Recently, some states, most notably Texas and Florida, have changed the time of their lethal injection executions to 6:00 p.m. to better accommodate the work schedules of prison personnel, judges, attorneys, witnesses, and journalists. Having executions at 6:00 p.m. also reduces the need for overtime pay for prison personnel and execution team members. Another possible reason for the earlier execution times in some states is that "executions have now become so routine in certain states, and meet so little public protest, that prison officials have little reason to hide, or appear to hide, them in the middle of the night."[135]

On execution day, the prison is gradually closed, and the only people allowed on the institution grounds are people who are directly involved with the execution or have a work assignment. A briefing is held for personnel involved with the execution. The execution paraphernalia is checked and rechecked. The inmate is given his (or her) last meal. Usually, a few hours before the execution the inmate is offered a sedative. The press and state witnesses are briefed on what to expect. Approximately 30 minutes before the execution the inmate is brought into the execution chamber and strapped down to the gurney. The IV is placed in the inmate's arm (sometimes IVs are placed in both arms), and a heart monitor is connected. The witnesses are escorted into the witness room or rooms. The inmate is allowed to make a final statement. The warden checks with the governor's and the attorney general's offices to make sure the execution should proceed. If there are no last-minute stays, the warden reads the death warrant and gives the order to commence the execution.

Normally, death occurs in approximately 4.5 minutes after the first chemical has been injected. A doctor, who has been watching the heart monitor, examines the inmate and pronounces him dead. The witnesses then are escorted out of the witness room or rooms, but before the official witnesses are dismissed, they are required to sign a notarized return warrant of execution, which attests to the execution having taken place. The inmate is disconnected from the IV, and the coroner comes in and takes the body.

A NOTE ON WITNESSING AN EXECUTION

Many death penalty states do not allow citizens to witness an execution unless they have a direct relationship to the case. However, in at least 16 death penalty states, state law requires that a certain number of people serve as official witnesses to ensure that the execution is carried out in a dignified and humane way. For example, North Carolina requires four witnesses, Pennsylvania requires six witnesses, Missouri requires eight witnesses, and Florida requires 12 witnesses. The average number of required civilian witnesses is six.[136] In 2009, 10 states allowed family members of the victim to witness the execution: Alabama, Delaware, Georgia, Illinois (which abolished its death penalty in 2011), North Carolina, Oregon, Pennsylvania, South Carolina, Texas, and Washington.[137] Some states, such as Texas, also allow the family members of the offender to witness the execution.

At Florida State Prison, the warden selects the witnesses to an execution. He allows 30 witnesses, but usually only one or two of them are from the waiting list. A dozen places are reserved for the news media—six for the print media and six for television and radio. The warden lets trade organizations such as the Florida Press Association select the media witnesses. The warden chooses the 12 official witnesses. His first priority is law enforcement officers and prosecutors who were involved in the case and victims' relatives. Other witnesses include prison personnel, state officials, and a medical staff member to care for witnesses who need medical attention. Typically, an inmate's attorney and religious advisor witness an execution but rarely are they counted as official witnesses. The few citizens selected from the waiting list in Florida do not have to provide a reason why they want to witness an execution.

Witnesses are generally asked to arrive anywhere from 20 minutes to 2 hours before the scheduled execution. Once they get to the prison, they are escorted into the witness room by prison guards. In Oklahoma, relatives of the victim are placed in a different room from relatives of the prisoner; in other death penalty states all the witnesses sit together. Some execution chambers have a one-way mirror that only allows the witnesses to see the condemned. Others have a clear window that allows the condemned to see the witnesses as well. Once the IVs are inserted into the prisoner's arms, the curtain or blind covering the window is opened. In California, a recent Ninth U.S. Circuit Court of Appeals ruling allows witnesses to "view executions from the moment the condemned is escorted into the execution chamber."[138] Complete silence in the witness area is required in some states. In some cases, the witness room is not large enough to hold all the relatives who want to witness the execution, so an overflow room in another part of the prison may be used to allow family witnesses to view the execution via closed-circuit TV. Once the execution is completed, the curtain or blind is closed and prison staff escort the witnesses out of the witness room. Official witnesses are then required to sign a document attesting to the fact that they witnessed the execution and that it took place. In some cases, members of the media and families may be taken to a press area for a press conference. The witnesses are then escorted out of the prison.[139]

CONCLUSION

Deborah Denno argues that if the Supreme Court were willing to hear Eighth Amendment challenges to all current execution methods, to consider available evidence demonstrating the cruelty of those methods, and to apply both the "death is different" and "evolving standards of decency" criteria, it would be forced to conclude that all current methods of execution are unconstitutional.[140] Denno believes that if the Court were to follow such a course, it would also have to declare the death penalty itself unconstitutional because no method of punishment could meet the required standards. Denno may be overly optimistic on the latter point.

In the future, death penalty jurisdictions may require executions to be conducted using methods designed (and possibly approved) for human euthanasia. For example, an execution during which the condemned prisoner dies by inhaling carbon monoxide from a mask and tank—a preferred method of euthanasia expert Dr. Jack Kevorkian—might meet the required criteria. Criminal justice futurist Gene Stephens predicts that executions may one day be conducted using ultrasound which would literally "dematerialize" the condemned inmate. An added benefit to ultrasound is that it would eliminate the costs of disposing of the body.[141] If the death penalty continues to be employed, the future will likely bring execution methods which are now beyond imagination.

DISCUSSION QUESTIONS

1. Do you agree with the Supreme Court's definition of "cruel and unusual punishment"? Why or why not?
2. Are any of the current execution methods cruel and unusual punishments? Why or why not?
3. Should execution methods be cruel (and/or unusual)?
4. Are long stays on death row cruel and unusual punishment? Why or why not?
5. Is execution of the elderly or infirm cruel and unusual punishment? Why or why not?
6. What conditions of death row confinement, if any, do you think constitute cruel and unusual punishment? Why?
7. Should we be concerned about botched executions? What should be done about them?
8. Would you change anything about the execution process? If yes, what would you change and why?
9. Would you like to witness an execution? Why or why not?

Notes

1. Bedau (1982, p. 14); also see Denno (1994, p. 566, n. 87).
2. Bedau (1982, p. 14); also see Denno (1994, p. 563).
3. Banner (2002, p. 71).
4. Ibid., p. 72.
5. Ibid.
6. Ibid., pp. 74–75.
7. Ibid., pp. 81–82.
8. Bedau (1982, p. 15).
9. *Weems v. United States* (217 U.S. 349, 1910), Meltsner (1973, pp. 173–175), and Paternoster (1991, p. 51).
10. Ibid.
11. Paternoster (1991, p. 52).
12. Ibid.; *Trop v. Dulles* (356 U.S. 86, 1958).
13. Paternoster (1991, p. 53); *Trop v. Dulles* (356 U.S. 86, 1958). Law professor Corinna Barrett Lain calls the "evolving standards" doctrine "a sham both in its inception and in its application" that allows the U.S. Supreme Court justices "to get where they want to go" [in terms of their ideological positions]. Lain (2010, pp. 677–678).
14. Banner (2002, p. 235); also see Denno (1997, 1998).
15. High court rejects killers' cases. (1999, November 9). *The Orlando Sentinel*, p. A7.
16. Federman and Holmes (2005, pp. 338–339).
17. Ibid., p. 328.
18. Alabama Inmate Becomes Oldest Executed Since '41. (2004).
19. Man Executed in Mississippi is the Oldest to Die Since 1970s. (2005).
20. Thompson (2006).
21. See *Hudson v. McMillian* (1992); *Helling v. McKinney* (1993); also see Johnson (1989, 1990, 2003), for a description of conditions on death row.
22. Ibid.
23. See *Hudson v. McMillian* (1992); *Wilson v. Seiter* (1991).
24. See *Farmer v. Brennan* (1994).
25. Word (2004b).
26. Dow (2002b, p. 12).
27. Bedau (1982).
28. Percentage calculated by dividing 16,000 hangings cited in Denno (1994, p. 680) by the more liberal 22,500 total execution estimate of Espy.
29. Banner (2002, pp. 62 and 64).
30. Ibid., p. 65.
31. Ibid.
32. Ibid.
33. Denno (1994, p. 679).
34. Ibid.
35. Ibid.
36. Banner (2002, p. 36).
37. Ibid.
38. Ibid.
39. Ibid.
40. Ibid.

41. Ibid., p. 37.
42. Denno (1994, p. 686); Death Penalty Information Center (June 3, 2002).
43. Denno (1994, p. 682).
44. . Snell (2010a, Table 2).
45. Denno (1994, p. 683).
46. Snell (2010a, Table 2).
47. See Denno (1994, pp. 687–688).
48. See, for example, Mailer (1979).
49. Hartman (2010).
50. Calculated from Espy and Smykla (1987) and Death Penalty Information Center (2010).
51. http://www.clarkprosecutor.org/html/death/updates.htm; Georgia bans the electric chair. (2001, October 6). *The Orlando Sentinel*, p. A19.
52. Electric chair in Alabama upheld. (2000, February 23). *The Orlando Sentinel*, p. A5.
53. In May 2000, a Nebraska district court judge upheld Nebraska's death penalty statute, but ruled that the procedure used during electrocutions constituted cruel and unusual punishment. The court objected to the practice of Nebraska prison officials of using four separate jolts of electricity to execute inmates. According to the statute, a current of electricity is to be administered continuously until the inmate dies. Procedure of execution ruled cruel and unusual. (May 9). *The Orlando Sentinel*, p. A6.
54. Denno (2009, p. 189).
55. Death Penalty Information Center (2010).
56. Snell (2010a, Table 2).
57. Ibid.
58. Convicted Killer Put to Death by Electric Chair in Virginia. (2006).
59. Snell (2010a, Table 2).
60. Paternoster (1991, p. 23).
61. Denno (1994, p. 557).
62. The following account is from Bedau (1982, pp. 15–16), Denno (1994), and Paternoster (1991, pp. 14–15); also see Moran (2002).
63. The Court made the Eighth Amendment applicable to the states in 1962; see *Robinson v. California* (370 U.S. 660).
64. The specific cause of death from electrocution is presumed to be extensive electrical damage to the nervous system.
65. It is interesting that electrocution is considered an acceptable method for human executions but unacceptable for animal euthanasia. According to the American Veterinary Medical Association, "electrocution [is] an unacceptable method unless it is preceded by an injury inducing immediate unconsciousness, such as a blow to the head, because electrocution alone will not lead to unconsciousness for 10-to-30 seconds or longer" (cited in Denno, 1997). For an explicit description of the execution by electrocution of John Evans in Alabama, see Canan (1989).
66. Denno (1997, Appendix 2A) provides descriptions of 14 botched electrocutions since 1976.
67. *The Anniston (Alabama) Star*, December 12, 1984.
68. Ibid., October 16, 1985. Heart death cannot be ensured with voltages of less than 2000 volts. Current exceeding 6 amps can cause excessive burning of the flesh; see Denno (1997).
69. *Charlotte (North Carolina) Observer*, May 10, 1990.
70. See Bedau (1982, p. 16).
71. Denno (1997).
72. Duffy (1962, pp. 101–106).
73. Snell (2010a, Table 10).

74. For detailed descriptions of executions by lethal gas at San Quentin in California, also see Kroll (1989).

75. *The Anniston (Alabama) Star*, October 22, 1979. Because of the pain and agony experienced by Jesse Bishop, Nevada changed its method of execution from lethal gas to lethal injection. As was the case with electrocution, it is interesting that lethal gas is considered an acceptable method for human executions but unacceptable for animal euthanasia. Dr Richard Traystman, Director of the Anesthesiology and Critical Care Medicine Research Laboratories at Johns Hopkins Medical School, states, "[W]e would not use asphyxiation, by cyanide gas or by any other substance, in our laboratory to kill animals that have been used in experiments—nor would most medical research laboratories in this country use it" (cited in Denno, 1997). For a description of eight botched executions by lethal gas since 1976, see Denno (1997, Appendix 2A).

76. See Bedau (1982, pp. 17–19).

77. Ibid., p. 17.

78. Denno (1997, 2002).

79. Ibid.

80. Ibid.

81. The cost of drugs used in lethal injections in the mid-1990s averaged about $70 per execution. See ibid.

82. Unless indicated otherwise, this account is from Lee (2008) and Denno (2007).

83. Martschukat (2009, p. 265).

84. Taylor and Stutzman (2000).

85. Recer (1994).

86. Some doctors willing to kill. (2001, November 20). *The Orlando Sentinel*, p. A15.

87. Denno (2007, p. 89) and Federman and Holmes (2005, p. 342).

88. Denno (2007, p. 77).

89. Ibid., pp. 89–90, n. 267.

90. Reinhold (1982).

91. Information about the differences in the ways lethal injections are administered among jurisdictions is from Kunerth (2000), Taylor and Stutzman (2000), and Denno (2002).

92. After Botched Execution, Ohio to Change Method. (2009); Williams (2009).

93. In 1953, the British Royal Commission on Capital Punishment concluded that lethal injection as a method of capital punishment was deficient for four reasons: (1) it "could not be administered to individuals with certain 'physical abnormalities' that make veins impossible to locate, and that even 'normal' veins can be flattened by cold or nervousness, conditions oftentimes characteristic of an execution setting"; (2) it "is difficult unless the subject fully cooperates and keeps 'absolutely still'"; (3) "although a qualified [*sic*] injection requires medical skill, the medical profession was opposed to participating in the process"; and (4) "because of all such problems, the Commission concluded that it was likely that executioners would have to implement intramuscular (rather than intravenous) injection even though the intramuscular method would be slower and more painful." Cited in Denno (1997).

94. Denno (1997, Appendix 2C) provides descriptions of 22 botched executions by lethal injection since 1976. For an update through October 1, 2010, see Radelet (2010).

95. *The Anniston (Alabama) Star*, December 13, 1988.

96. Denno (1997).

97. Lee (2008, pp. 103 and 107).

98. Koniaris, Zimmers, Lubarsky, and Sheldon (2005).

99. Ibid.

100. Bell (2007).

101. Koniaris et al. (2005).

102. Ibid.

103. Ibid.

104. See Groner (2005), Heath, Stanski, and Pounder (2005), and Weisman, Bernstein, and Weisman (2005).

105. Zimmers, Lubarsky, Sheldon, and Koniaris (2005).

106. Lytle and Kennedy (2006).

107. Executions by Lethal Injection. (2005).

108. Kravets (2006) and McCarthy (2006).

109. Denno (2009, p. 194).

110. Mullane (2010); State Calls Off Execution. (2010).

111. Three Men. (2006).

112. Federal Judge Requires... (2006).

113. Denno (2009, p. 196).

114. Ibid.

115. Lethal Injections. (2006).

116. Leusner and Tseng (2006).

117. Denno (2009, p. 196 and n. 94).

118. Ibid., pp. 196–197.

119. Ibid., p. 197.

120. Ibid.

121. Ibid., p. 202.

122. Ibid.

123. Ibid.

124. Ibid., p. 203.

125. Ibid.

126. Ibid.

127. Ibid.

128. 1st One-Drug Execution. (2009).

129. Goldman (2011).

130. Pickert (2008).

131. Information about the sodium thiopental problem is from Colarossi (2011a, 2011b); MacLaggan (2011); Schwartz (2011).

132. Snell (2010a, Table 2).

133. Death Penalty Information Center (2011).

134. Lifton and Mitchell (2002, p. 178).

135. Ibid., pp. 179–180.

136. Hansen (2000) and Taylor (2000); Who Is Eligible? (2010).

137. Can the Family of the Victim Witness an Execution? (2010).

138. Mintz (2002).

139. Howstuffworks: How Lethal Injection Works. (2002); also see Gillespie (2003, pp. 4–8).

140. Denno (1997, 1998); also see Gottlieb (1961).

141. Stephens (1990). Another possibility is the return to a method employed in antiquity. For example, in 399 BC, Socrates was condemned to drink a cup of hemlock, an execution method that produced a relatively dignified and presumably painless death.

General deterrence and the death penalty

The next several chapters consider rationales or justifications for capital punishment, as well as arguments against its use. Available evidence is presented and evaluated. This chapter examines general deterrence—the belief that people in general can be prevented from engaging in crime by punishing specific individuals and making examples of them. In the context of this book, the broad deterrence question is whether executions prevent people other than the person executed from committing capital crimes.[1]

Another type of deterrence is specific or special deterrence—the prevention of individuals from committing crime again by punishing them. Special or specific deterrence does not apply to capital punishment because execution precludes the determination of whether a punished individual returns to crime. When people want to forever prevent prisoners from reoffending, they desire incapacitation and not specific or special deterrence. Capital punishment ensures incapacitation, which is one of the most compelling rationales in support of the death penalty. Incapacitation is the subject of the next chapter. Subsequent chapters address the costs of capital punishment, miscarriages of justice, arbitrariness and discrimination in the death penalty's administration, retribution, and religious arguments. The last chapter is devoted to public opinion about the death penalty.

THE RELATIVE IMPORTANCE OF GENERAL DETERRENCE

At one time, general deterrence was the reason cited most often when people were asked why they supported the death penalty.[2] This was a curious finding because other research found that retribution was the primary basis of death penalty support.[3] Professors Phoebe Ellsworth and Lee Ross contend that the reason for the paradox is that deterrence is more scientific or socially desirable than retribution: "people mention it [deterrence] first because its importance is obvious, not because its importance is real."[4] The contention of Ellsworth and Ross is supported by their finding that compelling evidence of no deterrent effect would not have much effect on people's death penalty support. In other words, a majority of death penalty supporters would not change their opinion even if it were proven to them that their belief in general deterrence was wrong.

Deterrence no longer seems to be an important rationale for death penalty proponents. According to a 2010 national opinion poll, only 45 percent of respondents thought that the death penalty could help deter crime (43% thought otherwise and 13% were undecided).[5] When asked their most important reason for supporting the death penalty in a 2008 national opinion survey, only 9.7 percent of respondents chose deterrence—"To set an example to others who think of committing the same crime"; 21.4 percent of respondents chose "To set an example" as their second most important reason. By contrast, 54.6 percent chose retribution—"The punishment should fit the crime" (47.3%) or "They deserve it" (7.3%)—as their most important reason for supporting the death penalty; another 26.5 percent chose "retribution" as their second most important reason.[6]

ARGUMENTS AND COUNTERARGUMENTS

Philosopher Ernest Van den Haag explains why one should believe in the general deterrent effect of the death penalty. In the first place, he says, "our penal system rests on the proposition that more severe penalties are more deterrent than less severe penalties."[7] If this is true, he asserts, the corollary is that "the most severe penalty—the death penalty—would have the greatest deterrent effect."[8] He adds that "arguments to the contrary assume either that capital crimes never are deterrable (sometimes because not all capital crimes have been deterred), or that, beyond some point, the deterrent effect of added severity is necessarily zero."[9]

Van den Haag's first assumption—more severe penalties are more deterrent than less severe penalties—is generally correct. Beyond a point, though, added severity may reduce deterrence. In England during the eighteenth century, for example, there were about 150 capital crimes (some put the number at more than 200). Many of the crimes were so petty that juries chose not to convict clearly guilty defendants rather than having to condemn them to die. The practice is called jury nullification.[10] Such a practice likely reduces any general deterrent effect.

Van den Haag's corollary—the most severe penalty, the death penalty, would have the greatest deterrent effect—is based on a debatable assumption and a testable proposition with no scientific evidence to support it. Is the death penalty the most severe penalty? For many, it may be; but for others, it may not. The prospect of spending the rest of one's life in prison may be more terrifying to some people than death, as it apparently was for Gary Gilmore.

Taking the opposite position to Van den Haag, Cesare Beccaria, the eighteenth-century philosopher whose ideas are the basis of much of the criminal justice process in the United States today, claimed that life imprisonment (he called it "perpetual servitude") is probably a greater deterrent than death:

> To anyone raising the argument that perpetual servitude is as painful as death and therefore equally cruel, I will reply that, adding up all the moments of unhappiness of servitude, it may well be even more cruel; but these are drawn out over an entire lifetime, while the pain of death exerts its whole force in a moment. And precisely this is the advantage of penal servitude, that it inspires terror in the spectator more than in the sufferer, for the former considers the entire sum of unhappy moments, while the latter is distracted from the thought of future misery by that of the present moment.[11]

Although Beccaria could never have imagined the prolonged process now operative in the United States—a process that takes an average of more than 14 years to complete[12]—he still may be correct that life imprisonment is a more severe punishment (and better deterrent) than execution. In any case, he did not think much of capital punishment, calling it a "useless prodigality of torments" that "never made men better."[13] He believed that "the death penalty cannot be useful, because of the example of barbarity it gives men."[14]

Abolitionists maintain that the important question is not whether capital punishment is the severest punishment, but rather what punishment should be the severest allowed by law. As noted in the last chapter, not all punishments are legally allowed. The U.S. Constitution prohibits cruel and unusual punishments. Interestingly, how a person answers the question of what punishment should be the severest allowed by law may be what ultimately divides people on the death penalty issue.

Even if it were agreed that the death penalty is the severest penalty (and that at least some capital crimes are deterrable), the problem remains that there is no scientific evidence showing conclusively that the death penalty has any marginal effect. There is no evidence that capital punishment deters more than an alternative noncapital punishment, such as LWOP.[15] Instead, statistics indicate that capital punishment makes no discernible difference on homicide or murder rates.

EVIDENCE

When considering the deterrence question, it is useful to distinguish between pre- and post-1975 studies because, until 1975, there were no scientific data showing that capital punishment had a significant (or greater than a chance) effect on homicide or murder rates.[16] This finding held, despite more than 40 years of research and dozens of studies.

PRE-1975 STUDIES

The pre-1975 studies generally employed one of three basic research designs.[17] The first type compares murder rates of states with and without a capital punishment statute. For example, Thorsten Sellin compared the average annual homicide death rates (per 100,000 population) in contiguous states with and without capital punishment for the years 1920 through 1963.[18] If capital punishment had a marginal deterrent effect, one would expect that states without capital punishment would have higher homicide rates than states with capital punishment—all other things being equal. States next to each other were compared in an effort to control for other possibly influential factors. Sellin found no persuasive evidence of deterrence. The following are among his findings:

- The average annual homicide death rates for Michigan (without capital punishment), Indiana (with capital punishment), and Ohio (with capital punishment) during the time period were all 3.5.
- Rates for Minnesota (without capital punishment), Wisconsin (without capital punishment), and Iowa (with capital punishment) were 1.4, 1.2, and 1.4, respectively; rates for North Dakota (without capital punishment), South Dakota (with capital punishment), and Nebraska (with capital punishment) were 1.0, 1.5, and 1.8, respectively.
- Rates for Maine (without capital punishment), New Hampshire (with capital punishment), and Vermont (with capital punishment) were 1.5, 0.9, and 1.0, respectively.
- Rates for Rhode Island (without capital punishment), Massachusetts (with capital punishment), and Connecticut (with capital punishment) were 1.3, 1.2, and 1.7, respectively.

Again, these data fail to reveal a marginal deterrent effect for the death penalty.[19]

Sellin also employed his comparative method to the specific cases of police killings and prison murders.[20] Regarding police killings, Sellin wanted to test whether capital punishment provided police officers an added measure of protection. It was (and still is) assumed by many people that the threat of execution deters criminals from carrying guns and using them when they face arrest.[21] Sellin examined rates of municipal police killings for contiguous states per 10 years and 100,000 population for the years 1919 through 1954. As with his previous comparisons of general homicide rates for contiguous states, Sellin did not find that the availability of capital punishment had any discernible effect on the rate of police killings. Specifically, he reported that the rate of police killings in 82 cities in abolition states was 1.2, while the rate in 182 cities in death penalty states was 1.3.[22] Sellin observed in an editorial postscript to his study that from 1961 through 1963, 140 police officers were killed in the United States: nine in abolition states and 131 in death penalty states. When he computed the average annual risk for the 3 years per 10,000 police in abolition states and contiguous death penalty states, he found a rate of 1.312 in the abolition states and 1.328 for the bordering death penalty states—not a significant difference.[23]

With regard to prison murders, Sellin researched whether, if capital punishment were an effective deterrent to murder, it would be reasonable to assume that inmates and correctional staff in prisons in abolition states would be in greater jeopardy for their lives than inmates and correctional staff in prisons in death penalty states because in abolition states there is no death penalty threat to deter would-be killers. The answer he found was that the evidence did not support the intuitive belief.[24] To the contrary, in 1965, there were 61 prison killings in the 37 jurisdictions that responded to his survey—eight of the victims were staff members and 53 were inmates. All of the staff members and 85 percent of the inmates were killed in death penalty states. Wendy Wolfson, who examined prison killings in 52 jurisdictions in the United States in 1973, has reported similar findings.[25] Of the 124 prison killings in 1973, 11 of the victims were staff members and 113 were inmates. Ninety-one percent of the staff member victims and 95 percent of the inmate victims were killed in death penalty jurisdictions. These data clearly show that prison staff members and inmates are no safer in prisons in death penalty states than in prisons in abolition states. The threat of death does not seem to effectively deter prison killings.[26]

The principal criticism of studies such as Sellin's is that the comparative results are weak evidence of deterrence (or its absence) because contiguous states are not necessarily comparable in all important respects. In attempting to overcome the criticism, studies that compare several important factors that could affect the murder rates in the contiguous states have been conducted.[27] Examples of such factors include probability of apprehension, probability of conviction, labor force participation, unemployment rate, population aged 15 through 24, real per-capita income, nonwhite population, civilian population, per-capita government expenditures (state and local), and per-capita police expenditures (state and local).[28] When these factors are compared for the contiguous states, no apparent reason emerges for the absence of a deterrent effect for capital punishment. Still, the criticism remains that the early comparative studies fail to account for the simultaneous influence of the other possible influential factors. This criticism would later be addressed using newer, more powerful statistical analytic techniques.

A second type of research design compares murder rates before and after the abolition and/or reinstatement of the death penalty.[29] If capital punishment has a deterrent effect, one would expect higher murder rates in states following abolition of the death penalty or lower rates following its reinstatement—all other things being equal. But before-and-after studies reveal no apparent deterrent effect for capital punishment.

A particularly interesting example of the "before-and-after" methodology using cross-national comparisons is a study by Dane Archer, Rosemary Gartner, and Marc Beittel.[30] The researchers examined homicide rate changes for selected countries 1 year, 5 years (where possible), and the maximum possible years before and after abolition of the death penalty. The countries (dates of abolition, except for extraordinary crimes, are in parentheses) were Austria (1968), Canada (1967), Denmark (1930), England and Wales (1965), Finland (1949), Israel (1954), Italy (1890), Netherlands

Antilles (1957), Norway (1905), Sweden (1921), and Switzerland (1942). In some countries, homicide rates increased following abolition, and in other countries, the rates decreased, but there were more decreases than increases. In short, these data do not show that capital punishment has a consistent or, for that matter, any deterrent effect. Fluctuations in homicide rates before and after abolition are probably a function of factors other than capital punishment. A problem with before-and-after studies is that they fail to control for other possibly influential factors.

The third type of research design examines short-term murder trends just before and just after highly publicized executions of convicted murderers.[31] If capital punishment has a deterrent effect, one would expect murder rates to decrease after these executions—all other things being equal. Some of the studies do reveal a short-term deterrent effect,[32] but in no case does the decrease in homicides last very long. Moreover, replications and reanalyses of these studies tend to show brutalizing, rather than deterrent, effects of execution publicity (more about brutalizing effects later).[33] This method does not provide any evidence of a long-term deterrent effect for capital punishment. The major problem with this method, like the other two, is the failure to adequately control for other possibly influential factors on homicides or murders.

In sum, none of the studies using any of the three research designs produced evidence to support a belief in the (long-term) deterrent effect of the death penalty. If the death penalty were an effective deterrent to homicides or murders (or any other crimes), one might expect to see at least some supportive evidence in at least some studies.

EHRLICH FINDS A GENERAL DETERRENT EFFECT

In 1975, economics professor Isaac Ehrlich published the first scientific study to report a deterrent effect for capital punishment.[34] Ehrlich began his article with two major criticisms of Sellin's research. The first was that Sellin compared different states on the basis of whether they had death penalty statutes rather than on whether they actually employed the death penalty. The second was that Sellin failed to control for a variety of factors that could influence homicide or murder rates.

Ehrlich used a sophisticated statistical analytic technique—multiple regression analysis—to examine the simultaneous effect of several variables on homicide rates during the years 1933–1969. Among the variables were arrest and conviction rates for murder, unemployment rates, labor force participation rates, per-capita incomes, and proportions of the general population between 14 and 24 years of age. His key variable—execution risk—was measured by dividing the number of executions by convictions for murder in the United States during the time period selected. Ehrlich concluded that "an additional execution per year over the period in question may have resulted, on average, in seven or eight fewer murders."[35]

Ehrlich's findings drew considerable attention. For example, the solicitor general of the United States introduced Ehrlich's prepublished results in *Fowler v. North Carolina* (428 U.S. 904, 1976) as evidence in support of the death penalty.[36] The study was cited in the majority's opinion in *Gregg v. Georgia* (1976) to support the more modest contention that scientific evidence concerning the death penalty's general deterrent effect was "inconclusive."[37] Ehrlich's research continues to inform the opinions of some Supreme Court members who believe that capital punishment deters many types of murder.[38] Finally, Ehrlich's research inspired additional studies (see Cloninger, 1977; Layson, 1985; Wolpin, 1978; Yunker, 1976), including another one by Ehrlich (1977) himself, that have found a statistically significant general deterrent effect for the death penalty.[39] Each of these studies, however, is considered methodologically inferior to Ehrlich's first study.

Most of the attention devoted to Ehrlich's first study was critical, and numerous methodological flaws with his research were cited.[40] Among the problems were (1) the failure to compare the effectiveness of capital punishment with that of particular prison terms (the marginal effect issue), (2) his finding of a deterrent effect does not hold if the years between 1965 and 1969 are omitted from his statistical model, (3) his use of aggregate U.S. data ignores important regional differences, and (4) despite his criticism of Sellin's failure to control for possibly influential factors on homicide or murder rates, in accounting for the increase in homicides during the 1960s, Ehrlich fails to consider the possible influences of racial discord, the Vietnam conflict, the sexual revolution, and increased handgun ownership—to name only a few possible factors. Regarding the third and fourth problems, although the homicide rate in the United States did indeed increase during the 1960s, the increase was as great in the states with capital punishment as it was in the states without it. More generally, Ehrlich's model also omitted such variables as the decline in time served in prison for murder and the availability and quality of emergency medical care, both of which might significantly affect the murder rate.

One of the first and most forceful critiques of Ehrlich's research came from a panel established in 1975 by the National Academy of Sciences.[41] The panel's final report was based in part on several commissioned papers. One of the more influential was by Lawrence R. Klein, a past president of the American Economic Association, and his colleagues Brian Forst and Victor Filatov.[42] Most of the problems listed earlier, as well as several others, were first described in this paper. Klein and his colleagues were more generous than the full panel would be in their assessment of Ehrlich's research. They wrote, "The deterrent effect of capital punishment is definitely not a settled matter, and this is the strongest social scientific conclusion that can be reached at the present time."[43] The panel's report emphasized that Ehrlich's research provides "no useful evidence on the deterrent effect of capital punishment" and that "the current evidence on the deterrent effect of capital punishment is inadequate for drawing any substantive conclusions."[44] Although not all members agreed, the report concluded on a pessimistic note: "research on this topic is not likely to produce findings that will or should have much influence on policy makers."[45]

Critiques of Ehrlich's research have prompted a new wave of deterrence studies, many of them conducted by economists like Ehrlich, such as Dezhbakhsh, Rubin, and Shepherd (2003); Liu (2004); Mocan and Gittings (2001, 2003); Shepherd (2004, 2005); and Zimmerman (2004, 2006, 2009). All these econometric studies have found a deterrent effect for capital punishment.[46] Some of them have even found additional murders associated with pardons, commutations, and exonerations.[47] Testifying before Congress in 2003, Shepherd remarked that there is a "strong consensus among economists that capital punishment deters crime" and that "the studies are unanimous."[48] When asked by the committee chairman about "the findings of anti-death penalty advocates that are 180 degrees from your conclusion," she stated, "There may be people on the other side that rely on older papers and studies that use outdated statistical techniques or older data, but all of the modern economic studies in the past decade have found a deterrent effect. So I am not sure what the other people are relying on."[49] Recently, economics professor Bijou Yang and psychology professor David Lester conducted a meta-analysis of 104 studies of the deterrent effect of capital punishment published in peer-reviewed journals after 1975.[50] A meta-analysis is the statistical analysis of a large collection of analysis results for the purpose of integrating the findings. Of the 104 deterrence studies, only 95 had adequate data that allowed the researchers to report an effect size. Yang and Lester reported that 60 of the studies found a deterrent effect, while 35 of the studies discovered a brutalization effect (executions may cause murders rather than deter them—more about this later). They also noted that the presence of a deterrent effect depended on the type of study. Statistically significant effects were found most clearly for time-series and panel studies, while cross-sectional studies, studies of single executions, and studies of newspaper and television publicity gave mixed results, that is, deterrence and brutalization effects failed to reach statistical significance.[51] A time-series study is a longitudinal study that examines a series of observations on some variable over time. A panel study is also a longitudinal study in which data are collected from the same sample (the panel) at several points in time. A cross-sectional study, by contrast, is a study that is based on observations representing a single point in time.

Critical analyses of the newer econometric studies have faulted them for some of the same problems that invalidated Ehrlich's earlier research, plus some new ones.[52] First, the newer studies, like most of the older ones, generally do not distinguish between different types of murder. Included in the general category are crimes of passion and jealousy and intimate partner homicides, crimes that are less likely to be deterred. One study discovered that capital punishment was an especially effective deterrent to intimate partner homicides.[53] This finding contradicts what is known about homicide and fails to account for the steadily declining incidence of intimate partner homicide since the early 1970s, despite fluctuations in executions over the period.[54] Another new deterrence study showed that murders were more prevalent in rural areas than in cities, which is contrary to most evidence on the subject.[55] Second, none of the studies controls for autoregression, which is the tendency for results in time-series analyses to be influenced by what happened in preceding years. Thus, the best predictor of next year's murder rate is last year's murder rate, not the relatively few executions that occurred.[56] Third, few of the studies statistically control for law enforcement's ability to clear capital crimes. Many studies show that police effectiveness at detection and apprehension is far more important for deterrence than are a few poorly publicized executions.[57] Fourth, the studies ignore large amounts of missing data, which likely biases the results. For example, most of the studies use homicide rates from the FBI; yet, the FBI is missing Florida's homicide data for 4 years in the 1980s and another 4 years in the 1990s.[58] Fifth, all the studies are indirect tests of the deterrence hypothesis. None of them measures whether murderers were aware of the likelihood of execution in the state where the murder was committed, and the few studies that examine newspaper accounts of executions fail to ascertain whether murderers regularly read newspapers.[59] Sixth, the deterrent effect found in most of the studies disappears when Texas executions are eliminated from the model. Apparently, none of the other executing states has enough executions to make a difference.[60] Seventh, none of the studies determines the marginal effect of executions, that is, whether executions have a greater deterrent effect than LWOP. For the more than 100 death row inmates who since 1976 have voluntarily given up their appeals because they preferred death to LWOP, LWOP clearly was considered a harsher punishment. Furthermore, the dramatic recent decrease in homicide rates in New York, Texas, and California seems to demonstrate the deterrent superiority of LWOP over executions because in capital cases LWOP sentences are much more frequently given than death sentences. On January 1, 2009, for instance, 3,864 California inmates were serving LWOP sentences, while 678 inmates were awaiting execution on death row.[61] Eighth, the studies fail to consider alternate explanations for variations in the murder rate. For example, none of the studies controls for the differences between homicides committed with guns and those that are not committed with guns (the rate of nongun homicides has not varied much since the early 1970s), gun availability, and the influence of the crack cocaine epidemic in the late

1980s and early 1990s on gun violence.[62] Following their critique of the new econometric studies, Donohue and Wolfers state, "The only clear conclusion is that execution policy drives little of the year-to-year variation in homicide rates. As to whether executions raise or lower the homicide rate, we remain profoundly uncertain."[63]

Ehrlich's research also inspired numerous studies that failed to find a deterrent effect for the death penalty. Bowers and Pierce (1975); Decker and Kohfeld (1984, 1986, 1987, 1988, 1990); Forst (1977); Katz, Levitt, and Shustorovich (2003); Kohfeld and Decker (1990); Passell (1975); Sorensen, Wrinkle, Brewer, and Marquart (1999); and Bailey used Ehrlich's multiple regression analytic approach, but none of them found a statistically significant deterrent effect. William C. Bailey, a sociologist at Cleveland State University and one of the most prolific researchers in this area, has conducted numerous studies on the possible deterrent effect of capital punishment using multiple regression analysis. His research on the possible deterrent effect on first-degree murder reviewed (1) executions versus imprisonment (Bailey, 1974; 1977a); (2) the role of celerity or swiftness in the use of the death penalty (Bailey, 1980); (3) actual executions in each of five states—California, North Carolina, Ohio, Oregon, and Utah (Bailey, 1979a, 1979d, 1979b, 1979c, and 1978, respectively); (4) executions in Chicago and Washington, D.C. (Bailey, 1984a and 1984b, respectively); (5) executions during the 1950s (Bailey, 1983); (6) execution publicity (Bailey, 1990; Bailey and Peterson, 1989); and (7) executions for assaults against the police (Bailey, 1990; Bailey and Peterson, 1994). He also looked for a deterrent effect of executions on rape (Bailey, 1977b) and noncapital felonies (Bailey, 1991). In none of these studies did Bailey find a statistically significant deterrent effect.

One of the most vexing problems with death penalty deterrence studies, as noted above, is the limited number of executions conducted annually in the United States or in any of the executing states, including Texas. Thus, it is impossible to determine whether executions simply do not deter homicides at all—despite the evidence to the contrary—or whether too few executions make it impossible to detect a deterrent effect. This problem has recently been addressed in two studies. One of the studies examines homicides in Texas from January 1994 through December 2005, but instead of using the number of executions and homicides per year, the researchers use the number of executions and homicides per month.[64] The other study compares execution and homicide rates in Singapore and Hong Kong—two comparable cities with similar homicide trends but very different execution practices.[65]

In the first study, Land and his colleagues, using a very sophisticated statistical analysis, discovered a modest, short-term deterrent effect on homicides (not all of which were death-eligible homicides) in Texas in the months of or after executions. From 1994 through 2005, Texas averaged about 119 homicides (range = 76–199) and nearly two executions (range = 0–8) per month. The researchers report that each execution prevented from 0.5 to 2.5 homicides and that "some of the homicides deterred in the first month after an execution actually may be suppressed and displaced to a subsequent month."[66] Three points are worth noting. First, this study shows that for executions to have any deterrent effect a large number of executions must be conducted—more executions than any other executing state but Texas. Since executions resumed in 1977, Texas has executed more than four times as many people as the next most executing state, Virginia. Second, most of any deterrent effect of executions on homicides occurs soon after the execution is announced, and third, based on 10–20 executions a year and using the 0.5 homicides per month deterred, five to 10 homicides would be deterred per year—substantially fewer homicides than predicted by most of the econometric studies discussed previously, but still a significant number.

In the second study comparing execution and homicide rates in Singapore and Hong Kong, Zimring and his colleagues arrived at a much different conclusion, one that challenges the findings of Land and his colleagues.[67] Hong Kong has conducted no executions since 1967; it officially abolished capital punishment in 1993. Singapore, on the other hand, had a relatively stable and low execution rate until the early 1990s, when it experienced a huge increase that peaked in 1994 through 1996. At their peaks, the execution risk for murder was 24 times higher in Singapore than in Texas, and Singapore gained the reputation of being the "world execution capital." Over the next 10 years, Singapore's execution rate dropped by 92 percent, and by 2007, Singapore's execution rate was at its lowest level since 1981. Thus, Singapore's execution rate showed great variation during the study period. The peak rate in the mid-1990s was 35 times greater than the lowest rate in 2007. By contrast, Hong Kong's execution rate did not vary at all between 1981 and 2007 because it conducted no executions; yet, as noted at the onset, the homicide trends for Singapore and Hong Kong were similar between 1972 and 2007. Neither the surge in Singapore's execution rate nor the steep decline in its execution rate affected Singapore's homicide rate. Nor, for that matter, did the absence of executions in Hong Kong affect that city's homicide rate. If executions were a deterrent to homicide, one might expect to see evidence of that effect in the "world execution capital" but one does not.

FIVE COUNTERARGUMENTS TO STUDIES THAT SHOW NO GENERAL DETERRENT EFFECT

The first three counterarguments to studies that show no general deterrent effect of capital punishment are from a 1980 report by the Committee on the Judiciary of the U.S. Senate: "[T]he value of these [deterrence] studies is seriously diminished by the unreliability of the statistical evidence used, the contrary experience of those in the field of law enforcement, and the inherent logic of the deterrent power of the threat of death."[68] The fourth counterargument that undermines the value of the deterrence studies is the observation that, from the mid-1960s through the 1970s, the homicide rate increased as the number of executions decreased.[69] A fifth counterargument is that the death penalty's deterrent effect has been reduced to nothing in recent years (and thus does not show up in the research) because it has not been imposed often or quickly enough to have the desired effect.

Regarding the first point—that "the value of the studies is seriously diminished by the unreliability of the statistical evidence used"—the report noted that "those who are, in fact, deterred by the threat of the death penalty and do not commit murder are not included in the statistical data."[70] It added that "even those favoring abolition agree that the available evidence on the subject of deterrence is, at best, inadequate."[71]

That the available evidence on the subject of deterrence is, at best, inadequate may have been true in 1980, but it is no longer, as the previous section makes clear. As William J. Bowers explains:

> The evidence that capital punishment has no deterrent advantage over imprisonment is now stronger and more consistent than when the Court last considered this issue in Gregg. Indeed, a comprehensive review of previous studies and recent analyses of refined statistical data both support the contention that the death penalty has a "brutalizing" rather than a deterrent effect—that executions can be expected to stimulate rather than to inhibit homicides.[72]

In 1989, following a comprehensive review of death penalty research by a panel of distinguished scholars, the American Society of Criminology—the largest association of criminologists in the nation—passed a resolution condemning capital punishment and calling for its abolition. Among the reasons for the Society's position was the absence of "consistent evidence of crime deterrence through execution."[73] Additionally, a 1996 survey of 67 current and past presidents of the top three criminology professional organizations—the American Society of Criminology, the Academy of Criminal Justice Sciences, and the Law and Society Association—found that "about 80 percent of them believe that the death penalty is no greater a deterrent to homicide than long imprisonment."[74]

The second counterargument is that most law enforcement officials continue to favor capital punishment because they believe it is an effective deterrent to violent crime.[75] Law enforcement officials, it is assumed, are in the best position to judge the utility of capital punishment because they are the people "most frequently called upon to deal with murderers and potential murderers."[76] This second counterargument, however, appears to be wrong. Most police chiefs do not believe that the death penalty is an effective deterrent to violent crime. A 1995 Hart Research Associates poll found that two-thirds of U.S. police chiefs do not believe that the death penalty significantly reduces the number of homicides. The police chiefs rated the death penalty last among seven effective ways of reducing violent crime. Only 1 percent of the chiefs selected "expand death penalty." By contrast, 31 percent of the chiefs chose "reducing drug abuse," 17 percent selected "better economy, jobs," 16 percent opted for "simplifying court rules," 15 percent preferred "longer prison sentences," 10 percent wanted "more police officers," and 3 percent chose "reducing guns."[77] A 2008 poll of 500 randomly selected police chiefs in the United States found results similar to those in the 1995 poll.[78] Only 37 percent of the chiefs believed the death penalty significantly reduces homicides. Only 24 percent of the chiefs believed that murderers consider the range of punishments before committing their crimes. When asked to name one area as the most important for reducing violent crime, the chiefs ranked the death penalty last; only 1 percent of the chiefs named the death penalty. Ranking much higher were increasing the number of police officers, reducing drug abuse, and creating a better economy and more jobs. Chiefs considered the death penalty the least efficient use of taxpayers' money.

The third counterargument, which simply generalizes the second, is that "[t]here is an inherent logic in the deterrent power of the threat of death."[79] This logic, moreover, is frequently supported by anecdotal evidence. For example, in the mid-1990s, California Senator Dianne Feinstein said the following about a woman convicted of first-degree armed robbery in the 1960s:

> … I saw that she carried a weapon that was unloaded into a grocery store robbery. I asked her the question: "Why was the gun unloaded?" She said to me: "So I would not panic, kill somebody, and get the death penalty." That was firsthand testimony directly to me that the death penalty in place in California in the sixties was in fact a deterrent.[80]

During a bank robbery in New York in the 1970s, one of the robbers reportedly told FBI agents:

> I'll shoot everyone in the bank. The Supreme Court will let me get away with this. There's no death penalty. It's ridiculous. I can shoot everyone here, then throw my gun down and walk out and they can't put me in the electric chair. You have to have a death penalty, otherwise this can happen everyday.[81]

While the death penalty was suspended during the 1970s because of the *Furman* decision, a couple in Kansas were held as hostages during a bank robbery. Rather than leave them alive as potential witnesses, the robbers decided to kill them. The wife escaped and the husband survived after being shot in the head twice. Later, they commented, "Thank God that we lived so that we can tell you that capital punishment does make a difference."[82] During a debate in the mid-1990s, Harvard law professor Alan Dershowitz, a death penalty opponent, conceded, "Of course, the death penalty deters some crimes. That's why you have to pay more for a hitman in a death penalty state, than a non-death penalty state."[83] Contradicting the argument made previously about prison murders, five federal prison officials were murdered during the 1980s when the federal death penalty was suspended. Inmates already serving a life sentence for murder committed three of the prison killings. Norman Carlson, former director of the U.S. Bureau of Prisons, remarked:

> … in the case of someone serving a nonrevokable life sentence, execution is the only sanction which could possibly serve as a deterrent…. We must impose the death penalty on prisoners sentenced to life who murder guards or other inmates in order to bring some semblance of security to our Federal prison system.[84]

On the other hand, ample anecdotal evidence also points to the death penalty's impotence in deterring crime. For example, English history reveals that pickpockets plied their trade at public hangings even though detection meant they, too, probably would be hanged.[85] Also, as noted in Chapter 1, horse stealing in Virginia during the late eighteenth and early nineteenth centuries was a capital offense and the most frequently committed crime in the state.

Still, even without evidence, the deterrent power of capital punishment makes intuitive sense. Defense attorney Anthony Amsterdam agrees that "the real mainstay of the deterrence thesis … is not evidence but intuition" but argues that the intuitive belief is misguided:

> You and I ask ourselves: Are we not afraid to die? Of course! Would the threat of death then not intimidate us to forbear from a criminal act? Certainly! Therefore, capital punishment must be a deterrent. The trouble with this intuition is that the people who are doing the reasoning and the people who are doing the murdering are not the same people. You and I do not commit murder for a lot of reasons other than the death penalty.[86]

In addition, there are intuitive reasons for believing that capital punishment provokes violence and other calamities; it has a "brutalizing effect." For example, if persons are to be dissuaded from killing by fear of capital punishment, then why have executions been banned from public view since the late 1930s? Why are executions not televised? The first chapter noted that executions were hidden from public view to avoid the rowdiness and violence that frequently accompanied them; the same is said of televised executions.[87] Similarly, if capital punishment is an effective deterrent, then why are prison inmates not allowed to view executions? Until recently, executions were almost always scheduled for late at night when most inmates were asleep. The reason? To avoid violent reactions.[88] Bowers remarks, "Our experience is that those who should benefit most react instead with anger, resentment, and hostility, if not overt violence, to the 'lesson' of an execution."[89] With the advent of lethal injection, those sorts of inmate reactions are apparently rare.

The fourth counterargument—that because the homicide rate increased as the number of executions decreased from the mid-1960s through the 1970s, there must be a general deterrent effect—is also suspect. It underscores the need for rigorous scientific inquiry into conclusions based on common sense. Amsterdam states the problem with the counterargument succinctly:

This is ridiculous [as evidence for general deterrence] when you consider that crime as a whole has increased during this period; that homicide rates have increased about half as much as the rates for all other FBI Index crimes; and that whatever factors are affecting the rise of most noncapital crimes (which cannot include cessation of executions) almost certainly affect the homicide-rate rise also (emphasis in original).[90]

Bowers further notes, "[C]ompared with yearly changes in the national homicide rate from 1962 on, states with reduced executions tended to have reduced homicide rates and those with increased executions tended to have increased homicide rates."[91] Law professor and now U.S. District Court Judge Paul Cassell counters that states with increased homicide rates have greater numbers of executions simply because they need them more (for deterrence?) than states with much lower homicide rates.[92] Furthermore, when comparing 1966 and 1999 state murder rates—2 years when nationwide murder rates were about the same—Cassell reports that states that aggressively employed the death penalty during that period generally saw their murder rates decline, while states not using the death penalty generally saw their murder rates increase.[93]

The fifth and related counterargument is that the death penalty's deterrent effect has been reduced to nothing in recent years (and thus does not show up in the research) because it has not been imposed often or quickly enough to have the desired effect. In California, for example, only 10 of the 717 defendants (1.4%) sentenced to death between 1977 and 2004 have been executed. By contrast, 13 death row inmates committed suicide during this period.[94] Such critics claim that a return to the "good old days" of more frequent and swifter executions would produce deterrence.[95] Evidence from the good old days, however, belies this hope.

During the 1930s, for example, there were a total of 1,676 executions in the United States.[96] This represents 167 executions per year, 14 executions per month, and the most executions in any single decade of the twentieth century. The most executions in any single year since 1930, the first year records were kept by the U.S. government, were the 199 recorded in 1935.[97] Furthermore, although data on the celerity of executions are not available for this period, data on celerity for 1951–1960 show that the average time between death sentence and execution was 14.4 months (the range was from 4.6 to 46.1 months); the average for 2009 was 169 months.[98] If capital punishment had a deterrent effect, and the frequency and celerity of executions were important, then one might expect a relatively low murder rate for the decade. The evidence shows, though, that homicide rates were higher in the 1930s than in the 1940s, 1950s, and early to mid-1960s—decades that had fewer executions.[99] Historical evidence provides no reason to believe that increasing the frequency and celerity of executions would dramatically increase the death penalty's deterrent effect.[100]

ASSUMPTIONS AND PROBLEMS WITH DETERRENCE THEORY

According to Bowers, "Deterrence theory assumes that potential offenders exercise rational judgment in deciding whether to kill and that they are predictably sensitive to the actual range of variation in certainty and severity of legal punishment for murder at the time of the decision to act."[101] Additional assumptions of deterrence theory are that potential killers "know what constitutes a capital murder," "that they view death as less acceptable than the other punishments imposed for capital murder," and "that the deterrence message is not neutralized by other confounding or contrary messages conveyed by capital punishment."[102] "From what we know about murder," Bowers surmises, "there is reason to doubt these assumptions."[103] Nevertheless, studies based on economic models of crime, such as the aforementioned study by Ehrlich (1975), rest on some of these dubious assumptions.

Most murderers, especially capital murderers, probably do not rationally calculate the consequences of their actions before they engage in them. Many murderers who end up on death row killed someone during the course of an armed robbery. Many never intended to kill but did so because of unexpected circumstances. Any who may have calculated the consequences of their actions before engaging in their crimes probably did not consider that the punishment might be death. And even if would-be killers knew that execution was the possible penalty for their actions, it likely would not deter them anyway. As Bowers notes, "Police statistics reported to the Federal Bureau of Investigation and execution records from the National Bureau of Prisons indicate that only a small fraction of criminal homicides have resulted in executions—no more than two percent per year since 1930."[104] The chance of being executed for criminal homicide is very remote.

A problem is that the objects of deterrence theory—rational human beings—frequently do not calculate the consequences of their actions. The point is moot, however, because most people, whether they calculate consequence or not, do not kill. Without dismissing the tragedy of even a single murder victim, according to data from the FBI, in recent years there have been only about 16,000 murders and nonnegligent manslaughters committed annually in the United States. Precise figures are not available, but it is estimated that only 10–25 percent of them, or about 1,600–4,000, are capital crimes and thus death eligible.[105] In a well-armed country of more than 300 million people, one might expect many more murders. The point is that most people do not kill, and the reasons they do not kill generally do not include fear of the death penalty.

Those killers who do take into account the possible consequences of their actions commit crimes that usually are impossible for the police to detect.[106] When they are caught, the chances of their being convicted are small and their chances of being executed even less.[107] As noted earlier, 75–90 percent of all killers are not eligible for the death penalty. Consider the prototypical rational killer, the professional "hit person," who would be the most likely candidate for execution. According to a study by Sarah Dike, "during 1919–1968, there were 1,004 gangland murders in Chicago, 23 convictions, 4 sentences to life imprisonment, and no death sentences imposed."[108]

What about the killer who has already committed enough murders to guarantee the death penalty? Such an individual may rationally calculate that killing more people makes no difference in terms of consequences because no greater penalty can be imposed. He or she thus has an incentive to kill others to avoid capture.[109]

In some cases, the killer may know the consequences of his or her actions but not care about them or may even seek the death penalty. Cotton poses the following provocative questions:

> But what if the murderer has already lived a life that is worse than the worst punishment our laws employ? What if the so-called capital punishment of the society would actually serve as a relief from circumstances that have, to that point, been unbearable? Is there any deterrent value in those punishments at all for such people? Does it make sense to blame the murderer for his actions in such a way as to reward him with a penalty that actually alleviates the pain of his existence?[110]

Critics of the death penalty point out that even if the penalty deterred some would-be killers, it does not logically follow, nor does available evidence support, that capital punishment is a more effective deterrent to capital crimes than is an alternative, noncapital punishment.[111]

THE COUNTERDETERRENT OR BRUTALIZING EFFECT

Most of the replications of Ehrlich's research not only show no deterrent effect for the death penalty, but many of them actually found a counterdeterrent or brutalizing effect. In other words, the death penalty may actually cause murders rather than deter them! The idea that executions can provoke murders is an old one,[112] and for years, psychiatrists have provided anecdotal evidence of such an effect. One variant of this phenomenon is called the "suicide–murder syndrome," which is illustrated by the case of Pamela Watkins. Watkins was "a babysitter in San Jose who had made several unsuccessful suicide attempts and was frightened to try again. She finally strangled two children so that the state of California would execute her."[113] Another example was Leslie B. Gireth, a 37-year-old businessman from southern California. Not long after he hired Dorena Hammer, they began a love affair. Unfortunately for the couple, Gireth's wife found out about the affair and tried to break it up, but to no avail. When Gireth asked his wife for a divorce so he could marry Dorena, his wife refused. Gireth became depressed and began to neglect his business and his family. Finally, Gireth and Dorena agreed to a suicide pact. They went to dinner and then to a motel where Gireth fired two bullets through Dorena's heart. However, he could not kill himself. He telephoned the police who came and arrested him. Gireth refused a lawyer, pleaded guilty to first-degree murder, and requested the death penalty. His request was granted, and he eagerly went to his death knowing that he soon would be reacquainted with Dorena.[114] A third example is the case of Daniel Colwell, who, in October 1998, was sentenced to die in Georgia's electric chair. Colwell confessed that, unable to kill himself, he shot two strangers (Mitchell and Judith Bell) in a parking lot so that the state would help him commit suicide. Diagnosed as a paranoid schizophrenic, Colwell had been released from a mental health program just 2 days before he committed the 1996 murders.[115] A fourth example of the phenomenon is the case of John Blackwelder, who was executed in Florida on May 26, 2004. Blackwelder stated that he killed a fellow inmate so that he would get the death penalty because he couldn't stand the idea of spending the rest of his life in prison, and he could not commit suicide. Blackwelder was serving an LWOP sentence for a series of sex convictions. He was diagnosed as a pedophile who had impulse control disorder and antisocial personality disorder.[116] Gary Gilmore was probably a fifth example of this syndrome.

Another variant of the counterdeterrent or brutalizing effect has been termed the "executioner syndrome."[117] Those afflicted with the problem believe their killing performs a public service by eliminating a problem. Still another variant stems from the pathological desire to die by execution.[118] Finally, from what is known about capital murderers, it is likely that some of them kill to gain the attention and notoriety that being executed might bring: Their executions provide them a stage that would not be available to them under different circumstances. This certainly seems to be true about serial killer Danny Rolling, who was sentenced to die in 1994 for five murders, three rapes, and three burglaries in what became known as the "Gainesville [Florida] Student Murders." Rolling confessed he wanted to be a criminal "superstar" and the "world's greatest rapist."[119]

Among those who believe most strongly in the death penalty's counterdeterrent or brutalizing effect are William J. Bowers and Glenn L. Pierce. They attempted to replicate Ehrlich's research, and discovered that Ehrlich's finding of a deterrent effect for the death penalty appeared only "if the period of analysis is extended beyond 1965 to include years when executions had dwindled to one or two or had actually ceased, and only if logarithmic values of the variables are used, giving disproportionate weight to these recent years in the regression analysis."[120] When the analysis is limited to the period 1935–1963, however, a period when executions actually took place, their research revealed:

- that execution risk tends to make a positive contribution to the homicide rate as measured by the FBI ... and by the Census Bureau ...
- that the number of executions imposed (a better index of possible brutalizing effects) makes a stronger and more consistent positive contribution to the FBI homicide rate ... ; and
- that the evident brutalizing effects become even stronger and more statistically significant with the more reliable census measure of willful homicide.[121]

Later, in an analysis of the 692 executions and all of the homicides in New York state between 1906 and 1963, Bowers and Pierce found that each execution "adds roughly three more to the number of homicides in the next nine months of the year after the execution."[122]

Bowers provides the following explanation for his findings:

> The lesson of the execution ... may be to devalue life by the example of human sacrifice. Executions demonstrate that it is correct and appropriate to kill those who have gravely offended us. The fact that such killings are to be performed only by duly appointed officials on duly convicted offenders is a detail that may get obscured by the message that such offenders deserve to die. If the typical murderer is someone who feels that he has been betrayed, dishonored, or disgraced by another person—and we suggest that such feelings are far more characteristic of those who commit murder than is a rational evaluation of costs and benefits—then it is not hard to imagine that the example executions provide may inspire a potential murderer to kill the person who has greatly offended him. In effect, the message of the execution may be lethal vengeance, not deterrence.[123]

Bowers maintains that the brutalization effect requires a different type of identification process than does the deterrent effect. If executions are to achieve deterrence, would-be killers must identify with criminals who are executed. If they do not, deterrence cannot work. If executions brutalize, on the other hand, would-be killers must identify their victims with executed criminals and themselves with state-sanctioned executioners. Bowers describes the process:

> The potential murderer will not identify personally with the criminal who is executed, but will instead identify someone who has greatly offended him—someone he hates, fears, or both—with the executed criminal. We might call this the psychology of "villain identification." By associating the person who has wronged him with the victim of an execution, he sees that death is what his despised offender deserves. Indeed, he himself may identify with the state as executioner and thus justify and reinforce his desire for lethal vengeance.[124]

Bowers adds that capital punishment may provoke homicides in other ways, such as through the psychology of suggestion or imitation.[125] To this, Van den Haag counters, "It is possible that all displays of violence, criminal or punitive, influence people to engage in unlawful imitations. This seems one good reason not to have public executions. But it does not argue against executions."[126] Van den Haag seems to be implying that only the viewing of executions is suggestive, but knowledge of them is not. For Van den Haag, media representations of executions must be inconsequential, yet there is considerable evidence that the media influences many types of behavior, including criminal behavior.[127] Consequently, if displays of or knowledge of violence do influence people to engage in unlawful imitations, as Van den Haag concedes in part, then it seems reasonable to conclude that executions, as a form of violence, could provoke some people to commit violent acts. If Van den Haag is correct, then the imitation of violence may help account for the relatively high violent crime rate in the United States.

MURDER VERSUS CAPITAL PUNISHMENT

Beyond the imitation of violence, some people equate capital punishment with murder. Beccaria wrote, "It seems to me absurd that the laws, which are an expression of the public will, which detest and punish homicide, should themselves commit it, and that to deter citizens from murder, they order a public one."[128] Van den Haag's reply is that capital punishment is not murder:

> Legally imposed punishments ... although often physically identical to the crimes punished, are not crimes or their moral equivalent. The difference between crimes and lawful acts is not physical, but legal ... . [Finally,] whether a lawful punishment gives an "example of barbarity" depends on how the moral difference between crime and punishment is perceived. To suggest that its physical quality, ipso facto, morally disqualifies the punishment, is to assume what is to be shown.[129]

On the other hand, Amsterdam writes that "the advocates of capital punishment can and do accentuate their arguments with descriptions of the awful physical details of such hideous murders as that of poor Sharon Tate," who was brutally killed by members of the infamous Manson family.[130] He argues that there are two main problems with justifying capital punishment by citing the heinousness of murders:

> First, the murders being described are not murders that are being done by us, or in our name, or with our approval; and our power to stop them is exceedingly limited even under the most exaggerated suppositions of deterrence.... Every execution, on the other hand, is done by our paid servants, in our collective name, and we can stop them all. Please do not be bamboozled into thinking that people who are against executions are in favor of murders. If we had the individual or the collective power to stop murders, we would stop them all—and for the same basic reason that we want to stop executions. Murders and executions are both ugly, vicious things, because they destroy the same sacred and mysterious gift of life which we do not understand and can never restore. Second, please remember therefore that descriptions of murders are relevant to the subject of capital punishment only on the theory that two wrongs make a right, or that killing murderers can assuage their victims' sufferings or bring them back to life, or that capital punishment is the best deterrent to murder. The first two propositions are absurd, and [for the third] the evidence is overwhelmingly against it.[131]

Albert Camus, the French philosopher, once wrote that an execution

> ... is not simply death. It is just as different ... from the privation of life as a concentration camp is from prison.... It adds to death a rule, a public premeditation known to the future victim, an organization ... which is itself a source of moral sufferings more terrible than death ... . [Capital punishment] is ... the most premeditated of murders, to which no criminal's deed,

however calculated … can be compared…. For there to be an equivalency, the death penalty would have to punish a criminal who had warned his victim of the date at which he would inflict a horrible death on him and who, from that moment onward, had confined him at his mercy for months. Such a monster is not encountered in private life.[132]

Whether or not capital punishment is the same as murder, or—as Amsterdam and Camus argue— worse, is an ethical issue that likely defies a definitive answer. Yet, it seems a critical issue to resolve because how one stands on the issue probably determines, to a large extent, one's position on capital punishment in general.

CONCLUSION

In 2000, during the third presidential debate between Republican George W. Bush and Democrat Al Gore, the debate's moderator, Jim Lehrer, asked both candidates whether they believed the death penalty was a deterrent. Bush replied that he thought it was and added that it was the only reason to support the death penalty. Gore did not disagree with him.[133] Apparently, both candidates were unaware of the more than a half century of research and dozens of studies investigating the intuitively appealing belief in the death penalty's deterrent effect. Had they been, they would have known that, with the exception of a handful of thoroughly discredited older analyses and the newer studies that have also been criticized for various problems, no evidence existed of the hypothesized effect. They also may have known about evidence of a counterdeterrent or brutalizing effect. Still, in fairness to both men, perhaps capital punishment both deters and brutalizes, producing the absence of a discernible deterrent effect by canceling each other out. In the final analysis, none of this may matter if results of a recent opinion poll are to be believed: Less than one third of death penalty proponents polled selected deterrence as the most important (9.7%) or second most important (21.4%) reason for their position.

The irony is that although capital punishment has virtually no effect on crime, capital or otherwise, it continues to be a favored political "silver bullet"—a simplistic solution to the crime problem used by aspiring politicians and some law enforcement officials.[134] A problem is that, as long as politicians and law enforcement officials can gain political currency by perpetuating the belief in the death penalty's deterrent effect, attention will be diverted from more constructive and (it is hoped) more effective approaches to the prevention and control of violent behavior.[135] This may be yet another way that capital punishment contributes to an increase in violent crime rather than the expected decrease.

DISCUSSION QUESTIONS

1. Is the death penalty a greater general deterrent to capital crime than an alternative noncapital punishment such as LWOP?
2. Is the death penalty a general deterrent to noncapital crimes?
3. Regarding the first two questions, does it matter?
4. Is the death penalty the most severe penalty?
5. Does the death penalty provide an added measure of protection for police officers?

6. Does the death penalty provide an added measure of protection for correctional officers?
7. Why have executions been banned from public view since the late 1930s?
8. Why are executions not televised?
9. Why are prison inmates not allowed to view executions?
10. In what ways, if any, could the general deterrent power of capital punishment be increased?
11. Does the death penalty have a counterdeterrent or "brutalizing" effect? (Does the death penalty cause capital crimes?)
12. Is capital punishment murder?

Notes

1. Available evidence indicates that capital punishment does not deter noncapital felonies, specifically, murder and nonnegligent manslaughter, rape, assault, robbery, burglary, grand larceny, or vehicle theft; see Bailey (1991).
2. Ellsworth and Ross (1983, p. 121, n. 15).
3. See, for example, Bohm, Clark, and Aveni (1991), Gallup Report (1985), and Kohlberg and Elfenbein (1975).
4. Ellsworth and Ross (1983, p. 149).
5. Rasmussen telephone poll conducted from June 2–3, 2010. Retrieved November 29, 2010, from http://www.deathpenaltyinfo.org/national-polls-and-studies#rasjune.
6. Sharp (2008).
7. Van den Haag (1982, p. 326).
8. Ibid., p. 327.
9. Ibid.
10. O.J. Simpson's criminal trial jury was accused of jury nullification when they acquitted him.
11. Beccaria (1975, pp. 48–49).
12. Snell (2010a, Table 12).
13. Beccaria (1975, p. 45).
14. Ibid., p. 50.
15. See, for example, Glaser (1979), Conrad in Van den Haag and Conrad (1983, pp. 133–134), Paternoster (1991, chap. 7), Peterson and Bailey (2003), Waldo (1981), and Zimring and Hawkins (1986, Appendix).
16. Specifically, statistical significance refers to the unlikelihood that relationships observed in a sample, that is, a subset of a larger group, can be attributed to sampling error alone. Sampling error refers to the difference between the measure of a population (the larger group) and the measure of a sample (the subset of the larger group).
17. See Paternoster (1991, chap. 7), Peterson and Bailey (2003), Zeisel (1982), and Zimring and Hawkins (1986, Appendix).
18. Sellin (1967, pp. 135–138). Sellin also conducted a year-by-year comparative analysis of contiguous states from 1920 to 1955; see Sellin (1959).
19. Also see Bye (1919), Reckless (1969), Schuessler (1952), Sutherland (1925), and Vold (1932, 1952). For examples of a similar type of analysis using data for the 1973–1984 and 1980–1995 periods, see Peterson and Bailey (1988, 2003). Other recent examples using this methodology are Cheatwood (1993) and Harries and Cheatwood (1997), who examined comparable counties, and the Death Penalty Information Center, http://www.deathpenaltyinfo.org/facts-about-deterrence-and-death-penalty. These studies found no deterrent effect for capital punishment either.

20. Sellin (1959; 1967, pp. 138–154).
21. Sellin (1967, p. 138).
22. Sellin (1959, p. 55; 1967, p. 146).
23. Sellin (1967, pp. 152–153). For multivariate analyses that found the same nondeterrent results, see Bailey and Peterson (1987, 1994).
24. Sellin (1967, pp. 154–160).
25. Wolfson (1982, pp. 159–173).
26. Based on the results of a 1950 survey by the International Penal and Penitentiary Commission, Sellin (1959, p. 70) also notes that "countries without the death penalty reported no more serious disciplinary problems [in prisons] than the countries which had retained the penalty."
27. See, for example, Baldus and Cole (1975).
28. See Bedau (1982, p. 123, Table 4–2–2).
29. See, for example, Bailey (1998), Bye (1919), Cochran, Chamlin, and Seth (1994), Reckless (1969), Schuessler (1952), and Sellin (1959).
30. Archer Gartner, and Beittel (1983); also see Sellin (1959, pp. 38–50) for cross-national comparisons.
31. See, for example, Bailey (1990), King (1978), Peterson and Bailey (1991), Sellin (1959), and Thompson (1999).
32. See, for example, Dann (1935), McFarland (1983), Phillips (1980), Savitz (1958), and Stack (1987). Both Dann (1935) and Savitz (1958) overlooked seasonal variations in homicides; see Bowers (1988, p. 66). For a detailed critique of Phillips (1980), see Bowers (1988, pp. 72–79). McFarland (1983) attributed the short-term decline in homicides following Gary Gilmore's execution in Utah, which was confined to only certain parts of the United States, to the abnormally severe winter conditions in those parts of the country. Bailey and Peterson (1989) replicated Stack's research, correcting some of Stack's coding errors, and failed to find a statistically significant relationship between execution publicity and homicide rates.
33. See Bowers (1988).
34. See Ehrlich (1975).
35. Ibid., p. 414.
36. Zimring and Hawkins (1986, p. 175).
37. Bowers (1984, p. 281, n. 13).
38. Haney and Logan (1994, pp. 87–90) and Peterson and Bailey (2003). Some of the Supreme Court justices apparently are ignoring the bulk of the evidence showing that capital punishment has no marginal deterrent effect, see Haney and Logan (1994, p. 89), and the review of studies below.
39. Wolpin (1978) reported that each execution may deter four murders; Layson (1985), about 18; Ehrlich (1977), 20–24; Yunker (1976), 156; and Cloninger (1977), 560.
40. See, for example, Andersen (1983, p. 35), Barnett (1981), Beyleveld (1982), Bowers (1984, pp. 280–282, 332–333; 1988), Bowers and Pierce (1975), Forst (1977), Friedman (1979), Klein, Forst, and Filatov (1982), Passell and Taylor (1977), Paternoster (1991, chap. 7), Peterson and Bailey (2003), Waldo (1981), Zeisel (1982), and Zimring and Hawkins (1986, pp. 175–181). For Ehrlich's reply to Beyleveld's critique, see Ehrlich (1982).
41. See Zimring and Hawkins (1986, pp. 179–181).
42. Klein, Forst, and Filatov (1982).
43. Ibid., p. 158.
44. Cited in Zimring and Hawkins (1986, p. 180).
45. Ibid.
46. See Brumm and Cloninger (1996), Cloninger and Marchesini (2001), Dezhbakhsh, Rubin, and Shepherd (2003), Ehrlich and Liu (1999), Liu (2004), Mocan and Gittings (2001, 2003), Shepherd (2004, 2005), Yunker (2002), and Zimmerman (2004, 2006, 2009). Mocan and Shepherd claim to be death penalty opponents; see Liptak (2007).

47. Mocan and Gittings (2001, 2003).
48. Cited in Donohue and Wolfers (2005, p. 793, n. 11).
49. Ibid.
50. Yang and Lester (2008).
51. Ibid.
52. See Berk (2005), Cohen-Cole, Durlauf, Fagan, and Nagin (2009), Donohue and Wolfers (2005, 2009), Fagan (2005, 2006), Fagan, Zimring, and Geller (2006), Hjalmarsson (2009), Kovandzic, Vieraitis, and Boots (2009), and Zimring (2008).
53. Shepherd (2005).
54. Fagan (2005).
55. The study was by Dezhbakhsh et al. (2003) and the criticism by Turow (2003, p. 60).
56. Fagan (2005).
57. Ibid.
58. Ibid.
59. Ibid.
60. Ibid.; Berk (2005); also see Shepherd (2005).
61. California Department of Corrections and Rehabilitation, Fourth Quarter 2008 Facts and Figures; Death Row, USA (2009).
62. Fagan (2005).
63. Donohue and Wolfers (2005, p. 843).
64. Land, Teske, and Zheng (2009).
65. Zimring, Fagan, and Johnson (2009).
66. Land et al. (2009, p. 1038).
67. Zimring et al. (2009).
68. Committee on the Judiciary, U.S. Senate (1982, p. 312).
69. See, for example, King (1982), who recognizes that other factors were also involved.
70. Committee on the Judiciary, U.S. Senate (1982).
71. Ibid.
72. Bowers (1984, p. 190); also see Zimring and Hawkins (1986, Appendix).
73. Petersilia (1990, p. 1).
74. Radelet and Akers (1996). In 1975, the Massachusetts Supreme Judicial Court reviewed the deterrence literature, including Ehrlich's study, and concluded that "there is simply no convincing evidence that the death penalty is a deterrent superior to lesser punishments" (*Commonwealth v. O'Neal*, 339 N.E. 2d 676, 1975 at 252).
75. Committee on the Judiciary, U.S. Senate (1982).
76. Ibid. Another group that should have some expertise on the deterrent value of capital punishment is prison inmates. Professors Wilcox and Steele (2003, p. 475) found that only about 25 percent of the prison inmates they surveyed believed that the death penalty was a deterrent. Nearly 80 percent of the inmates who had committed more than three violent crimes did not believe the death penalty deterred violent crime (also see Steele and Wilcox, 2003).
77. Cited in the Death Penalty Information Center. Law enforcement and the death penalty. Retrieved December 17, 2010, from http://www.deathpenaltyinfo.org/law-enforcement-views-deterrence.
78. Dieter (2009b).
79. Committee on the Judiciary, U.S. Senate (1982).
80. Cassell (2004, p. 190).
81. Ibid., p. 191.
82. Ibid.

83. Ibid.
84. Ibid., p. 192.
85. Lawes (1969, p. 13).
86. Amsterdam (1982, p. 357).
87. Bowers (1988, p. 49). For a thoughtful discussion about televising executions, see Leighton (1999); also see Sarat (2002, pp. 187–208).
88. Bowers (1988).
89. Ibid.
90. Amsterdam (1982, p. 356); also see Bowers (1984, p. 333). A similar argument could be made about the observation that Harris County, Texas, sentences to death more capital defendants than 36 of the then-38 death penalty states and, as a result, its murder rate has fallen more than 70 percent in the past 20 years; see Marquis (2004, p. 126).
91. Bowers (1984); for a cross-national perspective, see Archer et al. (1983); also see Death Penalty Information Center.
92. Cassell (2004, p. 192).
93. Ibid., pp. 192–194.
94. Sundby (2005, p. 38).
95. Cited in Peterson and Bailey (2003).
96. See Schneider and Smykla (1991, p. 6, Table 1.1) and Zimring and Hawkins (1986, p. 30, Table 2.2).
97. Bedau (1982, p. 25, Table 1–3).
98. Peterson and Bailey (2003, p. 177) and Snell (2010a).
99. See Zahn (1989, p. 219, Figure 10.1).
100. However, Peterson and Bailey warn that "because the celerity question has received so little attention, we are not able to conclude, 'with confidence,' that prompt executions are/are not effective in preventing murder"; see Peterson and Bailey (2003, p. 274).
101. Bowers (1984, p. 272).
102. Bowers (1988, p. 50). Peterson and Bailey write that "deterrence theory rests upon the premise that individuals weigh the costs and rewards associated with alternative sanctions, and choose behaviors that yield the greatest gain at the least cost. Thus, crime occurs when illegal actions are perceived either as more profitable (rewarding) or less costly (painful) than conventional alternatives... . [M]urder is discouraged because the threat of one's own death presumably outweighs the rewards gained from killing another"; see Peterson and Bailey (2003, p. 252); also see Sellin (1959, p. 20).
103. Bowers (1984).
104. Ibid., pp. 272–273. Liebman, Fagan, and West (2000, p. 6) report that during the years 1973–1995 only 12 death sentences were imposed for every 1,000 homicides. Also, in a study conducted by researchers on behalf of the Commission on sentencing decisions in Illinois, it was found that during the study period (1988–1997) there were 5,310 cases in which an Illinois defendant was convicted of first-degree murder. Only 115 (about 2%) of these cases resulted in the imposition of a death sentence; see Governor's Commission on Capital Punishment (2002).
105. Andersen (1983, p. 32), Baldus, Woodworth, and Pulaski (1990, p. 22), and Fagan et al. (2006, p. 1811). Professors Paternoster and Brame (2003) found that 22 percent of the Maryland murders they reviewed were death eligible.
106. Van den Haag and Conrad (1983, p. 84).
107. As Henry Schwarzschild, former director of the American Civil Liberties Union Capital Punishment Project, observed: "the deterrent value [of capital punishment] (which very likely does not exist at all in any case) is reduced to invisibility by the overwhelming likelihood that one will not be caught, or not be prosecuted, or not be tried on a capital charge, or not be convicted, or not be sentenced to death, or have

the conviction or sentence reversed on appeal, or have one's sentence commuted," see Schwarzschild (1982, p. 366).

108. Cited in Van den Haag and Conrad (1983, p. 92).

109. Donohue and Wolfers (2005, p. 795, n. 19).

110. Cotton (2008, p. xii).

111. See, for example, Professor John Conrad: "Punishment certainly deters some potential offenders, but we must not rely on increasing severity to make a corresponding decrease in the number of crimes committed. If we cannot do more to reduce the economic and social causes of crime, we must increase the risks of apprehension by the police. With crime clearance rates as low as they are, it is idle to suppose that dramatic increases in the severity of punishment will seriously affect the incidence of any type of crime," see Van den Haag and Conrad (1983, p. 103).

112. See Bowers (1984, pp. 273–274; 1988, pp. 57–61) and Sellin (1959, pp. 65–69).

113. Amsterdam (1982, p. 357); also see Bedau (1982, p. 98) and Sellin (1959). Sellin remarks that such cases once must have been relatively frequent "because Denmark, by an ordinance of December 18, 1767, deliberately abandoned the death penalty in cases where 'melancholy and other dismal persons (committed murder) for the exclusive purpose of losing their lives'"; see Sellin, ibid., p. 67. In some cases, the motivation for such actions was religious, explains Sellin: "by murdering another person and thereby being sentenced to death, one might still attain salvation whereas if one were to take one's own life, one would be plunged into eternal damnation"; see Sellin, ibid.

114. Duffy (1962, pp. 166–174).

115. Georgia Killer Is Granted His Wish to Be Executed." (1998).

116. Word (2004a).

117. See Bedau (1982).

118. See Sellin (1959, p. 65).

119. Leusner (2006). For another example, see Cheever (2006, pp. 188–190).

120. Bowers (1984, p. 333).

121. Ibid.

122. Bowers and Pierce (1980, p. 481). Also see Bailey (1984a); Cochran et al. (1994), who found a brutalization effect for killings involving strangers; Cochran and Chamlin (2000); Shepherd (2005); and Thompson (1997). For a sophisticated analysis to find a brutalization effect involving different types of murders, see Bailey (1998).

123. Bowers (1984, p. 274).

124. Ibid.

125. Ibid., p. 275.

126. Van den Haag (1982, p. 328).

127. For a review of the literature on the subject, see Surette (1992, chap. 5).

128. Beccaria (1975, p. 50).

129. Van den Haag (1982, pp. 327–328).

130. Amsterdam (1982, p. 348).

131. Ibid., pp. 348–349.

132. Cited in Amsterdam (1982, pp. 347–348). By contrast, prisoners in Japan are informed of their execution only moments before they are hanged. They are given only enough time to clean their cells, write a final letter, and receive last rites. Relatives are informed of the execution only after the fact. They are given 24 hours to claim the body. French (2002).

133. Turow (2003, p. 57). At the end of 2005, President Bush remained convinced that the death penalty deters, see White House: Bush Thinks. (2005).

134. Philosopher Ernest Van den Haag claims that, beyond deterrence, capital punishment, or at least the threat of capital punishment, has some technical advantages that should not be overlooked: By threatening it, prosecutors may persuade accomplices to testify against murderers, or persuade the murderers themselves to plead guilty in exchange for a life sentence. Also, in a hostage situation police can promise the criminal that the prosecution will not ask for the death penalty if he releases his hostages. Without the death penalty the criminal can threaten to kill his victims, while police can only threaten incarceration. See Van den Haag (1998, p. 155).
135. Bowers (1984, p. 164).

Incapacitation and economic costs of capital punishment

CHAPTER 8

INCAPACITATION AND CAPITAL PUNISHMENT

Incapacitation refers to preventing convicted murderers (or other capital offenders) from killing (or committing other crimes) again by executing them. Though it is arguably the most defensible of all rationales in support of the death penalty, the Supreme Court considers it only a secondary consideration.[1] Furthermore, only 12.7 percent of recent supporters of capital punishment chose incapacitation—"To keep the offender from reoffending"—as the most important reason for their support; another 20.5 percent chose incapacitation as the second most important reason for their support. Incapacitation ranked well below retribution at more than 50 percent.[2]

ARE EXECUTIONS NECESSARY?

Death penalty opponents concede that capital punishment permanently removes a threat to society, but they question whether such a drastic measure is necessary. They argue that if an alternative penalty, such as LWOP, accomplishes the same purpose, it would be preferable because of the other costs associated with the death penalty (e.g., a possible brutalizing effect and execution of innocent persons).

A key question, then, is whether the death penalty is necessary to protect society from the possible future actions of those who have already committed capital crimes. For proponents of the penalty, the answer to the question is a resounding yes. They argue that "some criminals are incorrigibly anti-social and will remain potentially dangerous to society for the rest of their lives."[3] They add that "mere imprisonment offers these people the possibility of escape or, in some cases, release on parole through error or oversight."[4] And even if they are never released, prisoners still may pose a threat to the victims' survivors or others. For example, while imprisoned challenging his conviction and death sentence, the murderer of a woman's husband sent her a threatening letter telling her that if she did not stop speaking to the media about him he would "take care of her," and he knew people on the outside who would do it for him.[5] Although inmate correspondence is supposed to be censored, apparently sometimes it is not.

ESCAPES, ERRORS, OVERSIGHTS, AND OTHER MISTAKES

As for the possibility of escape, Marie Arrington, one of the two female *Furman*-commuted death row inmates, escaped from Florida's death row on March 1, 1969. The 34-year-old woman slid through a cell window and escaped in her pajamas. She was arrested almost 3 years later in New Orleans, where she was working as a cocktail waitress.[6] Six men escaped from Oklahoma's death row in 1972. All of them were caught and reincarcerated.[7] On July 28, 1980, four death row inmates disguised as corrections officers escaped from Georgia's maximum-security prison at Reidsville. Among them was Troy Leon Gregg, the appellant in *Gregg v. Georgia* (1976). Gregg and the other three inmates escaped by using a hacksaw to cut the bars on their fourth-floor cells and a window in an exercise area. They then walked along the ledge of the building and gained access to fire escapes. The escapees had altered their prison-issue blue pajamas to look like uniforms. On their way to the front gate, they were challenged by actual corrections officers but were allowed to continue on their way after saying they were making "security checks." Prison officials learned of the escape from a reporter for The *Albany Herald*, who Gregg had telephoned a couple hours later. Gregg told the reporter that they had to get out because they could not stand the inhuman conditions on death row anymore. He added that they would rather die than stay there another day. Three of the escapees were captured the next day in rural North Carolina. Gregg's body was found later that day in a lake a few miles away from where the other escapees were captured. Gregg had been beaten to death.[8] Another escape occurred on May 31, 1984. Six death row inmates, who had murdered a total of 17 people, took 13 prison personnel hostage, put on their corrections uniforms, and, using a fake bomb (actually a television set), bluffed their way out of Mecklenburg Correctional Center in Boydton, Virginia. All of the escapees—known collectively as the "Mecklenburg 6"—were recaptured without incident, the last of them after 19 days of freedom.[9] Death penalty proponents can also point to death row inmate Martin Gurule, who escaped from the Texas prison in Huntsville in November 1998. Gurule was the first Texas death row inmate to escape since 1934. Gurule and six other death row inmates cut through a fence surrounding an outdoor recreation yard and climbed to a rooftop. Prison officials did not notice that the men were missing because they had created dummies out of pillows and sheets that made them appear to be asleep in their bunks. A corrections officer noticed the men dropping from the rooftop about 12:20 a.m., immediately sounded an alarm, and fired as many as 20 rounds. When the shooting began, the six other inmates surrendered, but Gurule ran about 30 yards and scaled two 10-foot chain-link fences topped with rolled razor wire that rim the perimeter of the prison. Gurule was free for a week. His bloated corpse was found beneath a bridge about a mile from the prison. He probably drowned.[10] More recently, on November 3, 2005, convicted double murderer and death row inmate Charles Victor Thompson escaped from the Harris County Jail in Houston, Texas. He was awaiting return to death row after attending a resentencing hearing on October 28, where he was again sentenced to death. After meeting with an attorney in a jail visiting room, Thompson put on civilian clothes that authorities believe he wore during his hearing and somehow smuggled back to his cell. Thompson left the locked prisoner's booth in the visiting room and waved a fake ID badge as he passed at least four jail employees. Thompson was then let into the jail's visitor's lobby, from which he walked out the door and into the street. He was captured without incident outside of a liquor store 200 miles away in Shreveport, Louisiana, on November 6. He was drunk and talking on a pay phone.[11] Marie Arrington, the six Oklahoma death row inmates, Troy Gregg and the other three Georgia death row inmates, the "Mecklenburg 6," Gurule, and Thompson show that a few death row inmates have escaped.

As for release decisions made by parole-board members, it is ironic and perhaps somewhat hypo-critical that parole authorities are distrusted because of decision errors they have made.[12] A similar distrust is not generally voiced about prosecutors who decide whom to charge with capital crimes or with judges and juries who decide whether defendants charged with capital crimes are guilty and should be executed.

Mistakes made by any of these decision makers can cause and have caused the deaths of innocent people. Attorney Anthony Amsterdam asks the pertinent question and supplies a thoughtful answer:

> Are we really going to kill a human being because we do not trust other people—the people whom we have chosen to serve on our own parole boards—to make a proper judgment in … [a] case at some future time? We trust this same parole board to make far more numerous, difficult, and dangerous decisions: hardly a week passes when they do not consider the cases of armed robbers, for example, although armed robbers are much, much more likely statistically to commit future murders than any murderer is to repeat his crime. But if we really do distrust the public agencies of law—if we fear that they may make mistakes—then surely that is a powerful argument "against" capital punishment. Courts which hand out death sentences because they predict that a man will still be criminally dangerous 7 or 25 years in the future cannot conceivably make fewer mistakes than parole boards who release a prisoner after 7 or 25 years of close observation in prison have convinced them that he is reformed and no longer dangerous.[13]

As for mistakes made by courts in capital cases, remember that as a result of automatic appellate reviews, direct and discretionary appeals, collateral postconviction proceedings in state and federal courts, and occasional gubernatorial commutations, nearly 100 death row inmates have their sentences vacated each year.[14] From 1973 through 2009, 3,338 inmates were removed from death row, which represented 41 percent of the death sentences imposed during that period.[15]

WHY NOT EXECUTE ALL CAPITAL OFFENDERS?

To ensure that no convicted capital offender killed again, all convicted capital offenders would have to be executed. There are several problems with such a strategy. First, as will be described in detail in the next chapter, innocent people, wrongfully convicted of capital crimes, have been executed. If all convicted capital offenders were executed to prevent any one of them from killing again, it would be impossible to rectify the injustices done to the innocent people executed, their families and friends, and to a society that considered such acts immoral. At least 400 Americans were wrongly convicted of crimes punishable by death in the twentieth century, and 138 Americans have been released from death row in 26 states because of evidence of their innocence since 1973 (through November 30, 2010),[16] and all of them would have died if this strategy were implemented.

To prevent such miscarriages of justice and still retain the death penalty it is necessary to identify convicted capital offenders who are innocent and spare them from death. This is no easy task because nearly all convicted capital offenders claim they are innocent, even though only a small percentage of them really are. Generally, it is only after considerable effort that proof of innocence is ever discovered, and rarely is such effort expended on death row inmates. For those family members and friends who would like to try, the financial and psychological resources necessary for such an endeavor are often not available.

SELECTING THE VERY WORST

Some death penalty proponents argue that the chances of executing an innocent person could be greatly reduced if death eligibility were reserved for the "worst of the worst" among all those currently sentenced to die. The key issue, of course, is identifying the very worst. The Supreme Court has wrestled with this issue since it approved guided discretion statutes in 1976 and, as noted previously, has limited the death penalty almost entirely to people convicted of an aggravated murder. At the same time, the response of many state legislatures and Congress has been to expand death eligibility by increasing the number of aggravating factors or death-eligible crimes.

Suppose, nevertheless, that death eligibility was narrowed to reduce the chances of executing an innocent person. For what type of offender, or, specifically, what type of murderer should capital punishment be reserved? Law professor Robert Blecker has recently suggested a few ways to narrow death eligibility. His views are particularly interesting because they are based on the opinions of more than 100 imprisoned "street criminals," most of whom were murderers he interviewed in a Virginia prison from 1986 to 1999.[17]

From his interviews, Blecker, himself a qualified supporter of the death penalty, concludes that to narrow death eligibility, death penalty statutes need to be revised to eliminate the overly broad aggravating factor that has put more people on death row than any other: murder during the course of a robbery. He would substitute in its stead the following three aggravating factors: killing an unresisting victim, killing from a pecuniary motive, and killing to eliminate an innocent witness. He would also modify a standard mitigating factor that he and the inmates he interviewed consider too broad: killing under the influence of alcohol or any other drug. He argues that "mitigation should be limited to a drug that significantly diminished the killer's mental capacity and self-control [such as crack and PCP], and then only if the killer was not aware while sober of the drug's probable effect on him and did not get high to summon the courage to kill."

The Constitution Project recommends limiting the death penalty to five types of murder: (1) the murder of a police officer while engaged in official duties; (2) murder in a correctional facility; (3) multiple murders; (4) murder involving torture; and (5) murder affecting the judicial system, such as the murder of witnesses, jurors, judges, prosecutors, or investigators.[18]

Such revisions to current death penalty statutes likely would reduce the number of people sentenced to death and, in turn, the chances of executing an innocent person. However, there are no changes or revisions that would eliminate entirely the chances of executing an innocent person. Such a risk is inherent in the process.

LWOP AS AN ALTERNATIVE

An alternative to capital punishment, and one that eliminates entirely the possibility of executing an innocent person, is true LWOP. Ironically, neither death penalty opponents nor death penalty proponents are enthusiastic about LWOP. For many death penalty opponents, LWOP is the "lesser of two evils." It is endorsed only because it is a tolerable alternative to the death penalty.[19] Death penalty foe Henry Schwarzschild, former director of the American Civil Liberties Union Capital Punishment Project, described LWOP as "mindless," "humanly and economically wasteful," and "morally repellant in its very assumptions," and was willing to withhold his opposition to it only as "a reluctant gesture of legislative realism."[20] Opponents such as Joseph Ingle, a minister to death row inmates, believe that LWOP suffers from the same problem as the death penalty. Both penalties write off the offender as worthless and beyond redemption. Both penalties amount to human garbage disposal.[21] Hugo Bedau, another death penalty opponent who considers LWOP a politically expedient "trade-off," would substitute for both LWOP and the death penalty "life imprisonment without the probability of parole." He would allow persons convicted of capital crimes to be sentenced to no more than 10 years in prison before they became eligible for parole. He would also require them to work in prison industry and give half of their pay to a victim's family fund. Bedau maintains that the death penalty is unnecessary from a utilitarian perspective because there is no evidence that capital punishment has a marginal deterrent effect, and keeping most elderly offenders incarcerated is neither beneficial nor cost-effective.[22] Still, the availability of LWOP has reduced the number of death sentences sought and won. Prosecutors have used LWOP in plea negotiations as an inducement to get death-eligible defendants to plead guilty and avoid execution.[23]

For their part, proponents of capital punishment object to LWOP, claiming that "even if they [convicted capital offenders] are successfully imprisoned for life, prison itself is an environment presenting dangers to guards, inmates and others."[24] They argue that LWOP inmates, without the threat of the death penalty, would have nothing to lose if they killed in prison.

Available evidence suggests, however, that the threat posed by inmates serving life sentences is probably more imagined than real. Wardens and superintendents of correctional institutions in the United States have long held that "lifers are generally ... among the best behaved prisoners."[25] For example, Lewis Lawes, warden of Sing Sing Prison in New York from 1920 to 1941, commented, "During the past twenty years I have personally known a great many men who have been commuted from death to life imprisonment. There is a considerable group in Sing Sing today, and without exception they are quiet, dependable, trustworthy. Many are in places of responsibility and except for that one deed they are in every way fitted and worthy to be normal and useful members of society."[26] Amsterdam relates that "Warden Lawes of Sing Sing and Governor Wallace of Alabama, among others, regularly employed murder convicts as house servants because they were among the very safest of prisoners."[27] It is important to emphasize that this evidence may not apply to LWOP inmates because they have no hope of release (this is why Professor Sellin advises against LWOP sentences) nor to capital murderers—yet a 1996 study found that capital murderers sentenced to LWOP were no greater threat to other prisoners or correctional staff than death-sentenced inmates or other murderers sentenced to terms of imprisonment.[28]

The fact is that LWOP inmates do have something to lose if they kill or commit other infractions in prison. They have numerous privileges, which they could lose for violations. Among these privileges are visits from family and friends, access to mail and the telephone, being able to buy items from the commissary, being able to take educational and vocational classes, being able to participate in recreational activities, and so on. They also can be removed from the general prison population and placed in isolation cells. Correctional authorities attest to the effectiveness that the threat of lost privileges has in controlling LWOP inmates: "[E]xperience with LWOP inmates in the Alabama penal system has shown that they commit about one-half as many infractions as other inmates."[29] LWOP inmates behave in prison because it is the only life they have. They become "institutionalized to the routines and limits of prison life."[30]

Another reason to recommend LWOP as an alternative to the death penalty is that some death-sentenced inmates rehabilitate themselves while in prison and contribute to society. For example, San Quentin death row inmate and Crips street gang cofounder Stanley "Tookie" Williams was nominated for the 2001 Nobel Peace Prize. Williams, who was convicted in 1981 for killing four people, was nominated for his series of children's books and his international peace efforts. His latest book, *Life in Prison*, describes daily life behind bars in San Quentin. It is targeted at sixth-graders and intended to keep them out of street gangs. His Internet Project for Street Peace links at-risk California and South African youths through e-mail and chat rooms. The project allows these youths to share their experiences and transform their lives.[31] In 2005, Williams received a Presidential Call to Service Award from President Bush for his more than 4,000 hours of community service.[32] In December 2005, Williams was executed.

Death penalty opponents claim that historically only a small number of imprisoned capital offenders have killed other inmates and prison personnel. Inmates not sentenced to death, they contend, commit most prison killings. The available evidence suggests that such a contention is only partially true (depending on what offenses are considered capital and what is considered a small number).

For example, Sellin examined fatal and nonfatal prison assaults that occurred in 1965,[33] reporting that 603 victims were assaulted in the 37 jurisdictions that responded to his survey. Sixty-one of the assault victims died—eight staff members and 53 inmates. There were 59 killers, and 34 percent of them were serving time for capital offenses (11 for murder, six for robbery, one for assault, one for rape, and one for kidnapping). At the time, all the listed offenses were death eligible in at least some jurisdictions; today, only aggravated murder is. If the crimes that currently are not death eligible are excluded, the largest group of killers was inmates convicted of robbery, accounting for 32 percent of the total. The second largest group of killers, accounting for 27 percent of the total, was inmates convicted of murder (only 18% were convicted of capital murder). Therefore, even if convicted murderers do not account for the largest number of prison killings, at least in 1965 they did account for more than one in four of them (or about one in five if only capital murderers are included).

The problem with this knowledge, observes Sellin, is that it does not help in the prediction of which convicted murderers will kill in prison and which ones will not. Evidence shows that at least 90 percent of convicted capital offenders probably will not kill again. But to prevent all prison killings by convicted capital offenders, it would be necessary to execute all of them (before they could kill), even though that strategy would not have prevented nearly three out of every four of the prison killings in 1965.

The prediction problem has been addressed in a study of life-sentenced Texas capital murder defendants.[34] The study found that the likelihood of repeat murder by a life-sentenced Texas capital murder defendant was about 0.2 percent over a 40-year period. (Texas law at the time required capital murderers to serve at least 40 years of flat time before they become eligible for parole. Texas is now an LWOP state.) The likelihood of future assaultive behavior in general was approximately 16 percent. Six factors were significantly related to future violent behavior among the incarcerated murderers. Three of the factors were related to the circumstances of the offense and three factors were related to the characteristics of the offender. The offense factors were involvement in a robbery/burglary murder, the presence of multiple victims in the original offense, and a previously attempted murder or assault. The offender factors were prison gang membership, having served a prior prison term, and age at time of entering prison. The age factor was the most influential predictor of prison violence. The younger the inmate, the higher was the risk of violence.

Age was also the best predictor of male inmate misconduct among 145 LWOP-sentenced capital offenders who entered the Federal Bureau of Prisons from August 1991 through November 2005.[35] The inmates had served from 6 months to nearly 15 years; the average time served was 6.17 years. The researchers found that for each year older an inmate was at the time of his conviction, the likelihood of his committing a disruptive act decreased by 10 percent. Possession of a weapon and drug offenses were the most frequently committed offenses; none of the LWOP inmates killed another inmate; killed a member of the correctional staff; or participated in a riot, escape, or a hostage taking.[36] Although more than 70 percent of the LWOP inmates had been cited for at least one disciplinary infraction, of which about 20 percent were assaults and 9 percent were serious assaults, none of the assaults committed by the LWOP inmates resulted in life-threatening injuries. Also, none of the assaults was committed against a member of the correctional staff. The annual rate of serious or potentially violent offenses among the LWOP-sentenced capital offenders, in short, was not significantly different from the annual rate of other inmates serving time in high-security U.S. penitentiaries.

Similar results were found in a recent study of the 2003 disciplinary records of 51,527 inmates under custody of the Florida Department of Corrections.[37] Among them 9,586 were convicted of some degree of homicide. Note that in this study capital and noncapital homicide offenders were not differentiated. Nevertheless, the researchers found that inmates convicted of homicide did not have a higher rate of institutional violence compared with inmates convicted of other crimes. As in the previous study, the best predictor of prison violence was the age of the inmate. The researchers report that for each yearly increase in age, the number of violent acts an inmate is expected to commit decreases by more than 5 percent. This study also found that gang membership was important in predicting prison violence. Suspected or confirmed gang members were expected to commit 24 percent more violent acts in prison than were non–gang members. Prior prison incarceration was another important factor, increasing the likelihood of violent acts by 29 percent. Sentence length factored in as well. Inmates serving shorter sentences were more likely to commit a violent act, with each additional year of incarceration resulting in a decrease of nearly 1 percent in the number of violent acts. Time served had the opposite effect; that is, with each additional year of time served, the expected number of violent acts increased by nearly 1 percent.

A particularly interesting study examined the violent misconduct of 3,403 inmates confined at the Potosi Correctional Center (PCC) in Missouri between January 1991 and January 2002.[38] The study is interesting for two reasons. First, PCC is a maximum-security prison that houses only three types of inmates: those who have been sentenced to death ($N = 149$), those who have been sentenced to LWOP for first-degree murder ($N = 1,054$), and those who have been sentenced to a parole-eligible term ($N = 2,199$). Most of the inmates sentenced to a parole-eligible term were serving minimum sentences of 50 years. Second, the death-sentenced inmates were "mainstreamed" or fully integrated with the non–death-sentenced inmates in the general prison population. The researchers found that during the 11-year period of mainstreaming inmates, who otherwise would have been segregated on death row, none of the death-sentenced inmates killed or attempted to kill another inmate or staff member. Furthermore, the rates of major and minor assaults of death-sentenced inmates were no higher than the rates of LWOP inmates and were 20–25 percent lower than the rates of inmates serving parole-eligible terms. Findings of this study refute the idea that LWOP and death-sentenced inmates have "nothing to lose." They obviously respond favorably to the many incentives provided by the prison administration, such as preferable housing assignments (including the "honor dorm"), opportunities for interpersonal interactions, family contact, and meaningful activity. Mainstreaming death-sentenced inmates also provides substantial long-term savings. The researchers reported that the average daily cost of an inmate confined in the general prison population of the Texas Department of Criminal Justice (TDCJ) in 2002 was $40.71, while the cost of confining an inmate on the TDCJ death row, where inmates are housed in single cells in highly restrictive administrative segregation conditions, was $60.32. Thus, mainstreaming a Texas death-sentenced inmate would cost the state 50 percent less than confining that inmate on death row. Put differently, integrating death-sentenced Texas inmates in the general prison population would save the state more than $7,000 in additional expenses per death-sentenced inmate per year. In 2002, Texas had 448 death-sentenced inmates, so mainstreaming those death row inmates would have saved the state more than $3 million that year. By mainstreaming death row inmates, the psychologically debilitating conditions of death row confinement would be eliminated as well.

Another study examined the prison behavior of 39 former Indiana death row inmates who were transferred to the general prison population between 1972 and 1999 following modifications to their death sentences.[39] The average number of years served by the inmates was 16 years. During that period, 14 inmates (36%) were involved in 24 violent acts (3.8 per 100 inmates). Only seven of the violent acts caused serious injury. Six inmates committed them. There was one murder. About a quarter of the violent acts was committed on death row, and about 20 percent, including the murder, occurred in the general prison population. As was the case in the previously described Texas and Florida studies, the likelihood of prison violence decreased as the length of incarceration increased. Disciplinary records showed that more than 20 percent of the former death row inmates had no disciplinary write-ups following their transfer to the general prison population, and 60 percent had four or fewer disciplinary infractions. On the other hand, nearly 80 percent of the inmates had at least one disciplinary write-up while in the general prison population, and 40 percent had five or more disciplinary infractions. Not all former death row inmates make model prisoners.

Another problem with LWOP as an alternative to capital punishment is that it is unnecessary for most convicted capital offenders who will not kill again, even if they are released from prison. Based on the 1953 Report of the Royal Commission on Capital Punishment, Appendix 15, for foreign countries; a study of parolees from Pennsylvania from 1914 to 1952; and a study of parolees from California from 1945 to 1954, Sellin stated, "It is generally agreed that those who are allowed to return to the community after serving a term of years for a capital crime, behave themselves better than do other criminals similarly released."[40] He elsewhere noted, "The conclusion seems inescapable that the murderer who is not executed but instead sentenced to life imprisonment is not nearly so great a danger to the prison community, nor to the outside world when he is paroled or pardoned, as are many other classes of prisoners, who are regularly released after serving much shorter periods of imprisonment."[41]

Other data support Sellin's conclusion. For example, Bedau reports that of 2,646 murderers released in 12 states between 1900 and 1977, only 88 (approximately 3%) were reincarcerated after conviction for a subsequent felony and only 16 (approximately 0.6%) were reincarcerated after conviction for committing a subsequent criminal homicide.[42] He also used data from the National Council on Crime and Delinquency's Uniform Parole Reports to show that, between 1965 and 1975, 11,404 inmates originally convicted of "willful homicide" were released from prison nationwide. One year after release, only 170 (approximately 1.5%) were reincarcerated after conviction for the commission of a subsequent felony and only 34 (approximately 0.3%) after conviction for the commission of a subsequent criminal homicide.[43]

Admittedly, there are problems with these data. A problem with the figures from the National Council on Crime and Delinquency is that they only cover 1 year after release—certainly too short a time to draw any definitive conclusions about the future risks of released murderers (the amount of time on release in the first study cited above was not mentioned). A more recent study with a longer follow-up period discovered that 8 (4.9%) of 164 paroled Georgia murderers committed subsequent murders within 91 months of release.[44] A second problem is that the data include both capital and noncapital murderers. Without separating the two groups, it is impossible to know whether one group is a greater risk than the other of committing subsequent homicides. A third problem is that the data include only those recidivists who were caught and convicted. The actual number of released capital offenders who kill again, though probably very small, is unknown.

THE *FURMAN*-COMMUTED INMATES

The first and second problems just discussed can be meaningfully addressed, thanks to a natural experiment created by the Supreme Court in 1972. The *Furman* decision resulted in all death row inmates in the United States at that time receiving new sentences of life imprisonment, a term of years, or, in a few cases, new trials. Three hundred twenty-two of those 589 death row inmates have since been released from prison; the courts have exonerated seven of them.[45] They served, on average, 18 years and 3 months before being released on parole.[46] In June 1972, their average age was 31; in June 2005, their average age was 63.[47] By June 2005, at least 85 of the former death row inmates had died as free men.[48] More than half of the 322 released *Furman*-commuted death row inmates had successfully completed their paroles.[49] Of the former death row inmates not released from prison, approximately 94 died while being incarcerated; 10 committed suicide.[50] One hundred sixty-four of the inmates remain in prison and likely never will be paroled.[51] Thirty-two of these inmates killed police officers (37 of the paroled inmates killed police officers).[52] An examination of the *Furman*-commuted inmates' postrelease criminal behaviors can provide a relatively good measure of the risks posed by capital offenders who, but for the luck of *Furman*, might have been executed. Because each of the studies described below defines recidivism as reconviction or reincarceration, they share, with the previous data, the problem of not showing the proportion of subsequent killers who are not reconvicted or reincarcerated. Death penalty opponents assume the number is very small.

The most recent study of the 322 *Furman*-commuted death row inmates who had been released from prison found that, as of June 2005, 111 of them (34%) were reincarcerated either for a new crime or a parole violation.[53] Thirty-three of the 111 former inmates (30%) were "technical violators," whose offenses were so minor that they were either not returned to prison or were incarcerated for only a few months. The minor offenses included misdemeanor crimes, failure to notify a parole officer about a change of address before moving, being around places where alcoholic beverages were served, associating with people of "questionable" character, failure to pay parole administrative fees, or failure to pay several parking tickets.[54] The technical violators who were returned to prison had been free for an average of 4 years.[55] Seventy-eight of the 111 former inmates (70%) were returned to prison; 42 of them committed nonviolent crimes, such as alcohol or other drug offenses, burglary, or possession of a firearm; 29 committed violent offenses, such as armed robbery or aggravated assault, two were convicted of attempted murder, two were convicted of manslaughter, and three were convicted of murder. One parolee committed suicide before he was charged with murder.[56] Drug offenders who were returned to prison were free for an average of 5 years, those who committed serious felonies besides murder were free for an average of 10 years, and those who killed were free for only about 2 years.[57] Thus, of the 322 *Furman*-commuted death row inmates released from prison, 24 percent were returned to prison—most for a relatively short amount of time: 13 percent for nonviolent crimes and 11 percent for violent crimes. Less than 2 percent of them likely killed again (6/322). The recidivism rate of the *Furman*-commuted death row inmates is significantly lower than the recidivism rate of the general prison population.[58]

The 26 states that responded to a 1987 survey by the National Clearinghouse on Prisons and Jails reported 457 living *Furman*-commuted inmates, of whom 185 (40.6%) were paroled.[59] Eight parolees died during the 14-year period and are excluded from the following analysis, reducing the percentage of *Furman*-commuted inmates paroled to 38.7 percent. Only 35 (19.7%) of the paroled inmates recidivated (were reincarcerated). Of those who did recidivate, three (8.6%) had committed murder and eight (23%) had committed a violent crime (three murders, three robberies, one rape, and one kidnapping). The largest number of parolees was returned to prison for parole violations (12, or 34.3%). Other parolees were reimprisoned for burglary (6, or 17.1%), drug offenses (5, or 14.2%), and other property offenses (4, or 11.4%). Also worthy of note is that 29 (16.4%) of the 177 paroled *Furman*-commuted inmates successfully completed their parole terms and regained (in applicable states) their civil rights.

Another study tracked down 558 of the *Furman*-commuted inmates and discovered that only about 1 percent of them murdered again. Conversely, more than 98 percent of them did not kill again either in prison or in the free community upon release.[60]

A fourth study examined the postrelease behavior of 28 *Furman*-commuted inmates in Texas over the 14-year period of 1973–1986.[61] Only seven (25%) of the 28 recidivated. The average time they spent in the community was 4.1 years. One of the parolees (3.6%) committed a murder, four of them (14%) committed felonies (one murder, one rape, and two burglaries), and three of them (11%) were reincarcerated for technical parole violations. The one recidivist murderer killed his girlfriend and then committed suicide within 12 months of his release from prison.

A fifth study focused on the experiences of the 23 *Furman*-commuted death row inmates in Kentucky, of whom 17 were paroled.[62] The average follow-up period was 42 months. None of the parolees was rearrested for a murder; only two (12%) were rearrested for violent crimes (robberies) and four (24%) for any new crime (two for robbery, one for burglary, and one for drug possession). In all, 35 percent of the parolees were rearrested, 29 percent were reconvicted and reimprisoned, and 6 percent were put in jail. One of the parolees (6%) obtained his final release from parole supervision and 11 (65%) had been placed on inactive supervision.

More recently, Texas executed Kenneth McDuff, who is believed to be the only murderer ever freed from death row and then returned to it after killing again. McDuff was executed in 1998 for the 1992 rape and killing of a young woman whom he abducted from a convenience store. He was suspected of five to nine other murders. He originally was sent to death row in 1968 for the killing of three teenagers but was released in 1990 after being turned down for parole 14 times from 1976 through 1988. McDuff was one of 42,999 prisoners paroled from the Texas prison system because of a federal court order to reduce overcrowding. He was a *Furman*-commuted inmate.[63]

CONCLUSION

Three arguments for the execution of all capital offenders are (1) execution is the only way to guarantee they will not kill again; (2) life imprisonment provides opportunity for escape, parole, or additional murders; and (3) LWOP is costly.

The data just presented show that murderers, including capital murderers, do sometimes kill again even after having been imprisoned for many years, but the data also reveal that the number of such repeat killers is very small. A somewhat larger percentage of paroled death row inmates commit other offenses. However, most individuals are returned to prison for parole violations rather than for committing new crimes. Most convicted capital offenders will not kill again, even if they are released from prison, and a large majority of them will not be arrested for any new crimes.

For those who claim that life imprisonment provides the opportunity for escape or parole through error or oversight, or that life prisoners are a threat to other inmates and correctional personnel, Anthony Amsterdam responds, "You cannot tell me or believe that a society which is capable of putting a man on the moon is incapable of putting a man in prison, keeping him there, and keeping him from killing while he is there."[64]

Some people oppose LWOP because they believe it would be too costly; they assume that the death penalty is cheaper than LWOP. If they have in mind only the costs of the eventual execution, they are right, but if they consider the entire process of capital punishment, including trials, appeals, and executions, then they are wrong. The financial costs of capital punishment are the subject of the next section.

THE ECONOMIC COSTS OF CAPITAL PUNISHMENT VERSUS LIFE IMPRISONMENT[65]

One of the most common myths about capital punishment is that it is cheaper than alternative punishments such as life imprisonment without opportunity for parole. Political science professor John Culver claims, for example, that "the execution of an individual in his or her 30s is less expensive than maintaining that person in prison for 30 or more years until a natural death occurs."[66] Despite the myth, the cost issue apparently is not a particularly salient issue for death penalty proponents. In a recent national opinion survey, for example, only 4.1 percent of supporters of capital punishment selected "Save taxpayers money" as the most important reason for their support; another 6.5 percent selected the cost item as their second most important reason.[67] Furthermore, in an analysis of 3,939 *New York Times* stories about capital punishment published from 1960 through 2005, only 20 of the stories mentioned cost on either side of the debate.[68]

The principal purpose of this section is to compare the economic costs of capital punishment with the economic costs of alternative punishments. Implicit in the analysis are comparisons of three types: (1) capital punishment versus an alternative punishment applied after a successful plea bargain, (2) capital punishment versus an alternative punishment imposed after a trial only, and (3) capital punishment versus an alternative punishment imposed after a trial and postconviction review. Assuming the same alternative punishment, the comparisons are listed in descending order from largest to smallest cost differential. The first comparison reveals the largest cost differential because the costs of the alternative punishment do not include trial or postconviction review expenses, all of which are invariably incurred in capital cases (unless postconviction proceedings are waived). Also briefly discussed are past practices and their costs (which may help explain why some people believe in the myth), financial and other ramifications of recent efforts to streamline the process, the costs of mistakes, "start-up" costs for jurisdictions contemplating reinstatement of the death penalty, and some of the consequences if capital punishment were to be replaced with LWOP in the future.

ECONOMIC COSTS OF CAPITAL PUNISHMENT UNDER PRE-*FURMAN* STATUTES

Prior to the *Furman* decision in 1972, the economic costs of capital punishment were not an issue. The death penalty was not an expensive punishment relative to LWOP because capital cases were disposed of quickly, no extraordinary procedures were followed, reversals were relatively rare, and the costs associated with executions alone were minimal. Regarding the relatively quick disposal of capital cases, in 1934, for example, Doc Williams was executed in Florida 33 days following his apprehension and only 45 days after the crime was committed.[69] Data from 1956 to 1960 show that the average time between death sentence and execution was 14.4 months; however, by year-end 2009, the average had risen to 169 months.[70] A primary reason for the 1,074 percent increase in time between sentence and execution in capital cases is the super due process now required by the Supreme Court's "death is different" doctrine.[71] Super due process, as noted previously, refers to the unique procedural safeguards afforded to people charged with capital crimes. These safeguards apply primarily to the trial and postconviction stages of the process.

ECONOMIC COSTS OF CAPITAL PUNISHMENT UNDER POST-*FURMAN* STATUTES

Although the actual death-causing procedure may be relatively inexpensive, the process of getting to that point is quite costly under post-*Furman* statutes. The Supreme Court requires that defendants charged with capital crimes be provided with super due process, and super due process is expensive. Below are some recent estimates of the economic costs of capital punishment.

- The death penalty costs California taxpayers $137 million a year, compared to only $11.5 million per year for a comparable system that sentenced the same inmates to LWOP. Because California has executed only 13 people since it reinstated the death penalty in 1977, the cost for each execution is more than $250 million. The state has indicated that it needs $400 million for a new death row.[72]
- New Jersey's death penalty cost taxpayers at least $253 million since 1983, approximately $11 million a year, even though New Jersey has not executed anyone during that period. The $253 million is "over and above the costs that would have been incurred had the state utilized a sentence of life without parole instead of death." Since 1982 and through the end of 2005, New Jersey had conducted 197 capital trials and had imposed 60 death sentences, of which 50 were reversed. At the end of 2004, it was estimated that it took $2.3 million to $3.2 million to pursue a death prosecution in New Jersey.[73] New Jersey abolished its death penalty in 2007.
- In 2005, Indiana taxpayers spent an average of $741,000 over 16 years to execute a 30-year-old capital offender. The figure includes jails costs, prosecutor's and defender's fees from murder trial through appeals, and execution costs. It cost $622,000 to lock up the same person for life, estimated to be 47 years in prison. This includes appeals and health care costs. It cost $506,000 to imprison a person for 65 years with a 50 percent reduction for good behavior.[74]
- In the state of Washington between 1993 and 2003, a death penalty trial cost, on average, $432,000. This was more than twice as much as the average $153,000 cost of a non-death penalty trial.[75]
- In 2003, the average cost of a death penalty case in Kansas was $1.2 million. A life-without-parole sentence could save Kansas taxpayers between $400,000 and $500,000 per trial.[76]
- In Maryland, the estimated extra cost to taxpayers for each death penalty case prosecuted between 1978 and 1999 was $186 million. Based on the five executions conducted during this period, the cost per execution was $37 million.[77]

The average cost per execution in the United States (that is, the entire process) is estimated to range from about $2.5 million to $5 million (in 2000 dollars).[78] Extraordinary cases can cost much more. The state of Florida, for example, reportedly spent $10 million to execute serial murderer Ted Bundy in 1989.[79] Orange County, California, spent more than $10 million just to convict serial killer Randy Kraft the same year. (At this writing, Kraft remains on California's death row.)[80] As noted in Chapter 5, the federal government spent more than $100 million to execute mass murderer Timothy McVeigh in 2001.

If an inmate sentenced to LWOP lives 31 years,[81] and the average annual cost of imprisonment for the first 21 years is about $23,400 per inmate and the average annual cost of imprisonment for the last 10 years is $70,000 per inmate,[82] then the cost of that LWOP sentence is roughly $1 million (assuming the LWOP sentence was the result of a successful plea bargain), making capital punishment, on average, 2.5–5 times more expensive than LWOP imposed as a result of plea bargaining. If the LWOP sentence is imposed after a trial and includes other post-conviction proceedings, then the difference will be much smaller. Nevertheless, the costs of a death sentence will probably always be more expensive than the costs of an LWOP sentence because super due process is required only in capital cases.[83] In North Carolina in the early 1990s, for example, the cost differential between a capital case culminating in an execution and a noncapital case resulting in a 20-year sentence was estimated to be between $163,000 and more than $216,000.[84] Another consideration, as Richard Dieter, executive director of the Death Penalty Information Center, points out, is that "death penalty costs are accrued upfront, especially at trial and for the early appeals, while life-in-prison costs are spread out over many decades." "A million dollars spent today," Dieter notes, "is a lot more costly to the state than a million dollars that can be paid gradually over 40 years."[85]

Why is super due process so expensive? This question is answered in the next sections. It must be emphasized that many of the costs reported are estimates, that there can be great variation in the costs of specific services among different jurisdictions, that cost estimates are not available for every part of the process, and that not every cost or part of the process occurs in every case. Some costs can be duplicated when retrials or resentencings follow the vacation of a conviction or capital sentence on appeal or during the post-conviction review process. Another caveat is that some of the data come from studies conducted as long ago as the 1980s. They are presented for historical reference, and in some cases, they are the only data available. It is assumed that the current costs are higher, as indicated by more current data where available.

It should also be remembered that whenever a capital trial does not result in a death sentence and execution, the added costs associated with the death penalty process have been incurred without any "return" on the state's investment of resources. In other words, the enormous costs of capital punishment are not a product of the number of executions but rather the number of people death penalty jurisdictions attempt to execute.[86] This last point is an especially important one because, as Jon Sorensen argues, the high costs of capital punishment, such as the $11 million a year New Jersey spent on the sanction despite no executions, can be explained at least in part by the large number of capital trials that do not result in executions. Sorensen maintains that if 50 percent of death penalty trials produced executions, the cost savings of LWOP would "wash out" and capital punishment would be "cost-effective."[87] Whether Sorensen is right about this, the fact remains that the number of capital trials that produce executions is currently decreasing, not increasing.[88]

One final introductory point is that the death penalty's availability creates a pressure to seek it that is difficult to resist and would not exist in its absence. As Herbert Haines explains:

How is a prosecutor to explain to [a] grieving family why she decided to seek death for another accused murderer but not for the killer of their loved one? How is she to apply it sparingly, knowing that her opponent in some future election will accuse her of being soft on criminals? Elected officials striving to appear moderate sometimes call for limited death penalty laws intended only for the "worst of the worst" killers. But limited death penalties beg to be expanded, especially in election years. Capital punishment, then, often seems to have a built-in momentum that demands that it be used and drives up its cost.[89]

The following analysis is divided into five general stages of the capital punishment process: (1) pretrial, (2) trial, (3) posttrial, (4) imprisonment, and (5) execution.

The pretrial stage

The costs of capital punishment begin to mount soon after a potentially capital crime (in most cases, an aggravated murder) has been reported to the police. The investigation of potentially capital crimes tends to be more rigorous than the investigation of other felonies. When the crime may be a capital offense, forensic experts examine the crime scene more carefully, and this greater attention and time result in an added but unknown cost.[90]

Investigation of the case frequently continues through trial and can last several years.[91] The investigation of potentially capital crimes has been estimated to take three to five times longer than for other felonies, primarily because the prosecution as well as the defense must prepare for both stages of the bifurcated trial—the guilt and penalty phases.[92] Because defense counsel can present any relevant mitigating evidence during the penalty phase of a capital trial (see *Lockett v. Ohio*, 1978), a thorough investigation of possible mitigators is time-consuming and expensive. In the late 1980s, experienced private investigators, who frequently are hired by the defense, were paid between $75 and $200 an hour.[93] Investigators working for the state of North Carolina were paid $22.16 per hour in 1991–1992.[94] In 2002, the district attorney's office in Fulton County, Georgia, spent an additional $43,000 on overtime for investigators in a single case.[95] In 2003, investigation costs for death-sentence cases in Kansas were found to be about three times greater than for nondeath cases.[96] In 2010, defense investigators and mitigation specialists in an Arizona capital murder case submitted bills totaling $101,000 before the trial had even begun.[97]

Once a suspect has been identified and arrested, a bond hearing is held. The costs of those processes probably do not differ greatly for potentially capital crimes and other serious felonies, but estimates of the costs have not been reported. If bond is denied, however, and the suspect is incarcerated—which is nearly always more likely with potentially capital crimes—then additional costs will be incurred as a result of the tighter security that will be provided through the entire process.[98] There are no estimates for these extra security costs, either.

If the prosecutor believes that there is evidence to convict the suspect of the crime, and the crime is an aggravated murder (or another capital offense), then the prosecutor will seek an indictment for capital murder in jurisdictions that employ grand juries.[99] In jurisdictions that do not use grand juries, formal charges are filed through an indictment. The costs of each capital indictment are believed to be "enormous" (though no dollar figure has been cited) because each indictment must be prepared, even though in the late 1980s only about 20 percent of them reached trial.[100]

The most expensive part of the pretrial process frequently involves the motions filed in death penalty cases. Defense counsel has both a professional and an ethical obligation to represent his or her client's interests by filing nonfrivolous motions which, at a minimum, create and preserve the defendant's record for appeal.[101] Extensive amounts of time can be devoted to researching and writing pretrial motions. The prosecution must respond to the motions as well as prepare and file its own. In North Carolina, at least 34 different motions have been made in capital litigation, not to mention 11 more motions made during the penalty phase of the trial.[102] These motions are in addition to the more standard ones that are frequently filed by both sides in other felony cases.[103] Typical motions filed in capital cases involve voir dire, jury composition, death qualification process challenges, change of venue, and challenges to the death penalty's constitutionality in general and to the state's death penalty statute in particular.[104] In the 1980s, it was estimated that two to six times more motions were filed in death penalty cases than in other felony cases.[105] Between five and seven motions were typically filed in noncapital cases in New York in the early 1980s.[106] In a single North Carolina capital case in 1991, the cost of pretrial motions was $115,247.[107]

A big part of the expense of motions is the cost of experts who are paid for their research/consulting and for their testimony at trial. Both the defense and the prosecution employ experts. Among the experts used in capital cases are: (1) psychiatrists, who were paid $100–$150 an hour or $500–$1000 a day in the 1980s;[108] (2) medical examiners, who were paid $700–$1000 a day in the 1980s;[109] (3) polygraph experts, who were paid $200–$300 a day for courtroom testimony and $150–$250 per examination in the 1980s;[110] (4) experts on eyewitness identification, who were paid about $100 an hour or about $500 a day for courtroom testimony in the 1980s;[111] and (5) forensic scientists, juristic psychologists, and criminologists, who (in 1996) were paid a maximum of about $130 an hour in Florida (Orange County) unless special circumstances existed.[112] In the 1990s, it was estimated that defense expert witnesses alone could easily cost more than $40,000 in capital cases.[113] In 2005 and 2006, the cost of expert witnesses in North Carolina averaged about $35,700 per capital trial, about $20,900 per noncapital trial of a death-eligible defendant, and about $5,400 per noncapital trial of a non-death-eligible defendant.[114] Death-eligible defendant refers to a defendant whose crime made him eligible under state guidelines for the prosecutor to seek the death penalty. Not all death-eligible defendants are advanced to a capital trial.

As of October 2010, the pretrial costs in the Casey Anthony case in Florida amounted to about $425,000.[115] Her trial is set to begin May 9, 2011. Anthony is charged with the first-degree murder of her 2-year-old daughter, Caylee Marie. In March 2010, Anthony was declared indigent. Before then, Anthony's private funding totaled $275,000, including $200,000 paid by ABC News. Of the $275,000, $111,953.83 went to two attorneys and $10,000 to a media consultant. Since March 2010, Anthony has racked up the following costs: $38,672.38, including $8,118.92 to expert witness Dr. Henry Lee (made famous by the O.J. Simpson murder case); $11,123 to Jeremiah Lyons Investigations for interviewing witnesses, picking up law enforcement records, making public records requests, and consulting with attorneys; $6,413.88 for court reporting and transcription services; $68,629.40 for housing Anthony in the Orange County Jail since October 14, 2008; and $42,200.16 for prosecution costs, which does not include the salaries of the prosecutors working on the case (two of the prosecutors earn more than $100,000 a year).

The trial stage

Approximately 95 percent of criminal cases never reach trial, but instead are resolved through plea bargaining. Capital cases are an exception; they are rarely plea bargained.[116] Because "death is different," death penalty cases go to trial 10 times more often than do other felony cases.[117]

The most striking difference between a capital trial and trials for other serious felonies is that capital trials are bifurcated, that is, divided into two separate stages: a guilt phase and a penalty phase.

In bifurcated trials, all the expenses of the guilt phase can possibly be duplicated in the penalty phase.[118] Death penalty trials in Maryland between 1978 and 1999 were $664,000 more costly than noncapital trials of death-eligible defendants.[119] In his testimony before the Commission to Study the Death Penalty in New Hampshire on December 4, 2009, Richard Dieter, executive director of the Death Penalty Information Center, asserted that "for a single death penalty trial, the state may pay $1 million more than for a non-death penalty trial [b]ut [because] only one in every three capital trials may result in a death sentence ... the true cost of that death sentence is $3 million."[120] In a footnote to the written report of his testimony, Dieter, presumably using the data from the Maryland study, observed that the additional cost of a death penalty trial in Maryland was nearly $2 million.[121] In 2003, trial costs for death penalty cases in Kansas were about 16 times greater than those for non-death penalty cases. The average death penalty trial cost about $508,000, while the average trial in a non-death penalty case cost about $32,000. Trials involving a death sentence averaged 34 days, including jury selection; non-death penalty trials averaged about 9 days.[122] An average capital trial in California in 1983 was about 3.5 times or 30 days longer than an average noncapital murder trial, which required approximately 12 days.[123] A 1999 capital murder trial in Suffolk County, New York, cost 3.5 times what it would have cost had the death penalty not been sought.[124] The average death penalty trial in Texas in 1992 lasted 14 weeks and cost $265,640.[125] The cost difference in a death penalty trial compared to a non-death penalty trial in Harris County, Texas, in 2005, was estimated to be $57,000.[126] The average death penalty trial in North Carolina in 1991–1992 lasted 14.6 days and cost $84,099,[127] with the range being a low of $24,777 and a high of $179,736.[128] By contrast, the average noncapital murder trial in North Carolina lasted 3.8 days and cost $16,697,[129] with a range of $7,766–$30,952.[130] In 2005 and 2006, capital trials in North Carolina lasted 11.7 days longer than noncapital trials of death-eligible defendants and cost approximately $48,600 more.[131] The $48,600 figure is only for extra defense costs (a second defense attorney, the motions practice, and extra time to select the jury and to conduct the sentencing phase). Not included are the "opportunity costs" of the North Carolina courts and the North Carolina district attorney offices.[132] "Opportunity costs" refer to hidden costs such as the extra time district attorneys spend trying capital cases and the extra court time consumed by lengthy death trials. These opportunity costs affect other noncapital cases. For example, other serious cases receive less attention than they would otherwise, or cases that ordinarily would be tried are plea bargained, simply because there is not enough time to do otherwise.

The guilt phase of the bifurcated capital trial in North Carolina and Maryland was considerably more expensive than the penalty phase. The costs of the guilt phase in North Carolina in 1991–1992 ranged from $9,802 to $137,500; the average guilt phase cost $52,290 and lasted 10.6 days.[133] The guilt phase in North Carolina in 1991–1992, in other words, accounted for about 62 percent of the costs and 73 percent of the time spent on the entire trial. In Maryland between 1978 and 1999, the guilt phase of a capital trial was $517,000 more than the cost of a noncapital trial (of a death-eligible defendant), while the penalty phase (which does not occur in a noncapital trial) lasted an average of nearly 14 working days and increased the cost of the trial by "only" $147,000.[134] The cost of a capital trial's guilt phase in North Carolina and Maryland may be atypical, however. Paternoster claims that the penalty phase, and not the guilt phase, is "the single greatest cost inflator of a capital trial."[135] He explains that in most capital trials, the prosecutor's overwhelming evidence makes the defendant's guilt obvious, so there is little to contest. Law professor David Dow corroborates Paternoster's explanation by noting that during the 1990s, 99 percent of capital murder defendants in Houston, Dallas, and San Antonio were convicted; the conviction rate in Virginia, Alabama, Mississippi, and Louisiana ranged from more than 75 percent to more than 90 percent; and the conviction rate in Florida and California exceeded well over 50 percent.[136] Consequently, defense counsel focuses on saving his or her client's life in the penalty phase of the trial. To aid the effort, counsel is allowed to present mitigating evidence on his or her client's behalf, which requires a considerable, but unknown, amount of time.

Among the specific costs of the guilt phase of a capital trial are voir dire, attorney hours, expert testimony, witnesses, and court costs. Most of these expenses involve payments for time expended on the case. However, in a 2002 case conducted in Fulton County, Georgia, the district attorney's office spent about $34,000 for equipment, graphic design for court exhibits, and expert testimony.[137] Many prosecutors and defense attorneys believe that jury selection is the key element in a capital case. As an Erie County, New York, district attorney observed, "All you have to do is find one person that doesn't want to go for the death penalty, and you've defeated it."[138] It is estimated that voir dire during the selection of the jury takes five times longer in capital cases than in other felony cases [139] and, in 1985, increased the cost of a capital trial by nearly $90,000.[140] Jury selection in capital cases typically takes 6 weeks to complete and can take longer than the guilt phase of the trial.[141] However, in Maryland, the average length of voir dire for capital cases between 1978 and 1999 was 5 days compared to 2 days in noncapital cases.[142] In two capital cases in New York, jury selection took 10 weeks in the first case and 7 weeks in the second case.[143] The average cost of empaneling a jury in capital cases in Texas in 1992 was $17,220.[144] Jury costs for capital trials in North Carolina in 2005 and 2006 were about $7,746 more than jury costs in noncapital trials of death-eligible defendants, and this cost differential did not include reimbursement for parking and meals.[145] A survey of 20 California capital murder trials conducted in the early 1980s found that jury selection was the most expensive part of a capital trial.[146]

A major reason voir dire in capital cases is so costly is that many death penalty jurisdictions require that jurors not only be questioned individually but also remain sequestered until the full jury is selected or until they are dismissed.[147] Although an atypical case, Los Angeles County, California spent an estimated $9 million on O. J. Simpson's 1995 murder trial. An expensive part of that trial was the sequestering of jurors for 265 days.[148] In a 2002 case in Fulton County, Georgia, selecting and sequestering the jury cost $87,000, which included $63,600 for hotel rooms, dinners, and drinks for jurors; $6,000 for juror lunches and beverages; $2,500 for juror transportation; $765 for entertainment expenses; and $14,300 to copy the questionnaires used to select the jury. The amount did not include the overtime paid to sheriff's deputies who guarded the jury and the court.[149] Estimated jury costs for another atypical case, the Casey Anthony trial scheduled for May 9, 2011, in Orlando, Florida, are more than $360,000. The bulk of the costs are to house, feed, and transport 20 sequestered jurors (12 jurors and 8 alternates) for the estimated eight weeks of trial. Specific costs are $137,984 for hotel rooms, $48,800 for meals, $128,917.44 for court-clerk and security costs, $3,962.32 for jury selection, and $41,400 for other expenses such as juror wages and vans for transportation.[150] Many jurisdictions allow defendants to waive the individual questioning and sequestering of jurors requirements. Although data on the frequency of such waivers are not available, they are probably not requested very often. Other reasons that voir dire in capital cases takes longer and is more expensive are (1) the increased number of peremptory challenges allowed in capital cases,[151] (2) the increased number of jurors who are likely to be dismissed for cause,[152] (3) the increased number of jurors who try to disqualify themselves,[153] and (4) in some jurisdictions, the need to select jurors for both the guilt and penalty phases of the trial.[154]

Many states require that capital defendants have two attorneys; no state requires two attorneys in noncapital cases.[155] Attorneys can spend from 300 to 1,000 hours on capital cases.[156] In North Carolina in 1991–1992, for example, defense attorneys and prosecutors spent an average of 613 and 282 hours, respectively, on capital cases.[157] By contrast, they spent an average of 150 and 61 hours, respectively, on noncapital cases.[158] In North Carolina in 2005 and 2006, defense attorneys spent an average of 451.5 hours on capital cases and 157.4 hours on noncapital cases of death-eligible defendants.[159] The demands of capital cases can be so great, they can devastate an attorney's regular practice.[160]

In the early 1990s, public defenders in North Carolina were paid an average of $68.31 an hour; assistant public defenders received an average of $48.34 an hour.[161] District attorneys, on the other hand, were paid an average of $83.10 an hour and assistant district attorneys received an average of $55.63 an hour.[162] Based on these hourly rates, the average cost of a public defender in North Carolina capital cases in 1991–1992 was about $42,000 per case; the average cost of an assistant district attorney (assuming most capital cases are handled by assistant district attorneys) was about $16,000 per case (it would be about $23,000 if handled by a district attorney).[163] In 2002, the Fulton County, Georgia, district attorney assigned four prosecutors to a capital case. Not including time spent preparing for the case, the prosecutors' salaries exceeded $74,000 for the 2 months of trial and jury selection.[164] Also, in Maryland, in 2007, district public defender's were paid $53.83 an hour, and assistant public defenders were paid $41.47 an hour.[165] A Maryland state's attorney was paid $102 an hour in 2007, while an assistant state's attorney was paid $58 an hour.[166] Note that although prosecutors and public defenders are salaried state employees and work on any cases assigned to them, as noted previously, pursuit of the death penalty creates "opportunity costs" that would not exist in the penalty's absence.[167] That is, the extraordinary number of hours expended on death penalty cases could be devoted to many other important cases that do not get the attention they would otherwise receive if there were no death penalty cases.

The cost of defense counsel through sentencing in Maryland in 1982 was estimated to range from $50,000 to $75,000 per capital case.[168] In 2002, Fulton County, Georgia, paid a defense attorney in a capital case $164,000 in fees and expenses.[169] In 1993, the Connecticut Public Defender's Office spent $138 to defend an average noncapital case (this included plea bargains) and approximately $200,000 to defend each death penalty case.[170] Private defense fees in a California capital trial involving three defendants cost the state $1.1 million.[171] Florida increased its fees for appointed defense attorneys in capital cases in January 1998. The hourly rate for the lead attorney was raised from $50 to $120, while assisting attorneys may receive as much as $100 an hour.[172] Florida also set a $3,500 cap on the amount it would pay for defense services in capital cases.[173] Some states pay less. For example, in the 1990s, court-appointed attorneys in Alabama were being paid only $20 an hour for out-of-court time in capital cases, with a limit of $2,000 per case; Mississippi was limiting payment to $1000 a case.[174] In 2005, Alabama paid on average $20,416 for the defense of indigents charged with capital crimes, which included the costs of two defense attorneys, an investigator, and a mitigation specialist. This $20,416 average was about 16 times as much as the $1,300 average Alabama paid for indigent defense in class-A felony cases. Since 2000, Alabama taxpayers have paid more than $14 million to defend people charged with capital murder.[175] From 1995 through 1999, the New York Capital Defender's Office spent more than $34 million on 37 defendants charged with capital crimes. The costs included the defender office's annual budget and money paid to court-appointed defense attorneys, defense investigators, and defense experts. For fiscal year 1999, $14.75 million was allocated for capital defense costs.[176] In 1998, defense expenses in three capital cases cost Indiana taxpayers more than $2 million.[177] In two capital cases in New York in the 1990s, defense expenditures were nearly $600,000 and $900,000. The district attorneys in these cases spent nearly $800,000 and

$750,000, respectively.[178] An analysis of North Carolina data for the years 2005 and 2006 found that the extra defense costs for the 29 capital trials during the 2 years were about $13 million or about $454,496 per trial.[179] The costs included a second defense attorney, the motions practice, extra time to select the jury and to conduct the sentencing phase, the prorated budget of the Indigent Defense Services Office of the Capital Defender ($2.4 million), and the budget of the Center for Death Penalty Litigation ($1.2 million), which helps recruit and train defense attorneys for capital case representation. In the capital prosecutions of John Muhammad and Lee Boyd Malvo in Virginia, it was reported that Muhammad's attorneys were paid $790,726 and Malvo's attorneys more than $781,000 for their work and expenses. The costs did not include appeals.[180] The federal government spent $13.8 million in public funds to hire private attorneys and cover other costs to defend Timothy McVeigh.[181]

The hourly or daily rates of expert witnesses for in-court testimony were described previously and are not repeated here.

A larger number of witnesses are usually called in capital trials. These witnesses must be interviewed, their testimony must be prepared, and the other side must depose them. All this requires considerable attorney time. Total costs for two defense attorneys, three prosecutors, investigators, and expert witnesses in capital cases in Texas in 1992 averaged $150,452 ($112,400 for the two defense attorneys, investigators, and expert witnesses and $38,052 for the three prosecutors).[182]

Court costs are estimated to be 3.5 times greater in capital cases than they are in other felony cases.[183] Again, remember these are "opportunity costs." In North Carolina in 1991–1992, superior court judges were paid an average of $631 a day; in Maryland in 2007, circuit court judges were paid $803 a day.[184] Court reporters in North Carolina (1991–1992) were paid an average of $191 a day; court reporters in Maryland (2007) were paid $313 a day.[185] In North Carolina (1991–1992), deputy court clerks were paid $146 a day; court clerks in Maryland (2007) were paid $182 a day; and court law clerks in Maryland (2007) were paid $257 a day.[186] In North Carolina (1991–1992), bailiffs were paid $125 a day; in Maryland (2007), they were deputy sheriffs and were paid $278 a day.[187] Two bailiffs were generally assigned to each capital trial in North Carolina (1991–1992).[188] In Texas in 1992, the average cost per judge in a capital case was $23,968.[189] Courtroom space in North Carolina in 1991-1992 was estimated to cost $174 a day; in Maryland in 2007 the cost was $173 a day.[190] In addition, the daily cost of a jury room in Maryland in 2007 was $38.53, the daily cost of a judge's chamber was $61.14, and the daily cost of a jury pool room was $503.27.[191] The total per day cost of a capital trial in a North Carolina Superior Court in 1991–1992 was estimated to be $1,416; the cost of a capital trial per day in California in 1983 was approximately $2,186, not including extra security or transcript costs.[192] In 1999, a criminal court case in New York city cost about $3,800 per day. At this rate, court costs in two death penalty cases in Queens totaled approximately $725,000. In Suffolk County, where the daily rate was $3,556, the court costs in one capital case were almost $650,000.[193]

As mentioned earlier, all the expenses of the guilt phase could be duplicated in the penalty phase. The penalty phase will require, at a minimum, additional expenditures for attorney time, expert testimony, witnesses, and court costs.[194] Some jurisdictions require separate juries for the penalty phase of a capital trial, in which case the costs of voir dire also could be duplicated.

Capital trials can force local governments to make difficult choices. For example, a recent study in Illinois found that capital trials could increase county spending by as much as 1.8 percent per trial (Illinois abolished its death penalty in 2011). Such trials are often financed through increased property taxes or funds taken from police and highway appropriations.[195] A *Wall Street Journal* article reported that the Texas county where the three men convicted of the 1998 murder of James

Byrd were tried was forced to raise property taxes 6.7 percent for 2 years to cover trial costs.[196] During the early 1990s, two capital trials in Jefferson County, Florida, caused the county to put a freeze on employee raises and cut the library budget by 20 percent.[197] Some counties have almost been bankrupted by capital trial costs.[198] County officials in Kentucky and Georgia have been jailed for contempt because they refused to provide funding for expert defense testimony in capital cases.[199] In some death-eligible cases, prosecutors forego capital trials altogether rather than incur the expense. Some defense attorneys have used the high costs of capital trials as leverage when negotiating a plea deal for their clients.[200] The costs of capital punishment are thus a source of its arbitrary and discriminatory application (discussed in Chapter 10). Counties that can afford it may seek the death penalty in all cases that warrant it, while "poor" counties may have to pick and choose among death-eligible cases, pursuing the death penalty in only some cases or not at all. "Poor" counties simply may not be able to afford the death penalty.[201]

The posttrial stage

At least one authority believes the posttrial stage generally is the most expensive part of the entire process.[202] However, a 2003 report from Kansas found that pretrial and trial expenses accounted for 49 percent of the total costs, appeals accounted for 29 percent of the total, and the remaining 22 percent went for incarceration and execution costs.[203] Automatic appeal of conviction and/or death sentence to the state supreme court is required in nearly all jurisdictions with capital punishment statutes.[204] If the appellant wins, the costs of the original trial, or at least part of the costs, could be replicated at the retrial or resentencing.[205] In North Carolina in 2005 and 2006, three resentencing hearings cost $594,216 or nearly $200,000 each.[206] The cost of a direct appeal in North Carolina in 2005 and 2006 was $22,651 per capital case compared to $3,977 per case for direct appeals involving defendants sentenced to LWOP.[207] In North Carolina, defendants convicted by a jury and sentenced to LWOP have a right to an attorney for direct appeal but do not have a right to an attorney during state post-conviction proceedings.[208]

It is estimated that a typical capital appeal requires from 500 to 2000 hours of attorney time, not including travel, photocopying, etc.[209] In North Carolina, in 1991–1992, appellate defenders received an average of $61.89 an hour; assistant appellate defenders were paid an average of $43.80 an hour.[210] Appointed appellate defense attorneys in California received an average of $60 per hour in 1985.[211] North Carolina Supreme Court justices were paid an average of $96.92 an hour in 1991–1992, while their law clerks received an average of $28.02 an hour.[212] The average cost of a North Carolina Supreme Court justice in 1991–1992 for a capital appeal was estimated to be $1,887; the average cost of a court clerk was $2,083.[213] The average cost of the North Carolina attorney general for a capital appeal in 1991–1992 was estimated to be $5,261.[214] In Maryland, in 2007, a court of appeals chief judge earned $128.77 an hour, while a court of appeals associate judge earned $114.57 an hour.[215] The daily labor cost of judicial staff in Maryland's Court of Appeals was estimated to be $6,749.85.[216] The court of appeals is Maryland's state supreme court.

Some states also provide proportionality review, although the Supreme Court does not require it (see *Pulley v. Harris*, 1984). Proportionality review is a process whereby state appellate courts compare the sentence in the case being reviewed with sentences imposed in similar cases in the state.[217] Its purpose is to identify disparities in sentencing. To perform a proportionality review, data must be gathered and analyzed and a report must be written. In 2006, the New Jersey Administrative

Office of the Courts estimated that each proportionality review costs an average of $93,018 in additional salary costs for court staff (New Jersey abolished its death penalty in 2007).[218] Many death penalty states do not conduct proportionality reviews because of the expense.

Besides the automatic appellate review, capital defendants may contest their conviction and/or sentence through both state and federal postconviction proceedings. Including the automatic appeal, there are at least nine or 10 possible levels of review following the guilt and penalty phases of a capital trial.[219] The average cost of the state postconviction process for capital cases in Texas in 1992 was $94,240,[220] the biggest expense being for attorney time. The U.S. Constitution does not require the appointment of attorneys for indigent capital defendants beyond the automatic appeal, that is, for state postconviction collateral review (see *Murray v. Giarratano*, 1989), but many jurisdictions provide them anyway.[221] It has been estimated that attorneys spend an average of 700 – 1,000 hours on state postconviction proceedings in capital cases.[222] A 1986 American Bar Association survey found that lawyers spent an average of 963 hours on state postconviction appeals.[223] Specific cost averages in Texas were as follows:

1. Defense costs = $15,000,
2. Prosecution costs = $29,000,
3. Cost of reproducing the trial[224] = $20,000, and
4. Court of criminal appeals (3-day estimate) = $30,240.[225]

The cost of state postconviction proceedings in two North Carolina cases was considerably higher—$293,393 and $216,387 per case—although this may be due to the inclusion of stages such as clemency/commutation proceedings not included in the Texas costs.[226] Specific costs in the more expensive North Carolina case included the following (years in which expenses were incurred are in parentheses):

1. state motion for appropriate relief = $29,957 (1985–1987),
2. petition for certiorari to North Carolina Supreme Court = $6,188 (1987–1988),
3. state motion hearing = $2,057 (1988),
4. motion for stay of execution in North Carolina Supreme Court = $833 (1989),
5. motions in North Carolina Supreme Court = $3,642 (1990),
6. motions in North Carolina Superior Court = $115,247 (1991), and
7. clemency/commutation proceedings = $84,888 (1991–1992).[227]

In 2003, appeals in Kansas death penalty cases were 21 times more expensive than appeals in non-death penalty cases.[228] In Maryland between 1978 and 1999, the appellate process in a capital case was $201,000 more costly than a capital-eligible case in which no death penalty was sought.[229] In North Carolina in 2005 and 2006, defense representation for appeals cost $679,414 per capital case compared to $3,977 per case for appeals involving defendants sentenced to LWOP.[230] The $3,977 figure is for the direct appeal. Because they have no right to an attorney for state postconviction proceedings, defendants sentenced to LWOP rarely seek relief beyond the direct appeal.[231]

Federal postconviction proceedings for Texas capital appellants in the early 1990s averaged 6 years and cost about $1.7 million per appellant.[232] Unlike the situation for state postconviction proceedings, the federal government requires legal representation for capital defendants pursuing federal habeas corpus appeals.[233] The federal courts have (or had) three options in meeting this statutory requirement.[234] First, they may appoint attorneys from the private bar. These attorneys submit vouchers for payment to the Administrative Office of the United States Courts, which allocates funds according to provisions in the Criminal Justice Act (1994).[235] Although the act does not prescribe any limitation on the amount that can be paid for services, in *In re Berger* (1991), the Court limited appointed counsel representing capital defendants before the Supreme Court to $5,000 in fees. A second option is to appoint attorneys employed by federal public defender organizations, which are funded through grants made available by the Judicial Conference of the United States.[236] A problem with these two options is that neither one guarantees the appointment of attorneys with expertise in capital jurisprudence.[237]

The third and best option (for capital defendants) was the appointment of attorneys employed by Post-Conviction Defender Organizations (PCDOs), which were originally called Death Penalty Resource Centers. Congress created these agencies in 1988.[238] They dealt only with capital cases and related postconviction issues and employed full-time, salaried attorneys, investigators, and support staff.[239] In the mid-1990s, they operated in 20 of the then-38 death penalty states.[240] The Judicial Conference funded PCDOs through grants that were contingent upon the receipt of state funding for any state court work PCDOs did. In fiscal year 1994, the 20 PCDOs received nearly $20 million for their work on capital cases.[241]

Because of the success of PCDO attorneys in getting convictions and death sentences overturned, the agencies came under fire from death penalty proponents, who won the day. On January 6, 1996, President Clinton signed into law HR-1358 (Pub. L. No. 104–91, 110 Stat. 7). The law provided a budget of approximately $262 million for the Federal Judiciary's Defender Services but stipulated that none of the money was to be spent on PCDOs after April 1, 1996—to allow for an orderly end to the program.[242] After the 1996 fiscal year ended on September 30, no further federal funding of the PCDOs was to be provided.[243]

With the demise of PCDOs, the federal courts are left with only the first two options of providing attorneys for capital defendants pursuing federal habeas corpus relief. The debate in Congress suggested that the abolition of PCDOs would save the government about $20 million annually,[244] but the chief judge of the U.S. Court of Appeals for the Eighth Circuit, Richard Arnold, disagreed. He predicted "that elimination of the PCDOs will significantly increase delays in handling an ever-increasing death penalty caseload by creating an insufficient pool of qualified and experienced attorneys to handle the petitions."[245] He estimated that "the cost of representing death row inmates would rise from the current expenditure of $21.2 million to 'between $37 million and $51.1 million' with the elimination of the PCDOs."[246]

In the late 1980s, it was estimated that attorneys in capital cases spent an average of 700 to more than 1,000 hours on federal postconviction proceedings.[247] The 1986 American Bar Association survey found that lawyers spent an average of 1,037 hours on federal postconviction litigation.[248] In Texas, in the early 1990s, defense attorneys received an average of $92,300 for their federal postconviction work in capital cases, while it cost the Texas attorney general's office an average of $19,600 per capital case challenged on federal habeas corpus.[249] The remainder of the estimated $1.7 million per federal postconviction capital case went for court costs and outlays.[250]

Cost estimates of federal postconviction proceedings for North Carolina capital prisoners included the following (years on which estimates are based are in parentheses):

1. Certiorari petition to the U.S. Supreme Court = $7,885 (1984),
2. Motion for stay of execution in the federal district court = $757 (1989),
3. Federal district court habeas proceedings = $17,383 (1989–1990), and
4. Federal appellate proceedings = $24,556 (1990–1992).[251]

Imprisonment

Under current practices, convicted capital offenders serve a long prison term on death row (now averaging more than 14 years), in addition to being sentenced to death.[252] Put somewhat differently, because of super due process protections, capital offenders typically serve more than 20 percent of what otherwise might be a 50-year LWOP sentence before they are executed.

It almost certainly is more expensive to house inmates on death row than to confine them with the general population in a maximum-security prison.[253] Reasons are added security precautions, which include single-cell confinement. Although one source suggests that the difference in the annual costs of confinement is not great—approximately $1,000–$2,000 per inmate; in 2005, it cost the state of Florida $26,422 to house an inmate on death row and $18,108 to house an inmate in a major prison—a more than $8,300 difference. The difference in Texas was about $7,600, $22,477 on death row (in 2002) compared to $14,877 (in 2005) in the general population of a maximum-security prison. In 2005, it reportedly cost California about $90,000 more a year to house an inmate on death row than in the general prison population.[254] In 2006, the New Jersey Department of Corrections estimated that the state would save between $974,430 and $1,299,240 per inmate over each inmate's lifetime, if it were to abolish the death penalty (which it did). The department's figures were based on an annual cost of $72,602 to house an inmate on New Jersey's death row versus an annual cost of $40,121 to house an inmate in the general population of New Jersey's maximum-security prison. It was estimated that a life sentence would be 30–40 years.[255] A recent study in North Carolina found that, had the death penalty been abolished prior to 2005, the net savings in prison expenditures would have been $169,617 or $4,584 per inmate.[256] During 2005–2006, 151 inmates occupied North Carolina's death row. If the death penalty had been abolished, the 151 death row inmates would have had their sentences commuted to LWOP, and most of them would have been placed in close custody with maintenance costs similar to death row. However, 37 of these death row inmates had served more than 10 years and would be eligible to be transferred to a medium security facility, saving the state $5,297 per inmate. Additionally, 11 inmates had been executed during 2005–2006 at a cost of $180,059 or $16,369 per execution. Had these inmates not been executed, they would have cost the state an additional $206,400 or $18,764 per inmate. Thus, all told, North Carolina would have saved $4,584 per inmate had the death penalty been abolished prior to 2005.

An additional and unique cost of confinement for death row inmates involves the deathwatch—the period just before the execution, generally 24 hours, when the condemned inmate is watched by the guards who will also take part in the execution process.[257] The extra costs of the deathwatch have not been estimated.

Execution

Executions themselves are fairly inexpensive, regardless of the method employed. The electricity needed for an electrocution costs about 31 cents; the sodium cyanide pellets used in executions by lethal gas were about $250; and the chemicals needed for a lethal injection cost anywhere from $71.50 to $700.[258] In 2007, the cost of the drugs used in Texas executions was $86.08, the same as it cost in 2003.[259] The prices of the bullets and rope used in shooting and hanging executions have not been reported but must be minimal. The costs of the execution apparatuses also vary considerably and are not very expensive when averaged over a large number of executions. An electrocution system was about $35,000; the cost of a gallows, about $85,000; a gas chamber was around $200,000; and a lethal injection system was around $30,000. These costs do not include payments to the "execution technicians," which may range from $150 to $500 per execution.[260] In North Carolina in 2005 and 2006, 11 executions cost the state $16,369 per execution.[261]

One last cost of capital punishment involves disposal of the body—a potential cost for any inmate who dies in prison. If the family of the executed offender does not make final arrangements, burial or cremation is left to the state. This final cost has not been estimated, but it is unlikely to be very expensive.

STREAMLINING THE APPELLATE AND POSTCONVICTION PROCESS

Proponents of capital punishment argue that the costs of the penalty could be reduced significantly if the appellate and postconviction processes were streamlined. They contend that most of the legal challenges filed by death row inmates or their attorneys are without merit—that they are nothing more than desperate attempts to keep the inmate alive. The evidence presented in Chapter 3, however, shows that many of the habeas corpus petitions filed by death row inmates or their attorneys do have merit. Nevertheless, it is true that, until recently, it was possible for death row inmates to employ the dual system of collateral review numerous times, but this is no longer the case. The Supreme Court began placing restrictions on the federal review process in state capital cases in the 1980s.[262]

In addition, as explained in Chapter 5, the passage of the Antiterrorism and Effective Death Penalty Act of 1996 (and similar measures by state legislatures) has made access to both the federal and state courts during the postconviction process more difficult. However, while the recent restrictions on federal habeas corpus in capital cases may reduce costs at the federal level, they may not reduce costs overall. Costs likely will be shifted to the states and counties where postconviction motions in state courts will be litigated more extensively.[263]

THE COSTS OF MISTAKES

Mistakes made in capital cases (see Chapter 9) can add another monetary cost to the process. For example, Freddie Lee Pitts and Wilbert Lee were pardoned in Florida in 1975 after spending 12 years apiece on death row for a murder that somebody else committed.[264] In 1997, after years of failed efforts, Pitts and Lee received a few hundred thousand dollars each as compensation from the state for its mistakes. Bobby Joe Leaster, received a check from Massachusetts for $75,000 in 1992. The money was the first installment of the $1 million annuity the state pays him for wrongly imprisoning him for 15 years for a murder he did not commit.[265] Leaster was released from prison in 1986 after prosecutors declined to pursue a retrial. Because of the state's fiscal problems, it took several attempts before Massachusetts' legislators approved the indemnification measure. The Ford Heights Four won a $36 million settlement from the Illinois county that wrongfully convicted them. They had spent 18 years in prison before DNA tests exonerated them in 1996.[266] The state of Illinois paid nearly $65 million for wrongful convictions from 2000 through 2009.[267]

Twenty-seven states, the District of Columbia, and the federal government have statutory provisions for indemnifying the wrongly convicted (in capital and noncapital cases). Until recently, most of these states were far from generous. A list of compensating states and the amounts they allow is provided in Chapter 9. Until the end of 2004, when Congress passed the Innocence Protection Act, the federal government limited compensation to a maximum of $5,000 regardless of the amount of time served. The new law now provides a maximum of $100,000 a year. The law also recommends that states "should provide reasonable compensation to any person found to have been unjustly convicted of an offense against the State and sentenced to death."[268] Nevertheless, in many states that provide compensation, attorney expenses for preparing the necessary legal documents can take a third of the money. Getting the money from the state, even after it has been awarded, as noted previously, seldom is easy.[269] Regardless, mistakes made in capital cases can prove costly to the jurisdictions that make them.

"START-UP" COSTS

Another cost of capital punishment is the substantial start-up expense incurred when a jurisdiction decides to reinstate the death penalty. This expense is of three types: (1) building and facility costs, (2) judicial and attorney training costs, and (3) equipment costs.[270] Because the costs of execution equipment have been described previously, only the first two types of start-up costs are examined here.

Building and facility costs vary greatly, but jurisdictions can expect to spend hundreds of thousands and, in some cases, millions of dollars to construct death rows and execution chambers. For example, in 1993, the Wisconsin Department of Corrections estimated that "a new twelve-unit death row, including a lethal injection death chamber" would cost $1.4 million to construct.[271] An estimated $144,600 would have to be spent on one-time start-up overhead costs, and about $500,000 annually for security personnel.[272]

When New York reinstated the death penalty in 1995, the legislature appropriated a little more than $1 million for start-up costs: $389,000 for a 12-cell death row; $190,000 to convert an old correctional hospital into a three-cell death row for women; and $475,000 for a death chamber, injection room, and three holding cells.[273] Florida spent $9.5 million in 1992 to build a new 336-unit death row,[274] and in 1996 the federal government spent $500,000 to build a lethal injection chamber at the new federal death row in Terre Haute, Indiana.[275]

Because "death is different," special training is needed for judges and attorneys involved in death penalty cases. A few jurisdictions require such training. When the New York legislature reinstated capital punishment in 1995, it appropriated about $3.5 million for a new agency for training capital defense attorneys and another $2 million for the training of capital prosecutors.[276] Kansas reinstated the death penalty in 1994, then budgeted $1.4 million for a death penalty defense agency.[277] In 1995, the Wisconsin legislature contemplated the reenactment of capital punishment and considered spending $60,000–$70,000 to bring in national experts for a one-time seminar to train 50–100 lawyers.[278] It also estimated that attorney and judicial training costs for the first 2 years after reenactment would be about $400,000 and then $200,000 annually, thereafter.[279] In short, attorney and judicial training in capital jurisprudence involves both substantial start-up costs and ongoing expenses to keep both lawyers and judges abreast of changes in capital punishment law.

THE LWOP ALTERNATIVE

Currently, all 34 death penalty states plus the federal government and the U.S. military have LWOP.[280] As of the mid-1990s, LWOP was the only alternative to capital punishment in 16 death penalty jurisdictions in the United States; in 12 jurisdictions, the alternative to capital punishment was either LWOP or a lesser punishment, usually life imprisonment with parole eligibility.[281] The preceding discussion shows that it is less costly to sentence capital offenders to LWOP than it is to sentence them to death.

The greatest savings occur when LWOP sentences are imposed following a guilty plea (but see note 163). In such cases, the substantial costs of the bifurcated trial, the automatic appeal, and post-conviction processes are eliminated. The most expensive outcome is when lengthy and complicated death penalty trials are followed by a sentence of LWOP. This outcome is typical because the death penalty is frequently not imposed following a capital trial, and even when it is imposed, it is rarely carried out. For example, between July 1993 and December 2009, 37 Florida death row inmates were executed, while 39 Florida death row inmates died while awaiting execution.[282] As Dieter observes, "the death penalty without executions is just another name for life-without-parole; and this is the most expensive form of life-without-parole because the sentences that are obtained occur after the high costs of death penalty trials."[283]

If LWOP sentences were imposed after a non-death penalty trial (and postconviction review), they would be cheaper than capital punishment because the Supreme Court has ruled that LWOP sentences do not require the super due process procedures necessary when the penalty is death.[284] Thus, the replacement of death sentences with LWOP sentences would reduce financial expenditures considerably.

Critics fear that such a strategy would have the undesirable effect of exacerbating the current prison-overcrowding crisis, but this has not been a problem. For example, according to a recent study, only 2.8 percent of the nation's more than 1.6 million prison inmates in 2008 were serving LWOP sentences.[285] If all death sentences were changed to LWOP, the 106–122 offenders sentenced to death each year (from 2006 through 2009), together with the approximately 3,300 current death row inmates, would hardly be noticed among the more than 1.6 million inmates now confined in American prisons.

Another concern is the medical costs of an increasing number of elderly inmates if the death penalty were replaced with LWOP. At the end of 2009, there were 260 death row inmates aged 60 or older; by contrast, there were 110 death row inmates 60 or older in 2003.[286] The oldest person on death row, until recently, was probably LeRoy Nash, who was 94 years old when he died on February 12, 2010, on Arizona's death row. Nash, who had been in prison almost continually since he was 15 years old and was on Arizona's death row since 1983, was deaf and nearly blind and suffered from heart disease, arthritis, dementia, and mental illness.[287] In many states, elderly prisoners who are not on death row are housed in geriatric facilities inside prisons, or they are placed in "end of life" programs. These options are not available to death row inmates because current policy requires them to be segregated from the general prison population and housed in individual cells on death row.[288] This policy, of course, could be changed. Although the costs of medical care for elderly prison inmates is unknown (but presumably high), national estimates put the annual costs of elderly inmates at about $70,000 or about three times the approximately $23,400 per inmate regardless of age.[289] Thus, there certainly would be added medical expenses if the death penalty were replaced with LWOP, but, as above, the number of elderly LWOP inmates who otherwise would have been sentenced to death if the penalty were available represents only a tiny fraction of the overall prison population.

In sum, death sentences could be replaced with LWOP at considerable cost savings to the taxpayer, with negligible impact on the current prison overcrowding crisis. LWOP sentences would also allow for the correction of miscarriages of justice when they were discovered and would eliminate any brutalizing effect of capital punishment—to name just a few benefits. North Carolina passed legislation that allows prosecutors to offer capital defendants the chance to plead guilty and accept an LWOP sentence.[290] Prosecutors previously did not have this option. The legislation likely will save the state millions of dollars by eliminating the costs of a capital trial and appellate and postconviction review. Whether such a strategy is desirable for other reasons is another matter.

CONCLUSION

The evidence clearly shows that capital punishment systems in the United States are always more expensive than punishment systems without capital punishment because super due process is required in the former but not in the latter. Still, for some people, the cost issue is a red herring because, they argue, there are so few capital prosecutions. For example, they claim that before Illinois abolished its death penalty in 2011, it had only 10–15 capital prosecutions each year.[291] These cost critics contend that even if the costs of capital cases exceeded the costs of noncapital cases by $1 or $2 million, the overall annual cost to the state of Illinois would pale in comparison to its more than $50 billion annual state budget.[292] This might be true if there were really only 10–15 capital prosecutions each year in Illinois, but recent evidence indicates that there were more than 50 capital prosecutions per year in Illinois from 2000 through 2009 (and Cook County, Illinois, from 2000 through the first 6 months of 2010).[293] Furthermore, while Illinois conducted more than 500 capital prosecutions during this period, only 17 death sentences were imposed, making the cost of each death sentence extraordinarily expensive. If the ultimate penal sanction is supported because of the belief that it is cheaper than noncapital punishments, then this chapter establishes why such a belief is mistaken. Thus, a fair question in the capital punishment debate is whether the death penalty is worth the extra cost.

DISCUSSION QUESTIONS

1. Is the death penalty necessary to protect society adequately from the possible future actions of those who have already committed capital crimes?
2. Is the death penalty necessary to protect prison guards and other inmates?
3. Why not execute all capital offenders?
4. Do you agree with Blecker's strategy for narrowing death eligibility? Should death eligibility be narrowed?
5. Should Stanley "Tookie" Williams have been eligible for the Nobel Peace Prize? Why or why not?
6. Should capital punishment be replaced with LWOP?
7. Which costs more: capital punishment or LWOP? How much more? Why?
8. In a society with limited resources, is capital punishment worth the costs?
9. Why is "super due process" so expensive?
10. Could and should the costs of capital punishment be significantly reduced? (If answered in the affirmative, how?)
11. Should the cost of capital punishment matter?

Notes

1. Bowers and Steiner (1999, pp. 623–624).
2. Sharp (2008).
3. Committee on the Judiciary, U.S. Senate (1982, p. 315); also see Rosenbluth (2006) and Van den Haag (1982).
4. Ibid.
5. Levey (2006, p. 40–41); also see Wagner (2006, p. 77).
6. Cheever (2006, p. 218).
7. Ibid.
8. 4 in Death Row in Georgia Flee Jail in Disguise. (1980, July 29). *New York Times* (1857–Current file) [ProQuest Historical Newspapers *The New York Times* (1851–2003)], p. A10; 3 Convicted Killers Recaptured in North Carolina; 4th is Found Dead. (1980, July 31). *New York Times* (1857–Current file) [ProQuest Historical Newspapers *The New York Times* (1851–2003)], p. A12.
9. Escape from Death Row at http://www.courttv.com/onair/shows/thesystem/a_f_episodes/escape_death_row.html.
10. Man Escapes from Texas' Death Row. (1998, November 28). *The Orlando Sentinel*, p. A1; Fugitive Inmate Found Dead. (1998, December 4). *The Orlando Sentinel*, p. A6.
11. "Strenuous Security" as Escapee Returns to Jail at http://msnbc.msn.com/id/9922969/.
12. California has sentenced inmates to LWOP for more than 25 years, and not one inmate with such a sentence has ever been released from prison; see Dieter (1993, p. 13).
13. Amsterdam (1982, p. 354). Zimring (2003, p. 48) points out the irony in the death penalty position of political conservatives, who are more likely to support the death penalty than are political liberals: "If you do not trust government bureaucracies with your tax dollars and racial policies in public schools, how can you trust them to choose appropriate targets for death sentences and believe that government officials can protect against the execution of the innocent? If the government screws up every other major responsibility it administers, why should the death penalty be any different?"
14. Calculated from Bonczar and Snell (2005, pp. 8–9).
15. Calculated from Snell (2010a, Table 20).
16. Radelet, Bedau, and Putnam (1992); Death Penalty Information Center, retrieved November 30, 2010, from http://www.deathpenaltyinfo.org/innocence-and-death-penalty.
17. Material in this section is from Blecker (2001).
18. The Constitution Project (2005, pp. xxiv–xxv).
19. Haines (1996, pp. 139–140).
20. Cited in ibid., p. 227, n. 49.
21. Ibid., p. 138.
22. Cited in ibid., p. 139.
23. Ibid., p. 207.
24. Committee on the Judiciary, U.S. Senate (1982); also see Van den Haag (1982).
25. Sellin (1959, p. 72).
26. Lawes (1969, p. 51).
27. Amsterdam (1982).
28. Sorensen and Wrinkle (1996).
29. Paternoster (1991, p. 279).
30. Ibid.
31. Harris (2000). For additional examples of death row inmates who were rehabilitated, see Guin (2002); Cheever (2006).

32. Furillo (2005).
33. Sellin (1967, pp. 154–160).
34. Sorensen and Pilgrim (2000).
35. Cunningham, Reidy, and Sorensen (2008).
36. However, one inmate, not an LWOP-sentenced inmate but one who had been sentenced to death and had his sentence commuted, killed another inmate. Ibid., p. 61, n. 5.
37. Sorensen and Cunningham (2010).
38. Cunningham, Reidy, and Sorensen (2005).
39. Reidy, Cunningham, and Sorensen (2001).
40. Sellin (1959, p. 76).
41. Ibid., pp. 77–78.
42. Bedau (1982, p. 176, Table 4–5–1).
43. Ibid., p. 177, Table 4–5–2.
44. A.B. Heilbrun, L.C. Heilbrun, and K.L. Heilbrun (1978).
45. Cheever (2006, pp. 4 and 7). Different sources report different numbers of *Furman*-commuted inmates. The 589 number is used here because it was used for the data reported below.
46. Ibid., p. 71.
47. Ibid., p. 147.
48. Ibid., p. 36.
49. Ibid., p. 231.
50. Ibid.
51. Ibid., p. 42.
52. Ibid., p. 168.
53. Ibid., p. 56.
54. Ibid.
55. Ibid., p. 71.
56. Ibid., p. 56
57. Ibid., p. 71.
58. Ibid.
59. Vito, Koester, and Wilson (1991).
60. Marquart and Sorensen (1989, p. 26).
61. Marquart and Sorensen (1988).
62. Vito and Wilson (1988).
63. Killer Once Freed from Death Row Is Executed. (1998, November 18). *The Orlando Sentinel*, p. A16; also see Cheever (2006, chap. 12); but also see the cases of Robert Massie and Carl Bowles, who killed again following release or escape from prison to which they were sent for a previous murder or murders> Marquis (2005, pp. 518–519).
64. Amsterdam (1982).
65. A version of this section appeared as The Economic Costs of Capital Punishment: Past, Present, and Future, in Acker et al. (2003). It is reprinted with permission of the publisher.
66. Culver (1985, p. 574).
67. Sharp (2008).
68. Baumgartner, DeBoef, and Boydstun (2008, p. 45).
69. McGovern (1982, p. 10).
70. Peterson and Bailey (2003) and Snell (2010a, Table 12).
71. On "super due process," see Radin (1980).
72. Dieter (2009a, p. 5); Death Penalty Information Center, retrieved September 8, 2010, from http://www.deathpenaltyinfo.org/number-executions-state-and-region-1976.

73. Death Penalty Has Cost New Jersey Taxpayers $253 Million. (2005).

74. Indiana Editorial Calls for End to "Costly" Death Penalty. (2005). Also see Dickson (2006, p. 280).

75. Larranaga and Mustard (2004).

76. Kansas Study Concludes Death Penalty Is Costly Policy. (2003).

77. Dieter (2009a, p. 6); also see Roman, Chalfin, and Knight (2009), who estimated the additional cost of a death penalty case to be between about $650,000 and $1 million, and the overall cost to Maryland taxpayers between 1978 and 1999 to be in excess of $170 million.

78. Liebman, Fagan, and West (2000, n. 74); also see Cook and Slawson (1993), Dieter (1992), Garey (1985), Hoppe (1992), New York State Defenders Association (1982), Roman et al. (2009), and Spangenberg and Walsh (1989). Between 1995, the year New York reinstated the death penalty, and 1999, New York spent an estimated $68 million on 37 death penalty cases. More than half of these cases resulted in plea deals and life sentences. Eight cases were still pending. Of the nine trials completed, five ended with death sentences and four with LWOP. By the time the first death row inmate is executed, the costs to New York of the five cases could reach $238 million. See Death Penalty Expenses Adding Up. (1999). In 2004, the state supreme court ruled New York's death penalty unconstitutional. As of this writing, New York had not enacted new death penalty legislation.

79. Muwakkil (1989, p. 6).

80. "Hanging Judge" Calls for End to the Death Penalty. (2005).

81. Because of the conditions of prison life, such as violence, HIV and other diseases, poor diets, and poor health conditions, it has been estimated that an inmate sentenced to LWOP will live an average of 31 years in prison; see Brooks and Erickson (1996). At year-end 2009, the median age of a death row inmate at the time of admission to death row was 36 years (the median age of death row inmates was 44 years); see Snell (2010a, Table 5).

82. American Correctional Association 2005 Directory, p. 362; Brooks and Erickson (1996, p. 883); "Death Row Fact Sheet," Florida Department of Corrections at http://www.dc.state.fl.us/oth/deathrow/index.html; "'Hanging Judge' Calls for End to the Death Penalty" (2005); "Inmate Cost Per Day," Florida Department of Corrections at http://www.dc.state.fl.us/pub/statsbrief/cost.html; Villa (2005).

83. Paternoster (1991); also see *Harmelin v. Michigan*, 1991.

84. Cook and Slawson (1993, pp. 97–98).

85. Dieter (2005).

86. Haines (1996, p. 170).

87. Sorensen (2004).

88. See, for example, A Matter of Life and Death: The Effect of Life-Without-Parole Statutes on Capital Punishment. (2006); also see Death Penalty Information Center, retrieved December 2, 2010, from http://www.deathpenaltyinfo.org/death-sentences-year-1977-2009.

89. Haines (1996, p. 170).

90. Spangenberg and Walsh (1989); New York State Defenders Association (1982). Assistant district attorney for Harris County, Texas, Bill Hawkins (2006, p. 258) claims that the police investigation of a death-eligible homicide has "no impact on the criminal justice system," it "does not require more of or less of the police."

91. Garey (1985, p. 1252) and Spangenberg and Walsh (1989, p. 49).

92. Ibid.; Brooks and Erickson (1996, p. 893).

93. Spangenberg and Walsh (1989, p. 49).

94. Cook and Slawson (1993, p. 44, Table 5.3).

95. Georgia Judge Notes Expensive Bottom Line in Capital Cases. (2002).

96. Kansas Study Concludes Death Penalty Is Costly Policy. (2003).

97. Smith (2010).

98. Brooks and Erickson (1996, p. 901) and Spangenberg and Walsh (1989, p. 48).
99. Grand Juries are Involved in Felony Prosecutions in about Half the States and in the Federal System. See Bohm and Haley (2007, p. 296).
100. Spangenberg and Walsh (1989, p. 49).
101. Garey (1985, p. 1251, n. 134).
102. Cook and Slawson (1993, pp. 28–29, n. 47).
103. Ibid., p. 30, n. 47.
104. Cook and Slawson (1993, pp. 28–29, n. 47) and Garey (1985, pp. 1249–1250).
105. Garey (1985, p. 1248) and Spangenberg and Walsh (1989, p. 50).
106. New York State Defenders Association (1982, p. 12).
107. Cook and Slawson (1993, p. 81, Table 7.6).
108. Garey (1985, p. 1253) and Spangenberg and Walsh (1989).
109. Ibid.
110. Ibid.
111. Ibid.
112. Author's own experience.
113. Brooks and Erickson (1996, p. 895).
114. Cook (2009).
115. Colarossi (2010).
116. In some cases, the threat of the death penalty may encourage guilty pleas, thus providing substantial cost savings in comparison to capital cases that go to trial. However, the death penalty is not often used in this way, see Brooks and Erickson (1996, pp. 890–891), and a recent study shows that the threat of the death penalty does not increase defendants' overall propensity to plead guilty, although it does lead defendants to accept plea bargains with harsher terms; see Kuziemko (2006). In some states, state law restricts such plea bargains. Moreover, if this were an avowed purpose of the death penalty, it is unlikely "the courts would uphold the constitutionality of such an intentional interference with the right to trial." See Dieter (2005). If capital punishment were replaced with LWOP, on the other hand, it is unlikely that defendants would plead guilty to LWOP (what would they have to lose if they went to trial?). Consequently, in jurisdictions that provide for both capital punishment and LWOP sentences, the availability of capital punishment, as at least a threat, may sometimes reduce costs.
117. Cook (2009), Garey (1985, p. 1247, n. 114), Spangenberg and Walsh (1989).
118. Brooks and Erickson (1996, p. 897) and Spangenberg and Walsh (1989, p. 52).
119. Roman et al. (2009).
120. Dieter (2009a, p. 5).
121. Ibid., p. 5, n. 4.
122. Kansas Study Concludes Death Penalty Is Costly Policy. (2003).
123. Garey (1985, p. 1258, n. 175).
124. New York Death Penalty Trial 3.5 Times More Costly Than Non-capital Trial. (1999).
125. Hoppe (1992).
126. Hawkins (2006, p. 261).
127. Cook and Slawson (1993, pp. 59 and 61, Tables 6.2 and 6.3).
128. Ibid., p. 59, Table 6.2.
129. Ibid., pp. 59 and 61, Tables 6.2 and 6.3.
130. Ibid., p. 59, Table 6.2.
131. Cook (2009).
132. Ibid.

133. Cook and Slawson (1993, pp. 59 and 61, Tables 6.2 and 6.3).
134. Roman et al. (2009).
135. Paternoster (1991, p. 198); also see Garey (1985, p. 1259).
136. Dow (2002a, pp. 4–5).
137. Georgia Judge Notes Expensive Bottom Line in Capital Cases. (2002).
138. Death Penalty Expenses Adding Up. (1999).
139. Garey (1985, p. 1257) and Spangenberg and Walsh (1989).
140. Garey (1985, p. 1257).
141. Brooks and Erickson (1996, p. 896, n. 134); Assistant District Attorney for Harris County, Texas, Bill Hawkins (2006, p. 259) reports that jury selection in capital cases in his county averages close to 3 weeks, compared to 1 day in non-death capital cases. On taking longer than the guilt phase, see Leyte-Vidal and Silverman (2006, p. 271).
142. Roman et al. (2009).
143. Death Penalty Expenses Adding Up. (1999).
144. Hoppe (1992).
145. Cook (2009).
146. Kaplan (1983, p. 571).
147. Garey (1985, p. 1255) and Spangenberg and Walsh (1989, p. 51).
148. Colarossi (2011c).
149. Georgia Judge Notes Expensive Bottom Line in Capital Cases. (2002).
150. Colarossi (2011c).
151. Garey (1985, p. 1256) and Spangenberg and Walsh (1989, p. 52).
152. Garey (1985, p. 1256).
153. Ibid., p. 1257, n. 173.
154. Ibid.; Brooks and Erickson (1996, p. 897) and Spangenberg and Walsh (1989).
155. Cook and Slawson (1993, p. 15) and Spangenberg and Walsh (1989, p. 54).
156. Spangenberg and Walsh (1989, p. 53).
157. Cook and Slawson (1993, p. 61, Table 6.3).
158. Ibid.
159. Cook (2009).
160. Haines (1996, p. 172).
161. Cook and Slawson (1993, p. 44, Table 5.3).
162. Ibid.
163. Although the hourly costs of district attorneys, public defenders, judges, etc. are usually "fixed" (because they receive salaries) and would be the same whether the case was capital or noncapital, the costs of these participants in the process are provided for two reasons. First is to allow the reader to gauge the costs of a capital case (or any case) that goes to trial (and is further reviewed) in comparison to the costs of a capital case that is plea bargained to LWOP. Second is to help in the estimation of some of the "hidden costs" or "opportunity costs" of capital punishment. When district attorneys spend much of their time trying capital cases, when court time is consumed with lengthy death trials, and when appellate courts spend so much of their time reviewing death penalty appeals, other noncapital cases are affected. For example, other serious cases receive less attention than they would otherwise, or cases that ordinarily would be tried are plea bargained, simply because there is not enough time to do otherwise. On the latter point, see Haines (1996, pp. 171–172), for example.
164. Georgia Judge Notes Expensive Bottom Line in Capital Cases. (2002). Harris County, Texas Assistant District Attorney Bill Hawkins (2006, p. 259) reports that because of experience, "the prosecution of a capital death case does not significantly affect the ordinary operations of the office."

165. Roman et al. (2009).
166. Ibid.
167. Dieter (2009a, p. 9).
168. Garey (1985, p. 1258).
169. Georgia Judge Notes Expensive Bottom Line in Capital Cases. (2002).
170. Brooks and Erickson (1996, p. 892).
171. Ibid., p. 894.
172. Clary (2001).
173. Acker and Lanier (1999, pp. 448–449).
174. Bright (1997, p. 11).
175. Birmingham News Criticizes Costly, Arbitrary Death Penalty. (2005).
176. Death Penalty Expenses Adding Up. (1999).
177. Indiana Taxpayers Charged over $2 Million for Defense of Three Capital Cases. (1999).
178. Death Penalty Expenses Adding Up. (1999).
179. Cook (2009).
180. Partial Costs in the Virginia Trials of John Muhammad and Lee Malvo. (2004).
181. McVeigh Defense: $13.8 Million. (2001, June 30). *The Orlando Sentinel*, p. A17.
182. Hoppe (1992).
183. Garey (1985) and Spangenberg and Walsh (1989).
184. Cook and Slawson (1993, p. 46) and Roman et al. (2009).
185. Ibid.
186. Ibid.
187. Cook and Slawson (1993, p. 46, Table 5.4) and Roman et al. (2009).
188. Cook and Slawson (1993, p. 45).
189. Hoppe (1992).
190. Cook and Slawson (1993, p. 46) and Roman et al. (2009).
191. Roman et al. (2009).
192. Cook and Slawson (1993, p. 46) and Garey (1985, p. 1255). See note 152.
193. Death Penalty Expenses Adding Up. (1999).
194. Spangenberg and Walsh (1989, p. 52).
195. Cited in Governor's Commission on Capital Punishment (2002, p. 199); also see Haines (1996, p. 170).
196. Cited in Governor's Commission on Capital Punishment (2002, p. 199).
197. Costly Death Penalty Takes Toll on State Budgets. (2003).
198. Haines (1996, p. 171).
199. Ibid.
200. Ibid.
201. Dieter (2005).
202. Paternoster (1991, p. 212).
203. Kansas Study Concludes Death Penalty Is Costly Policy. (2003).
204. Spangenberg and Walsh (1989). At year-end 2005, the federal government was the only exception. In South Carolina, the defendant, if deemed competent, may waive right of sentence review. Idaho, Montana, Oklahoma, South Dakota, and Tennessee require only review of the sentence. Review of conviction in Idaho has to be filed through appeal or forfeited. An appeal of trial court error may be waived in Virginia but not a review of sentence for arbitrariness and proportionality. The right to waive an automatic review has not been addressed in Mississippi. Neither statute nor case law precludes a waiver of appeal in Wyoming. See Snell (2006, p. 3).
205. Brooks and Erickson (1996, pp. 897–898) and Spangenberg and Walsh (1989, p. 53).

206. Cook (2009).
207. Ibid.
208. Ibid.
209. Garey (1985, p. 1263), Paternoster (1991, p. 205), and Spangenberg and Walsh (1989, pp. 52–53), Roman et al. (2009) estimated attorney time in the appeals phase in Maryland to be 600 hours for the defense and 300 hours for the prosecution.
210. Cook and Slawson (1993, p. 48, Table 5.6).
211. Garey (1985).
212. Cook and Slawson (1993, p. 47, Table 5.5).
213. Ibid., p. 79, Table 7.5.
214. Ibid. See note 152.
215. Roman et al. (2009).
216. Ibid.
217. See, for example, Paternoster (1991, pp. 81–82).
218. New Jersey Death Penalty Study Commission Report (January 2007), p. 32, at http://www.njleg.state.nj .us/committees/dpsc_final.pdf.
219. Freedman (1998) and Garey (1985). See Chapter 3, note on the appellate process in capital cases.
220. Hoppe (1992).
221. Spangenberg and Walsh (1989, p. 54).
222. Ibid., p. 55, for both state and federal postconviction proceedings.
223. Paternoster (1991, p. 205).
224. In 2006, a study found that the typical trial record in a capital case in California was 9000 pages, see Death Penalty in California Is Very Costly. (2006). In Indiana, trial records in the initial appeal of a capital sentence typically consist of 3000–5000 pages, or more, and the record presented in subsequent collateral review appeals is usually twice the amount; Dickson (2006, p. 279). The cost for preparing 24 copies of the 22,000-page transcript of a 1999 capital trial in New York was $44,478.28; see Death Penalty Expenses Adding Up. (1999).
225. Hoppe (1992).
226. Cook and Slawson (1993, pp. 81–82, Tables 7.6 and 7.7).
227. Ibid., p. 81, Table 7.6. In California, state habeas corpus petitions typically average 200–300 pages, plus hundreds of pages of exhibits and declarations; see Gillette (2006, p. 264).
228. Kansas Study Concludes Death Penalty is Costly Policy. (2003).
229. Roman et al. (2009).
230. Cook (2009).
231. Ibid.
232. Hoppe (1992).
233. 21 U.S.C. S 848 (q)(4), 1994; also see Howard (1996).
234. See Howard (1996, p. 903).
235. 18 U.S.C. S 3006A, 1994.
236. 18 U.S.C. S 3006A(g)(2)(A), 1994; 28 U.S.C. S 605, 1994.
237. Howard (1996).
238. Ibid., p. 904.
239. Ibid.
240. Ibid.
241. Ibid.
242. Ibid., p. 914
243. Ibid.

244. Ibid., p. 915.

245. Ibid.

246. Ibid.

247. Spangenberg and Walsh (1989, p. 55) for both state and federal postconviction proceedings.

248. Paternoster (1991).

249. Hoppe (1992).

250. Ibid.

251. Cook and Slawson (1993, p. 81, Table 7.6).

252. Some death row inmates have served more than 30 years awaiting execution. For a description of the "living hell" that death row inmates experience, see Gillespie (2003, pp. 35–51) and Johnson (1989, 1990, 2003).

253. See Spangenberg and Walsh (1989, p. 56).

254. See Brooks and Erickson (1996, p. 883); Death Row Fact Sheet, Florida Department of Corrections at http://www.dc.state.fl.us/oth/deathrow/index.html; "Inmate Cost Per Day, Florida Department of Corrections at http://www.dc.state.fl.us/pub/statsbrief/cost.html; Hawkins (2006, p. 261); "Hanging Judge" Calls for End to the Death Penalty. (2005).

255. New Jersey Death Penalty Study Commission Report (2007).

256. Cook (2009).

257. See Johnson (1990, chap. 6).

258. Denno (1994, p. 655).

259. Death Row Facts, Texas Department of Criminal Justice. Retrieved June 20, 2006, and November 28, 2010, from http://www.tdcj.state.tx.us/stat/drowfacts.htm.

260. Denno (1994, p. 655). Denno notes that before 1990, states were increasingly buying "execution trailers" costing $100,000. The trailers included "a lethal-injection machine, a steel holding cell for the prisoner, and additional areas for witnesses, the chaplain, prison employees, and medical personnel," see Denno, ibid.

261. Cook (2009).

262. See, for example, *Barefoot v. Estelle*, 1983; *Saffle v. Parks*, 1990; *Clemons v. Mississippi*, 1990.

263. Brooks and Erickson (1996, pp. 900 and 902).

264. Amsterdam (1982, p. 349).

265. *The Charlotte Observer*, November 13, 1992.

266. Cohen (1999).

267. Bienen (2010, p. 25, Table 1).

268. Justice for All Act of 2004: Section-By-Section Analysis.

269. Scheck, Neufeld, and Dwyer (2001, pp. 297–298).

270. See Brooks and Erickson (1996).

271. Ibid., p. 886.

272. Ibid.

273. Ibid., p. 886, n. 62.

274. Ibid., p. 886.

275. Ibid., pp. 886 887.

276. Ibid., p. 887.

277. Ibid., p. 892.

278. Ibid., p. 887.

279. Ibid.

280. Death Penalty Information Center, retrieved December 3, 2010, from http://www.deathpenaltyinfo.org/life-without-parole. In addition, 14 of 15 states without the death penalty plus the District of Columbia have LWOP. Alaska is the only state without the death penalty not to have LWOP.
281. Acker and Lanier (1995, p. 55).
282. Colarossi (2009).
283. Dieter (2005).
284. *Harmelin v. Michigan*, 1991; Paternoster (1991, p. 279).
285. Nellis and King (2009) and Sabol, West, and Cooper (2009).
286. Snell (2010a, Table 5) and Growing Elderly Population on Death Row. (2005).
287. Death Penalty Information Center, retrieved November 21, 2010, from http://www.deathpenaltyinfo.org/time-death-row.
288. Growing Elderly Population on Death Row. (2005).
289. Villa (2005) and American Correctional Association 2005 Directory, p. 362.
290. Death Penalty Information Center at http://www.deathpenaltyinfo.org/Changes.html#NC.
291. Turow (2003, pp. 61–62).
292. Ibid.
293. Bienen (2010, p. 25, Table 1).

Miscarriages of justice and the death penalty

Austin Sarat writes about a "new abolitionism" that eschews moralistic arguments against the death penalty, as well as those that suggest the penalty is unconstitutional, in favor of arguments about the unfair and inequitable way in which capital punishment is administered. He argues that "new abolitionists" focus on the damage capital punishment has done to core legal values such as due process and equal protection and to the legitimacy of the law itself.[1] Law professor David Dow, who has represented more than 30 death row inmates, argues that the commanding issue for death penalty abolitionists today is innocence; that is, wrongfully convicting the innocent, sentencing the innocent to death, and executing them.[2] Innocence is an issue that exposes many of the injustices associated with capital punishment and is arguably the most unfair outcome of the process. Thus, for these new abolitionists (and old abolitionists, too!), when assessing the administration of capital punishment, it is important to distinguish between how the death penalty might be administered ideally and the way it is administered in practice. To support the death penalty is to support actual practice and not some unobtainable ideal. It is noteworthy, in this regard, that much of the Supreme Court's workload during the past 30+ years has been devoted to refining capital punishment procedures—to making the process work "right." The record of this effort clearly shows that the death penalty in the United States remains very much a work in progress.[3]

One of the enduring problems with capital punishment is that it "not merely kills people, it also kills some of them in error, and these are errors which we can never correct."[4] This irrevocability of capital punishment is one reason why "death is different" and why it requires "super due process."

Ironically, super due process sometimes creates a false sense of security. Some people believe that the chances of a miscarriage of justice in the administration of the death penalty (such as a wrongful arrest, a wrongful charge or indictment, a wrongful conviction, a wrongful sentence, or a wrongful execution) have been reduced to a mere possibility and probably do not occur in any case. The Committee on the Judiciary wrote: "The Court's decision with respect to the rights of the individual … have all but reduced the danger of error in these [capital] cases to that of a mere theoretical possibility. Indeed, the Committee is aware of no case where an innocent man has been put to death."[5] But miscarriages of justice are still a possibility because human beings are fallible. Had the committee examined the evidence, which at the time was anecdotal but, in many cases, persuasive, it could have drawn a different conclusion. For example, M. Watt Espy Jr, the capital punishment historian who has confirmed more than 19,000 legal executions in the United States since 1608, estimates that approximately 5 percent, or 950, of those executed were innocent.[6]

DEFINITIONS OF INNOCENCE

To determine whether any innocent people have been victims of miscarriages of justice in capital cases, it is necessary to settle on a definition of "innocence." There are several possibilities.[7] Probably the most conservative definition is one that includes only those cases in which a government official admitted error. A problem is that in the twentieth century, no government official in the United States had ever admitted to being involved in the execution of an innocent person. This does not mean that none had occurred.

The next most conservative definition of innocence includes only officially exonerated defendants who either were completely uninvolved in the capital crime for which they were convicted or were convicted of a capital crime that did not occur. Examples of the latter category are defendants who were convicted of capital rape (when rape was a capital crime) even though sexual relations were consensual or defendants convicted of capital murder even though the alleged victim was alive.[8] This was the definition of innocence employed by Bedau and Radelet (1987) in their research (which is discussed later) and the definition used in this chapter (unless indicated otherwise).

A more liberal definition of innocence might include capital defendants whose cases were dismissed or who were found not guilty at retrial. A problem with this definition is that such defendants may be legally innocent but factually guilty. Other definitions might include defendants convicted of capital crimes even though those crimes were accidental, committed in self-defense, or the product of mental illness. In none of these examples should the crime have been considered capital in the first place, even though in some cases it was. In short, a more liberal definition of innocence produces a larger number of such people, while a more conservative definition produces a smaller number.

It should also be noted that the best evidence of miscarriages of justice in capital cases is the release of convicted capital offenders prior to their executions. The reason is that once a person has been executed, there is usually little interest in pursuing his or her claim of innocence. Critics may complain that such "freed" individuals should not count because they were not executed, and, furthermore, they show that the system works. However, it should be remembered that, in each case, the freed individual was the victim of a miscarriage of justice (many of them spent years on death row despite their innocence) and in all likelihood would have been executed if not for sheer luck.

MISCARRIAGES OF JUSTICE IN PRE-*GREGG* (1976) CAPITAL CASES

BORCHARD'S RESEARCH

Yale law professor Edwin Borchard conducted the pioneering study of miscarriages of justice in the United States.[9] Responding to a challenge from the district attorney of Worcester County, Massachusetts, who contended that innocent men are never convicted, Borchard accumulated case studies of 65 people whose experiences with the justice system belied the district attorney's belief. The 65 miscarriages of justice included several cases in which men condemned to die were eventually exonerated. Borchard's research, which was published in 1932 in his classic book, *Convicting the Innocent*, exposed for the first time how frequently wrongful convictions occurred in the U.S. criminal justice system.

BEDAU'S RESEARCH

One of the first scholars to publish a study of miscarriages of justice exclusively in capital cases or potentially capital cases in the United States (in 1964) was Hugo Adam Bedau.[10] Bedau reported:

74 cases between 1893 and 1962 involving criminal homicide, and thus the possibility of a death sentence, in which the evidence suggested that the following major errors had occurred: In each of the 74 cases an innocent person was arrested and indicted; in 71, the innocent person was convicted and sentenced; in 30 (including 11 in states with no death penalty), there was a sentence to prison for life; in 31 cases, there was a sentence to death; in eight an innocent person was executed.[11]

Later, Bedau added 50 "new" cases to the 74 above. The new cases covered 1930–1980.

RESEARCH BY BEDAU AND RADELET

A more recent and ambitious attempt to document miscarriages of justice in capital cases is the joint effort by Bedau and Michael L. Radelet.[12] They have cataloged 416 cases involving 496 defendants who were convicted of capital or potentially capital crimes in the twentieth century, in many cases sentenced to death, and who were later found to be innocent.[13] The 416 cases represent those found through the summer of 1991, when the research was formally concluded. Among the innocent people wrongfully convicted were 23 people who were executed (about 5% of the total) and another 22 people who were reprieved within 72 hours of execution.[14]

Of the 496 people wrongfully convicted, 84 percent were convicted prior to 1976 and the implementation of super due process. All but one of the wrongful executions (96%) occurred before 1976. One should not infer from these percentages that super due process has significantly reduced miscarriages of justice in capital cases, however. The "prior-to-1976 data" are for 7.5 decades, while the "1976-and-after data" are for only about 1.5 decades. The average number of people wrongfully convicted of capital crimes in the first six decades of the twentieth century is 59 per decade. The number of wrongful convictions for the 1980s is also 59.[15] During the first 7.5 decades of the twentieth century, there was an average of six wrongful convictions in capital cases discovered each year. This was about the same number of discovered wrongful convictions per year during the 1980s with super due process. The yearly average is based on the number of wrongful convictions discovered by Bedau and Radelet, which, according to them, may represent only the "tip of the iceberg."

MISCARRIAGES OF JUSTICE IN POST-*GREGG* (1976) CAPITAL CASES DESPITE SUPER DUE PROCESS

Research by Bedau and Radelet reveals that 16 percent of the wrongful convictions in capital cases and one of the 23 wrongful executions occurred between 1976 and the summer of 1991—after the reimposition of the death penalty and super due process and the conclusion of their research. Between 1976 and 1979, 21 wrongful convictions were discovered (an average of seven per year); during the 1980s, 59 wrongful convictions were discovered (almost six per year); and in 1990, only one wrongful conviction was found. Under post-*Gregg* statutes and super due process, according to research by Bedau and Radelet, there has been an average of six or seven discovered wrongful convictions (excluding the one in 1990) in capital cases per year. This average is about the same as the one for the prior period.

Looked at somewhat differently, the Death Penalty Information Center reports that since 1973 (as of December 2010), 138 people in 26 states have been released from death rows because of evidence of their innocence. This represents about one death row inmate released for every nine that have been executed. The average number of innocent death row inmates being released has been increasing according to this source. Between 1973 and 1999 there was an average of 2.84 innocent death row inmates released per year. Between 1999 and 2010, on the other hand, there has been an average of 5.72 death row inmates released per year.[16]

Again, it must be remembered that the averages are based only on those wrongful convictions that have been discovered. It does not appear that super due process protections have made much of a difference in the incidence of wrongful convictions in capital cases.[17] The evidence shows that despite super due process safeguards, miscarriages of justice in capital cases continue. On the other hand, death penalty proponents argue that these data demonstrate that super due process works because it has dramatically reduced, if not eliminated altogether, wrongful executions.[18] None of the 138 people released from death row was executed. Indeed, death penalty proponents maintain that, among the more than 8,000 defendants sentenced to death under post-*Furman* statutes, there is no incontrovertible evidence that a single innocent person has been executed.[19] Furthermore, death penalty advocates claim that the vast majority of the released death row inmates were not "factually" innocent but rather the objects of procedural errors that required reviewing courts to order retrials and, for a variety of reasons, prosecutors elected not to retry the case.[20] Among the reasons that prosecutors might not retry a case are the following: (1) the prosecutor was barred from using some of the evidence against the defendant by the appellate court; (2) incriminating evidence against the defendant was misplaced or destroyed; (3) witnesses against the defendant, often coperpetrators, either have or have not received the prosecutor's incentive to testify and thus have no incentive to testify again; (4) key prosecution witnesses cannot be found or are deceased; (5) because of the passage of time, prosecution witnesses may have trouble recalling what occurred, thus injecting doubt into the prosecution's case; and (6) the public may no longer support a prosecution because their feelings about the case have changed or they are no longer interested.[21] In light of these allegations, what does the evidence show? Following are a few examples that have received some publicity.

EXAMPLES FROM NEWS ACCOUNTS

Wayne Williams, the so-called Atlanta child murderer, was arrested on June 21, 1981, and later convicted of killing two ex-felons (27 and 21 years old). He was sentenced to two life terms.[22] Police also linked Williams to 21 of 27 child murders, and these cases were then closed. Meanwhile, the unsolved murders of young blacks continued for three more years, until 1984. Police refused to say how many murders occurred following Williams's arrest, but the Fulton County medical examiner's log listed at least 23 that seemed to fit the pattern. Many people feel that Williams was a scapegoat.

In 1984, Larry Hicks of Gary, Indiana, won his freedom 2 weeks before his scheduled execution. Apparently an innocent bystander, Hicks had been convicted of murder on the testimony of one person in a trial that lasted only a day and a half.[23] Also in 1984, Earl Charles was nearly executed in Georgia for a double murder. He was freed after proving that he was in Florida at the time.[24]

Randall Dale Adams was released from a Texas prison in 1989 after serving more than 12 years following his 1977 conviction for the murder of a Dallas police officer.[25] Adams, the subject of an award-winning documentary, *The Thin Blue Line*, once came within 3 days of execution, despite steadfastly maintaining his innocence. In the documentary, the state's key witness against Adams, David Harris, all but confessed to the shooting for which Adams was convicted. The Texas Court of Criminal Appeals set aside Adams's conviction and noted that prosecutors had suppressed evidence and that witnesses had given perjured testimony in the case.

Also in 1989, Timothy Hennis walked away from a New Hanover County, North Carolina, courthouse a free man after serving 844 days on death row at Central Prison in Raleigh.[26] Hennis was convicted of three murders in July 1986. He was granted a new trial when the North Carolina Supreme Court ruled that the state's use of victim photographs may have inflamed the jury. The jury acquitted him at his second trial.

Leonel Torres Herrera was executed in Texas on May 12, 1993, for the murder of two police officers.[27] Prior to his execution, the Supreme Court rejected evidence (sworn statements) that his then-dead brother had committed the crimes. The Court ruled that Herrera and others like him are not entitled to federal hearings on belated evidence of innocence unless they meet an undefined "extraordinarily high" level of proof. The Court opined that relief in cases such as Herrera's should be sought through executive clemency.

In June 1993, Anson Avery Maynard's death sentence was commuted to life in prison by North Carolina Governor Jim Martin.[28] Maynard had been convicted of the 1981 killing of his thief-partner, Steven Henry. It was believed that Henry had made a deal to testify against Maynard and that Maynard had killed Henry to keep him silent. Maynard was convicted on the testimony of a man who swore he had witnessed the killing. No physical evidence tied Maynard to the crime. As Maynard awaited his execution, the wife of the man who had testified against him admitted she had lied during her part of the trial in order to protect her husband—who may have been Henry's killer in a drug deal gone bad. Several alibi witnesses then came forward, including a truck driver who corroborated Maynard's claim that he had hitchhiked a ride after his car broke down far from where the crime was committed.

In 1993, a Baltimore County, Maryland, circuit judge overturned Kirk Bloodsworth's conviction for the rape and murder of a 9-year-old girl and ordered him to be freed from prison.[29] Bloodsworth had served 9 years in prison, part of it on death row, despite his continued claim of innocence. His conviction was overturned after DNA testing of the semen on the girl's underpants indicated that someone else had committed the crime. Bloodsworth had been convicted on the testimony of three eyewitnesses who stated that they saw the defendant with the girl shortly before she disappeared. Bloodsworth insisted that he had never met the girl.

Jesse Dwayne Jacobs was executed in Texas on January 4, 1995. Two days prior to the execution, the Supreme Court denied his request for a stay of execution, even though the state of Texas conceded that he did not kill the victim of the kidnapping and murder for which he was convicted in 1987.[30] Jacobs originally confessed to the crime, but later recanted and told authorities that his sister, Bobbie Hogan, had committed the murder. He said that he confessed to the murder because he preferred death to spending the rest of his life in prison. Seven months after Jacobs was convicted of capital murder, his sister was tried and convicted of the same crime. During the sister's trial, the prosecutor, who had also prosecuted Jacobs, told the jury that the sister had pulled the trigger and that Jacobs did not even know that she had a gun. Jacobs was called to testify at his sister's trial and claimed that he was outside when the killing took place in an abandoned house. The Supreme Court has held (in *Enmund v. Florida*, 1982) that the Eighth Amendment prohibits the execution of a person who participated in a crime that led to murder when that person did not actually kill or intend for a killing to occur.

Don Paradis was set free in April 2000 after serving 21 years on Idaho's death row for a murder he did not commit. With the help of a New York City corporate attorney working pro bono for two decades, Paradis had his conviction overturned by a federal judge because of irrefutable evidence that the prosecution had concealed exculpatory evidence. Paradis's attorney estimates that the cost of securing justice for his client was more than $5 million.[31]

In January 2002, Juan Melendez was released from Florida's death row after serving nearly 18 years for a murder he did not commit. Melendez was convicted in 1983 of killing a cosmetology school owner based on the testimony of two witnesses. There was no physical evidence linking Melendez to the murder. After Melendez was convicted, the true killer, Vernon James, confessed to at least four investigators or attorneys, but the prosecutor in the case did not disclose the confession to Melendez's defense attorneys. Also, after Melendez's conviction, one of the witnesses recanted; the other witness is now dead. The witness who recanted was a paid police informant who had negotiated a deal in exchange for his testimony—a fact the prosecutor failed to disclose at the trial. During his prison stay, Melendez, who had always claimed that he was innocent, had lost several rounds of appeals and had his death sentence upheld by the Florida Supreme Court before James's confession to the killing was discovered in 1999.[32]

In April 2004, North Carolina Governor Mike Easley pardoned Darryl Hunt, after vacating the charges against him the previous month. Hunt had served 18 years in prison for a rape and a murder he did not commit. Hunt was freed from prison in December 2003, when DNA evidence led police to another man, Willard Brown, who confessed to the crimes and acting alone. Brown was charged with murder, rape, kidnapping, and robbery; pled guilty to the charges; and was sentenced to life in prison plus 10 years.[33] Two eyewitnesses had identified Hunt as the perpetrator in the 1984 crime. Two juries had convicted him and appellate courts upheld the convictions, even though DNA testing in 1994 proved that he was not the rapist. Only after Brown was arrested for Hunt's supposed crimes did the prosecutors turn over to Hunt's attorneys hundreds of pages of police reports they illegally withheld, including a two-page report of a 1986 interview with Brown, who the police briefly suspected was the perpetrator in the 1984 crimes. The eyewitnesses, not surprisingly, were mistaken.[34] One eyewitness picked Hunt out of a photograph lineup after spending hours with the lead detective. The second witness failed to identify Hunt in a live lineup but later picked him out in a photograph lineup.[35] Hunt's attorney observed, "… we always ran into so many obstacles, from the courts and the police, from district attorneys, … [o]ther attorneys were very skeptical, and most people in the community were very dubious about Darryl's innocence."[36]

In February 2006, the Florida Supreme Court unanimously overturned the conviction of death row inmate John Ballard and ordered his acquittal in the 1999 murders of two of his acquaintances. The court concluded that the circumstantial evidence against him was insufficient to sustain his conviction. The state's primary evidence was a hair and a fingerprint, both of which could have been left during his many visits to the victims' apartment. Bloody fingerprints and 100 other hair samples were found associated with the crime scene, but none of them belonged to Ballard, who always maintained his innocence. One of the victims was a known drug dealer and had been the target of gang violence in the past, but the state attorney never presented evidence ruling out gang violence or addressed the suspected motive of robbery. The court's acquittal was rare. Since 1976, the Florida Supreme Court has acquitted only three people of all charges.[37]

In May 2007, Curtis McCarty was released from prison after a district court judge ordered that the charges against him be dismissed. McCarty had spent the last 22 years in an Oklahoma prison, 16 of the years on death row. The judge ruled that the case against McCarty was tainted by the questionable testimony of former police chemist Joyce Gilchrist (more about Gilchrist later), who gave improper expert testimony about semen and hair evidence during McCarty's two trials. Gilchrist falsely testified that hairs and other biological evidence showed that McCarty could have been the rapist and killer of a police officer's daughter in 1982. Although Gilchrist's original notes revealed that hairs from the crime scene did not match McCarty, she changed her notes to say that the hairs did indeed match him. When the defense requested retesting, the hairs were lost. A judge has said that Gilchrist either destroyed or willfully lost the hairs. Recent DNA testing also showed that another person raped the victim. McCarty had maintained his innocence since his arrest.[38]

In July 2009, Ronald Kitchen was exonerated and released after spending 21 years in an Illinois prison, including 13 years on death row. Kitchen was one of the death row inmates whose sentence was commuted to LWOP by former Illinois Governor George Ryan in 2003. Kitchen and a codefendant had been found guilty of the murders of two women and three children in 1988. Kitchen's conviction was based primarily on a confession he gave to detectives under the command of discredited former Police Commander Jon Burge after hours of beatings and threats by police (more about Burge later). Prosecutors also relied on the testimony of the defendant's friend who was in prison for burglary. This witness later recanted his testimony, and the prosecutors withheld from the defense that they had released this witness from prison early in return for his testimony. Following a review of the case, the Illinois assistant attorney general told the trial judge that the state could not "sustain its burden of proof," and justice required the release of Kitchen and his codefendant.[39]

These are only a few of the many examples that could have been cited. Newspaper accounts of wrongful convictions are much more prevalent today than they were prior to 1991. Research shows that "exonerated defendants today receive more than ten times the number of [newspaper] stories, per individual, than those who were exonerated before 1991."[40] According to Baumgartner and his associates, before 1991, the "negative stereotyping of criminal defendants conspired with basic ignorance to produce mass-level denial about the fallibilities of the American justice system ... All this changed in the mid-1990s. Within a few short years ... [the public] was [e]xposed to a virtual flood of information about the risk of executing an innocent individual, [and] the public slowly began to see things from another point of view."[41]

WRONGFUL EXECUTIONS UNDER POST-*GREGG* (1976) STATUTES

Documenting cases of innocent persons executed is an extraordinarily difficult task. Once an alleged murderer is dead, it is almost impossible to right the record, so a degree of uncertainty nearly always characterizes such cases. Of particular interest are wrongful executions that have taken place under post-*Gregg* (1976) statutes and super due process. Bedau and Radelet report one (as of the summer of 1991): James Adams, a black man, convicted of first-degree murder in 1974 and executed in Florida in 1984. Following is the description of the facts of the case, as taken from the catalog of defendants of Bedau and Radelet:

> Witnesses located Adams' car at the time of the crime at the home of the victim, a white rancher. Some of the victim's jewelry was found in the car trunk. Adams maintained his innocence, claiming that he had loaned the car to his girlfriend. A witness identified Adams as driving the car away from the victim's home shortly after the crime. This witness, however, was driving

a large truck in the direction opposite to that of Adams' car, and probably could not have had a good look at the driver. It was later discovered that this witness was angry with Adams for allegedly dating his wife. A second witness heard a voice inside the victim's home at the time of the crime and saw someone fleeing. He stated this voice was a woman's; the day after the crime he stated that the fleeing person was positively not Adams. More importantly, a hair sample found clutched in the victim's hand, which in all likelihood had come from the assailant, did not match Adams' hair. Much of this exculpatory information was not discovered until the case was examined by a skilled investigator a month before Adams' execution. Governor Graham, however, refused to grant even a short stay so that these questions could be resolved.[42]

Critics have challenged the inclusion of James Adams by Bedau and Radelet. They contend that a reading of the trial transcript leaves little doubt that Adams was guilty of the crime for which he was executed. They attribute the mistake of Bedau and Radelet to their source of information, which was Adams's Petition for Executive Clemency (the only source they cited) written by his defense attorneys. The Florida Clemency Board found Adams's petition without merit, something that Bedau and Radelet failed to mention.[43] In a personal communication to this author, Radelet took exception to these criticisms.[44] He noted that the Florida Clemency Board, which comprises Florida Cabinet members, specifically, the governor, attorney general, chief financial officer, and commissioner of agriculture, is hardly an objective body. He also explained that, in addition to the clemency petition, his and Bedau's inclusion of Adams in their catalog was based on his reading of the entire trial transcript and all the appellate briefs for both the prosecution and defense; his conversation with Adams on Florida's death row; and conversations with Adams's minister, the retired Philadelphia police detective who investigated the case, his lead attorney, and other attorneys who worked on the case. Only the clemency petition was cited in the notes because, in Radelet's words, it was "the most concise treatment of the case" and "to cite everything else would have been … overkill."

Bedau and Radelet also cite the case of Edward Earl Johnson who was executed in Mississippi on May 20, 1987. Although they describe why they doubt his guilt, they did not include him in their catalog apparently because his case did not meet their conservative definition of innocence.

Besides Leonel Torres Herrera and Jesse Dwayne Jacobs, who were both executed in Texas in 1993 and 1995, respectively (both cases were described previously but were not included in the catalog of cases of Bedau and Radelet because their executions occurred after the summer of 1991 when the research by Bedau and Radelet was formally concluded), another post-*Gregg* (1976) execution involved Robert Sullivan, who was convicted in 1973 and executed in Florida in 1983. Enough questions were raised about Sullivan's guilt that Pope John Paul II made a personal plea to Florida Governor Graham to halt the execution. Other people executed after 1976 and the implementation of super due process, despite evidence of their innocence, include (state and date of execution in parentheses): Timothy Baldwin (Louisiana, 1984), Willie Jaspar Darden (Florida, 1988), Carlos DeLuna (Texas, 1989), Walter Blair (Missouri, 1993), Ruben Cantu (Texas, 1993), Robert Nelson Drew (Texas, 1994), Roy Stewart (Florida, 1994), Girvies L. Davis (Illinois, 1995), Barry Fairchild (Arkansas, 1995), Larry Griffin (Missouri, 1995), Bernard Bolender (Florida, 1995), Billy Gardner (Texas, 1995), Dennis Stockton (Virginia, 1995), Joseph O'Dell (Virginia, 1997), David Spence (Texas, 1997), Leo Jones (Florida, 1998), Wilburn Henderson (Arkansas, 1998), Troy Farris (Texas, 1999), Roy Roberts (Missouri, 1999), Bernie Demps (Florida, 2000), Gary Graham (Texas, 2000), Claude Jones (Texas, 2000), and Cameron Willingham (Texas, 2004).[45] It is important to emphasize that the evidence of wrongful execution in each of these cases is not definitive. For example, a previous member of this list, Roger Keith Coleman, who was executed in Virginia in 1992, has been removed. In January 2006, Virginia Governor Mark Warner announced the results of new DNA tests that confirmed Coleman's guilt. The new DNA tests used technology that was not available at the time of Coleman's execution.[46]

Not counting Coleman, as many as 26 people (and likely more) may have been executed in error in the United States since 1976 and the implementation of super due process. This represents about 2 percent of all executions through December 2010. How could these wrongful executions (and wrongful convictions) occur, especially within the context of super due process? This question is addressed shortly. First, however, it is important to distinguish between two general types of errors that occur in capital cases.

ERRORS IN CAPITAL CASES

Most errors in capital cases are probably never discovered, but of those that are there are two general types: "harmless" errors and "serious" or "prejudicial" errors.[47] A serious or prejudicial error is one that can be shown by the defendant to have likely affected the outcome of the trial or to be the type of error that generally results in reversals. In addition—and this is important—the error has to be properly preserved. A harmless error is one, which by proof beyond a reasonable doubt, did not contribute to the verdict. Appellate courts will reverse convictions and sentences only for serious or prejudicial errors that have been properly preserved.

Prior to the mid-1960s, nearly any mistake, especially a violation of a defendant's constitutional rights, was considered serious or prejudicial even if it did not affect the outcome of the trial. In cases tainted by such error, appellate courts almost always reversed convictions. Critics complained that the practice allowed clearly guilty criminal defendants to escape justice because of minor errors—"legal technicalities"—that probably did not adversely influence the trial's outcome. In 1967, the Supreme Court created the "Chapman rule" in *Chapman v. California* (386 U.S. 18). The rule provided that violations of a defendant's rights do not require remedy (reversal of conviction or sentence) unless the error or errors are serious or prejudicial.

At each appeal stage, what constitutes serious or prejudicial error becomes more restrictive mostly due to the requirement that error be properly preserved. For example, most state direct appeals courts will not grant relief based on error—even if the error affected the outcome of the trial—if three conditions are not met: (1) a timely objection was not made at trial, (2) a motion for a new trial based on the objection is not made in a timely fashion after the trial ends, and (3) the objection is not properly asserted in a timely appeal. Defendants may suffer even though the failure to properly preserve the error is entirely their defense attorneys' fault. Several capital defendants have been executed despite obvious prejudicial errors because of their lawyers' failure to properly preserve their objections (when objections were made in the first place). Even in the case of a claim of innocence based on new evidence, 33 death penalty states require that such a claim be made within 6 months of the final appeal. Virginia, which has the shortest deadline in the United States, requires the claim to be made within 21 days following conviction. Only seven states allow the motion at any time. Consequently, most prisoners who claim innocence based on new evidence can get state relief only by applying to the governor for executive clemency.[48]

At the state postconviction stage, serious or prejudicial error is properly preserved when it (1) meets the criteria of the direct appeals stage, (2) involves a state or federal constitutional issue, and (3) was not or could not have been raised on direct appeal. Today, most error discovered by state appellate courts in capital cases is considered harmless and does not result in reversals.

At the federal habeas corpus stage, serious or prejudicial error is properly preserved when the error (1) meets the criteria of the direct appeals stage, (2) violates the federal Constitution, (3) does not involve the Fourth Amendment's exclusionary rule, (4) is not based on a new rule of federal law if litigated in 1989 or later, and (5) if litigated in 1993 or thereafter, meets an especially high standard of prejudice or harmful error (that the error had "substantial and injurious effect or influence in determining the jury's verdict").

Given the restrictive requirements of serious or prejudicial error, one might suppose that the percentage of death sentences reversed on these grounds would be small. However, that was not the case, at least at first. According to a study of the fully reviewed state death sentences imposed between 1973 and 1995, two-thirds were reversed at one of the appeal stages because of serious or prejudicial errors.[49] The study found that in 82 percent of the reversals by state postconviction courts the defendant deserved a sentence other than death when the errors were cured on retrial and in 7 percent of the reversals the defendant was found to be innocent of the capital crime. Eighty percent of the reversals were due to ineffective assistance of counsel, prosecutor misconduct, unconstitutional jury instructions, and judge/jury bias. Yet, as noted in Chapter 3, the number of reversals in death penalty appeals has been decreasing dramatically in recent years, not because of greater fairness in the system or fewer constitutional errors, but rather because death row inmates are simply less likely to prevail. Nearly all constitutional errors today are subject to harm analysis and "proving that an error was harmful is difficult or impossible."[50] The irony, as Dow observes, is that "it is easier in our system to convict someone who did not commit a crime than to have that conviction set aside once we have evidence of the person's innocence."[51]

WHY WRONGFUL CONVICTIONS OCCUR IN CAPITAL CASES

As law professor Samuel Gross surmises, "The basic cause for the comparatively large number of errors in capital cases is a natural and laudable human impulse: We want murderers to be caught and punished."[52] Many of the errors that contribute to wrongful convictions in capital cases frequently occur long before the case goes to trial. Some of the sources of these errors are discussed in the following sections.

SHODDY INVESTIGATION AND MISCONDUCT BY THE POLICE

Many wrongful convictions in capital cases are a product of shoddy investigation by the police, who sometimes identify the wrong person as the criminal. According to Gross, "This is the critical stage, where most errors occur."[53] When a capital crime is committed, there is usually great pressure on the police to solve it. When the police are unable to do so within a reasonable amount of time, they sometimes cut corners and jump to conclusions. In particular jeopardy in such cases are people who are innocent of the crime being investigated but who have prior felony records. Individuals with prior felony records often become the focus of criminal investigations, especially when police do not have other leads. Unfortunately for such people, recent exploratory research has discovered that innocent (of the crime being investigated) people with prior felony records who have been wrongly convicted of a capital crime have a much greater chance of being executed than innocent people without prior felony records who have been wrongly convicted of capital crimes.[54]

Law enforcement officers (or others who aid them) may even go so far as to lose, destroy, or manufacture evidence against a suspect. For example, in 1993, the West Virginia Supreme Court of Appeals ruled as invalid hundreds of blood tests that West Virginia prosecutors had used over a 10-year period to link defendants to crime scenes.[55] The state police serologist in every case had lied about, made up, or manipulated evidence to win convictions. The practice of crime laboratory technicians fabricating results to support police suspicions without ever testing the evidence is called "dry labbing."[56] There was also evidence that the serologist's supervisors may have ignored or concealed complaints of his misconduct. At least 134 prisoners may have been entitled to new trials because of the falsified testimony that put them in prison.

More recently, an FBI investigation found that former Oklahoma City police crime laboratory chemist Joyce Gilchrist had misidentified or misinterpreted evidence or testified improperly in court in at least five of the eight cases reviewed. The investigation was prompted by DNA evidence that disproved her testimony against Jeffrey Pierce who was released from prison in May 2001, after serving 15 years on a rape conviction. Another state investigation focused on 23 capital trials in which her testimony helped gain convictions. Ten of these defendants had already been executed. Most controversial was the case of Malcolm Rent Johnson who was executed for rape and murder on January 6, 2000. At Johnson's trial, she testified that six samples of semen taken from the victim's bedroom were consistent with Johnson's blood type. However, when the evidence was reexamined after Johnson's execution, there was no semen present. Gilchrist, who was involved in about 3,000 cases from 1980 to 1993, had been criticized for years. (In 1994 she stopped doing laboratory work after she was promoted to a supervisory position.) In another case, two appellate courts ruled that Gilchrist gave false testimony about semen evidence in the 1992 rape and murder trial of Alfred Brian Mitchell. In August 2001, Mitchell's rape conviction was overturned because of her false testimony (his murder conviction was upheld). State officials and the FBI scrutinized her work in about 1200 cases, including the cases of three death row inmates. She was fired from her job in September 2001 after a hearing by an administrative panel into her alleged misconduct.[57] Note that in both these examples the errors were discovered (posthumously in Malcolm Johnson's case); how many such errors go undetected cannot be known. However, the results of a 2004 *Chicago Tribune* investigation of 200 DNA and death row exonerations nationwide between 1984 and 2004 found that in 55 cases with 66 defendants (more than 25% of the cases studied) original forensic testing or testimony was flawed.[58]

EYEWITNESS MISIDENTIFICATION AND PERJURY BY PROSECUTION WITNESSES

Eyewitness misidentification is the most important contributing factor to wrongful convictions in noncapital cases.[59] For example, a study of DNA exonerations by the Innocence Project discovered that 82 percent of the wrongful convictions were at least in part a result of mistaken identification by an eyewitness or victim.[60] Decades of research show that eyewitnesses are just not very good at identifying criminal offenders especially when the eyewitnesses are under stress or are attempting to identify offenders of a different race. Oftentimes the witnesses who are most certain of their identification are the least likely to be correct.[61] Eyewitness misidentification is probably less common in capital cases, but it still was the second most important factor, accounting for 16 percent of the errors in the capital cases discovered by Bedau and Radelet.

In noncapital cases, the crime victim is often able to identify the offender; in capital cases, this is not possible. Consequently, in capital cases, the police frequently must rely on evidence from other people, such as accomplices, jailhouse snitches, other disreputable characters, and even the defendant himself or herself. Some offenders implicate innocent people to divert suspicion from themselves. Other people, who may or may not have had a role in the crime, perjure themselves for money or for other favors from criminal justice officials, such as the dropping of charges in another unrelated case. It should come as no surprise, then, that perjury by prosecution witnesses is the foremost cause of wrongful convictions in capital cases. Bedau and Radelet identified witness perjury as a factor in 35 percent of the wrongful convictions that they discovered.[62] The Center on Wrongful Convictions at Northwestern University Law School also found that perjury by prosecution witnesses (jailhouse snitches) was the number-one cause of wrongful convictions in capital cases, accounting for 45.9 percent of 111 death row exonerations between 1977 and 2004.[63] Furthermore, recent exploratory research shows that when allegations of witness perjury are raised on appeal, innocent capital defendants are 27 times more likely to be exonerated and released from death row than are innocent defendants who did not raise perjury issues on appeal and are eventually executed.[64]

FALSE CONFESSIONS

The third most common cause of errors in capital cases is false confessions, which accounted for 14 percent of the errors in the cases discovered by Bedau and Radelet.[65] Police officers in the United States have powerful techniques for extracting confessions:

> They confuse and disorient the suspect, they lie about physical evidence, about witnesses, about statements by other suspects; they pretend that they already have their case sealed and are only giving the suspect a chance to explain his side of the story; they pretend to understand, to sympathize, to excuse; they play on the suspect's fears, his biases, his loyalty to family and friends, his religion; they exhaust the suspect and wear him down; in some cases, they use violence, even torture.[66]

By using such coercive and manipulative methods, the police are often successful in getting guilty defendants to confess. Sometimes, however, they get innocent people to confess, too.

One of the most egregious modern cases of police officers extracting false confessions involves former Chicago Police Commander Jon Burge, who, in June 2010, was found guilty in a civil trial in federal district court of obstruction of justice and perjury for lying about alleged torture during interrogations.[67] He could not be criminally prosecuted because the statute of limitations had expired on the cases. Burge was fired from the police force in 1993, because of mounting torture allegations. Burge, now 62 years old and retired, and his "Midnight Crew" allegedly tortured more than 200 black men in police interrogation rooms during the 1970s, 1980s, and early 1990s. Dozens of these men were sent to prison on the basis of false confessions, including several who were sent to death row. For example, after being tortured by Burge's detectives, Ronald Kitchen, as noted previously, falsely confessed to the 1988 killing of two women and three children inside their South Side home. Kitchen was exonerated in 2009 after spending 21 years in prison—13 of them on death row. Kevin Fox, who was suspected of sexually assaulting and murdering his 3-year-old daughter, had been interrogated in a small, windowless room for 14 hours. His request for a lawyer was denied, and he was told that if he did not confess, arrangements would be made for inmates to rape him in jail. Detectives screamed at him, showed him a picture of his daughter bound and gagged with duct tape, and told him his wife was planning to divorce him. Michael Tillman, serving a life sentence and seeking a new trial, was convicted of the rape and murder of a South Side woman in 1986. Tillman said that Burge's detectives coerced him to confess in a police interview room by putting a gun to his head and threatening him with death, repeatedly punching him in the stomach, holding a plastic bag over his head and suffocating him, and pouring 7-Up into his nose after forcing his head back in what his lawyers called a crude form of waterboarding. Cortez Brown sought a new trial in 2009 for his conviction in the 1990 killing of two men. He was sentenced to death but then-Governor George Ryan commuted his death sentence to life in prison in 2003. Brown maintains that Burge's detectives coerced him to falsely confess by beating him with their fists and a flashlight. In other cases, Burge and his detectives were accused of extracting false confessions with radiator burns, electric shocks, and putting a shotgun in a suspect's mouth.

Over the past two decades, the city of Chicago has paid about $10 million to defend Burge, itself, and other defendants in the torture scandal in an attempt to avoid worse potential court damages in dozens of related civil lawsuits. (The Fraternal Order of Police has also contributed to Burge's defense bills.) Nevertheless, in 2007, the city of Chicago agreed to pay nearly $20 million to settle lawsuits filed by four former death row inmates who claimed they were tortured by Burge and his detectives and falsely confessed. The four inmates—Aaron Patterson, Leroy Orange, Stanley Howard, and Madison Hobley—were pardoned by then-Governor Ryan in 2003. In addition, Chicago taxpayers paid more than $7 million for a report on Burge's alleged torturing of suspects. Special prosecutors took more than 4 years to investigate and complete the report released in 2006. Finally, during this entire time, the city has been paying Burge's pension of $3,768 a month for his years on the force.

GUILTY PLEAS BY INNOCENT DEFENDANTS

Another source of error in capital cases is guilty pleas by innocent defendants. Because of their fear of being executed, some innocent people charged with capital crimes plead guilty to lesser, noncapital offenses. Radelet and his colleagues list 16 cases of innocent people in the twentieth century who pled guilty to noncapital murder to avoid the possibility of execution.[68]

PROSECUTOR MISCONDUCT

Prosecutors are the most powerful people in the administration of justice.[69] Not only do they conduct the final screening of each person arrested for a criminal offense, deciding whether there is enough evidence to support a conviction, but in most jurisdictions they also have unreviewable discretion in deciding whether to charge a person with a crime and whether to prosecute the case. In other words, regardless of the amount (or lack) of incriminating evidence, and without having to provide any reasons to anyone, prosecutors have the authority to charge or not to charge a person with a crime and to prosecute or not prosecute a case. If they decide to prosecute, they also determine what the charge or charges will be. (The charge or charges may or may not be the same as the one or ones for which the person was arrested.)

For these reasons and others (such as their authority to decide which cases to "plea bargain" and what bargain to strike), prosecutors are the most powerful people in the capital punishment process. They are the gatekeepers of this process and alone decide whether to charge a suspect with a capital crime. (A committee of prosecutors sometimes makes the decision.) They sometimes try to minimize their awesome responsibility by saying that their role is only to give a judge or jury the opportunity to decide whether death is the appropriate punishment in a capital case. However, their role is much more pivotal. Prosecutors are the first authorities to determine who among those arrested is fit to live and who should die.

Ideally, prosecutors are supposed to charge an offender with a crime (capital or otherwise) and to prosecute the case if after full investigation three, and only three, conditions are met: (1) they find that a crime has been committed; (2) a perpetrator can be identified; and (3) there is sufficient evidence to support a guilty verdict. In capital cases, prosecutors must also find at least one statutorily enumerated aggravating factor.

On the other hand, prosecutors are not supposed to charge suspects with more criminal charges or for more serious crimes than can be reasonably supported by the evidence. They are not supposed to prosecute simply because an aroused public demands it. They are not supposed to be influenced by the personal or political advantages or disadvantages that might be involved in prosecuting or not prosecuting a case. Nor, for that matter, are they supposed to be swayed by their desire to enhance their records of successful convictions. It would be naive, however, to believe that these factors do not have at least some influence on some prosecutors' decisions in capital or potentially capital cases.[70] A recent study of death-eligible cases in Maryland found that prosecutors were significantly more likely to seek the death penalty in cases with an offender who had a history of alcohol problems and a troubled job history, and in cases with a white victim, a victim unable to defend himself or herself, an elderly victim, a victim who was a stranger to the offender, a victim murdered in his or her own home, a victim who was sexually assaulted by the offender, and a victim who the offender continued to assault after the victim's death was certain.[71]

A large body of evidence (presented in the next chapter) shows that prosecutor misconduct is a major source of arbitrary and discriminatory application of the death penalty. Prosecutor misconduct is also a principal cause of wrongful convictions. For example, in a study of the 88 cases under post-*Furman* statutes (through December 31, 2000) in which people were completely exonerated of crimes for which they were sentenced to die, 30 instances of prosecutor misconduct were discovered in 27 (31%) of the cases.[72] Fourteen instances of prosecutor misconduct involved withholding exculpatory evidence, 12 instances involved the subordination of perjury, and four instances involved the use of improper evidence.[73]

Prosecutors know that legal procedure prohibits them from withholding exculpatory evidence from the defense as was done in the case of Don Paradis, who was mentioned previously, and many others like him. Exculpatory evidence is evidence favorable to the accused that has an effect on guilt or punishment. Examples of possible exculpatory evidence are physical evidence, evidentiary documents (such as a defendant's recorded statements to police or reports of medical examinations or scientific tests), and lists of witnesses. A prosecutor's concealment or misrepresentation of evidence (typically referred to as a "Brady violation"; see *Brady v. Maryland*, 1963) is grounds for an appellate court's reversal of a conviction or sentence. In the study of the 88 exonerations cited above, withholding exculpatory evidence accounted for more than half of all instances of prosecutor misconduct and was a factor in about 16 percent of the 88 cases.[74]

Because suborning perjury is a criminal offense, it is hard to believe that many prosecutors know in advance that their witnesses are lying under oath. Yet, how can prosecutors ignore or not suspect the obvious motives of jailhouse snitches and the questionable incriminating evidence they provide?[75] It is also hard to believe that most prosecutors are not privy to inmate informer argot about their deceptive practices: "'Don't go to the pen—send a friend.' Or: 'If you can't do the time, just drop a dime.' [Or:] 'Trouble? You better call 1-800-HETOLDME.'"[76] Perjury by prosecution witnesses occurred in 13.6 percent of the cases in the aforementioned study of the 88 people sentenced to die who were exonerated. It accounted for nearly 45 percent of all cases of prosecutor misconduct.[77] And, as noted previously, Bedau and Radelet identified witness perjury as a factor in 35 percent of the wrongful convictions that they discovered.[78] In their study, it was the foremost cause of wrongful convictions in capital cases.

Sometimes prosecutors fail to dismiss capital charges against ostensibly innocent defendants. Prosecutors may be reluctant to dismiss charges even when the case is a weak one, especially when there is public clamor for a conviction. Much of this has to do with ego. A sign seen in the Dallas County, Texas, prosecutor's office reads: "Convicting the guilty is easy. It's the innocent that keep us working late."[79] The problem is that not only are some weak cases tried, but, as the quotation suggests, in some cases innocent defendants are convicted. In 20 of the 88 cases (22.7%) in which people sentenced to die were exonerated, lack of evidence was the primary reason for release.[80]

DNA analysis has proven to be an important tool in the successful investigation, prosecution, and exoneration of criminal defendants, including defendants facing the death penalty. In 10 (11.4%) of the 88 cases in the study cited above, DNA evidence was responsible for exoneration.[81] Yet, despite relatively easy access to the technology, many local prosecutors refuse to release crime evidence for DNA analysis unless litigation is threatened or filed. They point out that they have no legal obligation to cooperate because once a trial has been concluded, a convicted defendant has no absolute right to prove his or her innocence. They argue that the offender's interest in proving his or her innocence is outweighed by the state's interest in the finality of judgment.[82] Although refusing to release crime evidence for DNA analysis when possible innocence is at stake may not be prosecutor misconduct in a legal or technical sense, the belief that finality of sentence is more important than the preservation of innocent life is certainly debatable.

In some cases, following the exoneration of an innocent person who was wrongfully convicted and sentenced to death, prosecutors elect not to seek a death sentence when the actual perpetrator is found.[83]

Hopefully, most prosecutors follow the rules. Some do not. What happens to those prosecutors who get caught engaging in misconduct in capital cases? The answer is not much. In a study of 381 murder convictions since 1963 that were reversed because of police or prosecutor misconduct, not one of the prosecutors who broke the law was convicted or disbarred for his or her misconduct. Most of the time, they were not even disciplined. Current laws also protect prosecutors from civil suits even when they knowingly allowed perjured testimony or deliberately concealed evidence of innocence.[84]

JUDICIAL MISCONDUCT OR ERROR

In capital trials, judges are responsible for allowing the jury a fair chance to reach a verdict on the evidence presented. Judges must ensure that their behavior does not improperly affect the outcome of the case. Before juries retire to deliberate and reach a verdict, judges instruct them on the relevant law. This involves interpreting legal precedents and applying them to the unique circumstances of the case.

In her examination of Missouri clemency petitions, sociologist Cathleen Burnett found the following allegations of judicial misconduct or error:

1. not permitting the defense to present evidence of an alternative theory of the case;
2. not permitting the defense to present certain mitigating evidence;
3. denying the right of defense experts to offer evidence;
4. failing to order a psychiatric examination prior to trial;
5. prejudging the case;
6. incorrectly finding fact;
7. refusing to give certain jury instructions;
8. failing to admonish the prosecutor for an improper closing argument;
9. allowing a highly prejudicial photograph during the penalty phase;
10. failing to permit withdrawal of a guilty plea; and
11. not having jurisdiction.[85]

BAD DEFENSE LAWYERS

Gross claims that, despite some of the problems just cited, the capital trial "plays a comparatively minor role in the production of errors in capital cases."[86] Gross says the reason is that capital defendants (as compared to other felony defendants) usually have superior defense counsel: "Capital defendants ... may be better represented than other criminal defendants. The attorneys who are appointed to represent them may be more experienced and skillful, and their defenders may have more resources at their disposal."[87] The evidence, however, suggests that Gross may be wrong on this point.

Bedau relates that "experienced criminal trial attorneys ... say that 'no really capable defense lawyer should ever lose a capital case.'"[88] Research shows that "a lawyer's skill is the most important factor determining whether a defendant is sentenced to death or to life in prison."[89] Most capital defendants, though, are not represented by capable defense attorneys, but by those who are inexperienced, over-worked, understaffed, less resourceful, less independent, and who frequently lose capital cases.[90]

A good example is the case of John Spinkelink, the third person executed in the United States under post-*Gregg* (1976) statutes and the first person during that period executed against his will. Spinkelink's last appeal was based on a Sixth Amendment claim of counsel ineffectiveness. According to Ramsey Clark, former attorney general of the United States:

John Spinkelink's trial attorneys were court-appointed. They lacked sufficient resources to prepare and conduct the defense. One publicly stated that the case was beyond his competence. One was absent during part of the jury selection to be with his wife in childbirth. He had not sought a delay in the proceeding or permission of the court to be absent. Spinkelink's lawyers also failed to challenge the composition of the grand and petit juries. Both were later found to underrepresent blacks, women and young people—groups considered by most experienced attorneys to be favorable to the defense in capital cases. The lawyers failed to ask that Spinkelink be tried separately from his co-defendant who was acquitted. Severance was authorized under Florida law and would seem strategically important. Counsel failed to challenge excessive security measures in the courtroom, which are generally thought to be prejudicial to a defendant... . They [the prosecution] had (wrongly) informed the jury in their closing argument that the judge could not impose a more severe sentence than the jury recommended. This may have encouraged the jury to ask for a maximum sentence, leaving the judge the full range of punishment alternatives. Counsel failed to obtain a transcript of questions asked prospective jurors, which was necessary in determining if they were constitutionally selected. The Florida Supreme Court ruled that all objections had been waived. With their client facing death, counsel did not request oral argument on appeal in the Supreme Court of Florida.[91]

Spinkelink's experience is not uncommon. A Texas study by the governor's judicial council found that three-quarters of murderers with court-appointed attorneys were sentenced to death, while only about a third of those represented by private lawyers were so sentenced.[92] That study has been corroborated by a more recent study of 504 adult defendants indicted for capital murder in Harris County (Houston), Texas, from 1992 to 1999.[93] Harris County, Texas, as students of the death penalty know, is the capital punishment capital of the United States. If Harris County were a state, it would rank second only to Texas itself as the state with the most post-*Furman* executions. Harris County also is noteworthy for not having a public defender system. All criminal defendants with lawyers have either privately retained counsel or court-appointed counsel. Of the 504 defendants, the Harris County district attorney sought the death penalty in 129 cases, sought life imprisonment in 218 cases, and reached a plea bargain (sentence less than death) in 157 cases. The study showed that those defendants with privately retained counsel for the entire case ($N = 31$) were never sentenced to death, and defendants with privately retained counsel for a portion of the case ($N = 104$) were substantially less likely to be sentenced to death. This remained true after controlling for the crime's heinousness. A defendant might have privately retained counsel for a portion of the case if he were declared indigent and appointed counsel but later acquired funds to hire counsel, or the defendant hired counsel but exhausted his funds and had to be appointed counsel. The district attorney sought the death penalty for only 3 percent of defendants with hired counsel, 26 percent of defendants with "mixed" counsel, and 27 percent of defendants with appointed counsel. The 31 defendants with hired counsel escaped the death penalty primarily by reaching a plea deal with the district attorney. With one exception, all 504 of the capital defendants were poor. Some poor defendants were able to hire an attorney because their relatives and friends pooled resources. All other poor defendants were provided attorneys by the court. The only defendant to be acquitted was the lone wealthy defendant who was represented by a hired attorney for the entire case.

Another study that compared innocent capital defendants who were eventually exonerated and released from death row and innocent capital defendants who were later executed discovered that defendants with privately retained lawyers at trial were nine times more likely to be exonerated and released from death row than defendants with court-appointed attorneys.[94]

A 1990 *National Law Journal* study showed that criminal defendants in six states of the South—Alabama, Florida, Georgia, Louisiana, Mississippi, and Texas—often wound up on death row after being represented by inexperienced, unskilled, or unprepared court-appointed lawyers.[95] The study found that many poor defendants sentenced to death (and nearly all capital defendants are poor) had lawyers who had never handled a capital trial before, lacked training in life-or-death cases, made little effort to present evidence in support of a life sentence, or had been reprimanded, disciplined, or subsequently disbarred. An investigation published in the *Chicago Tribune* on June 11, 2000, found that in Texas, "attorneys in 40 capital cases 'presented no evidence whatsoever or only one witness during the trial's sentencing phase' [and that in] forty-three cases, the accused were represented by attorneys who were punished for professional misbehavior."[96] One notoriously incompetent Texas attorney, Ron Mock, had so many clients sentenced to death that people referred to a section of Texas's death row as the "Mock Wing."[97] In 2002, the U.S. Supreme Court upheld the death sentence of Gary Cone from Tennessee, even though his attorney presented no mitigating evidence and did not argue for his client's life. It was reported that the attorney was mentally ill and later committed suicide. Nevertheless, the Court ruled 8–1 that the attorney's inaction did not amount to a complete absence of representation and that the state court did not act unreasonably when it held that the attorney might have been making a tactical decision in not presenting evidence.[98] Consider the following additional examples from the *National Law Journal* study:

- Nine years after John Young was condemned to death in Georgia in 1976, his disbarred lawyer, Charles Marchman Jr, admitted that his drug use, the breakup of his marriage, the discovery of his homosexuality, and other factors prevented him from defending Young adequately.
- James Copeland, on Louisiana's death row, had a lawyer at his second trial who confessed that he never read the first trial's transcript and did little to uncover evidence for life imprisonment.
- Texas lawyer Jon Wood unsuccessfully defended Jesus Romero against the death penalty with 29 words, among them: "You've got that man's life in your hands. You can take it or not. That's all I have to say."

Even an attorney who sleeps through the trial is not necessarily considered ineffective, as is seen in the following description of a capital case in Houston, Texas:

Seated beside his client—a convicted capital murderer—defense attorney John Benn spent much of Thursday afternoon's trial in apparent deep sleep. His mouth kept falling open and his head lolled back on his shoulders, and then he awakened just long enough to catch himself and sit upright. Then it happened again. And again. And again.

Every time he opened his eyes, a different prosecution witness was on the stand describing another aspect of the Nov. 19, 1991, arrest of George McFarland in the robbery-killing of grocer Kenneth Kwan.

When state District Judge Doug Shaver finally called a recess, Benn was asked if he truly had fallen asleep during a capital murder trial. "It's boring," the 72-year-old longtime Houston lawyer explained.[99]

Attorney Benn's performance did "not offend the right to counsel guaranteed by the United States Constitution, the trial judge explained, because, '[t]he Constitution doesn't say the lawyer has to be awake.'"[100] Agreeing with the trial judge's assessment was the Texas Court of Criminal Appeals, which rejected McFarland's claim of ineffective assistance of counsel.[101]

Benn is not the only Texas attorney who has fallen asleep during a capital trial. Houston attorney Joe Frank Cannon, who is now dead, also had that reputation. He continually dozed off while defending Calvin Burdine, and the Texas Court of Criminal Appeals again held that "a sleeping attorney was sufficient 'counsel' under the Constitution."[102] However, in August 2001, the Fifth U.S. Circuit of Appeals, sitting en banc, reversed a three-judge federal panel, which earlier had upheld Burdine's death sentence. The full court ordered a new trial for Burdine because his lawyer dozed off frequently enough and for long enough stretches to deprive Burdine of his right to the effective assistance of counsel.[103] The Texas attorney general's office appealed the ruling to the U.S. Supreme Court, contending that Burdine had received a fair trial despite his attorney's lapses. In June 2002, the Supreme Court let stand the Fifth Circuit's earlier ruling, giving no reason for its refusal to intervene. The Houston district attorney's office planned to retry Burdine and again seek the death penalty.[104] On the other hand, when another one of Cannon's death penalty clients, Carl Johnson, eventually appealed to the U.S. Court of Appeals for the Fifth Circuit, the court ruled that Johnson was not denied the effective assistance of counsel "notwithstanding the sleeping lawyer."[105] At least the Texas Court of Criminal Appeals is empowered to consider claims of ineffective assistance of counsel; in most states, ineffective assistance of counsel claims cannot be heard on direct appeal.[106]

The *National Law Journal* study discovered a general failure of the states to provide effective assistance of counsel to capital defendants. Much has changed since 1990. As of December 6, 2010, 30 of the then-35 death penalty states had adopted minimum guidelines or standards for the appointment of counsel at either the trial or appellate level or both in capital cases.[107] The only death penalty states that have not are Mississippi, New Hampshire, Ohio, South Dakota, and Wyoming.[108] One state that adopted such minimum standards (on July 1, 2000) was Florida, whose guidelines resemble those created by the American Bar Association (ABA) in 1989.

The statement of purpose to Florida's new standards reads in part: "Counsel in death penalty cases should be required to perform at the level of an attorney reasonably skilled in the specialized practice of capital representation, zealously committed to the capital case, who has had adequate time and resources for preparation." Following are the minimum standards in Florida.[109]

A. List of Qualified Counsel
  1. Every circuit shall maintain a list of counsel qualified for appointment in capital cases in each of three categories:
    a. lead trial counsel;
    b. trial cocounsel; and
    c. appellate counsel.

No attorney may be appointed to handle a capital trial unless duly qualified on the appropriate list.

  2. The conflict committee for each circuit is responsible for approving and removing attorneys from the list pursuant to section 925.037, Florida Statutes. Each circuit committee is encouraged to obtain additional input from experienced capital defense counsel.
  3. No attorney may be qualified on any of the capital lists unless he or she has attended within the last year a continuing legal education program of at least ten hours' duration devoted specifically to the defense of capital cases. Continuing legal education programs meeting the requirements of this rule shall be offered by the Florida Bar or another recognized provider and should be approved for continuing legal education credit by the Florida Bar. The failure to comply with this requirement shall be cause for removal from the list until the requirement is fulfilled.
B. Appointment of Counsel. A court must appoint lead counsel and, upon written application and a showing of need by lead counsel, should appoint cocounsel to handle every capital trial in which the defendant is not represented by retained counsel or the Public Defender. Lead counsel

shall have the right to select cocounsel from attorneys on the lead counsel or cocounsel list. Both attorneys shall be reasonably compensated for the trial and sentencing phase. Except under extraordinary circumstances, only one attorney may be compensated for other proceedings.

C. Lead Counsel. Lead trial counsel assignments should be given to attorneys who:

1. are members of the bar admitted to practice in the jurisdiction or admitted to practice pro hac vice [for this occasion]; and

2. are experienced and active trial practitioners with at least five years of litigation experience in the field of criminal law; and

3. have prior experience as lead counsel in no fewer than nine jury trials of serious and complex cases which were tried to completion, as well as prior experience as lead defense counsel or cocounsel in at least two cases tried to completion in which the death penalty was sought. In addition, of the nine jury trials which were tried to completion, the attorney should have been lead counsel in at least three cases in which the charge was murder; or alternatively, of the nine jury trials, at least one was a murder trial and an additional five were felony jury trials; and

4. are familiar with the practice and procedure of the criminal courts of the jurisdiction; and

5. are familiar with and experienced in the utilization of expert witnesses and evidence, including but not limited to psychiatric and forensic evidence; and

6. have demonstrated the necessary proficiency and commitment which exemplify the quality of representation appropriate to capital cases.

D. Cocounsel. Trial cocounsel assignments should be given to attorneys who:

1. are members of the bar admitted to practice in the jurisdiction or admitted to practice pro hac vice; and

2. who qualify as lead counsel under paragraph (C) of these standards or meet the following requirements:

   a. are experienced and active trial practitioners with at least three years of litigation experience in the field of criminal law; and

   b. have prior experience as lead counsel or cocounsel in no fewer than three jury trials of serious and complex cases which were tried to completion, at least two of which were trials in which the charge was murder; or alternatively, of the three jury trials, at least one was a murder trial and one was a felony jury trial; and

   c. are familiar with the practice and procedure of the criminal courts of the jurisdiction; and

   d. have demonstrated the necessary proficiency and commitment which exemplify the quality of representation appropriate in capital cases.

E. Appellate Counsel. Appellate counsel assignments should be given to attorneys who:

1. are members of the bar admitted to practice in the jurisdiction or admitted to practice pro hac vice; and

2. are experienced and active trial or appellate practitioners with at least five years of experience in the field of criminal law; and

3. have prior experience in the appeal of at least one case where a sentence of death was imposed, as well as prior experience as lead counsel in the appeal of no fewer than three felony convictions in federal or state court, at least one of which was an appeal of a murder conviction; or alternatively, have prior experience as lead counsel in the appeal of no fewer than six felony convictions in federal or state court, at least two of which were appeals of a murder conviction; and

4. are familiar with the practice and procedure of the appellate courts of the jurisdiction; and

5. have demonstrated the necessary proficiency and commitment which exemplify the quality of representation appropriate in capital cases.

F. Exceptional Circumstances. In the event that the trial court determines that counsel meeting the technical requirements of this rule is not available and that exceptional circumstances require appointment of other counsel, the trial court shall enter an order specifying, in writing, the exceptional circumstances requiring deviation from the rule and the court's explicit determination that counsel chosen will provide competent representation in accord with the policy concerns of the rule.

Clearly, Florida's standards for the appointment of counsel in capital cases, as well as the standards created by other death penalty states, are better than no standards at all. However, none of the standards can be considered particularly rigorous; they are truly minimum standards.

In 2003, the ABA's House of Delegates approved a revised edition of its 1989 guidelines for the appointment and performance of defense counsel in death penalty cases. (These guidelines are provided in the Appendix.) The revised edition was created because of deficiencies in the older guidelines. One change in emphasis is illustrative. In the 1989 version, the stated purpose of the guidelines was to ensure "quality legal representation." In the 2003 guidelines, that was changed to "high-quality legal representation." However, as of December 2010, only three death penalty states— Kansas, Kentucky, and Oregon—explicitly followed the ABA guidelines.[110] The reason why more death penalty states do not explicitly follow the guidelines is twofold. First, according to critics of the guidelines, they are too expensive to implement.[111] Second, the Supreme Court has not required them. In fact, in *Strickland v. Washington* (466 U.S. 668, 1984), the case that provided a test for determining when counsel is ineffective, the Court adamantly refused to adopt performance guidelines for evaluating counsel in capital cases.[112] It gave three reasons for its position. First, the Court pointed out that the purpose of the effective assistance guarantee was "not to improve the quality of legal representation." Second, the Court opined that "no particular set of detailed rules for counsel's conduct can satisfactorily take account of the variety of circumstances faced by defense counsel or the range of legitimate decisions regarding how best to represent a criminal defendant." Third, the Court was concerned that the adoption of specific standards would encourage ineffectiveness claims, which would discourage many attorneys from representing defendants in capital cases.

In addition, and contrary to what Gross reports, defense counsel in capital cases (including those in states with minimum standards) rarely has the resources necessary to mount an effective defense. In the 1990s, for example, attorneys in Alabama were being paid only $20 an hour for out-of-court time in capital cases, with a limit of $2,000 per case; Mississippi was limiting payment to $1,000 a case.[113] As late as 2004, Florida had a $3,500 cap on the payment for defense services in capital cases, meaning that state-funded lawyers in Florida capital cases would be paid an estimated $3.00 an hour.[114] A paralegal working on a federal bankruptcy case is paid more per hour than a defense attorney in a capital case in Alabama, Georgia, Mississippi, and Virginia.[115] It is not unusual for attorneys in capital cases to be compensated at less than minimum wage, and states have been known to appoint attorneys in capital cases who submitted the lowest bids.[116] As Bowers explains:

Dollar-wise [an appointed attorney] peaks out before going to trial, meaning the trial is his gift to the defendant—it's free—that's his practice he's cutting into.... The cap makes hungry, inexperienced guys take cases but attorneys who can command fees can't afford to.[117]

In 1924, famed attorney Clarence Darrow observed, "No court ever interferes with a good lawyer's business by calling him in and compelling him to give his time" to a poor person facing criminal charges; "instead, judges appoint lawyers willing to take the case for what the courts pay."[118] This is as true today as when Darrow said it. Furthermore, some judges will not appoint capable defense attorneys to represent capital defendants even when they have the opportunity to do so. According to a Texas survey of trial judges, for about half the judges, a lawyer's reputation for moving cases quickly, regardless of the quality of the defense, was a factor in the decision to appoint a particular lawyer.[119] Some court-appointed attorneys may be less than zealous in their client's defense because they do not want to antagonize a judge and lose future business.[120] Some jurisdictions have attempted to provide more adequate resources in capital cases, but in none could the provision of these resources be considered generous. Most provide woefully inadequate resources. The Louisiana Supreme Court recently ruled that trial judges in death penalty cases could stop prosecutions of indigent defendants until the state provides the money to pay for an adequate defense.[121] (See Chapter 8 for the economic costs of capital punishment.)

Even if the necessary financial resources were provided, that would not compensate entirely for deficient intellectual resources. Defense attorneys, however, are not entirely to blame for this problem. Capital jurisprudence is a highly specialized area of the criminal law, and most attorneys have not received instruction in it.[122] Nevertheless, many judges will appoint any lawyer licensed to practice law to represent a capital defendant, even if the lawyer's practice is limited mostly to real estate or divorce law.[123] Consequently, even when they are conscientious, appointed attorneys in capital cases may make numerous mistakes.

Defense attorneys who lack experience in capital cases are often stymied at the penalty phase of the bifurcated trial. Many attorneys have experience pleading their client's innocence (the focus of the guilt phase), but only those lawyers who have tried several capital cases are experienced in making an affirmative case for their client's life in the penalty phase. As attorney Margot Garey relates:

> Many defense attorneys fail to make the transition and do not adequately prepare or effectively present the defendant's penalty phase trial. For example, a defense attorney may structure a guilt trial strategy that is inconsistent with the penalty phase theory. This situation may negate any effective defense at the penalty proceeding since a consistent trial strategy increases the defendant's believability and credibility. Should a guilty verdict be rendered in the guilt phase, it is imperative that the jury believe the defendant's mitigating circumstances proffered in the penalty phase. Therefore, the defense attorney cannot plan the theory of the guilt phase trial independent of the penalty phase. She must develop and structure a defense theory that will include the penalty phase. Because the preparation required for structuring a bifurcated proceeding is categorically different from that required for a noncapital trial, defense counsel who may be very competent in complex noncapital criminal trials may, without training, be ineffective in capital trials.[124]

An example of the problem of coordinating the guilt and penalty phases of a capital trial is provided by the case of *People v. Lane*.[125] In the guilt phase of Lane's trial, his attorney claimed that Lane was not the killer despite a videotape clearly showing Lane pulling the trigger at point-blank range. Lane's attorney contended that it was a case of mistaken identity, that Lane was not the person on the videotape. The jury found Lane guilty of capital murder. At the penalty phase, his attorney argued that Lane did the murder because of extenuating circumstances, which jurors took as just another attempt to deceive them (as Lane's attorney tried to do during the guilt phase). Lane's attorney also noted at the penalty phase that others, such as Hitler and Manson, were worse than his client—"assuming, of course, that he had done it." By first denying guilt then arguing mitigation, jurors viewed Lane as a "remorseless manipulator."[126] The jury sentenced Lane to death.

In sum, whether it is the result of a lack of training, experience, or heart, most capital defendants receive what appears to be ineffective legal representation. Critics cynically argue that in practice the courts use the "mirror test" in determining whether a defense attorney is effective in a capital case: If the mirror fogs up because the attorney is breathing, then the attorney is effective. This may be why the Supreme Court has rarely granted relief on the grounds of ineffective assistance of counsel.[127]

Proponents of capital punishment argue that the reason the Supreme Court rarely grants relief in ineffective assistance of counsel claims is that most capital defendants have superior defense attorneys, as death penalty opponent Gross suggested at the onset of this section. Proponents argue that death penalty abolitionists do not show that ineffectiveness of counsel is widespread and that the evidence of ineffectiveness is mostly anecdotal and "grossly outdated."[128] They add that just because some defense attorneys in some death penalty states may be ineffective the death penalty in the entire United States need not be abolished. They ask, Why should a state or the federal government, for that matter, that provides effective representation be penalized because of states that do not?[129] Their answer, of course, is they should not.

Furthermore, not all of the problems encountered in a capital defense are a defense attorney's fault. Some capital defendants refuse to cooperate or cooperate fully with their attorneys. For example, some defendants refuse to help their attorneys develop their life story to use as mitigation in the penalty phase. These defendants often want to protect their families from embarrassment by not revealing family secrets of child abuse and molestation. Sometimes defendants refuse to allow their attorneys to claim their clients suffer from mental illness, even when the evidence strongly supports such a claim. Some defendants simply want to be sentenced to death, placing a considerable burden on their attorneys who are required by law to zealously defend them.[130]

JURY PROBLEMS

Jury problems that may cause miscarriages of justice in capital cases are described in more detail in the next chapter on arbitrary and discriminatory application of the death penalty. Here only a few points are made. First, jurors are unlikely to find defendants innocent of their crimes after the police and prosecutors failed to do so. Jurors have less information and experience than the police and prosecutors. Consequently, jurors are less to blame for miscarriages of justice in capital cases than are the police and prosecutors.[131] Second, jurors are also less to blame for miscarriages of justice because most jurors are probably not up to the task of sitting in judgment of another human being; perhaps no one is. As Cotton relates:

> [H]ow do people judge other people's actions when they do not live in their head? The overwhelming task of having to sit and listen to a set of facts as they are told by people who did not witness the event, about people whom they have never met before, and about circumstances that most people have never experienced, is given to ordinary citizens: our system of justice requires it. Without any expertise, experience, general knowledge of, or predilection toward the events or people that they are being asked to judge, jurors are charged

with the responsibility of rendering a "reasonable" verdict. It is not so much the fact that this task is nearly impossible to accomplish (putting aside personal views and experiences to judge the very same in others), but rather the fact that most people put faith and confidence in this process is what offers a subject for scrutiny.[132]

Perhaps people would have less confidence in the process if they knew that jurors are frequently found to be "sleeping, daydreaming, grooming themselves, or doodling in notebooks" instead of paying attention to the proceedings.[133] Perhaps people would have less confidence in the process if they knew how attorneys manipulate jurors: "The facts of the case are presented by legal advocates who have been trained on how to pick a jury, how to persuade a jury, and how to present facts to a jury that lead to certain conclusions without arousing suspicion or prejudice. Such skills are repeatedly rehearsed in law school classes to be utilized on juries in criminal cases."[134] Perhaps people would have less confidence in the process if people knew that jurors are expected only to make a good-faith effort at deciding a case correctly and that despite this, they fail too often (no one knows how often) to make the correct decision.[135]

THE ILLUSIVE HOPE OF CLEMENCY

Clemency generally provides the final opportunity to consider whether a death sentence should be imposed.[136] All 50 states, the federal government, and the military have provisions for granting clemency.[137] They allow the governor of a state or the president of the United States, when federal or military law is violated, to exercise leniency or mercy. Many states have specialized administrative boards or panels authorized to assist the governor in making the clemency decision. In a few states, the governor is not authorized to grant clemency unless an administrative body has first recommended it.[138]

The granting of clemency was much more common in colonial America than it is today. For example, in the eighteenth century, more than half of all condemned prisoners in New York and one quarter to one third of condemned prisoners in Virginia escaped execution through clemency.[139] The reason was not that colonial Americans were more lenient than their contemporary counterparts, but rather that clemency had more purposes in the seventeenth and eighteenth centuries that, today, are accomplished in other ways. For instance, in colonial America, there were no criminal appeals so clemency was the only way to correct trial errors, such as the conviction of an innocent person. Today, appellate courts perform that function (in at least some cases).[140] Incidentally, the availability of automatic appellate review under post-*Furman* statutes has given governors a plausible excuse for denying clemency petitions. They can simply state that they are deferring judgments about constitutional issues to appellate court judges.[141] Second, during the colonial period, clemency was the only way to mitigate a death sentence. Today, mitigation is considered during sentencing.[142] Third, clemency served a law enforcement purpose in the colonial period that it does not serve today. It was sometimes granted to offenders who implicated their partners, something that is now accomplished through plea bargaining.[143] Thus, there were important practical reasons for the more liberal use of clemency during the colonial period.

In a recent study of governors' capital case commutation decisions in New York from 1900 to 1963, Harmon, Acker, and Rivera discovered that New York governors were more likely to commute death sentences "when defendants were younger than 21; when one or more court of appeals judges issued a dissenting opinion in the case's appeal; when the number of mitigating factors present in a case exceeded the number of aggravating factors; and when the offender was sentenced to death pursuant to a mandatory rather than a discretionary statute."[144] Research has consistently found a defendant's age to be an important determining factor in governors' decisions to commute death sentences.[145] New York governors were reluctant to permit the execution of young offenders. The importance of court of appeals judges' dissenting opinions on New York governors' commutation decisions probably derives from the unique authority of New York appeals courts to determine issues of fact as well as issues of law in capital cases. For New York governors, a dissenting opinion likely raised doubts about the factual and legal bases of capital convictions and death sentences. Further doubts on the credibility of capital convictions and death sentences probably arose when mitigating factors outnumbered aggravating factors. Finally, although mandatory death penalty statutes are no longer allowed (see *Woodson v. North Carolina*, 1976, and *Roberts v. Louisiana*, 1976), 85 percent of New York's death sentences from 1900 to 1963 were imposed under a mandatory statute. A problem with New York's mandatory death penalty statute was that it frequently precluded the sentencing authority (judge or jury) from considering mitigating circumstances that might have diminished the defendant's culpability and death eligibility. The researchers found no evidence that offenders' race, ethnicity, or socioeconomic status influenced New York governors' commutation decisions.

George W. Bush, in his autobiography, *A Charge to Keep*, wrote that decisions about executions are "by far the most profound" that a governor can make. He should know, having presided over 152 executions—by far the most by a governor in the United States under post-*Furman* statutes—during his 6 years as Texas governor.[146] Because Texas has conducted more than one third of all executions under post-*Furman* statutes and more than four times as many executions as its nearest contender, an examination of its clemency strategy may prove instructive though probably not representative.[147]

The state of Texas maintains the legal fiction that its governor, unlike governors of other states, does not have unfettered authority to grant clemency. In Texas, the governor can grant clemency only to those inmates recommended by the 18-member Board of Pardons and Paroles. Otherwise, the governor must either approve the execution or grant a 30-day stay. However, the governor can control the process because the governor appoints the board that is authorized to approve or deny all clemency applications.[148] A good example of this legal fiction in action involves the case of infamous serial killer Henry Lee Lucas, the only person to whom Bush granted clemency during his tenure as governor. Lucas, who had confessed falsely to hundreds of murders, had been convicted in the 1980s of nine murders for which he was serving six life sentences, two 75-year sentences, and one 60-year sentence. In yet another murder trial, Lucas was sentenced to death. After the trial and investigations by two successive state attorneys, it became apparent that Lucas was wrongly convicted of the murder for which he was sentenced to death because he had not been in the state of Texas when the victim was killed. When then-Governor Bush became aware of this fact, he let the Board of Pardons and Paroles know that he would not allow Lucas to be executed for a crime he did not commit. The Board of Pardons and Paroles subsequently voted 17–1 to commute Lucas's death sentence to life in prison, which Bush approved. Ironically, in denying Karla Faye Tucker's clemency petition, Bush, citing Texas law, stated that he could not commute Tucker's sentence from death to life in prison without the recommendation of the Board of Pardons and Paroles—something he somehow was able to get in the Lucas case.[149]

The Texas Board of Pardons and Paroles does not meet to discuss applications. Instead, members review cases separately and fax in their votes from across the state. The board operates without guidelines and does not have to give explanations for its decisions. The *Dallas Morning News* described the clemency process in Texas as "shrouded in secrecy." In 1999, Federal District Judge Sam Sparks ruled that the clemency system in Texas had the "minimal procedural safeguards" required by the U.S. Supreme Court. He added, however, that

> [i]t is abundantly clear the Texas clemency procedure is extremely poor and certainly minimal. Legislatively, there is a dearth of meaningful procedure. Administratively, the goal is more to protect the secrecy and autonomy of the system rather than carrying out an efficient legally sound system. The board would not have to sacrifice its conservative ideology to carry out its duties in a more fair and accurate fashion.[150]

Before Governor Bush made a final decision on clemency, usually on the morning of the day of the scheduled execution, he reviewed a document prepared by his legal counsel summarizing the facts of the case. His counsel then briefed him on these facts. Alberto Gonzales, who was the U.S. attorney general under President Bush, prepared the first 57 clemency memos given to then-Governor Bush. An examination of these memos and Bush's handling of them is revealing about the clemency process in Texas at that time.[151]

The clemency memos, which were only three to seven pages long, were the primary source of information used by the governor in making his clemency decisions. Each memo contained a brief description of the crime, one or two paragraphs about the defendant's personal background, and a short legal history. Rarely were recommendations made about whether to grant clemency, but many memos reflected a clear prosecutorial bias and an assumption that the governor had no good reason to revisit claims already rejected by appellate courts. Conspicuously missing from nearly all the memos was any reference to crucial issues in the case, such as ineffective counsel, conflict of interest, mitigating evidence, or evidence of actual innocence.

When speaking about the clemency process throughout his term of office, Bush repeatedly made statements like the following: "I take every death penalty case seriously and review each case carefully." "Each case is major, because each case is life or death." In his autobiography, he revealed, "I review every death penalty case thoroughly." Referring to his legal staff, he wrote, "For every death penalty case, they brief me thoroughly, review the arguments made by the prosecution and defense, raise any doubts or problems or questions." Bush touted the review as a "fail-safe" method for ensuring due process and certainty of guilt. During the 2000 presidential campaign, Gonzales was asked whether Bush ever read death row inmates' clemency petitions. He responded, "I wouldn't say that was done in every case … [b]ut if we felt there was something he should look at specifically—yes, he did look from time to time at what had been filed." However, a review of the clemency memos suggests that Governor Bush often allowed executions to proceed "based on only the most cursory briefings on the issues in dispute."

Three types of clemencies relevant to capital punishment are reprieve, commutation, and pardon. Reprieve is the most common type of clemency employed in capital cases and the most limited. A reprieve temporarily postpones an execution. It is typically used to allow a death row inmate the opportunity to complete a pending appeal or to give the governor a last-minute chance to review questions about the inmate's guilt.

Commutation involves the substitution of a lesser punishment for the one imposed by the court. A sentence of life imprisonment (with or without the opportunity for parole) is the sentence most likely to be substituted for a death sentence. Two broad types of commutations are commutations for humanitarian reasons and commutations for judicial expediency. The former includes doubts about the defendant's guilt or questions about the processes' legitimacy. Commutations for judicial expediency include cases in which courts have vacated or were likely to vacate a death sentence and a commutation would save the state the time and expense of a new sentencing proceeding, or cases in which a death sentence was imposed on a mentally retarded or juvenile offender despite Supreme Court rulings that such punishments are unconstitutional.[152] Sometimes commutations are contingent on certain conditions, such as the inmate waiving his or her right to a new trial or agreeing not to profit from the sale of an account of his or her crime. From 1976 through December 2010, 250 death row inmates had their sentences commuted for humanitarian reasons. This represents about 3 percent of all death sentences imposed during the period. Illinois governors granted about 69 percent of the commutations (172), including 167 in January 2003, by Illinois Governor George Ryan, just days before leaving office (more about this later).[153]

A pardon is the most expansive type of clemency. With a pardon, the prisoner's crime is erased and his or her punishment is terminated. A pardoned individual is freed entirely from the criminal justice system and is treated legally as if he or she had never been charged or convicted of a crime. Pardons are rarely granted to people convicted of capital crimes. From January 1, 1973, through December 2010, only seven pardons were granted to condemned inmates, including four by Governor Ryan in January 2003.[154]

Former Chief Justice Rehnquist considered executive clemency the "fail-safe" of the criminal justice system.[155] It is the last, best chance of rectifying miscarriages of justice. Unfortunately for those who would rely on clemency to correct errors made earlier in the process, recent experience contradicts the promise. In a bow to states rights, the federal courts are increasingly deferring to governors the job of correcting substantive problems with death sentences. Yet, governors are being effectively deterred from granting clemency. Few death sentences have been commuted under post-*Furman* statutes because of increased media attention devoted to capital clemency deliberations and the realization by governors that a decision to commute a death sentence is likely to lead to political suicide. The few commutations that have been granted have come mostly from governors not seeking reelection.[156] This is a change from the past. Prior to 1970, governors in death penalty states "routinely commuted up to a third of the death sentences that they reviewed," but since then, with the exception of the 167 death sentences commuted by Illinois Governor George Ryan in 2003, only about two death sentences a year (in the entire country) have been commuted.[157] The most common reasons given for granting clemency during the post-*Furman* period are the offender's mental retardation or mental illness, doubts about the offender's guilt, and equitable concerns about offenders who have received harsher sanctions than other participants in the same crime.[158]

WHAT CAN BE DONE?

The only sure way to put a stop to miscarriages of justice in capital cases is to abolish the death penalty. However, short of total abolition are reforms that could substantially reduce the incidence of miscarriages of justice in capital cases. The following sections describe some of these reforms.

GOOD DEFENSE ATTORNEYS CAN MAKE A DIFFERENCE

The most successful capital punishment defense attorney in American history was undoubtedly Clarence Darrow, who, in more than 100 capital trials, never had a client sentenced to death.[159] Most capital defendants do not have attorneys as talented as Darrow. Perhaps the Innocence Protection Act of 2004, which was described in Chapter 5, and the ABA's 2003 capital defense guidelines, which are listed in the Appendix, will help change that. Some death penalty states, as noted previously, have created minimum standards for defense attorneys in capital cases—that, too, is at least a start. It would also help if fees for court-appointed defense attorneys were raised to levels high enough to attract competent lawyers.[160] A handful of states have attempted to address the legal representation problem in capital cases by creating centralized state-funded agencies (capital defender offices or CDOs) comprising defense attorneys who specialize in capital cases. Attorneys in these agencies defend indigent clients charged with capital crimes as well as advise and assist other appointed counsel in capital cases.[161] Some of these agencies appear to be particularly effective in not only reducing the number of people sentenced to death but also the amount of capital litigation generally. Both situations likely reduce the number of wrongful convictions.

For example, in Colorado the CDO is part of the statewide Office of the Public Defender. So successful is the office that prosecutors in Colorado rarely seek the death penalty—only about three times a year on average. From 1975 (the year Colorado enacted its post-*Furman* death penalty statute) through 2010, there were fewer than 60 capital trials in Colorado, eight people were sentenced to death, and only one person was executed.[162] Connecticut also has a CDO within its public defender office. Although the death penalty is rarely sought in northeastern states, only one person has been executed in Connecticut in more than 37 years since it reinstated the death penalty.[163] New York reenacted its death penalty statute in 1995. The statute created a CDO that was considered one of the best. In 2000, it had a $15 million budget, 21 experienced trial lawyers, and 17 well-trained investigators. Between 1995 and 2000, there were more than 500 cases in which prosecutors either charged first-degree murder or went to court leaving open the possibility of that charge. However, in only 39 cases (as of February 2000) did prosecutors seek the death penalty, and in only five cases was a defendant sentenced to death. Not one of the five defendants was executed.[164] (In 2004, New York's death penalty statute was declared unconstitutional. As of this writing, New York had not reenacted a death penalty statute.) It may never be known for sure whether it is the CDOs or some other factor or factors that are responsible for reducing the number of people sentenced to death and death penalty litigation generally in those states with CDOs, but it is instructive that few death penalty states, especially those with the largest number of executions, have adopted the CDO model of legal representation in capital cases.

ADOPT THE ABA'S 2003 GUIDELINES FOR THE APPOINTMENT AND PERFORMANCE OF COUNSEL IN DEATH PENALTY CASES

Death penalty states should adopt the ABA's guidelines. The guidelines are listed in the Appendix.

PUNISH THE MISCONDUCT OF DEFENSE ATTORNEYS[165]

Most acts of misconduct by defense attorneys in capital cases should result in the attorney being disciplined by the state bar association. Where applicable, such disciplined attorneys should be removed from the roster of attorneys eligible to handle death penalty cases. For egregious cases of misconduct, defense attorneys should be disbarred.

IMPROVE POLICE INVESTIGATIONS, INTERROGATIONS, AND THE HANDLING OF EVIDENCE[166]

Police should keep an open and objective mind during investigations. They should investigate crimes rather than trying to build a case against a likely suspect. Once a suspect has been identified, the police should continue to pursue all reasonable leads, whether they point toward or away from the suspect. Police should be trained to avoid "tunnel vision" or "confirmatory bias" where the belief that a particular suspect has committed a crime often prevents an objective evaluation of whether there might be others who are actually guilty.

To reduce the number of false confessions, defense counsel should be provided to indigent suspects during police interrogation in potential death penalty cases. When there is doubt about whether the suspect is indigent, defense counsel should be provided. Police should also make a reasonable attempt to determine if a suspect is mentally retarded. If the suspect is deemed mentally retarded, the police should not ask leading questions (mentally retarded suspects are inclined to agree with the police version of events) and suggest that they believe the suspect is guilty.

In potential death penalty cases, the entire police custodial interrogation should be videotaped to help validate the interrogation and confessions. Where videotaping is not feasible during an interrogation, audiotaping should be substituted. Any nonrecorded statement by a homicide suspect, for example, in a patrol car on the way to the police station, should be repeated to the suspect on tape, and the suspect's comments recorded. Interviews with significant witnesses in homicide cases should also be electronically recorded.

To make sure that the police provide all the evidence in their possession to the prosecution, (1) all relevant evidence, including exculpatory evidence and its location, should be listed on schedules by the police, (2) specific police officers or employees should be assigned record-keeping responsibility, and (3) prosecutors should be given certified written copies of the schedules by the police.

IMPROVE EYEWITNESS IDENTIFICATION TECHNIQUES AND PROCEDURES[167]

Experts agree that the accuracy of eyewitness identifications could be greatly improved if the following policy reforms were adopted in all jurisdictions. First, videotapes should be made of all lineups, photograph spreads, and other identification processes so that later any biases, suggestions, or hints that infected the process could be exposed and evaluated. Second, eyewitnesses should be given explicit instructions that the suspected perpetrator might not be in the lineup or photograph spread, and therefore making an identification may not be possible. Third, independent examiners should conduct all lineups and photograph spreads. Fourth, to avoid dropping hints, examiners should not know who the suspect is. Fifth, eyewitnesses should be told that they should not assume that the examiner of the lineup or photograph spread knows which person is the suspect in the case. Sixth, when the examiner does not know who the suspect is, a sequential procedure should be used. With a sequential procedure the eyewitness views only one lineup member or photograph at a time, making a judgment ("yes it is" or "no it isn't" the perpetrator) about each person before looking at another lineup member or photograph. Seventh, nonsuspect lineup "fillers" should look like the witnesses' descriptions of the suspect and not the person who has been identified as the potential suspect. Eighth, witnesses should be required to rate the certainty of their identifications at the time they make them. This would provide fact finders important information weeks or months after the identifications were made. Ninth, police and prosecutors should be trained not to provide corroborating details to eyewitnesses. Such prompts tend to increase the certainty of identifications but to decrease their reliability. In addition, trial judges should inform jurors that eyewitness testimony should be judged in light of the other evidence in the case. Finally, convictions for murder based on the testimony of a single eyewitness or accomplice, without any other corroboration, should never be death eligible.[168]

IMPROVE THE WORK AND CREDIBILITY OF CRIME LABORATORY TECHNICIANS[169]

To promote greater credibility in the work of crime laboratory technicians, such laboratories and their budgets should be independent and not under the supervision of a police department or prosecutor's office as is now typically the case. Crime laboratories should also be accredited by professional organizations and subjected to regulatory oversight and external blind proficiency testing (in which samples are sent in as ordinary evidence to corroborate the validity of results). Prosecutors who introduce scientific evidence should be required to provide all underlying documentation that was used in writing the report as well as the name of the technician or technicians who performed the work. Fundamental questions should be asked about the reliability of the evidence: Have the scientific tests been replicated? What is the error rate of the procedure? Did any controls fail? Have the methods been published in peer-reviewed journals? Agent-technicians who make mistakes should be disciplined. The reports should indicate what, if any, exculpatory inferences can be derived from the evidence. Every public defender's office should have at least one attorney with scientific evidence expertise.

REQUIRE DNA TESTING[170]

DNA testing should be required in cases in which DNA evidence is available and there is a reasonable probability that the defendant could be exonerated based on it. The testing should be conducted in a timely manner, within 7–14 days of the crime, if possible, to ensure that innocent suspects are not incarcerated too long and to improve the chances of catching the guilty. In May 2000, only two states—Illinois and New York—gave inmates the right to use the latest DNA testing.[171] As of December 2010, 48 states gave inmates that right; only Massachusetts and Oklahoma did not (and Massachusetts does not have a death penalty).[172] The federal government and the states also should provide adequate funding for the creation of a comprehensive DNA database. Hopefully, the Innocence Protection Act of 2004, which was described in Chapter 5, is a step in that direction.

SET RIGOROUS STANDARDS FOR JAILHOUSE SNITCHES/INFORMANTS[173]

Before allowing a jailhouse snitch/informant to testify a committee of prosecutors should be able to provide satisfactory answers to the following questions: (1) Is there corroborating evidence to support the statement other than the testimony of another snitch? (2) Does the statement provide details of the crime or lead to evidence that could only be known by the perpetrator? (3) Could the incriminating evidence have been obtained from a source other than the accused, such as press accounts or legal proceedings? (4) Does the snitch/informant have a reputation for being dishonest? And (5) Does the snitch/informant regularly provide incriminating evidence? There should be a presumption that the testimony of a jailhouse snitch/informant is unreliable, and the prosecutor should be required to overcome that presumption before a jury is allowed to hear the evidence. Any deal that police officers or prosecutors make with a snitch/informant should be recorded, preferably videotaped. Additionally, trial judges should inform jurors of the potential hazards of relying on the testimony of a jailhouse snitch/informant. Finally, the uncorroborated testimony of a jailhouse snitch/informant witness about the confession or admission of the defendant should never be the sole basis for imposition of a death penalty.

IMPROVE POLICE TRAINING[174]

Training manuals should be developed, and police who work on homicide cases should receive periodic training in the following areas: (1) the risks of false testimony by in-custody informants (jailhouse snitches), (2) the risks of false testimony by accomplice witnesses, (3) the dangers of tunnel vision or confirmatory bias, (4) the risks of wrongful convictions in homicide cases, (5) police investigative and interrogation methods, (6) police investigating and reporting of exculpatory evidence, (7) forensic evidence, (8) the risks of false confessions, and (9) consular rights and the notification obligations during the arrest and detention of foreign nationals.

PUNISH POLICE MISCONDUCT[175]

Depending on the seriousness of the misconduct, offending police officers should be reprimanded, suspended without pay, decertified (if applicable), or terminated. Particularly serious misconduct by police officers should be prosecuted in the federal courts.

GUIDE PROSECUTORS' DECISIONS TO SEEK THE DEATH PENALTY[176]

Statewide written protocols should be developed to guide county prosecutors in making death penalty determinations. The guidelines should include the requirement that each county prosecutor establish within his or her office a committee to review homicide cases in which the death penalty may be sought, to assist the prosecutor in making the decision. The governor should appoint a statewide committee to review prior to trial death-eligibility decisions made by prosecutors. Where the committee decides that death is not the appropriate sentence in the case, the prosecutor should not be authorized to seek the death penalty. Committee authorization of the death penalty should be required by statute and mandatory.

IMPROVE DISCLOSURE REQUIREMENTS[177]

The prosecutor should be required to file a certificate with the court at least 14 days before the date set for the trial guaranteeing that all material that is required to be disclosed to the defense has been disclosed. Also, any discussions with a witness or the representative of a witness about benefits, potential benefits, or detriments given to a witness by any prosecutor, police official, corrections official, or anyone else should be put in writing and disclosed to the defense prior to trial. Both these requirements could occur in a case management conference before the trial judge. Following conviction, the prosecutor should have a continuing obligation to make timely disclosure to the defendant's counsel, or the defendant if not represented by counsel, of the existence of evidence known to the prosecutor that tends to negate the guilt of the defendant or mitigate the defendant's capital sentence.

PUNISH PROSECUTOR MISCONDUCT[178]

For extreme misconduct, prosecutors should be criminally prosecuted. At the least, statutes should be narrowed that grant prosecutors broad immunity from civil suits in cases of intentional misconduct. Another strategy is to create panels comprising bar association members who would review complaints against prosecutors. For egregious cases of misconduct, prosecutors should be disbarred.

BETTER TRAINING AND CERTIFICATION OF TRIAL JUDGES IN CAPITAL CASES[179]

Capital case training should be provided for all trial judges who preside over capital cases. The training should be required before a judge hears a capital case. A statewide bench manual covering capital cases should also be developed and used. A digest should be created and made available to trial judges and other participants in capital cases. The digest should contain information about relevant case law and other resources. Trial judges should be certified to hear capital cases by the state supreme court or the chief judges of judicial circuits. Certification should be based on experience and training. Only certified judges should hear capital cases.

GIVE TRIAL JUDGES VETO POWER[180]

The trial judge should have to indicate on the record whether he or she agrees with the jury's sentence of death. When the judge does not agree with the jury's death sentence, the defendant must not be sentenced to death. (In most cases, the defendant should be sentenced to LWOP.)

ELIMINATE TIME LIMITS AND OTHER CONSTRAINTS ON CLAIMS OF ACTUAL INNOCENCE[181]

Claims of actual innocence in capital cases based on newly discovered evidence should be heard by a court of record any time after conviction, without regard for other postconviction matters or timing. Also, state "closed discovery" laws should be repealed. These laws prevent defense attorneys or journalists from reviewing evidence following a conviction, thus making the detection of miscarriages of justice even more difficult.

IMPROVE THE CLEMENCY PROCESS[182]

To make officials more accountable in their decision making, clemency boards should hold public hearings to determine their recommendations to the governor. Governors should meet personally with attorneys and should be required to provide the public with an explanation of their clemency decisions. Better yet, to depoliticize the process, clemency decisions should not be made by governors but, instead, by respected three-judge panels.

COLLECT RELEVANT DATA[183]

To provide a complete understanding of how a capital punishment system is working, each death penalty jurisdiction should collect detailed and relevant information and create a statistical database about all first-degree murder cases in that jurisdiction, and not just the death penalty cases. These data could be used for proportionality reviews, to effectively monitor the system, and for other research purposes.

INNOCENCE PROJECTS AND INNOCENCE COMMISSIONS[184]

The first of what would become known as innocence projects is Centurion Ministries, founded in 1983, in Princeton, New Jersey, by former executive and now minister James McCloskey. The nonprofit organization is dedicated to identifying prison inmates who are innocent, freeing them from prison, and clearing their names. The ministries have helped exonerate inmates sentenced to death.[185] Nearly a decade later, in 1992, attorneys Barry Scheck and Peter Neufeld founded the Cardoza Innocence Project. It is a clinical law program for law students that operates out of the Benjamin N. Cardoza School of Law at Yeshiva University in New York City. The project provides pro bono legal services to inmates who are challenging their convictions based on DNA evidence. The project has represented or assisted more than 100 cases in the United States, including several death penalty cases, where convictions have been reversed or overturned. As of this writing, a national network of at least 80 loosely affiliated innocence projects is operating in all 50 states and the District of Columbia.[186] Most of these innocence projects are affiliated with major universities and are staffed with student volunteers. According to Baumgartner and his colleagues, this arrangement is the single most important factor in focusing the media's—and through the media, the public's—attention on the issue of innocence: "News that college students have helped to free an innocent man from prison tells a fundamentally different story than news that high-powered attorneys have accomplished the same feat.... if unfunded student-led organizations are able to find mistakes in the system, the public must wonder how many more mistakes might there be that simply have not been unearthed for lack of looking?"[187] Beyond advances in DNA technology, contends Baumgartner et al., "the spread of the innocence projects may be one of the most significant causes of the increased rate of exonerations."[188]

Innocence commissions are organizations created to monitor, investigate, and address errors in a jurisdiction's criminal justice system and, in this case, a jurisdiction's capital punishment system. When errors are discovered, the commissions should review the system's failures by asking the following questions: (1) What went wrong? (2) Was the error the result of an individual's mistake or a systemic error? (3) Was there any official misconduct? and (4) What can be done to correct the problem and prevent it from happening again? Innocence commissions are modeled after the National Transportation Safety Board, which investigates airline crashes. To operate properly, innocence commissions must have subpoena power, access to first-rate investigative resources, and political independence. North Carolina was the first state to create an innocence commission in 2002. California, Connecticut, and Virginia are other death penalty states that have established innocence commissions.

ASSISTANCE AND INDEMNITY[189]

When wrongfully convicted inmates and especially death row inmates are released from prison, they almost always need immediate financial assistance. Most of them also need help with such things as obtaining a driver's license, opening a bank account, and getting meaningful employment. In addition, there is generally a need for counseling to overcome stress, depression, and anger caused by wrongful incarceration. Death penalty jurisdictions should create mechanisms or expand existing ones to help with these needs.

As mentioned in Chapter 8, 27 states, the District of Columbia, and the federal government have statutory provisions for indemnifying the wrongly convicted (in capital and noncapital cases); 23 states have no such law. Eight of these compensating states (Iowa, Maine, Massachusetts, New Jersey, New York, Vermont, West Virginia, and Wisconsin) and the District of Columbia do not have a death penalty. Following is a list of death penalty states with compensation statutes and the amount or type of compensation provided (as of 2009).

- Alabama: Minimum of $50,000 for each year served; additional sum at discretion of legislature.
- California: $100 a day for each day served.
- Connecticut: Actual damages; reintegration expenses.
- Florida: $50,000 per year, $2 million maximum; attorney fees, waiver of tuition and fees for up to 120 hours of instruction.
- Louisiana: $15,000 per year served with a $150,000 maximum.
- Maryland: Actual damages.
- Mississippi: $50,000 per year, $500,000 maximum.
- Missouri: $50 per day served.
- Montana: Educational aid only.
- Nebraska: Any damages up to $500,000.
- New Hampshire: $20,000 maximum.
- North Carolina: $50,000 per year, $750,000 maximum; job skills training and education tuition waivers.
- Ohio: $40,330 per year of incarceration, attorney fees, lost wages.
- Oklahoma: $175,000 maximum.
- Tennessee: $1 million maximum.
- Texas: $80,000 per year, death row exoneree $100,000 per year, plus $25,000 per year spent on parole or registered as a sex offender, plus lifetime monthly annuity payments.
- Utah: Average annual Utah wage per year, maximum 15 years, plus damages up to $500,000.

- Virginia: 90 percent of the average Virginia income for up to 20 years plus a tuition award worth $10,000 in the state's community-college system.[190]

Prior to 2004, the federal government limited compensation to a maximum of $5,000 regardless of the amount of time served. However, the Innocence Protection Act of 2004 raised the amount of compensation in federal capital cases to $100,000 per year of incarceration.[191]

A major purpose of these compensation statutes is to protect the jurisdiction and its officials from frivolous claims. Most of them impose substantial barriers to recovery. One of these barriers is the requirement that the claimant did not by misconduct or neglect cause or bring about his or her own prosecution or enter a guilty plea. As described previously in this chapter, false confessions and guilty pleas by innocent defendants are common causes of errors in capital cases.

Currently, wrongfully convicted death row inmates may be compensated in one of four ways: filing a compensation claim, lawsuits, private legislation, or private donations. Simply filing a compensation claim is becoming more common. For example, Florida's new compensation law, which took effect in July 2008, allows the wrongfully convicted with no prior convictions to apply for compensation— $50,000 for every year spent in prison. To obtain compensation, an applicant must obtain a judge's order declaring the conviction was wrongful and then petition the state attorney general's office for the money—a potentially lengthy and complicated process that, for most people, requires the services of a lawyer. A problem is that the law does not provide reimbursement for attorney fees and legal costs related to the compensation process. Because the compensation is paid out in a long-term annuity, applicants have to use their own money—which most applicants do not have—to pay their legal costs unless they can find lawyers who will do the work for free or who are willing to wait until the applicant receives enough compensation to pay the legal fees and costs.[192]

Another problem with Florida's new compensation law, as noted, is that to qualify for compensation a claimant cannot have any prior convictions. This is the problem recently encountered by William Dillon, who spent 27 years in prison for a murder he did not commit.[193] Prior to his murder arrest, Dillon had been stopped while driving drunk and had a marijuana joint in his pocket. He was convicted, placed on probation, and fined $175. His conviction disqualifies him under the new law that speeds up the compensation process. Dillon must now find a state legislator who will file a claims bill on his behalf. This process involves an administrative hearing during which Dillon must prove his innocence and a decision by the legislature's presiding officers about whether to even hear the bill in the next legislative session. Ultimately, legislators will determine if Dillon receives compensation and what his time is worth.

Another common method is bringing a lawsuit against the state. Such lawsuits are rarely successful, however, primarily because government officials (and their jurisdictions) are generally immune from liability as long as they are acting in their official capacities, and they have not committed a constitutional violation—something that is very hard to prove.[194] Also, the wrongfully convicted who wants to file a lawsuit must hire an attorney, who will take a substantial amount of any compensation that is granted.

Other methods of litigation also can be pursued if intentional misconduct was the cause of the wrongful conviction and imprisonment. Simple error is not grounds for receiving state compensation in such cases. If it can be shown that the wrongful conviction and imprisonment were the result of a breach of duty, then a common law tort claim can be made. For example, on May 5, 2006, a federal jury awarded Earl Washington, Jr. $2.25 million from the estate of Virginia State Police investigator

Curtis Reese Wilmore, who died in 1994. The jury ruled that Wilmore deliberately fabricated Washington's confession to a 1982 rape and murder Washington did not commit. Washington's conviction and death sentence were based largely on his confession, in which he got several key details wrong. There was no forensic or physical evidence. Washington, with an IQ of 69, spent 18 years in Virginia prisons—nine and a half of those years on death row.[195] Washington was lucky because it is difficult to prove intentional misconduct and the burden of proof was on him, as it is in all such cases. Other possible grounds for litigation to obtain compensation are charging a criminal offense, claiming eminent domain, or alleging false imprisonment. None of these strategies is likely to prove successful.

Some states address wrongful convictions and imprisonment through a policy of strict liability. Strict liability does not depend on actual negligence or intent to harm but is based on the breach of an absolute duty.[196] Although the claimant does not have to prove fault in strict liability cases, he or she still has to prove his or her innocence and, as noted, has the burden of proving—if specified, by either clear and convincing evidence or a preponderance of the evidence—that the wrongful conviction was not in any way his or her fault.

If the claimant is successful in a strict liability case, a court or, in some states, a board of claims determines, within statutory limits, the amount of compensation to be awarded. As noted above, some states have cap limits on awards, while others do not. Some states require the governor to issue a pardon before awarding compensation; other states will award compensation only for DNA exonerations. Some states have time limits for filing claims. California, for example, has the shortest time limit, requiring claims to be filed within 6 months of release; most states require claims to be filed within 2 or 3 years of release. The state, however, currently does not have to inform the freed death row inmate of the statute or the deadline. In most cases, as noted above, attorney fees are deducted from the compensation. Some states also deduct the costs of housing, clothing, and feeding the claimant while he or she was imprisoned.

A third method for obtaining compensation is by private legislation. This compensatory method is discretionary and not an obligation of the state. It requires the claimant and/or his or her advocate to lobby the state legislature. This method, like lawsuits, is rarely successful for two principal reasons. First, a sympathetic legislator must be found, and there is little incentive and some political risk for getting involved. Second, with always scarce resources, there invariably are more worthy projects and causes (in the minds of legislators and the public) than indemnifying an innocent inmate who has spent many years on death row. Some state constitutions (e.g., Missouri's) expressly prohibit seeking compensation through private legislation. Two examples of a successful effort of obtaining compensation by private legislation are the cases, mentioned earlier, of Freddie Lee Pitts and Wilbert Lee, two black men who, in 1975, were finally pardoned by the Florida Cabinet.[197] Pitts and Lee had been tried and sentenced to death twice. They spent 12 years apiece on death row for a murder that somebody else committed. In the case of Pitts and Lee, it was not until 1997, after years of failed efforts, that they received a few hundred thousand dollars each as compensation from the state of Florida for its mistakes. That they received any compensation at all, as noted, is unusual.

Another fortunate exception is Bobby Joe Leaster who, in 1992, finally received a check for $75,000. The money was the first installment of the $1 million annuity the state of Massachusetts will pay him for wrongly imprisoning him for 15 years for a murder he did not commit.[198] Leaster was arrested in 1970 for the killing of a variety store owner during a holdup. After reading a newspaper article about Leaster, an eyewitness to the crime told police he knew the killer, and the killer was not Leaster. Leaster was released from prison in 1986 after prosecutors declined to pursue a retrial.

Because of the state's fiscal problems, it took several attempts before Massachusetts's legislators approved the indemnification measure.

A fourth method of obtaining compensation is through private donations. Like the other methods, this method has a number of problems. First, the released inmate is generally not psychologically prepared to seek private donations. Thus, to be successful, a released inmate must have devoted advocates willing to work for him or her. Second, the released inmate and his or her advocates must find a source of funding willing to donate. Possible sources are religious and civic organizations, as well as private foundations such as the Soros or Ford Foundations. These groups receive many requests to help fund worthy causes with which the freed death row inmate will have to compete. A problem with foundation funding is that the application process can be very complicated. Third, it is difficult to raise enough money to pay and sustain the costs of reintegration. Fourth, this method of compensation can have the undesirable effect of keeping the released inmate in a state of childlike dependence rather than promoting his or her independence.

A number of proposals have been made to improve the compensation process for the wrongfully convicted and imprisoned. Following are some of the better ideas. Compensation should be automatic; it should be a part of the release package. A death row inmate who has been freed because of his or her innocence should not have to prove again that he or she is innocent to receive compensation. Any judicial or executive order indicating that the claimant is innocent should suffice. Cathleen Burnett proposes to move the issue of compensation to wrongfully convicted and imprisoned inmates from the formal criminal justice process to a restorative justice process.[199] In restorative justice, the focus is on the miscarriage of justice victim and what he or she needs to have the harm repaired and to be reintegrated into society. A first step should be the creation of a state-level "Wrongful Conviction Office," with staff to help released innocent death row inmates from the moment they leave prison. However, the freed death row inmate should not have to participate, to be left alone, if he or she wishes. If the newly freed death row inmate elects to participate, the Wrongful Conviction Office staff member assigned to him or her will, in consultation with his or her client and other relevant stakeholders, prepare a plan or program for successful reintegration. A mediation setting and, if needed, an arbitration setting rather than a courtroom would be the forum for addressing compensation issues in a restorative justice framework. The specific administrative process could be modeled after the federal government's Victim Compensation Fund of 2001, which was used to assist the 9/11 victims. The case also should be turned over to an innocence commission (see the previous section) to investigate the causes of the miscarriage of justice, not for the purpose of assigning blame, but to prevent a similar calamity from happening in the future. The most difficult issues are probably the amount of compensation to be awarded and from where it comes. As for the first issue, what is the worth of years of a person's life lived in horrible prison conditions? Regarding the source of funds, they could come from the state attorney general's budget, since that office is ultimately responsible for the administration of justice in a particular state, or they could come from the state treasury. Whatever the source, the compensation funds should be tax-free at least at the state level so that the state does not benefit from its mistakes.

MORATORIUM

Short of total abolition, some observers, including some respected individuals who support the death penalty in principle, have called for a moratorium on executions until some of the more egregious problems with its administration are fixed. There have been three major moratorium movements during the modern death penalty era. The first moratorium movement was during the decade 1968–1977 and was characterized by the constitutional challenge to the death penalty. The second moratorium movement, characterized by the "discovery of innocence," spanned the mid-1990s through the mid-2000s, though its effects still linger today. The third and latest moratorium movement, characterized by the lethal injection controversy, began in the mid-2000s and effectively ended with the U.S. Supreme Court's *Baze v. Rees* decision in 2008, although its effects still linger as well. Since the first moratorium movement was thoroughly discussed in Chapter 3, and the third moratorium movement was addressed in Chapter 6, only the second moratorium movement, dealing with the subject of this chapter—miscarriages of justice in capital cases—and the discovery of innocence, is examined below.

The second moratorium movement was the result of a series of developments that began during the last few years of the twentieth century.[200] The movement started in Illinois with revelations that people convicted of capital crimes and sentenced to die were actually innocent (among the first were Rolando Cruz and Alejandro Hernandez and the Ford Heights Four). In some cases, investigations by Northwestern University journalism professor David Protess and his students provided the proof of innocence. The movement gained momentum in November 1998, when Northwestern University hosted the first National Conference on Wrongful Convictions and the Death Penalty. Attending were 35 former death row inmates. Some of them told their stories about almost being executed and how they were spared when evidence emerged showing that they had been wrongly convicted.[201]

The most publicized and influential miscarriage of justice in Illinois during this period was the Anthony Porter case. By sheer luck Porter's innocence was discovered, and he was exonerated and released from prison in February 1999, after spending 16 years on death row. He came within 2 days of his execution in 1998. Porter's attorneys were able to secure a stay of execution for him, arguing that he might be mentally incompetent to be executed because he was unable to understand that he was going to be executed and why. His IQ was 51. As a result of the stay, a Northwestern University journalism class that previously had decided not to investigate his case changed its decision. In a few months the students, Protess, and an investigator discovered the real killer and proved that Porter was innocent. The real killer confessed on videotape to the 1982 double murder for which Porter was convicted.[202]

Also in 1999, the *Chicago Tribune* published two major series. The first series documented prosecutor misconduct throughout the United States; the second series examined problems with Illinois's capital punishment system that contributed to such a large percentage of its death row inmates being exonerated because of their innocence. Based largely on the Anthony Porter case, the series by the *Chicago Tribune*, and the fact that Illinois had released 13 condemned inmates from death row since 1977 while executing 12, Republican Governor George Ryan, himself a proponent of the death penalty, imposed a moratorium on capital punishment in Illinois in January 2000. In May 2000, Governor Ryan charged a special commission he created with producing a comprehensive report on the administration of capital punishment in Illinois. In April 2002, Governor Ryan received the completed report, which contained 85 recommendations for changes in Illinois's capital punishment system.[203] Declaring the Illinois capital punishment system to be broken, in January 2003, just days before he was to leave office, Governor Ryan, as noted previously, pardoned four death row inmates and commuted the sentences, mostly to LWOP, of the remaining 167 inmates on Illinois's death row.[204]

A second important influence on the second moratorium movement was the ABA. In February 1997, the ABA adopted a resolution calling for a moratorium on the death penalty until problems with its administration could be resolved. Problems cited by the ABA included ineffective assistance of counsel, racial discrimination, imposition of the penalty on juveniles and the mentally retarded (which is no longer allowed; see *Roper v. Simmons*, 2005, and *Atkins v. Virginia*, 2002), and postconviction and habeas corpus concerns. Former ABA president Martha Barnett, a "reluctant supporter" of the death penalty, made the organization's moratorium effort a high priority. She maintained that defendants should not be executed unless there are guarantees that they received adequate legal representation and the sentence was not the result of racial discrimination. In March 2001, the ABA Section of Individual Rights and Responsibilities issued a group of protocols that identified factors that the section believed legislatures and commissions should consider when evaluating the fairness of death penalty laws and how these laws could be reformed. Finally, as noted previously, in 2003, the ABA's House of Delegates approved a revised edition of its 1989 guidelines for the appointment and performance of defense counsel in death penalty cases.

Third, besides the state of Illinois and the ABA, other governmental bodies and organizations joined the moratorium movement. For example, the Republican-controlled Nebraska legislature in 1999 voted for a moratorium on executions and for a study of the fairness of Nebraska's capital punishment system. Although Governor Mike Johanns vetoed the moratorium, the study was approved after legislators overrode the governor's veto of it. Similar studies have been undertaken in Illinois (as noted), Arizona, North Carolina, Maryland, and Indiana. In 1999, legislators in at least nine states introduced moratoria on executions (most were unsuccessful; besides Nebraska and Illinois, states that introduced moratoria bills were Connecticut, Maryland, Montana, New Jersey, North Carolina, Pennsylvania, and Washington).[205] In May 2002, Democratic Governor Parris Glendening imposed a moratorium on executions in Maryland until the state completed a study of whether there was racial bias in the use of the death penalty.[206] Despite the study's finding of racial bias, Glendening's successor, Republican Robert Ehrlich, resumed executions in 2004. In 2005, the New Jersey state legislature passed and Governor Richard Codey signed legislation that provided a 1-year moratorium on executions, thus becoming the first state to pass a moratorium legislatively, rather than by executive order.[207] (As noted previously, the New Jersey legislature and Governor Jon Corzine abolished the death penalty in 2007.) Additionally, more than 700 small towns and cities, church and religious groups, legal organizations, labor organizations, human rights groups, social service agencies, and business groups throughout the United States passed resolutions calling for a moratorium on the death penalty.[208]

Fourth, in May of 2000, the New Hampshire legislature voted to abolish the death penalty and thus became the first state to do so since the death penalty was reinstated in 1976. However, New Hampshire Democratic Governor Jeanne Shaheen vetoed the bill.[209]

A fifth development was the winter of 2000 publication and accompanying national publicity of Barry Scheck, Peter Neufeld, and Jim Dwyer's book, *Actual Innocence: Five Days to Execution, and Other Dispatches from the Wrongly Convicted*. The book documents numerous exonerations that resulted from after-the-fact DNA testing. Material in the book came from cases handled by the Innocence Project, which was described earlier.[210]

Sixth was the publication in June 2000 of a study by Columbia University law professor James S. Liebman and his colleagues Jeffrey Fagan and Valerie West. The study, discussed previously, showed that two thirds of the fully reviewed state capital cases between 1973 and 1995 were infected by serious, reversible errors. The study received major media attention. It was both lauded and criticized. Such reports embarrass the courts.

Seventh was the extensive media publicity surrounding the execution of Gary Graham in Texas on June 22, 2000. Though he claimed he was innocent, there was no DNA evidence to exonerate him. He was convicted on the testimony of a single eyewitness. Graham's execution also reignited the debate about the execution of juveniles.

Eighth were Juan Garza's impending execution by the federal government (the second federal execution under post-*Furman* statutes) and the national media publicity it generated. Just a day after Gary Graham's execution, the national media reported claims that the federal capital punishment system discriminated against minorities and that Garza's execution was being rushed. The White House leaked President Clinton's decision to stay Garza's execution at about the same time that the president stated at a news conference that he was disturbed about the racial distribution of the federal death row population. At about the same time The *Washington Post* did an expose on the racial disparities of Maryland's death row and several papers ran stories about recent miscarriages of justice in capital cases in Texas and Virginia. Then, in September 2000, a report issued by the Justice Department showed an apparent pattern of racial discrimination in the federal death penalty's imposition. This led to calls from a number of organizations, including the ABA, for a moratorium on federal executions. The Justice Department responded by announcing that it would hire outside experts to study the matter further.

Ninth, members of the U.S. Congress became active in the moratorium movement. For example, on October 26, 2000, the U.S. Senate passed a nonbinding resolution introduced by Vermont Democratic Senator Patrick Leahy. The resolution called for states to improve the quality of legal representation in capital cases and to provide wider access to postconviction DNA testing. On January 31, 2001, a bill to place a moratorium on executions by the federal government was introduced by Wisconsin Democratic Senator Russell Feingold. The bill urged states to do the same while a National Commission on the Death Penalty reviewed the death penalty's fairness. Senator Feingold together with Illinois Democratic Congressman Jesse Jackson, Jr. also introduced legislation that would give more time to death row inmates to gain access to DNA testing. On March 7, 2001, senators Leahy, Feingold, Gordon Smith (Oregon Republican), and Susan Collins (Maine Republican), joined representatives William Delahunt (Massachusetts Democrat) and Ray LaHood (Illinois Republican) to reintroduce the Innocence Protection Act in Congress. The bipartisan legislation sought to address problems of fairness in the death penalty in order to avoid the risk of wrongful convictions and executions. The bill required states to provide qualified and experienced attorneys to all defendants facing the death penalty and allowed for greater access to DNA testing.[211] Much of the bill was passed as the Innocence Protection Act of 2004, part of the Justice For All Act of 2004.

Tenth, long-time proponents of capital punishment began to express their misgivings about the penalty's administration. For example, former Florida Chief Justice and Miami Prosecutor Gerald Kogan called for a moratorium on the death penalty. Pat Robertson, head of the conservative Christian Coalition, and conservative commentator George Will also expressed their concerns. This development led to the creation of the National Committee to Prevent Wrongful Executions. On October 12, 2000, former President Jimmy Carter and his wife, Rosalynn, called for both a federal and state moratorium of the death penalty. As governor of Georgia, Carter had signed into law Georgia's post-*Furman* death penalty statute.

Two sitting Supreme Court justices voiced their concerns about the administration of the death penalty, especially the quality of legal representation. Justice Sandra Day O'Connor (who has since retired) believed that it was probably time to require minimum standards for lawyers in capital cases.

She also believed such lawyers should be adequately compensated. She remarked in a speech to a women's law group in Minneapolis that "if statistics are any indication, the system may well be allowing some innocent defendants to be executed."[212] Justice Ruth Bader Ginsburg, speaking at the University of the District of Columbia, acknowledged that she supported a proposed moratorium on the death penalty in Maryland. She observed that her experience with death row inmates who have asked the Court for last-minute reprieves demonstrated that not one of them received really good legal help at trial. She also criticized the "meager" amount of money spent to defend poor people. (Maryland lawmakers failed to pass the moratorium.[213])

Eleventh, the Catholic Church strongly and unequivocally opposed capital punishment and supported a moratorium. Toward the end of 1999, the Catholic Church together with the Reform and Conservative Jewish movements announced a joint campaign against capital punishment in the United States.

Twelfth, world opinion also seemed to be playing a role. See the discussion in Chapter 5.

Thirteenth, the media in the United States increasingly focused on problems with the death penalty and its administration. For example, "The Oprah Winfrey Show," the highest rated talk show in the country, devoted its entire September 2000 program to the death penalty issue. Oprah presented several innocent men who had been on death row as well as legal experts in favor of a death penalty moratorium.

All these affected public support for the death penalty in the United States, which appeared to be waning. In 26 national public opinion polls conducted between February 2000 and May 2006, only 62–69 percent of adults or registered voters nationwide were in favor of the death penalty for a person convicted of murder.[214] This was the lowest level of support recorded in a national poll in more than 20 years, and likely the first time the level of support had fallen below 70 percent during that period.[215] Fan and his colleagues found that the decline in death penalty support was a product of the media's attention on the condemnation of innocent persons (see the material that follows).[216] Moreover, for about a decade and a half, national public opinion polls had shown that when given a choice between the death penalty and LWOP, no more than about half and sometimes less of the public preferred the death penalty.[217]

The American public was also expressing greater concern about the way the death penalty was being administered, although recently this concern seems to be moderating somewhat. For example, a *USA Today*/Gallup poll conducted in June 2000 found that 41 percent of adults nationwide believed the death penalty was applied unfairly (51% believed it was applied fairly).[218] An NBC News/*Wall Street Journal* poll conducted in July 2000 found that 42 percent of registered voters nationwide thought that the death penalty was not applied fairly (42% believed it was applied fairly). Sixty-three percent of the respondents to this poll favored the suspension of the death penalty until questions about its fairness could be studied. Gallup polls conducted in May 2002, May 2003, May 2004, May 2005, and May 2006 discovered that 40, 37, 39, 35, and 35 percent of respondents, respectively, believed the death penalty was applied unfairly (53, 60, 55, 61, and 60%, respectively, believed the penalty was applied fairly). A *Newsweek* poll conducted in June 2000 found that more than 80 percent of adults nationwide thought that at least some innocent people had been wrongly executed since the death penalty was reinstated in the 1970s: 8 percent thought that "many" innocent people had been wrongly executed, 33 percent thought that only "some" innocent people had been wrongly executed, and 41 percent thought that only a "very few" innocent people had been wrongly executed. A Harris poll conducted in July 2000 revealed that 94 percent of adults nationwide thought that innocent people were sometimes convicted of murder. Perhaps even more telling, according to a CNN/*USA Today*/Gallup poll conducted in June 2000, 80 percent of adults nationwide thought that in the past 5 years a person had been executed who was, in fact, innocent of the crime with which he or she was charged. Gallup polls conducted in May 2003, May 2005, and May 2006 show that 73, 59, and 63 percent of respondents, respectively, believed an innocent person had been executed within the past 5 years.[219] The June 2000 *Newsweek* poll revealed that 82 percent of adults nationwide thought that states should make it easier for death row inmates to introduce new evidence that might prove their innocence, even if it might result in delays in the death penalty process. Ninety-five percent of adults nationwide thought that states should permit DNA testing in all cases where it might prove a person's guilt or innocence, and 88 percent of adults nationwide thought that the federal government should require states to permit DNA testing under these circumstances. To varying degrees, these suggestions have been implemented. It appears that revelations about the quality of justice in capital murder trials, the overturning of convictions as a result of DNA tests, and the resulting moratorium on executions in Illinois, among other factors, have had an impact on public opinions about the death penalty.

This conclusion has been corroborated by a recent study conducted in Florida—the state that leads the nation in death row exonerations.[220] Based on the responses of 543 people called to jury service in Hillsborough County (Tampa), Florida, during the spring of 2009, the researchers found that 86.5 percent of the potential jurors believed that there was at least a "minimal chance" that an innocent person would be wrongly executed; only 5.5 percent responded that there was "almost no chance" of such a miscarriage of justice. Nearly 53 percent of the respondents thought there was either a "moderately good chance" (30.5%) or a "near certain chance" (22%) of a wrongful execution. When asked to estimate the percentage of capital defendants wrongfully convicted, more than 87 percent of the respondents believed that between 2 and 20 percent of all capital defendants have been wrongfully convicted. Only 12.6 percent responded that there were no wrongful convictions in capital cases. About 41 percent of respondents believed that 2 percent of capital defendants were wrongfully convicted, 23.5 percent chose 5 percent, nearly 12 percent selected 10 percent, and 5.6 percent picked 20 percent.

Respondents were very supportive of most of the preventive or corrective remedies to miscarriages of justice (percentage supportive of the remedy in parentheses): better training/education for lawyers (98%), more qualified lawyers (96%), punish official misconduct (96%), independent crime laboratories (96%), videotaped police interrogations (94%), fully investigate innocent claims (93%), better compensation for lawyers (93%), continuous access to evidence (89%), compensation for wrongfully convicted (88%), unanimous jury decisions (81%), public clemency hearings (76%), higher degree of proof needed (74%), ban judicial overrides on jury sentence (69%), bar mentally ill from execution (59%), remove time restrictions on appeals (43%), and bar the elderly from execution (25%).

As noted, 96 percent of respondents were willing to punish official misconduct in capital cases. Nearly 32 percent of respondents were willing to seek criminal charges for officials responsible for miscarriages of justice, about 31 percent were willing to impose fines or civil sanctions, and approximately 20 percent wanted irresponsible officials fired from their jobs. Another 14 percent of respondents thought tainted evidence should be excluded from the trial, but only 3 percent believed the case should be dismissed because of official misconduct.

When asked about providing compensation to innocent persons wrongfully convicted in capital cases, respondents were quite generous. A plurality of respondents (22%) were willing to award wrongfully convicted innocent persons $50,000 per year incarcerated. The median response was $40,000 per year, and the mean response was $57,970 per year. Recently, Florida passed legislation that provides $50,000 per year incarcerated for wrongfully convicted individuals up to a maximum of $2 million, but only for those individuals with no prior felony convictions.[221] Perhaps surprisingly, nearly 80 percent of respondents would be willing to incur a tax increase to pay for this compensation. A plurality (36.3%) would support a 1 percent tax increase, followed by 24 percent who would support a 2 percent tax increase. The average tax increase supported by respondents was 1.74 percent.

Ironically, only 12.5 percent of respondents believed that the reforms listed above would eliminate errors, and despite the relatively large percentage of people who believed that miscarriages of justice in capital cases occur, nearly 40 percent of respondents would not change their support for the death penalty in light of this knowledge; 34.5 percent were less in favor, and only 11.6 percent were more opposed. Still, nearly 64 percent of the respondents favored a moratorium on the death penalty.

Also noteworthy is the dramatic decrease in the number of death sentences imposed annually and, to a somewhat lesser extent, the number of annual executions that coincided with the moratorium movement. Regarding death sentences, in 1999, 276 individuals were sentenced to death in the United States; in 2000, 235 individuals were sentenced to death; in 2001, 167; in 2002, 169; in 2003, 154; in 2004, 140; in 2005, 138; in 2006, 122; in 2007, 119; in 2008, 111; in 2009, 106; and in 2010, 114.[222] As for executions, in 1999, there were 98 executions in the United States; in 2000, 85; in 2001, 66; in 2002, 71; in 2003, 65; in 2004, 59; in 2005, 60; in 2006, 53; in 2007, 42; in 2008, 37; in 2009, 52; and in 2010, 46.[223]

CONCLUSION

Contrary to the beliefs of some death penalty proponents, miscarriages of justice in capital cases, including wrongful executions, do occur and, unfortunately, they happen with some regularity and frequency. Moreover, the evidence suggests that super due process requirements have not had the desired effect of significantly reducing these mistakes. Gross maintains that:

> The basic conclusion is simple. The steady stream of errors that we see in cases in which defendants are sentenced to death is a predictable consequence of our system of investigating and prosecuting capital murder.... . But what about what happens after trial? Everybody knows that direct and collateral review are more painstaking for capital cases than for any others. Isn't it likely that all these mistakes are caught and corrected somewhere in that exacting process? The answer, I'm afraid, is No. At best, we could do an imperfect job of catching errors after they occur, and in many cases we don't really try. As a result, most miscarriages of justice in capital cases never come to light.[224]

Some death penalty proponents argue that even if some innocent persons are executed, the mistakes, though regrettable, are justified nonetheless by the protection executions provide society.[225] Those who make the argument clearly believe that executions (whether of the guilty or the innocent) have a general deterrent effect. As shown in detail in Chapter 7, however, there is no credible evidence to support such a belief. The view is also misguided for another reason. Most miscarriages of justice in capital cases, especially wrongful convictions, mean that the actual killer has gone free and remains able to prey upon an unsuspecting public.

Finally, some death penalty proponents generalize the preceding argument and maintain that (unspecified) advantages of capital punishment morally justify miscarriages of justice in capital cases. Van den Haag writes:

> Most human activities—medicine, manufacturing, automobile and air traffic, sports, not to speak of wars and revolutions—cause the death of innocent bystanders. Nevertheless, if the advantages sufficiently outweigh the disadvantages, human activities, including those of the penal system with all its punishments, are morally justified.[226]

A Harris survey conducted in 2001 found that 67 percent of Americans supported the death penalty. Yet, the same survey discovered that 94 percent of Americans believed that innocent people were sometimes convicted of murder. Those surveyed believed that, on average, 12 percent of those convicted of murder were innocent.[227] Such findings would not have surprised long-time Sing Sing Prison Warden Lewis Lawes, who, in the 1920s, wrote: "The fact that innocent persons may occasionally be executed does not affect the public mind to a sufficient extent to result in a popular demand for the abolition of the death penalty. Such occurrences are too remote from the lives of the vast majority."[228]

One must wonder whether there is a threshold level for miscarriages of justice at which people who favor the death penalty in general would oppose it.[229] If other, less final punishments can achieve the same purposes as capital punishment—and can do so without the liabilities associated with capital punishment, such as miscarriages of justice—then, morally, the alternative punishments should be preferred.[230] Apparently, that is the position of Houston, Texas District Judge Kevin Fine, who, on March 5, 2010, ruled that the Texas death penalty was unconstitutional.[231] The ruling was made in response to a capital murder case pretrial motion and almost certainly will be overruled by an appellate court. Nevertheless, the ruling is noteworthy because Houston, Texas, and Harris County are notorious for being the capital punishment capital of the United States. If Harris County were a state, it would rank second only to Texas as the state with the most post-*Furman* executions.

DISCUSSION QUESTIONS

1. Have innocent people been wrongly convicted and executed under post-*Furman* statutes?
2. Do you agree with the harmless error rule? Why or why not?
3. How can wrongful convictions and executions occur, especially within the context of "super due process"?
4. To what type of defense should capital defendants be entitled?
5. Should attorneys who represent capital defendants be required to possess any special qualifications or training? What should the special qualifications or training be?
6. Should we trust capital defendants' lives to juries?
7. If not juries, who should make the decision of whether a convicted capital defendant should live or die?
8. What constitutes effective assistance of counsel?
9. What can be done about miscarriages of justice in capital cases? What do you consider to be the most important reform? Why?
10. Should the state be required to indemnify innocent people wrongly convicted of capital crimes when they have spent years in prison?

11. Should the state be required to indemnify the families of innocent people who have been executed?

12. Do you favor a moratorium on capital punishment? Why or why not?

13. Is the possibility of executing innocent people reason enough to abolish the death penalty?

14. How can the human sacrifice of innocent persons (any persons?) be morally justified in the first years of the twenty-first century?

Notes

1. Sarat (2002, pp. 246–260; 2005, pp. 9–10; 2006b).
2. Dow (2005); also see Baumgartner, DeBoef, and Boydstun (2008).
3. Professor David McCord (2006) makes an interesting argument that if the death penalty were subject to consumer protection laws, the public would have a cause of action for consumer fraud.
4. Amsterdam (1982, p. 349).
5. Committee on the Judiciary, U.S. Senate (1982, p. 317); also see Markman and Cassell (1988).
6. Personal communication between Espy and the author.
7. The following discussion is from Radelet and Bedau (2003).
8. In 20 of the 350 cases (6%) of wrongful convictions in capital cases catalogued by Bedau and Radelet (1987), no crime actually occurred, though a defendant was convicted of a capital offense.
9. See Scheck, Neufeld, and Dwyer (2001, p. 322).
10. But also see Bye (1919, pp. 80–81) and Sellin (1959, pp. 63–65).
11. Bedau (1982, p. 234).
12. Bedau and Radelet (1987); also see Radelet, Bedau, and Putnam (1992). The Bedau and Radelet study caused great consternation in the Reagan Justice Department. Attorney General Edwin Meese III requested Stephen J. Markman, assistant attorney general to Meese, and Paul G. Cassell, special assistant U.S. attorney, Eastern District of Virginia, and former associate deputy attorney general, to write a response. The first draft of their response was an 18-page Department of Justice internal memorandum. See Markman and Cassell (1988). For the rejoinder of Bedau and Radelet to the Markman and Cassell response, see Bedau and Radelet (1988).
13. Most of the information in this chapter about the Bedau and Radelet research is from Radelet et al. (1992). Note also that although Radelet et al. report 416 cases, the author's count of cases in their Inventory of Cases revealed only 375.
14. For an update of this study with additional cases, see Radelet, Lofquist, and Bedau (1996).
15. The specific number for each decade is as follows: 1900s = 30; 1910s = 93 (This total is misleading because one case had 51 defendants. The "crime"—a race riot between blacks and whites—occurred in Arkansas in 1919. All 51 of the defendants were black; no whites were charged with crimes. Excluding the 51 defendants in the 1910s, the average for the six decades was 51 and not 59.); 1920s = 64; 1930s = 69; 1940s = 41; 1950s = 31; and 1960s = 27. Between 1970 and 1976, before the reimposition of the death penalty and super due process, there were 60 wrongful convictions in capital cases.
16. Calculated from data at the Death Penalty Information Center, retrieved December 5, 2010, from http://www.deathpenaltyinfo.org/innocence-and-death-penalty#inn-yr-rc; also see Dieter (2004). Another source claims that only about 30 of these people are actually innocent, see Marquis (2005, p. 520).
17. Theoretically, one might assume that super due process protections would reduce the number of wrongful convictions in capital cases. On the other hand, one might reasonably argue that miscarriages of justice might be easier to detect and, therefore, more numerous the more recently they occur because of the "fresher trail" that is left.
18. See, for example, Sorensen (2004) (who may not be a proponent); Marquis (2005).

19. Ibid.

20. Ibid.

21. Ibid.

22. See *The Anniston [AL] Star*, September 9, 1984; Murders Still Haunt Atlanta. (1999, June 21). *The Orlando Sentinel*, p. 5.

23. *U.S. News and World Report*, December 17, 1984, p. 45.

24. Ibid.

25. See *The Anniston [AL] Star*, March 22 and 24, 1989.

26. *The Charlotte [NC] Observer*, September 5, 1989.

27. See *The Charlotte [NC] Observer*, January 26, 1993.

28. See *The Charlotte [NC] Observer*, June 27, 1993.

29. See *The Charlotte [NC] Observer*, June 29, 1993.

30. See *The Charlotte [NC] Observer*, January 3, 1995.

31. Herbert (2000).

32. Man Gets off Death Row. (2002, January 4). *The Orlando Sentinel*, p. C2; Man Leaves Death Row after 17 Years, Hoping to Find "Good things." (2002, January 6). *The Orlando Sentinel*, p. B3; Roman, I. (2002, January 27). Freed Man Relishes His 2nd Chance. *The Orlando Sentinel*, p. A1.

33. Holmes (2004).

34. The problem of eyewitness misidentification and what to do about it is discussed later in this chapter.

35. Problems with lineups and how they can be improved are discussed later in this chapter.

36. Zerwick (2004).

37. *Miami Herald*, February 24, 2006. Retrieved December 5, 2010, from http://www.deathpenaltyinfo.org/innocence-cases-2004-present.

38. *The Oklahoman*, May 11, 2007. Retrieved December 5, 2010, from http://www.deathpenaltyinfo.org/innocence-cases-2004-present.

39. *Chicago Sun-Times*, July 7, 2009. Retrieved December 5, 2010, from http://www.deathpenaltyinfo.org/innocence-cases-2004-present.

40. Baumgartner et al. (2008, p. 52).

41. Ibid., p. 54.

42. Bedau and Radelet (1987, p. 91). See Markman and Cassell (1988) for a critique of the conclusion of Bedau and Radelet (1988) for a rejoinder.

43. Cassell (2004, pp. 206–207).

44. Radelet (2006).

45. Harmon and Lofquist (2005) and Lehner (1996); Death Penalty Information Center, retrieved December 5, 2010, from http://www.deathpenaltyinfo.org/executed-possibly-innocent. For a detailed analysis of the Gary Graham case, see Welch and Burr (2002). For a detailed analysis of the Cameron Todd Willingham case, see Grann (2009).

46. Gelineau (2006); also see Marquis (2005).

47. Unless indicated otherwise, material in this section is from Coyne and Entzeroth (2001, p. 540); Liebman, Fagan, and West (2000).

48. Scheck et al. (2001, pp. 282 and 340).

49. See Liebman et al. (2000).

50. Dow (2005, pp. xxii–xxiii and 44).

51. Ibid., p. 133.

52. Gross (1996, pp. 499–500). Unless indicated otherwise, most of the information in this section is from Gross (1996), who based his analysis on data from Bedau and Radelet (1987) and Radelet et al. (1992).

53. Gross (1998, p. 133).

54. Harmon and Lofquist (2005, p. 514).
55. See *The Charlotte [NC] Observer*, November 12, 1993, p. 8A.
56. Baumgartner et al. (2008, p. 51).
57. Hastings (2001); Yardley (2001a, 2001b); Accusations Cost Chemist Job. (2001); for more examples, see Scheck et al. (2001, chap. 5).
58. Cited in Baumgartner et al. (2008, p. 70, Table 3.2).
59. Huff, Rattner, and Sagarin (1986) and Scheck et al. (2001).
60. Scheck et al. (2001, p. 95).
61. Ibid., p. 58.
62. Also see Harmon (2001).
63. Center on Wrongful Convictions (2004).
64. Harmon and Lofquist (2005, p. 511).
65. On the other hand, the discovery of most miscarriages of justice in capital cases is the result of a confession by the real criminal. On false confessions, also see Drizin and Leo (2004).
66. Gross (1998, p. 485); also see Dow (2005, p. 26) and Scheck et al. (2001, p. 116).
67. Information about Burge is from a series of *Chicago Tribune* articles retrieved on November 12, 2010, from http://articles.chicagotribune.com/keyword/jon-burge.
68. Radelet et al. (1992).
69. Bohm and Haley (2007, p. 278); also see McCord (2005, p. 822–823).
70. For additional reasons why prosecutors do not pursue death sentences in death-eligible cases, both merit based and non–merit based, see McCord (2005, pp. 856–864).
71. Roman, Chalfin, and Knight (2009).
72. Miller-Potter (2002); also see Burnett (2002), Harmon (2001), Liebman et al. (2000), and Scheck et al. (2001).
73. Miller-Potter (2002). Other forms of prosecutor misconduct in capital cases are overzealous and inappropriate arguments to the jury. See Burnett (2002, p. 43). For a theory of prosecutor misconduct, see Schoenfeld (2005).
74. Miller-Potter (2002); also see Liebman et al. (2000).
75. See Scheck et al. (2001, chap. 6).
76. Ibid., pp. 165–167.
77. Miller-Potter (2002).
78. Also see Harmon (2001).
79. Lehner (1996).
80. Miller-Potter (2002).
81. Ibid.
82. Scheck et al. (2001, pp. xxi–xxii).
83. Bright (2004, pp. 164–165).
84. Scheck et al. (2001, pp. 226 and 233).
85. Burnett (2002, p. 103).
86. Gross (1998, pp. 492–493).
87. Ibid., p. 496.
88. Bedau (1982, pp. 189–190).
89. Dow (2005, p. 7).
90. Bedau (1982, p. 190) and Bowers (1984, p. 339). Hammel (2002, p. 108) maintains that Texas capital defense attorneys frequently begin with a defeatist attitude and put on passive, reactive, and minimal defenses because they feel (and with good reason) it is inevitable that their clients will be convicted, sentenced to death, and executed.

91. Quoted in Bowers (1984, pp. 352–353).
92. Andersen (1983, p. 39); also see Harmon (2001).
93. Phillips (2009).
94. Harmon and Lofquist (2005, p. 511).
95. Coyle, Strasser, and Lavelle (1990); also see Mello and Perkins (1998, p. 268). These six states accounted for approximately 50 percent of all post-*Gregg* executions. See Burnett (2002, pp. 66–68) for attorney problems alleged in Missouri clemency petitions. For additional examples, see Dow (2002b, pp. 22–23; 2005).
96. Cited in Scheck et al. (2001, p. 336); also see Dow (2005, pp. 82–84) and Liebman et al. (2000).
97. Bright (2004, p. 160).
98. See *Bell v. Cone*, 2002.
99. Cited in Bright (1998, p. 130); also see Mello and Perkins (1998, p. 271).
100. Bright (1998, p. 130).
101. Ibid.
102. Ibid., pp. 130–131.
103. Court Backs Death-Row Man. (2001).
104. Weinstein (2002).
105. Bright (1998); also see Dow (2005, pp. 1–24).
106. Siegel (2009) and Tabak (2001, p. 756).
107. National Center for States Courts (2010).
108. Based on information in ibid.
109. See In re Amendment to Florida Rules of Criminal Procedure—Rule 3.112 Minimum Standards for Attorneys in Capital Cases, adopted July 1, 2000.
110. National Center for States Courts (2010).
111. Post (2004).
112. Williams (2005).
113. Bright (1997, p. 11).
114. Acker and Lanier (1999, pp. 448–449) and Williams (2005).
115. Bright (2004, p. 168).
116. Bright (1997b, pp. 816–821).
117. Bowers (1984).
118. Cited in Bright (2004, p. 168).
119. Ibid.
120. Ibid., pp. 168–169.
121. Death Penalty Prosecutions May Be Halted if Funding Is Inadequate. (2005).
122. To help remedy this problem, some states, such as Florida, have created capital punishment defense agencies. The attorneys who work in the agencies handle only capital punishment cases and, thus, are able to develop expertise. A problem is that most of the agencies are understaffed and underfunded and, consequently, have only the resources to handle appeals.
123. Bright (2004, p. 169).
124. Garey (1985, pp. 1240–1241); also see Wollan (1989) regarding the complexities of capital jurisprudence. Some inexperienced defense attorneys naively believe that their clients will be acquitted in the guilt stage and, therefore, do not bother to prepare for the penalty stage. See Burnett (2002, p. 36).
125. See Sundby (2005).
126. Ibid., p. 35.
127. Alter (2000a); *Wiggins v. Smith* (539 U.S. 510, 2003); *Rompilla v. Beard* (545 U.S. 374, 2005).
128. Cassell (2004, pp. 209–210).

129. Ibid., p. 209.
130. Sundby (2005, p. 77).
131. See Gross (1998, p. 145–146).
132. Cotton (2008, p. xiv).
133. Ibid., p. 150.
134. Ibid., p. xiv.
135. Ibid.
136. Unless indicated otherwise, material in this section is from Acker and Lanier (2000), Kobil (2003), and Sarat (2005).
137. Every judicial system in the world except China's provides for clemency; Sarat (2006a, p. 204, n. 2).
138. The governor in 35 states can make clemency decisions directly or in conjunction with an advisory board. Boards make clemency decisions in five states, and the decision is shared between the governor and an advisory board in 16 states; Sarat (2006a, p. 204, n. 2).
139. Banner (2002, p. 54).
140. Ibid., pp. 56–57.
141. Ibid., pp. 291–292.
142. Ibid., p. 58.
143. Ibid.
144. Harmon, Acker, and Rivera (2010).
145. See, for example, Heise (2003) and Pridemore (2000).
146. Berlow (2003).
147. For a description of the Missouri clemency process, see Burnett (2002, pp. 162–165).
148. Yardley (2000).
149. Berlow (2003).
150. Yardley (2000).
151. Material on the Texas clemency memos is from Berlow (2003).
152. Harmon et al. (2010).
153. Death Penalty Information Center, retrieved December 7, 2010, from http://www.deathpenaltyinfo.org/clemency.
154. Dieter (2010).
155. Cited in *Herrera v. Collins* (1993, p. 415).
156. Banner (2002, p. 291).
157. See Death Penalty Information Center, http://www.deathpenaltyinfo.org/article.php?>?did=126&scid=13, Acker and Lanier (2000, pp. 212–213, Table 1) and Baldus and Woodworth (1998, pp. 388–389) for the pre-1970s figure; also see Dieter (1996, p. 26). Palacios (1996, p. 347) claims that "the heyday of commutations was the early and mid-1940s, during which twenty to twenty-five percent of death penalties were commuted."
158. Acker and Lanier (2000, p. 215). For additional reasons, see Burnett (2002, pp. 158 and 169, n. 7); Radelet and Zsembik (1993).
159. Cited in Acker and Lanier (1999, p. 430).
160. Also see Burnett (2002, pp. 185–187).
161. Ibid., p. 437.
162. Perez-Pena (2000); data from 2000 through 2010 were generously provided by Michael L. Radelet.
163. Ibid; Death Penalty Information Center, retrieved December 8, 2010.
164. Perez-Pena (2000).
165. Material in this section is from the Governor's Commission on Capital Punishment (2002, pp. 191–192).
166. Material in this section is from Governor's Commission on Capital Punishment (2002, pp. 20, 22–25, 30–31); also see The Constitution Project (2005).

167. Material in this section is from Scheck et al. (2001, pp. 98–99); the Governor's Commission on Capital Punishment (2002, pp. 31–40, 129, 158); also see The Constitution Project (2005).

168. Dow (2005, p. 30) reports that Texas law, and the law of other states, makes it impossible to convict someone of a crime based solely on the testimony of a coconspirator. However, Texas law only requires minimal corroboration of accomplice testimony; ibid., p. 120.

169. Material in this section is from Scheck et al. (2001, pp. 158, 161–162, 212–213, 220); also see The Constitution Project (2005).

170. Unless indicated otherwise, material in this section is from Scheck et al. (2001, p. 351); Governor's Commission on Capital Punishment (2002, pp. 52–60); also see The Constitution Project (2005).

171. Alter and Miller (2000).

172. Innocence Project. Retrieved December 8, 2010, from http://www.innocenceproject.org/news/LawView2.php.

173. Material in this section is from Scheck et al. (2001, pp. 352–353); Governor's Commission on Capital Punishment (2002, pp. 131 and 158); also see The Constitution Project (2005).

174. Material in this section is from the Governor's Commission on Capital Punishment (2002, pp. 40–42); also see The Constitution Project (2005).

175. Material in this section is from Scheck et al. (2001, pp. 233–234, 355); Governor's Commission on Capital Punishment (2002, pp. 42–43).

176. Material in this section is from Governor's Commission on Capital Punishment (2002, pp. 82–85); also see The Constitution Project (2005).

177. Material in this section is from Governor's Commission on Capital Punishment (2002, pp. 118, 120, 168); also see The Constitution Project (2005).

178. Material in this section is from Scheck et al. (2001, pp. 233–234, 355).

179. Material in this section is from Governor's Commission on Capital Punishment (2002, pp. 94–99); also see The Constitution Project (2005).

180. Material in this section is from Governor's Commission on Capital Punishment (2002, p. 152); also see The Constitution Project (2005).

181. Material in this section is from Governor's Commission on Capital Punishment (2002, p. 172); also see The Constitution Project (2005).

182. Material in this section is from Burnett (2002, pp. 188–189).

183. Material in this section is from ibid., pp. 189–191.

184. Unless indicated otherwise, material in this section is from the Innocence Project at http://www.innocenceproject.org; also see The Constitution Project (2005); Gross, Jacoby, Matheson, Montgomery, and Patil (2004).

185. Baumgartner et al. (2008, p. 57, Table 3.1).

186. Ibid., p. 64.

187. Ibid., p. 63.

188. Ibid., p. 64.

189. Unless indicated otherwise, material in this section is from Burnett (2005) and Burnett (2002, pp. 194–195); also see Westervelt and Cook (2008).

190. Compensation Statutes Chart (2009).

191. Death Penalty Information Center. Retrieved from http://www.deathpenaltyinfo.org/article.php?>?scid=40&did=1234#subC.

192. Burstein (2009).

193. Deslatte (2009).

194. See, for example, the discussion of *Strickland v. Washington* (466 U.S. 668, 1984) in Chapter 4.

195. Jury: Freed Inmate to Get $2.25 Million. (2006); Markon (2006).

196. Garner (2000).
197. See Amsterdam (1982).
198. See *The Charlotte [NC] Observer*, November 13, 1992.
199. Burnett (2005).
200. Unless indicated otherwise, material in this section is from Tabak (2001).
201. See Alter (2000b) and Davis (1998); http://www.deathpenaltyinfo.org/IllinoisCCP.html.
202. http://www.deathpenaltyinfo.org/IllinoisCCP.html; also see Armbrust (2002).
203. Ibid.
204. Davey and Mills (2003). Ryan's critics are sure to point out that on September 6, 2006, Ryan was sentenced to 6.5 years in prison for 18 counts of racketeering, conspiracy, fraud, and other offenses involving favoritism and kickbacks for state contracts and property leases that enriched Ryan and his friends. Most of the charges were related to Ryan's 8 years as secretary of state during the 1990s. Ryan maintained his innocence throughout the trial, and the verdict is being appealed (Stern, 2006).
205. Cohen (1999); http://www.apbnews.com:80/cjsystem/justicenews/2000/02/04/moratorium0204_01.html.
206. Maryland Halts Executions. (2002, May 10). *The Orlando Sentinel*, p. A15.
207. Codey Signs Bill Suspending Executions in New Jersey, at http://www.njadp.org/forms/codeymor.html.
208. http://www.apbnews.com:80/cjsystem/justicenews/2000/02/04/moratorium0204_01.html.
209. Alter and Miller (2000).
210. http://www.cardozo.yu.edu/innocence_project.
211. http://www.deathpenaltyinfo.org/Changes.html.
212. Healy (2001).
213. Gearan (2002).
214. The polls can be found at the following sites: PollingReport.com, *Crime/law enforcement*, retrieved from http://www.pollingreport.com/crime.htm#Death; Death Penalty Information Center, *Summaries of recent poll findings*, retrieved from http://www.deathpenaltyinfo.org/article.php?scid=23&did=210#gallup200310.
215. In only five national Gallup polls during this period did public support for the death penalty exceed 69 percent: May 2002 (72%), October 2002 (70%), May 2003 (70 and 74%), and May 2004 (71%). Ibid.
216. Fan, Keltner, and Wyatt (2002).
217. For example, in a June 1991 Gallup poll, 53 percent of adults nationwide preferred the death penalty to LWOP; in an ABCNews.com poll conducted in January 2000, 48 percent of adults nationwide preferred the death penalty to LWOP; in a May 2001 Gallup poll, 52 percent of adults nationwide preferred the death penalty to LWOP; in a May 2002 Gallup poll, 52 percent of adults nationwide preferred the death penalty to LWOP; in a May 2003 Gallup poll, 53 percent of adults nationwide preferred the death penalty to LWOP; in a May 2004 Gallup poll, 50 percent of adults nationwide preferred the death penalty to LWOP, but in December 2004, a Quinnipiac University poll reported that only 42 percent of adults nationwide preferred the death penalty to LWOP (46% preferred LWOP); in an April 2005 CBS News poll, 39 percent of adults nationwide preferred the death penalty to LWOP (39% preferred LWOP); and in a May 2006 *USA Today*/Gallup poll, 47 percent of adults nationwide preferred the death penalty to LWOP (48% preferred LWOP). PollingReport.com, *Crime/law enforcement*, retrieved from http://www.pollingreport.com/crime.htm#Death; Gallup and Newport (1991); Jones (2006).
218. The following poll data can be found at PollingReport.com at http://www.pollingreport.com/crime.htm#Death.
219. Ibid; also see Unnever and Cullen (2005, pp. 14–15, 29), who found that 74.6 percent of Gallup poll respondents believed that an innocent person had been executed in the last 5 years. They also found that Americans were more likely to oppose the death penalty if they believed that the penalty was applied unfairly than if an innocent person had been executed. Finally, they discovered that the decrease in death penalty support among African Americans was much greater than it was for whites when either group believed an innocent person had been executed.

220. Bingham, Cochran, Heide, and Boots (2010).

221. Florida Statute 961 (2008).

222. The Death Penalty Information Center. Retrieved December 8, 2010, from http://www.deathpenaltyinfo .org/death-sentences-year-1977-2008.

223. The Death Penalty Information Center. Retrieved December 8, 2010, from http://www.deathpenaltyinfo .org/executions-year and December 23, 2010, from http://www.deathpenaltyinfo.org/documents/ 2010YearEnd-Final.pdf.

224. Gross (1996, p. 497).

225. See, for example, the Committee on the Judiciary, U.S. Senate (1982), and Markman and Cassell (1988).

226. Van den Haag (1982, p. 325).

227. Death Penalty Information Center, http://www.deathpenaltyinfo.org/Polls.Html#Harris7/01.

228. Lawes (1969, p. 5).

229. See Longmire (1996) for the finding that evidence of the execution of innocent persons is one of the most effective ways of changing the opinions of death penalty supporters to opponents.

230. Professor Bedau (1999, p. 47) offers this general substantive due process principle that might apply here: "Society, acting through the authority of its government, must not enact and enforce policies that impose more restrictive-invasive, harmful, violent-interference with human liberty, privacy, and autonomy than are absolutely necessary as the means to achieve legitimate and important social objectives." Bedau (2004, pp. 32–33) calls this the "Minimal Invasion principle." For Bedau, the death penalty always violates the principle.

231. Rogers (2010).

Arbitrariness and discrimination in the administration of the death penalty

10

In its *Furman* decision, two of the major problems the Supreme Court found with existing death penalty statutes were that they did not prevent the death penalty from being imposed arbitrarily and in a discriminatory fashion. Barry Nakell and Kenneth Hardy provide relevant definitions of the two key terms:

- Arbitrariness involves the question of whether discretion permits the death penalty to be applied randomly, capriciously, irregularly, or disproportionately among the qualified defendants without any evident regard for the legal criteria designed to determine the selection. Arbitrariness is random.[1]
- Discrimination involves the question of whether discretion permits the death penalty to be deliberately directed disproportionately against certain qualified defendants, not because of the nature of their crimes, but because they belong to a particular class or group, determined by such considerations as race, sex, nationality, religion, or wealth. Discrimination is deliberate.[2]

Recall from the discussion in Chapter 3 that the Supreme Court approved, on faith, the new guided discretion statutes enacted in the wake of *Furman*. The Court assumed, without any evidence, that the new statutes and other procedural reforms would rid the death penalty's administration of the problems cited in *Furman*, including arbitrariness and discrimination. The purpose of this chapter is to examine the evidence amassed since the Court's 1976 decision and to determine whether the Court's faith was justified.

ARBITRARINESS IN THE ADMINISTRATION OF THE DEATH PENALTY UNDER POST-*FURMAN* STATUTES

As evidence of arbitrary application of the death penalty under post-*Furman* statutes, critics point to the small percentage of all death-eligible offenders who are executed and to the patterns in which the death penalty has been applied across jurisdictions and over time. Sources of this arbitrariness have been identified as (1) post-*Furman* statutes that justify arbitrariness, (2) jurors' misunderstanding or underestimating their sentencing obligations, (3) rule changes by the Supreme Court, (4) problems in determining murderous intent, (5) the availability and use of plea bargaining, and (6) the appellate courts.

FEW DEATH-ELIGIBLE OFFENDERS ARE EXECUTED

Only 1–2 percent of all death-eligible offenders have been executed from 1930 to the present. Thus, not only is the vast majority of capital offenders able to escape execution, but there is no meaningful way to distinguish between the eligible offenders who were executed and those who were not. Even during the peak of executions in the United States in the 1930s, only 20 percent of all death-eligible offenders were executed.

The situation has not changed much under post-*Furman* statutes. Bowers found that:

> … of the first 607 sentences imposed on convicted murderers under Georgia's post-*Furman* capital statute—not counting guilty pleas resulting in life sentences—113 were death sentences…. That is to say, more than 80 percent of the death-eligible murderers in Georgia—the vast majority—were given life sentences. And Georgia is among the states most likely to impose death sentences; in most other states the percentage of death-eligible murderers receiving death sentences will be even less.[3]

One might assume that the few death-eligible offenders that are executed represent the "worst of the worst," but the "worst of the worst" sometimes escape execution, while murderers who clearly are not among the "worst of the worst" do not. Regarding the first category, in 2003, Gary Ridgeway, the so-called "Green River Killer," admitted to killing 48 women during a span of two decades. He was allowed to escape the death penalty by pleading guilty to the murders and, in doing so, gained the distinction of pleading guilty to more murders than any other serial killer in American history. He was sentenced to consecutive LWOP sentences for each murder. The prosecutor reluctantly agreed to the plea deal because investigators and victims' relatives wanted the murders resolved and cases closed. Had the victims not been prostitutes, drug addicts, and runaways, perhaps the prosecutor's decision might have been different. However, Ridgeway is not the only serial killer to escape the death penalty. Two more examples are Angelo Buono and Kenneth Bianchi, the so-called "Hillside Stranglers." Bianchi pleaded guilty to five murders, and Buono was found guilty of nine murders. All the murder victims were young women. Both Bianchi and Buono were sentenced to LWOP in 1983.[4]

APPLICATION OF THE DEATH PENALTY ACROSS JURISDICTIONS AND OVER TIME

Arbitrariness is evident in the way the death penalty has been applied across jurisdictions and over time. As Amsterdam, who has defended dozens of capital offenders, describes:

> [T]here is a haphazard, crazy-quilt character about the administration of capital punishment that every knowledgeable lawyer or observer can describe but none can rationally explain. Some juries are hanging juries, some counties are hanging counties, some years are hanging years; and men live or die depending on these flukes. However atrocious the crime may have been for which a particular defendant is sentenced to die, "experienced wardens know many prisoners serving life or less whose crimes were equally, or more atrocious."[5]

Consider, for example, the distribution of executions among death penalty jurisdictions. Although 36 jurisdictions in the United States (which includes 34 states, the U.S. government, and the U.S. military) have death penalty statutes, only 33 jurisdictions have executed at least one person under their post-*Furman* statutes (as of May 2011).[6] Kansas, New Hampshire, and the U.S. military have not conducted an execution under their post-*Furman* statutes (as of May 2011).[7] Between 1976 and 2006, only eight states executed more people than they did from 1945 through 1975: Texas, Oklahoma,

Virginia, Missouri, Delaware, Indiana, Arizona, and Montana. Every other state has dramatically reduced or completely abandoned executions.[8] More than 40 percent of the executing jurisdictions (16) have executed fewer than 10 people since executions resumed in 1977.[9] Bowers contends, "Capital punishment appears to be not an integral part of the criminal justice process in these states, but an occasional product of chance—an unpredictable occurrence."[10]

Only five of the 33 jurisdictions account for about two thirds of the 1,247 people executed under post-*Furman* statutes as of May 7, 2011; two states (Texas and Virginia) can lay claim to about 46 percent of the total; and one state (Texas) has executed more than 37 percent of the total.[11] Still, even Texas executes only a small percentage of its death-eligible offenders.

Regional variation in executions also suggests arbitrariness in application. Historically, capital punishment has been employed mostly in the South. Sixty percent of the approximately 4,000 persons legally executed under state authority in the United States between 1930 and 1980 were in the South. Between 1930 and 1980, the state of Georgia executed more people (366) than any other state.[12] The distribution by region is shown in Table 10.1.

During the period, 3.8 times more capital offenders were executed in the South than in any other region of the United States.[13] As of May 7, 2011, nearly seven times more capital offenders were executed in the South than in any other region of the United States under post-*Furman* statutes.[14] More than 80 percent of executions under post-*Furman* statutes have occurred in the South.[15] The post-*Furman* distribution by region is displayed in Table 10.2.

There is also regional variation within states. For example, in Florida and Georgia, the probability of receiving a death sentence for felony homicide (death-eligible murder) by judicial circuit or county varied greatly.[16] In Florida, a capital offender was more than four times more likely to be sentenced to death for a felony homicide in the panhandle area of the state than in either the northern or southern regions of the state, and more than twice as likely to be sentenced to death in the panhandle than in the central region of the state. Similarly, in Georgia, a capital offender was nearly nine times more likely to be sentenced to death in either the central or southwest regions than in Fulton County (Atlanta), more than four times more likely to be sentenced to death in either the central or southwest regions of Georgia than in the northern region, and twice as likely to be sentenced to death in the northern region than in Fulton County. A study of Virginia death-sentencing practices found that the strongest predictive factor was location of the prosecution. A death sentence was significantly more likely to be sought in lower density areas of the state than in high-density urban areas.[17]

These data do not necessarily indicate arbitrariness if it can be shown that a similar proportion of death-eligible murders are committed in the South or in a particular region of a state. However, in 2009, only 44.8 percent of (all) murders occurred in the South[18]—a smaller percentage than might be

Table 10.1 Pre-*Furman* Distribution of Executions by Region

Region	Distribution
South	2,307 (60%)
Northeast	602 (16%)
West	511 (13%)
North central	403 (11%)
Total	3,823

Region	Distribution
South	1,024 (82%)
Northeast	4 (0.3%)
West	71 (6%)
Midwest	148 (12%)
Total	1,247

Table 10.2 Post-*Furman* Distribution of Executions by Region

predicted, given that more than 80 percent of the executions occur in the South. But the 44.8 percent is for all murders and not just death-eligible murders, and data separating the two categories are not available. Thus, it is still possible, though improbable, that a much larger proportion of murders are death eligible in the South than in other regions of the country.

Such disparities are not limited to the South. A study in Nebraska also discovered significant differences in charging and plea bargaining in major urban and nonurban counties. In major urban counties prosecutors were more willing than their counterparts in nonurban counties to waive the death penalty unilaterally or by way of plea bargain. These practices produced a statewide "adverse disparate impact" on racial minorities, who were more likely to face a death sentence.[19] In Illinois (before it abolished its death penalty), defendants outside of Cook County were substantially more likely to receive a death sentence than defendants within Cook County. Specifically, after controlling for aggravating factors, 8.4 percent of first-degree murder convictions from rural counties in Illinois resulted in a death sentence. The corresponding percentages for urban counties, collar counties, and Cook County were, respectively, 3.4, 3.3, and 1.5 percent.[20] Similar geographical (county) disparities were found in Ohio and Maryland, in the latter even after controlling for numerous relevant case characteristics.[21]

Data of regional variation within states suggest that greater numbers of death-eligible homicides do not increase the overall probability of a death sentence, as one might expect. Rather, the data show that the odds of being sentenced to death are either greater in regions with fewer death-eligible homicides or not related to the number of death-eligible homicides at all. It may be that where capital murders are few, those that are committed receive harsher punishment. Another explanation, as noted in Chapter 8, has to do with the costs of capital punishment. Counties that can afford it may seek the death penalty in all cases that warrant it, while "poor" counties may have to pick and choose among death-eligible cases, pursuing the death penalty in only some cases or not at all. "Poor" counties simply may not be able to afford the death penalty.[22]

In Florida, for example, other regions had between 4.5 and nearly nine times more homicides than the panhandle, yet in the panhandle, the probability of a death sentence was two to four times greater than that in other regions of the state. This finding was the exception, however. The overall probability of a death sentence in the central region of Florida was at least twice as great as the probability in either the north or south regions, even though the number of death-eligible homicides in the central region (172) was more than the 140 in the north region and less than the 270 in the south region. In Georgia, the central and southwest regions were nearly nine times more likely than Fulton County to impose a death sentence, yet the 154 death-eligible homicides in Fulton County were greater than the 103 in the southwest region and fewer than the 162 in the central region. In

Texas, Harris County (Houston) alone accounts for nearly one third of the state's death row inmates, while Dallas, with a higher murder rate, has only about one quarter the number of Houston's death row inmates.[23]

A recent study found that only 10 percent of U.S. counties accounted for all death sentences imposed between 2004 and 2009, and 5 percent of U.S. counties accounted for all death sentences imposed between 2007 and 2009.[24] The concentration of death sentences in these counties was not a function of the heinousness of the murders committed or the incorrigibility of the offenders. Rather, in some counties prosecutors sought the death penalty, and in other counties in the same state they did not, even for the same or more aggravated death-eligible murders.[25] These combined data show that the application of the death penalty under post-*Furman* statutes, in the words of the Court in its *Furman* decision, has been "rare," "uncommon," and "freakish."

POST-*FURMAN* STATUTES JUSTIFY ARBITRARINESS

Bowers suggests that the post-*Furman* statutes may have an effect different from the one intended by the Court. Rather than reducing or eliminating arbitrary and discriminatory application, the new statutes may facilitate both problems, especially in states such as Texas. He further explains, "Perhaps explicitly enumerated aggravating circumstances do not serve to guide sentencing discretion as much as they become means of justifying arbitrary or discriminatory sentencing practices in places where social or political influences favor such practices."[26]

JURORS' MISUNDERSTANDING OR UNDERESTIMATING THEIR SENTENCING OBLIGATIONS

Another troublesome problem with post-*Furman* statutes—a problem that also contributes to arbitrary application—is the failure of many jurors to understand their statutory sentencing obligations. Research shows that jurors commonly misapprehend judges' capital sentencing instructions, especially those pertaining to mitigating circumstances.[27] Particularly troublesome is evidence from the Capital Jury Project indicating that nearly 75 percent of jurors "acknowledge that sentencing instructions did not guide their decision making on punishment but served instead as an after-the-fact façade for a decision made prior to hearing the instructions."[28] Many jurors inappropriately made their sentencing decisions before the sentencing phase of the trial began, and oftentimes these decisions were pro-death.[29] Data from the Capital Jury Project also reveal that jurors frequently have mistaken views about the alternatives to a death sentence and, consequently, vote for death even though they would vote for life if they were assured that the defendant would never be released from prison or would not be released for a long time. Many jurors do not believe that LWOP actually means that a defendant will be imprisoned for the rest of his or her life. Many capital jurors believe that murderers will be back on the streets far too soon; typically, in about 15 years or less.[30] Judges in many jurisdictions are legally barred from clarifying this issue for jurors.[31]

Many jurors also underestimate their sentencing responsibilities, seeming to believe that they are only to follow a prescribed formula in determining a sentence in capital cases. For them, it is "the law" or "legal instructions" that ultimately determine whether a capital defendant lives or dies. For some jurors, "the law" or "legal instructions" "authorize" them to impose the death penalty and, at the same time, relieve them of any personal responsibility in making the decision.[32] Other jurors assume that the sentence they impose is only preliminary and nonbinding since it will be reviewed and corrected, if necessary, by an appellate court.[33] In *Caldwell v. Mississippi* (1985), the Supreme Court opined that for jurors to believe that "the responsibility for any ultimate determination of death will rest with others" is an "intolerable danger." Such thinking on the part of capital jurors may lead to arbitrarily imposed death sentences.

RULE CHANGES BY THE SUPREME COURT

Arbitrariness is also inevitable whenever the Supreme Court changes the rules by which the penalty is imposed. This is especially true when the changes have a retroactive effect (i.e., when they are applied to earlier cases). An example is the Court's 1968 *Witherspoon* decision, which held as unconstitutional the practice of excluding people from capital juries simply because they generally opposed capital punishment. This ruling resulted in dozens of death row inmates having their death sentences set aside because of constitutional errors in jury selection. *Witherspoon* was welcome news to those inmates who received new trials, but the decision did nothing for the dozens who had been executed even though their trials were infected with identical errors.[34]

Similarly, the Court's 1977 *Coker* decision declared capital punishment for rape of an adult woman unconstitutional. *Coker* did nothing for the 455 men (405 of whom were black) who had been executed for rape in the United States since 1930.[35] Had they been tried under the *Coker* standard, they would have met a different fate. The same could be said for the mentally retarded before *Atkins v. Virginia* (2002) and for juveniles under the age of 18 before *Roper v. Simmons* (2005). There are numerous other such examples of changes in death penalty laws.

Supreme Court justices change their minds. They do not always follow precedent. Some of this is to be expected because of "evolving standard of decency," but they also do not follow precedent when they disagree with a precedent. Regarding "evolving standard of decency," for example, Justice Scalia has written, "having an evolving Constitution … means you don't have a Constitution at all. It means, ultimately, you're going to have a Constitution that means what the current society wants it to mean, which means it's useless."[36] Sometimes justices are simply inconsistent in their decisions, that is, inconsistent with their own reasoning in other cases. According to Miller and Niven, this is true of justices, such as Rehnquist, Scalia, and Thomas, who consider themselves "strict constructionists" (relying on the Constitution's text and its writers' original intent) and pride themselves on their consistency. Each of the justices believes that consistency in decision making is a primary source of the Court's legitimacy. Yet, writes Miller and Niven, these justices have rendered inconsistent decisions in at least three crucial areas: "the operative definition of cruel and unusual punishment, the independence of states, and the obligations of jurors."[37] Miller and Nixon claim "that a coherent link between Rehnquist, Scalia, and Thomas' decisions cannot be found in any method of constitutional interpretation but instead seems to reside only in their politically preferred outcome."[38] The more general point, however, is that whether or not an inmate is executed depends, in part, on chance—that is, whether his or her execution date came before or after a crucial Supreme Court decision.

PROBLEMS IN DETERMINING MURDEROUS INTENT

Another source of arbitrariness in the application of capital punishment involves the charge for which a defendant is prosecuted. Generally, whether a defendant is charged with first- or second-degree murder or capital or noncapital murder depends on such considerations as whether the defendant acted with "premeditation" or "criminal intent."[39] Determining what a person intended to do before he or she acted is a difficult, if not impossible, task. Former Supreme Court Justice Benjamin Cardoza underscored this dilemma when he wrote "that [he] did not understand the concept of premeditation after several decades of studying and trying to apply it as a judge."[40] Yet whether a defendant is tried for his or her life depends on just such a determination.

AVAILABILITY AND USE OF PLEA BARGAINING

A related source of arbitrariness involves whether a capital suspect is allowed to plea bargain to a noncapital offense. The plea bargain option creates a particular dilemma for the capital suspect who is innocent (or at least innocent of a capital offense). If the suspect pleads guilty to a noncapital offense and, thus, escapes the death penalty, he or she will still have to serve a prison sentence (in all likelihood), perhaps for a crime that he or she did not commit. On the other hand, if the innocent suspect (or suspect who did not commit a capital crime) elects to be tried for the capital charge, he or she risks the chance of being found guilty and executed. This scenario is more than hypothetical. Julian Bond recounts that "on the date of his death [May 25, 1979], [John] Spinkelink could have already been paroled if he had plea bargained and accepted the uncontested second-degree murder conviction offered him by the state [of Florida]."[41]

THE APPELLATE COURTS

As noted previously, at least 30 percent and as many as 68 percent of death sentences imposed under post-*Furman* statutes have been found legally faulty. Many people may believe that appellate review detects and corrects arbitrary and discriminatory application of capital punishment, and, in some cases, it does—at a considerable burden in time and other resources to the appellate courts. Sometimes, though, appellate review becomes another independent source of arbitrariness. The description of John Spinkelink's final appeal to the Eleventh U.S. Circuit Court illustrates how this occurs.[42] Bowers summarizes the lesson to be learned from Spinkelink's experience (as well as an unanticipated consequence):

> The final appeal of Spinkelink ... reveals arbitrariness at the highest levels of legal authority. Federal judges are not exempt from or immune to personal, social, or situational influences; they are subject to the same pressures and temptations as everyone else who handles capital cases.... It is a seductive illusion to believe that the highest courts can intercept arbitrariness wherever it occurs in the handling of capital cases.
>
> Indeed, [for some] the assumption that the federal appellate process can serve as a fail-safe mechanism against arbitrariness and discrimination now sustains the institution of capital

punishment in America. But the truth ... is that the federal courts themselves are an independent source or conduit of such arbitrariness.[43]

CONCLUSION

Perhaps it is impossible to eliminate arbitrary application of the death penalty completely because of human involvement in the process. Perhaps the Supreme Court, in *Gregg*, was naive to believe that the new guided discretion statutes and other procedural reforms would eliminate arbitrary imposition of the death penalty. Either way, faced with evidence from the post-*Gregg* experience, the Court would seem to have two alternatives. First, it could decide that some arbitrariness in the death penalty's application is tolerable (which may be its current unofficial and implicit position, anyway). However, if it were to officially recognize the arbitrariness, then it probably would have to determine how much arbitrariness it will allow. This task might lead down a slippery slope to the second alternative—the abolition of capital punishment. The Court might conclude that arbitrary application of capital punishment is inevitable (intolerable though it may be) as long as the penalty is administered.

DISCRIMINATION IN THE ADMINISTRATION OF THE DEATH PENALTY UNDER POST-*FURMAN* STATUTES

Only a select few of all murderers eligible for execution are ever actually executed. Consideration of the unique characteristics of those executed, the laws under which they are prosecuted, and the behavior of defense attorneys, prosecutors, and jurors reveals objectionable forms of discrimination. Before turning to evidence of discrimination, however, it is important to distinguish between disparity and discrimination.

DISPARITY VERSUS DISCRIMINATION

Disparity refers to numerical differences based on some characteristic, such as race. There has been a pattern of racial disparity in the imposition of the death penalty in the United States because the penalty has been imposed on blacks disproportionately to their numbers in the population.[44] The Supreme Court holds that as long as racial or other disparities can be justified by relevant legal factors (e.g., that blacks commit a disproportionate number of capital crimes), there is nothing inherently problematical with those disparities in the administration of capital punishment. For the most part, the Court considers it legally irrelevant that disparities may be either wholly or partially products of factors antecedent to the criminal act (e.g., growing up in a racist or psychologically impoverished environment).[45]

Discrimination is a violation of the equal protection clause of the Fourteenth Amendment and of special restrictions on the use of capital punishment under the Eighth Amendment. Discrimination is evident to the Court when the death penalty is intentionally or purposefully imposed on persons because of some characteristic, such as race, and not because of or in addition to legitimate sentencing considerations. Proving intentional discrimination in specific cases is an extremely difficult task.

DISCRIMINATION BASED ON SOCIAL CLASS AND THE DEFINITION OF MURDER

The FBI's Uniform Crime Reports show that, since 2000, approximately 16,000 murders and nonnegligent manslaughters have been committed each year. About 20 percent (or 3,200) of them are probably death eligible. A problem with the murders reported by the FBI is that they represent only a fraction of the people killed intentionally or negligently each year and an even smaller fraction of potentially death-eligible murders. For example, conservative estimates indicate that each year in the United States at least 12,000 lives are lost because of unnecessary surgeries, 98,000 to preventable medical errors, 37,500 to hospital personnel spreading infections in hospitals, 50,000 to occupational disease, 450,000 to tobacco-related diseases, and an unknown number to lethal industrial products.[46]

While the proximate decision makers and perpetrators in most of these deaths are not death eligible, because their actions or inactions are neither intentional nor criminally negligent, a small but significant fraction are. Yet, few of them are defined legally as murderers, especially death-eligible murderers. One reason is that few of the offenders are readily identifiable because their decisions are hidden by the complexities of the workplace environment or by the corporate chain of command. Another more cynical reason is that, by virtue of their class position, the perpetrators of these "white-collar crimes," no matter how malicious and heinous their actions, simply are not considered appropriate candidates for capital punishment in the United States. Justice Douglas wrote in his *Furman* decision, "One searches our chronicles in vain for the execution of any member of the affluent strata of this society."[47] Former San Quentin warden Clinton T. Duffy stated that he knew of no one of means who was ever executed.[48] Former Sing Sing (New York) warden Lewis Lawes elaborated, "The defendant of wealth and position, of influence, seldom goes to the electric chair. Through good counsel, through legal technicalities and delay, through influence, he manages to escape death while the man who is friendless and destitute pays the extreme penalty. This statement is borne out by an examination of the data concerning the men who have been executed in this state during the past thirty years."[49] Finally, attorney Bryan Stevenson has pointed out that capital punishment really means "them without the capital gets the punishment."[50] A major reason wealth matters, as Warden Lawes observed, is that the wealthy are able to hire the best attorneys. In many capital cases, the outcome depends more on an attorney's skill than what actually happened.[51]

That the wealthy are practically immune to the death penalty is supported by criminologist Scott Phillips's recent study of 504 adult defendants indicted for capital murder in Harris County (Houston), Texas, from 1992 to 1999.[52] As noted previously, Harris County, Texas, is notorious for being the capital-punishment capital of the United States. Harris County also is noteworthy because it does not have a public defender system. All criminal defendants are represented by privately retained lawyers or appointed counsel. Phillips reported that all but one of the 504 defendants were poor (based on the median household income of the defendant's neighborhood, i.e., census block group). The one exception was multimillionaire Robert Angelton, who was accused of hiring his brother to kill his wife. Not surprisingly, Angelton was acquitted of the capital murder at trial.

The point, however, is not to argue for the death penalty for such offenses and offenders, but to show that an unacceptable form of discrimination is created by the way death-eligible murders are defined.[53] If death-eligible murder also included the actions and inactions just listed that are particularly reprehensible, then the distribution of persons convicted of death-eligible murder would be more evenly divided among social classes.[54]

In another study using the same data, Phillips also discovered that the victim's social class or social status frequently determined whether the prosecutor sought and the jury imposed the death penalty.[55] He found that prosecutors were more likely to seek the death penalty and juries were more likely to impose the death penalty in cases of high-status victims than in cases of low-status victims. Phillips defined high-status victims as wealthy (based on median household income in victim's residential neighborhood), integrated (married or widowed), sophisticated (college degree), conventional (white or Hispanic), and respectable (clean criminal record). Low-status victims, on the other hand, were poor, marginal (separated, divorced, or single), unsophisticated (no college degree), unconventional (black or Asian), and disrespectable (prior criminal record). Thus, not only does the offender's social status determine death eligibility but so does the victim's social status.

DISCRIMINATION BY GENDER

The death penalty is rarely inflicted on women, even though women commit roughly one in 10 of all criminal homicides (where the gender of the offender is known).[56] (The percentage of women who commit death-eligible homicides is unknown.) Approximately 20,000 people have been legally executed in the United States since 1608, and about 3 percent (approximately 569) of them have been women. Most of them (nearly 90%) were executed prior to 1866.[57] Between 1930 and 1980, approximately 4,000 persons were executed by civil authority in the United States—32, or about 0.8 percent, were women.[58]

It has been estimated that under current death penalty laws, if women and men were treated equally, and that no factor other than offense was considered, women would receive between 4 and 6 percent of all death sentences.[59] Under post-*Furman* statutes, however, women have received about 2 percent of all death sentences—two to eight death sentences a year—167 between January 1, 1973, and late 2010.[60] The reason for the difference is that from arrest through execution, women are filtered from the process. Women account for about:

- 10 percent of murder arrests,
- 2 percent of death sentences imposed at trial,
- 1.7 percent of persons on death row, and
- 1 percent of persons executed under post-*Furman* statutes (1,247 executions as of May 4, 2011).[61]

Only 12 women have been executed under post-*Furman* statutes as of this writing. At least 14 years separated the first execution from the other 11. The women executed were Velma Barfield, who was executed in North Carolina on October 2, 1984; Karla Faye Tucker, who was executed in Texas on February 3, 1998; Judy Buenoano, who was executed in Florida on March 30, 1998; Betty Lou Beets, who was executed in Texas on February 24, 2000; Christina Riggs, who was executed in Arkansas on May 2, 2000; Wanda Jean Allen, who was executed in Oklahoma on January 11, 2001; Marilyn Plantz, who was executed in Oklahoma on May 1, 2001; Lois Nadean Smith, who was executed in Oklahoma on December 4, 2001; Linda Lyon Block, who was executed in Alabama on May 10, 2002; Aileen Wuornos, who was executed in Florida on October 10, 2002; Frances Newton, who was executed in Texas on September 14, 2005; and Teresa Lewis, who was executed in Virginia on September 23, 2010.[62]

Approximately 90 percent of the post-*Furman* women sentenced to death but no longer on death rows had their death sentences reversed.[63] As of late 2010, 55 women occupied death rows—about 1.7 percent of the total.[64] They ranged in age from 27 to 77 and had been on death row from less than 1 year to nearly 25 years.[65] Sixty-five percent of the female death row inmates were white, 22 percent were black, 11 percent were Hispanic, and 2 percent were Native American.[66] Fourteen of the women currently on death rows killed their husbands or boyfriends, 11 of them killed their children, one of them killed both her husband and children, and three other women killed a young niece, nephew, or child in their care.[67]

Law professor Victor Streib observes that the women who have been executed, both historically and in modern times, share certain distinctive characteristics:

> The executed females tended to be very poor, uneducated, and of the lowest social class in the community. Their victims tended to be white and of particularly protected classes, either children or socially prominent adults. Comparatively few executed females committed their crimes with a co-defendant, so they could not claim they were under the domination of another. Most of the executed females manifested an attitude of violence, either from past behavior or present acts, that countered any presumption of nonviolence. Finally, and perhaps most fatally for them, they committed shockingly "unladylike" behavior, allowing the sentencing judges and juries to put aside any image of them as "the gentler sex" and to treat them as "crazed monsters" deserving of nothing more than extermination.[68]

Streib is among the scholars who believe gender discrimination is evident in the application of the death penalty.[69] He identifies two principal sources of this discrimination: (1) the conscious or subconscious attitudes of key actors in the criminal justice process and (2) death penalty laws themselves.[70] Streib contends that the aggravating and mitigating circumstances enumerated in death penalty laws bias the application of the death penalty in favor of women. For example, among aggravating factors that generally advantage women over men charged with capital crimes are those that pertain to (1) previous criminal record (women are less likely than men to have one), (2) premeditation (homicides by women tend to be unplanned and sudden acts), and (3) felony murders (women are rarely involved in them).[71] Mitigating factors that tend to advantage women involve (1) committing a capital crime while under extreme mental or emotional disturbance (female murderers are perceived to be more emotionally disturbed than male murderers) and (2) acting under the substantial domination of another person (when both women and men are involved in a capital crime, the man is generally considered the principal actor).[72]

As for the key actors in the criminal justice process, judges (who are predominantly male) admit that, in general, they tend to be more lenient toward female offenders. They also tend to believe that women are better candidates for rehabilitation than are men. Jurors also tend to be more lenient toward female offenders, particularly in cases of serious crimes.[73]

Streib describes an ethical dilemma with the practice of reserving execution almost entirely for men:

> Making women ineligible for the death penalty, as Russia has done expressly and as the United States has done in practice, seems harder to defend. This practice, while explainable in some of

its dimensions, seems at bottom to be unvarnished gender bias—a queasiness among criminal justice officials for putting a woman to death. One need not be a supporter of the death penalty to observe that if men are eligible for it then women should be also. Otherwise, women are lumped in with children and the mentally retarded as not fully responsible human beings.[74]

In short, if women are to be accorded full dignity as human beings, and illegal discrimination is to be avoided, then, as Streib contends, women either must be executed for their capital crimes, or no one should be executed for a capital crime. Apparently, a large percentage of the American public agrees— at least with the first part. According to a 2002 Gallup Poll, 68 percent of Americans favor the death penalty for women, 29 percent oppose it, and 3 percent do not know or refused to answer. In the same poll, 72 percent of Americans favored the death penalty in general, 25 percent opposed it, and 3 percent did not know or refused to answer. Among subgroups, however, 72 percent of males but only 63 percent of females favored the death penalty for women, and 72 percent of whites but only 51 percent of nonwhites favored the death penalty for women.[75]

DISCRIMINATION BY AGE

About 2 percent (approximately 366) of the approximately 20,000 people executed in the United States since 1608 have been juveniles, that is, individuals who committed their capital crimes prior to their 18th birthday. As noted previously, on March 1, 2005, in the case of *Roper v. Simmons* (543 U.S. 551), the U.S. Supreme Court ruled, by a vote of 5–4, that the U.S. Constitution's Eighth and Fourteenth Amendments prohibited the execution of capital offenders under the age of 18. However, while the practice existed, juveniles, like women, were filtered from the process. They accounted for about:

- 8 percent of murder arrests,
- 3 percent of death sentences imposed at trial (before March 1, 2005),
- 0 percent of persons on death row (as of December 11, 2010), and
- about 2 percent of persons executed under post-*Furman* statutes (1,247 executions as of May 4, 2011).[76]

Only 23 juveniles—all but one of whom were 17 years old at the time they committed their crimes— have been executed under post-*Furman* statutes.[77] The one exception was Sean Sellers, who was executed in Oklahoma on February 4, 1999, for a crime he committed when he was 16 years old.[78] The last executed juvenile in the United States, who was younger than 17 years at the time of his crime, before Sellers, was 16-year-old Leonard Shockley, who was executed in Maryland on April 10, 1959.[79] The first juvenile executed under post-*Furman* statutes was Charles Rumbaugh, who was executed in Texas on September 11, 1985; the last was Scott Hain, who was executed in Oklahoma on April 3, 2003.[80] The age at execution of the 23 juveniles ranged from 23 to 38, reflecting the time they spent on death row.[81] Since 1990, the United States was one of only eight countries that had executed anyone under 18 years of age at the time of the crime; the others were China, the Democratic Republic of the Congo, Iran, Nigeria, Pakistan, Saudi Arabia, and Yemen.[82] During the mid-1980s, psychiatrist Dorothy Lewis and her colleagues evaluated 14 (40%) of the then 37 juvenile death row inmates in the United States.[83] They found that all of them had suffered head injuries as children; 12 of them had been abused physically, sexually, or both; 12 of them had IQ scores of 90 or less; 11 of them had below-average reading abilities; nine of them had major neuropsychological problems; seven of them had psychotic disorders since early childhood; seven of them had serious psychiatric disturbances; and five of them reported being sodomized by relatives. Between 1973 and the *Roper* decision in 2005, jurisdictions in the United States had imposed death sentences on 228 offenders under the age of 18 at the time of their crime,[84] but the chances of any of those juveniles actually being executed were remote. The reversal rate for juveniles sentenced to death under post-*Furman* statutes was about 90 percent.[85]

Whether juveniles should be subjected to capital punishment had been a controversial issue before the *Simmons* decision. A Gallup poll conducted in 2002 found that 72 percent of Americans favored the death penalty for people convicted of murder, 25 percent opposed it, and 3 percent did not know or refused to answer. However, as noted in Chapter 4, only 26 percent of respondents in that poll favored the death penalty for juveniles, 69 percent opposed it, and 5 percent did not know or refused to answer. Among subgroups, only 31 percent of males, 21 percent of females, 25 percent of whites, and 29 percent of nonwhites favored the death penalty for juveniles.[86] The level of support (or lack thereof) of the death penalty for juveniles in 2002 represented a dramatic change from the results of a Gallup poll conducted in 1994. In the 1994 poll, 60 percent of Americans thought that when a teenager commits a murder and is found guilty by a jury, he (the survey item did not address female teenage killers) should get the death penalty (compared with 80% who favored the death penalty for adults); 30 percent opposed the death penalty for teenagers; and 10 percent had no opinion.[87] Seventy-two percent of those who favored the death penalty for adults also favored it for teenage killers.

Among the reasons for not subjecting juveniles to capital punishment are the following:

- Our society, as represented by our legislatures, prosecutors, judges, and juries, has rejected the juvenile death penalty;
- Other nations, including many that share our Anglo-American heritage, have rejected the juvenile death penalty;
- The threat of the death penalty does not deter potential juvenile murderers because juveniles often do not consider the possible consequences prior to committing their murderous acts and because, even if they did consider these consequences, they would realize that very few juveniles actually receive the death penalty;
- Juveniles are especially likely to be rehabilitated or reformed while in prison, thus rendering the juvenile death penalty especially inappropriate;
- The juvenile death penalty does not serve a legitimate retributive purpose, since juveniles are generally less mature and responsible than adults, and should therefore be viewed as less culpable than adults who commit the same crimes.[88]

An additional reason for treating juveniles differently than adults in the administration of justice is that juveniles are already treated legally differently from adults in other areas of life, such as driving, voting, gambling, marriage, and jury service.[89]

On the other hand, some of the reasons for subjecting juveniles to capital punishment are:

- The evidence of a societal consensus against the juvenile death penalty is nonexistent or at least too weak to justify a constitutional ban (this no longer may be the case);
- The views of other nations are irrelevant to the proper interpretation of our Constitution, at least absent a consensus within our own society;
- The threat of the death penalty can deter potential juvenile murderers, or at least the judgments of legislatures and prosecutors to that effect deserve deference;

- The most heinous juvenile murderers, who are the only ones likely to receive the death penalty, are not good candidates for rehabilitation or reform;
- There are some juvenile murderers who are sufficiently mature and responsible to deserve the death penalty for their crimes, and thus the juvenile death penalty serves a legitimate retributive purpose.[90]

As for other areas of the law that distinguish between adults and juveniles, proponents of capital punishment for juvenile offenders stress that while juveniles may not vote conscientiously or drive safely, they do know that killing other human beings is wrong.[91]

Another reason for supporting the death penalty for at least some juvenile capital offenders, and what makes the current practice of excluding death-eligible juveniles from the death penalty discriminatory, is that the designation of "juvenile" is arbitrary and only a proxy for more relevant characteristics. It was not until the sixteenth and seventeenth centuries that the young began to be viewed as other than miniature adults or property.[92] Before that time, juveniles as young as 5 or 6 years were expected to assume the responsibilities of adults and, when they violated the law, were subjected to the same criminal sanctions as adults. Moreover, is there a significant difference on any relevant social characteristic between a 17- and 18-year-old, other than what has been created by law? Is it really meaningful to consider a 17-year-old a juvenile and an 18-year-old an adult?

In considering whether a person deserves the death penalty from a retributive standpoint, law professor Joseph Hoffmann points out that age is largely irrelevant. It is used because it serves as an imperfect proxy for more relevant social characteristics. Whether a murderer, regardless of age, deserves the death penalty depends, not on age, argues Hoffmann, but on maturity, judgment, responsibility, and the capability to assess the possible consequences of his or her actions.[93] Some juveniles possess these characteristics in greater quantity than some adults, or in sufficient quantities to be death eligible; some do not. The use of age as a basis for determining who is or is not death eligible is therefore discriminatory. Thus, the *Simmons* decision did nothing more than change the age at which death penalty states are allowed to discriminate.

Age plays a role in death penalty administration in another way. Research from Ohio shows that death-eligible offenders who were over 25 years old were more than twice as likely to be sentenced to death than were death-eligible offenders who were 25 years old or younger.[94]

RACIAL DISCRIMINATION

Post-*Furman* statutes also have failed to end racial discrimination in the imposition of the death penalty. In the past, discussions of racial discrimination have focused almost entirely on the race of those executed, and while race of offender is not the only form of racial discrimination, this issue is considered first.

As noted in Chapter 1, by 1860, no northern state punished by death any crime except for murder and treason. In the antebellum South, there was never much debate about abolishing the death penalty entirely but, by the Civil War, few whites were executed for any crime other than murder, even though penal codes continued to list other capital felonies.[95] In the case of Southern blacks, on the other hand, the death penalty was imposed for many crimes. For example, in 1856, Virginia had 66 capital crimes for slaves but only one (murder) for whites, and Mississippi had 38 capital crimes that applied exclusively to slaves.[96] In Texas, prior to the Civil War, the crimes of insurrection; arson; and if the victim were white, attempted murder, rape, attempted rape, robbery, attempted robbery, and assault with a deadly weapon were capital crimes if committed by slaves but were not capital crimes if committed by whites. Capital punishment in Texas was also reserved for free blacks who committed the crimes listed above as well as for the crime of kidnapping a white woman.[97] In Virginia, slaves were eligible to be executed for any crime for which a free person could be sentenced to prison for 3 years or more. If the victim were white in Virginia, rape, attempted rape, kidnapping a woman, and aggravated assault were capital crimes when committed by free blacks but were not when committed by whites.[98] The attempted rape of a white woman was a capital offense exclusively for blacks in Florida, Louisiana, Mississippi, South Carolina, Tennessee, Texas, and Virginia.[99] Black slaves were executed for the deterrent effect that Southerners reasoned could not be achieved by either incarceration or forced labor. It was widely believed that the latter two punishments were not much worse and sometimes better than slavery itself.[100] Free blacks were executed for numerous crimes because, it appears, they were simply black. In many southern states, "free blacks [also] could be enslaved for a period of years if they were convicted of one of a variety of offenses.[101] Whatever the reason, blacks were executed in the South disproportionately to their numbers in the population.

From 1800 to 2002, 50 percent of all persons executed in the United States were African Americans, even though they comprised only about 11 percent of the population.[102] Put differently, from the early eighteenth century through the mid-twentieth century, African American execution rates were, on average, about nine times higher than white execution rates.[103] Between 1930 and 1980, 3,862 prisoners were executed under civil authority in the United States: 1,754 (45%) were white and 2,066 (53%) were black.[104] Blacks constituted around 10 percent of the population during this period. Among the 3,862 persons executed were 455 convicted of rape. Of them, 48 (11%) were white and 405 (89%) were black. Ninety-seven percent (443) were executed in the South.[105] Wolfgang and Riedel reported in a 1975 study of 361 rape convictions from a sample of 25 Georgia counties from 1945 to 1965, "that the most important predictor of which among the 361 rapists would be sentenced to death was the racial combination of offender and victim,.,,, [b]lack offenders who raped white victims ... were significantly more likely to be sentenced to death in comparison to rapes involving all other racial combinations."[106]

The statistics on executions for the crime of rape indicate that the case for racial discrimination in the imposition of the death penalty is strongest for the South.[107] Recall that between 1930 and 1980, 60 percent of all executions in the United States occurred in the South. Of those executed, 28 percent were white and 72 percent were black.[108] Again, these figures do not necessarily indicate an undesirable form of racial discrimination if blacks committed a disproportionately greater number of death-eligible murders or rapes, but this was unlikely the case. From roughly 1973 through 1977, for example, 617 persons were arrested or suspected by police of death-eligible murder in Florida, 535 in Georgia, and 702 in Texas.[109] In Florida, 49 percent of the death-eligible murderers were black; in Georgia, 63 percent; and in Texas, 42 percent.[110] Racial distributions for rape were similar. These figures suggest the unlikelihood that 89 percent of the death-eligible rapists and 72 percent of the death-eligible murderers in the South were black.

According to an "evaluation synthesis" of 28 post-*Furman* studies prepared by the U.S. General Accounting Office (GAO) and published in 1990, "more than half of the studies found that race of defendant influenced the likelihood of being charged with a capital crime or receiving the death penalty ... [and in] more than three-fourths of the studies that identified a race-of-defendant effect ... black defendants were more likely to receive the death penalty."[111] An update of the GAO study prepared for the American Bar Association (ABA) by the premier researchers in this area, law professor David Baldus and statistician George Woodworth, showed that in nearly half of the death penalty states race of defendant was a significant predictor of who would receive a death sentence. In all but two of these states (Florida and Tennessee), black defendants were more likely to receive a death sentence.[112] Likewise, a 1994 study by the *Houston Post* found that in Harris County—which accounts for more post-*Furman* executions than any state other than Texas itself and more death sentences than most states—blacks were sentenced to death twice as often as whites.[113] A more recent study of Harris County, Texas, published in 2008 found that death sentences were still more likely to be imposed on black defendants than on white defendants.[114] In another study, Baldus and his colleagues studied a sample of death-eligible murderers in Philadelphia, Pennsylvania, between 1983 and 1993. They found that African Americans had a nearly four times greater chance of receiving a death sentence than similarly situated defendants, even after controlling for a variety of factors including severity of offense and background of defendant.[115] They also discovered that race made the most difference in "midrange" of severity or aggravation cases in which prosecutors and jurors exercise the most discretion in seeking and imposing the death penalty.[116] However, not all studies have discovered a race-of-defendant effect.[117]

In some cases,[118] but interestingly not in capital cases,[119] the Supreme Court has allowed racially discriminatory intent to be inferred from "a clear pattern, unexplainable on grounds other than race." Criteria of proof are more restricted in capital cases, but short of public admission of racially discriminatory intent or other unlikely happenstance, it is not clear how such intent on the part of participants in the administration of capital punishment could be shown.[120] Even when overt racially offensive remarks are made in capital trials, racial discriminatory intent is not always inferred. For example, in a 1985 capital case in Florida, the trial judge referred to the family of a black defendant as "niggers." The Florida Supreme Court did not strongly reprimand the judge for his remark; the court only reminded him that he must always maintain an "image of impartiality."[121] In Utah, two black men were sentenced to death by an all-white jury and executed, "even though jurors received a note which contained the words 'Hang the Nigger's' [*sic*] and a drawing of a figure hanging on a gallows."[122] According to attorney Stephen Bright, "No court, state or federal, even had a hearing on such questions as who wrote the note, what influence it had on the jurors, and how widely it was discussed by the jurors."[123] In a 1989 capital trial in Georgia, both the judge and the defense attorney referred to the black defendant as "colored" and "colored boy." The defense attorney stated that he used the racial slur, "nigger," jokingly. Two of the jurors who sentenced the defendant to death admitted after the trial to using the word "nigger" to describe the defendant. Again, appellate courts found no fault.[124] It may be that racially discriminatory outcomes are not generally the product of a conscious process and that participants in the administration of capital punishment do not "know" that their behavior is racially motivated.

Available evidence indicates that post-*Furman* statutes have not eliminated a second, less obvious form of racial discrimination: victim-based racial discrimination. Whether the death penalty is imposed continues to depend on the race of the victim. Research shows that the killers of whites, regardless of their race, are much more likely to be sentenced to death than are the killers of nonwhites. This is especially the case for the killers of white females, particularly if the victim had been degraded and humiliated.[125] On the other hand, the killers of black male victims are the least likely to be sentenced to death.[126] For example, between 1973 and 1977, under a post-*Furman* statute in Florida, the probability of a black person receiving the death penalty for the aggravated murder of a white was

32 percent (143 offenders; 46 persons sentenced to death). The probability of a white person receiving the death penalty for the aggravated murder of a white was 21.5 percent (303 offenders; 65 persons sentenced to death). The probability for a black who killed a black was 4 percent (160 offenders; seven persons sentenced to death), and the probability for a white who killed a black was 0 percent (11 offenders; no persons sentenced to death).[127]

In other words, a black person convicted of an aggravated murder of a white in Florida between 1973 and 1977 was more than seven times more likely to receive a death sentence than was a black who killed a black. A white person convicted of an aggravated murder of a white was almost five times more likely to receive a death sentence than was a black who killed a black. A person convicted of aggravated murder of a white, whether the killer was a black or a white, was more likely to receive the death penalty than was a person of either race convicted of aggravated murder of a black. Moreover, a white person convicted of aggravated murder of a black almost never received a death sentence (the total of such cases for Florida, Georgia, and Texas was 54; in three (5.5%) there was a death sentence).[128] A similar pattern was found in Georgia,[129] Texas,[130] South Carolina,[131] North Carolina,[132] Louisiana,[133] Alabama,[134] Mississippi,[135] Tennessee,[136] Kentucky,[137] California,[138] Illinois,[139] Missouri,[140] Oklahoma,[141] Maryland,[142] Virginia,[143] New Jersey,[144] Connecticut,[145] Ohio,[146] and Pennsylvania (Philadelphia).[147] The ABA study found evidence of race-of-victim disparities in 93 percent of death penalty states, and in all but one of the states (Delaware) white-victim cases were more likely to receive death sentences.[148]

The GAO evaluation synthesis further revealed that "in 82 percent of the studies, race of victim was found to influence the likelihood of being charged with capital murder or receiving the death penalty... . This finding was remarkably consistent across data sets, states, data collection methods, and analytic techniques."[149] The report also noted that "the race of victim influence was stronger for the earlier stages of the judicial process (e.g., prosecutorial decision to charge defendant with a capital offense, decision to proceed to trial rather than plea bargain) than in later stages."[150]

In the classic study used in the *McCleskey* case, Baldus and his colleagues found that in Georgia under its post-*Furman* statute "race-of-victim effects as was the case with race-of-defendant effects in their more recent Philadelphia study were particularly strong in the midrange of cases when prosecutors and juries have the greatest room for the exercise of discretion."[151] They estimated that the outcomes in more than one-third of the midrange (in aggravation) cases were determined by the race of the victim. At least in the aforementioned states, these findings suggest that the life of a black victim is valued less than the life of a white victim, regardless of the race of the offender.[152]

More recent data do not indicate any change in the situation. As of January 1, 2010, defendant–victim racial combinations for post-*Furman* executions were as indicated in Table 10.3 (based on 1,757 victims).[153] The data reveal that about 80 percent of the victims of those persons executed under post-*Furman* statutes have been white, and that only about 13 percent have been black. Yet, 56 percent of defendants executed have been white, 35 percent have been black, 7.15 percent have been Latino(a), 1.26 percent have been Native American, and 0.59 percent have been Asian.[154] Discrimination seems apparent because, historically, capital crimes have generally been intraracial.[155] For example, in 2009, 84 percent of white victims were murdered by white offenders, and 91 percent of black victims were murdered by black offenders (when race of victim and offender was known).[156] Still, uncertainty remains about whether the data show discrimination because only about 20 percent of murders and nonnegligent manslaughters are capital crimes.[157] It seems likely that the percentage of interracial murders may be somewhat greater for capital murders than it is for noncapital murders. In any event,

Table 10.3 Defendant–Victim Racial Combinations for Post-*Furman* Executions

Combination	Percent
White defendant/white victim	52.61
White defendant/black victim	1.26
White defendant/Asian victim	0.34
White defendant/Latino(a) victim	1.09
Black defendant/white victim	20.71
Black defendant/black victim	11.20
Black defendant/Asian victim	0.93
Black defendant/Latino(a) victim	1.43
Latino defendant/white victim	3.28
Latino defendant/Latino(a) victim	3.20
Latino defendant/Asian victim	0.17
Latino defendant/black victim	0.25
Native American defendant/white victim	1.09
Native American defendant/Native American victim	0.17
Asian defendant/Asian victim	0.42
Asian defendant/white victim	0.17

two major implications of these data are (1) "in places that currently treat black defendants more punitively than similarly situated non-black defendants, an evenhanded system would reduce the absolute number of black defendants sentenced to death … [and] the proportion of black defendants on death row," and (2) "if an evenhanded policy were applied to the black and white victim cases (at the current rate for either black or white victim cases), the 'proportion' of black defendants on death row would increase."[158]

Sources of racial disparity/discrimination

Studies that have found post-*Furman* racial disparity/discrimination have located the source of it predominantly in the discretionary actions of prosecutors and juries. (Evidence suggests that prosecutors and juries are also sources of arbitrariness in the death penalty's application.) Baldus and his colleagues declare that "the exercise of prosecutorial discretion [in seeking a death sentence] is the principal source of the race-of-victim disparities observed in the system."[159] In Georgia (and in other states) a capital sentencing hearing is a preliminary stage in the process that leads to a capital trial. Baldus and colleagues report that under Georgia's post-*Furman* statute, black defendants whose victims were white were advanced to a capital sentencing hearing by prosecutors at a rate nearly five times that of black defendants whose victims were black, and more than three times the rate of white defendants whose victims were black.[160] Other research found that prosecutors have sought the death penalty in 70 percent of cases involving black defendants and white victims and in only 35 percent of the cases involving other racial combinations.[161] A study of Maryland's death penalty found that, after controlling for relevant case characteristics, the killers of white victims, especially if they were black, were substantially more likely than the killers of nonwhites to be charged by prosecutors with a capital crime and for the charge to "stick," that is, not be withdrawn by the prosecutor once the death notification was filed.[162]

In Florida, prosecutors have "upgraded" and "downgraded" potential capital cases under post-*Furman* statutes by alleging aggravating circumstances, charging defendants with an accompanying felony, ignoring evidence in police reports, and withholding an accompanying charge depending on the race of the offender and of the victim.[163] Radelet and Pierce report that "cases in which blacks were accused of killing whites were the most likely to be upgraded and least likely to be downgraded."[164] Prosecutors have engaged in similar actions in South Carolina,[165] Kentucky,[166] and other states.[167] Prosecutors also have reduced death-eligible white-defendant or black-victim cases to noncapital ones through plea bargaining, or they have foregone a penalty trial and thus waived the death penalty, even when a defendant had been convicted by a jury of a capital offense.[168]

Historically, blacks are the demographic group most likely to oppose the death penalty[169] and thus are the group most likely to be excluded from jury service in capital cases. Even if blacks are not opposed to the death penalty categorically, they also can be underrepresented on capital juries by the prosecutor's exercise of peremptory challenges.[170] For example, if jurors express some opposition to the death penalty but not enough to exclude them for cause, they still can be eliminated through the prosecutor's peremptory challenge. In Texas, prosecutors have been found to have "shuffled" the venire panel (rearranging the order in which venire panel members were seated and questioned) to reduce the chances of blacks serving on a jury.[171] They also asked different questions to black and nonblack panel members about their views on the death penalty and minimum acceptable sentences to provide a basis for eliminating potential black jurors.[172] Finally, they used their peremptory challenges to exclude black venire members from juries—the latter a decades-old practice of the Dallas County District Attorney's Office.[173]

Data from the Capital Jury Project show that prosecutors are about twice as likely to ask the white covictims of white murder victims to present victim-impact evidence at trial than they are to ask the black covictims of black murder victims to do so.[174] Post-*Furman* evidence from two judicial circuits in Georgia show that blacks play only a small role in capital cases, except, of course, as defendants—a category in which they are overrepresented.[175] In the words of former Georgia state senator Gary Parker, "The classic death penalty case in Georgia remains a black person prosecuted by a white district attorney before a white judge and an all-white jury for a crime against a prominent white person."[176]

How black defendants in Georgia counties and other jurisdictions with black populations often exceeding 40 percent continue to be tried by all-white juries in light of the Supreme Court's *Batson* decision also points to racial discrimination. Recall from the discussion in Chapter 4 that *Batson v. Kentucky* (1986) required trial judges to determine whether prosecutors intended to discriminate against black defendants by using their peremptory jury strikes to eliminate black jurors. However, the relationship between many prosecutors and trial judges may make this determination a meaningless exercise. Many trial judges are former prosecutors who, themselves, may have violated *Batson* as prosecutors and are sympathetic to the illegal actions of current prosecutors. Many trial judges, when they were prosecutors, hired the prosecutors who appear before them. Trial judges also may be beholden to prosecutors who contribute money to their reelection campaigns. Thus, it may be difficult for judges with such relationships with prosecutors to reject a prosecutor's reasons for striking black jurors.[177] The evidence is quite clear that racial disparities continue to be produced through the exercise of prosecutorial discretion in capital or potentially capital cases.

These findings are truly ironic in light of the majority's response in *Gregg* that:

> Petitioner's argument that the prosecutor's decisions in plea bargaining or in declining to charge capital murder are standardless and will result in the wanton or freakish imposition of the death penalty condemned in Furman, is without merit, for the assumption cannot be made that prosecutors will be motivated in their charging decisions by factors other than the strength of their case and the likelihood that a jury would impose the death penalty if it convicts.[178]

Although perhaps not as critical as the prosecutor, juries also play a role in racial disparities (and arbitrary sentencing decisions) produced under post-*Furman* statutes. Many potential jurors are biased from the onset of a capital case because of exposure to the media's typical one-sided coverage.[179] The media provide potential jurors with a "framework for understanding" a capital crime.[180] The media tend to focus on the most dramatic and heinous aspects of the crime. Rarely are the offender and his or her crime put in historical or social context. The offender's personal history and background—factors that might "humanize" the offender and mitigate the crime—generally are ignored. Thus, potential jurors are exposed to portrayals of capital offenders as "animals" or "monsters," as something less than human, something to fear and despise. Not surprisingly, then, research shows that the more negative information about a capital offender a potential juror was exposed to by the media, the more likely the potential juror was willing to convict the offender prior to his or her death penalty trial.[181] The irony is that most murderers are not like the media portrayals of them. As David Dow, who, as previously noted, has represented more than 30 death row inmates, relates, "What is arresting about nearly all murderers is how ordinary they are, how unremarkable they appear."[182]

A remedy for the influence of pretrial publicity is a change of venue, but judges are reluctant to grant them even when prejudicial publicity has been extensive, community awareness of the crime is very high, and there is significant prejudgment of the case in the communities where the trial is to be held.[183] Judges are reluctant to grant change of venue motions because a change of venue is expensive when the trial is not held in the jurisdiction where most trial participants live. This is particularly true in capital cases, which are typically more complex and lengthier than other types of cases. The political risk of changing venues in capital cases is also a reason why elected judges are reluctant to grant them. When a highly publicized capital crime has been committed, judges, for political reasons, generally are more responsive to community sentiment to hold the trial in the jurisdiction where the crime was committed than they are to the constitutional rights of defendants.[184]

Another solution to the influence of pretrial publicity is the elimination of potential jurors affected by it during voir dire. However, biased jurors are hard to detect. This is especially true of "automatic death penalty" (ADP) jurors (jurors who would automatically vote for the death penalty following a guilty verdict in a capital case). Evidence from the Capital Jury Project suggests that an average of 14–30 percent of capital jurors—between about two and four persons on a 12-person jury—are ADPs.[185] Research reveals that potential jurors (ADPs and others) often claim that they can be impartial, even when they know they have been exposed to negative pretrial publicity that has prejudiced their opinion of the defendant.[186] Research also indicates that the biasing effects of pretrial publicity are not reduced by judicial instructions to ignore it.[187]

Research conducted by psychology professor Craig Haney and others demonstrates that voir dire and death qualification (as noted in Chapter 4, the process of excluding death penalty opponents from capital juries because they are opposed to the death penalty under any circumstances),[188] themselves, are independent sources of bias in capital cases (especially when jurors are questioned in a group rather than individually after being sequestered). These processes have been found to "'condition' jurors to a particular point of view or set of expectations."[189] Research shows, for example, that potential jurors can be prejudiced by the responses of other potential jurors during voir dire and, in an effort to be seated or excused, may structure their answers to questions based on the reactions of judges and trial attorneys to the responses to the same questions asked of other potential jurors.[190]

Haney and his colleagues also found that the prolonged discussion of penalty at the very start of the trial during voir dire and death qualification, a unique aspect of capital trials, predisposed potential jurors to believe that the defendant was guilty and that he would be convicted and sentenced to death, that judges and attorneys shared their guilt-prone views, and that the judge in the case favored the death penalty. These beliefs, in turn, divert jurors' attention from the presumption of innocence. The discussion of penalty at the onset of the trial also desensitized potential jurors to the prospect of imposing the death penalty. Additionally, because death penalty opponents are excluded from participating in capital trials, many potential jurors believed that the law disfavors death penalty opponents. Finally, because they are required to publicly affirm their commitment to capital punishment during voir dire, potential jurors were more likely to believe that the death penalty was the appropriate punishment when confronted with a hypothetical capital case. They also were more likely to vote to impose it.[191]

Another source of bias is the capital trial, itself. Capital trials are unique among criminal trials because only in capital trials are juries required to make the sentencing decision. Haney contends that "normal, law-abiding persons" who become jurors in capital cases must overcome a deep-seated inhibition to sentence someone to death. To do so, according to Haney, jurors must be able to "morally disengage" from the realities of their decision. The trial structure and sequencing of evidence, the formal, legalistic atmosphere of the trial, and various legal doctrines allow them to do this.[192]

Moral disengagement is facilitated by the dehumanization of the capital defendant. As noted previously, this starts with typical media portrayals of the capital offender as a "monster" or an "animal." The trial is structured so that the first opportunity to "humanize" the capital defendant comes at the end of the trial, during the penalty phase when mitigation evidence can be presented. Even then, court rules give the prosecution the opportunity to present its evidence of aggravation first. As noted previously, data from the Capital Jury Project show that jurors are more likely to be influenced by the victim-impact testimony of the white covictims of white murder victims than they are by the victim-impact testimony of the black covictims of black murder victims.[193] During the guilt phase, the jury hears only the prosecution's description of the crime's brutal details. Moreover, the prosecution's typical theory of the crime—that the defendant is an inherently evil person entirely responsible for his or her crime—usually coincides with jurors' stereotypical beliefs about crimes and punishment. Not surprisingly, then, before jurors are exposed to any mitigating evidence, they become frightened of the defendant (assuming they were not already frightened of him), which provokes punitive and vengeful feelings and a concern about the defendant's future dangerousness, whether or not the issue was explicitly raised at trial.

Oftentimes the defendant unwittingly jeopardizes his or her own chances during the trial. Many jurors pay more attention to a defendant's appearance, demeanor, and reactions than the evidence presented. For example, when jurors see a clean-cut defendant in a suit and tie at the defense table, they may conclude that the defendant is trying to deceive them following the prosecution's presentation of photographs showing the defendant as a totally different person being booked into jail with long hair, scruffy beard, and tattoos everywhere.[194] Also, a defendant frequently does a disservice to himself or herself in the eyes of jurors by failing to show signs of remorse and repentance during the trial. When a prosecutor, for instance, shows photographs of the victims' bodies and the defendant fails to show any emotion, jurors may decide there is little hope for redemption. A few tears shed by a defendant may mean the difference between a life and death sentence.[195] All these help explain why many capital jurors believe the defendant should be sentenced to death before the penalty phase of the trial begins. To effectively deal with this structural barrier, defense attorneys must be able to make a strong case for mitigation during the penalty phase and overcome what many jurors believe is common sense. However, as noted in the last chapter, many defense attorneys in capital cases lack the training, professional experience, time, and resources to do the job properly.[196] The "emotionally distant and decontextualized legal language by which the process proceeds" makes efforts at humanizing the capital defendant even more difficult.[197]

Also working against the capital defendant and contributing to moral disengagement is legal doctrine that forbids detailed discussion during the penalty phase of prison conditions or future prospects should the defendant be sentenced to LWOP.[198] If jurors were made aware of the high level of security characteristic of modern maximum-security prisons; the pains of imprisonment; evidence that the death penalty is no greater deterrent than LWOP; that defendants sentenced to LWOP only rarely engage in violent acts in prison, almost never escape or are released in error, sometimes are rehabilitated, and make positive contributions while in prison; and that LWOP is nearly always less expensive than the death penalty with all it entails, they might feel more comfortable sentencing convicted capital defendants to LWOP. Furthermore, legal doctrine prohibits telling jurors of the details of the execution the defendant may experience if sentenced to death and how that execution may affect his family and friends. This, too, contributes to moral disengagement. Haney points to the asymmetry this prohibition creates because there is no prohibition to exposing jurors to the violence and, oftentimes, gore of the capital crime and the consequences of the crime to surviving family and friends.[199] Prosecutors also are allowed to introduce evidence about a defendant's prior criminal convictions during the penalty phase to show that the defendant poses a future danger and the current crime was not an isolated event. Such evidence is generally not allowed during the guilt phase unless it has a direct bearing on the current crime.[200] Knowledge of the execution process, incidentally, may not matter anyway because research shows that most jurors are skeptical about an execution ever being carried out after a death sentence is imposed.[201] This skepticism is justified in states such as California, for example, where only 13 out of 927 defendants (1.4%) sentenced to death between 1973 and 2010 have been executed.[202]

Moral disengagement may also be the product of juror misunderstanding or confusion about their sentencing responsibilities. As described earlier in this chapter, a considerable amount of research shows that jurors frequently misapprehend judges' capital sentencing instructions, particularly those that apply to mitigation. Rather than correcting these misapprehensions, established legal doctrine presumes that jurors understand and follow judges' instructions, even when they do not. And when jurors ask questions, legal doctrine presumes that they understand the judge's answers, however unhelpful they may be. Many judges refuse to clarify instructions even when jurors make it clear they are confused and need help. At most, they simply repeat the original instructions. Long-standing legal doctrine also prohibits jurors from researching on their own the meanings of key terms about which they are confused.[203] In an attempt to overcome this latter problem some courts or legislatures have provided juries with definitions of confusing terms. However, in many cases, this has not helped. For example, the Virginia Supreme Court has provided the following definition for the term, "depravity," in the phrase "depravity of mind": "a degree of moral turpitude and psychical debasement surpassing that inherent in the definition of ordinary malice and premeditation."[204]

One of the issues about which jurors often seek clarification is the meaning of the phrase "life without parole." How a judge answers a jury's request for clarification can determine whether a jury returns a sentence of life or death. If a judge responds in unambiguous language that a defendant sentenced to LWOP will spend the rest of his or her natural life in prison, a jury is often likely to sentence a defendant to LWOP—frequently in a matter of minutes after receiving the judge's answer. On the other hand, if the judge responds in an ambiguous way by refusing to answer the question or by explaining to the jury that a governor has the power to commute sentences, the jury usually is quick to sentence a defendant to death.[205] Most jurors are reluctant to take risks with dangerous offenders.

The cumbersome and intimidating procedures in the way the court handles jurors' questions also are a disincentive for jurors to seek clarification. For example, in one case a juror during deliberations requested a witness's testimony to be reread to the jury. Before the judge granted the request, he first consulted with the prosecutor and defense attorney and then reconvened the court with all participants present, including the defendant, the lawyers, jurors, and court personnel. This process is typical, as judges guard against possible reversal on appeal by ensuring the defendant and attorneys are present whenever the jury is in the courtroom.[206] Such a time-consuming procedure discourages jurors from asking questions, assuming, of course, jurors even know they are confused and need help.

The misapprehension of jury instructions causes at least two significant and related problems. The first is that jurors may simply ignore the parts of the sentencing instructions they do not understand. For example, they may ignore mitigating evidence if they do not understand what mitigation means. Second, lacking guidance and left on their own, jurors are likely to resort to stereotypes and impermissible factors that, in turn, lead to arbitrary and discriminatory decision making—the very outcomes the sentencing instructions were supposed to help eliminate.[207] For example, Haney, reporting the results of his own research, observed that "being confused about the [judge's] instructions seemed to allow a greater amount of prejudice to come into play in the death-sentencing process, while high levels of comprehension appear to reduce or eliminate its effect."[208] Specifically, according to Haney, "our jurors regarded exactly the same mitigating and aggravating evidence very differently depending on whether it was offered in a case in which the defendant was white as opposed to one in which he was African American" (less so for aggravating evidence).[209] For instance, testimony that the defendant was abused as a child, had untreated psychological problems, and was a drug abuser was found to be significantly more mitigating for white defendants than it was for black defendants.[210] Furthermore, in some black defendant cases some jurors "inappropriately converted some of the mitigating factors [e.g., the defendant was abused as a child and had untreated psychological problems] into aggravating factors (by indicating that their presence in the case inclined them toward a death rather than life sentence)."[211] Another study found that when jury instructions were poorly understood, white defendants benefited from the incomprehension, while black defendants were punished for it.[212]

The dynamics of jury deliberations also play a major role in capital case sentencing decisions. The law in most death penalty jurisdictions requires a jury to decide unanimously whether a capital defendant lives or dies. If it does not reach a unanimous decision, the result is a hung jury, following which the judge declares a mistrial and the prosecutor must decide whether to retry the case. Judges want to avoid hung juries, if at all possible. In fact, they have jury instructions, variously referred to as "shotgun charges," "hammer charges," "third-degree charges," "dynamite charges," and "nitroglycerine charges" intended to encourage jurors to continue deliberating and reach a unanimous verdict.[213] Many jurors consider a hung jury as a failure on their part. The most heinous cases and the least heinous cases rarely present problems for juries. In the former, juries almost always return death sentences and, in the latter, they almost always return life sentences, regardless of the individual characteristics of jurors.[214] It is usually only the "middle-range" cases, those that are less clear-cut, that present problems.

When jurors begin deliberations, one of the first things they do is take a vote to determine where the jury stands on sentence. In most cases, jurors are not unanimous on the initial ballot. This is not surprising because jurors, although death qualified, still bring unique perspectives, experiences, and beliefs to jury deliberations often resulting in their reacting differently to the same evidence.[215] Consequently, it is always possible that another jury, with a different group of jurors, might decide the case differently.[216] Research shows that the initial vote often foretells the final vote. For example, as part of the Capital Jury Project, a study of South Carolina capital jurors by law professor Theodore Eisenberg and his colleagues discovered that if eight or more jurors vote for death on the first ballot, the jury invariably returns a death sentence. On the other hand, if fewer than eight jurors vote for death on the first ballot, the jury is almost guaranteed to choose a life sentence. In this study, a life sentence was easier to obtain than a death sentence.[217] The study also found that a juror's first vote is influenced by the juror's race, religion, and how strongly the juror believes death is the appropriate sentence in the case.[218] Black jurors were more likely than white jurors to vote for life on the first ballot, but not on the final one. In the end, all jurors generally voted with the initial majority and because black jurors rarely comprised a majority of jurors, majority rules usually meant white rule.[219] Additionally, jurors who identified themselves as Southern Baptists, of whom almost all are white, usually voted for death on the first ballot, as did jurors who felt strongly that death was the appropriate sentence in the case.[220]

In another study using data from the Capital Jury Project, Bowers, Steiner, and Sandys found the influence of race in jury decision making to be strongest in black defendant/white victim cases.[221] The racial composition of the jury made a difference. For example, on the first ballot in black defendant/white victim cases, two of every three white jurors believed the punishment should be death, while two of every three black jurors believed the punishment should be life imprisonment.[222] On the final vote, the jury was three times more likely to impose a death sentence if there were five or more white males on the jury than if there were four or fewer white males on the jury.[223] However, if there was at least one black male on the jury, the jury was twice as likely to impose a life sentence compared to juries that had no black members. Additional black male jurors only reduced the chances of a death sentence slightly.[224] The study revealed that white and black jurors in black defendant/white victim cases saw the same defendants, the same evidence, and the same arguments in the same cases very differently.[225] For instance, white jurors more often than black jurors saw black defendants as likely to pose a future danger to society and to return to the streets if not sentenced to death. Black jurors, on the other hand, were more likely than white jurors to see black defendants as remorseful and deserving of mercy. Black jurors were also more likely to wonder whether the black defendant was the actual killer or whether the killing was death eligible in the first place. On each of these issues, males of each race took a more extreme position than females; still, black females were closer in position to black males and white females were closer in position to white males. These findings were independent of socioeconomic status.[226] A reason that the presence of at least one male black juror significantly increases the likelihood of a life sentence in black defendant/white victim cases is that the black juror is sometimes able to help white jurors better understand and appreciate the defendant's life history and how it mitigates the crime.[227]

Research confirms that the way a jury ultimately reaches unanimity on sentence involves a complex social–psychological process. Classic psychological research shows that people have a desire to conform and fear being wrong.[228] People tend to trust a confident majority even when it is wrong because they do not trust their own judgment. However, if a person is joined by just one other person in his or her judgment, the power of the majority to alter a person's correct position is significantly reduced. If that one other person deserts to the majority's incorrect position, the other person's ability to resist the majority declines dramatically. This dynamic is especially likely to occur when people must announce their positions publicly and there are only two options from which to choose, as occurs in death penalty cases. The study of South Carolina jurors found that the more serious the crime, the less willing a juror was to switch his or her initial vote from death to life; conversely, the less serious the crime, the more willing a juror was to switch from death to life.[229] Also the more strongly a juror supported the death penalty, the less likely he or she would abandon his or her first vote, and the less strongly a juror supported the death penalty, the more likely he or she would abandon his or her initial vote.[230] Ironically, when asked, most people respond that they could resist the majority's influence and give the correct response. Yet, as noted, research shows that this is not true in many cases.

The ability to resist a majority's position, which is believed to be wrong, is further complicated by mental and physical fatigue, stress, depression, insomnia, nightmares, a sense of isolation, and other maladies as jury deliberations are drawn out.[231] Other jurors, in an attempt to get a holdout to change positions, may try to make the holdout feel guilty by demanding the holdout switch his or her focus from the defendant to the victim and the victim's family.[232] Some holdout jurors are subject to personal attacks, both physical and mental. Black jurors have complained of being ostracized, deceived, and intimidated by white jurors.[233] When a holdout juror succumbs to the pressure and changes position to conform to the majority, the juror sometimes describes the process as being "brainwashed." According to law professor Scott Sundby, life holdouts typically differ from death holdouts on their reasons for changing positions. To change positions, life holdouts generally have to be convinced by the majority that a death sentence is the only appropriate sentence and to holdout for life violates the law and his or her oath as a juror. If they view their position as a product of an honest understandable difference of opinion, life holdouts will rarely change position.[234] Death holdouts, on the other hand, are likely to change their positions to avoid a hung jury. They do not want to make the taxpayer finance another trial and do want to guarantee that the defendant will at least spend the rest of his life in prison. They rarely concede that a life sentence is a just outcome and often view their fellow jurors as "gutless" or "wimps."[235] If a juror later realizes he or she voted wrongly for death instead of life, there is little he or she can do to correct the mistake except petition the governor for clemency, an option which seldom succeeds.[236] Courts have an aversion to second-guessing jury decisions and allowing jurors to cast doubt on a verdict that has been rendered. Short of some external influence, such as an attempt to bribe a juror, courts do not allow participants in a legal proceeding to challenge a verdict.[237] As the preceding discussion reveals, structural and social–psychological factors create corrupting biases in the way the death penalty is administered. These biases affect all capital defendants to varying degrees, but they adversely affect black capital defendants even more, particularly when their victims are white.

Theories of racial discrimination in the administration of the death penalty

There are several plausible theories of racial discrimination in the administration of the death penalty. The first and more obvious theory is that prosecutors, judges, jurors, and even defense attorneys intentionally discriminate against black defendants and victims because blacks are feared, disliked, or both. Such an explanation certainly is believable, given the history of race relations in the United States, particularly in the South.[238] Recent evidence shows that death penalty support by many whites continues to be associated with prejudice against blacks.[239]

A second theory is that many actors in the legal system today, even in the South, believe they are not racially prejudiced or are not conscious that they are. Yet, racially discriminatory outcomes are produced through a sometimes unconscious psychological process of racial identification.[240] Haney calls the same phenomenon the "empathic divide."[241] Gross and Mauro describe the process of victim-based racial identification:

> We are more readily horrified by a death if we empathize or identify with the victim, or if we see the victim as similar to ourselves or to a friend or relative, than if the victim appears to us as a stranger. In a society that remains segregated socially if not legally, and in which the great majority of jurors are white, jurors are not likely to identify with black victims or to see them as family or friends. Thus jurors are more likely to be horrified by the killing of a white than of a black, and more likely to act against the killer of a white than the killer of a black. This reaction is not an expression of racial hostility but a natural product of the patterns of interracial relations in our society.[242]

Victim-based racial identification, or the empathic divide, also may affect judges, prosecutors, and defense attorneys.[243] Thus, if victim-based racial identification affects all the actors in the administration of capital punishment and, further, if nearly all the actors are white, then it follows that racial discrimination against black defendants, particularly those who are the killers of whites, may be a real, albeit unintended outcome of the process.[244]

Another unconscious psychological process by which racially discriminatory outcomes can be produced is through what has been variously called "modern racism," "symbolic racism," "subtle prejudice," and "aversive racism."[245] "Modern racism" has been described as "cool, distant, and indirect" and is manifested not by negative attributions toward out-group members (e.g., blacks) but rather by attributing more positive attributes to in-group members (e.g., whites). These "modern racists" still rely on cultural stereotypes but conceal their racism by expressing ostensibly non-prejudicial values and opinions that, in practice, prove damaging to out-group members (e.g., endorsing tough-on-crime policies, affirmative action bans, and immigration restrictions).[246]

A third theory is that racial disparities are the result of institutional racism. Institutional racism occurs when members of a race are subordinated, disadvantaged, or overrepresented in negative outcomes through the normal functioning of social institutions, whether or not that subordination, disadvantage, or overrepresentation is consciously or deliberately intended.[247] It is possible that the racial disparities are not so much a product of overt racial animus as they are of the pragmatic goals of the courtroom participants. Consider two prosecutor examples. First, prosecutors may not underrepresent blacks in capital jury pools because of racial prejudice *per se*, but rather because of the belief that blacks are more likely than whites to oppose the death penalty and to acquit capital defendants if they are jurors, particularly when the defendant is black and the victim is white. As noted previously, evidence from the Capital Jury Project shows that in black defendant/white victim cases, a death sentence is imposed more than twice as often if there are at least five white males on the jury. On the other hand, the presence of only one black male on the jury reduces the chances of a death sentence by nearly half.[248] Because prosecutors are constrained by limited resources and highly motivated to win their trials, they increase their odds of winning by excluding as many blacks as possible.

The second example may not be the result of overt racial enmity but rather of a political consideration. Elected prosecutors may believe that their key constituencies want their limited resources expended on white victim cases and not on black ones.[249] Prosecutors themselves may not be racially prejudiced (they would focus their efforts on the prosecution of any social group if it would win them votes), but they may bow to the racial prejudices of their voters. In sum, whether racial discrimination is the product of institutional racism or of intentional or purposeful action, its existence in the administration of capital punishment is odious and intolerable.

The Supreme Court has implicitly recognized the existence of institutional racism in some types of cases (e.g., housing, public accommodations, jury selection, and employment) and has held it to be impermissible. The Court has not been equally responsive to institutional racism in death penalty cases but, instead, requires proof of intentional or purposeful discrimination in individual cases. One reason for this was given by Justice Powell in the *McCleskey* decision:

> McCleskey's claim, taken to its logical conclusion, throws into serious question the principles that underlie our entire criminal justice system.... [I]f we accepted McCleskey's claim that racial bias has impermissibly tainted the capital sentencing decision, we could soon be faced with similar claims as to other types of penalty.[250]

Baldus and Woodworth provide two additional reasons why the Court may have rejected the claim of racial discrimination in McCleskey's particular case. First, "as a convicted murderer, McCleskey did not enjoy the same status of an 'oppressed minority' as would a blameless claimant seeking equal access to housing, employment, or schools."[251] Second, "McCleskey's claim primarily pointed not to discrimination on the basis of his race (over which he had no control) but rather to discrimination on the basis of the victim's race.... [I]t was McCleskey [however] who 'chose' his victim, a fact that weakened the moral appeal of his claim."[252] Finally, Hoffmann argues that in *McCleskey* the Court, in effect, conceded that comparative injustice (i.e., discrimination) was inevitable in any sentencing scheme, but decided that "none of the available alternative approaches to capital sentencing would be more 'just' than the guided discretionary approach employed in Georgia."[253]

Another theory suggests that the continuing practice of racial discrimination in the administration of the death penalty is evidence that capital punishment serves other latent purposes. According to this theory, it serves (1) as an instrument of minority group oppression ("to keep blacks in the South in a position of subjugation and subservience"), (2) as an instrument of majority group protection ("to secure the integrity of the white community in the face of threats or perceived challenges from blacks"), and (3) as a repressive response ("to conditions of dislocation and turmoil in ... time of economic hardship").[254] From this viewpoint, the death penalty as administered devalues the lives of blacks—particularly in the South—by using them as tools in a social (racial) and economic power struggle. Advocates of the theory contend that the death penalty in the United States is, at least in part, a race relations mechanism that controls blacks by extermination or, perhaps even more importantly, by threat of extermination.

Counterarguments to claims of racial discrimination

Many proponents of capital punishment claim that there is no longer any racial discrimination in its administration. The more sophisticated among them concede that there may have been racial discrimination in the past but that evidence under post-*Furman* statutes reveals racial disparities and not discrimination.[255]

Concerning victim-based racial discrimination, Judge Paul Cassell believes it is implausible "that a racist criminal justice system would look past minority defendants and discriminate solely on the more attenuated basis of the race of their victims." He asks, "If racists are running the system, why wouldn't they just discriminate directly against minority defendants?"[256] Furthermore, according to Cassell, what appears to be victim-based racial discrimination simply may be an artifact of the nature of interracial murders. As noted previously, the vast majority of murders are intraracial and occur in circumstances where the death penalty is likely inappropriate. Black-on-white murders, on the other hand, frequently occur during the course of a serious felony. For example, in Georgia, fewer than 10 percent of the black-on-black murders involve armed robbery compared to two thirds of the black-on-white murders.[257] Compared to murders involving other racial combinations, black-on-white murders are more likely to involve aggravating factors such as the killing of a law enforcement officer (75–80 percent of whom are white), kidnapping and rape, mutilation, execution-style killing, and torture.[258] Other factors that could explain what appears to be victim-based racial discrimination are the victim's socioeconomic status, defendant's failure to accept plea bargains in such cases, black victims' families not insisting on the state's pursuing the death penalty, and the victim's role in the prosecutor's decision not to seek the death penalty. In the latter case, the victim may have been a drug dealer, who was robbed and killed, or a rival gang member killed in a drive-by shooting.[259] Not all research has shown victim-based discrimination. For example, an examination of capital murders in Texas between 1974 and 1988 showed that prosecutors were more likely to seek the death penalty in white-victim cases when the defendant was white, and not when the victim was black.[260] Another study in Texas found that even if victim-based discrimination was a problem in the past, it has decreased significantly. The study revealed that the percentage of defendants sentenced to death for killing white victims in Texas has declined from more than 90 percent in the 1970s to less than 50 percent by 2003.[261] Research also has shown that the proportion of black-victim cases and white-victim cases resulting in death sentences was nearly identical when death-sentenced inmates were compared to homicide arrests in Texas between 1994 and 2001, and legally relevant variables were controlled.[262]

Perhaps most damning from a death penalty proponent's perspective is the judgment of U.S. District Court Judge J. Owen Forrester.[263] In reviewing Baldus's Georgia study, Judge Forrester observed that a race-of-victim effect was only evident in Baldus's summary models, ones that included only a few control variables. When additional control variables were added, he further noted, no statistically significant race-of-victim effects were found. When Baldus's model included all 430 control variables for which he had data, Forrester continued, no statistically significant evidence of racial discrimination was observed.[264] According to Baldus, however, Judge Forrester was wrong.[265] In personal correspondence to this author, Baldus wrote, "the race of victim effect was robust across all analyses of death sentences imposed among all death eligible cases."[266] He also noted that there was no 430-variable model. The largest model had 230 variables.

Another argument is that even if some post-*Furman* death sentences are a product of racial discrimination, society's interests in retribution, justice, and concern for crime victims and their families are more important, so that racial discrimination in the death penalty's application can be and should be ignored.[267] A related argument suggests that even if there is racial discrimination in the application of the death penalty, this in no way reduces either the blameworthiness of the guilty defendants who are sentenced to death for racial reasons or society's justification for executing them.[268] A final argument is that racial discrimination is inevitable and that it infects all social institutions, the death penalty being no exception. Hence, there is nothing that can be done about such racial discrimination short of abolishing the death penalty.[269] A problem with abolishing the death penalty for this reason, according to Louis Pojman, is that by the same logic it would also require the abolition of traffic laws and laws against murder, rape, and theft, for example, because these laws are applied to only some people who violate them.[270] He continues: "We should reform our practices as much as possible to eradicate unjust discrimination wherever we can, but if we are not allowed to have a law without perfect application, we will be forced to have no laws at all."[271] Proponents of capital punishment who make this argument clearly believe that the death penalty's administration can be reformed to significantly reduce discrimination, or that the merits of capital punishment outweigh any racial discrimination in its application.

CONCLUSION

The vote in the *McCleskey* decision was 5–4. Justice Lewis Powell, who wrote the majority opinion, cast the deciding vote. It was Powell's last year on the Court. Four years later, Powell's biographer asked him if he wished he could change his vote in any single case. Powell answered yes, in the *McCleskey* case. Powell, who had dissented in *Furman* and had regularly supported the death penalty in cases decided by the Supreme Court, opined, "I have come to think that capital punishment should be abolished … [because] it serves no useful purpose."[272]

The counterarguments of death penalty proponents notwithstanding, the Supreme Court has not and likely cannot rid the imposition of the death penalty from repugnant forms of racial discrimination. Yet, in *Zant v. Stephens* (1983), *McCleskey v. Kemp* (1987), and other cases, it has clearly indicated that either defendant-based or victim-based racial discrimination in the administration of capital punishment, whether overt or covert, is constitutionally impermissible.[273] Even under post-*Furman* statutes, Bowers and Pierce observe that:

> race is truly a pervasive influence on the criminal justice processing of potentially capital cases, one that is evident at every stage of the process … it is an influence that persists despite separate sentencing hearings, explicitly articulated sentencing guidelines, and automatic appellate review of all death sentences… .[274]

The same could also be said about social class, gender, and age discrimination.

DISCUSSION QUESTIONS

1. What does it mean to say that the death penalty has been imposed in an arbitrary and discriminatory way?
2. Are arbitrariness and discrimination acceptable in the administration of capital punishment?
3. Has the death penalty been administered in an unacceptably arbitrary and discriminatory way?
4. Is the death penalty currently administered in an unacceptably arbitrary and discriminatory way?
5. If the answer to the former question is yes, what are the sources of arbitrariness and discrimination?
6. Should powerful and wealthy capital offenders be able to escape capital punishment?
7. Should any of the harmful actions described in this chapter, for example, the production and distribution of known lethal products, that are not now capital crimes be made capital crimes?
8. Should the administration of capital punishment be different for females and males?
9. Is there a significant difference in any relevant social characteristic between a 17- and 18-year-old, other than what has been created by law?
10. Is it really meaningful to consider a 17-year-old a juvenile and an 18-year-old an adult?
11. Have post-*Furman* death penalty statutes and Court decisions had the effect desired by the Court's majority in *Furman*? Can death penalty statutes be made constitutionally acceptable?

Notes

1. Nakell and Hardy (1987, p. 16).
2. Ibid.
3. Bowers (1984, p. 191).
4. Tizon (2003); also see McCord (2005), who provides examples in both categories.
5. Amsterdam (1982, p. 351).
6. Death Penalty Information Center. Retrieved May 7, 2011, from http://www.deathpenaltyinfo.org/number-executions-state-and-region-1976.
7. Ibid.
8. Baumgartner, DeBoef, and Boydstun (2008, p. 31).
9. Death Penalty Information Center. Retrieved May 7, 2011, from http://www.deathpenaltyinfo.org/number-executions-state-and-region-1976.
10. Bowers (1984, p. 191).
11. Death Penalty Information Center. Retrieved May 7, 2011, from http://www.deathpenaltyinfo.org/number-executions-state-and-region-1976.
12. Meltsner (1973, p. 224).
13. See Bedau (1982, pp. 56–57). Banner (2002, p. 208) claims that before 1950 executions were primarily a northern phenomenon.
14. Calculated from data at Death Penalty Information Center. Retrieved May 7, 2011, from http://www.deathpenaltyinfo.org/number-executions-state-and-region-1976.
15. Ibid.
16. Bowers (1984, p. 236, Table 7–5) from the effective dates of those states' respective post-*Furman* statutes through 1977. Keil and Vito (2006) also found similar variation in Kentucky.
17. Joint Legislative Audit and Review Commission (2002); also see Willing and Fields (1999).

18. Federal Bureau of Investigation (2010), retrieved December 9, 2010, from http://www2.fbi.gov/ucr/cius2009/offenses/violent_crime/murder_homicide.html.
19. Baldus, Woodworth, Young, and Christ (2001, pp. 18–19).
20. Governor's Commission on Capital Punishment (2002, pp. 88 and 196); also see Radelet and Pierce (2006) and Willing and Fields (1999).
21. For Ohio, see Roberts (2005), Seewar (2005), Welsh-Huggins (2005), and Williams and Holcomb (2001); for Maryland, see Paternoster and Brame (2003).
22. Dieter (2005).
23. Willing and Fields (1999); also see Bright (2004, pp. 163–164).
24. Smith (2010).
25. Ibid.
26. Bowers (1984, p. 189).
27. Acker and Lanier (1998, p. 105), Blankenship, Luginbuhl, Cullen, and Redick (1997), Bowers and Foglia (2003), Bowers and Steiner (1998, pp. 311, 321, and 323), Eisenberg and Wells (1993–1994), Frank and Applegate (1998), Garvey, Johnson, and Marcus (1999–2000), Haney (2003, pp. 475–477), Haney, Sontag, and Costanzo (1994), and Sandys (1998, p. 304). Sentencing instructions in at least one California case were 30 pages long, see Sundby (2005, p. 49).
28. Bowers (1995) and Bowers and Steiner (1998, p. 328; 1999). "The Capital Jury Project (CJP) is organized as a consortium of university-based investigators ... specializing in the analysis of data collected in their respective states and collaborating to address the following objectives of the Project: (1) to examine and systematically describe jurors' exercise of capital sentencing discretion; (2) to identify the sources and assess the extent of arbitrariness in jurors' exercise of capital discretion; and (3) to assess the efficacy of the principal forms of capital statutes in controlling arbitrariness in capital sentencing." "Lengthy, in-person interviews with capital jurors are the chief source of data for this research"; see Bowers and Steiner (1999, p. 643, n. 185).
29. Bowers and Foglia (2003) and Bowers, Sandys, and Steiner (1998).
30. Bowers and Steiner (1999); also see Bowers and Foglia (2003), Eisenberg and Wells (1993–1994), Haney (2005, p. 83), Hood (1989), and Paduano and Smith (1987).
31. See, for example, *Simmons v. South Carolina*, 512 U.S. 154 (1994); *Ramdass v. Angelone*, 530 U.S. 156 (2000); *Weeks v. Angelone*, 528 U.S. 225 (2000). Georgia was the first state to bar jury consideration of parole or pardon by statute in 1955. Keeping such information from jurors has been justified by the separation of powers doctrine, the likely arbitrariness of unreliable speculation, and legislative intent. Such prohibitions have generally been considered a desirable protection for capital defendants and may have contributed to the decline in executions during the period. However, by the mid-1980s, this view began to be challenged. The claim was the jurors were substantially underestimating how long a person would remain in prison if not sentenced to die and the misperception made jurors more likely to impose the death penalty. Still, informing capital jurors about how long a capital defendant not sentenced to death would usually serve in prison also has its problems. In noncapital cases, the Supreme Court requires that jurors fully understand all available sentencing options. See Bowers and Steiner (1999, pp. 633–634, 715–716, and 717, n. 324).
32. Bowers and Foglia (2003), Haney (2005, pp. 179–180), Sundby (2005), and Weisberg (1983).
33. Acker and Lanier (1998), Bowers and Steiner (1998, pp. 320–321), and Hoffmann (1995).
34. Amsterdam (1982, p. 350).
35. Ibid.
36. Cited in Miller and Niven (2009, p. 9).
37. Ibid., p. 5.
38. Ibid, p. 13.

39. See Amsterdam (1982, p. 350).
40. Quoted in ibid.
41. Quoted in Bedau (1982, p. 190).
42. See Bowers (1984, pp. 368–370).
43. Ibid., p. 372; also see Burnett (2002, chap. 6).
44. Bedau (1982), Bowers (1984), and Schneider and Smykla (1991).
45. But see Haney (2003) for a discussion of the importance of antecedent factors in the penalty phase of capital trials.
46. Reiman (2007) and Simon (2006).
47. *Furman v. Georgia*, 1972, at 251–252.
48. Meltsner (1973, p. 70).
49. Lawes (1969, p. 10).
50. Stevenson (2004, p. 95).
51. Dow (2005, p. 7).
52. Phillips (2009).
53. See Reiman (2007) and Tifft (1982).
54. See Marquart, Ekland-Olson, and Sorensen (1994) for an examination of class effects on the death penalty in Texas.
55. Phillips (2010).
56. Federal Bureau of Investigation (2005) at http://www.fbi.gov/ucr/05cius/offenses/expanded_information/data/shrtable_03.html.
57. Schneider and Smykla (1991, p. 6, Table 1.1).
58. From data in Bedau (1982).
59. Rapaport (1993, p. 147).
60. Streib (2010). The largest number of women sentenced to death in 1 year during the modern era was 11 in 1989.
61. Ibid.; Death Penalty Information Center, retrieved May 7, 2011, from http://www.deathpenaltyinfo.org/number-executions-state-and-region-1976.
62. Streib (2010).
63. Extrapolated from Strieb (2003, p. 304).
64. Death Row, USA (2009).
65. Streib (2010).
66. Ibid.
67. Ibid.; also see Gillespie (2003, p. 28–30).
68. Streib (1993, p. 144).
69. See Marquart et al. (1994) for an examination of gender effects on the death penalty in Texas. Also see Rapaport (1993, p. 151), who argues "that the undervaluation of the heinousness of domestic murder is the most serious form of gender discrimination."
70. Streib (1993, p. 142).
71. Ibid., pp. 142–143.
72. Ibid., p. 143.
73. Ibid.
74. Streib (2003, p. 322); also see Rapaport (1993, p. 146).
75. Jones (2002).
76. Federal Bureau of Investigation (2005), Streib (2003); Death Penalty Information Center, retrieved December 8, 2010, from http://www.deathpenaltyinfo.org/number-executions-state-and-region-1976.
77. There is some dispute over Jose High's age at the time he committed the crime for which he was executed in Georgia on November 6, 2001. It is believed he was 17 years old at the time of his crime.

78. Death Row, USA (2007).
79. Streib (1998, p. 207).
80. Death Row, USA (2007).
81. Streib (2005).
82. Death Penalty Information Center. Retrieved December 20, 2010, from http://www.deathpenaltyinfo.org/execution-juveniles-us-and-other-countries.
83. Lewis et al. (1988).
84. Streib (2005).
85. Ibid.
86. Jones (2002); also see B.L. Vogel and R.E. Vogel (2003).
87. Moore (1994).
88. Hoffmann (1993, p. 117); also see Bradley (2006).
89. Hoffmann (1993, p. 117).
90. Ibid., pp. 117–118; also see Blecker (2006).
91. Hoffmann (1993, p. 118); also see Blecker (2006).
92. See Bohm and Haley (2007, p. 475).
93. Hoffmann (1993, pp. 118–119).
94. Williams and Holcomb (2001).
95. Banner (2002, pp. 139–140).
96. Ibid., p. 141. Steelwater (2003, p. 78) writes, "The state of Virginia around 1820 listed seventy-three capital offenses for slaves against only one—first degree murder—for white persons." Also see Vandiver et al. (2003) for a description of the Tennessee situation.
97. Banner (2002).
98. Ibid.
99. Ibid.
100. Ibid., p. 142.
101. Steelwater (2003, p. 78).
102. Baumgartner, DeBoef, and Boydstun (2008, p. 33).
103. Allen and Clubb (2008, p. 21).
104. See Bedau (1982, pp. 58–59).
105. Ibid., pp. 58–61.
106. Cited in Paternoster (1991, p. 127). As noted in Chapter 4, in *Coker v. Georgia* (433 U.S. 584, 1977), the Supreme Court effectively ended the possibility of a death penalty for rape of an adult woman where the victim is not killed.
107. See Hagan (1974), Kleck (1981), and Marquart et al. (1994).
108. See Bedau (1982).
109. See Bowers (1984, pp. 221–222) for methodology.
110. Ibid., p. 230.
111. U.S. General Accounting Office (1990, p. 6).
112. Baldus and Woodworth (1997).
113. Bright (1997, p. 4); also see Marquart et al. (1994) for an examination of race effects on the death penalty in Texas.
114. Phillips (2008).
115. Baldus, Woodworth, Zuckerman, Weiner, and Broffitt (1998).
116. Ibid.
117. For example, in a recent study of Maryland's death penalty, no significant race-of-defendant effect was found, Paternoster and Brame (2003); also see Williams and Holcomb (2001), who found no significant

race-of-defendant effect in Ohio; Brock, Cohen, and Sorensen (2000), who found similar results in four Texas counties.

118. See *Village of Arlington Heights v. Metropolitan Hous. Dev. Corp.*, 429 U.S. 252, 266 (1977).

119. See *McCleskey v. Kemp*, 481 U.S. 279 (1987); also see the discussion in Chapter 4.

120. Lawrence (1987, p. 387) has argued that "the intent requirement is a centerpiece in an ideology of equal opportunity that legitimizes the continued existence of racially and economically discriminatory conditions and rationalizes the superordinate status of privileged whites."

121. Radelet and Pierce (1985, p. 32).

122. Bright (1998, p. 131).

123. Ibid.

124. Bright (2002, pp. 47–48); also see Ogletree (2006, p. 64).

125. Holcomb, Williams, and Demuth (2004), Williams, Demuth, and Holcomb (2007), and Williams and Holcomb (2004); but see Stauffer, Smith, Cochran, Fogel and Bjerregaard (2006) for a different finding. For a discussion of a gendered form of racism in the treatment of capital rape-murders, see Crocker (2002).

126. Williams et al. (2007, p. 885).

127. Bowers (1984); also cf. Arkin (1980), Baldus, Pulaski, and Woodworth (1986), Foley (1987), Gross and Mauro (1984, 1989), Radelet (1981), Radelet and Pierce (1985, 1991), Radelet and Vandiver (1983), and Zeisel (1981).

128. Bowers (1984).

129. Baldus, Pulaski, and Woodworth (1983, 1986, 1990), Barnett (1985), Bowers (1984), and Gross and Mauro (1984).

130. Baldus et al. (1983, 1986), Bowers (1984), Brock, Cohen, and Sorensen (2000), and Ekland-Olson (1988).

131. Paternoster (1983, 1984, 1991), Paternoster and Kazyaka (1988), and McCord (2002).

132. Gross and Mauro (1984) and Nakell and Hardy (1987); but see Paternoster (1991), Stauffer et al. (2006), and Unah and Boger (2001).

133. Smith (1987).

134. Baldus et al. (1986).

135. Baldus et al. (1986) and Gross and Mauro (1984, 1989).

136. Baldus et al. (1986); also see Scheb and Lyons (2001), who found that race of the victim in relation to that of the defendant significantly predicted the prosecutor's decision to seek the death penalty but not the jury's decision to impose a death sentence.

137. Keil and Vito (1989, 1990, 1995) and Vito and Keil (1988).

138. Baldus et al. (1986), Klein and Rolph (1991), and Pierce and Radelet (2005).

139. Baldus et al. (1986), Governor's Commission on Capital Punishment (2002), Gross and Mauro (1984, 1989), Murphy (1984), and Radelet and Pierce (2006).

140. Baldus et al. (1986).

141. Gross and Mauro (1984, 1989).

142. Baldus et al. (1986) and Paternoster and Brame (2003, 2008).

143. Baldus et al. (1986).

144. Bienen, Weiner, Denno, Allison, and Mills (1988).

145. *State v. Cobb*, 663 A.2d 948 (1995).

146. Roberts (2005), Seewar (2005), Welsh-Huggins (2005), and Williams and Holcomb (2001).

147. Baldus et al. (1998).

148. Baldus and Woodworth (1997).

149. U.S. General Accounting Office (1990, p. 5).

150. Ibid.; also see Paternoster and Brame (2003), who found the same pattern in Maryland.

151. Baldus et al. (1990, p. 185).
152. See, for example, McAdams (1998, p. 165).
153. Death Row, USA (2010).
154. Ibid.
155. See Zahn (1989) for homicide trends during the twentieth century; also see Federal Bureau of Investigation (2001, p. 14).
156. Federal Bureau of Investigation. (2010). Expanded homicide data table 6. Retrieved December 12, 2010, from http://www2.fbi.gov/ucr/cius2009/offenses/expanded_information/data/shrtable_06.html.
157. Baldus and Woodworth claim that "in most death sentencing states only about 10 to 15 percent of defendants arrested for homicide have committed death-eligible crimes"; see Baldus and Woodworth (1998, pp. 395–396). Note that Baldus and Woodworth are referring to homicide arrests and not to murders and nonnegligent manslaughters committed.
158. Baldus and Woodworth (1998), p. 402.
159. Baldus et al. (1990, p. 403).
160. Baldus et al. (1983).
161. Bright (1997).
162. Paternoster and Brame (2003).
163. Bowers (1984, pp. 340–341), Radelet (1981), and Radelet and Pierce (1985); Dow (2005, p. 120) reports that circumstantial evidence has been the basis for about one sixth of all death penalty convictions. Circumstantial evidence is based on inference and not on personal knowledge or observation. It is evidence not provided by testimony.
164. Radelet and Pierce (1985, p. 601).
165. Jacoby and Paternoster (1982), Paternoster (1984), and Paternoster and Kazyaka (1988).
166. Vito and Keil (1988).
167. Baldus et al. (1990), Gross and Mauro (1989), and Sorensen and Wallace (1999).
168. Baldus et al. (1990), p. 398.
169. Bohm (1991).
170. See Bright (1995) and Hans (1988).
171. *Miller-El v. Dretke*, 125 S. Ct. 2007 (2005).
172. Ibid.
173. Ibid.
174. Karp and Warshaw (2006, p. 284).
175. Bohm (1994); also see Pokorak (1998) who shows that 98 percent of chief district attorneys in death penalty states are white.
176. Parker (1991, p. 505).
177. Bright (2002, pp. 54–55).
178. *Gregg v. Georgia*, 1976 at 157.
179. The following discussion is not limited to just racial prejudices.
180. Haney (2005).
181. Ibid., p. 62.
182. Dow (2005, p. 183).
183. Ibid.
184. Ibid., pp. 97–98 and 113.
185. Ibid., p. 287, n. 53.
186. Ibid., p. 63.
187. Ibid.
188. See *Lockhart v. McCree*, 1986, and the discussion in Chapter 4.

189. Haney (2005, p. 117); also see Bowers and Foglia (2003).
190. Haney (2005).
191. Ibid., pp. 120–132.
192. Ibid., pp. 141–143; also see Weisberg (1983).
193. Karp and Warshaw, 2006, p. 287.
194. Sundby (2005, p. 31).
195. Ibid., pp. 32–33.
196. Haney (2005, pp. 146–147 and 151).
197. Ibid., p. 146.
198. Ibid., p. 154.
199. Ibid., pp. 156 and 159.
200. Sundby (2005, p. 17).
201. Ibid., p. 157.
202. Snell (2010a, Tables 17 and 20).
203. Sundby (2005, pp. 183–184 and 50).
204. Ibid., pp. 10–11.
205. Ibid., pp. 147–148.
206. Ibid., p. 66.
207. Haney (2005, pp. 187–188).
208. Ibid., p. 206.
209. Ibid.; also see Bowers, Steiner, and Sandys (2001).
210. Haney (2005, p. 206).
211. Ibid., pp. 206–207; also see Bowers et al. (2001).
212. Lynch (2006, pp. 195–196).
213. Sundby (2005, p. 154).
214. Eisenberg (2001, p. 278).
215. Sundby (2005, pp. 133–134).
216. Ibid., p. 134.
217. Eisenberg, Garvey, and Wells (2001, pp. 303–304).
218. Ibid., p. 277.
219. Ibid.
220. Ibid., pp. 303–304.
221. Bowers et al. (2001).
222. Ibid., p. 260.
223. Ibid., p. 259.
224. Ibid.
225. Ibid., p. 260.
226. Ibid.
227. Sundby (2005, p. 151).
228. Ibid., pp. 81–84, citing the research of Solomon Asch and others.
229. Eisenberg et al., 2001, p. 304.
230. Ibid., pp. 303–304.
231. Sundby (2005, pp. 87 and 168–169).
232. Ibid., p. 88.
233. Bowers et al. (2001, p. 261).
234. Sundby (2005, p. 156).
235. Ibid., pp. 156–157.

236. Ibid., p. 102.

237. Ibid., pp. 100–101.

238. Although the prevalence of racial discrimination in the United States probably has declined over the past few decades, it has not disappeared. A 1979 study by the National Conference of Christians and Jews found that 74 percent of blacks felt that they were discriminated against in white-collar jobs, 68 percent in blue-collar jobs, and 58 percent in finding decent housing; only 39 percent of blacks believed that the government was committed to equality, see Facts on File (1979). The National Opinion Research Center's 1988 General Social Survey shows that 25 percent of white respondents believed that there should be laws against interracial marriages, 37 percent would not attempt to change the rules of racially segregated social clubs so that blacks could join, 24 percent agreed [strongly (8%) or slightly (16%)] that white people have a right to keep blacks out of their neighborhoods, 46 percent are living in racially segregated neighbor-hoods, and 44 percent of all respondents attended racially segregated churches; see Niemi (1989).

239. Barkan and Cohn (1994), Soss, Langbein, and Metelko (2003), Unnever and Cullen (2007a, 2007b, 2010a), and Unnever, Cullen, and Jonson (2008). Young (2004) discovered that racially prejudiced white Americans are more likely to favor executing innocent people than freeing the guilty.

240. See, for example, Baldus et al. (1990, p. 79, n. 59). For two explanations (one based on Freudian theory, the other on cognitive psychology) of the unconscious nature of racially discriminatory beliefs and actions in American society today, see Lawrence (1987, pp. 329–344).

241. Haney (2005, p. 203).

242. Gross and Mauro (1989, p. 113); also see Sundby (2005, p. 40). At least theoretically, the process of victim-based racial identification may apply as well to the white killers of white victims, though white actors in the legal system may show more sympathy for white killers than for black killers. The possibility of offender-based racial identification is a potentially fertile area for future research. For a discussion of "villain identification" by the capital offender, see Bowers (1988, p. 54). For a review of the extensive literature on the process of identification, see Gross and Mauro (1989, chap. 7).

243. Gross and Mauro (1989, p. 114); regarding prosecutors, see Baldus et al. (1990, p. 184).

244. The discussion of victim-based racial identification is not intended to imply that intentional discrimination does not operate in the process. It is likely that some combination of the two account for racial discrimination where it exists. Either way, white hegemony in the administration of capital punishment could produce the same results through either process.

245. Lynch (2006, p. 185).

246. Ibid.

247. See Carmichael and Hamilton (1967).

248. Bowers and Foglia (2003).

249. See, for example, McAdams (1998, p. 166), Schoenfeld (2005), and Willing and Fields (1999).

250. *McCleskey v. Kemp*, 1987 at 315–316.

251. Baldus and Woodworth (1998, p. 408).

252. Ibid.

253. Hoffmann (1993, p. 125).

254. Bowers (1984, pp. 131–132); also see Douglas in *Furman v. Georgia*, 1972; Baldus and Woodworth (1998, p. 386), Fleury-Steiner (2006), Kaufman-Osborn (2006), Lynch (2006), and Rusche and Kirchheimer (1968).

255. See, for example, Wilbanks (1987). For a graphic example of blatant post-*Furman* racial discrimination, see the description of the *Walter McMillian* case, Stevenson (2004, pp. 79–82).

256. Cassell (2004, p. 203).

257. Ibid.

258. Ibid., pp. 203–204.

259. Sorensen (2004).

260. Ibid.

261. Ibid.

262. Ibid.

263. See *McCleskey v. Zant*, 580 F. Supp. 338, 368. M.D. Ga. (1984).

264. See Cassell (2004, p. 204).

265. See Baldus et al. (1990, Appendix B).

266. Baldus (2006).

267. See, for example, Van den Haag (1982).

268. Ibid.

269. Apparently this was the position of Justice Scalia, as indicated by a memo he wrote while *McCleskey* was pending in the Court, see Baldus and Woodworth (1998, p. 409).

270. Pojman (2004, p. 71).

271. Ibid.

272. Cited in Radelet and Borg (2000, p. 48).

273. See Baldus and Woodworth (1998, p. 389) and Baldus et al. (1990).

274. Bowers and Pierce (1982, p. 220); also see Gross and Mauro (1984, 1989).

Retribution, religion, and capital punishment

11

Retribution appears to be the primary basis of support for the death penalty in the United States.[1] In a 2008 national opinion survey, 54.6 percent of respondents chose retribution, that is, "The punishment should fit the crime" (47.3%) or "They deserve it" (7.3%) as the most important reason for supporting the death penalty; another 26.5 percent chose retribution as their second most important reason for supporting the death penalty.[2] The second most important reason for supporting the death penalty after retribution was incapacitation: "To keep the offender from reoffending" (12.7%). Law professor Joseph Hoffmann claims that the basic principles of retributive justice are now the principal guide by which the Supreme Court evaluates whether the death penalty, either in a single case or in a category of cases, is cruel and unusual punishment in violation of the Eighth Amendment.[3] These developments would have surprised long-time prison warden Lewis Lawes, who, in the 1920s, wrote:

> The idea of punishment of any type solely as retribution is gradually disappearing, together with other of the older conceptions and theories of criminology. This idea is yielding to the more modern, progressive and scientific attitude, that retribution, a more euphonious word for revenge, is not justification for any system of punishment nor are its results beneficial. It is repressive, not reformative; it ignores social responsibility and disregards all possibility of individualization.[4]

Retributive motives or feelings are, at least to some extent, a product of religious teachings. This chapter examines the subjects of retribution, religion, and capital punishment. In the section on retribution, the effects of the death penalty on the families of murder victims and death row and executed inmates are also addressed.

RETRIBUTION AND CAPITAL PUNISHMENT

As a theoretical term, the concept of retribution is imprecise.[5] Philosopher John Cottingham argues that "the term 'retributive' as used in philosophy has become so imprecise and multivocal that it is doubtful whether it any longer serves a useful purpose."[6] Justice Thurgood Marshall, in *Furman v. Georgia* (1972), wrote that "the concept of retribution is one of the most misunderstood in all of our criminal jurisprudence."[7] As a result, law professor Margaret Radin notes that "retributivism is espoused by both [political] liberals and conservatives; it is seen as both a new way to limit inhumane practices and to exorcise permissiveness and coddling of criminals."[8]

The different meanings of retribution cause two problems: (1) disagreements over retribution's effects on death penalty opinions and (2) disagreements about the acceptability of retribution as a justification for capital punishment. Justice Potter Stewart, who voted with the majority in the

Furman decision, held that retribution was psychologically necessary for maintaining social stability,[9] while Justice Marshall equated retribution with vengeance and argued that neither was compatible with decent and civilized conduct.[10] Did the justices really have in mind the same definition of retribution?

MEANINGS OF RETRIBUTION

Some scholars believe retribution and revenge are virtually synonymous.[11] Others say there is an important difference between the two terms. Radin maintains that "revenge occurs when one person, with the idea of retaliation, injures someone she believes is responsible for an injury either to herself or to someone she cares about."[12] Revenge, for Radin, "is a private act between one person or group and another" and may or may not be justified.[13] On the other hand, she defines retribution as "a public act" or, more specifically, "the formal act of a community against one of its members, and is carried out in the manner and for the reasons that are justified under the political constitution of the community."[14] The purpose of retribution, argues Radin, is to prevent personal revenge, which she calls "revenge–utilitarianism."[15]

Law professor Herbert Packer describes two versions of retribution: "revenge theory" and "expiation theory."[16] Revenge theory is captured in the idea of *lex talionis* ("an eye for an eye"), while expiation theory is based on the premise that only through suffering punishment can an offender atone for his or her crime.[17]

Criminologist James Finckenauer similarly distinguishes two versions of retribution.[18] In one version (the bad version, in some people's view), the criminal is paid back. This is retribution as revenge and vindictiveness. In a second version (the seemingly acceptable one, according to the Supreme Court and some scholars of punishment philosophy), retribution means that the criminal pays back for the harm he or she has done. The desert theorists call this "just deserts." What is confusing, explains Finckenauer, is that in research examining the relationship between retributive feelings and death penalty support, the concepts of desert and retribution have generally been employed interchangeably.[19]

Cottingham has prepared the most exhaustive list of meanings, identifying and critiquing nine "theories" of punishment that have been labeled retributive.[20] First, and the one he argues captures the fundamental notion of retribution, is repayment theory. Although ostensibly similar to Packer's expiation theory (with elements of revenge theory), Cottingham claims that there can "not be an atonement theory of punishment; atonement is something voluntarily undertaken, punishment something exacted."[21] Another problem Cottingham has with a repayment theory of punishment is the unexplained question of "how or why suffering something unpleasant … should count as payment for an offence?"[22]

A second variety of retribution is desert theory: the idea that punishment is imposed because it is deserved.[23] This theory, taken literally, rests on the idea that an offender receives punishment as a reward for wrongdoing.[24] Recall Finckenauer's assertion that just deserts is one of two versions of retribution, the other being revenge.[25] Finckenauer argues that the principal difference between just deserts and revenge has to do with who repays whom, that is, whether the offender repays society (just deserts) or society repays the offender (revenge).[26] The distinction is specious for at least three reasons. First, just deserts, as Finckenauer defines it, is indistinguishable from restitution. Second, Finckenauer's conception of just deserts appears very similar to Packer's expiation theory and, as Cottingham reasons, as long as punishment is not voluntarily undertaken, it is not atonement. Few offenders volunteer to repay society. Third, Finckenauer proposes that in just deserts the offender is the subject, that is, "the active party," and in revenge the offender is the object, that is, "the passive target of society's actions."[27] It is not clear, however, how the punished offender can be, except perhaps in a hypothetical way, the subject or active party. The offender does not voluntarily seek to be punished to repay society in most cases; the offender is coerced. Moreover, how are the intentions of the offender in regard to punishment to be discerned? In either case, as Cottingham points out, it is not clear why suffering punishment should count as repayment for an offense.

A variation of desert theory, as some death penalty proponents interpret it, holds that "some crimes are so heinous [and] some criminals so evil, that no other sentence can satisfy justice."[28] In other words, justice simply requires capital punishment for some crimes and some offenders. This view, of course, begs the question, why? Why cannot justice be achieved by a punishment other than death? Non-death penalty jurisdictions in the United States and throughout the world apparently are able to achieve justice without capital punishment. Why cannot current death penalty jurisdictions do likewise?

A third variety of retribution is penalty theory, which is associated with the classical Kantian notion that an offender is punished automatically simply because he or she has committed a crime.[29] This idea implies both proportionality and deserts in punishment. In other words, a "punishment must fit the crime and must not be more or other than the person deserves" in order to respect a person's status as an autonomous moral entity.[30] Despite the emphasis on respecting a person's autonomy, penalty theory is still based on repayment, albeit circumscribed repayment.

Fourth is minimalism, which refers to the idea that "no one should be punished 'unless' he is guilty of a crime and culpable."[31] Minimalism is dismissed by Cottingham, who asks, "What on earth is supposed to be distinctly 'retributivist' about [this] thesis?"[32]

Fifth is satisfaction theory, which is similar to repayment theory and rests on a view of reciprocity: "A man is rightly punished because his punishment brings satisfaction to others."[33] However, as Cottingham notes, "if the underlying idea here is that the penal system provides a substitute for private revenge," then satisfaction theory is not a theory of retribution at all but rather one of social utility, furthering the goal of social stability.[34]

A sixth variety is fair play theory, which assumes that "failure to punish is unfair to those who practise self-restraint and respect the rights of others."[35] This theory, however, turns out to be a form of repayment theory as the offender is made to pay "for the unfair advantage he has obtained" by his or her criminal acts.[36]

Seventh is placation theory, which is captured by Kant's famous passage that "even if a civil society were to dissolve itself by common agreement … the last murderer remaining in prison must first be executed so that … the blood guilt thereof will not be fixed on the people."[37] Cottingham points out that this theory "looks forward to the desired result of appeasing the wrath of God" and, thus, "is unlikely to have much appeal to present-day thinkers concerned to provide a secular justification for punishment."[38]

An eighth variety is annulment theory, which, according to Cottingham confuses retribution with restitution. Annulment theory is based on the idea that "we are obliged to punish because to do so is 'to annul the crime which otherwise would have been held valid, and to restore the right.'"[39]

A ninth and final variety of retribution is denunciation theory, that is, punishment is inflicted to denounce a crime.[40] Cottingham maintains that denunciation theory is not uniquely retributivist because there are other ways, besides punishment, of denouncing crime.[41] At the end of his exercise, Cottingham admits that most of the theories that he has described share much in common with the notion of retribution as repayment. Indeed, one must strain to identify differences.

SOURCES OF RETRIBUTION

Because of the presumed universality of retributive emotions, some writers have suggested that retributive motives have a biological basis.[42] Others have argued that retributive emotions are derived from the socialization process and "are the psychological representations of more overt social and socialpsychological processes."[43]

Vidmar and Miller are among those who believe that the socialization process is the principal source of retributive emotions. They argue that retribution "derives from the individual's attachment to the group, internalization of group values, and perception of the offense as a threat to those values."[44] Retribution also may be a means of obtaining social acceptance about the moral rightness of the violated rule.[45] Vidmar and Miller found that retributive punishment reactions increased with the increasing importance of the violated rule and the increasing seriousness of the outcome.[46] Thus, for example, a greater retributive punishment would be expected in a case in which a murderer cannibalized or otherwise mutilated the victim's body than in a case in which the murderer did not.

More recently, Unnever and Cullen tested three explanations of the public's punitiveness, which is assumed here is analogous to the public's desire for retribution.[47] They label the first explanation the "crime-distrust model." In this model, retributive sentiments are attributed to a perception that crime is increasing and that increasing crime will disrupt a person's way of life, and to a loss of faith in the government's (especially the court's) ability to protect people from crime.[48] The second explanation is called the "moral decline model." This model attributes retributive sentiments to a feeling that society is in a state of moral decline and that harsh punishments (such as the death penalty) are a way of restoring social cohesion.[49] The third explanation is dubbed the "racial animus model." Retributive sentiments in this model are based on racial and ethnic intolerance or negative views about minority group members.[50] Although the crime-distrust model and the moral decline model were partially supported by the data, the racial animus model was the most strongly supported model of Americans' punitiveness (and retributive sentiments). Research by Unnever and Cullen suggests that the public's retributive support for the death penalty is rooted in race and racism.

PROBLEMS WITH RETRIBUTION AS REVENGE

Revenge for death-eligible crimes is an emotional, though quite understandable, reaction. A problem with revenge as a justification for capital punishment is that a decision as important as the intentional taking of a life by the state should be based more on reason than on emotion. Opponents of the death penalty point out that it is largely emotion that makes people want to punish in kind. As the father of a murder victim expressed it: "For many months after the bombing I could have killed Timothy McVeigh myself. Temporary insanity is real, and I have lived it. You can't think of enough adjectives to describe the rage, revenge, and hate I felt."[51] The brother of a murder victim put it this way: "Murder drives even the most loving and compassionate people to the edge of that fine line that separates our respect for life from our violent potentials."[52] As for punishing in kind, no other crime is punished in kind; the literal interpretation of the eye-for-an-eye maxim is not imposed for any other offense. For example, the state does not burn down the homes of arsonists, cheat people who defraud, or rape people who rape.[53] Why, then, opponents ask, is it necessary to kill people who kill? Their answer is that it is not. In practice, only a select few among all those who are death eligible are executed in the name of revenge.

Criminologist Edna Erez claims that the eye-for-an-eye (*lex talionis*) formula has frequently been misinterpreted[54]—that the famous formula was never intended to be taken literally but was meant as a warning against applying punishment in a discriminatory way. The conclusion to the biblical dictate of "an eye for an eye" is "You shall have one manner of law, as well for the stranger, as for your own country."[55] This has been interpreted to mean that the eye of a peasant is just as worthy as the eye of a noble; thus, the victim and the offender should be treated alike, without consideration of social status. The eye-for-an-eye formula was intended to require monetary compensation and not the trading of body parts.[56] Similarly, law professor Joseph Hoffmann points out that proportional punishment—a goal of retributive justice—does not require payment in kind, but instead needs only to "be defined in terms of whatever the particular society views as appropriate for the crime."[57] The key is that the proportional punishment be applied proportionately and not in a discriminatory way.

Thus, even assuming that revenge is a legitimate rationale, opponents of the penalty argue that there is no reason why revenge could not be served by another noncapital punishment. On this point rests what may be the quintessential difference between proponents and opponents of the death penalty: Proponents sometimes misunderstand that opponents of the penalty do not want capital offenders to escape punishment or justice; indeed, most of them want such offenders to be punished to the severest degree allowed by law. The only difference between the two groups is what the severest punishment allowed by law should be.

Supporters of capital punishment maintain that by allowing the state to seek revenge, relatives and friends of the victim(s) are relieved of the need to do so. An implication is that with the abolition of capital punishment, relatives and friends of a victim are more likely to seek personal revenge. However, as Justice Brennan observed in his *Furman* decision, "There is no evidence whatever that utilization of imprisonment rather than death encourages private blood feuds and other disorders."[58] During the hiatus in capital punishment in the United States between 1968 and 1977, there was no apparent increase in personal revenge, nor do states without capital punishment have elevated levels of personal revenge. The 139 countries that have abolished capital punishment in law or practice suffer no apparent problems either.[59] This seems proof that a need for revenge can be satisfied by an alternative punishment, such as life imprisonment.

Vindictiveness notwithstanding, the family or the friends of a victim—the "covictims"—as well as others, may support capital punishment for the catharsis, finality, or closure it may bring to their loss.[60] However, whether executions provide covictims closure is a controversial issue. On the one hand, a 2001 public opinion poll showed that 60 percent of Americans believed that the death penalty was fair because "it gives satisfaction and closure to the families of murder victims."[61] However, a 2008 national opinion survey found that closure ("It will give the victim's family closure") was chosen only by 3.8 percent of respondents as their most important reason for supporting the death penalty; another 10.3 percent of respondents chose closure as their second most important reason for supporting the death penalty.[62] Nevertheless, describing his decision to grant clemency to all Illinois death row inmates following discussions with covictims, Governor George Ryan said, "To a family they talked about closure…. They pleaded with me to allow the state to kill an inmate in its name to provide the families with closure."[63] On the other hand, the meager research on capital crime victims' families reveals covictims, including some who support capital punishment, who bristle at the contention that executions bring closure. For them, executions produce an outcome, but never closure.[64] As the daughter of a murder victim explained, "I get sick when death-penalty advocates self-righteously prescribe execution to treat the wounds we live with after homicide…. Those who hold out an event— execution—as the solution to pain have no understanding of healing. Healing is a process, not an event."[65] Similarly, the mother of a murder victim complains, "I don't know why the powers that be have come up with the word 'closure.' There is no closure, and there never, never will be."[66]

Law professor Franklin Zimring maintains that in the past couple of decades "closure" has replaced "revenge" as a primary purpose of capital punishment.[67] It was not until 1989, he discovered, that the term "closure" was first used by the printed mass media to describe a major objective of the death penalty.[68] This symbolic and linguistic shift in emphasis from revenge to closure, according to Zimring, has been a "public relations godsend" for death penalty proponents that has transformed capital trials and executions, at least in the minds of the public, into politically palatable processes that serve the personal interests of homicide survivors.[69] He observes that the penalty stage of death penalty trials, for example, has become a "status competition" between the offender and those who were injured by the crime.[70] This shift in rhetoric has been especially important in retaining the support of people who distrust government because, for them, it is much easier to support executions as a public service, such as garbage collection or street cleaning, than it is to contend with arguments that executions represent the excessive use of power by and for the government.[71] As a public service, the death penalty is a private right and not a show of governmental power, which, for Zimring, is consistent with the American tradition of community control of punishment and vigilante justice.[72]

Research on covictims emphasizes their immense suffering and loss.[73] Professor Margaret Vandiver summarizes some of the results of the research:

- The loss of a close relative to homicide is a shatteringly traumatic event. The pain, disruption, and trauma caused by homicide cannot be overstated.
- The trauma and difficulty of adjusting to loss due to homicide is such that survivors often experience posttraumatic stress disorder–like symptoms. Many survivors report losing their sense that there is any justice or safety in the world; many feel that life itself has lost all meaning.
- Survivors can expect to encounter difficulties in many other areas of their lives, including their marriages, relationships with children, friendships, and work.
- The experience of bereavement moves through several stages, including denial, anger, grief, and ultimately, resolution. These stages are necessarily distinct and do not always occur in the same sequence.
- The process of recovery takes years, if not decades. Expectations of quick grieving and recovery are unrealistic and damaging. Even after survivors resolve their grief, it is unlikely that their emotional lives will ever be the same as before the crime.
- Survivors often are not helped, and sometimes are further victimized, by the criminal justice system. Both formal and informal supports for homicide victims' survivors are dreadfully inadequate.
- The experience of isolation is very common—at the time they most need contact and support, families often feel the most isolated. The opposite situation of intrusion is often a problem

as well, with unwelcome contacts from the criminal justice system, the media, and curiosity seekers.

- There seems to be much potential for advancing the process of healing through nonjudgmental, ongoing, emotionally involved listening, without suggestions as to how the survivors should feel or what they should do.[74]

Some family members do not want their relative's killer executed. Among their reasons are the following:

- A general opposition to the death penalty;
- An execution would diminish or belittle the memory of their relative;
- A desire to avoid the prolonged contact with the criminal justice system that the death penalty requires;
- A desire to avoid the public attention an impending execution bestows on the condemned prisoner;
- A preference for the finality of a sentence of life imprisonment without the possibility of parole and the obscurity into which the defendant will quickly fall, over the continued uncertainty and publicity of the death penalty;
- A desire for the offender to have a long time to reflect on his or her deed, and perhaps to feel remorse for it;
- A hope that someday there can be some sort of mediation or reconciliation between the family and the offender;
- And if the offender is a relative, for obvious reasons.[75]

Another reason covictims do not want their relative's murderer executed is that they do not want the murderer to "win." As the daughter of a murder victim explains, "If we let murderers turn us to murder, we give them too much power. They succeed in bringing us to their way of thinking and acting, and we become what we say we abhor."[76]

Some death penalty proponents argue that life imprisonment or a lesser punishment, rather than execution, may not provide the psychological relief deserved by victims' suffering survivors. For some families, anything less than an execution may be taken as a slight, "an indication that society does not value their relative or understand the magnitude of their loss."[77] For them, it is unfair that their loved one's killer will continue to experience many of the small joys of life, such as seeing the sun rise and set, celebrating birthdays, experiencing holidays, and visiting with loved ones, while their loved one cannot.[78] Opponents respond in three ways. First, they acknowledge that an execution may indeed relieve feelings of profound loss, but assume that, in many cases, the relief may be only temporary. In the long run, they presume (there is no systematic research on the subject), an execution may make the burden more difficult to bear because the desire for revenge appeases only the basest and most primitive characteristics of human beings.

It is instructive that only one quarter of the approximately 1,100 people eligible to view Timothy McVeigh's execution chose to do so. (U.S. Attorney General John Ashcroft approved closed-circuit television viewing for the survivors and relatives of victims of the 1995 Oklahoma City bombing.) Reasons for not viewing the execution included being opposed to capital punishment and not wanting to watch someone die. Many of those choosing not to watch the execution believed that they had healed physically, psychologically, and spiritually. Viewing the execution for them was an unnecessary diversion. They also feared that McVeigh's final statement might haunt them.[79]

Second, opponents note that the family members and friends of many criminal homicide victims are likely to be disappointed and, in many cases, offended by the "justice" they receive. Very few of them will receive any of the presumed benefits of capital punishment because 98–99 percent of criminal homicide offenders are never executed. In the vast majority of criminal homicides, a death sentence is not even sought. Thus, many homicide victims' family members and friends will feel that they and the homicide victim are unworthy and have been devalued by the justice system because the killer of their loved one or friend did not receive the maximum penalty allowed by law.[80]

Third, opponents point out that even if an execution did make a loss easier to endure for the relatives of the victim, this advantage would have to be weighed against the effects of the execution on the relatives of the perpetrator. This attempt to balance the death penalty's effects on both families raises two key questions posed nicely by Vandiver:

> Given that the crime cannot be undone, what can the criminal justice system offer to the victim's family? And what kind of sentence can be imposed on a defendant found guilty of first degree murder that is commensurate to the crime, protects society, and yet does not destroy the defendant's family in turn?[81]

In the 1920s, prison warden Lewis Lawes provided the following insight about capital punishment and the families of death row inmates:

> It is a punishment, too, that falls most severely on the family of the offender. The mental and physical suffering of the murderer himself is soon over. Many are of the stoic type, or of such low intellectual development that they are susceptible of little feeling. The mothers, the wives, the sisters are the ones who suffer and for them this suffering continues for months before and for months after the execution. I yield to no one in acknowledging the duty we owe the family of the murderer's victim. But I have very grave doubt whether we have the right to inflict this terrible burden on the innocent family of the murderer, believing as I do that the punishment itself serves no useful purpose either in its primary object of deterring others or its secondary object of reformation or expiation.[82]

There is even less research on the families of death row or executed inmates than there is on victims' families. The research that is available, though, indicates that the effects of capital punishment on death row or executed inmates' families can be as profound as it is for victims' families. Families of death row or executed inmates are different from the families of victims of any other kind of violent death in some important ways. Vandiver lists four of the differences:

- The families of condemned prisoners know for years that the state intends to kill their relatives and the method that will be used. They experience a prolonged period of anticipatory grieving, complicated by the hope that some court or governor will grant relief.
- Their relatives' deaths will come about as the result of the actions of dozens of respected and powerful persons. Their deaths will not be caused by a breakdown in social order but by a highly orchestrated and cooperative effort of authority.
- Their relatives are publicly disgraced and shamed; they have been formally cast out of society and judged to be unworthy to live.
- The deaths of their relatives are not mourned and regretted the way other violent deaths are; rather, the death is condoned, supported, and desired by many people, and actively celebrated by some.[83]

In a footnote, Vandiver adds a fifth important difference and its ironic consequence:

Family members of capital defendants frequently have been victims of violent crime themselves; indeed, it is not unusual for these families to have lost relatives to homicide. Yet, because of class and racial inequities in sentencing, it is unlikely their relatives' deaths were punished with much severity. How ironic for these families that when a relative encounters the criminal justice system as a defendant rather than a victim, the system turns from leniency to severity.[84]

Other problems experienced by families of death row inmates (some of which they share with the families of victims) are stress (both economic and psychological), grief (only the families of death row inmates experience anticipatory grief), depression and other medical illnesses, self-accusation, social isolation, powerlessness, demoralization, and family disorganization.[85] Since the families of both the victim and the perpetrator are usually "innocent," the infliction of pain and suffering on one group to relieve the pain and suffering of the other group is hard to justify.

The death penalty also affects police officers, attorneys, judges, jurors, witnesses, correctional personnel, and other persons who find themselves involved in the process by choice or by duty. Unfortunately, there is a dearth of research on the death penalty's impact on these people's lives.[86]

Supporters of capital punishment cite retributive grounds in suggesting that legal vengeance is a way of enhancing social solidarity and of sanctifying the importance of innocent life.[87] Assuming the argument has merit, there would seem to be other ways than capital punishment of achieving those ends (e.g., noncapital punishments or, better yet, more positive measures). Moreover, it is difficult to understand how the taking of a life, even of a person guilty of aggravated murder, in any way sanctifies life. Henry Schwarzschild, former director of the Capital Punishment Project of the American Civil Liberties Union, asked, "How can a thoughtful and sensible person justify killing people who kill people to teach that killing is wrong?"[88]

Research shows that the public supports the death penalty primarily for vindictive revenge.[89] This raises two important questions. First, is the satisfaction of the desire for vindictive revenge a legitimate penal purpose? Second, does legitimizing this desire for vindictive revenge contribute to the violent social relationships that pervade our nation? Justice Marshall observed in his *Furman* decision:

Retaliation, vengeance, and retribution have been roundly condemned as intolerable aspirations for a government in a free society. Punishment as retribution has been condemned as intolerable by scholars for centuries, and the Eighth Amendment itself was adopted to prevent punishment from becoming synonymous with vengeance.[90]

A principal source of the desire for vindictive revenge (the eye-for-an-eye variety) is religion; however, religious support for vindictive revenge and for the death penalty is puzzling, as the Bible is ambiguous on both subjects. (This discussion applies only to those religions that use the Bible, either the Old or the New Testament, as their basis of authority.)

RELIGION AND CAPITAL PUNISHMENT

The leaders of most organized religions in the United States no longer support the death penalty, and many actually openly favor its abolition.[91] For example, the National Conference of Catholic Bishops has declared its opposition, arguing that capital punishment is "uncivilized," "inhumane," "barbaric," and an assault on the sanctity of human life.[92] Religious leaders have argued that capital punishment is inconsistent with efforts "to promote respect for human life, to stem the tide of violence in our society and to embody the message of God's redemptive love."[93] Capital punishment is believed to institutionalize retribution and revenge and to exacerbate violence by giving it official sanction.[94]

A recent survey of religious organizations in the United States found that of the 126 religious organizations that responded to the survey, 61 percent (77) officially oppose capital punishment, 17 percent (22) officially support capital punishment, and 21 percent (27) leave it up to individual congregations or individual religious leaders to determine their own position on capital punishment.[95] The religious organizations that officially oppose capital punishment are: African Methodist Episcopal Church, African Methodist Episcopal Zion Church, American Association of Lutheran Churches, American Baptist Association, American Ethical Union, American Unitarian Conference, Anabaptist Groups, Anglican Catholic Church, Anglican Church, Anglican Church in America, Apostolic Christian Churches of America, Apostolic Faith Mission of Portland, OR, Apostolic Lutheran Church of America, Association of Free Lutheran Congregations, Brethren in Christ Church, Buddhist Information Network, Catholic Apostolic Church in North America, Christ Catholic Church International, Christian Methodist Episcopal Church, Church of All Worlds, Church of the Brethren, Church of God (Cleveland), Church of God of Prophecy, Church of the Lutheran Brethren, Church of the Lutheran Confession, Church of the United Brethren in Christ, Creation 7th Day Adventist Church, Disciples of Christ, Episcopal Church, Episcopal Missionary Church, Evangelical Community Church–Lutheran, Evangelical Covenant Church, Evangelical Friends International, Evangelical Lutheran Church in America, Evangelical Methodist Church, Friends General Conference, Friends United Meeting, Greek Orthodox Archdiocese of America, Holy Eastern Orthodox Catholic and Apostolic Church in North America, The Independent Celtic Church, International Church of the Foursquare Gospel, Lutheran Church–Missouri Synod, official, Lutheran Orthodox Church, Malankara Archdiocese of the Syrian Orthodox Church in North America, Mennonite Brethren Churches, United States Conference, Mennonite Church USA, Mennonite–Conservative Mennonite Conference, Mennonite–The Evangelical Mennonite Conference, Mennonite Information Center, Missionary Church USA, Moravian Church in America, National Association of Evangelicals, National Council of Churches, National Spiritualist Association of Churches, Old Roman Catholic Church in North America, Orthodox Catholic Church of America, Orthodox Church in America, Orthodox Presbyterian Church, The Pagan Federation, Presbyterian Church in America, Presbyterian Church (USA), Primitive Baptist Church, Primitive Methodist Church in the USA, Reform Judaism–Union for Reformed Judaism, Reformed Church in America, Reformed Episcopal Church, Religious Society of Friends, Roman Catholic, U.S. Catholic Conference, Seventh Day Adventists, Sikhism Home Page, The Southern Episcopal Church, Swedenborgian Church, Taoism Information Page, Unitarian Universalist Association, United Church of Christ, and United Methodist Church.

The religious organizations that officially support capital punishment are: American Carpatho-Russian Orthodox Diocese of the USA, American Evangelical Christian Churches, Association of Reformed Baptist Churches of America, Baha'i–The Baha'i Faith, Church of Illumination, Church of Jesus Christ of Latter-day Saints, Conservative Judaism–United Synagogue of Conservative Judaism, Conservative Baptist Association of America, Conservative Congregational Christian Conference, Evangelical Congregational Church, Evangelical Presbyterian Church, Free Methodist Church of North America, General Association of Regular Baptist Churches, Islamic Society of North America, Nation of Islam, Russian Orthodox Church outside of Russia, Separate Baptists in Christ, Southern

Baptist Convention, Sovereign Grace Baptist Association, Syrian Orthodox Church: Eastern Vicariate of North America, United Synagogue of Conservative Judaism, and Wisconsin Evangelical Lutheran Synod.

It is important to note that, despite the official positions of their religious organizations, a majority of people in the United States who profess a religious belief, whether Protestant, Catholic, or Jewish, appear to support capital punishment. According to a 2006 Gallup poll, for example, 67 percent of all Christians were in favor of the death penalty for a person convicted of murder, as were 68 percent of Protestants, 67 percent of Christians other than Protestants, 67 percent of Catholics, 55 percent of non-Christians, and 56 percent of those who had no religious preference.[96] However, a survey conducted among more than 1,000 U.S. Catholics in March 2005 found that 48.5 percent supported capital punishment and 48.4 percent opposed it.[97] Another survey of U.S. Catholics in 2007 discovered that 60 percent of all Catholics favored the death penalty (35% opposed it and 5% had no opinion); 66 percent of white Catholics favored the penalty (28% opposed it and 6% had no opinion), but only 47 percent of Hispanic Catholics favored the penalty (40% opposed it and 13% had no opinion).[98] Among U.S. Catholics who attended church weekly, 55 percent favored the penalty (39% opposed it and 6% had no opinion), while those who attended church less than weekly, 73 percent favored the penalty (22% opposed it and 5% had no opinion).

The relationship between religious belief and death penalty opinion is more complex than the general poll data suggest. For example, recent research by Unnever and his colleagues revealed that Americans with a personal relationship with a loving–forgiving God are less likely to support the death penalty for convicted murderers than are those who believe in a wrathful–punitive God.[99] Grasmick and his colleagues discovered that "evangelical/fundamentalist" Protestants were more likely to favor the death penalty than were "liberal/moderate" Protestants.[100] Britt found that black fundamentalists were less likely to support the death penalty than were white fundamentalists.[101]

CAPITAL PUNISHMENT IN THE OLD TESTAMENT

Religious leaders who oppose capital punishment concede that the Old Testament prescribes the death penalty for many offenses. They are:

- Murder (Exodus 21:12–13; Leviticus 24:17; Numbers 35:16ff; Deuteronomy 19:11ff)
- Manslaughter (Numbers 35:9–28)
- Bearing false witness on a capital charge (Deuteronomy 19:18–21)
- Kidnapping or stealing a man (Exodus 21:16; Deuteronomy 24:7)
- Cursing God (Exodus 22:28; Leviticus 24:10–16)
- Idolatry (Exodus 20:3–5, 22:20; Deuteronomy 13:1–11, 17:2–7)
- Disobedience of religious authority (Deuteronomy 17:8–13)
- Laboring on the Sabbath (Exodus 31:14–15, 35:2)
- False prophecy in the name of God (Deuteronomy 18:20–22)
- Child sacrifice (Leviticus 20:2)
- Striking, cursing, or rebelling against a parent (Exodus 20:12ff, 21:17; Leviticus 19:3, 20:9; Deuteronomy 21:18–21)
- Adultery and unnatural vice (Leviticus 18:23, 20:10–16; Deuteronomy 22:22)
- Prostitution or harlotry under certain circumstances (Leviticus 21:9; Deuteronomy 22:20–24)

- Sorcery (Exodus 22:18; Leviticus 20:27)
- Incest (Leviticus 18:6–18, 20:14; Deuteronomy 27:20, 23)
- Sodomy and bestiality (Leviticus 18:22ff, 20:13ff); and
- Keeping an ox known to be dangerous, if it kills a person (Exodus 21:29)[102]

Offenders were executed by stoning—the standard method of judicial execution in biblical times (Leviticus 24:14, 16; Deuteronomy 22:24; 1 Kings 21:13; Numbers 15:35)—and, in some cases, burning (Leviticus 20:14, 21:9; Genesis 38:24), beheading (2 Kings 6:31–32; 2 Samuel 16:9), strangling (not listed in the Old Testament, but contained in the Tractate on the Sanhedrin in the Mishnah), and shooting with arrows (Exodus 19:13). Occasionally, corpses of executed lawbreakers were hung in public as an example to others (Deuteronomy 21:22, 23), and sometimes, the corpse of the executed person was mutilated (2 Samuel 4:12).[103]

More scriptural support for capital punishment in the Old Testament includes Genesis 9:6, which commands, "Who sheddeth man's blood, by man shall his blood be shed," and 25 verses after "Thou shalt not kill," in Exodus 21:12, one finds, "He that smiteth a man so that he may die, shall be surely put to death."[104] Leviticus 24:17 states, "He who kills a man shall be put to death," and in Numbers 35:30–31, "If anyone kills a person, the murderer shall be put to death on the evidence of witnesses…. Moreover, you shall accept no ransom for the life of a murderer who is guilty of death; but he shall be put to death… ."[105]

It appears that the ancient Hebrews were a vengeful and barbaric people; however, in practice, Hebrew law made it very difficult to execute a capital offender. Some of the legal requirements and procedures were:

- The court was composed of 23 members (as opposed to three members in monetary matters): a majority of one was needed to acquit the defendant, but a majority of two was needed to convict;
- Men lacking in compassion and mercy were not to be appointed to the court (among those excluded were the very old, the impotent or castrated, or the childless, all of whom were believed to have good reason for their lack of compassion and mercy);
- Adjudication had to begin and be completed in the daytime;
- Adjudication could be completed the same day if the defendant was acquitted, but was to be postponed until the following day if the defendant was convicted (to provide the opportunity of discovering favorable evidence);
- Two capital cases could not be adjudicated on the same day, to allow enough time to thoroughly present the defendant's case;
- The court was expected to act in the defendant's defense (an adversarial system was not employed in capital cases);
- If members of the court witnessed the capital crime, they could not be involved in the case's adjudication because they could not argue in favor of the defendant;
- If the court began its adjudication process with a unanimous vote against the defendant, acquittal was mandated because such a vote could only mean that the court had not done its job defending the defendant (it was assumed that at least one argument could always be made on behalf of the defendant);
- Adjudication began with arguments in favor of the defendant;
- Those who argued against the defendant were allowed to change their minds; those who argued in favor of the defendant could not;
- Everyone was allowed to argue in favor of the defendant, but only certain people could argue against the defendant;

- The defendant was not allowed to argue against himself or herself (conviction in capital cases could not be based solely on a confession);
- Ignorance of the law was a valid defense (the death penalty could not be imposed unless witnesses warned the offender just prior to the commission of the crime that the act was punishable by death and the offender acknowledged the warning and admitted knowing the punishment for the crime) (originally this was a means of distinguishing between intentional and accidental murder);
- Trustworthy testimony had to be given by two qualified eyewitnesses, who were together at the time and scene of the crime and observed the crime from the same place (witnesses had to be free adults, to be of sound mind and body, to be of unquestioned integrity, and to have no personal interest in the case);
- Evidence from those people related by blood or marriage was not admissible;
- Circumstantial evidence was excluded;
- Witnesses were warned not to testify to anything that was based on inference or hearsay;
- Witnesses were interrogated separately about the exact time, place, and persons involved in the offense, and any material discrepancies resulted in an acquittal;
- Witnesses were warned that false testimony would make them liable to the accused's penalty if the accused was convicted.[106]

Furthermore, according to one authority:

> there was a saying that a Sanhedrin [in ancient times, the supreme council and highest court of the Hebrew nation] which put one man to death in seven years might be called murderous. Rabbi Eliezer ben Azarya said that it [the Sanhedrin] would be called murderous if it executed one man in seventy years. And Rabbi Akiba and Rabbi Tryphon said if they had been present, they would always have had some way of making it impossible to pass the death sentence.[107]

Two additional points about capital punishment in the Old Testament relevant to contemporary practice are important. First, the majority of the capital offenses of the ancient Hebrews are not capital offenses today, and few Americans would sanction the death penalty for most of them. Second, rabbis have concluded that the Torah ("the five books of Moses") suggests that different and more appropriate punishments may be used, as historical circumstances dictate.[108]

Finally, there is the Sixth Commandment's admonishment in the Old Testament, "Thou shalt not kill." Death penalty opponents who base their opposition primarily on their religious beliefs cite the Sixth Commandment as a scriptural basis for their position. Proponents of the penalty counter that in the original Hebrew, the Sixth Commandment translates as "Thou shalt not commit murder."[109] Thus, the Sixth Commandment presumably prohibits only murder and not capital punishment or killing in "just" wars. Catholic scholar Father James Reilly indicates that, according to the Roman Catechism of the Council of Trent promulgated by Pope Pius V in 1566, the death penalty is a morally permissible way to punish murderers.[110] This view, as noted previously, has since been superseded.

CAPITAL PUNISHMENT IN THE NEW TESTAMENT

The New Testament provides many references that ostensibly argue against capital punishment. Followers of Jesus were asked to love their enemies (Matthew 5:44) and to forgive those who trespass against them (Matthew 6:14–15), and while he was on the cross, Jesus forgave his executioners because of their lack of knowledge and understanding. In Matthew 5:38–40, he provided an alternative to violence: "You have heard the commandment, 'An eye for an eye, a tooth for a tooth,' but what I say to you is: Offer no resistance to injury. When a person strikes you on the right cheek, turn and offer him the other." As evidenced by his ministry to outcasts and his acceptance of sinners, Jesus expressed a love and mercy for all people, regardless of their worth or merit. He was not, however, "soft on crime," but believed that ultimate judgment rested with God (Matthew 25:31–46). As St Paul warned in Romans 12:19, "Vengeance is mine, says the Lord. I will repay."[111]

During the twelfth and thirteenth centuries (the Middle Ages) when the Catholic Church dominated social life in Western Europe, capital punishment began to be used widely for religious crimes—despite New Testament references seemingly against it. Before then, pre-Christian legal codes listed fewer crimes and milder punishments than those imposed later under religious auspices.[112]

Religious authorities created some of the more barbaric methods of execution. They included the rack, the wheel, the iron maiden, burning at the stake, and impaling in the grave. A primary purpose of these execution methods was to cause prolonged suffering before death so that in the interim, heretics had the opportunity to confess, repent, and receive salvation.[113]

Thus, even though the official position of the Catholic Church today is against capital punishment, traditional Catholic teaching supported it. Thomas Aquinas cited the following passage from Corinthians:

> Now every individual person is compared to the whole community, as part to whole. Therefore, if a man be dangerous and infectious to the community on account of some sin [crime], it is praiseworthy and advantageous that he be killed in order to safeguard the common good, since "little leaven corrupts the whole lump."[114]

Traditional thinking of the Catholic Church further held that capital punishment is the best deterrent to crime.[115] Paul wrote in Romans 13:4, "It is not without purpose that the ruler carries the sword. He is God's servant, to inflict his avenging wrath upon the wrongdoer."[116] Therefore, if capital punishment is the only effective way to protect society from predatory behavior, it is considered both legitimate and necessary. The arguable issue, of course, is whether capital punishment is the only effective way to prevent crime.

Protestant scholar and journalist Reverend G. Aiken Taylor states that "most Christians tend to confuse the Christian personal ethic with the requirements of social order … we tend to apply what the Bible teaches us about how we—personally—should behave toward our neighbors with what the Bible teaches about how to preserve order in society."[117] This presumed difference between a personal and a social ethic is what may ultimately divide Christians on the subject of capital punishment. But before the ethical division is accepted, several questions must be addressed: (1) "Does God, then, have two different sets of rules by which he wants people to live?" (2) "Does he have one code for individuals as Christians and another for persons acting together, as they do in government?" (3) "Does he have one ethic for Christians and another for rulers and politicians?" (4) "What happens when Christians become part of their society's decision-making process, as in the case of a democracy?"[118] Answers to these questions may enable some Christians to reconcile their differences regarding capital punishment.

Protestant clergy member and scholar Reverend Reuben Hahn writes, "Not to inflict the death penalty is a flagrant disregard for God's divine law which recognizes the dignity of human life as a product of God's creation. Life is sacred, and that is why God instituted the death penalty—as a way to protect innocent human life."[119] The problem with this argument, counters legal scholar Charles Black, is that, "though the justice of God may indeed ordain that some should die, the justice of man is altogether and always insufficient for saying who these may be."[120]

CONCLUSION

The public's retributive feelings toward capital offenders are what ultimately may sustain the institution of capital punishment in the United States. The reason many people support the death penalty is vindictive revenge—they want to pay back offenders for what they have done. Death penalty opponents ask why capital offenders cannot be paid back with a noncapital punishment such as life imprisonment without opportunity of parole. They point out that no other crime is punished in kind.

A principal source of vindictive revenge is religion: The phrase "an eye for an eye," comes from the Bible. Yet, religious support for vindictive revenge, and for the death penalty, is puzzling because the Bible appears to be ambiguous on both subjects. An interesting question is how people, particularly people whose lives are governed by the Bible, can endorse revenge, support or oppose capital punishment, and use the Bible as a basis of their support or opposition, when they know the Bible is ambiguous on the subjects. Apparently not many people base their death penalty opinions on the Bible. When asked for their most important reason for favoring the death penalty for persons convicted of murder, only 3.2 percent of death penalty proponents in a 2008 national opinion survey responded, "The Bible says it is right," while 8.6 percent of death penalty opponents answered, "Religious convictions" as their most important reasons for opposing the death penalty.[121]

Still, religious support for capital punishment may be underestimated because public opinions, established over a long period of time, are difficult to change and probably lag behind changes in the official doctrines of organized religions. Moreover, in certain regions of the United States, religion may have more influence over death penalty opinions than in other regions. In the South, for example, religion may continue to exert an extraordinary influence on support for the death penalty, especially since the Southern Baptist Convention is one of the religious organizations that continues to support capital punishment.

Continued support for the death penalty, at least among some Christian groups, may be related to capital punishment's key role in the creation of Christianity. As New York state senator James Donovan is reported to have asked in a letter to a church group opposed to the state's enactment of a death penalty statute, "Where would Christianity be today had 'Jesus got 8 to 15 years with time off for good behavior'?"[122]

DISCUSSION QUESTIONS

1. What is retribution?
2. Is retribution an acceptable basis for supporting the death penalty?
3. Why do so many people seek retribution for crimes, in general, and capital crimes, in particular?
4. How or why does suffering something unpleasant count as payment for a criminal offense?
5. How are the intentions of the offender in regard to punishment to be discerned?
6. Why is it necessary to kill people who kill?

7. Given that the crime cannot be undone, what can the criminal justice system offer to the victim's family?
8. What kind of sentence can be imposed on a defendant found guilty of first-degree murder that is commensurate to the crime, protects society, and yet does not destroy the defendant's family in turn?
9. How can a thoughtful and sensible person justify killing people who kill in order to teach that killing is wrong?
10. Is the satisfaction of the desire for vindictive revenge a legitimate penal purpose?
11. Does pandering to or legitimizing the desire for vindictive revenge contribute to the violent social relationships that pervade our nation?
12. Does the Bible (both Old and New Testaments) support the death penalty? Does it matter?
13. How can people, particularly people schooled in the Bible, endorse revenge, support or oppose capital punishment, and use the Bible as the basis of their support or opposition, when they know the Bible is ambiguous on these subjects?
14. Should a religious person support the death penalty?

Notes

1. Bohm, Clark, and Aveni (1991), Finckenauer (1988), Firment and Geiselman (1997), Harris (1986), Kohlberg and Elfenbein (1975), Lotz and Regoli (1980), Sarat and Vidmar (1976), Vidmar (1974), and Warr and Stafford (1984). Most of the section on retribution is from Bohm (1992b).
2. Sharp (2008).
3. Hoffmann (1993, p. 124).
4. Lawes (1969, p. 9).
5. Cottingham (1979), Finckenauer (1988), Packer (1968), and Radin (1980).
6. Cottingham (1979, p. 238).
7. *Furman v. Georgia*, 408 U.S. 238, 1972 at 342.
8. Radin (1980, p. 1165).
9. *Furman v. Georgia*, 408 U.S. 238, 1972 at 308.
10. Ibid., at 332.
11. For example, see Jacoby (1983, p. 1).
12. Radin (1980, p. 1169).
13. Ibid.
14. Ibid.
15. Ibid.
16. Packer (1968, pp. 37–38).
17. Ibid.
18. Finckenauer (1988, p. 92).
19. Ibid., p. 93.
20. Cottingham (1979).
21. Ibid., p. 238.
22. Ibid.
23. Ibid., p. 239; also see Finckenauer (1988), Gale (1985), and Gibbs (1978).
24. Cottingham (1979).
25. Finckenauer (1988, p. 92).

26. Ibid., p. 91.
27. Personal correspondence with the author (1990).
28. See, for example, Marquis (2004, p. 149).
29. Cottingham (1979).
30. Radin (1980, p. 1164); also see Hoffmann (1993) on retribution and the death penalty for juveniles.
31. Cottingham (1979, p. 240).
32. Ibid., p. 241.
33. Ibid.
34. Ibid., p. 242.
35. Ibid.
36. Ibid., p. 243.
37. Ibid.
38. Ibid., pp. 243–244. The need for a secular rather than a religious justification of punishment may not be as strong today as it was when Cottingham originally wrote his analysis.
39. Ibid., p. 244.
40. Ibid., p. 245.
41. Ibid.
42. On the universality of retributive emotions, see Heider (1958) and Kelsen (1943); on the biological basis of retributive emotions, see Trivers (1971).
43. See, for example, Vidmar and Miller (1980, p. 581).
44. Ibid., p. 570.
45. Ibid., p. 571.
46. Ibid., p. 592.
47. Unnever and Cullen (2010b).
48. Ibid., p. 102.
49. Ibid., p. 104–105.
50. Ibid., p. 106–107.
51. Cited in Levey (2006, p. 38).
52. Ibid., p. 36.
53. Amsterdam (1982).
54. Erez (1981, p. 32).
55. Leviticus 24:22.
56. Exodus 21:23; Erez (1981, p. 37).
57. Hoffmann (1993, p. 120).
58. *Furman v. Georgia*, 408 U.S. 238, 1972 at 303.
59. More than 70 percent of the world's countries (139) have now abolished capital punishment in law or practice. More than 50 countries have abolished the penalty since 1990. Fifty-eight countries have retained it, although only a few execute in a given year. In 2009, for example, about 700 prisoners were executed in 18 countries. This does not count China, which does not report executions but is believed to have executed thousands. Amnesty International, retrieved November 24, 2010, from http://www.amnesty.org/en/death-penalty.
60. Vandiver reports the finding that approximately 16.4 million American adults have lost (1) immediate family members to homicide (5 million; includes vehicular homicide), (2) other relatives (6.6 million), or (3) close friends (4.8 million); see Vandiver (2003, p. 615). One covictim observes that the resolution of a capital case provides three benefits: (1) it holds perpetrators accountable for their heinous crimes; (2) it provides some degree of "judicial closure," that is, at least the perpetrator is imprisoned during what may be a lengthy appellate process; and (3) "it allows victims to begin to construct a 'new sense of normal'"; Levey (2006).

61. Cited in Zimring (2003, p. 61).
62. Sharp (2008).
63. Cited in Sarat (2006a, p. 220, n. 30).
64. On the meager research on covictims, see Acker and Karp (2006) and Vandiver (2006). On the issue of closure, see Acker (2006), Coleman (2006), Levey (2006), Roper (2006), Rosenbluth (2006), and White (2006).
65. Cited in Levey (2006, p. 44).
66. Cited in Ellis, Ho, and Seymour (2006, p. 436).
67. Zimring (2003, pp. 57–63).
68. Ibid., p. 58.
69. Ibid., pp. 51–52.
70. Ibid., p. 55.
71. Ibid., p. 62.
72. Ibid.
73. For a more detailed description of the effects of the death penalty on the families of homicide victims, see Bohm (2010) and Vandiver (2003).
74. Vandiver (2003, pp. 616–617); also see Bohm (2010) and Reed and Blackwell (2006).
75. Vandiver (2003, pp. 635–636); for the personal accounts of "covictims," see Coleman (2006), Cushing (2002), Kimble (2006), Levey (2006), Roper (2006), Rosenbluth (2006), Wagner (2006), Welch (2002), and White (2006). Professor Borg (1998) found significant variation in support of the death penalty among what she called "vicarious victims." Vicarious victims who were black, female, and non-evangelicals were less likely to support the death penalty than were whites, males, and evangelicals.
76. Cited in Levey (2006, p. 44).
77. King (2006) and Vandiver (2003, p. 638).
78. Turow (2003, pp. 52–53).
79. Some Won't Watch When McVeigh Dies. (2001, April 22). *The Orlando Sentinel*, p. A3.
80. Acker and Mastrocinque (2006, p. 149); also see Zimring (2003, pp. 55–57).
81. Vandiver (2003, p. 613).
82. Lawes (1969, pp. 10–11).
83. Vandiver (2003, pp. 624–625).
84. Ibid. p. 624.
85. Beck, Britto, and Andrews (2007), Radelet, Vandiver, and Barado (1983), Smykla (1987), and Vandiver (1989, 2003); also see Eschholz, Reed, Beck, and Leonard (2003), Ingle (1989), Kaczynski and Wright (2006), King (2006), Prejean (1993), and Sharp (2005).
86. However, see Bohm (2010); on correctional personnel, see Abramson and Isay (2002), Cabana (1996), and Johnson (1998); on judges, see Dickson (2006), Hintze (2006), and Leyte-Vidal and Silverman (2006); on prosecutors or state attorneys, see Gillette (2006) and Hawkins (2006); on defense attorneys, see Ottinger (2002), Stafford-Smith (2002), and Walker (2006); on jurors, see Antonio (2006).
87. See Committee on the Judiciary, U.S. Senate (1982), Van den Haag and Conrad (1983), and Vidmar and Miller (1980).
88. Schwarzschild in Bedau (1982).
89. See Bohm (1992b). The desire for vindictive revenge is not shared by all covictims. As the daughter of a murder victim explains, "I think people don't actually want vengeance. They would like to end their pain. Sometimes they think it's a zero-sum game: if they can make someone else feel pain, theirs will go away. I just don't think it works that way." Cited in Levey (2006, pp. 44–45). Also, research indicates that few jurors who return death sentences do so because of vengeful feelings. For example, in one study only 1 percent of death-returning jurors responded that "feelings of vengeance or revenge" were "very

important" to their decision; an additional 4 percent stated that it was "fairly important." Cited in Sundby (2005, p. 200, n. 5). These jurors are more likely to say that a defendant convicted of a capital crime creates a moral imbalance that can only be remedied by sentencing the defendant to death. A life sentence, on the other hand, cannot right the imbalance in part because prison life is too easy. Sundby, ibid., p. 127.

90. *Furman v. Georgia*, 1972 at 343.
91. Bedau (1982, pp. 305–306).
92. Gow (1986, p. 80).
93. Religious Leaders in Florida (1986, p. 87).
94. Ibid.
95. The survey was conducted in August and September of 2006. Originally, 193 religious organizations in the United States were identified from a listing provided by the Hartford Institute for Religion Research at http://hirr.hartsem.edu/org/faith_denominations_homepages.html. For various reasons, 67 of the organizations did not respond (22 of the organizations had invalid contact information), leaving 126 organizations that did respond (a 65% response rate, or a 74% response rate if the organizations with invalid contact information are excluded). My thanks to Gavin Lee for conducting the survey.
96. Demographic data from the 2006 death penalty poll were obtained directly from the Gallup Organization. My thanks to Maura A. Strausberg, Data Librarian, for her help. Also see Carroll (2004).
97. Ostling (2005).
98. A Portrait of American Catholics on the Eve of Pope Benedict's Visit to the U.S. (2008).
99. Unnever, Cullen, and Bartkowski (2006); also see Applegate, Cullen, Fisher, and Ven (2000).
100. Grasmick, Cochran, Bursik, and Kimpel (1993).
101. Britt (1998); also see Young (1992).
102. Kehler et al. (1985, pp. 5–6) and Religious Leaders in Florida (1986, p. 88). Haines (1996, p. 103) claims that as many as 33 offenses in the Old Testament may have been punished by death.
103. Erez (1981, p. 29), Kehler et al. (1985, p. 6), and Religious Leaders in Florida (1986, p. 88). Erez reports that Hebrew law forbade the mutilation of an executed person's body.
104. Cited in Gow (1986, p. 84).
105. Ibid.; also see Kania (1999) for additional passages supporting capital punishment in the Old Testament, as well as in the Koran.
106. Erez (1981, pp. 33–36) and Kehler et al. (1985, pp. 57–58).
107. Cited in Kehler et al. (1985, p. 8); also see Haines (1996, p. 104).
108. Religious Leaders in Florida (1986); also see Kehler (1985, pp. 1–2) for a similar Christian perspective.
109. Koch in Gow (1986, p. 81).
110. Gow (1986, p. 82).
111. Kehler et al. (1985) and Religious Leaders in Florida (1986, pp. 88–89).
112. Bowers (1984, pp. 132–133).
113. Ibid., p. 133.
114. Cited in Gow (1986, p. 83).
115. Ibid.
116. Ibid., p. 84.
117. Ibid.
118. Kehler et al. (1985, p. 12).
119. Cited in Gow (1986, p. 85).
120. Black (1974, p. 96).
121. Sharp (2008).
122. Quoted in Bedau (1982, p. 305).

American death penalty opinion[1]

Nearly 40 years after the Supreme Court's decision in *Furman v. Georgia* (1972)—the ruling that temporarily halted capital punishment in the United States—64 percent of adult Americans indicated that they favor the death penalty for persons convicted of murder. This level of support is substantially lower than the 80 percent that favored the death penalty in a 1994 poll, which was the highest level of support in more than 70 years of scientific opinion polling.[2] However, it is considerably higher than in 1966—the year that death penalty support fell to 42 percent, its lowest level ever.[3] In 1994, only 16 percent of respondents opposed the death penalty and 4 percent had no opinion; in 1966, 47 percent of respondents opposed the death penalty and 11 percent had no opinion. In no year for which polls are available has a majority of Americans opposed capital punishment.

WHY AMERICAN DEATH PENALTY OPINION IS IMPORTANT

American death penalty opinion is important because such opinion, perhaps more than any other factor, probably accounts for the continued use of capital punishment in many jurisdictions in the United States. If most citizens in death penalty jurisdictions opposed capital punishment, it is unlikely the penalty would be employed. In the 1980s, attorney David Bruck predicted that the death penalty's "political potency" could be effectively neutralized if only a quarter to a third of death penalty proponents could be convinced to oppose the penalty.[4] Strong public support may contribute to the continued use of capital punishment in at least five ways. First, it probably sways legislators to vote in favor of death penalty statutes (and against their repeal).[5] Few politicians are willing to ignore the preferences of most of their constituents.[6] Support of capital punishment is also a rather easy way for politicians to signal and demonstrate their more conservative "law and order" credentials.

Second, strong public support likely influences some prosecutors to seek the death penalty for political rather than legal purposes in cases where they might ordinarily plea bargain. As White relates from his interviews with defense attorneys:

Some prosecutors are more reluctant to plea bargain now than they were a few years ago, because they feel that in today's climate failure to seek the death penalty in certain types of cases could have a devastating effect on their political careers.[7]

Third, to retain their positions, some trial-court judges feel public pressure to impose death sentences in cases in which such is inappropriate, and some appellate-court judges may uphold death sentences on appeal when they should not.[8] Among judges removed from office following their unpopular death penalty decisions were: Chief Justice Rose Bird and justices Cruz Reynoso and

Joseph Grodin of the California Supreme Court, Tennessee Supreme Court Justice Penny White, Mississippi Supreme Court Justice James Robertson, Justice Charles Campbell of the Texas Court of Criminal Appeals, Texas District Court Judge Norman Lanford, and Washington Supreme Court Justice Robert Utter.[9]

Fourth, some governors may be dissuaded from vetoing death penalty legislation and commuting death sentences because of strong public support for the penalty. With regard to commutations, it is instructive to note that prior to 1970, governors in death penalty states "routinely commuted up to a third of the death sentences that they reviewed.... Today, however, commutations of death sentences by governors [and review boards] are rare events."[10] Few governors are willing to ignore what they perceive are their constituents' preferences.[11] Furthermore, support of capital punishment generally defines for his or her constituents much of a governor's political agenda—at least the part that concerns crime.

Fifth, and arguably most important, strong public support might be used, at least indirectly, by justices of both state supreme courts and the U.S. Supreme Court as a measure of evolving standards of decency regarding what constitutes cruel and unusual punishment in state constitutions and under the Eighth Amendment of the U.S. Constitution.[12] Decline in public support was cited as such a measure in the *Furman* decision.[13] Regarding the US Supreme Court, Baumgartner and his colleagues claim that "the majority opinion in each major death penalty decision in the last century cited polling data by Gallup or other major survey houses in support of the ruling, whether for or against capital punishment."[14]

This chapter is divided into three major sections. First is the history of American death penalty opinion. This section describes what is called here "the too simple and, therefore, misleading death penalty opinion question period." The second section surveys the present period and chronicles what is called "the more complex and revealing death penalty opinion question period." This section begins with a description of research that tested the hypothesis that death penalty support is largely a product of ignorance about the way capital punishment is actually administered. The final section addresses the future of American death penalty opinion and the effect it may have on the practice of capital punishment in the United States.

THE HISTORY OF AMERICAN DEATH PENALTY OPINION: THE TOO SIMPLE AND, THEREFORE, MISLEADING DEATH PENALTY OPINION QUESTION PERIOD

The American Institute of Public Opinion, producer of the Gallup polls, conducted interviews for the first scientific death penalty opinion poll in the United States in December 1936.[15] The poll gauged public sentiment about the death penalty in light of the unprecedented media attention given to the execution of Bruno Hauptmann, the alleged kidnapper and murderer of the Lindbergh baby. The poll showed that 61 percent of the 2,201 adults interviewed "believe[d] in the death penalty for murder" and 39 percent did not.[16] The category of "no opinion" or "don't know" was not included as an option. Since the first poll, dozens of surveys of American death penalty opinion have been conducted.[17]

The most recent Gallup poll on death penalty opinion in the United States, conducted in 2010, found that 64 percent of Americans were in favor of the death penalty for a person convicted of murder,

29 percent opposed, and 7 percent did not know or refused to respond.[18] Note the slight difference in the wording of the questions in the 1936 and 2010 polls. In the 1936 poll, respondents were asked, "Do you believe in the death penalty for murder?" (In the 1937 and later Gallup polls, respondents were asked, "Do you favor or oppose capital punishment for murder?") Respondents to the 2010 poll answered the question, "Are you in favor of the death penalty for a person convicted of murder?" It is doubtful that the subtle differences significantly altered the resulting opinions, but even a small change in the wording of questions and response categories can make an important difference in the distribution of opinions.[19]

Over the past 74 years or so, support of and opposition to capital punishment have varied substantially.[20] However, when the increases and decreases are plotted over time, a "v" shape can be observed (with a slight downward tail in recent years). Viewing the "v" shape from left to right, in 1936, 61 percent of respondents favored the death penalty; in 1966, only 42 percent of respondents favored it; but by 2010, 64 percent of respondents supported it. Put differently, between 1936 and 2010 there has been an overall 3 percentage point increase in support and a 10 percentage point decrease in opposition to the death penalty. The 7 percentage point difference between overall support and opposition is a function of the respondents with "no opinion" or who refused to respond in the 2010 poll (the "no opinion" or "refused to respond" categories were not included in the 1936 poll). When the 74-year period is divided into the 1936–1966 and the 1966–2010 periods, the relatively precipitous decrease then increase in support (or increase then decrease in opposition) for the penalty is readily apparent. Support of capital punishment between 1936 and 1966 decreased 19 percentage points, while opposition increased 8 percentage points (the difference is due to the 11 percent of "no opinion" responses in the 1966 poll). On the other hand, between 1966 and 2010, support of the death penalty increased 22 percentage points, while opposition decreased 18 percentage points (again, the difference is attributable to changes in "no opinions" or "refused to responds").

A detailed analysis of the 52 percent increase in death penalty support since 1966 has yet to be written. It appears, however, that the *Furman* decision played an important part. As noted, 1966 marked the nadir in death penalty support in the United States; yet by 1967, support for the penalty had risen to 53 percent and opposition had decreased to 39 percent—an 11 percentage point increase in support and an 8 percentage point decrease in opposition.[21] The increase in support was relatively short-lived because by the end of 1971 death penalty support had fallen to 49 percent.[22] The Court's decision in *Furman v. Georgia* was announced on June 29, 1972. Two 1972 Gallup polls asked about death penalty opinions, one before the *Furman* announcement (interviews March 3 through 5) and one after it (interviews November 10 through 13).[23] In the pre-*Furman* poll, 50 percent of respondents favored the death penalty, 42 percent opposed it, and 9 percent had no opinion. The poll conducted post-*Furman* showed that 57 percent of respondents supported capital punishment, only 32 percent opposed it, and 11 percent had no opinion.[24] In short, between March and November 1972, approximately 4 months before and 4 months after the announcement of the *Furman* decision, support for the death penalty increased 7 percentage points and opposition dropped 10 percentage points. Although other factors may have had an effect, it appears that significant public discontent with the *Furman* decision was decisive.

Following the *Furman* decision, public support for the death penalty trended upward for the next two decades peaking in 1994 at 80 percent. By 1996, however, death penalty support began a downward trajectory, as the media stepped up its reporting "of legal action based on DNA evidence and concerns about the possible innocence of death row inmates and the fallibility of the system."[25] The Death Penalty Information Center (DPIC) would report that the year 2000 "was perhaps the most significant single year affecting death penalty opinion in United States history. A broad change in the way the American public views capital punishment was precipitated by a steady sequence of eye-opening events, including releases from death row, reports on the unfairness of the process, and governmental action to limit or halt the death penalty."[26] Adding to this momentum, the DPIC's report noted:

> Former supporters of the death penalty joined long-time critics in raising concerns about the accuracy and fairness of capital punishment in America. More conservative voices, such as those of Rev. Pat Robertson, Oliver North, new Congressman Tom Osborne of Nebraska, columnist George Will, and others voiced strong criticisms of the death penalty. The risk of taking innocent lives and the gross inequities in the way the death penalty is applied have led to a new consensus that the system is seriously broken.[27]

DEMOGRAPHIC CHARACTERISTICS OF RESPONDENTS

Recent polls have included a greater variety of questions about death penalty opinions, whereas earlier polls focused primarily on the percentage distribution of opinions themselves and the percentage distribution of opinions by demographic characteristics of respondents.[28] Most of the Gallup polls provide information on the following 10 demographic characteristics: (1) gender, (2) race, (3) age, (4) politics, (5) education, (6) income or socioeconomic status (SES), (7) occupation, (8) religion, (9) city size, and (10) region of the country.[29]

During the first half century of Gallup polling, between 1936 and 1986, five of the demographic characteristics varied substantially and five of them did not.[30] Characteristics showing greatest variation, in order of the magnitude of the variation, were race, income or SES, gender, politics, and region of the country. In other words, between 1936 and 1986, whites, wealthier people, males, Republicans, and Westerners tended to support the death penalty more than blacks, poorer people, females, Democrats, and Southerners.[31] The characteristics showing much less variation over the 50 years were age, education, occupation, religion, and city size.

A majority of people in all demographic categories, except race, supported the death penalty in the 1986 poll, but there was substantial variation within categories for all the demographic characteristics except religion. City size was not a category in the 1986 poll. Blacks, females, people under 30 years, Democrats, college graduates, people in the bottom income or SES category, manual laborers, Easterners, and Southerners were less likely to support or more likely to oppose the death penalty than were whites, males, Republicans, high school graduates, people in the top income category, clerical and sales workers, Westerners, and Midwesterners.[32]

In the 2006 poll (the most recent one available that reports demographic characteristics), death penalty support exceeded 50 percent in every social category examined except race, with "only" 49 percent of nonwhites favoring the death penalty.[33] (67% of nonwhites favored the death penalty in the 2002 poll.) Although separate data for blacks were not reported in the 2006 poll, nearly 60 percent of blacks have supported the penalty in recent years. Black support in the past has been much lower. A recent study found that black proponents are hardly distinguishable in other characteristics from their white counterparts. Black proponents tend to be male, married, politically conservative, have high incomes, come from middle- and upper-class backgrounds, live in urban areas and the South, are afraid of crime, have never been arrested, and perceive that the courts are too lenient with criminals.[34]

The 2006 poll included information about eight of the 10 demographic characteristics reported in the earlier polls plus seven additional ones. The categories of occupation and city size were omitted. Characteristics showing the greatest variation, in order of the magnitude of that variation, were ideology, political party, race, sex/age, education, marital status, religion, sex, income, region of the country, age, and type of community. Thus, in 2006, conservatives, Republicans, whites, males 50 years or older, people with some college education, married people, Protestants, males, people with annual incomes of $30,000–$74,999, Southerners, people age 50–64, and rural residents favored the death penalty more than liberals, Democrats, nonwhites, females 50 or older, people with postgraduate educations, unmarried people, non-Christians, females, people with annual incomes of less than $20,000, Easterners, people age 65 or older, and urban residents. The characteristics with insignificant variation were employment, church attendance, and having children under 18 years.[35] The characteristics (for which there are comparable data) that have consistently distinguished death penalty opinions from 1936 through 2006 are race, sex, political party, and income. That is, over the 70 years from 1936 through 2006, whites, males, Republicans, and wealthier people have been more likely to support the death penalty than nonwhites, females, Democrats, and poorer people.

In a recent analysis, Baumer and his colleagues found that death penalty opinion was a function of both the characteristics of individuals and the social environment.[36] They discovered significant community-level variation in support of the death penalty, while controlling for standard demographic characteristics. Some areas had very high levels of support, other areas had more modest levels of support, and in some areas, a majority of residents opposed the death penalty.[37] Residents of local areas with higher levels of homicide, a larger proportion of blacks (but much less than a majority), and a more conservative political climate were more likely to support the death penalty.[38]

These data show that there is much variation in death penalty opinions within various groups and not just between them.[39] With regard to religious belief in general and Protestant support for the death penalty in particular, for example, recent research by Unnever and his colleagues found that Americans who believe in a wrathful-punitive God are more likely to support the death penalty for convicted murderers than those with a personal relationship with a loving-forgiving God.[40] In another study, Unnever and his associates also found that less empathetic individuals were more likely than more empathetic individuals to support the death penalty. They defined empathy as "the imaginative transporting of oneself into the thinking, feeling, and acting of another and by doing so viewing the world as the person does."[41] Grasmick and his colleagues discovered that "evangelical/fundamentalist" Protestants were more likely to favor the death penalty than were "liberal/moderate" Protestants.[42] And Britt reported that white fundamentalists were more likely to support the death penalty than were black fundamentalists.[43]

In the case of regional variation, a recent study using General Social Survey data by Barkan and Cohn found that before 1993, Southern whites were no more likely to support capital punishment than were non-Southern whites. However, since 1993, and through 2006, Southern whites have been somewhat more likely to support the death penalty than have non-Southern whites. Conversely, since 1993, Northeastern whites have been somewhat less likely than non-Northeastern whites to support the death penalty.[44]

Still, for the most part, the same sorts of people continue to favor the death penalty the most strongly. Based on findings from the most recent Gallup poll then, it is not much of an exaggeration to state that most Americans favor the death penalty—or so it seems.

THE PRESENT: THE MORE COMPLEX AND REVEALING DEATH PENALTY OPINION QUESTION PERIOD

Little critical scrutiny of the figures presented in various death penalty opinion polls existed prior to the *Furman* decision in 1972. The reported percentages of support and opposition were generally accepted as accurate indicators of public sentiment. One of the first people to question the validity of death penalty opinion poll results, albeit indirectly, while at the same time emphasizing their importance, was former Supreme Court Justice Thurgood Marshall.

THE MARSHALL HYPOTHESES

Justice Marshall stressed in his opinion in *Furman v. Georgia* the importance of public opinion with respect to the constitutionality of the death penalty. He identified several standards by which to judge whether a punishment is cruel and unusual. One such standard was: "where a punishment is not excessive and serves a valid legislative purpose, it still may be invalid if popular sentiment abhors it."[45] Thus wrote Marshall, "It is imperative for constitutional purposes to attempt to discern the probable opinion of an informed electorate."[46] He stressed that the public's choice about the death penalty must be "a knowledgeable choice."[47]

Like many other opponents, Marshall believed that, given information about it, "the great mass of citizens would conclude … that the death penalty is immoral and therefore unconstitutional."[48] He assumed that support of the penalty is a function of a lack of knowledge about it and that opinions are responsive to reasoned persuasion. The one exception to his assumption was that if the underlying basis of support for the penalty was retribution, then knowledge would have little effect on opinions. Though some of his colleagues on the Court disagreed with him, Marshall maintained that retribution "is a goal that the legislature cannot constitutionally pursue as its sole justification for capital punishment."[49] He added, "I cannot believe that at this stage in our history, the American people would ever knowingly support purposeless vengeance."[50]

Social scientists did not take long to subject Marshall's assertions to empirical investigation. Two of the first three studies that systematically tested all or part of what have become known as "Marshall's hypotheses" were conducted in the United States; the third was conducted in Canada. A fourth study employing Stanford University undergraduates as subjects, although not a direct test of Marshall's hypotheses, is nevertheless relevant and will be discussed shortly. In one of the American studies, subjects were from the San Francisco Bay area, and the data were collected in 1974.[51] In the other, subjects were from Amherst, Massachusetts, and data were collected in 1975.[52] The Canadian study does not indicate when data were collected.[53] Three of the four studies support all or part of the Marshall hypotheses,[54] although possible problems relating to social conditions at the times data were collected and to methodology render the findings potentially inapplicable to current experience and generally invalid.

Following the *Furman* decision in 1972, there was a flurry of activity as 36 states moved to adopt new death penalty statutes that would meet the Supreme Court's requirements. Thus, at the times the Marshall hypotheses data were being collected in 1974 and 1975, the theory of the death penalty was receiving much media and public attention. A distorting factor in the research, though, was that no one had been executed in the United States since 1967, and no one in Canada since 1962. This moratorium made the issue of capital punishment "abstract" in that the respondents had no recent experience with it. Public opinion about the death penalty is sometimes dramatically different when people consider it in "concrete" situations (at times when people are being executed) rather than in the abstract.

A methodological dilemma for all studies of this type is operationalizing the concept of "informed" or "knowledgeable about the death penalty." According to Justice Marshall, for "the average citizen" (excepting those who base their opinion on retribution), some knowledge is "critical" to an informed opinion and "would almost surely convince [the average citizen] that the death penalty was unwise."[55] For Marshall, an informed citizen would know some of the following:

> that the death penalty is no more effective a deterrent than life imprisonment; that convicted murderers are rarely executed, but are usually sentenced to a term in prison; that convicted murderers usually are model prisoners, and that they almost always become law-abiding citizens upon their release from prison; that the costs of executing a capital offender exceed the costs of imprisoning him for life; that while in prison, a convict under sentence of death performs none of the useful functions that life prisoners perform; that no attempt is made in the sentencing process to ferret out likely recidivists for execution; and that the death penalty may actually stimulate criminal activity … capital punishment is imposed discriminatorily against certain identifiable classes of people; there is evidence that innocent people have been executed before their innocence can be proved; and the death penalty wreaks havoc with our entire criminal justice system.[56]

What Marshall fails to stipulate is how much of this information a citizen must know in order to be informed. Must one know all of it or will 50–60 percent suffice? Without setting a standard, Marshall leaves unanswered the key question of what it means to be informed or knowledgeable about the death penalty.

Results of the fourth study, the one using Stanford University undergraduates as subjects, differed dramatically from the results of the other three studies. The authors of the fourth study discovered that knowledge or information can have an entirely different effect on death penalty opinions than the one supposed by Marshall.[57] Lord and his colleagues found that information about the death penalty polarized opinions, instead of changing them from in favor to opposed or vice versa.[58] In other words, subjects who initially favored the death penalty tended to favor it more strongly after receiving information about it, while subjects who initially opposed the death penalty tended to oppose it even more after becoming informed. The researchers attributed polarization to biased assimilation, that is, subjects interpreted evidence so as to maintain their initial beliefs:

> Data relevant to a belief are not processed impartially. Instead judgments about the validity, reliability, relevance, and sometimes even the meaning of proffered evidence are biased by the apparent consistency of that evidence with the perceiver's theories and expectations. Thus individuals will dismiss and discount empirical evidence that contradicts their initial views and will derive support from evidence, of no greater probativeness, that seems consistent with their views.[59]

Ellsworth and Ross believe that biased assimilation is a probable explanation for the effect of knowledge on opinions in their study:

> [We] are tempted to infer that the attitude [opinion] comes first and the reasons second.... It looks very much as though our respondents simply went down the list of reasons, checking whatever side of the scale was compatible with their general attitude [opinion] toward capital punishment. The picture that emerges is one of an emotionally based attitude [opinion], tempered by a sense of social desirability.[60]

In short, contrary to expectations held by Justice Marshall and many other opponents, information about the death penalty may not significantly reduce the public support that currently exists for capital punishment. Notwithstanding the support for Marshall's hypotheses, if the results of the Lord study are reliable, the effect of exposing people to information about the death penalty may be to polarize them on the issue.

Two other methodological problems with the studies are related to the validity of the experimental stimulus and the experimental manipulation. The first problem involves the form that "knowledge" takes, and the second has to do with the way "knowledge" is imparted to subjects. In the 1976 study by Sarat and Vidmar, the experimental conditions involved reading two 1,500-word essays that described "scientific and other information" about the death penalty. The experimental manipulation was preceded by a pretest and followed by a posttest. The entire operation took only 1 hour. Sarat and Vidmar are candid about the inadequacies of the manipulation:

> Without question our information manipulations had limited potential for developing truly informed opinion about the death penalty—the issues are intricate and complex while the essays are short and simple; furthermore, exposure to the information took place in a brief interview session without time for reflection, discussion, or clarification.[61]

The experimental manipulation proved somewhat successful, nevertheless. On the pretest, 62 percent of the (181 randomly selected adult) experimental subjects favored the death penalty, 27 percent opposed it, and 10 percent were undecided. On the posttest, 42 percent favored the death penalty, 38 percent opposed it, and 21 percent were undecided. The experimental stimulus did not produce a majority of subjects opposed to the death penalty, but it did decrease support and increase opposition and indecision.

The 1981 study by Vidmar and Dittenhoffer improved the validity of the experimental manipulation in Sarat and Vidmar by increasing the opportunity for subjects to assimilate information about the death penalty. In this study, subjects were asked to read a 3,500-word essay on the death penalty (emphasizing the Canadian experience) and a series of eight articles. The articles contained representative material intended to augment the essay. The subjects also had the option of reading two books—Sellin's *Capital Punishment* (1967) and Bedau's *The Death Penalty in America* (1967)—and were invited to pursue any other related reading. After 2 weeks, subjects met in small, unsupervised discussion groups to "freely discuss the facts and issues involved in the capital punishment debate and to try to reach a final decision within an hour."[62] The experimental manipulation was preceded by a pretest and was followed by a posttest.

The results of the Vidmar and Dittenhoffer study indicate that the experimental manipulation was effective. On the pretest, 48 percent of the experimental subjects favored the death penalty, 33 percent were opposed to it, and 19 percent were undecided. On the posttest, 24 percent were in favor, 71 percent opposed, and 5 percent were undecided. The experimental stimulus of Vidmar and Dittenhoffer, unlike the one used by Sarat and Vidmar, did produce a majority of subjects opposed to the death penalty.

Despite the improvement of the experimental manipulation of Vidmar and Dittenhoffer over the one used by Sarat and Vidmar, the study by Vidmar and Dittenhoffer still had serious deficiencies. First, the experimental group consisted of only 21 nonrandomly selected students (18 in the control group). Second, the experimenters had to assume that the subjects did indeed read the assigned material. Third, even if subjects did read the material, it was not possible to determine how much of the material was comprehended. As to the discussion groups, Vidmar and Dittenhoffer are probably correct that discussion should enhance conditions for opinion change because active learning is presumed to be more conducive to opinion change than passive learning.[63] However, without supervision, the experimenters could not be sure of what happened in the groups. Was the death penalty in fact discussed? Did one member of the group dominate discussion? Were some of the group members intimidated or angered by others? Furthermore, a discussion of only 1 hour was probably not long enough for such an "intricate and complex" topic. Subjects were not given sufficient opportunity to reflect upon contradictory beliefs or to research information about which they disagreed. A discussion of only 1 hour also allowed a persuasive speaker to have extraordinary influence. In short, a discussion period of only 1 hour was probably not long enough to produce the intended effects of the experimental manipulation.

For these and other reasons, Bohm and his colleagues, beginning in the mid-1980s, conducted a series of studies that used an experimental manipulation that provided subjects with more information, provided greater control over the circumstances in which the information was acquired, and allowed subjects more time to evaluate and integrate the information into their own systems of beliefs. The experimental stimulus employed by Bohm and his colleagues was a college class on the death penalty.[64]

A death penalty class generally met a total of 40 hours a semester. Bedau's *The Death Penalty in America*, third edition (1982), was the assigned text for the course. Coursework included lectures by the instructor, presentations by guest speakers, videos, and discussion. Topics discussed were the history of the death penalty in the United States, with special emphasis on relevant Supreme Court cases, public opinion, evidence about general deterrence and incapacitation, religious and retribution arguments, and information on the administration of the death penalty (e.g., sources of arbitrariness and discrimination, executions of innocent persons, and costs).

In most of the experiments, subjects completed questionnaires at the beginning and the end of the semester. Although their content varied somewhat from semester to semester, the questionnaires, at minimum, generally sought information about the three principal variables in Marshall's hypotheses: opinions toward the death penalty, knowledge about the death penalty, and desire for retribution. The questionnaires also asked for demographic information about the subjects.

Bohm and his colleagues measured death penalty opinions with four questions because they believed that the general opinion question asked in the Gallup and other polls did not accurately reflect the complexity of public sentiment about the penalty. Each of the questions represented a different type of support or nonsupport for the death penalty. The first question was: "Which of the following statements best describes your position toward the death penalty for all persons convicted of first-degree murder?"[65] Only 28.3 percent of less-informed subjects opposed the death penalty for all persons convicted of first-degree murder (24.7% of males, 31.1% of females, 18.3% of whites, 37.6%

of blacks), but 46.6 percent of well-informed subjects were opposed to it (41.2% of males, 51.1% of females, 32.3% of whites, 60% of blacks).[66]

A second question asked subjects whether they favored the death penalty for "some people convicted of first-degree murder." This question is the one that is most similar to the general death penalty opinion question asked in the Gallup and other polls. Results for this question are similar to those for the previous one: 28 percent of less-informed subjects opposed the death penalty (24.7% of males, 30% of females, 22.6% of whites, 30.6% of blacks), but 49.5 percent of well-informed subjects opposed it (49.5% of males, 50% of females, 40.9% of whites, 56.6% of blacks).[67]

The third and fourth questions were asked because prior research has found that support for the death penalty is greatly reduced when a distinction is made between support in the abstract and support in concrete situations.[68] The first concrete question was: "If you served on a jury in a trial where the defendant, if found guilty, would automatically be sentenced to death, could you convict that defendant?" Only 22.5 percent of less-informed subjects could not convict (14.4% of males, 30% of females, 5.4% of whites, 23.5% of blacks), while 34.4 percent of well-informed subjects could not convict (30% of males, 38% of females, 21.5% of whites, 47.1% of blacks).[69]

The second concrete question was: "If asked to do it, could you pull the lever that would result in the death of an individual convicted of first-degree murder?" On this question, 47.2 percent of less-informed subjects could not pull the lever (45.4% of males, 55.5% of females, 37.6% of whites, 64.7% of blacks), while 49.6 percent of well-informed subjects could not pull the lever (50.5% of males, 62.2% of females, 40.9% of whites, 72.9% of blacks).[70]

Another reason for asking subjects four different death penalty questions was to ascertain whether subjects had a "coherent moral position" toward capital punishment. As Radin explains:

> The reason it is often suggested that one ought to look to what people do rather than what they say, or even more pointedly, that those who favor the death penalty should be asked whether they would be willing to pull the switch themselves, is that a person is more likely to have reached a coherent moral position if she is going to be required to transform her beliefs into action.[71]

Although Bohm and his colleagues wondered how people could have a coherent moral position toward the death penalty when they were ignorant about the subject, they nevertheless examined whether responses to the four questions formed a Guttman scale and thus were indicative of a coherent moral position. To their surprise, the findings suggested that their subjects did indeed hold coherent moral positions toward the death penalty, whether they were informed or not.[72] When they used subjects' Guttman scale coefficients as measures of opposition to capital punishment, Bohm et al. found that while only 34.7 percent of less-informed subjects opposed capital punishment, 56.3 percent of well-informed subjects opposed it.[73] This was the only measure that produced a majority of all subjects opposed to the penalty.

In sum, results of this research provided at least qualified support for all three of Marshall's hypotheses.[74] Subjects generally lacked knowledge about the death penalty and its administration prior to exposure to the experimental stimulus but were more informed following it. To the degree that retribution provided the basis for support of the death penalty, knowledge had little effect on opinions. The hypothesis that an informed public would generally oppose the death penalty was supported in one test but not in others. (In some tests, a majority of black males and a majority of black females and white females opposed the death penalty.) Thus, even though support for the death penalty might decline after subjects have been informed, the reduction may not be great enough to create a majority opposed to the death penalty.[75] This may hold true even when subjects are asked diverse death penalty opinion questions, such as "personal involvement" questions.[76]

Other findings of this research include the following:

- Exposure to death penalty information may result in the polarization of opinions (favoring or opposing more strongly);[77]
- It may be more difficult for subjects to change their positions if they have to publicly announce their death penalty opinions;[78]
- Initial beliefs about the death penalty and such issues as deterrence, revenge, and incapacitation generally are not affected by giving people information about those issues;[79] and
- When opinions about the death penalty do change, it is most likely because of administrative reasons such as racial discrimination or execution of innocent people.[80]

However, when the death penalty opinions of subjects in the 1988 and 1989 classes were examined 2 and 3 years later, it was discovered that opinions on the two abstract death penalty opinion questions (i.e., "Do you favor or oppose the death penalty for all and for some people convicted of first-degree murder?") had rebounded to near their initial pretest positions.[81] Opinions on the two concrete death penalty opinion questions (i.e., could you convict? and could you pull the lever?) did not change significantly for the 1988 and 1989 classes at any of the three points in time (pretest, posttest, or follow-up).[82] Another follow-up study of the 1988 and 1989 death penalty classes more than 10 years after students completed the class revealed small increases in support of the death penalty from the first follow-up period on the abstract opinion measures.[83] However, as was the case in the first follow-up study, the personal involvement measures did not change significantly in the second follow-up study.[84] Results of the follow-up studies also do not appear to be a function of a loss of knowledge, the irrelevancy of the death penalty class, or the influence of the instructor.[85] Why, then, did opinions rebound? Perhaps it was because death penalty opinions are based primarily on emotion rather than on cognition and that, in the long run, cognitive influences on death penalty opinions give way to emotional factors.

Results of the follow-up studies suggest that most death penalty opinions may not be significantly influenced by increased knowledge about the penalty or may be influenced only temporarily, at least if that knowledge is obtained in a college classroom.[86] If Justice Marshall had in mind a stimulus like the one employed in the research by Bohm and his colleagues, then Marshall's belief that death penalty opinions can be changed substantially (by increasing knowledge about the subject) may be wrong. This does not mean that the opinions are intransigent. Opinions do change, as evidenced by the more than 70-year history of public opinion polls on the death penalty in the United States. It means only that classroom knowledge may not be an effective way of changing these opinions.

ASKING ABOUT ALTERNATIVES TO THE DEATH PENALTY

Perhaps more important than the amount of accurate knowledge a person has about the death penalty is the way in which the death penalty opinion question is asked. A critical problem with the general opinion question (e.g., Do you favor or oppose the death penalty for first-degree murder?) is that there is either no context to the question or the context is ambiguous. For example, when people are asked whether they favor or oppose the death penalty or, for that matter, whether they favor or oppose the death penalty for all people or for some people convicted of first-degree murder, it is left to the imagination of each individual as to whether that means:

- The death penalty or no penalty at all;
- The death penalty or a too lenient alternative penalty such as 5 or 10 years in prison;
- The death penalty or a severe penalty such as a lengthy prison sentence but with opportunity for parole;
- The death penalty or an alternative severe penalty such as life imprisonment with no possibility of parole; or perhaps
- The death penalty and some other alternative.

With the exception of their latest studies, Bohm and his colleagues did not fully anticipate this possibility.[87]

It still appears that many people support the death penalty because they fear an alternative penalty will not be punitive enough or that it may be inappropriate, given the severity of the crime. Several studies show that 25–60 percent of the public believes that "the average prison term served by someone sentenced to life imprisonment is 10 years or less," even though the statement is false.[88] Another problem is that the public frequently fails to consider alternatives when asked the general death penalty opinion question because the media do a woeful job of publicizing them.[89]

Support of capital punishment drops, though, when the death penalty question is asked and a harsh and meaningful alternative is provided. In a 2010 Gallup poll, for example, when respondents were asked what they believed was the better penalty for murder, 49 percent chose the death penalty, 46 percent chose life imprisonment with absolutely no possibility of parole (LWOP), and 6 percent were unsure.[90] In a 2006 Gallup poll, when the same question was asked, 47 percent of respondents preferred the death penalty, 48 percent favored LWOP, and 5 percent had no opinion.[91] In many polls less than half of the public supported the death penalty when given the options of it and LWOP.[92] When given the options of the death penalty and life imprisonment with absolutely no possibility of parole and the payment of restitution by the offender (who would work in prison industry) to the victim's family or the community (LWOP+), even less of the public (only 19–43%) prefers the death penalty over the alternative.[93] Thus, on the surface, a majority of the public appears receptive to replacing capital punishment with a harsh and meaningful alternative such as LWOP or LWOP+. This is especially true of nonwhites, people 65 years of age or older, women, especially women 50 years of age or older, Easterners, people with a postgraduate education, Democrats, and the unemployed.[94]

A reason why even a larger percentage of the public does not favor LWOP or LWOP+ over capital punishment is that many people are very skeptical about the ability of correctional authorities to keep capital murderers imprisoned for life. A national survey showed that only 11 percent of registered voters believed that an offender sentenced to life imprisonment without possibility of parole would never be released from prison.[95] So, although the public might say it prefers the alternative of LWOP or LWOP+ over capital punishment, in practice it may not want to make the substitution due to fears that the alternative cannot guarantee protection from the future actions of convicted capital murderers.

Another problem with the LWOP+ alternative is that many murder victims' families find the idea of restitution repugnant, especially if it is received directly from the murderer.[96] They view restitution as "blood money" and reject the idea that it could satisfy them or bring them closure.[97] However, some of them support the idea of forcing murderers to work in prison and requiring them to put their earnings into a fund to pay the social debt they owe society or into a general survivors' compensation fund. For some murder victim family members, forced labor and paying reparations are better alternatives than having murderers idling in prison at taxpayers' expense.[98]

ASKING ABOUT DIFFERENT TYPES OF DEATH-ELIGIBLE MURDERS

Another ambiguity with general death penalty opinion questions is the type of murder, or first-degree murder, the pollsters have in mind. Not all death-eligible murders are the same. To address this issue, Durham, Elrod, and Kinkade presented people with 34 different murder scenarios, which varied by aggravating and mitigating circumstances.[99] Murders in some scenarios were death eligible, and murders in others were not. Respondents were asked what they thought was the appropriate punishment.

The researchers found that people's willingness to impose the death penalty may be greater than public opinion polls indicate. Only 13 percent of respondents would sentence all the murderers to death, but about 95 percent would sentence at least one to death.[100] There was also a huge variation in the willingness of people to impose the death penalty on different types of murderers. For one scenario, more than 90 percent of respondents thought death was the appropriate punishment, while for another, fewer than 25 percent of respondents believed so.[101] Even people in groups historically most opposed to the death penalty were likely to believe the death penalty was appropriate for at least some types of murderers. Although people's willingness to impose the death penalty was generally greatest for first-degree and felony murders, an unexpected finding was that several felony murders drew little death penalty support.[102] Durham and his colleagues also discovered that aggravating circumstances were more influential on sentencing decisions than were mitigating circumstances.[103] Finally, when the researchers compared their data with information obtained from the prosecutor's office, they found that the people they surveyed were more willing to impose the death penalty than was the prosecutor or than the law would have allowed.[104] These data suggest that death penalty support in the United States, for at least some types of murders, may be every bit as strong as recent public opinion polls suggest, and it may be even stronger for specific types of death-eligible murders.

OTHER DEATH PENALTY OPINION QUESTIONS

As noted previously, recent polls have included a greater variety of questions about the death penalty than did earlier polls. In fact, much more information is available about annual death penalty opinions today than at any time in the history of death penalty opinion polling. Some of this information was explored in previous chapters of this book. Besides questions about the death penalty versus LWOP and different types of death-eligible murders, recent polls have included questions about the administration of the death penalty, such as whether it is applied fairly, how often an innocent person has been executed, and whether poor people are more likely to receive the death penalty than people of average or above average income. Questions have been asked about the frequency with which the death penalty is imposed (too often, not enough, right amount) and whether the death penalty should be imposed on certain categories of offenders, such as the mentally retarded, the mentally ill, juveniles, and women. Additional questions address whether the death penalty is morally acceptable, whether it acts as a deterrent, and whether there should be a moratorium on it. Reasons for favoring the death penalty also have been sought. Finally, death penalty polls have included questions about the appropriateness of the death penalty for specific offenders, such as Timothy McVeigh, Terry Nichols, Juan Raul Garza, and Andrea Yates.

CONCLUSION: THE FUTURE OF AMERICAN DEATH PENALTY OPINION AND THE DEATH PENALTY

One of the more ambitious attempts to explain death penalty opinion in the United States was based on the results of a 20-year longitudinal study of the development of moral judgment in American males. From the study, Kohlberg and Elfenbein concluded that "nonfactual cognitive components of attitudes [opinions] toward capital punishment are determined by developing moral standards," as opposed to "irrational, purely emotional factors."[105] Since the American public generally is not well-informed about the death penalty, one might assume, following Kohlberg and Elfenbein, that death penalty opinions are primarily the product of "developing moral standards." Kohlberg and Elfenbein posited six moral stages and explained that as society progressed "through the universal, invariant sequence of moral stages," there is "a radical decline in support for capital punishment."[106] At Stage 6, to which society had yet to "progress," no person could support capital punishment.[107]

Kohlberg and Elfenbein observed that:

A gradual socio-moral evolution is evidently taking place in the United States that can be described and theoretically explained as moral stage development across social institutions and individuals over time. In large part, this evolution takes the form of a movement from Stage 4 to Stage 5.[108]

According to Kohlberg and Elfenbein, then, society is morally developing to a stage where the public will not support the death penalty. This observation, however, was published in 1975 during the hiatus on capital punishment in the United States and after a period of decline in support. Subsequent developments, such as increasing public support for the death penalty (until recently) and an increase in the number of death sentences and executions (until recently), indicate that Kohlberg and Elfenbein relied on a faulty theory, that they were wrong in their assessment of the moral evolution of American society, or that the American public is/was regressing in its moral development.

Public opinion about capital punishment, or at least public support, may prove to be irrelevant if and when the penalty is ever abolished in the United States. As Zimring and Hawkins have observed, "Successful and sustained abolition [of capital punishment] has never been a result of great popular demand."[109] Most countries that have abolished the death penalty continued to have a majority of citizens who supported retention at the time of abolition and shortly thereafter. Only gradually did death penalty support decline until opposition dominated public opinion.[110] In short, abolition of capital punishment, where it has occurred, generally has been achieved despite relatively strong public support for retention. In a sense, then, as Judge Cassell has observed, European countries do not have the death penalty because they are less democratic, or at least more insulated from public opinion, than the United States.[111] Zimring and Hawkins surmise that politicians and other opinion-makers probably will have to lead the public on this issue if capital punishment is ever to be abolished in the United States.

Harcourt agrees and adds that "elite political leadership" in retentionist states is likely to be aided by ordinary acts of resistance.[112] By ordinary acts of resistance, Harcourt is referring to people's efforts—a county courthouse clerk, a police department employee, a secretary in the prosecutor's office—to impede the death penalty process. They do so because they are consciously or unconsciously uncomfortable with capital punishment or because they are outright opposed to it.[113] They may stall the system, for example, by simply hiding a transcript or ignoring a case. In many states, such acts of minor sabotage make the death penalty process look ineffectual and sap its moral legitimacy by undermining some of its justifications, such as deterrence, finality, or moral equivalence (*jus talionis*).[114] Harcourt predicts that as the number of abolitionist states increases, coupled with increased international legal and political opposition to capital punishment, the more likely the U.S. Supreme Court is to ban capital punishment as a federal constitutional matter. Harcourt believes that international law will play an increasingly greater role in the Court's interpretation of the Eighth Amendment's "evolving standard of moral decency."[115]

The inherent danger in constitutional litigation, according to Steiker and Steiker, is the insulation and entrenchment of capital punishment if the constitutional challenges are brought and rejected, especially by the U.S. Supreme Court.[116] If constitutional litigation were to succeed, the U.S. population might respond as it did following the *Furman* decision and mobilize in support of the potent symbolic issue. Steiker and Steiker suggest that a waiting strategy may be safer and more effective. They believe that such a strategy would make the death penalty an increasingly marginalized outlier practice in a few jurisdictions.[117] Another strategy suggested by Steiker and Steiker is simply to continue the current path of substantive regulation of the death penalty process. With additional decisions such as *Atkins* (excluding the mentally retarded) and *Simmons* (excluding juveniles), capital punishment may become too constricted and costly to survive in a robust way.[118] A problem with both of these strategies is that a spectacularly gruesome crime could undermine the death penalty's marginalization and constriction and cause its expansion.[119]

On the other hand, a well-publicized and indisputable case of an innocent person wrongfully executed could have the opposite effect and rally support for the abolition of the death penalty. Indeed, research shows that the "reframing" of an issue can create important changes in political outcomes and the aggregate opinions that support those outcomes.[120] Baumgartner and his colleagues contend that the "discovery of innocence" in the mid-1990s has reframed the death penalty debate away from traditional morality-based and constitutional arguments and has effectively changed U.S. public opinion and public policy about the death penalty, as evidenced by reduced public support for the death penalty (especially when respondents are provided with the option of LWOP) and by declining numbers of death sentences and executions.[121] Their research shows that the cultural shift to the "innocence frame" is "1) unprecedented in its strength compared with previous understandings of this issue, 2) powerful in its effects on public opinion as well as on policy outputs, and 3) *more* powerful in these effects even than underlying social trends, such as the murder rate or other reasonable rival explanations."[122] For example, they report that the media effects of the shift to the innocence frame "alone account for a decline of more than 100 death sentences per year in recent years; the number attributable to declining homicide rates is about one quarter as much."[123] They conclude: "As long as attention continues to focus on issues of innocence, trends will continue toward less and less public support and official sanction of the practice."[124] They warn, however, "if attention were to shift to other topics [such as the morality question], the tone of discussion could easily tip back in a pro-death penalty direction, as it did in the 1970s and 1980s."[125]

Baumgartner et al. remind us that aggregate change in death penalty opinion is a slow process for two reasons. First, the death penalty is not a salient issue for most people; discussions about the death penalty are not in the news very often, and the death penalty does not directly affect the lives of most

Americans.[126] Second, Americans' views on the death penalty are closely tied to their moral and religious beliefs, and these beliefs do not change much over time.[127] Still, as Baumgartner et al. maintain, Americans' death penalty opinions do change, as they respond to events and interpretations of these events.[128] From their research, they discovered, for example, that, over the long run, "for every 1,000 homicides in the country, the level of opinion in equilibrium goes up by an average of 3.4 percentage points [and] for every ten additional net pro-death penalty stories ... the level of opinion [is expected] to move 1.5 percentage points in the pro-death penalty direction."[129] They also found that executions have no effect on death penalty opinions; exonerations may have a small, short-run effect; and death penalty opinion change is expedited when the question "moves from the theoretical to the individual" (as when a juror is asked to impose the death penalty).[130]

Based on my own analysis of the dramatic reversal in death penalty opinion in the United States beginning in the 1966–1967 period, this author has concluded, as have Baumgartner et al., that "the key to understanding temporal variations in death penalty opinions probably lies in the fear and anxiety engendered by the social events of an era."[131] The strength of death penalty support and opposition appears to be both a psychological barometer of the level of dread and angst in a society and a symbolic marker of the social landscape. In particular, levels of support and opposition seem to demarcate the threshold level of people's tolerance of media-reported crime and, at the same time, serve as an indicator of people's threshold tolerance of social change. As one student of the subject put it, death penalty support declined in the 1960s because, "as practiced, many people found [the death penalty] to be glaringly inconsistent with the ascendant ideas of the times."[132] It seems reasonable to assume "that historical changes, such as a political shift away from the conservative social policies of the last [two and a half decades or so], are apt to either produce a dramatic shift in future death penalty opinions or to be marked by changed death penalty opinions as the political shift passes a certain threshold level."[133] Either way, it is unlikely that the practice of capital punishment could be sustained if a majority of American citizens were to oppose it.

DISCUSSION QUESTIONS

1. How strongly does the American public support the death penalty?
2. Do you support the death penalty for all persons convicted of first-degree murder? Why or why not?
3. Do you support the death penalty for some people convicted of first-degree murder? Why or why not?
4. If you served on a jury in a trial where the defendant, if found guilty, would automatically be sentenced to death, could you convict that defendant? Why or why not?
5. If asked to do it, could you pull the lever that would result in the death of an individual convicted of first-degree murder? Why or why not?
6. Would you support the death penalty if the alternative were life imprisonment with absolutely no possibility of parole? Why or why not?
7. Would you support the death penalty if the alternative were life imprisonment with absolutely no possibility of parole and the payment of restitution by the offender (who would work in prison industry) to the victim's family or the community (LWOP+)? Why or why not?
8. Should public opinion be used in determining whether capital punishment is an acceptable or a constitutional form of punishment?

9. Does the public's opinion about the death penalty matter? Should it matter?

10. Have the new death penalty statutes and their procedural reforms rid the death penalty's administration of the problems cited in *Furman*?

11. Can death penalty statutes be made constitutionally acceptable?

12. Why do people oppose capital punishment? How could they be so wrong?

13. Why do people support capital punishment? How could they be so wrong?

14. Will the death penalty ever be abolished in all jurisdictions in the United States? If yes, what will cause its abolition?

Notes

1. A version of this chapter appeared as "American death penalty opinion: Past, present, and future," in J. R. Acker, R. M. Bohm, and C. Lanier (Eds.), (2003), *America's Experiment with Capital Punishment: Reflections on the Past, Present and Future of the Ultimate Penal Sanction* (2nd ed.). Durham, NC: Carolina Academic Press. Reprinted with permission.

2. See Newport (2010), for the most recent poll data. Unless indicated otherwise, figures reported in this chapter are from the Gallup polls, which are the oldest and most sustained effort to measure American death penalty opinion; see Bohm (1991). However, see the appendix to Ellsworth and Gross (1994) for a list of 90 death penalty opinion surveys conducted in the United States between 1936 and July 1993, the text of the questions asked, and the proportions of respondents providing each recorded answer. For more recent polls, see the Death Penalty Information Center website. Although some of these polls measure opinions about the death penalty for certain other categories of persons, such as juveniles and the mentally retarded, for certain other types of crimes, such as rape or kidnapping, and for certain kinds of death sentences, such as mandatory versus discretionary, this chapter focuses primarily on death penalty opinions for capital or aggravated murder. All post-*Furman* executions have involved capital or aggravated murderers.

3. Erskine cites a Harris Survey released on July 3, 1966, that showed that only 38 percent of respondents favored the death penalty, 47 percent were against, and 15 percent had no opinion; see Erskine (1970, p. 295).

4. Cited in Haines (1996, p. 164).

5. On Tennessee legislators, see Whitehead (1998); on Indiana legislators, see McGarrell and Sandys (1996); but see Sandys and McGarrell (1994). Evidence indicates that public opinion has affected policy making in the United States in other areas, such as civil rights, see Oskamp (1977, p. 241); also cf. Erikson (1976), Monroe (1979), Page and Shapiro (1983), Page, Shapiro, and Dempsey (1987), and Weissberg (1976).

6. See Dieter (1996). With regard to the death penalty, former New York governors Hugh Carey and Mario Cuomo and former California Governor Jerry Brown are three notable exceptions. Each governor vetoed death penalty legislation despite strong public support for the penalty.

7. White (1987, p. 17); also see Callahan, Acker, and Cerulli (2000) and Dieter (1996).

8. Bright (1998), Bright and Keenan (1995), Dickson (2006, p. 281), and Dieter (1996).

9. Bright (1998, pp. 123–124) and Dieter (1996, pp. 2–4).

10. Baldus and Woodworth (1998, pp. 388–389); also see Burnett (2002), Dieter (1996), and Kobil (2003).

11. A recent study found that "states are approximately 25 percent more likely to conduct executions in gubernatorial election years than in other years." It also discovered that "elections have a larger effect on the probability that an African-American defendant will be executed in a given year than on the probability that a white defendant will be executed and that the overall effect of elections is largest in the South." See Kubik and Moran (2003).

12. On state constitutions, see Bedau (1987, chap. 8); on the Eighth Amendment, see Marshall in *Furman v. Georgia* (1972, p. 329); also in *Furman*: Douglas (p. 242), Brennan (pp. 269–270), Burger (p. 383), and Powell (p. 409); *Trop v. Dulles* (1958, p. 101); *Weems v. United States* (1910, pp. 349, 373); *Robinson v. California* (1962, p. 666); also cf. *Estelle v. Gamble* (1976, p. 102); *Roberts v. Louisiana* (1976, pp. 336, 352); *Woodson v. North Carolina* (1976, p. 301); *Gregg v. Georgia* (1976, pp. 173, 227). But see Justice Rehnquist's dissent in *Atkins v. Virginia*, 2002, where he is highly critical of using public opinion as a measure of evolving standards of decency.

13. *Furman v. Georgia* (1972, p. 329).

14. Baumgartner, DeBoef, and Boydstun (2008, p. 169).

15. Bohm (1991).

16. Ibid., p. 115.

17. See note 2.

18. Newport (2010).

19. Bohm, Clark, and Aveni (1991), Bowers (1993), Ellsworth and Ross (1983), Harris (1986), Jones (1994), McGarrell and Sandys (1996), Sandys and McGarrell (1995), Sarat and Vidmar (1976), Unnever et al. (2005), and Williams, Longmire, and Gulick (1988).

20. The six most volatile short-term periods between 1936 and 2006 were (1) 1953–1957 (23% decrease in support, 5% increase in opposition, and 17% increase in "no opinions" or "don't knows"), (2) 1960–1966 (11% decrease in support and 11% increase in opposition), (3) 1966–1967 (11% increase in support and 8% decrease in opposition), (4) 1971–1976 (16% increase in support and 12% decrease in opposition), (5) 1978–1995 (15% increase in support, 14% decrease in opposition, and 9% decrease in "no opinions"), and (6) 1995–2003 (13% decrease in support, 19% increase in opposition, and 6% decrease in "no opinions" or "don't knows"); see Bohm (1991) and recent Gallup polls. With the exception of an analysis of the 1966–1967 period (see Bohm, 1992a), there have been no attempts, of which this author is aware, to explain the volatile periods.

21. See Bohm (1991, p. 116). For an analysis of the historical circumstances, that is, the social events and economic trends, that contributed to the dramatic reversal in death penalty support and opposition between 1966 and 1967, see Bohm (1992a).

22. See Bohm (1991).

23. Ibid.

24. Ibid.

25. Baumgartner (2008, p. 180).

26. Dieter (2000).

27. Ibid.

28. Death penalty opinion research published prior to 1975, when death penalty support was more moderate than it generally has been since then (until recently), frequently attributed support of capital punishment to some rather unflattering social psychological characteristics such as dogmatism, authoritarianism, and racism. Proponents of capital punishment were less likely than opponents to approve of gun registration laws or to favor open housing legislation and more likely to favor restrictive abortion laws, approve of the John Birch Society, move if blacks moved into their neighborhoods, and support such things as restrictions on civil liberties, discrimination against minority groups, and violence for achieving social goals (see Vidmar and Ellsworth, 1974); also see Bohm (1987). However, in light of the dramatic increase in death penalty support since 1975 (until recently), one might have hoped that such a distinctive personality profile of death penalty proponents no longer applied. Unfortunately, recent evidence suggests otherwise. Support of capital punishment by many whites continues to be associated with prejudice against blacks, see Barkan and Cohn (1994), Bobo and Johnson (2004), Bohm (1994), Borg (1997), Johnson (2001, 2003), Unnever and Cullen (2007a, 2007b, 2010b), Unnever, Cullen, and Jonson (2008), and U.S. General Accounting Office (1990). In a recent cross-national study, Unnever and Cullen found "that the link between support

for capital punishment and racial and ethnic animus may occur universally in countries with conflicted racial and ethnic relations." Unnever and Cullen (2010a).

29. Bohm (1991); also see Boots, Cochran, and Heide (2003), Fox, Radelet, and Bonsteel (1990–1991), and Longmire (1996).

30. See Bohm (1991).

31. Borg (1997) found significant variation among Southerners' views of the death penalty. Southerners who were racially prejudiced toward blacks, religious fundamentalists, and politically conservative were more likely to support the death penalty than Southerners who did not possess these characteristics.

32. Bohm (1991).

33. Demographic data from the 2006 death penalty poll were obtained directly from the Gallup Organization. My thanks to Maura A. Strausberg, Data Librarian, for her help.

34. Arthur (1998). For one interesting and detailed position on the death penalty offered by a black man, see Jackson (1996). Cochran and Chamlin (2006) found that the race/ethnicity difference in death penalty opinions held after controlling for the effects of SES, religion/religiosity, political ideology, positions on right-to-life and other social issues, fear of crime and victimization experience, experience with the criminal justice system, philosophies of punishment, and attribution styles. Also see Bobo and Johnson (2004) and Johnson (2001, 2003).

35. See note 33.

36. Baumer, Messner, and Rosenfeld (2003).

37. Ibid., p. 866.

38. Ibid., p. 844; also see Soss, Langbein, and Metelko (2003).

39. This appears to hold true even among prison inmates; see Steele and Wilcox (2003) and Wilcox and Steele (2003).

40. Unnever, Cullen, and Bartkowski (2006); also see Applegate, Cullen, Fisher, and Ven (2000).

41. Unnever et al. (2005).

42. Grasmick, Cochran, Bursik, and Kimpel (1993); but see Wozniak and Lewis (2009).

43. Britt (1998); also see Young (1992).

44. Barkan and Cohn (2010).

45. *Furman v. Georgia*, 1972 at 332.

46. Ibid., at 362, fn. 145.

47. Ibid. Elaborating on this point, Marshall wrote that "the question with which we must deal is not whether a substantial proportion of American citizens would today, if polled, opine that capital punishment is barbarously cruel, but whether they would find it to be so in the light of all information presently available": see *Furman v. Georgia*, 1972 at 362. For Marshall, however, "this is not to suggest that with respect to this test of unconstitutionality people are required to act rationally; they are not [and often do not – author's addition]. With respect to this judgment, a violation of the Eighth Amendment is totally dependent on the predictable subjective, emotional reactions of informed citizens" (at 362). Even if the American people were adequately informed about the death penalty and its effects, Radin is but one scholar who believes that public opinion polls should not be relied on in constitutional adjudication (see Radin, 1978). She argues that public opinion polls should not be used because they (1) "show that the majority of the public favors few of the protections embodied in the Bill of Rights" … [and] "the purpose of the Bill of Rights is to protect certain rights of individuals from an overreaching majority," (2) "are subject to methodological errors," and (3) "may record frivolous or ill-considered answers, or answers influenced by intrinsic factors"; see Radin (1978, pp. 1035–1036).

48. *Furman v. Georgia*, 1972 at 363. In his dissent in *Furman*, Justice Powell disagreed with Marshall and argued that the public would not oppose the death penalty if it were informed about its administration; see *Furman v. Georgia*, 1972 at 430–446.

49. *Furman v. Georgia*, 1972 at 363. In *Furman*, Justice Stewart, who voted with the majority, opined that retribution was psychologically necessary for maintaining social stability; see *Furman v. Georgia*, 1972 at 308.

50. *Furman v. Georgia*, 1972 at 363. Disagreement over the legitimacy of retribution as a purpose of capital punishment may be the product of confusion over what retribution actually means. For a discussion of the different meanings of retribution, see Chapter 11.

51. Ellsworth and Ross (1983).

52. Sarat and Vidmar (1976).

53. Vidmar and Dittenhoffer (1981).

54. The study by Ellsworth and Ross (1983) examined only opinions and knowledge about the death penalty. It did not examine whether knowledge about the death penalty would change opinions. Also see Longmire (1996) for the effects of knowledge about the death penalty on the opinions of death penalty proponents, opponents, and undecideds.

55. *Furman v. Georgia*, 1972 at 362–363.

56. Ibid., at 362–364.

57. Lord, Ross, and Lepper (1979).

58. Lord et al. presented 24 proponents and 24 opponents of the death penalty (all subjects were undergraduate students) "first with the results and then with procedural details, critiques, and rebuttals for two studies dealing with the deterrent efficacy of the death penalty—one study confirming their initial beliefs and one study disconfirming their initial beliefs"; see Lord et al. (1979, pp. 2100–2101), for more detail.

59. Ibid., p. 2099.

60. Ellsworth and Ross (1983, p. 152); also see Roberts (1984) and Tyler and Weber (1982). The concepts "attitudes" and "opinions" are often used synonymously, especially when discussing the death penalty. However, according to at least one authority (see Oskamp, 1977), opinions should be equated with beliefs, which are primarily cognitive, while attitudes are more emotion-laden. This distinction is ignored in this chapter, which employs the concepts "opinion" or "opinions" except in direct quotes (in which case the concepts are bracketed).

61. Sarat and Vidmar (1976, p. 183, fn. 59).

62. Vidmar and Dittenhoffer (1981, p. 49).

63. Ibid., pp. 45–46.

64. There are at least two potential problems with the experimental design of Bohm and his colleague. First is the use of student subjects. Whether students are representative of the general public with regard to death penalty opinion is questionable. In the 2006 Gallup poll, 65 percent of all respondents supported the death penalty, 66 percent of respondents with a high school education or less supported it, 69 percent of respondents with some college education supported it, and 62 percent of respondents with a college education supported it. Only respondents with postgraduate educations deviated significantly from the percentage of all respondents who favored the death penalty (only 54 percent of respondents with postgraduate educations supported the death penalty); see note 33. Variation in other years, however, has been both greater and smaller; see Bohm (1991, pp. 131–132) and more recent polls. In any case, the reason for using student subjects was that it was one of the only ways to employ a prolonged stimulus experimentally. Brevity of exposure to the experimental stimulus was a weakness of previous research (cf. Lord et al., 1979; Sarat and Vidmar, 1976; Vidmar and Dittenhoffer, 1981). A second potential problem with the experimental design of Bohm and his colleagues is the influence of the instructor. A charismatic teacher could have a significant influence over his or her students' opinions. The instructor in the death penalty classes was always forthright about his strong opposition to the death penalty but emphasized that his opinion should not influence the opinion of anyone else. Despite his personal opinion, both sides of all issues were presented, and no preference was shown intentionally for either side. Also, the instructor played "devil's advocate" to the positions taken by students to provoke thoughtful consideration of the

issues. Students were fully aware from the outset that their grade in the class was independent of their views. Informal feedback from all the classes and results of 2- and 3-year and more than 10-year follow-up studies of the 1988 and 1989 classes indicate that "demand characteristics" had negligible effects (Bohm and Vogel, 2004; Bohm, Vogel, and Maisto, 1993, p. 42).

65. As discussed in Chapter 4, although, in 1976, in the cases of *Woodson v. North Carolina* and *Roberts v. Louisiana*, the Supreme Court rejected mandatory statutes that automatically imposed death sentences for defined capital offenses, a question about the death penalty for all persons convicted of first-degree murder remains instructive. Not only does it give an indication of people's opinions in light of the Supreme Court decisions, but it also serves as a basis of comparison for other questions about the death penalty considered in this research.

66. Bohm, Clark, and Aveni (1991, pp. 373–375, Tables 2–4).

67. Ibid.

68. See Ellsworth and Ross (1983) and Jurow (1971). The distinction made between abstract questions and questions involving concrete situations is somewhat artificial. As is well known, what people say and what people do are often very different. Research indicates that correlations between people's attitudes [opinions] and their behavior are "rarely above .30, and often are near zero"; see Wicker (1969). The largest correlations are typically found when the researcher focuses on a specific attitude [opinion] toward a well-defined situation. Conversely, when the attitude [opinion] is a very general one that is presumed to influence a variety of different situations, much less consistency between attitude [opinion] and behavior is found; see Crespi (1971). Thus, what people say about the death penalty in general and what they would do as jurors in a capital murder trial, for example, probably are not the same. For that matter, what people say they would do if they served as jurors in a capital murder trial and what they would do if they actually served may not be the same. This, of course, is a problem with all survey research.

69. Bohm et al. (1991).

70. Ibid.

71. Radin (1978, p. 1041).

72. Bohm et al. (1991, pp. 368–369).

73. Ibid., p. 375.

74. See Bohm et al. (1991); also see Bohm (1989, 1990), Bohm, Clark, and Aveni (1990), and Bohm and Vogel (1994).

75. Bohm (1989), Bohm and Vogel (1994), Bohm et al. (1991), and Lambert and Clarke (2001).

76. Bohm et al. (1991) and Bohm, Vogel, and Maisto (1993); but see Murray (2003).

77. Bohm (1990) and Bohm et al. (1990).

78. Bohm (1990).

79. Bohm and Vogel (1994) and Bohm et al. (1993).

80. Bohm (1989), Bohm and Vogel (1994), Bohm et al. (1991, 1993), Clarke, Lambert, and Whitt (2000–2001), Lambert and Clarke (2001), and Sandys (1995).

81. Bohm et al. (1993).

82. Ibid. There was some significant change in opinions on the concrete questions in some of the tests.

83. Bohm and Vogel (2004).

84. Ibid.

85. Bohm and Vogel (2004) and Bohm et al. (1993, p. 42).

86. Also see Patenaude (2001) and Vollum and Buffington-Vollum (2010); but see Cochran and Chamlin (2005) and Sandys (1995).

87. See Bohm and Vogel (2004) and Wright, Bohm, and Jamieson (1995).

88. Bohm et al. (1991, p. 371), Ellsworth and Ross (1983), Hood (1989), Paduano and Smith (1987), and Wright et al. (1995); also see Bowers (1993), Bowers and Steiner (1998), and McGarrell and Sandys (1996).

89. See, for example, Niven (2002).
90. Newport (2010).
91. Jones (2006).
92. See, for example, Gallup and Newport (1991, p. 44); also see Boots et al. (2003), Bowers (1993), Bowers, Vandiver, and Dugan (1994), and Ellsworth and Gross (1994).
93. See Bowers (1993), McGarrell and Sandys (1996), and Sandys and McGarrell (1995). Bowers notes that there is evidence suggesting that "a majority of the public would also be willing to accept parole after a fixed term of at least 25 years in preference to the death penalty on the condition that it was coupled with a restitution requirement and that the defendant had fully met the restitution requirement," see Bowers (1993, p. 168).
94. Jones (2002, 2006). Vogel (2003) found that the only demographic characteristic (that she examined) that distinguished the views of death penalty supporters about LWOP was wealth. Wealthier death penalty supporters were less likely to favor LWOP than other death penalty supporters.
95. Cited in McGarrell and Sandys (1996, p. 509).
96. Kay (2006, p. 335).
97. Ibid., p. 338.
98. Ibid., pp. 340–342.
99. Durham, Elrod, and Kinkade (1996); also see Boots et al. (2003).
100. Durham et al. (1996, p. 726).
101. Ibid., p. 727.
102. Ibid.
103. Ibid.
104. Ibid.
105. Kohlberg and Elfenbein (1975, p. 617).
106. Ibid., pp. 637–638.
107. Ibid., p. 637.
108. Ibid., p. 638.
109. Zimring and Hawkins (1986, p. 12). Zimring (2003, pp. 23–24) notes that death penalty abolition in most European countries came during politically liberal administrations but, when they were replaced with politically conservative administrations, the death penalty was never reinstated. After abolition, he adds, the death penalty ceased to be an important political issue.
110. Ibid.
111. Cassell (2004, p. 200).
112. Harcourt (2009, p. 77).
113. Ibid., p. 78.
114. Ibid., pp. 90–91.
115. Ibid., p. 77; also see Steiker and Steiker (2009).
116. Steiker and Steiker (2009, p. 131).
117. Ibid.
118. Ibid., p. 133.
119. Ibid., pp. 132–133.
120. See Baumgartner et al. (2008, p. 12).
121. Ibid., pp. 8–9.
122. Ibid., p. 14.
123. Ibid., p. 21.
124. Ibid.
125. Ibid.

126. Ibid., p. 182–183.
127. Ibid., p. 184.
128. Ibid.
129. Ibid., p. 187.
130. Ibid., pp. 193 and 198.
131. Bohm (1992a, p. 539).
132. Haines (1996, p. 161).
133. Bohm (1992a); also see Zimring (2003).

American Bar Association 2003 guidelines for the appointment and performance of defense counsel in death penalty cases*

Despite some overlap, Guidelines 1.1–10.1 primarily describe how jurisdictions should create a capital case defense services delivery system, and Guidelines 10.2–10.15.2 primarily provide performance standards outlining counsel's duties in these cases.

GUIDELINE 1.1—OBJECTIVE AND SCOPE OF GUIDELINES

A. The objective of these Guidelines is to set forth a national standard of practice for the defense of capital cases in order to ensure high quality legal representation for all persons facing the possible imposition or execution of a death sentence by any jurisdiction.

B. These Guidelines apply from the moment the client is taken into custody and extend to all stages of every case in which the jurisdiction may be entitled to seek the death penalty, including initial and ongoing investigation, pretrial proceedings, trial, post-conviction review, clemency proceedings and any connected litigation.

GUIDELINE 2.1—ADOPTION AND IMPLEMENTATION OF A PLAN TO PROVIDE HIGH QUALITY LEGAL REPRESENTATION IN DEATH PENALTY CASES

A. Each jurisdiction should adopt and implement a plan formalizing the means by which high quality legal representation in death penalty cases is to be provided in accordance with these Guidelines (the "Legal Representation Plan").

B. The Legal Representation Plan should set forth how the jurisdiction will conform to each of these Guidelines.

C. All elements of the Legal Representation Plan should be structured to ensure that counsel defending death penalty cases are able to do so free from political influence and under conditions that enable them to provide zealous advocacy in accordance with professional standards.

---

*"American Bar Association Guidelines for the Appointment and Performance of Defense Counsel in Death Penalty Cases," Revised February 2003. A Joint Project by the American Bar Association's Standing Committee on Legal Aid & Indigent Defendants and the Special Committee on Death Penalty Representation, published online at http://www.abanet .org/legalservices/downloads/sclaid/indigentdefense/deathpenaltyguidelines2003.pdf © 2003 by the American Bar Association. Reprinted with permission.

GUIDELINE 3.1—DESIGNATION OF A RESPONSIBLE AGENCY

A. The Legal Representation Plan should designate one or more agencies to be responsible, in accordance with the standards provided in these Guidelines, for:

1. ensuring that each capital defendant in the jurisdiction receives high quality legal representation, and

2. performing all the duties listed in Subsection E (the "Responsible Agency").

B. The Responsible Agency should be independent of the judiciary and it, and not the judiciary or elected officials, should select lawyers for specific cases.

C. The Responsible Agency for each stage of the proceeding in a particular case should be one of the following:

Defender Organization

1. A "defender organization," that is, either:

   a. a jurisdiction-wide capital trial office, relying on staff attorneys, members of the private bar, or both to provide representation in death penalty cases; or

   b. a jurisdiction-wide capital appellate and/or post-conviction defender office, relying on staff attorneys, members of the private bar, or both to provide representation in death penalty cases; or

Independent Authority

2. An "Independent Authority," that is, an entity run by defense attorneys with demonstrated knowledge and expertise in capital representation.

D. Conflict of Interest:

1. In any circumstance in which the performance by a defender organization of a duty listed in Subsection E would result in a conflict of interest, the relevant duty should be performed by the Independent Authority. The jurisdiction should implement an effectual system to identify and resolve such conflicts.

2. When the Independent Authority is the Responsible Agency, attorneys who hold formal roles in the Independent Authority should be ineligible to represent defendants in capital cases within the jurisdiction during their term of service.

E. The Responsible Agency should, in accordance with the provisions of these Guidelines, perform the following duties:

1. recruit and certify attorneys as qualified to be appointed to represent defendants in death penalty cases;

2. draft and periodically publish rosters of certified attorneys;

3. draft and periodically publish certification standards and procedures by which attorneys are certified and assigned to particular cases;

4. assign the attorneys who will represent the defendant at each stage of every case, except to the extent that the defendant has private attorneys;

5. monitor the performance of all attorneys providing representation in capital proceedings;

6. periodically review the roster of qualified attorneys and withdraw certification from any attorney who fails to provide high quality legal representation consistent with these Guidelines;

7. conduct, sponsor, or approve specialized training programs for attorneys representing defendants in death penalty cases; and

8. investigate and maintain records concerning complaints about the performance of attorneys providing representation in death penalty cases and take appropriate corrective action without delay.

GUIDELINE 4.1—THE DEFENSE TEAM AND SUPPORTING SERVICES

A. The Legal Representation Plan should provide for assembly of a defense team that will provide high quality legal representation.

   1. The defense team should consist of no fewer than two attorneys qualified in accordance with Guideline 5.1, an investigator, and a mitigation specialist.

   2. The defense team should contain at least one member qualified by training and experience to screen individuals for the presence of mental or psychological disorders or impairments.

B. The Legal Representation Plan should provide for counsel to receive the assistance of all expert, investigative, and other ancillary professional services reasonably necessary or appropriate to provide high quality legal representation at every stage of the proceedings. The Plan should specifically ensure provision of such services to private attorneys whose clients are financially unable to afford them.

   1. Counsel should have the right to have such services provided by persons independent of the government.

   2. Counsel should have the right to protect the confidentiality of communications with the persons providing such services to the same extent as would counsel paying such persons from private funds.

GUIDELINE 5.1—QUALIFICATIONS OF DEFENSE COUNSEL

A. The Responsible Agency should develop and publish qualification standards for defense counsel in capital cases. These standards should be construed and applied in such a way as to further the overriding goal of providing each client with high quality legal representation.

B. In formulating qualification standards, the Responsible Agency should insure:

   1. That every attorney representing a capital defendant has:

      a. obtained a license or permission to practice in the jurisdiction;

      b. demonstrated a commitment to providing zealous advocacy and high quality legal representation in the defense of capital cases; and

      c. satisfied the training requirements set forth in Guideline 8.1.

   2. That the pool of defense attorneys as a whole is such that each capital defendant within the jurisdiction receives high quality legal representation. Accordingly, the qualification standards should insure that the pool includes sufficient numbers of attorneys who have demonstrated:

a. substantial knowledge and understanding of the relevant state, federal, and international law, both procedural and substantive, governing capital cases;
b. skill in the management and conduct of complex negotiations and litigation;
c. skill in legal research, analysis, and the drafting of litigation documents;
d. skill in oral advocacy;
e. skill in the use of expert witnesses and familiarity with common areas of forensic investigation, including fingerprints, ballistics, forensic pathology, and DNA evidence;
f. skill in the investigation, preparation, and presentation of evidence bearing upon mental status;
g. skill in the investigation, preparation, and presentation of mitigating evidence; and
h. skill in the elements of trial advocacy, such as jury selection, cross-examination of witnesses, and opening and closing statements.

GUIDELINE 6.1—WORKLOAD

The Responsible Agency should implement effectual mechanisms to ensure that the workload of attorneys representing defendants in death penalty cases is maintained at a level that enables counsel to provide each client with high quality legal representation in accordance with these Guidelines.

GUIDELINE 7.1—MONITORING; REMOVAL

A. The Responsible Agency should monitor the performance of all defense counsel to ensure that the client is receiving high quality legal representation. Where there is evidence that an attorney is not providing high quality legal representation, the Responsible Agency should take appropriate action to protect the interests of the attorney's current and potential clients.
B. The Responsible Agency should establish and publicize a regular procedure for investigating and resolving any complaints made by judges, clients, attorneys, or others that defense counsel failed to provide high quality legal representation.
C. The Responsible Agency should periodically review the rosters of attorneys who have been certified to accept appointments in capital cases to ensure that those attorneys remain capable of providing high quality legal representation. Where there is evidence that an attorney has failed to provide high quality legal representation, the attorney should not receive additional appointments and should be removed from the roster. Where there is evidence that a systemic defect in a defender office has caused the office to fail to provide high quality legal representation, the office should not receive additional appointments.
D. Before taking final action making an attorney or a defender office ineligible to receive additional appointments, the Responsible Agency should provide written notice that such action is being contemplated, and give the attorney or defender office opportunity to respond in writing.
E. An attorney or defender office sanctioned pursuant to this Guideline should be restored to the roster only in exceptional circumstances.
F. The Responsible Agency should ensure that this Guideline is implemented consistently with Guideline 2.1(C), so that an attorney's zealous representation of a client cannot be cause for the imposition or threatened imposition of sanctions pursuant to this Guideline.

GUIDELINE 8.1—TRAINING

A. The Legal Representation Plan should provide funds for the effective training, professional development, and continuing education of all members of the defense team.

B. Attorneys seeking to qualify to receive appointments should be required to satisfactorily complete a comprehensive training program, approved by the Responsible Agency, in the defense of capital cases. Such a program should include, but not be limited to, presentations and training in the following areas:

1. relevant state, federal, and international law;
2. pleading and motion practice;
3. pretrial investigation, preparation, and theory development regarding guilt/innocence and penalty;
4. jury selection;
5. trial preparation and presentation, including the use of experts;
6. ethical considerations particular to capital defense representation;
7. preservation of the record and of issues for post-conviction review;
8. counsel's relationship with the client and his family;
9. post-conviction litigation in state and federal courts;
10. the presentation and rebuttal of scientific evidence, and developments in mental health fields and other relevant areas of forensic and biological science.

C. Attorneys seeking to remain on the roster or appointment roster should be required to attend and successfully complete, at least once every two years, a specialized training program approved by the Responsible Agency that focuses on the defense of death penalty cases.

D. The Legal Representation Plan should insure that all non-attorneys wishing to be eligible to participate on defense teams receive continuing professional education appropriate to their areas of expertise.

GUIDELINE 9.1—FUNDING AND COMPENSATION

A. The Legal Representation Plan must ensure funding for the full cost of high quality legal representation, as defined by these Guidelines, by the defense team and outside experts selected by counsel.

B. Counsel in death penalty cases should be fully compensated at a rate that is commensurate with the provision of high quality legal representation and reflects the extraordinary responsibilities inherent in death penalty representation.

1. Flat fees, caps on compensation, and lump-sum contracts are improper in death penalty cases.
2. Attorneys employed by defender organizations should be compensated according to a salary scale that is commensurate with the salary scale of the prosecutor's office in the jurisdiction.
3. Appointed counsel should be fully compensated for actual time and service performed at an hourly rate commensurate with the prevailing rates for similar services performed by retained counsel in the jurisdiction, with no distinction between rates for services performed in or out of court. Periodic billing and payment should be available.

C. Non-attorney members of the defense team should be fully compensated at a rate that is commensurate with the provision of high quality legal representation and reflects the specialized skills needed by those who assist counsel with the litigation of death penalty cases.

    1. Investigators employed by defender organizations should be compensated according to a salary scale that is commensurate with the salary scale of the prosecutor's office in the jurisdiction.

    2. Mitigation specialists and experts employed by defender organizations should be compensated according to a salary scale that is commensurate with the salary scale for comparable expert services in the private sector.

    3. Members of the defense team assisting private counsel should be fully compensated for actual time and service performed at an hourly rate commensurate with prevailing rates paid by retained counsel in the jurisdiction for similar services, with no distinction between rates for services performed in or out of court. Periodic billing and payment should be available.

D. Additional compensation should be provided in unusually protracted or extraordinary cases.

E. Counsel and members of the defense team should be fully reimbursed for reasonable incidental expenses.

GUIDELINE 10.1—ESTABLISHMENT OF PERFORMANCE STANDARDS

A. The Responsible Agency should establish standards of performance for all counsel in death penalty cases.

B. The standards of performance should be formulated so as to insure that all counsel provide high quality legal representation in capital cases in accordance with these Guidelines. The Responsible Agency should refer to the standards when assessing the qualifications or performance of counsel.

C. The standards of performance should include, but not be limited to, the specific standards set out in these Guidelines.

GUIDELINE 10.2—APPLICABILITY OF PERFORMANCE STANDARDS

Counsel should provide high quality legal representation in accordance with these Guidelines for so long as the jurisdiction is legally entitled to seek the death penalty.

GUIDELINE 10.3—OBLIGATIONS OF COUNSEL RESPECTING WORKLOAD

Counsel representing clients in death penalty cases should limit their caseloads to the level needed to provide each client with high quality legal representation in accordance with these Guidelines.

GUIDELINE 10.4—THE DEFENSE TEAM

A. When it is responsible for designating counsel to defend a capital case, the Responsible Agency should designate a lead counsel and one or more associate counsel. The Responsible Agency should ordinarily solicit the views of lead counsel before designating associate counsel.

B. Lead counsel bears overall responsibility for the performance of the defense team, and should allocate, direct, and supervise its work in accordance with these Guidelines and professional standards.

  1. Subject to the foregoing, lead counsel may delegate to other members of the defense team duties imposed by these Guidelines, unless:

   a. The Guideline specifically imposes the duty on "lead counsel," or

   b. The Guideline specifically imposes the duty on "all counsel" or "all members of the defense team."

C. As soon as possible after designation, lead counsel should assemble a defense team by:

  1. Consulting with the Responsible Agency regarding the number and identity of the associate counsel;

  2. Subject to standards of the Responsible Agency that are in accord with these Guidelines and in consultation with associate counsel to the extent practicable, selecting and making any appropriate contractual agreements with non-attorney team members in such a way that the team includes:

   a. at least one mitigation specialist and one fact investigator;

   b. at least one member qualified by training and experience to screen individuals for the presence of mental or psychological disorders or impairments; and

   c. any other members needed to provide high quality legal representation.

D. Counsel at all stages should demand on behalf of the client all resources necessary to provide high quality legal representation. If such resources are denied, counsel should make an adequate record to preserve the issue for further review.

GUIDELINE 10.5—RELATIONSHIP WITH THE CLIENT

A. Counsel at all stages of the case should make every appropriate effort to establish a relationship of trust with the client, and should maintain close contact with the client.

B. Barring exceptional circumstances, an interview of the client should be conducted within 24 hours of initial counsel's entry into the case.

  1. Promptly upon entry into the case, initial counsel should communicate in an appropriate manner with both the client and the government regarding the protection of the client's rights against self-incrimination, to the effective assistance of counsel, and to preservation of the attorney–client privilege and similar safeguards.

  2. Counsel at all stages of the case should re-advise the client and the government regarding these matters as appropriate.

C. Counsel at all stages of the case should engage in a continuing interactive dialogue with the client concerning all matters that might reasonably be expected to have a material impact on the case, such as:

  1. the progress of and prospects for the factual investigation, and what assistance the client might provide to it;

  2. current or potential legal issues;

  3. the development of a defense theory;

  4. presentation of the defense case;

5. potential agreed-upon dispositions of the case;
6. litigation deadlines and the projected schedule of case-related events; and
7. relevant aspects of the client's relationship with correctional, parole, or other governmental agents (e.g., prison medical providers or state psychiatrists).

GUIDELINE 10.6—ADDITIONAL OBLIGATIONS OF COUNSEL REPRESENTING A FOREIGN NATIONAL

A. Counsel at every stage of the case should make appropriate efforts to determine whether any foreign country might consider the client to be one of its nationals.
B. Unless predecessor counsel has already done so, counsel representing a foreign national should:
    1. immediately advise the client of his or her right to communicate with the relevant consular office; and
    2. obtain the consent of the client to contact the consular office. After obtaining consent, counsel should immediately contact the client's consular office and inform it of the client's detention or arrest.
        a. Counsel who is unable to obtain consent should exercise his or her best professional judgment under the circumstances.

GUIDELINE 10.7—INVESTIGATION

A. Counsel at every stage have an obligation to conduct thorough and independent investigations relating to the issues of both guilt and penalty.
    1. The investigation regarding guilt should be conducted regardless of any admission or statement by the client concerning the facts of the alleged crime, or overwhelming evidence of guilt, or any statement by the client that evidence bearing upon guilt is not to be collected or presented.
    2. The investigation regarding penalty should be conducted regardless of any statement by the client that evidence bearing upon penalty is not to be collected or presented.
B. Counsel at every stage have an obligation to conduct a full examination of the defense provided to the client at all prior phases of the case.
    1. This obligation includes at minimum interviewing prior counsel and members of the defense team and examining the files of prior counsel.
    2. Counsel at every stage have an obligation to satisfy themselves independently that the official record of the proceedings is complete and to supplement it as appropriate.

GUIDELINE 10.8—THE DUTY TO ASSERT LEGAL CLAIMS

A. Counsel at every stage of the case, exercising professional judgment in accordance with these Guidelines, should:
    1. consider all legal claims potentially available; and
    2. thoroughly investigate the basis for each potential claim before reaching a conclusion as to whether it should be asserted; and

3. evaluate each potential claim in light of:
   a. the unique characteristics of death penalty law and practice, and
   b. the near certainty that all available avenues of post-conviction relief will be pursued in the event of conviction and imposition of a death sentence; and
   c. the importance of protecting the client's rights against later contentions by the government that the claim has been waived, defaulted, not exhausted, or otherwise forfeited; and
   d. any other professionally appropriate costs and benefits to the assertion of the claim.
B. Counsel who decide to assert a particular legal claim should:
   1. present the claim as forcefully as possible, tailoring the presentation to the particular facts and circumstances in the client's case and the applicable law in the particular jurisdiction; and
   2. ensure that a full record is made of all legal proceedings in connection with the claim.
C. Counsel at all stages of the case should keep under consideration the possible advantages to the client of:
   1. asserting legal claims whose basis has only recently become known or available to counsel; and
   2. supplementing claims previously made with additional factual or legal information.

GUIDELINE 10.9.1—THE DUTY TO SEEK AN AGREED-UPON DISPOSITION

A. Counsel at every stage of the case have an obligation to take all steps that may be appropriate in the exercise of professional judgment in accordance with these Guidelines to achieve an agreed-upon disposition.
B. Counsel at every stage of the case should explore with the client the possibility and desirability of reaching an agreed-upon disposition. In so doing, counsel should fully explain the rights that would be waived, the possible collateral consequences, and the legal, factual, and contextual considerations that bear upon the decision. Specifically, counsel should know and fully explain to the client:
   1. the maximum penalty that may be imposed for the charged offense(s) and any possible lesser included or alternative offenses;
   2. any collateral consequences of potential penalties less than death, such as forfeiture of assets, deportation, civil liabilities, and the use of the disposition adversely to the client in penalty phase proceedings of other prosecutions of him as well as any direct consequences of potential penalties less than death, such as the possibility and likelihood of parole, place of confinement, and good-time credits;
   3. the general range of sentences for similar offenses committed by defendants with similar backgrounds, and the impact of any applicable sentencing guidelines or mandatory sentencing requirements;
   4. the governing legal regime, including but not limited to whatever choices the client may have as to the fact finder and/or sentencer;
   5. the types of pleas that may be agreed to, such as a plea of guilty, a conditional plea of guilty, or a plea of nolo contendere or other plea which does not require the client to personally acknowledge guilt, along with the advantages and disadvantages of each;
   6. whether any agreement negotiated can be made binding on the court, on penal/parole authorities, and any others who may be involved;

7. the practices, policies, and concerns of the particular jurisdiction, the judge and prosecuting authority, the family of the victim, and any other persons or entities which may affect the content and likely results of plea negotiations;

8. concessions that the client might offer, such as:
    a. an agreement to waive trial and to plead guilty to particular charges;
    b. an agreement to permit a judge to perform functions relative to guilt or sentence that would otherwise be performed by a jury or vice versa;
    c. an agreement regarding future custodial status, such as one to be confined in a more onerous category of institution than would otherwise be the case;
    d. an agreement to forego in whole or part legal remedies such as appeals, motions for post-conviction relief, and/or parole or clemency applications;
    e. an agreement to provide the prosecution with assistance in investigating or prosecuting the present case or other alleged criminal activity;
    f. an agreement to engage in or refrain from any particular conduct, as appropriate to the case;
    g. an agreement with the victim's family, which may include matters such as: a meeting between the victim's family and the client, a promise not to publicize or profit from the offense, the issuance or delivery of a public statement of remorse by the client, or restitution;
    h. agreements such as those described in Subsections 8(a)–(g) respecting actual or potential charges in another jurisdiction;

9. benefits the client might obtain from a negotiated settlement, including:
    a. a guarantee that the death penalty will not be imposed;
    b. an agreement that the defendant will receive a specified sentence;
    c. an agreement that the prosecutor will not advocate a certain sentence, will not present certain information to the court, or will engage in or refrain from engaging in other actions with regard to sentencing;
    d. an agreement that one or more of multiple charges will be reduced or dismissed;
    e. an agreement that the client will not be subject to further investigation or prosecution for uncharged alleged or suspected criminal conduct;
    f. an agreement that the client may enter a conditional plea to preserve the right to further contest certain legal issues;
    g. an agreement that the court or prosecutor will make specific recommendations to correctional or parole authorities regarding the terms of the client's confinement;
    h. agreements such as those described in Subsections 9(a)–(g) respecting actual or potential charges in another jurisdiction.

C. Counsel should keep the client fully informed of any negotiations for a disposition, convey to the client any offers made by the prosecution, and discuss with the client possible negotiation strategies.

D. Counsel should inform the client of any tentative negotiated agreement reached with the prosecution, and explain to the client the full content of the agreement along with the advantages, disadvantages and potential consequences of the agreement.

E. If a negotiated disposition would be in the best interest of the client, initial refusals by the prosecutor to negotiate should not prevent counsel from making further efforts to negotiate. Similarly, a client's initial opposition should not prevent counsel from engaging in an ongoing effort to persuade the client to accept an offer of resolution that is in the client's best interest.

F. Counsel should not accept any agreed-upon disposition without the client's express authorization.

G. The existence of ongoing negotiations with the prosecution does not in any way diminish the obligations of defense counsel respecting litigation.

GUIDELINE 10.9.2—ENTRY OF A PLEA OF GUILTY

A. The informed decision whether to enter a plea of guilty lies with the client.

B. In the event the client determines to enter a plea of guilty:
1. Prior to the entry of the plea, counsel should:
   a. make certain that the client understands the rights to be waived by entering the plea and that the client's decision to waive those rights is knowing, voluntary, and intelligent;
   b. ensure that the client understands the conditions and limits of the plea agreement and the maximum punishment, sanctions, and other consequences to which he or she will be exposed by entering the plea;
   c. explain to the client the nature of the plea hearing and prepare the client for the role he or she will play in the hearing, including answering questions in court and providing a statement concerning the offense.
2. During entry of the plea, counsel should make sure that the full content and conditions of any agreements with the government are placed on the record.

GUIDELINE 10.10.1—TRIAL PREPARATION OVERALL

As the investigations mandated by Guideline 10.7 produce information, trial counsel should formulate a defense theory. Counsel should seek a theory that will be effective in connection with both guilt and penalty, and should seek to minimize any inconsistencies.

GUIDELINE 10.10.2—VOIR DIRE AND JURY SELECTION

A. Counsel should consider, along with potential legal challenges to the procedures for selecting the jury that would be available in any criminal case (particularly those relating to bias on the basis of race or gender), whether any procedures have been instituted for selection of juries in capital cases that present particular legal bases for challenge. Such challenges may include challenges to the selection of the grand jury and grand jury forepersons as well as to the selection of the petit jury venire.

B. Counsel should be familiar with the precedents relating to questioning and challenging of potential jurors, including the procedures surrounding "death qualification" concerning any potential juror's beliefs about the death penalty. Counsel should be familiar with techniques: (1) for exposing those prospective jurors who would automatically impose the death penalty following a murder conviction or finding that the defendant is death-eligible, regardless of the individual circumstances of the case; (2) for uncovering those prospective jurors who are unable to give meaningful consideration to mitigating evidence; and (3) for rehabilitating potential jurors whose initial indications of opposition to the death penalty make them possibly excludable.

C. Counsel should consider seeking expert assistance in the jury selection process.

GUIDELINE 10.11—THE DEFENSE CASE CONCERNING PENALTY

A. As set out in Guideline 10.7(A), counsel at every stage of the case have a continuing duty to investigate issues bearing upon penalty and to seek information that supports mitigation or rebuts the prosecution's case in aggravation.

B. Trial counsel should discuss with the client early in the case the sentencing alternatives available, and the relationship between the strategy for the sentencing phase and for the guilt/innocence phase.

C. Prior to the sentencing phase, trial counsel should discuss with the client the specific sentencing phase procedures of the jurisdiction and advise the client of steps being taken in preparation for sentencing.

D. Counsel at every stage of the case should discuss with the client the content and purpose of the information concerning penalty that they intend to present to the sentencing or reviewing body or individual, means by which the mitigation presentation might be strengthened, and the strategy for meeting the prosecution's case in aggravation.

E. Counsel should consider, and discuss with the client, the possible consequences of having the client testify or make a statement to the sentencing or reviewing body or individual.

F. In deciding which witnesses and evidence to prepare concerning penalty, the areas counsel should consider to include the following:

1. Witnesses familiar with and evidence relating to the client's life and development, from conception to the time of sentencing, that would be explanatory of the offense(s) for which the client is being sentenced, would rebut or explain evidence presented by the prosecutor, would present positive aspects of the client's life, or would otherwise support a sentence less than death;

2. Expert and lay witnesses along with supporting documentation (e.g., school records, military records) to provide medical, psychological, sociological, cultural, or other insights into the client's mental and/or emotional state and life history that may explain or lessen the client's culpability for the underlying offense(s); to give a favorable opinion as to the client's capacity for rehabilitation or adaptation to prison; to explain possible treatment programs; or otherwise support a sentence less than death; and/or to rebut or explain evidence presented by the prosecutor;

3. Witnesses who can testify about the applicable alternative to a death sentence and/or the conditions under which the alternative sentence would be served;

4. Witnesses who can testify about the adverse impact of the client's execution on the client's family and loved ones.

5. Demonstrative evidence, such as photos, videos, and physical objects (e.g., trophies, artwork, military medals), and documents that humanize the client or portray him positively, such as certificates of earned awards, favorable press accounts, and letters of praise or reference.

G. In determining what presentation to make concerning penalty, counsel should consider whether any portion of the defense case will open the door to the prosecution's presentation of otherwise inadmissible aggravating evidence. Counsel should pursue all appropriate means (e.g., motions in limine) to ensure that the defense case concerning penalty is constricted as little as possible by this consideration, and should make a full record in order to support any subsequent challenges.

H. Trial counsel should determine at the earliest possible time what aggravating factors the prosecution will rely upon in seeking the death penalty and what evidence will be offered in support thereof. If the jurisdiction has rules regarding notification of these factors, counsel at all stages of the case should object to any non compliance, and if such rules are inadequate, counsel at all stages of the case should challenge the adequacy of the rules.

I. Counsel at all stages of the case should carefully consider whether all or part of the aggravating evidence may appropriately be challenged as improper, inaccurate, misleading, or not legally admissible.

J. If the prosecution is granted leave at any stage of the case to have the client interviewed by witnesses associated with the government, defense counsel should:

1. carefully consider

   a. what legal challenges may appropriately be made to the interview or the conditions surrounding it, and

   b. the legal and strategic issues implicated by the client's cooperation or non-cooperation;

2. insure that the client understands the significance of any statements made during such an interview; and

3. attend the interview.

K. Trial counsel should request jury instructions and verdict forms that ensure that jurors will be able to consider and give effect to all relevant mitigating evidence. Trial counsel should object to instructions or verdict forms that are constitutionally flawed, or are inaccurate, or confusing and should offer alternative instructions. Post-conviction counsel should pursue these issues through factual investigation and legal argument.

L. Counsel at every stage of the case should take advantage of all appropriate opportunities to argue why death is not suitable punishment for their particular client.

GUIDELINE 10.12—THE OFFICIAL PRESENTENCE REPORT

A. If an official presentence report or similar document may or will be presented to the court at any time, counsel should become familiar with the procedures governing preparation, submission, and verification of the report. In addition, counsel should:

1. where preparation of the report is optional, consider the strategic implications of requesting that a report be prepared;

2. provide to the report preparer information favorable to the client. In this regard, counsel should consider whether the client should speak with the person preparing the report; if the determination is made to do so, counsel should discuss the interview in advance with the client and attend it;

3. review the completed report;

4. take appropriate steps to ensure that improper, incorrect, or misleading information that may harm the client is deleted from the report;

5. take steps to preserve and protect the client's interests where the defense considers information in the presentence report to be improper, inaccurate, or misleading.

GUIDELINE 10.13—THE DUTY TO FACILITATE THE WORK OF SUCCESSOR COUNSEL

In accordance with professional norms, all persons who are or have been members of the defense team have a continuing duty to safeguard the interests of the client and should cooperate fully with successor counsel. This duty includes, but is not limited to:

A. maintaining the records of the case in a manner that will inform successor counsel of all significant developments relevant to the litigation;
B. providing the client's files, as well as information regarding all aspects of the representation, to successor counsel;
C. sharing potential further areas of legal and factual research with successor counsel; and
D. cooperating with such professionally appropriate legal strategies as may be chosen by successor counsel.

GUIDELINE 10.14—DUTIES OF TRIAL COUNSEL AFTER CONVICTION

A. Trial counsel should be familiar with all state and federal post-conviction options available to the client. Trial counsel should discuss with the client the post-conviction procedures that will or may follow imposition of the death sentence.
B. Trial counsel should take whatever action(s), such as filing a notice of appeal, and/or motion for a new trial, will maximize the client's ability to obtain post-conviction relief.
C. Trial counsel should not cease acting on the client's behalf until successor counsel has entered the case or trial counsel's representation has been formally terminated. Until that time, Guideline 10.15.1 applies in its entirety.
D. Trial counsel should take all appropriate action to ensure that the client obtains successor counsel as soon as possible.

GUIDELINE 10.15.1—DUTIES OF POST-CONVICTION COUNSEL

A. Counsel representing a capital client at any point after conviction should be familiar with the jurisdiction's procedures for setting execution dates and providing notice of them. Post-conviction counsel should also be thoroughly familiar with all available procedures for seeking a stay of execution.
B. If an execution date is set, post-conviction counsel should immediately take all appropriate steps to secure a stay of execution and pursue those efforts through all available fora.
C. Post-conviction counsel should seek to litigate all issues, whether or not previously presented, that are arguably meritorious under the standards applicable to high quality capital defense representation, including challenges to any overly restrictive procedural rules. Counsel should make every professionally appropriate effort to present issues in a manner that will preserve them for subsequent review.

D. The duties of the counsel representing the client on direct appeal should include filing a petition for certiorari in the Supreme Court of the United States. If appellate counsel does not intend to file such a petition, he or she should immediately notify successor counsel if known and the Responsible Agency.

E. Post-conviction counsel should fully discharge the ongoing obligations imposed by these Guidelines, including the obligations to:
   1. maintain close contact with the client regarding litigation developments; and
   2. continually monitor the client's mental, physical, and emotional condition for effects on the client's legal position;
   3. keep under continuing review the desirability of modifying prior counsel's theory of the case in light of subsequent developments; and
   4. continue an aggressive investigation of all aspects of the case.

GUIDELINE 10.15.2—DUTIES OF CLEMENCY COUNSEL

A. Clemency counsel should be familiar with the procedures for and permissible substantive content of a request for clemency.

B. Clemency counsel should conduct an investigation in accordance with Guideline 10.7.

C. Clemency counsel should ensure that clemency is sought in as timely and persuasive a manner as possible, tailoring the presentation to the characteristics of the particular client, case, and jurisdiction.

D. Clemency counsel should ensure that the process governing consideration of the client's application is substantively and procedurally just and, if it is not, should seek appropriate redress.

References

Abramson, S., & Isay, D. (2002). The stopping point: Interview with a tie-down officer. In D. R. Dow, & M. Dow (Eds.), *Machinery of death: The reality of America's death penalty regime* (pp. 169–173). New York: Routledge.

Accusations cost chemist job. (2001, September 26). *The Orlando Sentinel* A13.

Acker, J. R. (1996). The death penalty: A 25-year retrospective and a perspective on the future. *Criminal Justice Review, 21,* 139–160.

Acker, J. R. (2006). The myth of closure and capital punishment. In R. M. Bohm, & J. T. Walker (Eds.), *Demystifying crime and criminal justice* (pp. 167–175). Los Angeles: Roxbury.

Acker, J. R., & Karp, D. R. (2006). Introduction. In J. R. Acker, & D. R. Karp (Eds.), *Wounds that do not bind: Victim-based perspectives on the death penalty* (pp. 3–14). Durham, NC: Carolina Academic Press.

Acker, J. R., & Lanier, C. S. (1995). Matters of life or death: The sentencing provisions in capital punishment statutes. *Criminal Law Bulletin, 31,* 19–60.

Acker, J. R., & Lanier, C. S. (1998). Beyond human ability: The rise and fall of death penalty legislation. In J. R. Acker, R. M. Bohm, & C. S. Lanier (Eds.), *America's experiment with capital punishment: Reflections on the past, present and future of the ultimate penal sanction* (pp. 77–115). Durham, NC: Carolina Academic Press.

Acker, J. R., & Lanier, C. S. (1999). Ready for the defense? Legislative provisions governing the appointment of counsel in capital cases. *Criminal Law Bulletin, 35,* 429–477.

Acker, J. R., & Lanier, C. S. (2000). May God—or the governor—have mercy: Executive clemency and executions in modern death-penalty systems. *Criminal Law Bulletin, 36,* 200–237.

Acker, J. R., & Mastrocinque, J. M. (2006). Causing death and sustaining life: The law, capital punishment, and criminal homicide victims' survivors. In J. R. Acker, & D. R. Karp (Eds.), *Wounds that do not bind: Victim-based perspectives on the death penalty* (pp. 141–160). Durham, NC: Carolina Academic Press.

Acker, J. R., Bohm, R. M., & Lanier, C. S. (Eds.) (2003). *America's experiment with capital punishment: Reflections on the past, present and future of the ultimate penal sanction* (2nd ed.). Durham, NC: Carolina Academic Press.

After botched execution, Ohio to change method. (2009, November 14). *The Orlando Sentinel,* p. A11.

Alabama inmate becomes oldest executed since '41. (2004, August 6). *The Orlando Sentinel,* p. A4.

Allen, H. W., & Clubb, J. M. (2008). *Race, class, and the death penalty.* Albany: State University of New York Press.

Alter, J. (2000a, July 3). A reckoning on death row. *Newsweek,* 31.

Alter, J. (2000b, June 12). The death penalty on trial. *Newsweek,* 24–34.

Alter, J., & Miller, M. (2000, May 29). A life or death gamble. *Newsweek,* 23–27.

A matter of life and death. (2006). The effect of life-without-parole statutes on capital punishment. *Harvard Law Review, 119,* 1838–1854, Retrieved from http://www.harvardlawreview.org/issues/119/april06/notes/capital_punishment.pdf.

American Bar Association. (2003). Guidelines for the appointment and performance of defense counsel in death penalty cases in the Summer 2003 [Electronic version]. *Hofstra Law Review, 31*(4), 913–1090.

American Bar Association. (2006). Evaluating fairness and accuracy in state death penalty systems: The Georgia death penalty assessment report. The report can be found at the Death Penalty Information Center website. http://www.deathpenalty info.org.

American Correctional Association 2005 Directory. (2005). *Adult and juvenile correctional departments, institutions, agencies and probation and parole authorities.* Lanham, MD: American Correctional Association.

Amnesty International. (2010). UN moratorium on the use of the death penalty December 2008. Retrieved November 24, 2010, from. http://www.amnesty.org/en/death-penalty/international-law/moratorium/2008-resolution.

Amnesty International Website Against the Death Penalty. (2002). Facts and figures on the death penalty. Retrieved from http://www.amnesty.org.

Amsterdam, A. G. (1982). Capital punishment. In H. A. Bedau (Ed.), *The death penalty in America* (3rd ed.). (pp. 346–358) New York: Oxford University Press.

Ancel, M. (1967). The problem of the death penalty. In T. Sellin (Ed.), *Capital punishment* (pp. 3–21). New York: Harper & Row.

Andersen, K. (1983, January 24). An eye for an eye. *Time* 28–39.

Antonio, M. E. (2006). Jurors' emotional reactions to serving on a capital trial. *Judicature, 89,* 282–288.

A portrait of American Catholics on the eve of Pope Benedict's visit to the U.S. (2008, March 27). The Pew Forum on Religion and Public Life. Retrieved December 12, 2010, from http://pewforum.org/Christian/Catholic/A-Portrait-of-American-Catholics-on-the-Eve-of-Pope-Benedicts-Visit-to-the-US-(3).aspx.

Applegate, B. K., Cullen, F. T., Fisher, B. S., & Vander Ven, T. (2000). Forgiveness and fundamentalism: Reconsidering the relationship between correctional attitudes and religion. *Criminology, 38,* 719–753.

Archer, D., Gartner, R., & Beittel, M. (1983). Homicide and the death penalty: A cross-national test of a deterrence hypothesis. *Journal of Criminal Law and Criminology, 74,* 991–1013.

Arkin, S. D. (1980). Discrimination and arbitrariness in capital punishment: An analysis of post-Furman murder cases in Dade County, Florida, 1973–1976. *Stanford Law Review, 33,* 75–101.

Armbrust, S. (2002). Chance and the exoneration of Anthony Porter. In D. R. Dow, & M. Dow (Eds.), *Machinery of death: The reality of America's death penalty regime* (pp. 157–166). New York: Routledge.

Arthur, J. (1998). Proximate correlates of black's support for capital punishment. *Journal of Crime and Justice, 21,* 159–172.

Atwell, M. W. (2004). *Evolving standards of decency: Popular culture and capital punishment.* New York: Peter Lang.

Bailey, W. C. (1974). Murder and the death penalty. *Journal of Criminal Law and Criminology, 65,* 416–423.

Bailey, W. C. (1977a). Imprisonment v. the death penalty as a deterrent to murder. *Law and Human Behavior, 1,* 239–260.

Bailey, W. C. (1977b). Deterrence and the violent sex offender: Imprisonment vs. the death penalty. *Journal of Behavioral Economics, 6,* 107–144.

Bailey, W. C. (1978). Deterrence and the death penalty for murder in Utah: A time-series analysis. *Journal of Contemporary Law, 5,* 1–20.

Bailey, W. C. (1979a). The deterrent effect of the death penalty for murder in California. *Southern California Law Review, 52,* 743–764.

Bailey, W. C. (1979b). The deterrent effect of the death penalty for murder in Ohio: A time-series analysis. *Cleveland State Law Review, 28,* 51–81.

Bailey, W. C. (1979c). Deterrence and the death penalty for murder in Oregon. *Willamette Law Review, 16,* 67–85.

Bailey, W. C. (1979d). An analysis of the deterrent effect of the death penalty in North Carolina. *North Carolina Central Law Journal, 10,* 29–52.

Bailey, W. C. (1980). Deterrence and the celerity of the death penalty: A neglected question in deterrence research. *Social Forces, 58,* 1308–1333.

Bailey, W. C. (1983). The deterrent effect of capital punishment during the 1950s. *Suicide, 13,* 95–107.

Bailey, W. C. (1984a). Disaggregation in deterrence and death penalty research: The case of murder in Chicago. *Journal of Criminal Law and Criminology, 74,* 827–859.

Bailey, W. C. (1984b). Murder and capital punishment in the nation's capital. *Justice Quarterly, 1,* 211–233.

Bailey, W. C. (1990). Murder and capital punishment: An analysis of television execution publicity. *American Sociological Review, 55,* 1308–1333.

Bailey, W. C. (1991). The general prevention effect of capital punishment for non-capital felonies. In R. M. Bohm (Ed.), *The death penalty in America: Current research* (pp. 21–38). Cincinnati: Anderson Publishing Co.

Bailey, W. C. (1998). Deterrence, brutalization, and the death penalty: Another examination of Oklahoma's return to capital punishment. *Criminology, 36*, 711–733.

Bailey, W. C., & Peterson, R. D. (1987). Police killings and capital punishment: The post-Furman period. *Criminology, 25*, 1–25.

Bailey, W. C., & Peterson, R. D. (1989). Murder and capital punishment: A monthly time-series analysis of execution publicity. *American Sociological Review, 54*, 722–743.

Baile,ly, W. C., & Peterson, R. D. (1994). Murder, capital punishment, and deterrence: A review of the evidence and an examination of police killings. *Journal of Social Issues, 50*, 53–74.

Baldus, D. C. (2006, April 26). Personal correspondence with the author.

Baldus, D. C., & Cole, J. W. L. (1975). Statistical evidence on the deterrent effect of capital punishment: A comparison of the work of Thorsten Sellin and Isaac Ehrlich on the deterrent effect of capital punishment. *Yale Law Journal, 85*, 17–186.

Baldus, D. C., & Woodworth, G. (1997). Race discrimination in America's capital punishment system since Furman v. Georgia (1972). The evidence of race disparities and the record of our courts and legislatures in addressing this issue. Report prepared for the American Bar Association [Cited in Dieter, R.C. (1998). The death penalty in black & white: Who lives, who dies, who decides. Death Penalty Information Center. Retrieved from http://www.deathpenaltyinfo.org/racerpt.html].

Baldus, D. C., & Woodworth, G. (1998). Racial discrimination and the death penalty: An empirical and legal overview. In J. R. Acker, R. M. Bohm, & C. S. Lanier (Eds.), *America's experiment with capital punishment: Reflections on the past, present and future of the ultimate penal sanction* (pp. 385–415). Durham, NC: Carolina Academic Press.

Baldus, D. C., Pulaski, C., & Woodworth, G. (1983). Comparative review of death sentences: An empirical study of the Georgia experience. *Journal of Criminal Law and Criminology, 74*, 661–753.

Baldus, D. C., Pulaski, C., Jr., & Woodworth, G. (1986). Arbitrariness and discrimination in the administration of the death penalty: A challenge to state Supreme Courts. *Stetson Law Review, 15*, 133–261.

Baldus, D. C., Woodworth, G. G., & Pulaski, C. A. (1990). *Equal justice and the death penalty: A legal and empirical analysis.* Boston: Northeastern University Press.

Baldus, D. C., Woodworth, G., Young, G. L., & Christ, A. M. (2001). The disposition of Nebraska capital and non-capital homicide cases (1973–1999): A legal and empirical analysis. The Nebraska Commission on Law Enforcement and Criminal Justice. Retrieved from. http://www.nol.org/home/crimecom/homicide/homicide.htm.

Baldus, D. C., Woodworth, G., Zuckerman, D., Weiner, N. A., & Broffitt, B. (1998). Race discrimination and the death penalty in the post-Furman era: An empirical and legal overview, with preliminary findings from Philadelphia. *Cornell Law Review, 83*, 1638–1770.

Banner, S. (2002). *The death penalty: An American history.* Cambridge: Harvard University Press.

Barkan, S. E., & Cohn, S. F. (1994). Racial prejudice and support for the death penalty by whites. *Journal of Research in Crime & Delinquency, 31*, 202–209.

Barkan, S. E., & Cohn, S. F. (2010). Contemporary regional differences in support by whites for the death penalty: A research note. *Justice Quarterly, 27*, 458–471.

Barnett, A. (1981). The deterrent effect of capital punishment: A test of some recent studies. *Operations Research, 29*, 346–370.

Barnett, A. (1985). *Some distribution patterns for the Georgia death sentence.* University of California Davis Law Review 18. 1327–1374.

Baumer, E. P., Messner, S. F., & Rosenfeld, R. (2003). Explaining spatial variation in support for capital punishment: A multilevel analysis. *American Journal of Sociology, 108*, 844–875.

Baumgartner, F. R., DeBoef, S. L., & Boydstun, A. E. (2008). *The decline of the death penalty and the discovery of innocence*. New York: Cambridge University Press.

Beccaria, C. (1975). *On crimes and punishments*. (H. Paolucci, Trans., with an introduction). Indianapolis, IN: Bobbs-Merrill.

Beck, E., Britto, S., & Andrews, A. (2007). *In the shadow of death: Restorative justice and death row families*. New York: Oxford University Press.

Bedau, H. A. (Ed.) (1967). *The death penalty in America: An anthology* (Rev. ed.). Chicago: Aldine.

Bedau, H. A. (Ed.) (1982). *The death penalty in America* (3rd ed.). New York: Oxford University Press.

Bedau, H. A. (1987). *Death is different: Studies in the morality, law, and politics of capital punishment*. Boston: Northeastern University Press.

Bedau, H. A. (1997). *The death penalty in America: Current controversies*. New York: Oxford University Press.

Bedau, H. A. (1999). Abolishing the death penalty even for the worst murderers. In A. Sarat (Ed.), *The killing state: Capital punishment in law, politics, and culture* (pp. 40–59). New York: Oxford University Press.

Bedau, H. A. (2004). An abolitionist's survey of the death penalty in America today. In H. A. Bedau, & P. G. Cassell (Eds.), *Debating the death penalty: Should America have capital punishment? The experts on both sides make their best case* (pp. 15–50). New York: Oxford.

Bedau, H. A. (2009). Racism, wrongful convictions, and the death penalty. *Tennessee Law Review, 76*, 615–624.

Bedau, H. A., & Radelet, M. L. (1987). Miscarriages of justice in potentially capital cases. *Stanford Law Review, 40*, 21–179.

Bedau, H. A., & Radelet, M. L. (1988). The myth of infallibility: A reply to Markman and Cassell. *Stanford Law Review, 41*, 161–170.

Bell, M. (2007, April 24). Study: Lethal injection flawed. *The Orlando Sentinel*, p. B7.

Berk, R. (2005). New claims about executions and general deterrence: Déjà vu all over again? Retrieved from http://preprints.stat.ucla.edu/download.php?paper=396.

Berlow, A. (2003, July/August). The Texas clemency memos. *The Atlantic Monthly*, 91–96.

Beyleveld, D. (1982). Ehrlich's analysis of deterrence. *The British Journal of Criminology, 22*, 101–123.

Bienen, L. B. (1996). The proportionality review of capital cases by state high courts after Gregg: Only 'The Appearance of Justice'? *Journal of Criminal Law and Criminology, 87*, 130–314.

Bienen, L. B. (2010). Capital punishment in Illinois in the aftermath of the Ryan commutations: Reforms, economic realities, and a new saliency for issues of cost. Northwestern Public Law Research Paper No. 10–72. Retrieved December 7, 2010, from SSRN: *Journal of Criminal Law and Criminology, 100*(4) http://ssrn.com/abstract=1704833.

Bienen, L. B., Weiner, N. A., Denno, D. W., Allison, P. D., & Mills, D. L. (1988). The reimposition of capital punishment in New Jersey: The role of prosecutorial discretion. *Rutgers Law Review, 41*, 27–372.

Bingham, A., Cochran, J. K., Heide, K., & Boots, D. P. (2010, October 1). *Public support for preventive/corrective remedies against miscarriages of justice in capital cases*. Paper presented at the annual meeting of the Southern Criminal Justice Association, Clearwater, FL.

Birmingham news criticizes costly, arbitrary death penalty. (2005, December 7). *The Birmingham News*. Retrieved from http://www.deathpenaltyinfo.org/article.php?scid=7&did=851.

Black, C. L., Jr. (1974). *Capital punishment: The inevitability of caprice and mistake*. New York: W. W. Norton & Co.

Blankenship, M. B., Luginbuhl, J., Cullen, F. T., & Redick, W. (1997). Jurors' comprehension of sentencing instructions: A test of the death penalty process in Tennessee. *Justice Quarterly, 14*, 325–346.

Blecker, R. (2001, January 7). The U.S. needs to rethink how it applies death penalty. *The Orlando Sentinel*. (from The Washington Post), p. G1.

Blecker, R. (2006). A poster child for us. *Judicature, 89*, 297–301.

Bobo, L. D., & Johnson, D. (2004). A taste for punishment: Black and white Americans' views on the death penalty and the war on drugs. *Du Bois Review, 1*, 151–180.

Bohm, R. M. (1987). American death penalty attitudes: A critical examination of recent evidence. *Criminal Justice and Behavior, 14*, 380–396.

Bohm, R. M. (1989). The effects of classroom instruction and discussion on death penalty opinions: A teaching note. *Journal of Criminal Justice, 17*, 123–131.

Bohm, R. M. (1990). Death penalty opinions: Effects of a classroom experience and public commitment. *Sociological Inquiry, 60*, 285–297.

Bohm, R. M. (1991). American death penalty opinion, 1936–1986: A critical examination of the Gallup polls. In R. M. Bohm (Ed.), *The death penalty in America: Current research* (pp. 113–145). Cincinnati: Anderson Publishing Co.

Bohm, R. M. (1992a). Toward an understanding of death penalty opinion change in the United States: The pivotal years, 1966 and 1967. *Humanity and Society, 16*, 524–542.

Bohm, R. M. (1992b). Retribution and capital punishment: Toward a better understanding of death penalty opinion. *Journal of Criminal Justice, 20*, 227–236.

Bohm, R. M. (1994). Capital punishment in two judicial circuits in Georgia: A description of the key actors and the decision-making process. *Law and Human Behavior, 18*, 319–338.

Bohm, R. M. (2010). *Ultimate sanction: Understanding the death penalty through its many voices and many sides.* New York: Kaplan.

Bohm, R. M., & Haley, K. N. (1997). *Introduction to criminal justice.* New York: McGraw-Hill.

Bohm, R. M., & Haley, K. N. (2007). *Introduction to criminal justice* (4th ed.). New York: McGraw-Hill. Update.

Bohm, R. M., Clark, L. J., & Aveni, A. F. (1990). The influence of knowledge on death penalty opinions: An experimental test. *Justice Quarterly, 7*, 175–188.

Bohm, R. M., Clark, L. J., & Aveni, A. F. (1991). Knowledge and death penalty opinion: A test of the Marshall hypotheses. *Journal of Research in Crime & Delinquency, 28*, 360–387.

Bohm, R. M., & Vogel, R. E. (1994). A comparison of factors associated with uninformed and informed death penalty opinions. *Journal of Criminal Justice, 22*, 125–143.

Bohm, R. M., & Vogel, B. L. (2004). More than ten years after: The long-term stability of informed death penalty opinions. *Journal of Criminal Justice, 32*, 307–327.

Bohm, R. M., Vogel, R. E., & Maisto, A. A. (1993). Knowledge and death penalty opinion: A panel study. *Journal of Criminal Justice, 21*, 29–45.

Bonczar, T. P., & Snell, T. L. (2005, November). *Capital punishment 2004.* US Department of Justice. Bureau of Justice Statistics Bulletin.

Boots, P. D., Cochran, J. K., & Heide, K. M. (2003). Capital punishment preferences for special offender population. *Journal of Criminal Justice, 31*, 553–565.

Borg, M. J. (1997). The southern subculture of punitiveness? Regional variation in support for capital punishment. *Journal of Research in Crime & Delinquency, 34*, 25–46.

Borg, M. J. (1998). Vicarious homicide victimization and support for capital punishment: A test of Black's theory of law. *Criminology, 36*, 537–567.

Bowers, W. J. (1988). The effect of executions is brutalization, not deterrence. In K. C. Haas, & J. A. Inciardi (Eds.), *Challenging capital punishment: Legal and social science approaches* (pp. 49–89). Newbury Park, CA: Sage.

Bowers, W. J. (1993). Capital punishment and contemporary values: People's misgivings and the court's misperceptions. *Law and Society Review, 27*, 157–175.

Bowers, W. J. (1995). The Capital Jury Project: Rationale, design, and preview of early findings. *Indiana Law Journal, 70*, 1043–1102.

Bowers, W. J., & Foglia, W. D. (2003). Still singularly agonizing: Law's failure to purge arbitrariness from capital sentencing. *Criminal Law Bulletin, 39*, 51–86.

Bowers, W. J., & Pierce, G. L. (1975). The illusion of deterrence in Isaac Ehrlich's research on capital punishment. *Yale Law Journal, 85*, 187–208.

Bowers, W. J., & Pierce, G. L. (1980). Deterrence or brutalization: What is the effect of executions? *Crime & Delinquency, 26,* 453–484.

Bowers, W. J., & Pierce, G. L. (1982). Racial discrimination and criminal homicide under post-*Furman* capital statutes. In H. A. Bedau (Ed.), *The Death Penalty in America* (3rd ed.). (pp. 206–224) New York: Oxford University Press.

Bowers, W. J., Pierce, G. L., & McDevitt, J. F. (1984). *Legal homicide: Death as punishment in America, 1864–1982.* Boston: Northeastern University Press.

Bowers, W. J., Sandys, M., & Steiner, B. D. (1998). Foreclosed impartiality in capital sentencing: Jurors' predispositions, guilt-trial experience, and premature decision making. *Cornell Law Review, 83,* 1476–1556.

Bowers, W. J., & Steiner, B. D. (1998). Choosing life or death: Sentencing dynamics in capital cases. In J. R. Acker, R. M. Bohm, & C. S. Lanier (Eds.), *America's experiment with capital punishment: Reflections on the past, present and future of the ultimate penal sanction* (pp. 309–349). Durham, NC: Carolina Academic Press.

Bowers, W. J., & Steiner, B. D. (1999). Death by default: An empirical demonstration of false and forced choices in capital sentencing. *Texas Law Review, 77,* 605–717.

Bowers, W. J., Steiner, B. D., & Sandys, M. (2001). *Death sentencing in black and white: An empirical analysis of the role of jurors' race and jury racial composition.* University of Pennsylvania. Journal of Constitutional Law 3:171-274.

Bowers, W. J., Vandiver, M., & Dugan, P. H. (1994). A new look at public opinion on capital punishment: What citizens and legislators prefer. *American Journal of Criminal Law, 22,* 77–150.

Bradley, C. M. (2006). The right decision on the juvenile death penalty. *Judicature, 89,* 302–303, 305.

Brier, S., & Feinberg, S. (1980). Recent econometric modeling of crime and punishment: Support for the deterrence hypothesis? *Evaluation Research, 4,* 147–191.

Bright, S. B. (1995). Discrimination, death and denial: The tolerance of racial discrimination in the infliction of the death penalty. *Santa Clara Law Review, 35,* 433–483.

Bright, S. B. (1997a). *Capital punishment on the 25th anniversary of Furman v.* Georgia. Atlanta, GA: Southern Center for Human Rights.

Bright, S. B. (1997b). Neither equal nor just: The rationing and denial of legal services to the poor when life and liberty are at stake. *Annual Survey of American Law, 1997,* 783–836.

Bright, S. B. (1998). The politics of capital punishment: The sacrifice of fairness for executions. In J. R. Acker, R. M. Bohm, & C. S. Lanier (Eds.), *America's experiment with capital punishment: Reflections on the past, present and future of the ultimate penal sanction* (pp. 117–135). Durham, NC: Carolina Academic Press.

Bright, S. B. (2002). Discrimination, death, and denial: Race and the death penalty. In D. R. Dow, & M. Dow (Eds.), *Machinery of death: The reality of America's death penalty regime* (pp. 45–78). New York: Routledge.

Bright, S. B. (2004). Why the United States will join the rest of the world in abandoning capital punishment. In H. A. Bedau, & P. G. Cassell (Eds.), *Debating the death penalty: Should America have capital punishment? The experts on both sides make their best case* (pp. 152–182). New York: Oxford.

Bright, S. B. (2006). Discrimination, death, and denial: The tolerance of racial discrimination in infliction of the death penalty. In C. J. Ogletree, Jr., & A. Sarat (Eds.), *From lynch mobs to the killing state: Race and the death penalty in America* (pp. 211–259). New York: New York University Press.

Bright, S. B., & Keenan, P. J. (1995). *Judges and the politics of death: Deciding between the Bill of Rights and the next election in capital cases.* Boston University. Law Review 75:pp. 759–835.

Britt, C. L. (1998). Race, religion, and support for the death penalty: A research note. *Justice Quarterly, 15,* 175–191.

Brock, D., Cohen, N., & Sorensen, J. (2000). Arbitrariness in the imposition of death sentences in Texas: An analysis of four counties by offense seriousness, race of victim, and race of offender. *American Journal of Criminal Law, 28,* 43–71.

Bronson, E. J. (1970). *On the conviction proneness and representativeness of the death-qualified jury: An empirical study of Colorado veniremen.* University of Colorado Law Review 42 1–32.

Brooks, J., & Erikson, J. H. (1996). The dire wolf collects his due while the boys sit by the fire: Why Michigan cannot afford to buy into the death penalty. *Thomas M. Cooley Law Review, 13,* 877–905.

Brumm, H. J., & Cloninger, D. O. (1996). Perceived risk of punishment and the commission of homicides: A covariance structure analysis. *Journal of Economic Behavior and Analysis, 31,* 1–11.

Brunsvold, M. L. (2004). Medicating to execute: Singleton v. Norris. *Chicago-Kent Law Review, 79,* 1291–1311.

Burnett, C. (2002). *Justice denied: Clemency appeals in death penalty cases.* Boston: Northeastern University Press.

Burnett, C. (2005). Restorative justice and wrongful capital convictions: A simple proposal. *Journal of Contemporary Criminal Justice, 21,* 272–289.

Burstein, J. (2009, November 2). Wrongly jailed man isn't taking state compensation. *The Orlando Sentinel* p. A21.

Bye, R. T. (1919). *Capital punishment in the United States.* Philadelphia: The Committee of Philanthropic Labor of Philadelphia Yearly Meeting of Friends.

Cabana, D. A. (1996). *Death at midnight: The confession of an executioner.* Boston: Northeastern University Press.

California Department of Corrections and Rehabilitation. Fourth quarter 2008 facts and figures. Retrieved November 29, 2010, fromhttp://www.cdcr.ca.gov/Adult_Operations/docs/Fourth_Quarter_2009_Facts_and_Figures.pdf

California Department of Corrections and Rehabilitation. Lethal injection procedures. Retrieved March 31, 2006, from http://www.cya.ca.gov/ReportsResearch/lethalInjection.html

Callahan, L., Acker, J. R., & Cerulli, C. (2000). Accommodating death penalty legislation: Personal and professional views of assistant district attorneys toward capital punishment. *American Journal of Criminal Justice, 25,* 15–29.

Camp, C. G., & Camp, G. M. (1994). *The corrections yearbook 1994.* South Salem, NY: Criminal Justice Institute.

Can the family of the victim witness an execution? (2010). CriminalDefenselawyer.com. Retrieved November 28, 2010, from http://www.criminaldefenselawyer.com/resources/criminal-defense/felony-offense/can-family-victim-witness-execution.

Canan, R. F. (1989). Burning at the wire: The execution of John Evans. In M. L. Radelet (Ed.), *Facing the death penalty: Essays on a cruel and unusual punishment* (pp. 60–80). Philadelphia: Temple University Press.

Carmichael, S., & Hamilton, C. V. (1967). *Black power: The politics of liberation in America.* New York: Vintage Books.

Carroll, J. (2004, November 16). Who supports the death penalty? The Gallup Organization. Retrieved from http://www.deathpenaltyinfo.org/article.php?scid=23&did=1266

Carter, D. T. (1969). *Scottsboro: A tragedy of the American South.* New York: Oxford University Press.

Cassell, P. G. (2004). In defense of the death penalty. In H. A. Bedau, & P. G. Cassell (Eds.), *Debating the death penalty: Should America have capital punishment? The experts on both sides make their best case* (pp. 183–217). New York: Oxford.

Cavender, G. (1995). Joining the fray: An interview with William J. Bowers. *American Journal of Criminal Justice, 20,* 113–136.

Center on Wrongful Convictions. (2004). *The snitch system: How snitch testimony sent Randy Steidl and other innocent Americans to death row.* Northwestern University School of Law. Retrieved October 24, 2010, from http://www.innocenceproject.org/docs/SnitchSystemBooklet.pdf.

Cheatwood, D. (1993). Capital punishment and deterrence of violent crime in comparable counties. *Criminal Justice Review, 18,* 165–181.

Cheever, J. M. (2006). *Back from the dead: One woman's search for the men who walked off America's death row.* West Sussex, England: Wiley & Sons.

Clarence Edward Hill. (2010). Retrieved November 25, 2010, from http://www.clarkprosecutor.org/html/death/US/hill1047.htm

Clarke, A. W., Lambert, E., & Whitt, L. A. (2000–2001). Executing the innocent: The next step in the Marshall hypotheses. *Review of Law and Social Change, 26*, 309–345.

Clary, S. (2001, December 1). Killer's defense cost will set record. *The Orlando Sentinel,* p. C1.

Cloninger, D. O. (1977). Death and the death penalty: A cross-sectional analysis. *Journal of Behavioral Economics, 6*, 87–106.

Cloninger, D. O., & Marchesini, R. (2001). Execution and deterrence: A quasi-controlled group experiment. *Applied Economics, 33*, 569–576.

Cochran, J. K., & Chamlin, M. B. (2000). Deterrence and brutalization: The dual effect of executions. *Justice Quarterly, 17*, 685–706.

Cochran, J. K., & Chamlin, M. B. (2005). Can information change public opinion? Another test of the Marshall hypotheses. *Journal of Criminal Justice, 33*, 573–584.

Cochran, J. K., & Chamlin, M. B. (2006). The enduring racial divide in death penalty support. *Journal of Criminal Justice, 34*, 85–99.

Cochran, J. K., Chamlin, M. B., & Seth, M. (1994). Deterrence or brutalization? An impact assessment of Oklahoma's return to capital punishment. *Criminology, 32*, 107–134.

Cochran, J. K., Sanders, B., & Chamlin, M. B. (2006). Profiles in change: An alternative look at the Marshall hypotheses. *Journal of Criminal Justice, 17*, 205–226.

Cohen, S. (1999, August 15). Mistakes refocus death-penalty debate. *The Orlando Sentinel* p. A4.

Cohen-Cole, E., Durlauf, S., Fagan, J., & Nagin, D. (2009). Model uncertainty and the deterrent effects of capital punishment [Electronic version]. *American Law and Economics Review, 11*, 335–369, Retrieved September 22, 2010.

Colarossi, A. (2009, December 1). Killer of 6 in Palm Bay dies before execution. *The Orlando Sentinel,* p. B3.

Colarossi, A. (2010, October 29). How much has Casey Anthony's case cost so far. *The Orlando Sentinel,* p. B1.

Colarossi, A. (2011a, January 26). Drug's demise snags Florida executions. *The Orlando Sentinel,* p. A1.

Colarossi, A. (2011b, February 22). Maker says Florida told: Drug not for executions. *The Orlando Sentinel,* p. A1.

Colarossi, A. (2011c, March 17). The $360K jury. *The Orlando Sentinel,* p. A1.

Cole, R. (1984, November 22). Florida's execution lead is attributed to history. *The Anniston [AL] Star.*

Coleman, C. (2006). Matters of life or death. In J. R. Acker, & D. R. Karp (Eds.), *Wounds that do not bind: Victim-based perspectives on the death penalty* (pp. 17–32). Durham, NC: Carolina Academic Press.

Committee on the Judiciary, US Senate. (1982). Capital punishment as a matter of legislative policy. In H. A. Bedau (Ed.), *The death penalty in America* (3rd ed.). (pp. 311–318) New York: Oxford University Press.

Compensation statutes chart. (2009). Life After Exoneration Program. Retrieved October 13, 2010, from http://www.exonerated.org/content/index.php?option=com_content&view=article&id=103&Itemid=55.

Convicted killer put to death by electric chair in Virginia. (2006, July 21). *The Orlando Sentinel* A15.

Cook, P. J. (2009). Potential savings from abolition of the death penalty in North Carolina [Electronic version]. *American Law and Economics Review, 11*, 498–529, Retrieved September 15, 2010.

Cook, P. J., Slawson, D. B., & Gries, L. A. (1993). *The costs of processing murder cases in North Carolina.* Raleigh, NC: North Carolina Administrative Office of the Courts.

Costly death penalty takes toll on state budgets. (2003, December 14). Lakeland Ledger. Retrieved from http://www.deathpenaltyinfo.org/article.php?scid=7&did=851

Cottingham, J. (1979). Varieties of retributivism. *Philosophical Quarterly, 29*, 238–246.

Cotton, A. M. (2008). *Effigy: Images of capital defendants.* Lanham, MD: Rowman & Littlefield.

Council of Europe. (2010). The Council of Europe's relations with non-member states. Retrieved November 25, 2010, from. http://www.coe.int/t/der/nonmemberstates_EN.asp.

Court backs death-row man. (2001, August 14). *The Orlando Sentinel* p. A7.

Cowan, C., Thompson, W. C., & Ellsworth, P. C. (1984). The effects of death qualification on jurors' predisposition to convict and on the quality of deliberation. *Law and Human Behavior, 8*, 53–79.

Cox, A. (1987). *The court and the Constitution*. Boston: Houghton Mifflin.

Cox, D. (1999, September 4). Provenzano loses again. *The Orlando Sentinel*, p. D1.

Coyle, M., Strasser, F., & Lavelle, M. (1990, June 11). Fatal defense: Trial and error in the nation's death belt. *The National Law Journal, 12*(40), 30–44.

Coyne, R., & Entzeroth, L. (1994). *Capital punishment and the judicial process*. Durham, NC: Carolina Academic Press.

Coyne, R., & Entzeroth, L. (1998). *Capital punishment and the judicial process: 1998 supplement*. Durham, NC: Carolina Academic Press.

Coyne, R., & Entzeroth, L. (2001). *Capital punishment and the judicial process* (2nd ed.). Durham, NC: Carolina Academic Press.

Crespi, I. (1971). What kinds of attitude measures are predictive of behavior? *Public Opinion Quarterly, 35*, 327–334.

Crocker, P. L. (2002). Is the death penalty good for women? In D. R. Dow, & M. Dow (Eds.), *Machinery of death: The reality of America's death penalty regime* (pp. 195–224). New York: Routledge.

Culbert, J. L. (2008). *Dead certainty: The death penalty and the problem of judgment*. Stanford, CA: Stanford University Press.

Culver, J. H. (1985). The states and capital punishment: Executions from 1977–1984. *Justice Quarterly, 2*, 567–578.

Cunningham, M. D., Reidy, T. J., & Sorensen, J. R. (2005). Is death row obsolete? A decade of mainstreaming death-sentenced inmates in Missouri. *Behavioral Sciences and the Law, 23*, 307–320.

Cunningham, M. D., Reidy, T. J., & Sorensen, J. R. (2008). Assertions of 'future dangerousness' at federal capital sentencing: Rates and correlates of subsequent prison misconduct and violence. *Law and Human Behavior, 32*, 46–63.

Cushing, R. (2002). Amazing grace: Reflections on justice, survival, and healing. In D. R. Dow, & M. Dow (Eds.), *Machinery of death: The reality of America's death penalty regime* (pp. 283–287). New York: Routledge.

Dann, R. H. (1935). The deterrent effect of capital punishment. *Friends Social Service Series, 29*, 1–20.

Davey, M., & Mills, S. (2003, January 12). Illinois governor sweeps inmates from death row. *The Orlando Sentinel* p. A1.

Davis, K. (1998, November 13). Hope sought for innocents sentenced to die. *USA Today* 14A.

Death penalty expenses adding up. (1999, October 20). *New York Daily News*. Retrieved from http://www.th-record.com/1999/10/20/executio.htm.

Death penalty has cost New Jersey taxpayers $253 million. (2005, November 21). Newsday. Retrieved from http://www.deathpenaltyinfo.org/article.php?scid=7&did=85.

Death penalty in California is very costly. (2006, March 11). *Lodi News-Sentinel*. Retrieved from http://www.deathpenaltyinfo.org/newsanddev.php?scid=7.

Death Penalty Information Center (2010, 2011). Retrieved from http://www.deathpenaltyinfo.org

Death penalty prosecutions may be halted if funding is inadequate. (2005, April 15). *ABA Journal*. Retrieved from http://www.deathpenaltyinfo.org/article.php?scid=7&did=851.

Death Row, U.S.A. (1996). New York, NY: NAACP Legal Defense and Educational Fund, Inc.

Death Row, U.S.A. (1998, Spring). New York, NY: NAACP Legal Defense and Educational Fund, Inc.

Death Row, U.S.A. (2002, Spring). *Criminal Justice Project*. New York, NY: NAACP Legal Defense and Educational Fund, Inc.

Death Row, U.S.A. (2006, Summer). *Criminal Justice Project*. New York, NY: NAACP Legal Defense and Educational Fund, Inc.

Death Row, U.S.A. (2006, Winter). *Criminal Justice Project*. New York, NY: NAACP Legal Defense and Educational Fund, Inc.

Death Row, U.S.A. (2007, Winter). *Criminal Justice Project*. New York, NY: NAACP Legal Defense and Educational Fund, Inc.

Death Row, U.S.A. (2009, Summer). *Criminal Justice Project*. New York, NY: NAACP Legal Defense and Educational Fund, Inc.

Death Row, U.S.A. (2010, Winter). *Criminal Justice Project*. New York, NY: NAACP Legal Defense and Educational Fund, Inc.

Decker, S. H., & Kohfeld, C. W. (1984). A deterrence study of the death penalty in Illinois, 1933–1980. *Journal of Criminal Justice, 12*, 367–379.

Decker, S. H., & Kohfeld, C. W. (1986). The deterrent effect of capital punishment in Florida: A time series analysis. *Criminal Justice Policy Review, 1*, 422–437.

Decker, S. H., & Kohfeld, C. W. (1987). An empirical analysis of the effect of the death penalty in Missouri. *Journal of Crime and Justice, 10*, 23–45.

Decker, S. H., & Kohfeld, C. W. (1988). Capital punishment and executions in the Lone Star State: A deterrence study. *Criminal Justice Research Bulletin, 3*, 1–6.

Decker, S. H., & Kohfeld, C. W. (1990). The deterrent effect of capital punishment in the five most active execution states: A time-series analysis. *Criminal Justice Review, 15*, 173–191.

DeFronzo, J. (1979). In search of the behavioral and attitudinal consequences of victimization. *Sociological Spectrum, 25*, 23–39.

Denno, D. W. (1994). Is electrocution an unconstitutional method of execution? The engineering of death over the century. *William and Mary Law Review, 35*, 551–692.

Denno, D. W. (1997). Getting to death: Are executions constitutional? *Iowa Law Review, 82*, 319–464, [citations are from a draft copy].

Denno, D. W. (1998). Execution and the forgotten Eighth Amendment. In J. R. Acker, R. M. Bohm, & C. S. Lanier (Eds.), *America's experiment with capital punishment: Reflections on the past, present and future of the ultimate penal sanction* (pp. 547–577). Durham, NC: Carolina Academic Press.

Denno, D. W. (2002). When legislatures delegate death: The troubling paradox behind state uses of electrocution and lethal injection and what it says about us. *Ohio State Law Journal, 63*, 63–260. Retrieved from http://moritzlaw.osu.edu/lawjournal/issues/ volume63/number1/denno.html.

Denno, D. W. (2007). The lethal injection quandary: How medicine has dismantled the death penalty. *Fordham Law Review, 76*, 49–128.

Denno, D. W. (2009). For execution methods challenges, the road to abolition is paved with paradox. In C. J. Ogletree, Jr., & A. Sarat (Eds.), *The road to abolition? The future of capital punishment in the United States* (pp. 183–214). New York: New York University Press.

Deslatte, A. (2009, November 3). Freed inmate wants $1.35 M. *The Orlando Sentinel*, p. B1.

Dezhbakhsh, H., Rubin, P. H., & Shepherd, J. M. (2003). Does capital punishment have a deterrent effect? New evidence from post-moratorium panel data. *American Law and Economic Review, 5*, 344–376.

Dickson, B. E. (2006). Effects of capital punishment on the justice system: Reflections of a state Supreme Court justice. *Judicature, 89*, 278–281.

Dieter, R. C. (1992). *Millions misspent: What politicians don't say about the high costs of the death penalty*. Washington, DC: The Death Penalty Information Center.

Dieter, R. C. (1993). *Sentencing for life: Americans embrace alternatives to the death penalty*. Washington, DC: The Death Penalty Information Center.

Dieter, R. C. (1996). *Killing for votes: The dangers of politicizing the death penalty process*. Washington, DC: The Death Penalty Information Center.

Dieter, R. C. (2000). *2000 Year end report: A watershed year of change*. Washington, DC: The Death Penalty Information Center.

Dieter, R. C. (2004). *Innocence and the crisis of the American death penalty.* Washington, DC: The Death Penalty Information Center.

Dieter, R. C. (2005, January 25). Costs of the death penalty and related issues. Retrieved from. *Testimony before the New York State Assembly: Standing Committees on Codes, Judiciary, and Correction.* http://www.deathpenaltyinfo.org ("Costs").

Dieter, R. C. (2009a). *Smart on crime: Reconsidering the death penalty in a time of economic crisis.* Retrieved September 8, 2010, from. Washington, DC: The Death Penalty Information Center. http://www.deathpenaltyinfo.org/documents/CostsRptFinal.pdf.

Dieter, R. C. (2009b). *Testimony before the commission to study the death penalty in New Hampshire.* Washington, DC: The Death Penalty Information Center.

Dieter, R. C. (2010, December 8). Executive Director, The Death Penalty Information Center. Personal communication.

Dillehay, R. C., & Sandys, M. R. (1996). Life under Wainwright v. Witt: Juror dispositions and death qualification. *Law and Human Behavior, 20,* 147–165.

Dinnerstein, L. (1968). *The Leo Frank case.* New York: Columbia University Press.

Donohue, J. J., III, & Wolfers, J. (2005). Uses and abuses of empirical evidence in the death penalty debate [Electronic version]. *Stanford Law Review, 58,* 791–846, Retrieved September 22, 2010.

Donohue, J. J., III, & Wolfers, J. (2009). Estimating the impact of the death penalty on murder [Electronic version]. *American Law and Economics Review, 11,* 249–309, Retrieved September 20, 2010.

Dow, D. R. (2002a). Introduction: The problem of 'innocence'. In D. R. Dow, & M. Dow (Eds.), *Machinery of death: The reality of America's death penalty regime* (pp. 1–8). New York: Routledge.

Dow, D. R. (2002b). How the death penalty really works. In D. R. Dow, & M. Dow (Eds.), *Machinery of death: The reality of America's death penalty regime* (pp. 11–35). New York: Routledge.

Dow, D. R. (2005). *Executed on a technicality: Lethal injustice on America's death row.* Boston: Beacon Press.

Drizin, S. A., & Leo, R. A. (2004). The problem of false confessions in the post-DNA world. *North Carolina Law Review, 82,* 891–1007.

Duffy, C. T., & Hirshberg, A. (1962). *88 Men and 2 women.* London: Victor Gollancz.

Durham, A. M., Elrod, H. P., & Kinkade, P. T. (1996). Public support for the death penalty: Beyond Gallup. *Justice Quarterly, 13,* 705–736.

Ehrlich, I. (1975). The deterrent effect of capital punishment: A question of life and death. *American Economic Review, 65,* 397–417.

Ehrlich, I. (1977). Capital punishment and deterrence: Some further thoughts and additional evidence. *Journal of Political Economy, 85,* 741–788.

Ehrlich, I. (1982). On positive methodology, ethics, and polemics in deterrence research. *British Journal of Criminology, 22,* 124–139.

Ehrlich, I., & Liu, Z. (1999). Sensitivity analysis of the deterrence hypothesis: Let's keep the econ in econometrics. *Journal of Law and Economics, 42,* 455–488.

Einwechter, J. E. (1998). *Material graciously provided to the author in August.* [Major Einwechter is a professor of Criminal Law at The Judge Advocate General's School, Charlottesville, VA.].

Eisenberg, T., Garvey, S. P., & Wells, M. T. (2001). Forecasting life and death: juror race, religion, and attitude toward the death penalty. *Journal of Legal Studies, 30,* 277–311.

Eisenberg, T., Garvey, S. P., & Wells, M. T. (2006). Victim characteristics and victim impact evidence in South Carolina capital cases. In J. R. Acker, & D. R. Karp (Eds.), *Wounds that do not bind: Victim-based perspectives on the death penalty* (pp. 297–321). Durham, NC: Carolina Academic Press.

Eisenberg, T., & Wells, M. T. (1993–1994). Deadly confusion: Juror instructions in capital cases. *Cornell Law Review, 79,* 1–17.

Ekland-Olson, S. (1988). Structured discretion, racial bias and the death penalty: The first decade after Furman in Texas. *Social Science Quarterly, 69,* 853–873.

Ellis, C. A., Ho, K., & Seymour, A. (2006). The impact of the death penalty on crime victims and those who serve them. In J. R. Acker, & D. R. Karp (Eds.), *Wounds that do not bind: Victim-based perspectives on the death penalty* (pp. 431–444). Durham, NC: Carolina Academic Press.

Ellsworth, P. C., & Gross, S. R. (1994). Hardening of the attitudes: Americans' views on the death penalty. *Journal of Social Issues, 50,* 19–52.

Ellsworth, P. C., & Ross, L. (1983). Public opinion and capital punishment: A close examination of the views of abolitionists and retentionists. *Crime & Delinquency, 29,* 116–169.

Erez, E. (1981). Thou shalt not execute: Hebrew law perspective on capital punishment. *Criminology, 19,* 25–43.

Erikson, R. S. (1976). The relationship between public opinion and state policy: A new look at some forgotten data. *American Journal of Political Science, 20,* 25–36.

Erskine, H. (1970). The polls: Capital punishment. *Public Opinion Quarterly, 34,* 290–307.

Eschholz, S., Reed, M. D., Beck, E., & Leonard, P. B. (2003). Offenders' family members' responses to capital crimes: The need for restorative justice initiatives. *Homicide Studies, 7,* 154–181.

Espy, M. W., & Smykla, J. O. (1987). *Executions in the United States, 1608–1987: The Espy file. Machine-readable data file.* Ann Arbor, MI: Inter-University Consortium for Political and Social Research.

Executions by lethal injection being challenged around the country. (2005). The Death Penalty Information Center. Retrieved from http://www.deathpenaltyinfo.org/newsanddev.php?>?scid=8&scyr=2005.

Facts on File. (1955). Facts on file yearbook. In L. A. Sobel (Ed.). New York: Facts on File, Inc.

Facts on File. (1956). Facts on file yearbook. In L. A. Sobel (Ed.). New York: Facts on File, Inc.

Facts on File. (1957). Facts on file yearbook. In L. A. Sobel (Ed.). New York: Facts on File, Inc.

Facts on File. (1958). Facts on file yearbook. In L. A. Sobel (Ed.). New York: Facts on File, Inc.

Facts on File. (1959). Facts on file yearbook. In L. A. Sobel (Ed.). New York: Facts on File, Inc.

Facts on File. (1960). Facts on file yearbook. In L. A. Sobel (Ed.). New York: Facts on File, Inc.

Facts on File. (1961). Facts on file yearbook. In L. A. Sobel (Ed.). New York: Facts on File, Inc.

Facts on File. (1979). Facts on file yearbook. In L. A. Sobel (Ed.). New York: Facts on File, Inc.

Fagan, J. (2005, January 21). Deterrence and the death penalty: A critical review of new evidence. Retrieved from. *Testimony to the New York State Assembly Standing Committee on Codes, Assembly Standing Committee on Judiciary and Assembly Standing Committee on Correction, Hearings on the Future of Capital Punishment in the State of New York.* http://www.deathpenaltyinfo.org/article.php?scid=12&did=167.

Fagan, J. (2006). Death and deterrence redux: Science, law and causal reasoning on capital punishment. *Ohio State Journal of Criminal Law, 4,* 255–299.

Fagan, J., Zimring, F. E., & Geller, A. (2006). Capital punishment and capital murder: Market share and the deterrent effects of the death penalty. *Texas Law Review, 84,* 1803–1867.

Fan, D. P., Keltner, K. A., & Wyatt, R. O. (2002). A matter of guilt or innocence: How news reports affect support for the death penalty. *International Journal of Public Opinion Research, 14,* 439–451.

Federal Bureau of Investigation. (1997). *Crime in the United States 1996.* Washington, DC: U.S. Department of Justice. GPO.

Federal Bureau of Investigation. (2001). *Crime in the United States 2000.* Washington, DC: U.S. Department of Justice. GPO.

Federal Bureau of Investigation. (2005). *Crime in the United States 2004.* Washington, DC: U.S. Department of Justice. GPO. Retrieved from http://www.fbi.gov/ucr/05cius/.

Federal Bureau of Investigation. (2010). *Crime in the United States 2009.* Washington, DC: U.S. Department of Justice. GPO Retrieved from http://www2.fbi.gov/ucr/cius2009/index.html.

Federal judge requires medically trained personnel for North Carolina lethal injection. (2006). Death Penalty Information Center. http://www.deathpenaltyinfo.org/news anddev.php?scid=8 Retrieved from.

Federman, C., & Holmes, D. (2005). Breaking bodies into pieces: Time, torture and bio-power. *Critical Criminology, 13,* 327–345.

Filler, L. (1967). Movements to abolish the death penalty in the United States. In T. Sellin (Ed.), *Capital punishment* (pp. 104–122). New York: Harper & Row.

Finckenauer, J. O. (1988). Public support for the death penalty: Retribution as just deserts or retribution as revenge? *Justice Quarterly, 5*, 81–100.

Firment, K. A., & Geiselman, E. (1997). University students' attitudes and perceptions of the death penalty. *American Journal of Forensic Psychology, 15*, 65–89.

1, 2009 1st one-drug execution. (2009, December 9). *The Orlando Sentinel*, p. A12.

Fitzgerald, R., & Ellsworth, P. C. (1984). Due process vs. crime control: Death qualification and jury attitudes. *Law and Human Behavior, 8*, 31–51.

Fleury-Steiner, B. (2006). Death in 'Whiteface': Modern race minstrels, official lynching, and the culture of American apartheid. In C. J. Ogletree, Jr., & A. Sarat (Eds.), *From lynch mobs to the killing state: Race and the death penalty in America* (pp. 150–181). New York: New York University Press.

Foley, L. (1987). Florida after the Furman decision: the effect of extralegal factors on the processing of capital offense cases. *Behavioral Sciences & the Law, 5*, 457–465.

Forst, B. E. (1977). The case against capital punishment: A cross-state analysis of the 1960's. *Minnesota Law Review, 61*, 743–767.

Fox, J. A., Radelet, M. L., & Bonsteel, J. L. (1990–1991)*Death penalty opinion in the post-Furman years*. New York University Review of Law and Social Change, *18*, 499–528.

Frank, J., & Applegate, B. K. (1998). Assessing juror understanding of capital-sentencing instructions. *Crime & Delinquency, 44*, 412–433.

Freedman, E. M. (1998). Federal habeas corpus in capital cases. In J. R. Acker, R. M. Bohm, & C. S. Lanier (Eds.), *America's experiment with capital punishment: Reflections on the past, present and future of the ultimate penal sanction* (pp. 417–436). Durham, NC: Carolina Academic Press.

Freedman, M. H. (2003). The professional obligation to raise frivolous issues in death penalty cases. *Hofstra Law Review, 31*, 1167–1180.

French, H. W. (2002, June 30). Japanese keep executions secret. *The Orlando Sentinel*, p. A25.

Friedman, L. (1979). The use of multiple regression analysis to test for a deterrent effect of capital punishment: Prospects and problems. In S. Messinger, & E. Bittner (Eds.), *Criminology review yearbook* (pp. 61–87). Beverly Hills, CA: Sage.

Furillo, A. (2005, November 21). Life of gang founder in Schwarzenegger's hands. *The Orlando Sentinel*, p. A6.

Gaddis, T. (1979). *Birdman of Alcatraz*. Ithaca, NY: Comstock Book Distributors.

Gale, M. E. (1985). *Retribution, punishment, and death*. In: *Davis Law Review, 18*. University of California. pp. 973–1035.

Galliher, J. F., Koch, L. W., Keys, D. P., & Guess, T. J. (2002). *America without the death penalty: States leading the way*. Boston: Northeastern University Press.

Galliher, J. F., Ray, G., & Cook, B. (1992). Abolition and reinstatement of capital punishment during the Progressive Era and early 20th century. *The Journal of Criminal Law and Criminology, 83*, 538–576.

Gallup, A., & Newport, F. (1991, June). Death penalty support remains strong. *The Gallup Poll Monthly*.

Gallup, G., Jr. (1995, June). *The Gallup Poll Monthly*. No. 357. Princeton, NJ: The Gallup Poll.

Gallup Report. (1985). *Support for death penalty highest in half-century*. Princeton, NJ: The Gallup Report.

Garey, M. (1985). *The cost of taking a life: Dollars and sense of the death penalty*. University of California. Davis Law Review 18:1221–1273.

Garner, B. A. (Ed.) (2000). *Blacks law dictionary* (abridged 7th ed.). St. Paul, MN: West.

Garvey, S. P., Johnson, S. L., & Marcus, P. (1999–2000). Correcting deadly confusion: Responding to jury inquiries in capital cases. *Cornell Law Review, 85*, 627–655.

Gearan, A. (2002, March 26). Supreme Court takes up claim of poor defense in death cases. *The Orlando Sentinel* p. A11.

Gelineau, K. (2006, January 13). DNA confirms guilt of man executed in '92. *The Orlando Sentinel*, p. A5.

Georgia judge notes expensive bottom line in capital cases. (2002, May 12). Atlanta Journal-Constitution. Retrieved from. http://www.deathpenaltyinfo.org/article.php?scid=7&did=851.

Georgia killer is granted his wish to be executed. (1998, October 14). *The Orlando Sentinel,* p. A14.

Gibbs, J. P. (1978). The death penalty, retribution and penal policy. *Journal of Criminal Law and Criminology, 69,* 291–299.

Gibson, W. E. (2002, April 23). Justices weigh case that could affect up to 870 on death row. *The Orlando Sentinel,* p. A1.

Gillespie, L. K. (2003). *Inside the death chamber: Exploring executions.* Boston: Allyn and Bacon.

Gillette, D. R. (2006). Defending death penalty judgment. *Judicature, 89,* 262–264.

Glaser, D. (1979). *Capital punishment—Deterrent or stimulus to murder? Our unexamined deaths and penalties.* University of Toledo Law Review, 10, 317–333.

Goldberg, F. (1970). Toward expansion of Witherspoon: Capital scruples, jury bias, and use of psychological data to raise presumptions in the law. *Harvard Civil Rights–Civil Liberties Law Review, 5,* 53–69.

Goldman, R. (2011). Ohio executes convict using single controversial drug. ABC News/U.S. Retrieved from http://abcnews.go.com/US/ohio-executes-convict-single-controversial-drug/story?id=13104642.

Gorecki, J. (1983). *Capital punishment: Criminal law and social evolution.* New York: Columbia University Press.

Gottlieb, G. H. (1961). Testing the death penalty. *Southern California Law Review, 34,* 268–281.

Governor's Commission on Capital Punishment. (2002). State of Illinois. http://www.idoc.state.il.us/ccp/ccp/reports/commission_reports.html.

Gow, H. B. (1986). Religious views support the death penalty. In B. Szumski, L. Hall, & S. Bursell (Eds.), *The death penalty: Opposing viewpoints* (pp. 79–85). St. Paul, MN: Greenhaven.

Grann, D. (2009, September 7). Trial by fire: Did Texas execute an innocent man? *The New Yorker.* Retrieved October 14, 2010, from http://www.newyorker.com/reporting/2009/09/07/090907fa_fact_grann.

Grasmick, H. G., Cochran, J. K., Bursik, R. J., Jr., & Kimpel, M. (1993). Religion, punitive justice, and support for the death penalty. *Justice Quarterly, 10,* 289–314.

Grimes, R.-E. M (1996). Walnut Street Jail. In M. D. McShane, & F. P. Williams, III (Eds.), *Encyclopedia of American prisons* (pp. 493–497). New York and London: Garland.

Groner, J. I. (2005). Inadequate anaesthesia in lethal injection for execution. *The Lancet, 366.* Retrieved from http://www.sciencedirect.com.

Gross, S. R. (1984). Determining the neutrality of death-qualified juries: Judicial appraisal of empirical data. *Law and Human Behavior, 8,* 7–30.

Gross, S. R. (1996). The risks of death: Why erroneous convictions are common in capital cases. *Buffalo Law Review, 44,* 469–500.

Gross, S. R. (1998). Lost lives: Miscarriages of justice in capital cases. *Law and Contemporary Problems, 61,* 125–152.

Gross, S., Jacoby, K., Matheson, D. J., Montgomery, N., & Patil, S. (2004). Exonerations in the United States, 1989 through 2003. Retrieved from http://www.umich.edu/NewsAndInfo/exonerations-in-us.pdf.

Gross, S. R., & Mauro, R. (1984). Patterns of death: An analysis of racial disparities in capital sentencing and homicide victimization. *Stanford Law Review, 37,* 27–153.

Gross, S. R., & Mauro, R. (1989). *Death and discrimination: Racial disparities in capital sentencing.* Boston: Northeastern University Press.

Growing elderly population on death row. (2005, February 10). *USA Today.* Retrieved from http://www.deathpenaltyinfo.org/article.php?&did=1708.

Guin, C. C. (2002). An eagle soars: The legacy of Mr. Smile. In D. R. Dow, & M. Dow (Eds.), *Machinery of death: The reality of America's death penalty regime* (pp. 225–240). New York: Routledge.

Haas, K. C., & Inciardi, J. A. (Eds.) (1988). *Challenging capital punishment: Legal and social science approaches.* Newbury Park, CA: Sage.

Hagan, J. (1974). Extra-legal attributes and criminal sentencing: An assessment of a sociological viewpoint. *Law and Society Review, 8*, 357–383.

Haines, E. (2006, April 29). Civil-rights-era crimes receive renewed focus. *The Orlando Sentinel,* p. A25.

Haines, H. H. (1996). *Against capital punishment: The anti-death penalty movement in America, 1972–1994.* New York: Oxford University Press.

Hammel, A. (2002). Jousting with the juggernaut. In D. R. Dow, & M. Dow (Eds.), *Machinery of death: The reality of America's death penalty regime* (pp. 107–126). New York: Routledge.

Haney, C. (1984). On the selection of capital juries: The biasing effects of the death-qualification process. *Law and Human Behavior, 8*, 121–132.

Haney, C. (2003). Mitigation and the study of lives: On the roots of violent criminality and the nature of capital justice. In J. R. Acker, R. M. Bohm, & C. S. Lanier (Eds.), *America's experiment with capital punishment: Reflections on the past, present and future of the ultimate penal sanction* (2nd ed.). (pp. 469–500) Durham, NC: Carolina Academic Press.

Haney, C. (2005). *Death by design: Capital punishment as a social psychological system.* New York: Oxford University Press.

Haney, C., & Logan, D. D. (1994). Broken promise: The Supreme Court's response to social science research on capital punishment. *Journal of Social Issues, 50*, 75–100.

Haney, C., Sontag, L., & Costanzo, S. (1994). Deciding to take a life: Capital juries, sentencing instructions, and the jurisprudence of death. *Journal of Social Issues, 50*, 149–176.

'Hanging judge' calls for end to the death penalty. (2005, June 24). Orange County Register. Retrieved from http://www.deathpenaltyinfo.org/article.php?scid=7&did=851

Hans, V. P. (1988). Death by jury. In K. C. Haas, & J. A. Inciardi (Eds.), *Challenging capital punishment: Legal and social science approaches* (pp. 149–175). Newbury Park, CA: Sage.

Hansen, M. (2000, July 21). Dearth of volunteers: 16 States require civilian witnesses to ensure dignity at execution. *American Bar Association Journal.* Retrieved from http://www.abanet.org/journal/current/nwitns.html.

Harcourt, B. E. (2009). Abolition in the United States by 2050: On political capital and ordinary acts of resistance. In C. J. Ogletree, Jr., & A. Sarat (Eds.), *The road to abolition? The future of capital punishment in the United States* (pp. 72–96). New York: New York University Press.

Harmon, T. R. (2001). Predictors of miscarriages of justice in capital cases. *Justice Quarterly, 18*, 949–968.

Harmon, T. R., Acker, J. R., & Rivera, C. (2010). The power to be lenient: Examining New York governors' capital case clemency decisions. *Justice Quarterly, 27*, 742–764.

Harmon, T. R., & Lofquist, W. S. (2005). Too late for luck: A comparison of post-Furman exonerations and executions of the innocent. *Crime & Delinquency, 51*, 498–520.

Harries, K., & Cheatwood, D. (1997). *The geography of execution: The capital punishment quagmire in America.* Lanham, MD: Rowman and Littlefield.

Harris, P. W. (1986). Oversimplification and error in public opinion surveys on capital punishment. *Justice Quarterly, 3*, 429–455.

Harris, R. (2000, November 19). Former gangster nominated for peace prize. *The San Francisco Examiner,* p. C2.

Harrison, P. M., & Beck, A. J. (2006, May). *Prison and jail inmates at midyear 2005.* US Department of Justice. Bureau of Justice Statistics Bulletin.

Hartman, K. I. (2010, June 18). Witness shares experience of watching execution by firing squad. *Digital Journal.* Retrieved November 27, 2010, from http://www.digitaljournal.com/article/293587.

Hastings, D. (2001, August 30). Facts disputed in execution case. *The Orlando Sentinel,* p. A3.

Hawkins, B. (2006). Capital punishment and the administration of justice: A trial prosecutor's perspective. *Judicature, 89*, 258–261.

Healy, T. (2001, July 4). Swing Justice O'Connor expresses qualms about death penalty. *The Orlando Sentinel,* p. A4.

Heath, M. J. S., Stanski, D. R., & Pounder, D. J. (2005). Inadequate anaesthesia in lethal injection for execution. *The Lancet* 366. Retrieved from http://www.sciencedirect.com.

Heider, F. (1958). *The psychology of interpersonal relations*. New York: Wiley.

Heilbrun, A. B., Jr., Heilbrun, L. C., & Heilbrun, K. L. (1978). Impulsive and premeditated homicide: An analysis of subsequent parole risk of the murderer. *Journal of Criminal Law and Criminology, 69*, 108–114.

Heise, M. (2003). Mercy by the numbers: An empirical analysis of clemency and its structure. *Virginia Law Review, 89*, 239–310.

Herbert, B. (2000, April 16). What if you're not guilty? *The New York Times*.

Hintze, & Michael. (2006). Tinkering with the machinery of death: Capital punishment's toll on the American judiciary. *Judicature, 89*, 254–257.

Hjalmarsson, R. (2009). Does capital punishment have a 'local' deterrent effect on homicides? [Electronic version]. *American Law and Economics Review, 11*, 310–334, Retrieved September 22, 2010.

Hoffmann, J. L. (1993). On the perils of line-drawing: Juveniles and the death penalty. In V. L. Streib (Ed.), *A capital punishment anthology* (pp. 117–132). Cincinnati: Anderson Publishing Co.

Hoffmann, J. L. (1995). Where's the buck?—Juror misperception of sentencing responsibility in death penalty cases. *Indiana Law Journal, 70*, 1137–1160.

Holcomb, J. E., Williams, M. R., & Demuth, S. (2004). White female victims and death penalty disparity research. *Justice Quarterly, 21*, 877–902.

Holmes, W. L. (2004, April 17). Man is cleared in 1984 slaying. *The Orlando Sentinel* A9.

Hood, R. (2002). *The death penalty: A worldwide perspective* (3rd ed.). New York: Oxford University Press.

Hood, W.W., III (1989). The meaning of 'life' for Virginia jurors and its effect on reliability in capital sentencing. Virginia Law Review 75:1605–1637. Retrieved from web.lexis-nexis.com.ucfproxy.fcla.edu/universe/document?_m=41ffaeccc13ad4707b82ddbeb9613e00&_docnum=1&wchp=dGLbVzz-zSkVA&_md5=ce4ed8343380cb42d1d64b9aa47cfee3

Hoppe, C. (1992, March 22). Life in jail, or death? Life term is cheaper. *The Charlotte [North Carolina] Observer* 12A.

Horowitz, I. A., & Seguin, D. G. (1986). The effects of bifurcation and death qualification on assignment of penalty in capital cases. *Journal of Applied Social Psychology, 16*, 165–185.

Howard, R. C., Jr. (1996). The defunding of the post conviction defense organizations as a denial of the right to counsel. *West Virginia Law Review, 98*, 863–921.

Howstuffworks: How lethal injection works (2002). Retrieved from http://www.howstuffworks.com/lethal-injection2.htm

Huff, C. R., Rattner, A., & Sagarin, E. (1986). Guilty until proven innocent: Wrongful conviction and public policy. *Crime & Delinquency, 32*, 518–544.

Indiana editorial calls for end to 'costly' death penalty. (2005, June 22). *Fort Wayne Journal Gazette*. Retrieved from http://www.deathpenaltyinfo.org/article.php?scid=7&did=85.

The Indiana Law Blog. (2005, November 29). Ind. Law—How in the Modern Media Age can a notorious defendant accused of a heinous crime get a constitutionally fair trial? Retrieved from http://indianalawblog.com/archives/2005/11/ind_law_how_in.html

Indiana taxpayers charged over $2 million for defense of three capital cases. (1999, February 7). *Indianapolis Star/News*. Retrieved from http://www.deathpenaltyinfo.org/article.php?scid=7&did=851.

Ingle, J. B. (1989). Ministering to the condemned: A case study. In M. L. Radelet (Ed.), *Facing the death penalty: Essays on a cruel and unusual punishment* (pp. 112–122). Philadelphia: Temple University Press.

Innocence Project. Retrieved from http://www.innocenceproject.org

Jackson, J., & Jackson, J., Jr. (1996). *Legal lynching: Racism, injustice and the death penalty*. New York: Marlowe.

Jacobs, D., Carmichael, J., & Kent, S. (2005). Vigilantism, current racial threat, and death sentences. *American Sociological Review, 70*, 656–677.

Jacoby, J., & Paternoster, R. (1982). Sentencing disparity and jury packing: Further challenges to the death penalty. *Journal of Criminal Law and Criminology, 73*, 379–387.

Jacoby, S. (1983). *Wild justice: The evolution of revenge.* New York: Harper and Row.

Johnson, D. (2001). Punitive attitudes on crime: Economic insecurity, racial prejudice, or both? *Sociological Focus, 34*, 33–54.

Johnson, D. (2003). *Set in stone? Support for capital punishment among white and black Americans.* Paper presented at the annual meeting of the Academy of Criminal Justice Sciences.

Johnson, R. (1989). *Condemned to die: Life under sentence of death.* Prospect Heights, IL: Waveland.

Johnson, R. (1990). *Death work: A study of the modern execution process.* Pacific Grove, CA: Brooks/Cole.

Johnson, R. (1998). *Death work: A study of the modern execution process* (2nd ed.). Belmont, CA: West/ Wadsworth.

Johnson, R. (2003). Life under sentence of death: Historical and contemporary perspectives. In J. R. Acker, R. M. Bohm, & C. S. Lanier (Eds.), *America's experiment with capital punishment: Reflections on the past, present and future of the ultimate penal sanction* (2nd ed.). (pp. 647–671) Durham, NC: Carolina Academic Press.

Joint Legislative Audit and Review Commission of the Virginia General Assembly. (2002, January 15). Final Report. Retrieved from http://jlarc.state.va.us/pubs_rec.htm.

Jones, J. M. (2001). Two-thirds of Americans support the death penalty. The Gallup Organization. Retrieved from http://www.gallup.com/poll/releases/pr010302.asp.

Jones, J. M. (2002). Slim majority of Americans say death penalty applied fairly. The Gallup Organization. Retrieved from http://www.gallup.com/poll/releases/pr020520.asp.

Jones, J. M. (2006). Two in three favor death penalty for convicted murderers. The Gallup Organization. Retrieved from http://poll.gallup.com/content/?ci=23167asp.

Jones, P. R. (1994). It's not what you ask, it's the way that you ask it: Question form and public opinion on the death penalty. *The Prison Journal, 74*, 32–50.

Jurow, G. L. (1971). New data on the effect of a 'death qualified' jury on the guilt determination process. *Harvard Law Review, 84*, 567–611.

Jury. (2006, May 6). Freed inmate to get $2.25 million. *The Orlando Sentinel*, p. A2.

Justice For All Act of 2004: Section-by-section analysis. Retrieved from http://leahy.senate.gov/press/ 200410/SectionbySectionDNA.htm

Kaczynski, D., & Wright, G. (2006). Building a bridge. In J. R. Acker, & D. R. Karp (Eds.), *Wounds that do not bind: Victim-based perspectives on the death penalty* (pp. 85–101). Durham, NC: Carolina Academic Press.

Kania, R. R. E. (1999). The ethics of the death penalty. *The Justice Professional, 12*, 145–157.

Kansas study concludes death penalty is costly policy. (2003, December). Performance audit report: Cost incurred for death penalty cases: A K-goal audit of the Department of Corrections. Retrieved from http://www.deathpenaltyinfo.org/article.php?scid=7&did=851.

Kaplan, J. (1983). *The problem of capital punishment.* Law Review 3. University of Illinois. pp. 555–577.

Karp, D. R., & Warshaw, J. B. (2006). Their day in court: The role of murder victims' families in capital juror decision making. In J. R. Acker, & D. R. Karp (Eds.), *Wounds that do not bind: Victim-based perspectives on the death penalty* (pp. 275–295). Durham, NC: Carolina Academic Press.

Katz, L., Levitt, S. D., & Shustorovich, E. (2003). Prison conditions, capital punishment, and deterrence. *American Law and Economics Review, 5*, 318–343.

Kaufman-Osborn, T. V. (2006). Capital punishment as legal lynching? In C. J. Ogletree, Jr., & A. Sarat (Eds.), *From lynch mobs to the killing state: Race and the death penalty in America* (pp. 21–54) New York: New York University Press.

Kay, J. W. (2006). Is restitution possible for murder?—Surviving family members speak. In J. R. Acker, & D. R. Karp (Eds.), *Wounds that do not bind: Victim-based perspectives on the death penalty* (pp. 323–347). Durham, NC: Carolina Academic Press.

Kehler, L., Sawatzky, S., Huebner, H., Dueck, L., Epp, E., & Epp, C. (1985). *Capital punishment study guide: For groups and congregations.* Winnipeg: Mennonite Central Committee Canada.

Keil, T. J., & Vito, G. F. (1989). Race, homicide severity, and application of the death penalty: A consideration of the Barnett Scale. *Criminology, 27,* 511–535.

Keil, T. J., & Vito, G. F. (1990). Race and the death penalty in Kentucky murder trials: An analysis of post-Gregg outcomes. *Justice Quarterly, 7,* 189–207.

Keil, T. J., & Vito, G. F. (1995). Race and the death penalty in Kentucky murder trials: 1976–1991. *American Journal of Criminal Justice, 20,* 17–36.

Keil, T. J., & Vito, G. F. (2006). Capriciousness or fairness? Race and prosecutorial decisions to seek the death penalty in Kentucky. *Journal of Ethnicity in Criminal Justice, 4,* 27–49.

Kelsen, H. (1943). *Society and nature.* Chicago: University of Chicago Press.

Kimble, M. (2006). My journey and the riddle. In J. R. Acker, & D. R. Karp (Eds.), *Wounds that do not bind: Victim-based perspectives on the death penalty* (pp. 127–138). Durham, NC: Carolina Academic Press.

King, D. R. (1978). The brutalization effect: Execution publicity and the incidence of homicide in South Carolina. *Social Forces, 57,* 683–687.

King, G. D. (1982). On behalf of the death penalty. In H. A. Bedau (Ed.), *The death penalty in America* (3rd ed.). (pp. 308–311) New York: Oxford University Press.

King, R. (2006). The impact of capital punishment on families of defendants and murder victims' family members. *Judicature, 89,* 292–296.

Kleck, G. (1981). Racial discrimination in criminal sentencing: A critical evaluation of the evidence with additional evidence of the death penalty. *American Sociological Review, 46,* 783–805.

Klein, L. R., Forst, B., & Filatov, V. (1982). The deterrent effect of capital punishment: An assessment of the evidence. In H. A. Bedau (Ed.), *The death penalty in America* (3rd ed.). (pp. 138–159) New York: Oxford University Press.

Klein, S. P., & Rolph, J. E. (1991). Relationship of offender and victim race to death penalty sentences in California. *Jurimetrics, 32,* 33–48.

Kobil, D. T. (2003). The evolving role of clemency in capital cases. In J. R. Acker, R. M. Bohm, & C. S. Lanier (Eds.), *America's experiment with capital punishment: Reflections on the past, present and future of the ultimate penal sanction* (2nd ed.). (pp. 673–692) Durham, NC: Carolina Academic Press.

Kohfeld, C. W., & Decker, S. H. (1990). Time series, panel design and criminology: A multi-state, multi-wave analysis of the effect of the death penalty in contiguous states. In K. L. Kempf (Ed.), *Measurement issues in criminology* (pp. 198–240). New York: Springer-Verlag.

Kohlberg, L., & Elfenbein, D. (1975). The development of moral judgments concerning capital punishment. *American Journal of Orthopsychiatry, 45,* 614–640.

Koniaris, L. G., Zimmers, T. A., Lubarsky, D. A., & Sheldon, J. P. (2005). Inadequate anaesthesia in lethal injection for execution. *The Lancet, 365.* Retrieved from http://www.sciencedirect.com.

Kovandzic, T., Vieraitis, L. M., & Boots, D. P. (2009). Does the death penalty save lives? New evidence from state panel data, 1977 to 2006. *Criminology and Public Policy, 8,* 803–843.

Kravets, D. (2006, February 22). Doctors refuse to help execute California killer. *The Orlando Sentinel,* p. A3.

Kroll, M. A. (1989). The fraternity of death. In M. L. Radelet (Ed.), *Facing the death penalty: Essays on a cruel and unusual punishment* (pp. 16–26). Philadelphia: Temple University Press.

Kubik, J. D., & Moran, J. R. (2003). Lethal elections: Gubernatorial politics and the timing of executions. Retrieved from. *The Journal of Law and Economics, 46.* http://web.lexis-nexis.com.

Kunerth, J. (2000, January 3). Lethal injection has its problems, too. *The Orlando Sentinel,* p. A1.

Kuziemko, I. (2006). Does the threat of the death penalty affect plea bargaining in murder cases? Evidence from New York's 1995 reinstatement of capital punishment. *American Law and Economics Review, 8,* 116–142, Retrieved from September 22, 2010.

Lain, C. B. (2007a). Deciding death. *Duke Law Journal, 57*, 1–83.

Lain, C. B. (2007b). Furman fundamentals. *Washington Law Review, 82*, 1–74.

Lain, C. B. (2010). Lessons learned from the evolution of 'evolving standards.' *Charleston Law Review, 4*, 661–678.

Lambert, F., & Clarke, A. (2001). The impact of information on an individual's support of the death penalty: A partial test of the Marshall hypothesis among college students. *Criminal Justice Policy Review, 12*, 215–234.

Land, K., Teske, R. H. C., Jr., & Zheng, H. (2009). The short-term effects of executions on homicides: Deterrence, displacement, of both? *Criminology, 47*, 1009–1043.

Lanier, C. S., & Breslin, B. (2006). Extinguishing the victims' Payne or acquiescing to the 'demon of error': Confronting the role of victims in capital clemency proceedings. In J. R. Acker, & D. R. Karp (Eds.), *Wounds that do not bind: Victim-based perspectives on the death penalty* (pp. 179–201). Durham, NC: Carolina Academic Press.

Larranaga, M. A., & Mustard, D. (2004). Washington's death penalty system: A review of the costs, length, and results of capital cases in Washington State. Retrieved from http://www.deathpenaltyinfo.org/article.php?scid=7&did=85.

Lawes, L. E. (1969). *Man's judgement of death: An analysis of the operation and effect of capital punishment based on facts, not on sentiment.* Montclair, NJ: Patterson Smith. (Original work published 1924).

Lawrence, C. R., III (1987). The id, the ego, and equal protection: Reckoning with unconscious racism. *Stanford Law Review, 39*, 317–388.

Layson, S. K. (1985). Homicide and deterrence: A reexamination of the United States time-series evidence. *Southern Economy Journal, 52*, 68–89.

Leahy, P. (2004a, October 9). Statement of Senator Patrick Leahy: The Justice For All Act of 2004. Retrieved from http://leahy.senate.gov/press/200410/100904B.html

Leahy, P. (2004b). Justice For All Act of 2004: Section-by-section analysis. Retrieved from http://leahy.senate.gov/press/200410/100904E.html

Lee, G. (2008). A painless cocktail? The lethal injection controversy. In R. M. Bohm (Ed.), *The death penalty today* (pp. 93–110). Boca Raton, FL: CRC Press.

Lehner, P. (1996). Abolition now!!!. Retrieved from http://www.abolition-now.com.

Leighton, P. S. (1999). Televising executions: Primetime 'Live'? *The Justice Professional, 12*, 191–207.

Lethal injections: Some cases stayed, other executions proceed. (2006). Death Penalty Information Center. Retrieved from http://www.deathpenaltyinfo.org/article.php?did=1686&scid=64.

Leusner, J. (2006, October 22). Horrors relived. *The Orlando Sentinel* p. A1.

Leusner, J., & Tseng, N.-H. (2006, September 21). Execution sends message to other death-row inmates. *The Orlando Sentinel* p. A1.

Levey, D. (2006). Feelings from the heart. In J. R. Acker, & D. R. Karp (Eds.), *Wounds that do not bind: Victim-based perspectives on the death penalty* (pp. 33–47). Durham, NC: Carolina Academic Press.

Lewis, D. O., Pincus, J. H., Bard, B., Richardson, E., Prichep, L. S., Feldman, M., & Yeager, C. (1988). Neuropsychiatric, psychoeducational, and family characteristics of 14 juveniles condemned to death in the United States. *American Journal of Psychiatry, 145*, 584–589.

Leyte-Vidal, H., & Silverman, S. J. (2006). Living with the death penalty. *Judicature, 89*, 270–273.

Liebman, J. S. (2007). Slow dancing with death: The Supreme Court and capital punishment, 1963–2006. *Columbia Law Review, 107*, 1–130.

Liebman, J. S., Fagan, J., & West, V. (2000). A broken system: Error rates in capital cases, 1973–1995. The Justice Project. Retrieved from http://www.justice.policy.net/jpreport.html.

Lifton, R. J., & Mitchell, G. (2002). *Who owns death? Capital punishment, the American conscience, and the end of executions.* New York: Perennial.

Lilly, J. R. (1993, October). *Race and capital punishment in the military: WWII.* Paper presented at the annual meeting the American Society of Criminology, Phoenix, AZ.

Lilly, J. R. (1996). Dirty details: Executing U.S. soldiers during World War II. *Crime & Delinquency, 42*, 491–516.

Lilly, J. R. (1997). Military justice: A neglected topic. *ACJS Today, 15*, 11.

Lilly, J. R., Davies, P., & Ball, R. A. (1995, November). *Dirty details: Executing U.S. soldiers during World War II*. Paper presented at the annual meeting the American Society of Criminology, Boston, MA.

Lindsey, S. (2005, August 6). Man found competent—Execution set. *The Orlando Sentinel*, p. A20.

Liptak, A. (2007, November 18). Does death penalty save lives? A new debate. Retrieved November 9, 2010, from *The New York Times*. http://www.nytimes.com/2007/11/18/us/18deter.html.

Liptak, A. (2008, January 19). Lawyer reveals secret, toppling death sentence. Retrieved November 9, 2010, from *The New York Times*. http://www.nytimes.com/2008/01/19/us/19death.html.

Liptak, A. (2010, January 5). Group gives up death penalty work. *The New York Times*. Retrieved from http://topics.nytimes.com/top/reference/timestopics/people/l/adam/adam_liptak/index.html?inline=nyt-per.

Liu, Z. (2004). Capital punishment and the deterrence hypothesis: Some new insights and empirical evidence. *Eastern Economic Journal, 30*, 237–258.

Locke, J. (1988). Two treatises of government. In P. Laslett (Ed.), New York: Cambridge University Press. (Original work published 1690).

Lofquist, W. S. (2002). Putting them there, keeping them there, and killing them: An analysis of state-level variations in death penalty intensity. *Iowa Law Review, 87*, 1505–1557.

Logan, W. A. (2006). Victims, survivors, and the decisions to seek and impose death. In J. R. Acker, & D. R. Karp (Eds.), *Wounds that do not bind: Victim-based perspectives on the death penalty* (pp. 161–177). Durham, NC: Carolina Academic Press.

Longmire, D. R. (1996). Americans' attitudes about the ultimate sanction capital punishment. In T. J. Flanagan, & D. R. Longmire (Eds.), *Americans view crime and justice: A National Public Opinion Survey* (pp. 93–108). Thousand Oaks, CA: Sage.

Lord, C. G., Ross, L., & Lepper, M. R. (1979). Biased assimilation and attitude polarization: The effects of prior theories on subsequently considered evidence. *Journal of Personality and Social Psychology, 37*, 2098–2109.

Lotz, R., & Regoli, R. M. (1980). Public support for the death penalty. *Criminal Justice Review, 5*, 55–66.

Luginbuhl, J., & Middendorf, K. (1988). Death penalty beliefs and jurors' responses to aggravating and mitigating circumstances in capital trials. *Law and Human Behavior, 12*, 263–281.

Lundy, S., & McClure, V. (2009, February 20). Did these men escape justice? *The Orlando Sentinel,* p. A1.

Lynch, M. (2006). Stereotypes, prejudice, and life-and-death decision making: Lessons from laypersons in an experimental setting. In C. J. Ogletree, Jr., & A. Sarat (Eds.), *From lynch mobs to the killing state: Race and the death penalty in America* (pp. 182–207). New York: New York University Press.

Lytle, T., & Kennedy, J. (2006, January 26). Top court halts killer's execution. *The Orlando Sentinel* A1.

MacLaggan, C. (2011, March 19). For executions, Texas switches of drug used on animals. *The Orlando Sentinel* p. A6.

Maguire, K., & Pastore, A. L. (Eds.) (1997). *Sourcebook of criminal justice statistics 1996*. Washington, DC: US Department of Justice, Bureau of Justice Statistics. GPO.

Maguire, K., & Pastore, A. L. (Eds.) (2001). *Sourcebook of criminal justice statistics 2000*. Washington, DC: US Department of Justice, Bureau of Justice Statistics. GPO.

Retrieved September 15, 2006, from. In Maguire, K., & Pastore, A. L. (Eds.), *Sourcebook of criminal justice statistics*. http://www.albany.edu/sourcebook.

Mailer, N. (1979). *The executioner's song*. Boston: Little Brown.

Man executed in Mississippi is oldest to die since 1970s. (2005, December 15). *The Orlando Sentinel,* p. A8.

Mandery, E. J. (2005). *Capital punishment: A balanced examination*. Sudbury, MA: Jones and Bartlett.

Markman, S. J., & Cassell, P. G. (1988). Protecting the innocent: A response to the Bedau–Radelet study. *Stanford Law Review, 41*, 121–160.

2006Markon, J. (2006, May 6). Wrongfully jailed man wins suit: Va. officer falsified confession, jury rules. Washingtonpost.com. Retrieved from http://www.washingtonpost.com/wp-dyn/content/article/2006/05/05/AR2006050501617.html

Marquart, J. W., Ekland-Olson, S., & Sorensen, J. R. (1994). *The rope, the chair, and the needle: Capital punishment in Texas, 1923–1990*. Austin: University of Texas Press.

Marquart, J. W., & Sorensen, J. R. (1988). Institutional and postrelease behavior of Furman-commuted inmates in Texas. *Criminology, 26*, 677–693.

Marquart, J. W., & Sorensen, J. R. (1989). A national study of the Furman-commuted inmates: Assessing the threat to society from capital offenders. *Loyola of Los Angeles Law Review, 23*, 101–120.

Marquis, J. K. (2004). Truth and consequences: The penalty of death. In H. A. Bedau, & P. G. Cassell (Eds.), *Debating the death penalty: Should America have capital punishment? The experts on both sides make their best case* (pp. 117–151). New York: Oxford.

Marquis, J. (2005). The myth of innocence. *The Journal of Criminal Law & Criminology, 95*, 501–521.

Martschukat, J. (2009). No improvement over electrocution or even a bullet: Lethal injection and the meaning of speed and reliability in the modern execution process. In C. J. Ogletree, Jr., & A. Sarat (Eds.), *The road to abolition? The future of capital punishment in the United States* (pp. 252–278). New York: New York University Press.

McAdams, J. C. (1998). Racial disparity and the death penalty. *Law and Contemporary Problems, 61*, 153–170.

McCaffrey, S. (2002, October 22). Justices refuse to review execution of juveniles. *The Orlando Sentinel*, p. A3.

McCarthy, M. (2006). Lethal injection challenged as 'cruel and unusual' fate. Retrieved from *The Lancet, 367*. http://www.sciencedirect.com.

McCord, D. (2000). State death sentencing for felony murder accomplices under the Enmund and Tison standards. *Arizona State Law Journal, 32*, 843–896.

McCord, D. (2002). A year in the life of death: Murders and capital sentences in South Carolina, 1998. *South Carolina Law Review, 53*, 250–359.

McCord, D. (2005). Lightning still strikes: Evidence from the Popular Press that death sentencing continues to be unconstitutionally arbitrary more than three decades after Furman. *Brooklyn Law Review, 71*, 797–927.

McCord, D. (2006). If capital punishment were subject to consumer protection laws. *Judicature, 89*, 304–305.

McFarland, S. G. (1983). Is capital punishment a short-term deterrent to homicide? A study of the effects of four recent American executions. *Journal of Criminal Law and Criminology, 74*, 1014–1030.

McGarrell, E. F., & Sandys, M. (1996). The misperception of public opinion toward capital punishment: examining the spuriousness explanation of death penalty support. *American Behavioral Scientist, 39*, 500–513.

McGovern, J. R. (1982). *Anatomy of a lynching: The killing of Claude Neal*. Baton Rouge: Louisiana State University Press.

Mello, M. (1989). Another attorney for life. In M. L. Radelet (Ed.), *Facing the death penalty: Essays on a cruel and unusual punishment* (pp. 81–91). Philadelphia: Temple University Press.

Mello, M., & Perkins, P. J. (1998). Closing the circle: the illusion of lawyers for people litigating for their lives at the Fin de Siecle. In J. R. Acker, R. M. Bohm, & C. S. Lanier (Eds.), *America's experiment with capital punishment: Reflections on the past, present and future of the ultimate penal sanction* (pp. 245–284). Durham, NC: Carolina Academic Press.

Meltsner, M. (1973). *Cruel and unusual: The Supreme Court and capital punishment*. New York: Random House.

Michel, L., & Herbeck, D. (2001). *American terrorist: Timothy McVeigh & the Oklahoma City bombing*. New York: Regan Books.

Miller, K. W., & Niven, D. (2009). *Death justice: Rehnquist, Scalia, Thomas, and the contradictions of the death penalty*. El Paso, TX: LFB Scholarly Publishing.

Miller, K. S., & Radelet, M. L. (1993). *Executing the mentally ill: The criminal justice system and the case of Alvin Ford*. Newbury Park, CA: Sage.

Miller-Potter, K. S. (2002). Death by innocence: Wrongful convictions in capital cases. *The Advocate: A Journal of Criminal Justice Education and Research, 24*, 21–29.

Mintz, H. (2002, August 3). Public has right to see executions, court rules. *The Orlando Sentinel,* p. A12.

Mocan, H.N., & Gittings, R. K. (2001). Pardons, executions and homicide. Retrieved from http://econ.cudenver. edu/mocan/papers.htm.

Mocan, H. N., & Gittings, R. K. (2003). Getting off death row: Commuted sentences and the deterrent effect of capital punishment. *Journal of Law and Economics, 46,* 453–478.

Monroe, A. D. (1979). Consistency between public preferences and national policy decisions. *American Politics Quarterly, 7,* 3–19.

Montgomery, L. (1994, April 3). Rising outrage over crime puts U.S. back in the execution business. *The Charlotte [NC] Observer,* p. 2A.

Moore, D. W. (1994, September: 2–5). Majority advocate death penalty for teenage killers. *The Gallup Poll Monthly.*

Moran, G., & Comfort, J. C. (1986). Neither 'tentative' nor 'fragmentary': Verdict preference of impaneled felony jurors as a function of attitude toward capital punishment. *Journal of Applied Psychology, 71,* 146–155.

Moran, R. (2002). *Executioner's current: Thomas Edison, George Westinghouse, and the invention of the electric chair.* New York: Alfred A. Knopf.

Mullane, N. (2010, September 28). Witness to an execution: Witnesses prepare as judge reconsiders a stay of execution. KALW News. Retrieved November 27, 2010, from kalwnews.org/blogs/ericamu/2010/09/28/witness-execution-witnesses-prepare-judge-reconsiders-stay-execution_612847

Murphy, E. (1984). The application of the death penalty in Cook County. *Illinois Bar Journal, 93,* 90–95.

Murray, G. R. (2003). Raising considerations: Public opinion and the fair application of the death penalty. *Social Science Quarterly, 84,* 753–770.

Muwakkil, S. (1989, May 24–June 6). The death penalty and the illusion of justice. *In These Times, 13*(26), 6.

Nakell, B., & Hardy, K. A. (1987). *The arbitrariness of the death penalty.* Philadelphia: Temple University Press.

National Center for States Courts. (2010, December 6). Indigent defense. Retrieved December 6, 2010, from http://www.ncsc.org/topics/access-and-fairness/indigent-defense/state-links.aspx?cat=Capital%20Case%20Representation.

The National Coalition to Abolish the Death Penalty. (2002). Retrieved from http://www.ncadp.org/html/factsandstats.html.

Nellis, A., & King, R. S. (2009, July). No exit: The expanding use of life sentences in America. *The Sentencing Project.* Retrieved December 3, 2010, from http://www.sentencingproject.org/doc/publications/publications/inc_noexitseptember2009.pdf.

New Jersey Death Penalty Study Commission Report. (2007). Retrieved December 19, 2010, from http://www.njleg.state.nj.us/committees/dpsc_final.pdf.

Newport, F. (2010, November 8). In U.S., 64% support death penalty in cases of murder. Retrieved December 12, 2010, from http://www.gallup.com/poll/144284/support-death-penalty-cases-murder.aspx.

New York death penalty trial 3.5 times more costly than non-capital trial. (1999, July 12). Newsday. Retrieved from http://www.deathpenaltyinfo.org/article.php?scid=7&did=851.

New York State Defenders Association. (1982). *Capital losses: The price of the death penalty for New York State.* Albany, NY: New York State Defenders Association, Inc.

New York Times series examines life sentences. (2005, October 2–3). *New York Times.* Retrieved from http://www.deathpenaltyinfo.org/article.php?&did=1708.

Niemi, R. (1989). *Trends in public opinion: A compendium of survey data.* New York: Greenwood Press.

Niven, D. (2002). Bolstering an illusory majority: The effects of the media's portrayal of death penalty support. *Social Science Quarterly, 83,* 671–689.

Ogletree, C. J., Jr. (2006). Making race matter in death matters. In C. J. Ogletree, Jr., & A. Sarat (Eds.), *From lynch mobs to the killing state: Race and the death penalty in America* (pp. 55–95). New York: New York University Press.

Online Sunshine View Statutes. (2010a). The 2010 Florida statutes. Retrieved December 15, 2010, from http://www.leg.state.fl.us/statutes/index.cfm?mode=View%20Statutes&SubMenu=1&App_mode=Display_Statute&Search_String=death+penalty&URL=0900-0999/0921/Sections/0921.141.html.

Online Sunshine View Statutes. (2010b). The 2010 Florida statutes. Retrieved December 15, 2010, from http://www.leg.state.fl.us/statutes/index.cfm?App_mode=Display_Statute&Search_String=&URL=0900-0999/0924/Sections/0924.055.html.

Oskamp, S. (1977). *Attitudes and opinions*. Englewood Cliffs, NJ: Prentice Hall.

Ostling, R. N. (2005, March 22). Bishops rally against death for inmates. *The Orlando Sentinel,* p. A3.

Ottinger, S. (2002). Representing Robert Sawyer. In D. R. Dow, & M. Dow (Eds.), *Machinery of death: The reality of America's death penalty regime* (pp. 249–266). New York: Routledge.

Owens, Sh., M. (2002, January 29). Execution may hinge on killer's mental condition. *The Orlando Sentinel,* p. D1.

Packer, H. L. (1968). *The limits of the criminal sanction*. Stanford: Stanford University Press.

Paduano, A., & Smith, C. A. S. (1987). Deathly errors: Jurors misperceptions concerning parole in the imposition of the death penalty. *Columbia Human Rights Law Review, 18*, 211–257.

Page, B. I., & Shapiro, R. Y. (1983). Effects of public opinion on policy. *American Political Science Review, 77*, 175–190.

Page, B. I., Shapiro, R. Y., & Dempsey, G. R. (1987). What moves public opinion? *American Political Science Review, 81*, 23–43.

Palacios, V. (1996). Faith in fantasy: The Supreme Court's reliance on commutation to ensure justice in death penalty cases. *Vanderbilt Law Review, 49*, 311–372.

Parker, G. (1991). *Prepared statement of Gary Parker, Georgia State Senator, Fifteenth Senatorial District, Columbus, GA*. Hearing before the Subcommittee on Civil and Constitutional Rights of the Committee on the Judiciary, House of Representatives, One Hundred First Congress, Second Session on H.R. 4618 Racial Justice Act of 1990, etc., May 3 and 9, 1990. Serial No. 125. Washington, DC: US Government Printing Office.

Partial costs in the Virginia trials of John Muhammad and Lee Malvo. (2004, February 14). The Washington Post. Retrieved from http://www.deathpenaltyinfo.org/article.php?scid=7&did=851.

Passell, P. (1975). The deterrent effect of capital punishment: A statistical test. *Stanford Law Review, 28*, 61–80.

Passell, P., & Taylor, J. B. (1977). The deterrent effect of capital punishment: Another view. *American Economic Review, 67*, 445–451.

Patenaude, A. L. (2001). May God have mercy on your soul! Exploring and teaching a course on the death penalty. *Journal of Criminal Justice Education, 12*, 405–425.

Paternoster, R. (1983). Race of victim and location of crime: The decision to seek the death penalty in South Carolina. *Journal of Criminal Law and Criminology, 74*, 754–785.

Paternoster, R. (1984). Prosecutorial discretion in requesting the death penalty: The case of victim-based discrimination. *Law and Society Review, 18*, 437–478.

Paternoster, R. (1991). *Capital punishment in America*. New York: Lexington.

Paternoster, R., & Brame, R. (2003). An empirical analysis of Maryland's death sentencing system with respect to the influence of race and legal jurisdiction. Final Report. Study commissioned by the Maryland governor. Retrieved from. http://www.urhome.umd.edu/newsdesk/pdf/finalrep.pdf.

Paternoster, R., & Brame, R. (2008). Reassessing race disparities in Maryland capital cases. *Criminology, 46*, 971–1007.

Paternoster, R., & Deise, J. (2011). A heavy thumb on the scale: The effect of victim impact evidence on capital decision making. *Criminology, 49*, 129–161.

Paternoster, R., & Kazyaka, A. M. (1988). The administration of the death penalty in South Carolina: Experiences over the first few years. *South Carolina Law Review, 39*, 245–414.

Perez-Pena, R. (2000, February 13). The death penalty: When there's no room for error. *The New York Times*, p. 3.

Petersilia, J. (1990). Death penalty resolution debated and endorsed. *The Criminologist, 15*, 1.

Peterson, R. D., & Bailey, W. C. (1988). Murder and capital punishment in the evolving context of the post-Furman era. *Social Forces, 66*, 774–807.

Peterson, R. D., & Bailey, W. C. (1991). Felony murder and capital punishment: An examination of the deterrence question. *Criminology, 29*, 367–395.

Peterson, R. D., & Bailey, W. C. (2003). Is capital punishment an effective deterrent for murder? An examination of social science research. In J. R. Acker, R. M. Bohm, & C. S. Lanier (Eds.), *America's experiment with capital punishment: Reflections on the past, present and future of the ultimate penal sanction* (2nd ed.). (pp. 251–282) Durham, NC: Carolina Academic Press.

Phillips, D. P. (1980). The deterrent effect of capital punishment: New evidence on an old controversy. *American Journal of Sociology, 86*, 139–147.

Phillips, S. (2008). Racial disparities in the capital of capital punishment. *Houston Law Review, 45*, 807–840.

Phillips, S. (2009). Legal disparities in the capital of capital punishment. *Journal of Criminal Law and Criminology, 99*, 717–755.

Phillips, S. (2010). Status disparities in the capital of capital punishment [Electronic version]. *Law and Society Review, 43*, 807–837.

Pickert, K. (2008, June 25). Lethal injection: A brief history. *Time*. Retrieved from http://www.time.com/time/printout/0, 8816, 1815535,00.html.

Pierce, G. L., & Radelet, M. L. (2005). The impact of legally inappropriate factors on death sentencing for California homicides, 1990–1999. *Santa Clara Law Review, 46*, 1–47.

Pojman, L. P. (2004). Why the death penalty is morally permissible. In H. A. Bedau, & P. G. Cassell (Eds.), *Debating the death penalty: Should America have capital punishment? The experts on both sides make their best case* (pp. 51–75). New York: Oxford.

Pokorak, J. J. (1998). Probing the capital prosecutor's perspective: Race of the discretionary actors. *Cornell Law Review, 83*, 1811–1820.

Post, L. (2004). ABA death penalty guidelines languish [Electronic version]. *The National Law Journal, 26*. (accessed online, address not reproduced because of its length).

Prejean, H. (1993). *Dead man walking: An eyewitness account of the death penalty in the United States*. New York: Random House.

Pridemore,Alex, W. (2000). An empirical examination of commutations and executions in post-Furman capital cases. *Justice Quarterly, 17*, 159–183.

Radelet, M. L. (1981). Racial characteristics and the imposition of the death penalty. *American Sociological Review, 46*, 918–927.

Radelet, M. L. (2006, April 24). Personal communication to Robert M. Bohm.

Radelet, M. L. (2009). The executioner's waning defenses. In C. J. Ogletree, Jr., & A. Sarat (Eds.), *The road to abolition? The future of capital punishment in the United States* (pp. 19–45). New York: New York University Press.

Radelet, M. L. (2010, October 1). Some examples of post-Furman botched executions. Retrieved December 16, 2010, from http://www.deathpenaltyinfo.org/some-examples-post-furman-botched-executions

Radelet, M. L., & Akers, R. L. (1996). Deterrence and the death penalty: The view of the experts. *Journal of Criminal Law and Criminology, 87*, 1–16.

Radelet, M. L., & Bedau, H. A. (2003). The execution of the innocent. In J. R. Acker, R. M. Bohm, & C. S. Lanier (Eds.), *America's experiment with capital punishment: Reflections on the past, present and future of the ultimate penal sanction* (2nd ed.). (pp. 325–344) Durham, NC: Carolina Academic Press.

Radelet, M. L., Bedau, H. A., & Putnam, C. E. (1992). *In spite of innocence: Erroneous convictions in capital cases*. Boston: Northeastern University Press.

Radelet, M. L., & Borg, M. J. (2000). The changing nature of death penalty debates. *Annual Review of Sociology, 26*, 43–61.

Radelet, M. L., Lofquist, W. S., & Bedau, H. A. (1996). Prisoners released from death rows since 1970 because of doubts about their guilt. *Thomas M. Cooley Law Review, 13*, 907–966.

Radelet, M. L., & Pierce, G. L. (1985). Race and prosecutorial discretion in homicide cases. *Law and Society Review, 19*, 587–621.

Radelet, M. L., & Pierce, G. L. (1991). Choosing those who will die: Race and the death penalty in Florida. *Florida Law Review, 43*, 1–34.

Radelet, M. L., & Pierce, G. L. (2006). The role of victim's race and geography on death sentencing: Some recent data from Illinois. In C. J. Ogletree, Jr., & A. Sarat (Eds.), *From lynch mobs to the killing state: Race and the death penalty in America* (pp. 117–149). New York: New York University Press.

Radelet, M., & Vandiver, M. (1983). The Florida Supreme Court and death penalty appeals. *Journal of Criminal Law and Criminology, 74*, 913–926.

Radelet, M. L., Vandiver, M., & Barado, F. M. (1983). Families, prisons, and men with death sentences. *Journal of Family Issues, 4*, 593–612.

Radelet, M. L., & Zscmbik, B. A. (1993). Executive clemency in post-Furman capital cases. *University of Richmond Law Review, 27*, 289–314.

Radin, M. J. (1978). The jurisprudence of death: Evolving standards for the cruel and unusual punishment clause. University of Pennsylvania Law Review, 126, 989–1064.

Radin, M. J. (1980). Cruel punishment and respect for persons: Super due process for death. *Southern California Law Review, 53*, 1143–1185.

Ralph, P. H. (1996). Benjamin Rush. In M. D. McShane, & F. P. Williams, III (Eds.), *Encyclopedia of American prisons* (pp. 412–413). New York and London: Garland.

Rankin, J. H. (1979). Changing attitudes toward capital punishment. *Social Forces, 58*, 194–211.

Rapaport, E. (1993). The death penalty and gender discrimination. In V. L. Streib (Ed.), *A capital punishment anthology* (pp. 145–152). Cincinnati: Anderson Publishing Co.

Recer, P. (1994, March 20). Professional groups want doctors out of executions. *The Charlotte [NC] Observer*, p. 17A.

Rcckless, W. C. (1969). The use of the death penalty. *Crime & Delinquency, 15*, 43–56.

Reed, M. D., & Blackwell, B. S. (2006). Secondary victimization among homicide families of homicide victims: The impact of the justice process on co-victims' psychological adjustment and service utilization. In J. R. Acker, & D. R. Karp (Eds.), *Wounds that do not bind: Victim-based perspectives on the death penalty* (pp. 253–273). Durham, NC: Carolina Academic Press.

Reidy, T. J., Cunningham, M. D., & Sorensen, J. R. (2001). From death to life: Prison behavior of former death row inmates in Indiana. *Criminal Justice and Behavior, 28*, 62–82.

Reiman, J. (2007). *The rich get richer and the poor get prison: Ideology, class, and criminal justice* (8th ed.). Boston: Allyn & Bacon.

Reinhold, R. (1982, December 7). Chemical injection executes Texas killer. *The Anniston [AL] Star*, p. 1A.

Religious Leaders in Florida. (1986). Religious views denounce the death penalty. In B. Szumski, L. Hall, & S. Bursell (Eds.), *The death penalty: Opposing viewpoints* (pp. 86–91). St. Paul, MN: Greenhaven.

Roberts, J. V. (1984). Public opinion and capital punishment: The effects of attitudes upon memory. *Canadian Journal of Criminology, 26*, 283–291.

Roberts, K. (2005, May 8). *Capital cases hard for smaller counties*. Retrieved from the Death Penalty Information Center website. Associated Press http://www.deathpenaltyinfo.org/newsanddev.php?scid=71&scyr=2005.

Rogers, B. (2010, March 5). Judge declares death penalty unconstitutional: Maverick jurist grants pretrial motion. Retrieved April 31, 2010, from *Houston Chronicle*. http://www.chron.com/disp/story.mpl/metropolitan/6897252.html.

Roman, J. K., Chalfin, A. J., & Knight, C. R. (2009). Reassessing the cost of the death penalty using quasi-experimental methods: Evidence from Maryland. *American Law and Economics Review, 11*, 530–574, Retrieved September 13, 2010.

Roper, R. (2006). Finding hope: One family's journey. In J. R. Acker, & D. R. Karp (Eds.), *Wounds that do not bind: Victim-based perspectives on the death penalty* (pp. 111–125). Durham, NC: Carolina Academic Press.

Rosenbluth, S., & Phyllis. (2006). Accidental death is fate, murder is pure evil. In J. R. Acker, & D. R. Karp (Eds.), *Wounds that do not bind: Victim-based perspectives on the death penalty* (pp. 103–109). Durham, NC: Carolina Academic Press.

Rothman, D. J. (1980). *Conscience and convenience: The asylum and its alternatives in progressive America*. Boston: Little, Brown.

Rusche, G., & Kirchheimer, O. (1968). *Punishment and social structure*. New York: Russell and Russell.

Sabol, W. J., West, H. C., & Cooper, M. (2009, December). *Prisoners in 2008*. Bureau of Justice Statistics Bulletin. US Department of Justice. Retrieved December 3, 2010, from http://bjs.ojp.usdoj.gov/content/pub/pdf/p08.pdf.

Sandys, M. (1995). Attitudinal change among students in a capital punishment class: It may be possible. *American Journal of Criminal Justice, 20*, 37–55.

Sandys, M. (1998). Stacking the deck for guilt and death: The failure of death qualification to ensure impartiality. In J. R. Acker, R. M. Bohm, & C. S. Lanier (Eds.), *America's experiment with capital punishment: Reflections on the past, present and future of the ultimate penal sanction* (pp. 285–307). Durham, NC: Carolina Academic Press.

Sandys, M., & McGarrell, E. F. (1994). Attitudes toward capital punishment among Indiana legislators: Diminished support in light of alternative sentencing options. *Justice Quarterly, 11*, 651–677.

Sandys, M., & McGarrell, E. F. (1995). Attitudes toward capital punishment: Preferences for the penalty or mere acceptance? *Journal of Research in Crime & Delinquency, 32*, 191–213.

Santich, K. (2001, June 9). Last man to die: Who was Victor Feguer. *The Orlando Sentinel*, p. E1.

Sarat, A. (Ed.) (1999). *The killing state: Capital punishment in law, politics, and culture*. New York: Oxford University Press.

Sarat, A. (2002). *When the state kills: Capital punishment and the American condition*. Princeton, NJ: Princeton University Press.

Sarat, A. (2005). *Mercy on trial: What it means to stop an execution*. Princeton, NJ: Princeton University Press.

Sarat, A. (2006a). Putting a square peg in a round hole; victims, retribution, and George Ryan's clemency. In J. R. Acker, & D. R. Karp (Eds.), *Wounds that do not bind: Victim-based perspectives on the death penalty* (pp. 203–232). Durham, NC: Carolina Academic Press.

Sarat, A. (2006b). The rhetoric of race in the 'new abolitionism'. In C. J. Ogletree, Jr., & A. Sarat (Eds.), *From lynch mobs to the killing state: Race and the death penalty in America* (pp. 260–284). New York: New York University Press.

Sarat, A., & Vidmar, N. (1976). Public opinion, the death penalty, and the Eighth Amendment: Testing the Marshall hypothesis. *Wisconsin Law Review, 17*, 171–206.

Savitz, L. (1958). A study in capital punishment. *Journal of Criminal Law, Criminology and Police Science, 49*, 338–341.

Scalia, J. (1997). *Prisoner petitions in the federal courts, 1980–96*. Washington, DC: US Department of Justice, Office of Justice Programs, Bureau of Justice Statistics. GPO.

Scheb, J. M., II, & Lyons, W. (2001, April). *Race, aggravating factors and prosecutorial discretion: Analyzing the death penalty in Tennessee*. Paper presented at the annual meeting of the Academy of Criminal Justice Sciences, Washington, DC.

Scheck, B., Neufeld, P., & Dwyer, J. (2001). *Actual innocence: When justice goes wrong and how to make it right*. New York: Penguin Putnam.

Schneider, V., & Smykla, J. O. (1991). A summary analysis of executions in the United States, 1608–1987: The Espy file. In R. M. Bohm (Ed.), *The death penalty in America: Current research* (pp. 1–19). Cincinnati: Anderson Publishing Co.

Schoenfeld, H. (2005). Violated trust: Conceptualizing prosecutorial misconduct. *Journal of Contemporary Criminal Justice, 21*, 250–271.

Schuessler, K. F. (1952). The deterrent effect of the death penalty. *The Annals, 284*, 54–62.

Schwarz, J. B. (1999). Personal correspondence. Associate Reference Librarian, Virginia Historical Society [from the Minutes of the Council and General Court of Colonial Virginia (for June 14, 1632), edited by H.R. McIlwaine].

Schwartz, J. (2011, April 13) Seeking execution drug, states cut legal corners. *The New York Times.* Retrieved from http://www.nytimes.com/2011/04/14/us/14lethal.html.

Schwarzschild, H. (1982). In opposition to death penalty legislation. In H. A. Bedau (Ed.), *The death penalty in America* (3rd ed.). (pp. 364–370) New York: Oxford University Press.

Seewar, J. (2005, May 9). *Two killers; one spared.* Retrieved from the Death Penalty Information Center website. Associated Press. http://www.deathpenaltyinfo.org/newsanddev.php?scid=71&scyr=2005.

Sellin, T. (1959). *The death penalty.* Philadelphia: The American Law Institute.

Sellin, T. (Ed.) (1967). *Capital punishment.* New York: Harper & Row.

Sharp, S. F. (2005). *Hidden victims: The effects of the death penalty on families of the accused.* Piscataway, NJ: Rutgers University Press.

Sharp, S. F. (2008). *Death penalty attitudes.* University of Oklahoma Public Opinion Learning Laboratory. (Thanks to Professor Sharp for generously providing these data.).

Shepherd, J. M. (2004). Murder of passion, execution delays, and the deterrence of capital punishment. *Journal of Legal Studies, 33*, 283–321.

Shepherd, J. M. (2005). Deterrence versus brutalization: Capital punishment's differing impacts among states. *Michigan Law Review, 104*, 203–256.

Siegel, D. M. (2009, February). The role of trial counsel in ineffective assistance of counsel claims: Three questions to keep in mind. Retrieved December 6, 2010, from. *The Champion.* http://www.nacdl.org/public.nsf/0/31d142160aba75a2852575860069b997?OpenDocument.

Simon, D. R. (2006). *Elite deviance* (8th ed.). Boston: Allyn & Bacon.

Simon, J., & Spaulding, C. (1999). Tokens of our esteem: Aggravating factors in the era of deregulated death penalties. In A. Sarat (Ed.), *The killing state: Capital punishment in law, politics, and culture* (pp. 81–113). New York: Oxford University Press.

Smith, K. (2010, September 28). Defense costs grow in Arivaca killing case. *Arizona Daily Star.* Retrieved December 2, 2010, from http://azstarnet.com/news/local/crime/article_78b100ec-a70d-56ce-a761-220005dc9dc8.html.

Smith, M. D. (1987). Patterns of discrimination in assessments of the death penalty: The case of Louisiana. *Journal of Criminal Justice, 15*, 279–286.

Smith, R. (2010). Arbitrariness as ever: Only 10% of counties in the country have imposed a death sentence in the last 6 years. Second Class Justice. Retrieved December 8, 2010, from http://www.secondclassjustice.com/?p=116.

Smith, T. W. (1975). A trend analysis of attitudes toward capital punishment, 1936–1974. In J. E. Davis (Ed.), *Studies of social change since 1948, Vol. II.* (pp. 257–318). Chicago: University of Chicago National Opinion Research Center.

Smykla, J. O. (1987). The human impact of capital punishment: Interviews with families of persons on death row. *Journal of Criminal Justice, 15*, 331–347.

Snell, T. L. (1997, December). *Capital punishment 1996.* US Department of Justice. Bureau of Justice Statistics Bulletin.

Snell, T. L. (2006, December). *Capital punishment 2005.* US Department of Justice. Bureau of Justice Statistics Bulletin.

Snell, T. L. (2006, December). *Capital punishment, 2005—Statistical tables.* Statistical Tables. US Department of Justice, Bureau of Justice Statistics. Retrieved December 9, 2010, from http://bjs.ojp.usdoj.gov/index.cfm?ty=pbdetail&iid=415.

Snell, T. L. (2007, December). *Capital punishment, 2006—Statistical tables*. Statistical Tables. US Department of Justice, Bureau of Justice Statistics. Retrieved December 9, 2010, from http://bjs.ojp.usdoj.gov/index.cfm?ty=pbdetail&iid=689.

Snell, T. L. (2008, December). *Capital punishment, 2007—Statistical tables*. Statistical Tables. US Department of Justice, Bureau of Justice Statistics. Retrieved December 9, 2010, from http://bjs.ojp.usdoj.gov/index.cfm?ty=pbdetail&iid=687.

Snell, T. L. (2009, December). *Capital punishment, 2008—Statistical tables*. Statistical Tables. US Department of Justice, Bureau of Justice Statistics. Retrieved December 9, 2010, from http://bjs.ojp.usdoj.gov/index.cfm?ty=pbdetail&iid=1757.

Snell, T. L. (2010a, December). Capital punishment, 2009-Statistical tables. US Department of Justice, Bureau of Justice Statistics, Statistical Tables. Retrieved December 9, 2010, from http://bjs.ojp.usdoj.gov/content/pub/pdf/cp09st.pdf

Snell, T. L. (2010b, December 16) US Department of Justice, Bureau of Justice Statistics. Personal correspondence.

Sorensen, J. (2004). The administration of the capital punishment. *ACJS Today, 29*(2), 1, 4, 5, 7.

Sorensen, J., & Cunningham, M. D. (2010). Conviction offense and prison violence: A comparative study of murderers and other offenders. *Crime & Delinquency, 56*, 103–125.

Sorensen, J., & Wallace, D. H. (1999). Prosecutorial discretion in seeking death: An analysis of racial disparity in the pretrial stages of case processing in a midwestern county. *Justice Quarterly, 16*, 559–578.

Sorensen, J. R., & Pilgrim, R. L. (2000). An actuarial risk assessment of violence posed by capital murder defendants. *Journal of Criminal Law and Criminology, 90*, 1251–1270.

Sorensen, J., & Wrinkle, R. D. (1996). No hope for parole: Disciplinary infractions among death-sentenced and life-without-parole inmates. *Criminal Justice and Behavior, 23*, 542–552.

Sorensen, J., Wrinkle, R., Brewer, V., & Marquart, J. (1999). Capital punishment and deterrence: Examining the effect of executions on murder in Texas. *Crime & Delinquency, 45*, 481–493.

Soss, J., Langbein, L., & Metelko, A. R. (2003). Why do white Americans support the death penalty? *Journal of Politics, 65*, 397–421.

Spangenberg, R. L., & Walsh, E. R. (1989). Capital punishment or life imprisonment? Some cost considerations. *Loyola of Los Angeles Law Review, 23*, 45–58.

Stack, S. (1987). Publicized executions and homicide, 1950–1980. *American Sociological Review, 52*, 532–540.

Stafford-Smith, C. (2002). Killing the death penalty with kindness. In D. R. Dow, & M. Dow (Eds.), *Machinery of death: The reality of America's death penalty regime* (pp. 269–273). New York: Routledge.

State calls off execution of childkiller Albert Greenwood Brown after legal setbacks. (September 29). KTLA.com. Retrieved November 27, 2010, from http://www.ktla.com/news/landing/ktla-albert-greenwood-brown,0, 1845806.story

Stauffer, A. R., Smith, M. D., Cochran, J. K., Fogel, S. J., & Bjerregaard, B. (2006). The interaction between victim race and gender on sentencing outcomes in capital murder trials. *Homicide, 10*, 98–117.

Steele, T., & Wilcox, N. (2003). A view from the inside: The role of redemption, deterrence, and masculinity on inmate support for the death penalty. *Crime & Delinquency, 49*, 285–312.

Steelwater, E. (2003). *The hangman's knot: Lynching, legal execution, and America's struggle with the death penalty*. Boulder, CO: Westview Press.

Steiker, C. S. (2002). Capital punishment and American exceptionalism. *Oregon Law Review, 81*, 97–130.

Steiker, C. S., & Steiker, J. M. (1998). Judicial developments in capital punishment law. In J. R. Acker, R. M. Bohm, & C. S. Lanier (Eds.), *America's experiment with capital punishment: Reflections on the past, present and future of the ultimate penal sanction* (pp. 47–75). Durham, NC: Carolina Academic Press.

Steiker, C., & Steiker, J. (2006). The effect of capital punishment on American criminal law and policy. *Judicature, 89*, 250–253.

Steiker, C., & Steiker, J. (2009). The beginning of the end? In C. J. Ogletree, Jr., & A. Sarat (Eds.), *The road to abolition? The future of capital punishment in the United States* (pp. 97–138). New York: New York University Press.

Stephan, J. J., & Snell, T. L. (1996). *Capital punishment 1994.* Bureau of Justice Statistics Bulletin. Annapolis Junction, MD: US Department of Justice. BJS Clearinghouse.

Stephens, G. (1990, July–August). High-tech crime: The threat to civil liberties. *The Futurist,* 20–25.

Stern, A. (2006). Ex-Illinois governor gets prison sentence. M and C News. Retrieved from http://news. monstersandcritics.com/northamerica/article_1198669.php/Ex-Illinois_governor_gets_prison_sentence

Stevens alters stance on lethal-injection methods. (2008, May 11). *The Orlando Sentinel* A7.

Stevenson, B. (2004). Close to death: Reflections on race and capital punishment in America. In H. A. Bedau, & P. G. Cassell (Eds.), *Debating the death penalty: Should America have capital punishment? The experts on both sides make their best case* (pp. 76–116). New York: Oxford.

Stinchcombe, A. L., Adams, R., Heimer, C. A., Scheppele, K. L., Smith, T. W., & Taylor, D. G. (1980). *Crime and punishment—Changing attitudes in America.* San Francisco: Josey-Bass.

Streib, V. L. (1987). *Death penalty for juveniles.* Bloomington and Indianapolis: Indiana University Press.

Streib, V. L. (1988). Imposing the death penalty on children. In K. C. Haas, & J. A. Inciardi (Eds.), *Challenging capital punishment: Legal and social science approaches* (pp. 245–267). Newbury Park, CA: Sage.

Streib, V. L. (1989). Juveniles' attitudes toward their impending executions. In M. L. Radelet (Ed.), *Facing the death penalty: Essays on a cruel and unusual punishment* (pp. 38–59). Philadelphia: Temple University Press.

Streib, V. L. (1993). Death penalty for female offenders. In V. L. Streib (Ed.), *A capital punishment anthology* (pp. 142–145). Cincinnati: Anderson Publishing Co.

Streib, V. L. (1998). Executing women, children, and the retarded: Second class citizens in capital punishment. In J. R. Acker, R. M. Bohm, & C. S. Lanier (Eds.), *America's experiment with capital punishment: Reflections on the past, present and future of the ultimate penal sanction* (pp. 201–221). Durham, NC: Carolina Academic Press.

Streib, V. L. (2002). Capital Punishment of Female Offenders: Present Female Death Row Inmates and Death Sentences and Executions of Female Offenders, January 1, 1973, to October 9, 2002 (October) at www.law. onu.edu/faculty/streib).

Streib, V. L. (2003). Executing women, juveniles, and the mentally retarded: Second class citizens in capital punishment. In J. R. Acker, R. M. Bohm, & C. S. Lanier (Eds.), *America's experiment with capital punishment: Reflections on the past, present and future of the ultimate penal sanction* (2nd ed). (pp. 301–323). Durham, NC: Carolina Academic Press.

Streib, V. L. (2005). The juvenile death penalty today: Death sentences and executions for juvenile crimes, January 1, 1973–December 31, 2004. Retrieved from. http://www.law.onu.edu/faculty/streib/juvdeath. htm.

Streib, V. L. (2006). Death penalty for female offenders January 1, 1973, through December 31, 2005. Retrieved from http://www.law.onu.edu/faculty/streib/femdeath.htm.

Streib, V. (2010). Death penalty for female offenders, January 1, 1973, through October 31, 2010. Retrieved December 11, 2010, from http://www.deathpenaltyinfo.org/documents/femaledeathrow.pdf.

Sturrock, T. (2006). Man behind historic death penalty case back in jail. Macon.com. Retrieved September 25, 2006, from. http://www.macon.com/mld/macon/15568709.htm.

Sullivan, D. H. (2006). Killing time: Two decades of military capital litigation. *Military Law Review, 189,* 1–50.

Sundby, S. E. (2005). *A life and death decision: A jury weighs the death penalty.* New York: Palgrave Macmillan.

Surette, R. (1992). *Media, criminal crime, and justice: Images and realities.* Pacific Grove, CA: Brooks/Cole.

Supreme Court of the United States. A brief overview of the Supreme Court. In About the Supreme Court. Retrieved from http://www.supremecourtus.gov/about/about.html

Supreme Court of the United States. The court and constitutional interpretation. In About the Supreme Court. Retrieved from http://www.supremecourtus.gov/about/about.html

The Supreme Court Historical Society. The Chase Court, 1864–1873. In History of the court. Retrieved from http://www.supremecourthistory.org/02_history/subs_history/02_c06.html

Sutherland, E. H. (1925). Murder and the death penalty. *Journal of Criminal Law and Criminology, 15*, 522–529.

Tabak, R. J. (2001). Finality without fairness: Why we are moving towards moratoria on executions and the potential abolition of capital punishment. *Connecticut Law Review, 33*, 733–763.

Taylor, G. (2000, May 8). Dozens seek front-row seat for executions. *The Orlando Sentinel*, p. C3.

Taylor, G., & Stutzman, R. (2000, February 23). Appeals run out—Sims set for death. *The Orlando Sentinel*, p. A1.

Texas Defender Service. (2004). *Deadly speculation: Misleading Texas capital juries with false predictions of future dangerousness*. Retrieved from. Houston and Austin, TX: Texas Defender Service. http://www.texasdefender.org/publications.htm.

The Constitution Project. (2005). *Mandatory justice: The death penalty revisited*. Washington, DC: The Constitution Project Death Penalty Initiative. Retrieved from http://www.constitutionproject.org/deathpenalty/article.cfm?messageID=136&categoryId=2.

Thomas, C. W., & Foster, S. C. (1975). A sociological perspective on public support for capital punishment. *American Journal of Orthopsychiatry, 45*, 641–657.

Thompson, D. (2006, January 18). California executes man despite protests about age. *The Orlando Sentinel*, p. A4.

Thompson, E. (1997). Deterrence versus brutalization: The case of Arizona. *Homicide Studies, 1*, 110–128.

Thompson, E. (1999). Effects of execution on homicides in California. *Homicide Studies, 3*, 129–150.

Thompson, E. P. (1975). *Whigs and hunters: The origin of the Black Act*. New York: Pantheon.

Thompson, W. C. (1989). Death qualification after Wainwright v. Witt and Lockhart v. McCree. *Law and Human Behavior, 13*, 185–215.

Three men facing federal execution receive stays. (2006). The Death Penalty Information Center. Retrieved from http://www.deathpenaltyinfo.org/newsanddev.php?scid=8.

Tifft, L. (1982). Capital punishment research, policy, and ethics: Defining murder and placing murderers. *Crime and Social Justice, 17*, 61–68.

Tizon, T. A. (2003, November 6). I killed the 48 women. *The Orlando Sentinel*, p. A1.

Totenberg, N. (2010, October 4). Justice Stevens: An open mind on a changed court. NPR Retrieved October 5, 2010, from http://www.deathpenaltyinfo.org/

Trivers, R. L. (1971). The evolution of reciprocal altruism. *Quarterly Review of Biology, 46*, 35–57.

Turner, A., & Ruiz, R. (2008, July 17). Texas still plans to execute killer despite U.N. order. Retrieved November 8, 2010, from *The Houston Chronicle*. http://www.chron.com/disp/story.mpl/front/5890690.html.

Turney, P. H. (2000). New developments in military capital litigation: Four cases highlight the fundamentals. *The Army Lawyer (May)*, 103–114.

Turow, S. (2003). *Ultimate punishment: A lawyer's reflections on dealing with the death penalty*. New York: Picador.

Tyler, T, R., & Weber, R, (1982). Support for the death penalty: Instrumental response to crime, or symbolic attitude? *Law and Society Review, 17*, 21–45.

Unah, I., & Boger, J. C. (2001). Race and the death penalty in North Carolina, an empirical analysis: 1993–1997. Retrieved from http://www.deathpenaltyinfo.org/NCRaceRpt.html.

Unnever, J. D., & Cullen, F. T. (2005). Executing the innocent and support for capital punishment implications for public policy. *Criminology & Public Policy, 4*, 3–38.

Unnever, J. D., & Cullen, F. T. (2007a). The racial divide in support for the death penalty: Does white racism matter? *Social Forces, 85*, 1281–1301.

Unnever, J. D., & Cullen, F. T. (2007b). Reassessing the racial divide in support for capital punishment: The continuing significance of race. *Journal of Research in Crime & Delinquency, 44*, 1–35.

Unnever, J. D., & Cullen, F. T. (2010a). Racial–ethnic intolerance and support for capital punishment: A cross-national comparison. *Criminology, 48*, 831–864.

Unnever, J. D., & Cullen, F. T. (2010b). The social sources of Americans' punitiveness: A test of three competing models. *Criminology, 48*, 99–129.

Unnever, J. D., Cullen, F. T., & Bartkowski, J. P. (2006). Images of God and public support for capital punishment: Does a close relationship with a loving God matter? *Criminology, 44*, 835–866.

Unnever, J. D., Cullen, F. T., & Fisher, B. S. (2005). Empathy and support for capital punishment. *Journal of Crime & Justice, 28*, 1–34.

Unnever, J. D., Cullen, F. T., & Jonson, C. L. (2008). Race, racism, and support for capital punishment. In M. H. Tonry (Ed.), *Crime and justice: A review of research, vol. 37.* (pp. 45–96). Chicago: Chicago University Press.

Unnever, J. D., Cullen, F. T., & Roberts, J. V. (2005). Not everyone strongly supports the death penalty: Assessing weakly-held attitudes about capital punishment. *American Journal of Criminal Justice, 29*, 187–216.

US General Accounting Office. (1990). *Death penalty sentencing: Research indicates pattern of racial disparities.* Report to Senate and House Committees on the Judiciary. Washington, DC: GAO.

Van den Haag, E. (1982). In defense of the death penalty: A practical and moral analysis. In H. A. Bedau (Ed.), *The death penalty in America* (3rd ed.). (pp. 323–341) New York: Oxford University Press.

Van den Haag, E. (1998). Justice, deterrence and the death penalty. In J. R. Acker, R. M. Bohm, & C. S. Lanier (Eds.), *America's experiment with capital punishment: Reflections on the past, present and future of the ultimate penal sanction* (pp. 139–156). Durham, NC: Carolina Academic Press.

Van den Haag, E., & Conrad, J. P. (1983). *The death penalty: A debate.* New York: Plenum.

Vandiver, M. (1989). Coping with death: Families of the terminally ill, homicide victims, and condemned prisoners. In M. L. Radelet (Ed.), *Facing the death penalty: Essays on a cruel and unusual punishment* (pp. 123–138). Philadelphia: Temple University Press.

Vandiver, M. (2003). The impact of the death penalty on the families of homicide victims and of condemned prisoners. In J. R. Acker, R. M. Bohm, & C. S. Lanier (Eds.), *America's experiment with capital punishment: Reflections on the past, present and future of the ultimate penal sanction* (2nd ed.). (pp. 613–645) Durham, NC: Carolina Academic Press.

Vandiver, M. (2006). The death penalty and the families of victims: An overview of research issues. In J. R. Acker, & D. R. Karp (Eds.), *Wounds that do not bind: Victim-based perspectives on the death penalty* (pp. 235–252). Durham, NC: Carolina Academic Press.

Vandiver, M., Giacopassi, D. J., & Curley, M. S. (2003). The Tennessee slave code: A legal antecedent to inequities in modern capital cases. *Journal of Ethnicity in Criminal Justice, 1*, 67–89.

Vick, K. (1996, January 21). Delaware readies gallows as rare form of execution draws near. *The Washington Post*, p. B4.

Vidmar, N. (1974). Retributive and utilitarian motives and other correlates of Canadian attitudes toward the death penalty. *Canadian Psychologist, 15*, 337–356.

Vidmar, N., & Dittenhoffer, T. (1981). Informed public opinion and death penalty attitudes. *Canadian Journal of Criminology, 23*, 43–56.

Vidmar, N., & Ellsworth, P. (1974). Public opinion and the death penalty. *Stanford Law Review, 26*, 1245–1270.

Vidmar, N., & Miller, D. T. (1980). Social psychological processes underlying attitudes toward legal punishment. *Law and Society Review, 14*, 565–602.

Vila, B., & Morris, C. (Eds.) (1997). *Capital punishment in the United States: A documentary history.* Westport, CT: Greenwood.

Villa, J. (2005, May 8). Aged inmates' care puts stress on state. Retrieved from. *The Arizona Republic.* http://www.azcentral.com/specials/special21/articles/0508prisonaging01.html.

Visger, M. A. (2005). The impact of Ring v. Arizona on military capital sentencing. *The Army Lawyer* (September) 54–77.

Vito, G., & Keil, T. (1988). Capital sentencing in Kentucky: An analysis of the factors influencing decision making in the post-Gregg period. *Journal of Criminal Law and Criminology, 79*, 483–508.

Vito, G. F., Koester, P., & Wilson, D. G. (1991). Return of the dead: An update on the status of Furman-commuted death row inmates. In R. M. Bohm (Ed.), *The death penalty in America: Current research* (pp. 89–99). Cincinnati: Anderson Publishing Co.

Vito, G. F., & Wilson, D. G. (1988). Back from the dead: Tracking the progress of Kentucky's Furman-commuted death row population. *Justice Quarterly, 5*, 101–111.

Vogel, B. L. (2003). Support for life in prison without the possibility of parole among death penalty supporters. *American Journal of Criminal Justice, 27*, 263–275.

Vogel, B. L., & Vogel, R. E. (2003). The age of death: Appraising public opinion of juvenile capital punishment. *Journal of Criminal Justice, 31*, 169–183.

Vold, G. B. (1932). Can the death penalty prevent crime? *Prison Journal, 12*, 3–8.

Vold, G. B. (1952). Extent and trend of capital crimes in the United States. *The Annals, 284*, 1–7.

Vollum, S., & Buffington-Vollum, J. (2010). An examination of social–psychological factors and support for the death penalty: Attribution, moral disengagement, and the value-expressive function of attitudes. *American Journal of Criminal Justice, 35*, 15–36.

Wagner, S. (2006). The death sentence: For criminals or victims? In J. R. Acker, & D. R. Karp (Eds.), *Wounds that do not bind: Victim-based perspectives on the death penalty* (pp. 69–83) Durham, NC: Carolina Academic Press.

Waldo, G. P. (1981). The death penalty and deterrence: A review of recent research. In I. L. Barak-Glantz, & C. R. Huff (Eds.), *The mad, the bad, and the different: Essays in honor of Simon Dinitz* (pp. 169–178). Lexington, MA: Heath.

Walker, R. N. (2006). How the malfunctioning death penalty challenges the criminal justice system. *Judicature, 89*, 265–268.

Warr, M., & Stafford, M. (1984). Public goals of punishment and support for the death penalty. *Journal of Research in Crime & Delinquency, 21*, 95–111.

Weinstein, H. (2002, June 4). Court backs inmate with sleepy lawyer. *The Orlando Sentinel*, p. A5.

Weisberg, R. (1983). Deregulating death. In P. B. Kurland, G. Casper, & D. J. Hutchinson (Eds.), *The Supreme Court review, 1983* (pp. 305–395). Chicago: University of Chicago Press.

Weisman, R. S., Bernstein, J. N., & Weisman, R. S. (2005). Inadequate anaesthesia in lethal injection for execution. *The Lancet, 366*. Retrieved from http://www.sciencedirect.com.

Weissberg, R. (1976). *Public opinion and popular government*. Englewood Cliffs, NJ: Prentice Hall.

Welch, B. (2002). Speaking out against the execution of Timothy McVeigh. In D. R. Dow, & M. Dow (Eds.), *Machinery of death: The reality of America's death penalty regime* (pp. 275–281). New York: Routledge.

Welch, M., & Burr, R. (2002). The politics of finality and the execution of the innocent: The case of Gary Graham. In D. R. Dow, & M. Dow (Eds.), *Machinery of death: The reality of America's death penalty regime* (pp. 127–143). New York: Routledge.

Welsh-Huggins, A. (2005, May 7). *Death penalty unequal*. Retrieved from the Death Penalty Information Center website. Associated Press. http://www.deathpenaltyinfo.org/newsanddev.php?scid=71&scyr=2005.

Westervelt, S. D., & Cook, K. J. (2008). Coping with innocence after death row. *Contexts, 7*, 32–37.

White, L. L. (2006). A tiger by the tail: The mother of a murder victim grapples with the death penalty. In J. R. Acker, & D. R. Karp (Eds.), *Wounds that do not bind: Victim-based perspectives on the death penalty* (pp. 49–68). Durham, NC: Carolina Academic Press.

White, W. S. (1987). *The death penalty in the eighties: An examination of the modern system of capital punishment*. Ann Arbor: University of Michigan Press.

White House. (2005, December 3). Bush thinks death penalty is deterrent. *The Orlando Sentinel*, p. A10.

Whitehead, J. T. (1998). Good ol' boys and the chair: Death penalty attitudes of policy makers in Tennessee. *Crime & Delinquency, 44*, 245–256.

Who is eligible to be legal witness to execution? (2010). CRIMINALDEFENSELAWYER.com. Retrieved November 27, 2010, from http://www.criminaldefenselawyer.com/resources/criminal-defense/criminal-defense-case/who-eligible-be-legal-witness-execution.

Wicker, A. W. (1969). Attitudes versus actions: The relationship of verbal and overt behavioral responses to attitude objects. *Journal of Social Issues, 25*, 41–78.

Wilbanks, W. (1987). *The myth of a racist criminal justice system.* Monterey, CA: Brooks/Cole.

Wilcox, N., & Steele, T. (2003). Just the facts: a descriptive analysis of inmate attitudes toward capital punishment. *The Prison Journal, 83,* 464–482.

Williams, C. J. (2009, September 21). *Is 2nd try at lethal injection too cruel? The Orlando Sentinel* p. A3.

Williams, F. P., Longmire, D. R., & Gulick, D. B. (1988). The public and the death penalty: Opinion as an artifact of question type.". *Criminal Justice Research Bulletin, 3,* 1–5.

Williams, K. (2005). Ensuring the capital defendant's right to competent counsel: It's time for some standards. Retrieved from. *The Wayne Law Review, 51,* 129–161. http://web.lexis-nexis.com (Full web address too long to reproduce here).

Williams, M. R., Demuth, S., & Holcomb, J. E. (2007). Understanding the influence of victim gender in death penalty cases: The importance of victim race, sex-related victimization, and jury decision making. *Criminology, 45,* 865–891.

Williams, M. R., & Holcomb, J. E. (2001). acial disparity and death sentences in Ohio. *Journal of Criminal Justice, 29,* 207–218.

Williams, M. R., & Holcomb, J. E. (2004). The interactive effects of victim race and gender on death sentence disparity findings. *Homicide Studies, 8,* 350–376.

Willing, R., & Fields, G. (1999, December 20). Geography of the death penalty. *USA Today,* p. 1A.

Wilson, R. J. (2003). The influence of international law and practice on the death penalty in the United States. In J. R. Acker, R. M. Bohm, & C. S. Lanier (Eds.), *America's experiment with capital punishment: Reflections on the past, present and future of the ultimate penal sanction* (2nd ed.). (pp. 147–165) Durham, NC: Carolina Academic Press.

Wolfgang, M. E., & Riedel, M. (1975). Rape, race and the death penalty in Georgia. *American Journal of Orthopsychiatry, 45,* 658–668.

Wolfson, W. P. (1982). The deterrent effect of the death penalty upon prison murder. In H. A. Bedau (Ed.), *The death penalty in America* (3rd ed.). (pp. 159–173) New York: Oxford University Press.

Wollan, L. A., Jr. (1989). Representing the death row inmate: The ethics of advocacy, collateral style. In M. L. Radelet (Ed.), *Facing the death penalty: Essays on a cruel and unusual punishment* (pp. 92–111). Philadelphia: Temple University Press.

Wolpin, K. I. (1978). Capital punishment and homicide in England: A summary of results. *American Economic Review, 68,* 422–427.

Woodward, B., & Armstrong, S. (1979). *The brethren: Inside the Supreme Court.* New York: Simon and Schuster.

Word, R. (2002, November 18). Federal cases rarely end in death penalty. *The Orlando Sentinel,* p. B3.

Word, R. (2004a, May 27). Killer put to death after delay. *The Orlando Sentinel,* p. B5

Word, R. (2004b, August 10). Death row not too hot for inmates. *The Orlando Sentinel,* p. B5

Wozniak, K. H., & Lewis, A. R. (2009, November 5). *Christian religion and support for the death penalty: A comparison of measurement strategies.* Paper presented at the annual meeting of the American Society of Criminology, Philadelphia, PA.

Wright, H. O., Jr., Bohm, R. M., & Jamieson, K. M. (1995). A comparison of uninformed and informed death penalty opinions: A replication and expansion. *American Journal of Criminal Justice, 20,* 57–87.

Wyble, D. W. (1985). Capital punishment in the military. *Military Police (Winter)* 36–37.

Yang, B., & Lester, D. (2008). The deterrent effect of executions: A meta-analysis thirty years after Ehrlich. *Journal of Criminal Justice, 36,* 453–460, Retrieved September 27, 2010.

Yardley, J. (2000, January 7). On the record: Texas' busy death chamber helps define Bush's tenure. *The New York Times.* Retrieved from http://www.crimelynx.com/bushdp.html.

Yardley, J. (2001a, September 2). Oklahoma takes close look at evidence in capital cases. *The Orlando Sentinel,* p. A5

Yardley, J. (2001b, May 2). Oklahoma inquiry focuses on scientist used by prosecutors. *The New York Times,* p. A1

Young, R. L. (1992). Religious orientation, race and support for the death penalty. *Journal for the Scientific Study of Religion, 31*, 76–87.

Young, R. L. (2004). Guilty until proven innocent: Conviction orientation, racial attitudes, and support for capital punishment. *Deviant Behavior, 25*, 151–167.

Yunker, J. A. (1976). Is the death penalty a deterrent to homicide: Some time-series evidence. *Journal of Behavioral Economics, 5*, 1–32.

Yunker, J. A. (2002). A new statistical analysis of capital punishment incorporating U.S. postmoratorium data. *Social Science Quarterly, 82*, 297–311.

Zahn, M. A. (1989). Homicide in the twentieth century: Trends, types, and causes. In T. R. Gurr (Ed.), *Violence in America: The history of crime, Vol. 1.* (pp. 216–234). Newbury Park, CA: Sage.

Zeisel, H. (1981). Race bias in the administration of the death penalty: The Florida experience. *Harvard Law Review, 95*, 456–468.

Zeisel, H. (1982). The deterrent effect of the death penalty: Facts v. faith. In H. A. Bedau (Ed.), *The death penalty in America* (3rd ed.). (pp. 116–138) New York: Oxford University Press.

Zerwick, P. (2004, December 16). Hunt case leads to legal reform. Retrieved from. *Winston-Salem Journal.* http://darrylhunt.journalnow.com/epilogue.html.

Zimmerman, P. R. (2004). State executions, deterrence, and the incidence of murder. *Journal of Applied Economics, 7*, 163–193.

Zimmerman, P. R. (2006). Estimates of the deterrent effect of alternative execution methods in the United States: 1978–2000 [Electronic version]. *American Journal of Economics and Sociology.* Retrieved from http://findarticles.com/p/articles/mi_m0254/is_4_65/ai_n16819418/?tag=content;col1.

Zimmerman, P. R. (2009). Statistical variability and the deterrent effect of the death penalty [Electronic version]. *American Law and Economics Review, 11*, 370–398, Retrieved September 22, 2010.

Zimmers, T. A., Lubarsky, D. A., Sheldon, J. P., & Koniaris, L. G. (2005). Inadequate anaesthesia in lethal injection for execution—Authors' reply. *The Lancet, 366.* Retrieved from http://www.sciencedirect.com.

Zimring, F. E. (2003). *The contradictions of American capital punishment.* New York: Oxford University Press.

Zimring, F. E. (2008). Criminology and its discontents: The American Society of Criminology 2007 Sutherland Address. *Criminology, 46*, 255–266.

Zimring, F. E., Fagan, J., & Johnson, D. T. (2009). Executions, deterrence and homicide: a tale of two cities. Columbia Public Law Research Paper No. 09–206; CELS 2009 4th Annual Conference on Empirical Legal Studies Paper. Retrieved from SSRN http://ssrn.com/abstract=1436993.

Zimring, F. E., & Hawkins, G. (1986). *Capital punishment and the American agenda.* Cambridge: Cambridge University Press.

Zinn, H. (1990). *A people's history of the United States.* New York: Harper Perennial.

Subject Index

Note: Page numbers followed by "t" denote tables.